An Introduction to the Study of Education

This fully updated fourth edition of *An Introduction to the Study of Education* provides a comprehensive and reflective introduction to the study of education, inviting students to question what education is, who it is for and what purpose it serves. Taking the reader from the early years through to lifelong learning, it examines all forms of education and learning.

This new edition includes ten completely new chapters and a step-by-step guide to essay writing. There is also a companion website to accompany the book, featuring additional chapters, which can be visited at www.routledge.com/cw/matheson. This fully updated fourth edition provides:

- a full exploration of the historical, sociological, philosophical and psychological roots of education;
- a clear focus on the individual levels of education – preschool, compulsory, post-compulsory and lifelong learning;
- the latest debates within special educational needs;
- an in-depth examination of learning styles;
- insights into the historical development of education and the role of, and background to, research in education;
- a focus on current educational practice and diversity across the United Kingdom and Ireland.

Written in a clear and accessible style, this is the essential core text for all beginning students on undergraduate and postgraduate courses in Education Studies and all those interested in education today, where it came from and where it is going.

David Matheson has published widely across the field of education in areas such as medical education, teacher training, lifelong learning, comparative education and cultural identity in education. He has extensive experience as an educator and researcher in higher education, adult education and secondary education.

An Introduction to the Study of Education

Fourth edition

Edited by David Matheson

Routledge
Taylor & Francis Group

LONDON AND NEW YORK

Fourth edition published 2015
by Routledge
2 Park Square, Milton Park, Abingdon, Oxon OX14 4RN

and by Routledge
711 Third Avenue, New York, NY 10017

Routledge is an imprint of the Taylor & Francis Group, an informa business

First edition published by David Fulton Publishers 1999
Third edition published by Routledge 2008

British Library Cataloguing in Publication Data
A catalogue record for this book is available from the British Library

Library of Congress Cataloging in Publication Data
A catalog record for this book has been requested

ISBN: 978-0-415-62309-4 (hbk)
ISBN: 978-0-415-62310-0 (pbk)
ISBN: 978-0-203-10545-0 (ebk)

Typeset in Palatino
by Wearset Ltd, Boldon, Tyne and Wear

Printed and bound by CPI Group (UK) Ltd, Croydon, CR0 4YY

Dedicated to the memory of

Elsa Monnet-Rossetti
My mother-in-law

1927–2013

Adrian Hastings
Colleague and friend

1953–2013

Contents

Figures

Tables

Contributors

Dr Abdeljalil Akkari, University of Geneva.

Professor Gert Biesta, University of Luxembourg.

Dr Colin Brock, University of Oxford.

Professor Trevor Corner, Middlesex University.

Professor Reg Dennick, University of Nottingham.

Dr Carmel Gallagher, General Teaching Council of Northern Ireland.

Professor Nigel Grant, late, of the University of Glasgow.

Professeur Dominique Groux, Université des Antilles et de la Guyane.

Dr Adrian Hastings, late, of Leicester University.

Professor Louise Hayward, University of Glasgow.

Dr Tim Heywood, University of Nottingham.

Dr Mary Kellett, Open University.

Professor Jane Martin, Institute of Education, University of London.

Dr Catherine Matheson, University of Southampton/Oxford Brookes University/Open University.

Dr David Matheson, Leeds Metropolitan University/Open University.

Professor Ian Menter, University of Oxford.

Dr Graham Mitchell, University of Northampton.

Alice Mongiello, University of the Highlands and Islands.

Alison Murphy, Cardiff Metropolitan University.

Dr Raúl Pardíñas-Solís, University of Oxford.

Professor John Pelley, Texas Tech University.

Dr Deirdre Raftery, University College Dublin.

Heather Rai, University of Nottingham.

Dr Martina Relihan, University College Dublin.

Dr John Stanley, Instituto Universitário da Maia, Portugal.

Dr Bernard Wentzel, Haute Ecole Pédagogique – Berne/Jura/Neuchâtel, Bienne.

Dr Philip Woodward, Toton College, Southampton.

Dr Michael Wyness, University of Warwick.

Professor Dominic Wyse, Institute of Education, University of London.

What is education?

David Matheson

Don't let schooling interfere with your education.

Mark Twain

Introduction

There are some notions which most of us *think* we know what they are and assume that others share the same or similar ideas. These can include ideas such as fairness, equality and justice. They are terms which are easy to use and to feel that we understand what we mean by them, but notoriously difficult to explain to others, other than by appealing to common sense and asserting that 'everyone' knows what justice, fairness, equality and so on actually are. Some terms, such as professionalism, are even best described by their absence. To define professionalism per se is notoriously difficult, but *unprofessional* somehow appears easier, even if in reality unprofessional is more often exemplified than defined. In this morass of potential confusion, there are phenomena which we recognise when we see them but would be hard put to describe in anything even vaguely resembling objective terms.

Among these slippery concepts is that of education. Education is what might be termed an *essentially contested concept* (Winch and Gingell 1999). It is one with a vast range of definitions, none of which is totally satisfactory. For example, we have the common equation between education and school. In this case, what about higher education? Where does further education fit in? And, for that matter, where do we place things we teach ourselves? We can discuss education that includes all of these arenas for learning or we can exclude at least some of them. We may even do as Abbs (1979) does and claim that 'education and school can refer, and often do refer, to antithetical activities' (p. 90). Or we can go even further and align ourselves with Illich (1986) and assert that school is not only the antithesis of education but that its main function is to provide custodial day care for young people.

This chapter has its function to consider what education might be. I intend to do this by considering a well-known attempt at defining education. I will then consider some of the things that education can be for and, lastly, I will consider what it might mean to be educated before briefly considering Education Studies itself.

Defining education

The literature is replete with attempts at defining education and so, at most, I will succeed here in merely scratching the surface. First, there is what we might term the 'elastic' sense of education. This is one, in a manner akin to the manner in which Lewis Carroll's Humpty Dumpty ascribes any meaning he wants to a word, where education means precisely what the speaker, though within limits unknown to Humpty, wants it to mean. This approach capitalises on the kudos attached to the term *education* and seeks to ascribe it to whatever the speaker wants to give it. The result is a very loose approach wherein terms like *education* and *learning* are used interchangeably and the whole notion of education gets diluted to vanishing point. Despite this, as Lawson (1975) says, to call an activity or process 'educational' is typically to vest it with considerable status.

It is a commonplace that humans are learning machines. As Malcolm Tight puts it, 'Learning, like breathing, is something everyone does all of the time' (Tight 1996: 21). A first step, then, in trying to get a definition of education that is worth the bother is to exclude some activities. Unfortunately this is exactly where the problems start. As soon as we exclude activities from the list of what constitutes education we have to exercise a value judgement and we have to find a good reason for doing so. Nonetheless, at least by going about it this way, if we do decide that education equals school – an all too common assumption – then we have hopefully begun with a definition of education into which school fits, rather than beginning with school and making our definition of education fit into it.

The synonymous use of school and education is, however, hardly surprising when we consider that most of us will have experienced in schools what is arguably the most important part of our formal education. After all, it is there that most of us will have learned to read, developed our skills in social interaction, encountered authority which does not derive from a parent and we will have been required to conform to sets of rules, some of which might have been explained, some of which might not. School leaves its mark on us and on our personal conception of education, but this risks rendering us at least myopic to other possibilities.

A popular approach to the definition of education, at least in Anglophone countries, is that proposed by Richard Peters. Peters' (1966) contention is that 'education implies that something worthwhile is being or has been intentionally transmitted in a morally acceptable manner' (p. 25). He manages to encompass two significant components: there is not only the end product, there is also means adopted to achieve it.

Peters' definition suggests several areas for exploration:

1. intentionality and the 'something';
2. the notion of transmission;
3. the criteria for ascertaining whether the something is worthwhile;
4. the basis upon which moral acceptability is to be judged.

Intentionality and the 'something'

For Peters, education cannot come about by accident. In this he concurs with Hamm's (1991) claim that 'learning is an activity that one engages in with purpose and intention to come up to a certain standard' (p. 91). This implies, *inter alia*, that those things which we learn incidentally cannot count and hence stands at odds with Tight's contention that 'Learning, like breathing, is something everyone does all of the time' (1996: 21). Equally, it implies that the person fulfilling the function of teacher has some clear notion of what is to be transmitted to the learners.[1] This may take the form of some specific material to be learned or it may take the form of attitudes to be acquired and opinions to be formed. A question to be asked concerns whether we can ever separate what is being transmitted from the manner in which the transmission occurs. In other words, can the message stand alone from the medium that carries it? Or is it the case, as Marshall Mcluhan (1967) claimed, that the medium *is* the message?[2]

For Peters, the 'something' refers to knowledge and understanding (and this can reasonably be extended to include skills and attitudes).[3] This, in turn, leads to several other questions, not least of which is to consider exactly what we mean by knowledge. Knowledge consists of several components. Most notably these consist in their turn of: knowing *how* to do things (procedural knowledge) and knowing *that* (prepositional knowledge) certain things exist or are true or have happened and so on. There is also the rather thorny question of how we know that we know something and just what knowledge is, but this is perhaps beyond the scope of this book.[4]

Understanding is important for Peters since this takes us beyond simply knowing and into the realms where we become better equipped to grasp underlying principles, are able to explain why things are the way they are or why they happen the way they do, and so on. The role of knowledge and understanding in defining education becomes even more crucial when one considers Peters' view on what it means to be educated (see Barrow and Woods 1995: ch. 1). For Peters, becoming educated is an asymptotic process: we can move towards it but we can never fully attain it. For Peters, 'this understanding should not be too narrowly specialised' (1970: 4). Just how narrow is too narrow is open to speculation, but this is a point best dealt with later as we consider what it means to be educated.

Transmission

Transmission creates in the mind an image of something passing from one place to another. However, we have to take care to understand just what Peters means by the term. In an age dominated by broadcast media, there is a tendency to equate 'broadcast' with 'transmission'; in other words, one may transmit but we never know who will receive or indeed exactly what they will receive. If Peters equates 'transmission' with 'broadcast' then he clearly is referring to teaching rather than to learning. On the other hand, if by transmission he actually means what we might nowadays term 'successful transmission' (i.e. when the message sent is equal to the message received), then he refers to both teaching *and* learning. Indeed, the etymology of 'transmission' would clearly indicate the latter. We need only look at the manner in which 'transmission' was employed in the days before our present media age (in terms, for example, of a vehicle's transmission, which transfers movement from the engine to the wheels – which certainly brooks no ambiguity as to the 'message' sent being the same as the 'message' received, although there is energy lost along the way – in the case of mechanical devices most often as sound and/or heat) to see the justification for this claim. Nonetheless, we do live in a media age; transmission has adopted a range of meanings; and so, perhaps Peters' definition might be better altered to use the term 'successful transmission'.

In any case the need for transmission in Peters' definition of education brings with it the idea that, first, one cannot educate oneself by means of discovery, although one can by means of educational materials such as books, since in this latter case it is the ideas of the writer of the book which are being transmitted via the book. Second, there is an implication of a deficiency model of education whereby the teacher has 'something' that the learner does not and hence the teacher's task is, at least in part, to remedy deficiencies on the part of the learner.[5] This is a view of education which stands at odds with Freire (1972) and Rogers and Freiberg (1993), who see personal growth *from within* as a central tenet of education and for whom 'transmission' of any 'something' is in effect anathema. For each of these writers, an educator may facilitate learning but nothing more.

Worthwhile and worthless knowledge

There are various criteria we might use to mark out *educationally* worthwhile or valuable knowledge from that which is worthless. We might do this in terms of need, but in doing so one must take care not to confuse *needs* with *wants*. What I want is not necessarily what I need and vice versa, and this goes for everything I could possibly want or need, including knowledge. Again, it is a matter of perspective and relative importance. With this in mind, needs can be defined in terms of societal needs or individual needs. The question arises as to whether the needs of society are necessarily compatible with the needs of the individual. The answer one gives is very much contingent on one's view of the social goal of education and whether one views society as composed of individuals or whether one sees individuals subsumed into society.

There is also the cultural aspect of knowledge to consider. Whether we seek cultural replication, maintenance or renovation, or even replacement, will play a major role in one's definition of educationally worthwhile knowledge. Our view, not only of the society we have now, but also of the society we want to have, is critical both in determining educationally worthwhile knowledge and in determining what counts as knowledge at all. This is exemplified, in all too many parts of the world, by the way in which some minority (and sometimes even majority[6]) languages have been proscribed in schools. This happened, for example, to Welsh, Scottish Gaelic, Scots, Swiss and French patois, Breton and Catalan, to name but a few cases in Europe. These languages were effectively designated as educationally (and often politically) unacceptable knowledge in often vicious bids to extirpate them.

Moral acceptability

Peters contends that education must be conducted in a morally acceptable manner. If there were consensus as to what constitutes morality then this exigency would present few, if any, problems. Unfortunately in our present society we see what are termed moral values being challenged on a regular basis. No longer is the teacher seen, if ever she or he were, as an absolute authority on moral matters and this is the case across the whole range of teaching and learning. Our society increasingly recognises itself as multicultural (as indeed it has been in reality since at least the dawn of recorded history – see Grant 1997) and, as such, acknowledges that there can exist a multiplicity of value systems within one society. This poses the major problem of defining 'morally acceptable'. There are, however, some points of agreement within our society that certain 'educational' methods are simply unacceptable. At the extreme this precludes inflicting physical pain as a means of encouraging learning. Yet it was only in 1985 that corporal punishment was finally outlawed in state schools in the UK. While in theory in its latter years this punishment was reserved for recalcitrant miscreants, in practice it could be used, and was used, as an 'aid' to learning whereby, for example, a pupil might be hit for not spelling a word correctly.[7] Moral torture in the form of denigration, however officially decried, still continues as a not uncommon means of pupil regulation. This can range from sarcasm to denigration of speech patterns and the learners' cultural roots.

The literature, however, tends to highlight *indoctrination* as an immoral means of encouraging learning. Indoctrination is defined as the intentional implantation of unshakeable beliefs regardless of appeals to evidence (Barrow and Woods 1995). A good example of indoctrination in action is what Anthony Flew (1975) called the *No True Scotsman* argument – see the final chapter in this volume for details on this and other sophistical devices – whereby the subject of an assertion is modified in the face of evidence which challenges the validity of the original assertion.

Indoctrination is seen as running counter to the very idea of education as it 'necessarily involves lack of respect for an individual's rationality [and hence] is morally unacceptable' (Barrow and Woods 1995: 80). These same writers illustrate their opposition to indoctrination by means of an imaginary Catholic school where all the teachers endeavour to have the pupils wholeheartedly and unequivocally share their belief in Catholicism. The fact that Barrow and Woods demonstrate some remarkable ignorance about Catholicism[8] is beside the point. Their focus is on major areas of belief, on whole-life beliefs, on what one might term *macro*-beliefs. What about the lesser ones, the *meso*-beliefs and the *micro*-beliefs? How did we learn that science is objective? That experts are to be trusted? That reading is a necessary prerequisite for any modern society? It does not demand much imagination to determine a welter of beliefs which we usually hold unshakeably and which have been intentionally transmitted to us. There is also the question of the level at which intentionality occurs. While a teacher may not intend to indoctrinate his or her learners, it is quite conceivable and indeed likely that the socio-political system within which that teacher operates demands that certain values and beliefs be transmitted (this is a theme returned to in the next chapter). If we are not only indoctrinated but also conditioned, then perhaps the very thoughts we are capable of thinking are restrained and constrained.[9] In addition, the very language we use and words we employ reflect power dynamics and whose version of language holds sway at that moment (Corson 1998: 5).

In Chapter 16 of this volume Trevor Corner and Nigel Grant remind us that we are generally better at identifying when others are indoctrinating. When it happens in our own education system we are more liable to call it 'moral education' or 'citizenship'. The question of moral (un)acceptability remains unanswered.

Perhaps a better question to ask is whether one can avoid *all* indoctrination in an educational process. Can one always present a learner with rationales as to why things are as we say they are? Will one always have learners who are capable of understanding such rationales? How does one rationalise to a three-year-old that to stick one's finger in the fire is not a good idea? By explaining the basic theories of thermodynamics and what happens when there is an interaction between skin and hot surfaces? By slightly scorching the child's finger? By telling the child that it will hurt and hope that one's authority as an adult/parent will be enough to have the child always believe that sticking a finger in the fire is not a good idea? Simply presenting notions as truth is much simpler than explaining them and may be much preferable to demonstrating possible consequences of an action one wishes the learner to avoid. Explanation demands a level of understanding which may simply not exist in the learner. However, even rationalising everything might be construed as 'indoctrination', in that one is presenting the learner and encouraging in him/her a pattern of behaviour and hence beliefs as to its acceptability. One's force of argument may give one such an advantage over the learner that the latter simply succumbs to the belief being proposed. As a teacher one may feel that the learner has agreed with the reasonableness of the belief and has agreed to share it. As a learner one might just feel ground down.

In passing, it can be worth reminding ourselves that 'acquiring a belief is like catching a cold' (Heil 1999: 47). No matter how I might contrive to 'catch' whatever metaphorical virus transmits a belief, no matter how I might believe myself willing to acquire the said belief, it is only when conditions are just right that I will acquire it. However, repetition and reinforcement that the proposed belief is true will help enormously in engendering these conditions. This point, known as *argumentum ad nauseam*, is illustrated by the way in which media stories can achieve a life of their own, regardless of how true they are and frequently in the face of powerful evidence to the contrary (Miller *et al.* 1998; Moore 2002). This notion of repetition is tied in with an approach used in psychiatry whereby the patient with depression learns to act as if they did not have depression. In this way, they may put a spring in their step, talk in an upbeat manner and basically conduct themselves as if they were fine. They are circumventing the depression and acting as if they believe themselves to be fine. The aim is to set in train a habitual behaviour and in effect change their belief about themselves. 'Fake it until you make it' requires a suspension of disbelief in order to modify expectations and hence belief. It is widely used in addiction therapies as well as in treatment of mood disorders (Demaree *et al.* 2004: 21).

It seems that the teacher is in a cleft stick if she or he decides to avoid *all* indoctrination. Giving no teaching implies to budding learners either that learning has a low value or that they themselves have. If we offer teaching, we are offering a complete package of beliefs that go with it and implying, if not insisting upon, its acceptability and desirability and hence 'indoctrinating' (Sutherland 1994).

On the other hand, perhaps there is a major argument in favour of critical thinking. Indeed, if one's position is that indoctrination *in all its forms and regardless of the intent* is immoral (i.e. if one accepts that Peters' definition of what constitutes education is valid at least in this respect) then the encouragement of critical thinking is essential. This does, however, require a conundrum whereby the learner has to be convinced of the value of critical thinking in order to acquire or develop the tools necessary for critical thinking. Hence, in order to avoid indoctrination, one needs to employ indoctrination.

Expressed at its least subtle we have Postman and Weingartner's notion of 'crap-detection' whereby the 'crap detector ... is not completely captivated by the arbitrary abstractions of the community in which he [*sic*] happened to grow up in' (1976: 18). In other words, the crap detector is able to look past the symbolism and theatricals of his or her society and adopt a critical perspective. This is a notion which is most often associated with Paulo Freire and his idea of conscientisation. In dealing with Freire a word of caution is needed: Freire wrote in Portuguese and used the term *conscienciza-ção* which, since the Portuguese words for conscience and consciousness are the same, could be translated into English as either *conscience-raising* or *consciousness-raising*, so there is an element of ambiguity about the concept. However, Freire, a gifted linguist, was probably aware of this and hence the double meaning is very likely to be deliberate.

Conscientisation is a means of empowerment whereby the learner decides what is to be learned and does so in terms of what is meaningful to his or her own existence. The goal of this education is to make the learner more critically aware of the area under discussion, and hence more critically aware of himself or herself and his or her environment. The political implications of such an educational goal and its associated pedagogy are immense. In this view of education, there is no received wisdom and everything is open to question. Nonetheless, the quandary outlined above remains, whereby offering teaching in any shape or form, or not at all, constitutes indoctrination but perhaps the development of the critical faculty is the most moral of options in that it encourages the learner to question even the basic premise upon which the learning experience is based (Akkari and Perez 2000).

What is education for?

What education is for is clearly dependent on how we choose to define education and how we determine the relationship between education and the society in which it operates. For the purposes of this section, where we look at some of the social goals of education, we shall concentrate on the formal domain. Formal education is above all associated with school, further education and higher education. It tends to aim, at least at some levels, at a qualification and is often associated in the public mind with younger people. Non-formal education requires no entrance qualifications (such as school certificates or degrees, but it may require a certain level of knowledge and/or expertise in the domain in question), may result in no exit qualifications and is more usually associated with adults. The boundaries between formal and non-formal education were never very strict and are becoming even more blurred as time goes on.

Since time immemorial, formal education has been used with a social goal in mind. Every society seeks to replicate itself and finds ways of transmitting what it considers worthwhile to its young and sometimes its not-so-young citizens. In Ancient Greece, for example, the Spartans used a formal school system to instil into their young men the ideas of absolute obedience to their military commanders, extreme courage and resistance to pain as well as, what were for the time, some of the most advanced notions of military strategy. The young women were trained in domestic arts and motherhood. By the same token, it was not uncommon for commentators to complain, as did Seneca during the Roman Empire, that 'we are training children for school, not for life'.[10] From this it becomes clear that it has been held for a very long time that school *ought* to have a social function and that this social function has not always been clear and well-defined.

Since the Reformation, at least, the idea that formal education can be used to reproduce society, mould society or create a new society has been widely discussed and written about in the West. The Reformers sought to create a society based around the *reading* of the Bible which distinguished them from their Roman Catholic predecessors, who emphasised the *interpretation* of the Bible given by the Old Church. The social upheaval of the Reformation was accompanied by attempts to literally create a new society based on a literate population. To this end, John Knox *et al.* (1560), in their *First Book of Discipline*, proposed the creation of schools in every centre of population whose aims would be not only to teach basic skills such as reading and writing, but also to act as a means whereby the more able boys and girls would learn sufficiently to allow entry to higher education. In this way, the intelligentsia would be kept in contact with the rest of the population and the upper echelons of society would be revitalised by new blood.

This idea of using education for social engineering has echoes in Robert Owen (1835), who states in his *New View of Society* that:

> Any general character, from the best to the worst, from the most ignorant to the most enlightened, may be given to any community, even to the world at large, by the application of proper means; which means are to a great extent at the command and under the control of those who have influence in the affairs of men.
>
> (Owen 1835 [1965]: 85)

It is important to underline here that *character* refers not to individuals but to the communities that they form. The essential point, however, is that for Owen education had the power to shape collections of individuals into communities and to determine the nature of those communities. In other words, education has a major socialising function. This theme is taken up by Durkheim, for whom 'education consists of the methodical socialisation of the young generation' (Durkheim 1956: 71). Durkheim also sees education as a means for social reproduction: 'Education, far from having as its unique or principle object the individual and his interests, is above all the means by which society perpetually recreates the conditions of its existence' (Durkheim 1956: 123). Part of the recreation of itself is the need for economic sustenance if not growth. However, until recently there seemed to be a certain coyness about openly espousing the view that 'the economic aims of education are as legitimate as any other' (Winch 2002: 101). Yet, if education – whether a lifelong activity or as Winch puts it 'broadly but not exclusively concerned with preparation for life' (2002: 101) – does not have economic aims, then why is so much money spent on it? In point of fact, it is fairly easy to establish that the economic aims of education are paramount, *especially* when education is viewed as a preparation for life or as a means of coping with changes in one's economic circumstances.

Formal education serves many functions besides those outlined above. It contains examinations and assessments of various kinds which serve to decide, in part at least, the choice of next destinations the learner can move on to. Depending on one's perspective, these can be seen as an opportunity for social mobility or as a means for further entrenching social divides and further ossifying the existing social structure. Formal education may liberate or enslave, expand horizons or confirm feelings of personal failure. But let us note that formal education is seen as a right but seldom as a privilege despite general consensus that it is essential in order for a person to learn how to function within our society.

What does it mean to become educated?

Becoming educated carries with it a number of notions such as the acquisition of *depth*, whereby a person understands (increasingly) the underlying principles within an 'area of knowledge'. The educated person will acquire *breadth* in the sense that she or he will develop a cognitive perspective *within* an area of knowledge and *between* areas of knowledge. This implies the creation of linkages across the area of knowledge and into areas which may adjoin or not. This not only serves to distinguish knowledge from information, but serves to encourage the adoption of differing perspectives on the same domain (an almost essential prerequisite to creative problem-solving). Indeed, for Peters, 'being educated is incompatible with being narrowly specialised' (1970: 4).

An area of knowledge is, by definition, not an amorphous mass, but has certain rules to bind it together. In this view of education, the educated person has to abide by these rules when acquiring knowledge, when handling knowledge and when using knowledge. To take one example, when learning another language, one accepts that the grammar and syntax of that language are rules to be obeyed (as best one can) if one wishes to communicate effectively in that language. Failure to obey the rules may make communication difficult, if not altogether impossible. Against this has to be set the notion that fundamental creativity often comes about when the accepted rules in an area of knowledge are bent or ignored and a new, revised set has to be put in place.[11]

We are used in our culture to measure 'being educated' against, for example, level of qualification or extent of acquaintance with some domain or other. In this way, the capacity to expound upon and employ the literary canon, or some other set of knowledge, may be the scale against which one's being educated is measured. Barrow (1999) draws this together with the development of criticality mentioned above and states that 'it is to have a developed mind, which means a mind that has developed understanding such that it can discriminate between logically different kinds of questions and exercise judgment, critically and creatively, in respect of important matters' (p. 139). Such discrimination and judgement inevitably need to be based upon a significant amount of knowledge. Just how much is significant and about what sort of knowledge we are talking is, of course, open to debate and will vary according to circumstances. My being educated in horticulture may be of little use when faced with a burst pipe in my living room.

All this implies that, while we may wax about general education, the sheer scope of knowledge and skills which are there to be acquired, at least in theory, is such that we must forcibly remain uneducated in at least some, if not many, domains. However, Barrow's argument, in company with many others, implies very strongly that education is the antithesis of indoctrination, although, as suggested above, education must perforce contain elements of indoctrination, if only to convince some learners of its own worth.

Education suffers from a variety of definitional problems, not least of which is the frequently false equation between education and studying (compounded by a similarly false equation between learning and studying[12]). Studying implies some sort of examination, if only self-examination. Learning does not. Whether education makes a similar implication is dependent on how one chooses to define it. However, we might do well to distinguish between *education* and *being educated.* If *education* runs into such problems through its simultaneously being a process and a product, then why not dispense with the one and concentrate on the other? In this way, discussion of what it means *to be educated* can potentially be more fruitful since the term implies not a process, with all the pitfalls and traps that await even the more astute such as Richard Peters, but rather a product. In this way, it is immaterial how we have acquired the components of being educated; what counts is that we have indeed acquired them.

With this idea in mind, it is worthwhile taking a moment to consider those things which, in your opinion, every person should know and those things which every person should be able to do. Should we value some knowledge and skills over others? If so, which ones? And, as importantly, why should these knowledge and skills be more important than others? By asking questions such as this, we can begin to establish a canon of basic knowledge – which might be quite sophisticated – as well as establishing a hierarchy of knowledge. Critical in this venture, though, is establishing the rationale for such a set of affairs. In the end we may arrive at the same conclusion as Maskell (1999), who argues that those whom we might term 'educated' are all too often themselves in want of an education, suffering as they do from limited horizons and narrow ranges of knowledge.

We might even arrive at the notion of the *educated public* which, as Wain (1994) tells us, can take a variety of forms but which in all of them seems to imply some sort of community of persons endowed not just with knowledge and understanding across a wide range of spheres, but with critically and a capacity to communicate effectively with each other.

Some different kinds of knowing

It seems fairly obvious that there are various things that we learn in different ways, regardless of our general preferences for learning. For example, it is hard to conceive of learning to sing without opening one's mouth and actually trying to sing. Equally, one could hardly train a surgeon (or should that be *educate*?) without expecting them to acquire knowledge not only of what to do but also of how to do it, as well as giving them supervised practice in actually doing it. This is tied in with the notion of developing expertise such as in the Dreyfus and Dreyfus (1985) model of skills acquisition, which takes the learner from novice to expert: novices rely on rules since they do not have the experience and insight that allow them to gauge the applicability of the rules, whereas the expert has an intuitive grasp of situations based on a deep tacit understanding. In this way, the expert may know something without knowing how they know it. In effect, they can know the answer on the basis of experience and knowledge deeply held. Linked to this is the conscious competency model (Table 1.1).

TABLE 1.1 The conscious competency model

	Incompetence	Competence
Unconscious	**Level 1: unconscious incompetence** The person is unaware that they are deficient in the skill or knowledge needed.	**Level 4: unconscious competence** The skill or knowledge set is so practised that active application is not realised or necessary. It is a 'second nature' response.
Conscious	**Level 2: conscious incompetence** The person is aware that they are deficient in the skill or knowledge needed. Practice will move the person to the conscious competence stage.	**Level 3: conscious competence** The skill or knowledge do not need assistance to be performed or recalled, but does require thought or concentration, and is not an automatic action.

Source: Roland and Matheson (2012: 144).

Donald Rumsfeld, as Secretary of Defense under George W. Bush, famously stated in 2002:

Reports that say that something hasn't happened are always interesting to me, because as we know, there are known knowns; there are things we know we know. We also know there are known unknowns; that is to say we know there are some things we do not know. But there are also unknown unknowns – the ones we don't know we don't know. And if one looks throughout the history of our country and other free countries, it is the latter category that tends to be the difficult ones.

(Federal News Service 2002)

Rumsfeld was frankly lampooned by the press and broadcast media. However, if we present Rumsfeld's comment in tabular form and add a fourth category and some notes of explanation, it becomes more clear (Table 1.2).

TABLE 1.2 Known knowns, and so on

	Known	Unknown
Known	**Known knowns** Things that I know I know – e.g. knowing that I speak certain languages.	**Known unknowns** Things that I know I don't know – e.g. knowing that I do not speak certain languages.
Unknown	**Unknown knowns** Things that I know but am unaware of my knowing them – tacit knowledge.	**Unknown unknowns** Things that I think I know but in fact don't – e.g. skills I could once execute but can no longer do, but I remain convinced that my former competence remains.

Source: Roland and Matheson (2012: 145).

In addition, we might consider *how* we know. A typical classification is as shown by Miller (1990) when he considered how to assess various types of competence in medical practitioners (Figure 1.1).

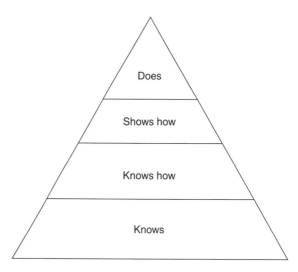

FIGURE 1.1 Miller's triangle (source: Miller 1990: S63).

The lowest level in Miller's triangle – *knows* – refers to *propositional knowledge*; that is, knowledge of facts, legislation, policies and so on. This is akin to learning for the theory part of a driving test. The second lowest level – *knows how* – refers to *procedural knowledge*; that is, knowing how to use the knowledge from the lowest level. This is like being able to describe how to drive a car. The third level – *shows* – refers to being able to demonstrate what one has learned in the lower levels. In other words, to be able to carry out practical tasks under supervision. This is like being accompanied by an experienced driver when learning to drive. Of course, during this time, one might well be continuing to acquire both procedural and propositional knowledge and, if one reflects on the practical work, one will be using that to add to both of these types of knowledge. The highest level is *does* and this is where one can work alone and unsupervised. This is like when one has passed the driving test and is able to get out on the road alone.

We can add a further level to Miller's triangle (Figure 1.2).

Shows others refers to teaching. In order to teach effectively, one needs to be able to bring forth the tacit knowledge that one has in order to be able to explain to learners. This entails breaking tasks down into component parts and empathising with the learner and the challenges that she or he faces. The expert has a dexterity that the novice usually lacks and so what is easy to the expert may be very difficult for the novice.

The move from unconscious competence back to conscious competence to be aware of the things one does automatically and without thinking can be difficult and even impossible for some people to achieve, at least in some instances.[13] Hence, for some, the further level of Miller's triangle might well be *Can't show others*. This is without mentioning those for whom the further level might well be entitled *Won't show others* as they jealously guard whatever skills they possess, perhaps for fear that the rising generation might usurp them.

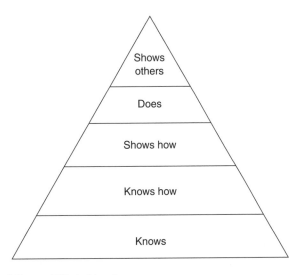

FIGURE 1.2 Matheson's variation on Miller's triangle.

There is also the phenomenon whereby one can recognise good performance without being able to perform to the level one is observing. Related to this is the sports coach who can advise players how to improve their game and yet cannot himself or herself play as well as the players she or he is coaching.

What is the study of education?

Education is unlike most other academic disciplines in that there is no agreement as to what it actually is. In consequence the study of education is somewhat diverse. It begins inevitably from the concept of education held by those directing the study – whether through their role as course managers, as researchers or as funders of research projects.

From the student's point of view?

If one succumbs to the notion that education equals school, then one's view of what constitutes knowledge of education worthy of study (for who really wants to study useless knowledge?) will be somewhat different from knowledge considered worthwhile by one who believes that education is a lifelong process. Unfortunately, there is a widespread tendency to do just that, despite the fact that it closes one's mind to the educational experiences that occur in the longer part of one's life. The excuse given, as Gutmann (cited in Wain 1994) reminds us, is that 'an exhaustive study of the other potential educational agencies in society would be exhausting if not impossible' (p. 155). This is doubtless true, but one could just pick and choose as has occurred in the present text and try at least to be representative of what is available.

At least two attempts have been made to establish what students of Education Studies might study and these were undertaken for the Quality Assurance Agency for Higher Education. The result is the *Benchmark Statements for Education Studies* (QAA 2000, 2007), which seek to state what a student completing a Single Honours programme in the subject will be capable of doing. Joint and Combined Honours students would be expected to show capability in a relevant selection of the areas.

The benchmark statements represent a compromise between those who argue that Education Studies is a discipline in its own right[14] and those who see it as an offshoot of teacher training. Equally, the statements have to accommodate those who emphasise one methodological approach, be this sociological, historical, psychological, philosophical, some combination of these or some other approach entirely.

> Education Studies is concerned with understanding how people develop and learn throughout their lives. It facilitates a study of the nature of knowledge, and a critical engagement with a variety of perspectives, and ways of knowing and understanding, drawn from a range of appropriate disciplines. There is diversity in Education Studies courses at undergraduate level, but all involve the intellectually rigorous study of educational processes, systems and approaches, and the cultural, societal, political and historical contexts within which they are embedded.
>
> (QAA 2000: 4)

In the second edition of the benchmark statements for Education Studies, this had evolved into:

> Education studies is concerned with understanding how people develop and learn throughout their lives, and the nature of knowledge and critical engagement with ways of knowing and understanding. It offers intellectually rigorous analysis of educational processes, systems and approaches, and their cultural, societal, political, historical and economic contexts. Many courses include the study of broader perspectives such as international education, economic relationships, the effects of globalisation and the role of education in human rights and ecological issues. They all include critique of current policies and practice and challenge assumptions.
>
> (QAA 2007: 1)

What is perhaps most remarkable is that, other than the definitions given above, the statements never explicitly state what topics need be studied. This should come as no surprise: if there can be no consensus on what constitutes education, there can surely be none on what constitutes Education Studies.

Despite this, Education Studies is perhaps unique among academic disciplines in that all students can bring directly to bear their own experiences and their own process of education. Since we have all found ourselves in situations which involve teaching and learning (and in studying Education Studies we are continuing to do so), then we all have experience which is relevant. In this respect, perhaps the only other domain which comes close in terms of universalised experience is Medicine, since we have all been sick at least once in our lives.

From the researcher's point of view?

The various chapters of this book, including this one, together with their references lists, give some indication of the wide diversity of subjects studied by researchers in Education Studies. Fundamentally, one can say that if a topic involves teaching or learning in any shape or form whatsoever, whether in a classroom or in the school of life or wherever, then it is fair game to be researched. Not that one would necessarily get funding, of course.

Conclusion

In essence, this chapter has been about ideas regarding education and its purpose, as well as briefly considering Education Studies. Ideas when formalised into practice naturally have material impacts and some of these are picked up in later chapters. A negative perspective on such an impact is given by Common, who presents us with perhaps the most cynical view of formal education as social control:

> We learn reading and boredom, writing and boredom, arithmetic and boredom, and so on according to the curriculum, till in the end it is quite certain you can put us in the most boring job there is and we'll endure it.
>
> (Common in Meighan 1986: 75)

Notes

1. It also implies some sort of examination to see if the learner has come up to the 'standard'. Examination may of course be self-examination, rather than some sort of test imposed or conducted by a third party.
2. A master of aphorisms and puns, Mcluhan deliberately entitled his book on this subject *The Medium is the Massage*.
3. Indeed, if one follows Bloom's (1969) *Taxonomy of Educational Objectives*, then one has to include at least some skills since the hierarchy of cognitive objectives is as follows, and the last three listed are clearly skills to be acquired:

   - knowledge
   - comprehension
   - application
   - analysis
   - synthesis
   - evaluation.

   Similarly, following Bloom's affective objectives will mean including attitudes in our 'something'.
4. For discussion of the nature of knowledge, the reader is referred to the *Blackwell Companion to Epistemology*. For a counter-argument to the commonly held belief that knowledge is justified, true belief, see the Gettier Problem which tackles the inconsistency in the JTB approach with humour and panache. See http://en2.wikipedia.org/wiki/Gettier_problem.
5. Being unable to educate oneself by means of discovery stands at odds with Donald Schön's (1984) work on the reflective practitioner, which has been extremely influential in the UK and elsewhere in terms of how not only teachers but also medical practitioners, engineers, architects and various other professionals are trained. Schön discusses, among other things, the development of the expert touch, that tacit knowledge that allows us to make adjustments to our practice on the hoof. It is a type of knowing that we see in every skilled craftsperson who knows by apparent intuition just what to do in a given situation. It is a skill which, like any skill, is learned, but it is essentially one which, although a teacher may help one on one's way, one teaches oneself.
6. Majority is a very relative term. In the UK, English speakers are in the majority but they are very much in the minority in Europe, however we want to define Europe – for this too is a relative term: do we mean the European Union? If so, then what about Switzerland and Norway? If Europe is that part of the world west of the Urals which sits on the European Continental Shelf (a traditional definition of Europe) then what about Iceland? The Icelanders consider themselves European and yet their country is a volcanic island in the middle of the Atlantic and very definitely not on the European Continental Shelf. Similarly, minority is relative. Both terms can also be considered in terms of power.
7. This was the standard practice in the primary school I attended in the 1960s.
8. This they do, among other things, by insisting that Catholics believe that the Pope is infallible (p. 70). The reality is that the Pope is held under the doctrine of infallibility to be able to make infallible statements under certain circumstances and only on matters of doctrine.
9. See Matheson and Matheson (2000) for a discussion of discourse and the limitations that language can set on our thinking.
10. *Non vitae sed scholae discimus.*
11. One can also contrast the way adults tend to learn languages compared with children. Adults aim more for accuracy in grammar etc., children for communication in just the same way as they learned their native tongue. Children use a new language for the purpose for which language was intended (i.e. to communicate) and only as a secondary consideration do they learn how to structure it. Compare the success rates of children and adults in language acquisition to judge the relative efficacy of the two approaches.
12. See http://s860.photobucket.com/user/chattahoochee1/media/reading-but-not-studying.gif.html (and elsewhere) for the very wonderful cartoon *reading but not studying*.
13. Parents who attempt to teach their offspring how to drive do not always find this to be an easy task, as the breaking down of automatisms into their component parts can render their execution challenging, if not impossible.
14. I once heard Education Studies being described as parasitic and proud of it!

References

Abbs, P. (1979) *Reclamations*. London: Heinemann.

Akkari, A. and Perez, S. (2000) 'Education and empowerment', in Matheson, C. and Matheson, D. (eds) *Educational Issues in the Learning Age*. London: Continuum.

Barrow, R. (1999) 'The higher nonsense: some persistent errors in educational thinking', *Journal of Curriculum Studies* 31 (2): 131–142.

Barrow, R. and Woods, R. (1995) *An Introduction to the Philosophy of Education*. London: Routledge.

Bloom, B.S. (1969) *Taxonomy of Educational Objectives: The Classification of Educational Goals*. London: Longman.

Corson, D. (1998) *Changing Education for Diversity*. Buckingham: Open University Press.

Demaree, H., Robinson, J., Everhart, J.E. and Schmeichel, B.J. (2004) 'Resting RSA is associated with natural and self-regulated responses to negative emotional stimuli', *Brain and Cognition* 56: 14–23.

Dreyfus, H. and Dreyfus, S. (1985). *Mind Over Machine: The Power of Human Intuition and Expertise in the Era of the Computer*. New York: Free Press.

Durkheim, E. (1956) *Education and Sociology*. New York: The Free Press.

Federal News Service. (2002) 'DoD News Briefing – Secretary Rumsfeld and Gen. Myers'. In: *Defense USDo*. www.defense.gov/transcripts/transcript.aspx?transcriptid=2636, last accessed 2 December 2011.

Flew, A. (1975) *Thinking About Thinking: Do I Sincerely Want to Be Right?*. London: Collins Fontana.

Freire, P. (1972) *The Pedagogy of the Oppressed*. Harmondsworth: Penguin.

Grant, N. (1997) 'Intercultural education in the United Kingdom', in Woodrow, D., Gajendra, K., Rocha-Trindade, M., Campani, G. and Bagley, C. (eds), *Intercultural Education: Theories, Policies and Practice*. Aldershot: Ashgate.

Hamm, C. (1991) *Philosophical Issues in Education: An Introduction*. London: Falmer.

Heil, J. (1999) 'Belief', in Dancy, J. and Sosa, E. (eds) *A Companion to Epistemology*. Oxford: Blackwell.

Illich, I. (1986) *Deschooling Society*. Harmondsworth: Pelican.

Lawson, K.H. (1975) *Philosophical Concepts and Values in Adult Education*. Nottingham: University of Nottingham.

Mcluhan, M. (1967) *The Medium is the Massage*. New York: Bantam Books.

Maskell, D. (1999) 'What has Jane Austen to teach Tony Blunkett?', *Journal of Philosophy of Education* 33 (2): 157–174.

Matheson, C. and Matheson, D. (2000) 'Educational spaces and discourses', in Matheson, C. and Matheson, D. (eds) *Educational Issues in the Learning Age*. London: Continuum.

Meighan, R. (1986) *A Sociology of Educating*, 2nd edn. London: Cassell.

Miller, D., Kitzinger, J. and Williams, K. (1998) *The Circuit of Mass Communication: Media Strategies, Representation and Audience Reception in the AIDS Crisis*. Thousand Oaks, CA: SAGE.

Miller, G. (1990) 'The assessment of clinical skills/competence/performance', *Academic Medicine* 65, supplement: S63–S67.

Moore, M. (2002) *Bowling for Columbine*. Dog Eat Dog Films Production.

Owen, R. (1835 [1965]) *A New View of Society and Report to the County of Lanark* (Gatrell, V.A.C. (ed.)). Harmondsworth: Pelican.

Peters, R.S. (1966) *Ethics and Education*. London: Allen and Unwin.

Peters, R. (1970) 'Education and the educated man', *Journal of Philosophy of Education* 4: 5–20.

Postman, N. and Weingartner, C. (1976) *Teaching as a Subversive Activity*. Harmondsworth: Pelican.

QAA (Quality Assurance Agency for Higher Education) (2000) *Education Studies*. Available at www.qaa.ac.uk/crntwork/benchmark/education.pdf, accessed 20 December 2003.

QAA (Quality Assurance Agency for Higher Education) (2007) *Education Studies*. Available at www.qaa.ac.uk/Publications/InformationAndGuidance/Documents/Education07.pdf, accessed 22 April 2014.

Rogers, C. and Freiberg, H.J. (1993) *Freedom to Learn*, 3rd edn. New York: Merrill.

Roland, D. and Matheson, D. (2012) 'New theory from an old technique: the Rolma matrices', *The Clinical Teacher* 9: 143–147.

Schön, D. (1984) *The Reflective Practitioner: How Professionals Think in Action*. New York: Basic Books.

Sutherland, M. (1994) *Theory of Education*. Harlow: Longman.

Tight, M. (1996) *Key Concepts in Adult Education and Training*. London: Routledge.

Wain, K. (1994) 'Competing conceptions of the educated public', *Journal of Philosophy of Education* 28 (2): 149–159.

Winch, C. (2002) 'The economic aims of education', *Journal of Philosophy of Education* 36 (1): 101–117.

Winch, C. and Gingell, J. (1999) *Key Concepts in the Philosophy of Education*. London: Routledge.

2

Ideology in education in the United Kingdom

Catherine Matheson

To 'idéologues' one must attribute all the misfortunes which have befallen France.
   Do you know what fills me most with wonder? The powerlessness of force to establish anything.... In the end the sword is always conquered by the mind.

Napoleon Bonaparte

Introduction

Every concept in education has varying and various interpretations, but perhaps none more so than ideology. As this chapter will show, it is used in a variety of senses and to a variety of ends. To do this, we begin with a discussion of the concept of ideology and show how it has had multiple meanings from the time it was first coined. We then move on to discuss ideology in education and show some of the types of ideology that are used in understanding education, before illustrating some of these types.

The concept of ideology

Ideology is a 'highly ambiguous concept' (Meighan and Siraj-Blatchford 1998: 179), a 'most equivocal and elusive concept' (Larrain 1979: 13) which has many meanings and usages and can be conceived either negatively and critically as a 'false consciousness' or positively as a 'world view'. The former has a restricted meaning and tends to be used in a pejorative manner to describe a set of undesirable and even distorted beliefs, while the latter has a looser meaning and is used by philosophers and social scientists in neutral and analytical ways. Ideology can also be viewed as a subjective psychological phenomenon emphasising the role of individuals and groups or as a more objective social phenomenon 'impregnating the basic structure of society' (Larrain 1979: 14). Ideology can also be seen either, restrictively, as part of, or more loosely, as equal to, the whole of the cultural sphere or ideological superstructure of society.

The word 'ideology' originated with that group of *savants* or intellectuals in the French Revolution who were entrusted by the Convention of 1795 with the founding and management of a new centre of revolutionary thought. These people were located within the newly established Institut de France, which was committed to the ideas of the French Enlightenment and thus the practical realisation of freedom of thought and expression (Lichtheim 1967).

In its original sense, the word 'ideology' was first used in 1796 by the French philosopher Destutt de Tracy, a member of the *Institut de France* and one of the directors of the highly influential French literary review *Mercure de France*. It was, in the words of one of the *Mercure's* regular contributors, Joseph-Jérôme Le François de Lalande, nothing more than a name for the 'science of ideas, their rules and their origins' (Lalande in Rey and Rey-Debove 1990: 957). Deriving ideas from sensations, Destutt de Tracy undertook to study the 'natural history of ideas' in his *Eléments d'idéologie* (1801–1815). He wanted to unmask the historicity of ideas by tracing their origins and setting aside metaphysical and religious prejudices, but also wanted this unmasking to reveal a true and universal knowledge of human nature (Hall 1978). Ideology was presented as a science and set in opposition to prejudice and false beliefs because scientific progress was possible only if these could be avoided.

From the start, however, ideology was to have pejorative connotations, one reason being that de Tracy and those who practised it, the ideologues or *'idéologistes'*, were concerned with two logically incompatible concepts of 'ideology': the relation between history and thought and the promotion of 'true' ideas which would be true regardless of the historical context. Following Helvétius, who believed that education could do everything, the ideologues shared his enthusiasm for it (Larrain 1979). After the years of revolution they wanted to educate the French people and, above all, the young people so that a just and happy society could be established. De Tracy wanted his book to be a study programme for youngsters and explicitly acknowledged that a motive for writing it was the new law (1801) introducing public education.

The other reason for the pejorative connotation of ideology was Napoleon, who was the first to use the term in a truly negative sense. Initially he shared the objectives and goals of the Institut de France and even became an honorary member in 1797 (Lichtheim 1967). The Institut then facilitated Bonaparte's accession to power, which he achieved in 1799, by helping him win the support of the educated middle class (Hall 1978). However, he abandoned the ideologues in 1803 when he signed his Concordat with the Church and deliberately set out to destroy the core of the Institut, the liberal and republican ideas of which greatly influenced the educational establishment. From then on the *'idéologistes'* were ridiculed as utopian visionaries under the name of *'idéologues'* (Dancy and Sosa 1993: 191) After the defeat in Russia in 1812, Napoleon turned on them forcefully and attributed all of France's misfortune to the ideologists, or *'idéologues'* as he disparagingly called them, whom he considered unrealistic, doctrinaire and ignorant of political practice (Lichtheim 1967). (It is worth noting that English language has reversed the pejorative and non-pejorative use of the term.) Nonetheless, after Napoleon's demise, the Comte de Tracy, who became a well-known personality in France and outside France, held an influential salon where writers and scientists met.

It is from this pejorative use of ideology as an undesirable or misguided set of ideas that many modern uses of the word have grown. Continuing this tendency, Marx and

Engels used ideology pejoratively to mean a false belief or illusion. In *The German Ideology*, written in 1845–1847 but only published in 1927, Marx and Engels, although not clearly defining the concept, use ideology to deride the proposition of the belief in the power of ideas to determine reality. For Marx (and Marxists) ideology was thus often seen as an attempted justification of a distorted set of ideas which consciously and/or unconsciously concealed contradictions in the interests of the dominant class or of a group, and served to maintain disproportionate allocation of economic and political power to the ruling class or dominant groups (Marx and Engels [1845–1847] 1970). Elsewhere Marx uses the term less pejoratively and gives a sociological interpretation of ideology (Marx 1859 in Meighan and Siraj-Blatchford 1998), in which ideology can be defined as a broad, interlocked set of ideas and beliefs about the world held by a group of people operating at various levels in society and in various contexts and which is demonstrated in their behaviour. This adds to the ambiguity of the concept of ideology not only because of the competing definitions, but also because the set of beliefs operates with several layers of meaning (Meighan and Siraj-Blatchford 1998).

After a period of disuse the word was revived with the publication in 1927 of Marx's and Engels' previously unpublished *The German Ideology*, which reinforced the Marxist and central sociological tradition view of ideology as 'distortion of reality' (Bullock *et al.* 1988). The classical Marxist position claims that ideological misconceptions cannot be dispelled by confronting with the 'truth' those under their spell since ideologies contain standards of evidence and argumentation that prevent the recognition of reality as it is (Dancy and Sosa 1993). For Gramsci and other Marxists, however, ideology is explained in terms of its social role, it is neither true nor false but 'the "cement" which holds together the *structure* [in which economic class struggle takes place] and the realm of the complex superstructures' (Hall 1978: 53). In other words, ideologies are those beliefs which are generated by a particular mode of production or economic structure. For Althusser, ideologies are non-scientific beliefs related more closely to social practice than to theoretical enquiry (Summer 1979). Lack of space precludes discussion of scientific beliefs as the only true beliefs and hence being free from ideological constraints; however, the reader is referred to Sokal and Bricmont (1998) for a discussion of the nature of scientific belief and reality. More recently, the concept of ideology has seen a renewed (implicit rather than explicit) interest, particularly in feminism, cultural studies and post-modernism in general, for the 'unmasking relations of power and domination implicit in culturally dominant forms of theoretical and social discourse' (Dancy and Sosa 1993: 193).

For my purposes I shall consider ideology in its broad sense of a set of beliefs as opposed to the narrow sense of a set of undesirable or misguided beliefs. Within contemporary sociology one distinguishes between 'particular' ideologies concerning specific groups and 'total' ideologies concerning a total commitment to a way of life. Every ideology is composed of three ingredients: (1) an invariable mythological structure, (2) an alternating set of philosophical beliefs and (3) a historically determined chosen group of people (Feuer 1975). Where ideologies exist in competition there are several outcomes: domination, incorporation and legitimation. In the first instance, we have cultural domination or hegemony. In the second, we have radical ideas incorporated into the traditional ideology. In the last instance, an ideology may achieve acceptance of its beliefs by direct repression or by more indirect means of institutional control, such as those of the media, education, religion, law or economy (Meighan and Siraj-Blatchford 1998).

Ideology, knowledge and the curriculum

A curriculum as a package of ideas, together with the manner in which it is delivered (its pedagogy) certainly fits the bill as an ideology. Curriculum heritage is the product of a philosophical tradition which can be traced through historical and contemporary curriculum practice, and in which we find the European triad of humanism (Plato, Erasmus and Locke), rationalism (Plato and Descartes) and naturalism (Rousseau). The first two elements of the triad underline, respectively, the importance of the human character and especially the feelings and the importance of reason, but with both understanding is sought by submission of the individual to an external body of knowledge, while the third seeks understanding in the private, concrete and the natural (McLean 1995). As in much in ideology, the triad's elements are not mutually exclusive.

It is these first two approaches that have dominated curriculum development across Europe, and, as a consequence of European influence, across much of the world. In France there is the rational encyclopaedic educational ideology with state prescription of national occupational needs (McLean 1995). In this collectivist tradition upper secondary schooling is subordinated to economic and social planning and general and vocational education are linked in content and control (collectivism). In the pluralist tradition we move towards an individualist and humanist approach such as exists in the UK and Germany, with a clear separation between general education and vocational training, though in Germany the curriculum is more infiltrated with rational encyclopaedic ideology than in the UK. We also have generalism (as in France and Germany) versus specialism or, as some say, elitism in England and to a lesser extent in Scotland (McLean 1995). Naturalism, however, as we shall shortly see, is very present and has been highly influential, especially in primary schools.

Educational ideologies

An educational ideology is any package of educational ideas held by a group of people about formal arrangements for education, typically expressed by contrasting two patterns of opposed assumptions such as teacher-centred and child-centred methods (the *Plowden Report* – DES 1967) or traditional and progressive methods (Bennett 1976). Going beyond dichotomies, Davies (1969) and Cosin (1972) outline four ideologies of education: (1) conservative or elitist, which maintains cultural hegemony; (2) revisionist or technocratic, which is concerned with vocational relevance; (3) romantic or individualist or psychological, which focuses on individual development and derives from the work of Pestalozzi, Froebel, Herbart, Montessori and Piaget; and (4) democratic socialist or liberal tradition or egalitarian, which seeks equality of opportunity and the progressive elimination of elitist values (Meighan and Siraj-Blatchford 1998). These categories are not hermetic, nor are they entirely mutually exclusive; they overlap and indeed an educational ideology might belong to several categories simultaneously. Assuming one accepts these categories as valid at all, the category(ies) to which a particular ideology might be assigned is often a matter of perspective.

Any ideology can be compared with others on the basis of a series of theories functioning as part of an aspect of knowledge, learning, teaching resources, organisation, assessments and aims. The concept of ideology can be used as an analytical tool to compare various patterns of education. Ideologies operate at different conceptual levels and, if categorised into levels of operations, can be compared along the lines of whole education systems, competing ideologies within a national system, ideologies within formal education and ideologies of classroom practice. Ideologies are usually linked: for example, ideologies of classroom practice may be linked to other parts of the educational and political network. The levels at which ideologies operate can be seen nationally in terms of Education Acts; regionally in terms of Local Education Authorities; locally at the levels of educational establishments, rival groups within educational establishments, classroom, teacher–learner interaction, and rival groups within the classroom (Meighan and Siraj-Blatchford 1998).

One could also distinguish between ideologies of legitimation or implementation, the former concerning goals, values and ends and the latter the means, and it can be a worthwhile exercise to consider the ideologies outlined below in this light.

Educational ideologies and politics

By definition education is a political activity in the broad sense, although this does not necessarily mean that it is a party political activity. Politics has to do with power and the distribution of power. Education has to do with knowledge (whether in terms of knowing that or knowing how). If knowledge is power, then education is political. If Gramsci's theory of hegemony (see Chapter 1) is accurate, then politics is an educational activity and education is a political activity. All educators have an ideology, whether formally articulated or not, or whether they are aware of having an ideology. To subscribe to a particular view of the aims of education is to subscribe to an educational ideology. Debate about the nature and purpose of education is therefore 'bound to be not only ideological but, in the broad sense, political as well' (Winch and Gingell 1999: 111).

Often people think, it would seem, that there is a correlation between political views and educational views. The correlation is usually that left-wing political views and support for child-centred or progressive education go hand in hand. This may have been more true at particular times, but it need not necessarily be so. Three examples illustrate the fact that political and educational ideologies cannot necessarily be subsumed into each other, although they certainly overlap.

The first example concerns two Labour personalities who had different educational ideologies. In his Ruskin speech of 1976 the Labour prime minister James Callaghan acknowledged his indebtedness to R.H. Tawney, who had been one of the originators of the Labour Party programme on education many years previously. Ironically, Callaghan and Tawney had very different views on most educational issues. Tawney defended liberal values, teacher autonomy and social democratic meritocracy. Callaghan, in his speech, advocated greater state control, teacher accountability and parentocracy, that is, more power to parents and less to the teachers. Callaghan aimed at increasing state control over education and over the curriculum, whereas Tawney had fought to remove central government's hold on the curriculum. He feared that government might abuse its power over the curriculum to serve the interests of industry or political ideologies instead of serving the interests of the pupils, who were best served by the professional judgement of the teachers. Callaghan questioned the power of the teachers over the curriculum and thought that teachers should be more accountable to parents and to industry (Brooks 1991).

The second example is that of a Marxist who had nothing but contempt for progressive educational ideologies. Antonio Gramsci, who thought that education had the power to affect political consciousness, advocated conservative schooling for radical politics (Entwistle 1979) and there could be no time for what he considered to be the playful experimentation approach of progressive educational methods. Instead, as much as possible of literacy, numeracy, history, politics and economics and science had to be learned as quickly as possible. In order to be in a position to counteract the dominant hegemony one had to learn what the dominant hegemony learned through education and much more. Learning had to be done in a concentrated systematic and disciplined intellectual way. Incidentally, the surfeit of playful experimentation and the opening up of the imagination was one of the major reasons behind the erstwhile Soviet Union abandoning in 1931 the very progressive and child-centred Dalton Plan that had been introduced from the United States shortly after the Russian Revolution. The Soviet Union needed to industrialise rapidly and discovery methods with self-directed learning were simply not delivering the expertise quickly enough (Grant 1979).

A third example is that a form of selective secondary schooling for all was introduced in the UK by a Labour government after the Second World War, which is currently associated with right-of-centre politics; and the Conservative Party has, over many years, much criticised comprehensive education that was widely introduced from the end of the 1960s onwards, replacing state-funded selective schooling in many areas but not all. The Conservative government, however, did not stop the spread of comprehensive schools but accelerated it. In 1967, the Conservative Party leader, Edward Heath, stated that 'it has never been a Conservative principle that in order to achieve [selection or grouping by ability] children have to be segregated in different institutions' (Heath in Finn *et al.* 1978: 176).

Political ideas and ideologies evolve and their expression in educational circumstances evolves too. Indeed, the apparently same educational ideology can be adopted simultaneously or consecutively by different political ideologies. This is the case not only with selective and comprehensive schools, but also with standards and achievement or equality of opportunity and, more recently, the application of market principles to education and the idea of 'privatisation' not only not rejected by Labour, but taken even further and then endorsed by the coalition government elected in 2010 (see Chapter 13).

Some examples of educational ideologies

An elitist ideology: the public school ethos

Perhaps the best illustration of an elitist ideology is the sort which is held to underpin the education of a country's ruling class. This kind of ideology is important not only for the way in which it might be held to form the ideas and behaviour of the ruling class, but also for the influence it has on the education of the non-ruling class.

Everyone knows something of the public school ethos or public school spirit. The largely autobiographical novel *Tom Brown's School Days*, whether faithful portrayal or 'romantic fiction and expurgated fact' (Chandos 1984: 45), has helped reinforce the mystique of the public school ethos, the 'pragmatic, almost unsupervised, trial-and-error, sink-or-swim test for survival in a self-governing community of male juveniles' (Chandos 1984: 38).

Its principal values are those of character over intellect and the importance of physicality. School is a place to train character. It is what came to distinguish the English public school from all other Western approaches to education or educational institutions. It is what 'impresses and amazes foreigners' (Gathorne-Hardy 1977: 75).

In France, Germany and even Scotland schools not only drew from the wider social spectrum, but were academic institutions only; character was left to the family (Vaizey 1977). Examples of the public school ethos can be found in *Tom Brown's School Days*. The first example is from the point of view of Tom's father:

> Shall I tell him to mind his work, and say he's sent to school to make himself a good scholar? Well, but he isn't in school for that – at any rate, not for that mainly. I don't care a straw for Greek particles, or the digamma, no more does his mother. What is he sent to school for? … If only he'll turn out a brave, helpful, truth-telling Englishman, and a gentleman, and a Christian, that's all I want.
>
> (Hughes [1857] 1963: 71–72)

The second example demonstrates that Tom himself seems to have fully internalised the importance of physicality and that character mattered more than intellectual achievement, which constitutes the fundamental values of the public school ethos:

> I want to be A1 at cricket and football, and all the other games, and to make my hands keep my head against any fellow, lout or gentleman. … I want to carry away just as much Latin and Greek as will take me through Oxford respectably.
>
> (Hughes [1857] 1963: 262)

Public schools pre-date the emergence of the British Empire. The most distinguished date from the High Medieval period. The public school ethos is therefore a package of ideas, values and associated practices that have grown up over time. However, it was in the Imperial period that their role, nature and ethos became most clearly defined. The main aim of the education of those who attended public schools was to develop a certain sort of character. This would be one in which self-control and 'stiff upper lip' would be of the greater importance as it gave clear imperial advantage. It was well suited to the needs of the army but equally suited to other forms and aspects of imperial service, from missionary work to exploration and administration (Matheson and Limond 1999).

Henry Newbolt's poem 'Vitai Lampada' from *Poems Old and New* (1912) linked together Empire and the public school: 'The sand of the desert is sodden/Red with the wreck of a square that broke;/the river of death has brimmed his banks,/ … But the voice of the schoolboy rallies the ranks: "Play up! Play up! and play the game".' The Empire is no more but the public school ethos endures, be it in modified form. *Tom Brown's School Days* gave rise to the public school novel and the public school memoirs. The magic derives from the myth and the myth derives from literature.[1] The public school ethos survives not just because the public school mystique has a firm hold on popular imagination, but also and most especially because the public school continues to educate the ruling class.

The Clarendon Commission (1864), an investigation of the nine leading public schools, found that

> The average school boy was almost ignorant of geography and of the history of his own country, unacquainted with any modern language but his own and hardly competent to write English correctly, to do a simple sum; a total stranger to the laws which govern the physical world.
>
> (Quoted in Martin 1979: 60)

Nonetheless, the public schools were praised for 'their public spirit, their vigour and manliness of character' as well as 'their love of healthy sport and exercise' and above all the fact that 'they have had perhaps the largest share in moulding the character of an English gentleman' (quoted in Martin 1979: 65).

Today the public school ethos endures, not only in about the tenth or so of English schools that are independent schools, both day and boarding schools, and are thus not financed by the state, but it also permeates to some extent the whole of the English education system. More particularly, the public school ethos endures in what are allegedly 'education's best kept secret' (Hackett 2001: 10): that there remains in England about 36 state boarding schools where one can get what amounts to a public school place for between one-third and half of what it would cost to send one's child(ren) to an independent school. The government pays for the teaching and parents for food and accommodation, at around £10,000.[2] Such schools are praised and prized for their discipline, importance given to team sports and excellent exam results (Hackett 2001). Such importance given to academic achievement is a more recent development within the ideology of the public school ethos.

Some romantic or psychological ideologies

The romantic or psychological ideology, derived from the naturalism of Rousseau, was central to the establishment of progressive schools and has had considerable influence on some forms of curriculum revision and on primary schools. Working within this ideology was perhaps the greatest influence upon the modern primary school curriculum: John Dewey, who argued against the subservience of the child to a curriculum devised for him/her by adults, with its logical division of subject matters and little notice taken of the child's interest. For him, 'the child is the starting point, the centre, the end. His[/her] development, his[/her] growth, is the ideal' (Dewey 1906: 21 in Curtis 1965: 162). This centrality of the child to the schooling process can perhaps be said to have reached its peak in the UK, and especially in England, with the *Plowden Report* (DES 1967).

In its own terms, Plowdenism emphasises such things as, 'Learning … [but] not [by] … direct teaching … [and] working harmoniously according to an unfolding rather than a preconceived plan' (Maclure 1973: 313). Plowden's was the pedagogy of learning by doing and following one's interests or enthusiasms. It was influenced by developmental psychology such as that of Piaget, Dewey and Montessori. A long time before Plowden it had been officially approved as an educational ideology in England. The Report of the Consultative Committee on *The Primary School* (1931: 75) backed the idea that 'the curriculum is to be thought in terms of activity and experience, rather than of knowledge to be acquired and facts to be stored'. The aim of education was to open up the imagination. The cramming of factual or propositional knowledge (knowing that) was condemned, but experience and activity or procedural knowledge (knowing how) were advocated instead. Schooling would be based on scientific ideas of how the child grows and changes. The purpose was to meet the needs of those processes because anything else would be counterproductive in practice, if not also morally wrong. Just as the Reports of the Consultative Committee on *The Primary school* (1931) and on *The Nursery School* (1933) were full of metaphors about growth and nurture and psychological needs, so was the *Plowden Report*, which stressed that education should foster flexibility and adaptability to an economically changing world. Such an ideology saw the aims of education as psychological harmony and saw intellectualism as detrimental to that psychological harmony. The importance of getting on with others and understanding them was stressed, along with psychological balance:

> They will need as always to be able to live with their fellows, appreciating and respecting their differences, understanding and sympathizing with their feelings.… They will need to be well balanced, with neither the emotions nor the intellect giving ground to each other.
>
> (DES 1967, §§494–496)

In the 1960s there was an increasing commitment to child-centred education as local authorities moved away from the 11+ examinations and the number of comprehensive schools increased (Brooks 1991). The *Plowden Report* deplored that some teachers 'still used books of English exercises and of mechanical computation' (DES 1967 quoted in Brooks 1991: 92). However, the Black Papers regarded Plowdenism as a libertarian charter and Callaghan's Ruskin Speech denounced progressivism. The prime minister seemed to have accepted much of the Black Papers propaganda about declining standards, but the ideology promulgated in Plowdenism was far from being what was actually happening in English schools (Brooks 1991).

Although often half-heartedly implemented, Plowdenism can nevertheless be seen as the British, or more specifically English, culmination of the romantic or individualist/psychological tradition (Matheson and Limond 1999). So Plowden had arguably a non-negligible influence in British primary classrooms until the advent in England and Wales of the National Curriculum, with its emphasis on cognitive performance. To its critics it is misguided and even a libertarian charter that promulgates the pursuit of 'relevance' to oneself as the essential criterion of intellectual worth. To its supporters it is 'a truth which has never been fully tested in practice because it has often been misunderstood or overlaid only very thinly as a veneer on existing practices and principles' (Matheson and Limond 1999: 22).

In all, Plowdenism bears a striking resemblance to Montessorism, the theories of Maria Montessori articulated in *The Montessori Method* (1912) and *The Advanced Montessori Method* (1917). The former deals with mentally or socially disabled children and the latter applies the deriving principles to non-disabled children. In other words, Maria Montessori advocates a psychological method implying that 'the educative process is adapted to the stage of mental development of the child, and to his/her interests and is not wholly subordinated to the necessities of a curriculum or to the teacher's scheme of work' (Rusk 1954: 262). Like that of Plowdenism, Montessori's own child-centred progressive pedagogy, with emphasis on freedom and auto-education, is associated with the names of Rousseau, Pestalozzi, Froebel, Herbart, Dewey and Piaget. Such a pedagogy aims to replace traditional pedagogy, whereby the teacher maintains discipline and immobility and engages in loud and continual discourse, 'by didactic material which contains within itself the control of errors' and thus 'makes auto-education possible to each child' (Montessori 1912: 371). She later added that 'to make the process one of self-education, it is not enough that the stimulus should call forth activity, it must also direct it' (Montessori 1917: 71).

Montessori's emphasis on interest as a driving force for the learner finds a modern echo in Malcolm Knowles' (1998) idea of andragogy (although, unlike Montessori, Knowles thought primarily of adult learners). Interest as a motivator has, however, a much longer heritage and was defined as 'the doctrine of interest' by Herbart, who derived the idea from Rousseau but expanded upon it (Herbart 1816 in Rusk 1954: 210).

Herbart asserts that 'that which is too simple must be avoided' and 'instruction must be comprehensible and yet difficult rather than easy, otherwise it causes *ennui* [boredom]' (Herbart 1901 quoted in Rusk 1954: 225). Herbart further asserts that 'the principle of interest braces [pupils] up to endure all manner of drudgery and hard work, the idea being 'of making drudgery tolerable by giving it a meaning' (Adams quoted in Rusk 1954: 225). The doctrine of interest, however, is to be found in Plato's

Republic, Rousseau's *Emile* and Pestalozzi's correspondence. Herbart also advocated the principle of recapitulation or spiral curriculum, which is a doctrine common to many educators from Plato to Montessori and Dewey. For Herbart, there is no education without instruction and conversely no instruction which does not educate (Rusk 1954). Paradoxically, for an educational ideologist in the romantic tradition, Herbart ascribes to the teacher a centrality which is largely absent from those whose ideas derived from his (Dewey 1923).

A revisionist ideologist: Herbert Spencer

Herbert Spencer challenged the traditional curriculum and 'liberal education' by classifying the subjects, with scientific subjects being seen as the most important because the knowledge which enables one to earn a living should come first in the curriculum and literary subjects should occupy the 'lowest place on the scale' (Curtis 1965). Spencer further asserted that 'education of whatever kind, has for its proximate end to prepare a child for the business of life – to produce a citizen who, while he [she] is well conducted, is also able to make his [her] way in the world' (Spencer 1911 in Curtis 1965: 154).

Spencer presents several facets of the doctrine of relevancy (i.e. relevant to the economy and relevant to the learner's future quality of life). The importance of this former facet in educational and economic debate should not be understated. Other than its returning to the forefront of debates with a great frequency (e.g. in Callaghan's 1976 Ruskin College speech), the doctrine suggests a great number of questions. How might it be determined *how* a learner is going to earn his/her living? How can we know what economic needs there will be in the future? To what extent does formal education not already instil *pre*-vocational skills? Spencer wrote at a time of economic stability, when the future appeared largely to be a direct continuation of the present, which itself flowed seamlessly from the past. Our future now appears much more uncertain – but is this reason sufficient to discard Spencer's ideas? Even relevancy to the economy is relative, as is discussed at length by White (1997). There are also questions which arise out of the second facet: the business of life also appears to be in mutation but are there underlying skills and values which the learner needs to acquire in order to be successful (by some measure or other) in the ways of the world? We no longer have the consensual moral frameworks that we arguably had at times in the past. Therefore, what skills or values need the learner acquire? And who is to decide these? In sum, to apply the doctrine of relevance, be it to the economy's future (or actual) needs or to the learner's future (or actual) needs, we are obliged to decide who is to decide these needs, on what basis (i.e. on what criteria) and to what end(s). Fundamentally, we need decide what education is for.

Liberal or egalitarian ideology

The democratic intellect

The philosophical underpinning of the Scottish education system appears to stand in opposition to the English education system. Both ideologies associated with the dominant values of each system are linked to the history of education in each country. For Scots of the nineteenth century, education had become a badge of national identity, instead of being associated with the privileged ruling class. Education was 'a potent symbol of Scottishness and one of the ways in which a sense of nationhood was preserved without in any way threatening the basic structure of the union with England' (Devine 1999: 389). This 'national' education system had been established by John Knox and his fellow reformers in the *Book of Discipline* in the sixteenth century. Its ideology remained a guiding principle for Scottish education. It was not only meritocratic, but according to some, even egalitarian, resting on a ladder of opportunity going from parish schools to burgh schools and then universities, although burgh schools could be bypassed and it was possible for a boy who had talent to go from the parish school to university after he had been given some post-elementary education by the parish schoolmaster in mathematics and Latin (Stephens 1998).

Although not an autobiographical novel, as was *Tom Brown's School Days*, Ian Maclaren's novel *Beside the Bonnie Briar Bush* exemplifies and reinforces an educational tradition and hence its ideology. The teacher who 'could detect a scholar in the egg, and prophesied Latinity from a boy who was only fit to be a cowherd' (Maclaren 1940: 8) is the leader of the local community. His function is to spot likely talent for intellectual endeavour and then persuade the family to live frugally to save up, and the better-off members of the community to give their help to put together the money for the university fees.

The term 'democratic intellectualism' was coined in 1919 by Walter Elliot, then Conservative Secretary of State for Scotland, and is associated with the works of George Elder Davie. The term is used to characterise Scotland's post-Reformation and Enlightenment history (Davie 1961: 75) in terms of thoughtful citizenship, reasoned participation and thriving intellectual debate derived from the fact that until the middle of the nineteenth century Scottish universities nurtured and promoted a set of highly distinctive academic values. The main mechanism of this nurturing and promotion was their concentration on teaching philosophy in a system that only went into decline when forced to change from the 1840s and 1850s (Bell and Grant 1977).

Davie was a lecturer in philosophy at Edinburgh University. He argued that the true nature of Scotland's educational tradition was democratic intellectualism and deplored the way this true nature had been eroded by closer contact with England (Davie 1993). He argued that Scotland's educational ideology fitted broadly into a European tradition of generalist curriculum and philosophy-centred higher education. This was contrasted to the insular and eccentric English narrowness of curriculum and specialised 'Honours' courses. Not only was there wider access to universities in Scotland, but also a wider and more balanced curriculum with the study of philosophy firmly at its centre (Bell 2000). To understand this point fully it is necessary to think of philosophy not as an academic subject, but as a way of encouraging students to inquire into issues and ideas, morals and metaphysics. In English universities (and at the start of the nineteenth century England had only two, while Scotland, with a tenth of the population, had four) the emphasis was on teaching a precise grasp of Latin and Greek grammar through studying Latin and Greek authors. In Scotland, by contrast, the emphasis was more on understanding what these authors had said rather than how they expressed themselves. (It was thus far more acceptable in Scottish universities to read classical authors in translation.) The ideas expressed in their words were of greater importance than the words themselves, thus the Scottish interest was philosophical rather than literary (Matheson and Limond 1999). The common sense of the subject was put before questions of detail. An understanding of ancient civilisation was preferable to textual study (Davie 1961). Asking and answering philosophical questions was always of prime importance, as was enlightenment over erudition, hence more morals and metaphysics than literature and language (Beveridge and Craig 1989). There was specific teaching of philosophy as a compulsory subject in its own right, but the weaving of philosophical concerns into all other subjects was of far greater significance (Matheson and Limond 1999).

Social democracy

In the period 1944 to 1970, educational policy was based upon the ideology of 'social democracy' constructed by three social groups who formed a coalition: the Labour Party (although supported in much of this by the Conservative Party), educationalists working in sociology and economics and the teaching profession. The key features of the ideology of 'social democracy' were: a commitment to educational progress through state policy and a concern with access and equality of opportunity. Reform was via the state (the state being seen as neutral) and was for the benefit of all sections of society, especially the underprivileged. A focus of attention in social democracy was working-class under-achievement and wastage of ability and, as a consequence, the idea of non-selective comprehensive schools slowly emerged. Teachers, for their part, pursued professional status and demanded autonomy and control of the curriculum. The notion was promoted, and accepted, that teachers knew what was best for their pupils.

A clarion call of social democracy was equality of opportunity in education, a notion fraught with conceptual difficulties. In a simple form, equality of opportunity can be seen as open and fair competition for economic rewards and social privileges. The problems arise when one tries to determine what is open and fair. The way in which this meaning shifted in the UK is demonstrated by the move by socialists from supporting selective secondary schools in the 1940s and 1950s to calling for a total end to selection for secondary school from the 1960s onwards. Both the generalisation of selective secondary school and the abolition of selective secondary school were justified on the grounds of equality of opportunity. However, coupled with equality of opportunity was also equality per se (Finn et al. 1978). Arguably, equality of opportunity equalises the chances people have to become unequal. It is therefore incompatible with any notion of equality as reducing privilege, except perhaps privilege of birth. Equality of opportunity does, however, give rise to the notion of the meritocracy, whereby everyone has, in theory, the same chances to go as far as their talents will take them. As this inevitably leads to the creation or at least the sustenance of an elite, it is perhaps best described as an elitist ideology hiding away in an apparently egalitarian one. This only goes to show the lack of mutual exclusivity of the four categories of educational ideology mentioned above.

In the 1970s the ideology of social democracy was finally challenged, largely because of its failure to promote economic growth and growing concerns about falling standards and indiscipline in schools. James Callaghan's 1976 speech in Ruskin College, Oxford effectively sounded the death knell for social democracy in education. Callaghan called for more control of teachers and more accountability from schools. Education, he claimed, should be seen as a means for training young people for work. The effect was the official beginning of the process that led to the National Curriculum in England and Wales, with its concomitant national testing, OfSTED and the full trappings of direct state control over schools (Chitty 1993).

The best of all worlds or neither one thing nor another

The Third Way

In 1998 Anthony Giddens came up with a new political ideology, the Third Way. (He borrowed much of his ideas from the New Democrats in the United States who, a few years before New Labour, wanted to be seen to have moved away from the Left and towards the Right to attract votes.) Giddens' book provoked a storm of interest and controversy (Giddens 1998). He wrote a response to his critics two years later (Giddens 2000).

The Third Way is an attempt to find a path between the New Right and the Old Left as there is a need to move away from the sterile debate between Left and Right, or between those who favour either the state or the free market doing everything. It was brought about by the realities of the modern world, that is, the dissolution of the welfare consensus, the rapid technological changes of the Information Age, globalisation and the discrediting of Marxism. It aims to combine social solidarity with a dynamic economy, to stress equality of opportunity, not of outcome, and to concentrate on the creation of wealth and not its redistribution (Giddens 1998). What does this really mean in theory and in practice? Its critics say it is an empty concept without any real content, an intellectual cover for those whose principles are sufficiently flexible to accommodate any type of wealth creation and a betrayal of left-wing ideals.

In terms of education, this new ideology is based on the idea that there is no viable alternative to the market economy. So the Third Way is really Social Democracy, because social justice and equality of opportunity are encouraged, but instead of the state paying the full cost of this, market principles are necessary to lessen state ownership, state funding and state intervention, and to encourage private initiatives to play their part in the educational process. The Third Way wants to encourage the less talented to succeed as the exclusion of the less able is feared as much as the withdrawal of the most able. This has to be prevented by improving education to such an extent, with the help of market forces, that someone with money will chose not to pay for their child(ren)'s education. Critics have ridiculed this idea by underlining that this would mean that the state must take so much in tax from everyone in order to afford to offer a state education that would attract those who previously chose to send their child(ren) to independent schools, and who now would become a burden to the taxpayer by no longer doing this!

Conclusion

This has only been a brief look at the role of ideology in education and, of necessity, it has been an eclectic look. There is a multitude of other educational ideologies that might equally merit inclusion, but space does not permit this. I have not specifically discussed the ideological precepts which underpin the National Curriculum or the development of academies in England, although some of these are dealt with in other chapters. I have omitted the ideology of the market which has set schools and universities in competition with each other in a bid to attract students and other sources of funding. I have not considered the ideology of 'privatisation'. Other chapters in this volume take up again the theme of ideology in education under different guises. There are educational ideologies based on gender, 'race', social class, age, culture and the nature of learning itself, to name but a few that are touched upon.

It is, however, worth remembering that few, if any, ideologies actually bear the name openly. Rather, we have various collections of notions, ideas and beliefs which may apply better to one level of education than to another (and this can mean, for example, applying better to a macro-perspective than to a micro-perspective) by which not only is behaviour influenced or even determined, but the very ways in which we think about phenomena may themselves be set. In this light, it can be worth wondering why comprehensive *secondary* school can rouse so much passion but comprehensive *primary* school never has. Is this through a rational choice on our part or is it through our internalising of an ideological precept which precludes the stimulation of heated debates over the possibility of non-comprehensive primary school?

Ideologies are not static. They evolve and they may expire, as did Scottish Democratic Intellectualism, although arguably until the re-establishment of the Scottish Parliament in 1999 this ideology had a few remaining vestiges in the form of the Scottish Ordinary degree which, unlike its English counterpart, is not (usually) a failed Honours degree but a general, as opposed to a specialised, degree. One of the first concerns of the Scottish Parliament was to set out to abolish university fees, as this was seen to go against a tradition and ideology articulated within a country that was not only proud of having a wider social intake in higher education than England, but wanted to be seen to promote the accessibility of higher education better than England. The more important role of the teacher within Democratic Intellectualism can also be seen in the fact that the Scottish Parliament decided to substantially increase teachers' salaries.

In terms of the public school ethos, the discourse of excellence and achievement, or rather of 'league tables' and 'exam results', is more marketable and resonates better than that of character. The importance of character formation gave way to psychological well-being, which was the cornerstone of progressive education. Recently there has been a revival of character education in Britain. The White Paper *Schools: Achieving Success* (DES 2001) talked of 'education with character' and linked this with the promotion of citizenship education.

Whether any of these, or the other ideologies mentioned, were ever true (or valid as the case may be) is another issue, but one we shall not pursue. Truth/validity depends on perspective. What is important in all these ideologies is not their truth or validity, but rather the impact they have had, and in some cases continue to have.

Notes

1. Of course there has in more recent years been the influence of the Harry Potter books and films, where magic and myth come together and which have engendered a greater interest from children in attending boarding schools and public school.
2. See www.sbsa.org.uk.

References

Bell, R. (2000) Scottish Universities, *Comparative Education*, 36 (2), 163–175.

Bell, R. and Grant, N. (1977) *Patterns of Education in the British Isles*. London: Unwin Education Books.

Bennett, S.N. (1976) *Teaching Styles and Pupils' Progress*. London: Open Books.

Beveridge, C. and Craig, R. (1989) *The Eclipse of Scottish Culture*. Edinburgh: Polygon.

Brooks, R. (1991) *Contemporary Debates in Education: A Historical Perspective*. London and New York: Longman.

Bullock, A., Stallybrass, O. and Trombley, S. (eds) (1988) *The Fontana Dictionary of Modern Thought*. London: Fontana Press.

Chandos, J. (1984) *Boys Together: English Public Schools 1800–1864*. Newhaven, CT and London: Yale University Press.

Chitty, C. (1993) *The Education System Transformed*. London: Baseline Books.

Clarendon Commission (1864) *On the Principal Public Schools*. London: HMSO.

Cosin, B. (1972) *Ideology*. Milton Keynes: Open University Press.

Curtis, S.J. (1965) *Introduction to the Philosophy of Education*. Foxton: University Tutorial Press.

Dancy, J. and Sosa, E. (eds) (1993) *A Companion to Epistemology*. Oxford and Cambridge, MA: Blackwell.

Davie, G.E. (1961) *The Democratic Intellect: Scotland and her Universities in the Nineteenth Century*. Edinburgh: Edinburgh University Press.

Davie, G.E. (1993) The Importance of the Ordinary MA, *Edinburgh Review*, 90, 61–69.

Davies, I. (1969) Education and Social Science, *New Society*, 8 May.

Department for Education and Skills (DES) (2001) *Schools: Achieving Success*. London: The Stationery Office.

Department of Education and Science (DES) (1967) *Children and their Primary Schools (The Plowden Report)*. London: HMSO.

Devine, T. (1999) *The Scottish Nation 1700–2000*. London: Penguin.

Dewey, J. (1906) *The School and the Child*. Glasgow: Blackie.

Dewey, J. (1923) *Democracy and Education*. New York: Macmillan.

Entwistle, H. (1979) *Conservative Schooling for Radical Politics*. London: Routledge.

Feuer, L.S. (1975) *Ideology and the Ideologists*. Oxford: Basil Blackwell.

Finn, D., Grant, N. and Johnson, R. (1978) Social Democracy, Education and the Crisis. In Centre for Contemporary Cultural Studies, *On Ideology*. London: Hutchinson.

Gathorne-Hardy, J. (1977) *The Public School Phenomenon 597–1977*. London: Hodder and Stoughton.

Giddens, A. (1998) *The Third Way: The Renewal of Social Democracy*. Cambridge: Polity Press.

Giddens, A. (2000) *The Third Way and its Critics*. Cambridge: Polity Press.

Grant, N. (1979) *Soviet Education*. Harmondsworth: Penguin.

Hackett, G. (2001) Boarders on a Budget, *Sunday Times*, 23 September, 10–11.

Hall, S. (1978) The Hinterland of Science: Ideology and the 'Sociology of Knowledge'. In Centre for Contemporary Cultural Studies, *On Ideology*. London: Hutchinson.

Hughes, T. ([1857] 1963) *Tom Brown's School Days*. London and Glasgow: Collins.

Knowles, M. (1998) *The Adult Learner*. Houston, TX: Gulf Publishing.

Larrain, J. (1979) *The Concept of Ideology*. London: Hutchinson University Library.

Lichtheim, J. (1967) *The Concept of Ideology and Other Essays*. New York: Vintage.

Lockhart Walker, A. (1994) *The Revival of the Democratic Intellect*. Edinburgh: Polygon.

McLean, M. (1995) *Education Traditions Compared*. London: David Fulton.

Maclure, J.S. (1973) *Educational Documents England and Wales 1816 to the Present Day*. London: Methuen.

Martin, C. (1979) *A Short History of English Schools 1750–1965*. Hove: Wayland.

Marx, K. and Engels, F. ([1845–1847] 1970) *The German Ideology*. London: Lawrence & Wishart.

Matheson, C. and Limond, D. (1999) Ideology in Education in the UK. In D. Matheson and I. Grosvenor (eds), *An Introduction to the Study of Education*, 1st edn. London: David Fulton.

Meighan, R. and Siraj-Blatchford, I. (1998) *A Sociology of Educating*, 3rd edn. London: Cassell.

Montessori, M. (1912) *The Montessori Method*. London: Heinemann.

Montessori, M. (1917) *The Advanced Montessori Method*. London: Heinemann.

Newbolt, H. (1912), *Poems: Old and New*. London: John Murray.

Report of the Hadow Consultative Committee (1931) *The Primary School*. London: HMSO.

Reports of the Consultative Committee (1933) *Infant and Nursery Schools*. London: HMSO.

Rey, A. and Rey-Debove, J. (1990) *Le Petit Robert*. Paris: Dictionnaires Le Robert.

Rusk, R.R. (1954) *The Doctrines of the Great Educators*. London: Macmillan.

Sokal, A. and Bricmont, J. (1998) *Intellectual Impostures*. London: Profile Books (UK); *Fashionable Nonsense*. New York: Picador.

Stephens, W.B. (1998) *Education in Britain 1750–1914*. London: Macmillan.

Summer, C. (1979) *Reading Ideologies*. London: Academic Press.

Vaizey, L. (1977) Facts, Theories and Emotions. In G. Macdonald-Fraser (ed.), *The World of the Public School*. London: Weidenfeld and Nicholson.

White, J. (1997) *Education and the End of Work*. London: Cassell.

Winch, C. and Gingell, J. (1999) *Key Concepts in the Philosophy of Education*. London and New York: Routledge.

3

Theories of learning

Constructive experience

Reg Dennick

There is nothing more practical than a good theory.

Kurt Lewin

Introduction and outline

This chapter first of all outlines what is meant by 'theory' in the context of education and learning and then describes some of the major theories. In addition, it attempts to make connections between what are often seen as separate theoretical areas by identifying some unifying concepts and relationships. By doing so, a synthesis will be revealed giving these areas a coherence that will be practically useful for teachers and educators.

I propose to briefly describe the nature of scientific theory and its relationship to educational/sociological theory. I will then examine a number of key educational theories in more detail, explaining their origins, assumptions and structure. I will look first at constructivist theories of learning as I believe they have the widest application to all modes of learning, whether in the classroom, the lecture theatre, online or in the workplace. Next, I will examine theories associated with experiential learning, as they have particular relevance to learning in professional, working, environments. Both of these two theories are strongly associated with the scientific method and I will attempt to unify these theories by showing that the way the scientific community creates new knowledge, in its broadest and multidisciplinary sense, is mirrored in the cognitive processes of the individual. Finally, I will outline how humanistic theories of the individual learner can connect to and support these learning theories.

When describing and explaining the above three theories I will make connections to a variety of other educational frameworks, which will be briefly mentioned, and attempt to show that they are all related to elements of the main theories. Finally, I will attempt to synthesise these theories into what I will term 'constructive experience'. I will outline connections between all these theoretical frameworks by demonstrating that the mechanism of experiential learning is consistent with a constructivist model of learning and that humanistic theories of the individual can underpin both of these models. A unifying principle will be the scientific method in its broadest aspect, encompassing the hard and social sciences, which not only socially creates new knowledge, but from a constructivist perspective is arguably a model of the learning process in the individual.

What is a theory?

In common usage the term 'theory' is often merely used to refer to a conjecture or idea used to explain an event or situation. In addition it frequently has the connotation of something which is not necessarily true, as in 'it's only a theory'. However, the concept of a theory has a deeper meaning in the context of scientific thinking (Chalmers 1999). Scientific usage implies a much more elaborate framework, often constructed after a whole series of hypotheses have been proposed, tested and supported by empirical evidence. This produces a set of concepts, ideas and facts that together provide a coherent framework for describing and predicting the properties and behaviour of some specified phenomena or domain of reality. A theory has often been derived via empirical observation and deliberate experimentation, and its presentation is sometimes formalised by mathematical notation. A theory is therefore much more than just an idea.

Importantly, a theory can be disproved. Nevertheless, because many theories have stood the test of time, for example quantum theory, relativity theory, evolutionary theory, they do achieve a high truth status. This status is achieved by virtue of the fact that each theory more or less corresponds to an area of reality and is capable of explaining and predicting it, frequently with great accuracy. A theory's ability to explain and predict provides support to the view that somehow it is mirroring 'reality'. One commonly held interpretation of the scientific method and the epistemology of science assumes that there is a real, objective world 'out there' that can be understood and modelled by scientific theories. Their truth value is measured by how well they map onto the reality they purport to describe, but they can be falsified and refuted by the presence of observations and anomalies that do not fit or contradict their predictions, or by rational and logical analysis. As will be explained, a feature of a 'good' scientific theory is that it should be capable of refutation or falsification by rational or empirical evidence.

The domain of education and learning, however, is predominantly the realm of the social sciences; conventional scientific theories, as described above, do not necessarily map onto the facts, experiences and relationships found in these areas. Many of the assumptions underpinning the scientific method itself are seen as problematic. For example, the very existence of an objective, social and interpersonal world that exists independently of our assumptions, prejudices and biases is called into question, as is the idea that observations of social systems can be carried out objectively. In addition, in many cases it is impossible to manipulate and experiment on social systems in the way that the natural sciences might do as there are profound methodological differences and ethical difficulties to consider. This does not prevent the creation of social and educational theories, but the criteria used to determine their validity and truth value do not have the same 'objective' status as those used for scientific theories. Some of the more extreme versions of social theorising, such as might be found in 'critical theory' and postmodernism, may not even be related to any form of empirical observations or evidence at all. (For a useful review of contemporary sociology theorising, see Benton and Craib 2001.)

There is no unifying theory of education or learning[1] and different areas are explored and studied by different disciplines. Useful general references for exploring educational theory are Curzon (1997), Jarvis *et al.* (1998), Knowles *et al.* (1998), Jarvis (2006) and Merriam *et al.* (2007). Unlike the 'hard' sciences, where theories are abandoned once they have been refuted by empirical evidence and become of interest only to historians of science, educational theories largely do not undergo this culling process, leading to a plurality of competing and complementary frameworks that co-exist. Elements from a variety of educational theories and their associated practices are frequently combined to help understand and optimise learning in many areas of teaching. It also seems to be the case that educational theories sometimes appear to be created by people in different disciplines or different educational traditions, and are then developed in isolation from each other. Some theories are virtually identical to other theories and yet the authors appear to be oblivious of each other's work. Other theories appear to be outgrowths or extensions of elements in another theory, again without the authors necessarily acknowledging this. Consequently, educational 'theory' contains a spectrum of frameworks ranging from the more empirical behaviourist theories through developmental and constructivist psychology and humanistic interpersonal frameworks to the unempirical and epistemologically relative end of the social sciences. However, if learning ultimately takes place in the brain, it has to be acknowledged that we are still a long way from providing a theory which connects overt human behaviour with 'objective' neurophysiology. The theories of learning described here use concepts and structures in a metaphorical way, their connections to underlying cerebral anatomy and processes as yet undefined.

Educational theories can be used to explain the structure of the curriculum and how it can be designed, whether for children or focused on higher education. There are also theories explaining how social, cultural and political factors influence the types of education existing in the world today in different countries and societies. The main theories described and explained here all have practical uses in the classroom, the lecture theatre, in working environments and in adult education. A feature of these particular theories is that they make predictions about what teachers and learners should do in order to optimise learning in given situations.

Constructivist models of learning

As the name implies, the constructivist view of learning is concerned with how learners *build* an understanding of the world. Implicit in the concept is that meaning and understanding are built up in a process that depends on the specific knowledge foundations and cognitive operations of each individual and the learning activities they engage in. Genuine understanding cannot be simply transmitted or copied from one brain to another without the receiving brain actively engaging in the process. Experience must be filtered through the learner's own personal knowledge constructs, to be assimilated into their conceptual frameworks in a process that enables the individual to find meaning in the world. Crucially, this process also involves modifying, demolishing and accommodating mental frameworks that no longer provide an adaptive advantage. Constructivist theory is associated with an evolutionary perspective that sees learning and the creation of mental models as an adaptation to the environment. Useful general references for exploring constructivist theory are Waltzlawick (1984), Tobin (1993), Fensham *et al.* (1994) Philips (1995) and Steffe and Gale (1995).[2]

In order to understand the nature of constructivist theory it is necessary to briefly describe the history of epistemology, that branch of philosophy that deals with the nature of knowledge. By understanding the origins of constructivist ideas in their historical context it will be seen that some of its underlying assumptions and concepts still play a very important role in contemporary educational theory.

Philosophical background

Two important epistemological strands can be traced back to the Greeks (Kelly 1986). Plato taught that true knowledge was located in, and could be generated by, the rational, thinking mind. He postulated that our minds were born with ideal 'forms' of knowledge and that the aim of human development was to understand these ideal and universal forms in areas such as beauty, truth, goodness and geometrical and logical reasoning. Reason was seen as a higher faculty than emotions or feelings. The world of sensory experiences, by contrast, was seen as a world of error, incompleteness and uncertainty, and knowledge derived from it was not to be trusted. This conception, that our minds contain innate knowledge and that new knowledge can be created by means of reason alone, is known as *rationalism*.

The other major strand, which can be traced back to Aristotle and his interest in the natural world, stressed the senses as the ultimate origin of knowledge and is known as *empiricism*.

These two epistemological theories became prominent by coming into conflict in the seventeenth century when the Christian world view in Western civilisation, with its political and religious dogma, started to break down and fragment, due in part to the empirical discoveries of Kepler, Copernicus, Galileo and ultimately Newton. During this period, known as the Enlightenment, empiricist philosophers such as Locke and Hume asserted that the mind was a *tabula rasa*, a blank slate written on by sensory experience. Empiricists asserted that there was nothing in the mind that was not previously presented to the senses and that thinking and reasoning was simply a process of connecting and relating ideas and thoughts that ultimately came from sensory experience. Supporting the development of science was the conception that new knowledge could be obtained by deliberate manipulation and experimentation on the external world. Empiricists, in contrast to rationalists, did not have a problem with the fact that the world of sensory experience was uncertain. They actively supported the idea that knowledge was tentative and provisional and encouraged an attitude of scepticism.

On the other hand, rationalist philosophers such as Descartes, Leibniz and Spinoza re-asserted the Platonic idea that the human mind was an intrinsic source of reason that could generate knowledge by thought alone, without the need for any sensory input. They were supported in this view by their belief that knowledge could be acquired through the application of reason, logic and mathematics. They assumed that as the world was God's creation, then God's laws would be embedded in our minds and hence reason alone should be able to understand God's world. Reflecting Plato's legacy, rational knowledge was considered to have a higher status than knowledge derived from the senses since it was certain knowledge of purity and truth.

It was the philosopher Immanuel Kant, in the eighteenth century, who synthesised these two epistemological positions (Kant 1983). Kant argued that knowledge could be created by combining these two processes and that our knowledge of the world is constructed from sensory experience filtered through and structured by the rational processes of the mind. Although the empiricists had stressed that human knowledge was constructed from sensations, because Kant asserted that there is an interaction between reason and sensory experience to build up knowledge of the world he can be seen as the father of modern constructivism. He further asserted that because knowledge of the world is mediated by innate rational processes, or 'intuitions' plus certain mental frameworks or 'categories' we see the world through space, time and causality tinted spectacles and we can never actually know the real world or 'things-in-themselves'. As will be seen, this view underpins 'radical' constructivism.

Educational implications of rationalism and empiricism

It is worthwhile looking at how the rationalist and empiricist traditions have developed as they have a bearing on a number of educational theories. They have essentially evolved into the two poles of the 'nature' and 'nurture' debate in contemporary thinking. Rationalism asserts an innate human nature which all human beings possess and which in today's understanding is a product of genetics. The empiricist tradition is dominated by the idea that human beings are fundamentally a product of their environment or nurture.

The empiricist tradition can be most clearly traced to Marxism and to twentieth-century sociological theories. The underlying connection here is that these philosophies share the concept that the individual is born into the world as a 'blank slate'. This implies that all human beings are products of their environment, of their nurture, and hence that changing their experiences and their environment will change the person. 'It is not the consciousness of men that determines their being, but, on the contrary, their social being that determines their consciousness' (Marx 1859: 1). The political implications of this philosophy are well known: Stalin, Mao Tse-tung and Pol Pot all believed that a communist society could be created by doing away with capitalist and bourgeois economic systems and the people who supported them. The proletariat, no longer influenced by capitalism, would then create the pure communist society. The consequences of this viewpoint have led to some of the worst genocides of the twentieth century. Sociologists have adopted a similar, but less draconian approach arguing that human behaviour, attitudes and thought are a direct creation of the economic and ideological structure of society. To many sociologists and postmodernists the idea of a human nature is anathema and human beings are considered to be mere puppets manipulated by external forces.

The empiricist perspective in education rejects the notion that some knowledge comes a priori from the rational mind, independently of the experience of the senses. It sees knowledge as uncertain and hypothetical and asserts that values are relative and human-made or 'socially constructed'. Its view of education and learning, therefore, is a tentative one. It sees the *development* of the individual as the central concern of education and the selection of knowledge content as subsidiary and subordinate to that. Its approach lends itself to adaptation and development. The educational implications of empiricism influenced Dewey's educational theorising, as will be discussed later.

The higher status of rationalism over empirical experience is reflected in the history of education. The study of ancient history and the rote learning of the grammar of ancient languages dominated the 'grammar school' curriculum into the late nineteenth century, when more experiential and practical scientific subjects began to be taught. Its resultant approach to education is one which is largely knowledge based and where academic or intellectual pursuits are intrinsically superior to others. In our society there was until quite recently a problem concerning the lower status of practical subjects such as engineering and science in comparison to the arts and humanities.

The rationalist theme has been influenced in the twentieth century by genetics, by theories of language acquisition and more recently by ideas coming from neuropsychology and evolutionary biology. In principle the idea of a human 'nature' might lead to a universal respect for an individual's human rights. Unfortunately, the history of the twentieth century demonstrated that almost the opposite occurred, with fascist dictators and nationalists persuading populations that one particular human nature or 'race' was superior to others. The development of 'eugenics' and other racist theories in the nineteenth century was the forerunner for the rise of Nazi ideology, the Holocaust, Apartheid in South Africa and, more recently, 'ethnic cleansing'.

Despite these dreadful aberrations in the interpretation of genetic ideas, modern socio-biology and evolutionary psychology have continued to explore the influence of genetics on individual psychology and learning behaviour and there is now a rich scientific literature in this area: Pinker (1994), Plotkin (1994, 2004), Mithen (1996) and Carruthers and Chamberlain (2000). The rationalist approach is also found in 'innatist' views of cognitive development such as the work of Chomsky (1988) and Fodor (1975, 1983), who assert that certain mental processes are built into the brain from birth and provide, for example, the deep structure of language and a range of innate mental concepts.

Constructivist education

In the nineteenth and early twentieth centuries the American thinkers Charles Pierce, William James and John Dewey all made significant contributions to constructivist thought (Buchler 1955; James 1901; Dewey 1938). Dewey, for example, derived a view from his pragmatist philosophical theory which stressed that the individual learner should be an 'actor' rather than a 'spectator'. Thus learners should not be seen as simply vessels to be passively filled with received and unchallenged knowledge, but should be actively engaged in constructing knowledge for themselves. However, by far the largest contribution came from the child psychologists Piaget and Vygotsky, who built up a large body of empirical and theoretical work supporting the constructivist position (Flavell 1963; Chapman 1988; Wertsch 1985), some of which is still being actively built on and interpreted today (Wood 1998; Karmilloff-Smith 1996).

Piaget's main conception was that the human mind constructed and internalised a model of how the world works, through experience, and that this was an inherent, biological, adaptive process. From birth to adulthood the brain sought to identify the rules under which external reality functioned as a means of survival. The developing cognitive system attempted to maintain 'equilibrium' with the external world by using two contrasting cognitive processes: assimilation and accommodation. Assimilation involves taking in the evidence of sensory experience and extracting meaning from it; it is the incorporation of the external world into cognitive structures. However, in order for this assimilation process to take place, the cognitive structures sometimes have to change, adjust or accommodate themselves. Accommodation thus means changing the developing conceptual framework or model to cope with new or anomalous experiences. Cognitive adaptations are thus seen as a constant dialectical interaction between these two processes. For Piaget, cognitive development is an iterative process moving from lower to higher levels of sophistication and integration. The developing individual is seen as a hypothesis-testing machine trying to make sense of the world and build up an internal mental representation of the world by discovering the rules of reality. In simple terms, intelligent activity involves 'assimilating the new to the old and accommodating the old to the new' (Flavell 1963: 72). We will later see that David Kolb uses these concepts in his theory of experiential learning.

Piaget's theory is often referred to as a structuralist theory, since it assumes that there are underlying mental systems of wholeness, self-regulation and transformation involved in the developmental process (Piaget 1970a). In addition, Piaget's theory is also described as a 'genetic epistemology' because it asserts that the epistemological framework of the individual is actually changing during development and that there is the spontaneous emergence and construction of cognitive complexity (Piaget 1970b).

The stages of cognitive development described and explained by Piaget have been well described and critically evaluated in the literature and will not be discussed further here (Flavell 1963; Donaldson 1978; Richardson 1998). The final 'logical operational' stage, which occurs from age 11 to adulthood, is characterised by fully mature thinking and the ability to manipulate abstract concepts. Problems are now solved by deliberate investigation involving an awareness of all factors that might influence the result. The ability to think in the abstract, logically and to be able to manipulate variables and all possible causes characterises scientific thinking – an underlying theme which connects some of the major theories of learning described here.

The work of Vygotsky in many ways complements that of Piaget, although they worked in different countries and traditions. Vygotsky's work largely supports much of Piaget's thinking, although there are some key differences. His important contribution to constructivist learning theory was to stress that learning is not just an individual event, it is also a social and cultural process mediated through a culture's symbols and language and that social interaction and the role of teachers and facilitators is of vital importance. He argued that the social 'collective memory' is internalised in the individual. Piaget also stressed social and cultural influences on cognition in his later works (Richardson 1998). Social cognitive theory (Bandura 1977) and theories of situated cognition (Lave and Wenger 1991) can be traced directly to the work of Vygotsky and his stress on the social, contextual and constructivist nature of learning.

His concept of the zone of proximal development (ZPD) emphasised that the learner could be actively helped to construct knowledge and understanding by means of 'scaffolding' mediated by appropriate educational experiences and teaching interventions. The ZPD was defined as the gap between the child's level of unaided cognition or problem-solving ability and what could be achieved under teacher guidance. This scaffolding process, according to Vygotsky, is fundamentally helped by the learner's social interactions and by their immersion in the shared cultural tools of their society (Wertsch, 1985). Thus, for Vygotsky and for social cognitive theory and situated cognition theory understanding is not just constructed by the individual, it is constructed by the group, the society and the culture.

In the latter half of the twentieth century, the work of Ros Driver and others (Driver 1983. Driver and Oldham 1986; Fensham *et al.* 1994; White 1988) in constructivist educational theory contributed towards the development of science education. Driver's work led to the development of frameworks for understanding how children's constructions can often get in the way of learning scientific ideas and for classroom techniques to deal with these problems. Piaget's theory had identified that the child passed through stages where they had inappropriate conceptions of physical reality, exemplified by their inability to deal with and conserve a variety of spatial, numerical, class and causal concepts (Flavell 1963; Richardson 1998). However, Driver and other constructivists showed that even older children, who have passed through Piaget's stages and are nominally logical operators, create and retain their own conceptions which often contradict reality. These conceptions have been termed 'student's conceptions', 'alternative frameworks', 'children's science', 'children's mini-theories' and 'misconceptions' (Driver *et al.* 1994; Duit and Treagust 1995). They do not always resolve themselves naturally and children can persist with incorrect concepts which, if undiagnosed and unchallenged by good teaching practice, can interfere and inhibit further learning.[3]

Driver emphasised the view that children can be seen as 'scientists' who have created their own theories explaining reality by generating and testing hypotheses (Driver 1983). They have done this by trying to extract meaning from their experiential world, a view of the child frequently alluded to by Piaget. The theory explains why children are full of hypotheses and explanations for why the world is the way it is even if these hypotheses can often be wrong and based on erroneous views of reality. The good science teacher finds out what the misconceptions are and devises experiential or logical challenges to help build correct conceptions.

The process of challenging mental conceptions, models and frameworks had been famously studied by the work of Festinger, who coined the term 'cognitive dissonance' to describe the feeling that a person might have when confronted with experiential evidence that contradicted or challenged an assumption about their world (Festinger 1957). This process became a fundamental constructivist teaching technique in the science classroom and was extensively studied by Driver and colleagues (Driver and Oldham 1986).

With respect to the 'child as scientist' concept, reference should also be made to the work of Kelly on personal construct theory in adults. Kelly conceived that individuals develop a set of personal constructs based on their life experience, which they use to anticipate events. Kelly importantly theorised that individuals were like scientists: 'Every man is, in his own particular way, a scientist' (Kelly 1955: 5). Kelly's theory of 'man-the-scientist' was developed into a method of understanding how individuals construct meanings in their life, how they gain control over their personal environment and how they can maintain mental health (Kelly 1955). Further extensions of constructivism into adult learning can be seen in work on 'lay theories'. All of us have constructed a world view that enables us to more or less survive in the physical, biological and social world. We have all constructed our own theoretical frameworks or mental models which help us make sense of the world. In some cases our own theories are alternatives to the 'standard' theories of science, sociology, economics or politics (Furnham 1988).

Finally, one of the most important concepts that underpins constructivism is that articulated by Ausubel in his famous quotation: 'The most important factor influencing learning is what the learner already knows. Ascertain this and teach accordingly' (Ausubel 1968: vi). This statement not only emphasises that learning is a building or a constructive process, rather than a simple didactic, transmission process, but also places the learner rather than the teacher at the heart of the learning process. Hence the constructivist approach is essentially a learner-centred approach beginning with the needs of the learners rather than the prescriptions of teachers.

Ausubel also acknowledged the importance of misunderstanding to learning: 'the unlearning of preconceptions might well prove to be the most determinative single factor in the acquisition and retention of subject matter knowledge' (Ausubel 1968: 336).

The idea of understanding where the learner is coming from, finding out what their existing knowledge, lack of knowledge or misunderstanding is and then designing an appropriate learning experience is fundamental to good teaching. The practice of beginning from the learner and acknowledging their individual constructs derives its rationale directly from constructivist theory and makes a direct connection to humanistic theories of learning, to be discussed later.

Constructivism and science

Science is not just a collection of laws, a catalogue of facts, it is a creation of the human mind with its freely invented ideas and concepts. Physical theories try to form a picture of reality and to establish its connections with the wide world of sense impressions.

(Einstein and Infield 1938: 46)

That the constructivist theory of learning has parallels with the scientific method has already been mentioned. In science, experiences, observations and 'facts' are incorporated into existing or new theoretical frameworks by the process of induction. Deductions derived from new or existing theory become hypotheses which are tested by empirical methods, creating new experiences which can be used to test the fit of the theoretical framework. Individual learning is analogous to the historical and social development of scientific knowledge in which theories are conjectured and either supported or refuted by experience and experiment (Popper 1972). The individual literally behaves like a scientist seeking the best theoretical framework to help make sense of their world. Experience is assimilated into cognitive frameworks; cognitive frameworks are accommodated to make sense of experience.

The effect of 'cognitive dissonance', when experience does not fit with an individual's conceptual framework, is seen as extremely important in this process. This is the moment when the individual is forced to reflect on and re-evaluate their understanding of the world. It may act as a powerful motivating factor for self-directed learning, as in problem-based learning. It may involve 'digging up' and discarding erroneous conceptions. This process also underpins the accommodative process described by Piaget. There is a strong analogy here with Thomas Kuhn's description of 'paradigm shifts' within the history of science (Kuhn 1970); the individual may literally undergo a 'scientific revolution'. A model of the hypothetico-deductive method is shown in Figure 3.1.

An important issue is where science 'begins' in the cycle depicted in Figure 3.1. One of the earliest views of science was that of Roger Bacon, who, in the thirteenth century, suggested that an accumulation of observations led to the construction of theories. There is no doubt that this collection of 'facts', termed 'naïve inductivism' (Chalmers 1999), is a feature of the scientific method, but it is a rather simplistic view of science. Most science actually begins with problems and with the testing of theories by deliberate experimentation and the creation of observations. This view of scientific method has implications for constructivist pedagogy in science education and beyond (Millar and Driver 1987). For example, in problem-based learning learners are confronted with problems which generate learning hypotheses to be tested by group discussion and investigation in the literature (Savin-Baden and Major 2004).

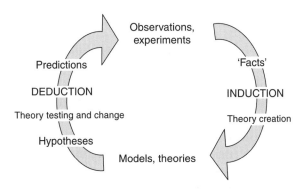

FIGURE 3.1 The hypothetico-deductive scientific method.

We will return to the relationship between scientific method and educational theory when we look at experiential learning.

The range of constructivist theories

The epistemology underlying constructivism has influenced many areas of contemporary thought. The fundamental idea that our knowledge is not the simple internalisation of some outside stimulus but is a mental model constructed from within which more or less has a correspondence with reality has been interpreted in a variety of ways that have led to a spectrum of constructivist positions. For example, in Berger and Luckman's *The Social Construction of Reality* (1991) it is implied that reality itself is very much a social construction and that there is no single, coherent, real world. This postmodern viewpoint asserts that individuals experience reality as multifaceted and contradictory, and rejects scientific 'objectivity'. Thus there is philosophical, educational and sociological constructivism (Matthews 1997) and there is personal, radical and social constructivism (Steffe and Gale 1995). Two ways in which these varieties of constructivism differ is in the status they ascribe to reality and the degree to which knowledge is an individual or social construct (Geelan 1997). For example, the personal constructivism of Piaget, Driver and Kelly accepts that the individual learner actively constructs a mental model and works out the rules of an objective world. However, the radical constructivism of von Glasersfeld suggests that the individual constructs knowledge as an adaptation to enhance survival and that the constructed model is entirely subjective and relative (von Glasersfeld 1984). He argues that its constructions do not have to necessarily map onto an 'objective' representation of the real world. However, it can be argued that a mental model that does not in some sense map onto 'reality' will not have high survival value.

Social constructivists (Solomon 1994; Gergen 1995) and Vygotsky (Wertsch 1985) assert that individual construction is fundamentally influenced by social and linguistic factors. Gergen goes so far as to suggest that knowledge does not only reside in the individual, but is located in societies, language and interpersonal 'dialogue'.[4]

Philips, in his analysis of constructivist positions, also sees an individual–social dimension, but in addition identifies a dimension moving from an empiricist to rationalist standpoint (Philips 1995). The key question here is whether knowledge is constructed by the human mind or whether it is created by 'instructions' from nature; is knowledge made or discovered?

This widening of the boundaries of constructivist thought enables it to encompass a range of educational theories that might be thought to be unrelated. For example, the social and interpersonal influences and learning from the modelling of others seen as important factors in Bandura's social cognitive theory can also be seen as inherent features of constructivist models of learning (Bandura 1977). Mezirow's theory of transformative learning (Mezirow 1991) also emphasises radical personal change as a result of cognitive dissonance, a constructivist process. As Merriam points out (Merriam *et al.* 2007) Vygotsky's social constructivist concepts can also be seen as the foundation for situated cognition (Lave and Wenger 1991). Here, the importance of culture, context and the constructivist principle of active learning are seen as important influences. In adult education, situated learning, reflective practice and communities of practice are seen as related to constructivist models, particularly in relation to frameworks for continuing professional development (Wenger 1998).

Constructivist implications for teaching

A feature of a good theoretical framework is that it predicts what will happen in particular situations and it enables judgements to be made concerning the choice of actions. A good educational theory should therefore suggest pedagogical interventions and techniques. The constructivist theory of learning provides a coherent set of teaching methods which are outlined below.

1. Ascertain prior knowledge

If learning is about building on existing knowledge then an effective teacher needs to be aware of the background knowledge of their students. This may be found out from an overall familiarity with the curriculum and from knowledge of pre-requisite qualifications for a course. It is also readily uncovered by good questioning technique at the beginning of a teaching session.

2. Activate prior knowledge

Students may have prior knowledge but could be unaware of it or have forgotten it. An effective teacher activates students' prior knowledge at the beginning of a teaching session by reviewing previous work or by asking pertinent questions. This process brings relevant knowledge to the surface and places it on the 'mental desktop'. It is an important implication of the constructivist approach to recognise that activating prior knowledge may bring *incorrect* conceptual understanding to the surface, which will have to be dealt with and maybe challenged later.

3. Build on existing knowledge

The acquisition of new knowledge can only be mediated by existing knowledge; the unknown can only be made sense of in terms of the known. Therefore, it is essential that teachers introduce and explain new concepts using knowledge that students already possess and by using analogy and metaphor to help build scaffolding and bridges to new understanding. In this respect the context and 'situation' of learning is extremely important. Not only should teachers make cognitive connections to new learning, but the importance and relevance of the learning should be emphasised to ensure that personal and affective connections are made.

4. Challenge existing knowledge and misconceptions

Some of the most powerful learning occurs when students are in a state of uncertainty. This leads to 'cognitive dissonance' and a desire to resolve conflict and achieve a sense of mental equilibrium (Festinger 1957). Challenge should lead to curiosity and investigation. Teachers should structure learning situations in such a way that erroneous or outmoded conceptions are challenged and confronted by empirical evidence, demonstrations or alternative frameworks with greater explanatory power. Students should be given specifically designed problems or scenarios, as in problem-based learning, that force them to question, abandon, elaborate or refine their existing understanding.

5. Facilitate the social construction of meanings; use group work

The work of Vygotsky and the later Piaget stressed the importance of the interpersonal and social nature of learning. By means of social interaction and the use of language, learners develop and elaborate their cognitive skills. Vygotsky argued that the 'collective memory' becomes a feature of the individual's psychology. This implies that individual understanding, making sense of the world and searching for meaning, is facilitated by interpersonal communication and learning together in groups. Students should therefore be given oral tasks that encourage them to use new terminology and concepts in group situations, elaborating and refining their conceptual understanding by critically exploring the views of others.

6. Stress the context and the 'situation'

The social context of learning is of paramount importance. Learning is a function of the interaction between the individual, other people and the environment (Bandura 1977). The relevance of the learning needs to be brought out and teachers and mentors need to model appropriate behaviour.

7. Encourage 'metacognition'

The construction of understanding is facilitated by reflecting on the process of learning itself, a task known as 'metacognition'. Different disciplines have their own ways of thinking, their own 'rules of the game' or 'ways of seeing'. Scientific, historical and critical thinking all involve particular ways of looking at the world and constructing meanings within their respective contexts. It is important that students are given opportunities to be inducted into these epistemological frameworks.

8. Use active learning techniques

The activation of prior learning by means of questioning, the generation of cognitive dissonance and its resolution by investigation, the importance of group work, social interaction and discussion all point in the direction of active learning techniques. Constructivist theory implies that effective learning should be learning by doing, applying knowledge and problem solving.

9. Give learners responsibility for their learning

If, as Ausubel stated, the most important factor in learning is what the learner already knows, then the learner is at the heart of learning, not the teacher. If effective learning involves personal construction, then learners must take responsibility for this fundamental process. This is essentially the most important 'metacognitive' concept that learners need to accept and it should lead to an attitude of personal responsibility towards learning. This idea needs to be discussed with and assimilated by learners who should abandon a passive, 'spoon-feeding' attitude and adopt a more collaborative, active approach to learning with their teachers.

Experiential learning theory

> Learning is the process whereby knowledge is created through the transformation of experience.
>
> (Kolb 1984: 38)

Ignoring the extremes of rationalist epistemology, in principle, all learning is ultimately derived from sensory experience. Experiential learning theory (ELT), developed by Kolb (1984), attempts to provide a mechanism for how experience can be transformed into knowledge, skills and attitudes. If constructivism is a general theory of learning, then ELT provides a mechanism for how learning takes place. ELT has a theory of cognitive development and contains elements of Piagetian theory, but it usually focuses on mature adult learning. It is frequently but not exclusively used to explain how learning takes place and can be optimised in environments where deliberate teaching and instruction are not taking place. For example, ELT is very useful in making sense of how learning occurs in professional working environments where learners are working or shadowing and engaged in an educational programme at the same time. The theory will be described in more detail below, but briefly one interpretation of Kolb is that learning is initiated with 'concrete experience' which is transformed into 'abstract conceptualisation' by a process of 'reflective observation' and 'active experimentation'. As will be shown, there are parallels with the constructivist theory of learning as well as the process of scientific thinking.

Origins of ELT and influences on it

Kolb traces the origins of ELT to the ideas of Dewey, Lewin and Piaget, but it is also influenced by Carl Jung and Carl Rogers. Dewey put forward a theory of learning that emphasised the fundamental role of 'inner experience' and activity. Traditional (nineteenth- and early twentieth-century) education in his view was inspired by rationalism and dominated by imposition from above, external discipline, learning from texts and teachers, the repetition of isolated skills and drills, preparation for a remote future and static aims. The more dynamic learning that Dewey espoused, on the other hand, was concerned with the expression and cultivation of individuality, free activity, learning through experience in relevant contexts and learning for a changing world. For Dewey, learning was also meant to be a democratic process and knowledge itself was seen as tentative and capable of change and revision. Dewey also stressed the importance of the acknowledgement of prior experience in vocational and adult education and the importance of recognising learners' personal histories and their learning styles.

Lewin's work on group dynamics, action research and organisational behaviour was based on his pioneering involvement with 'T-groups' (training groups) in the 1940s, which developed many of the small-group teaching techniques we use today (e.g. structured group exercises, simulations, case studies, games and role-plays). He used these methods to confront and challenge groups of learners, to make them experience conflict and the tension between theory and practice that leads to deep learning: 'Learning is best facilitated in an environment where there is dialectic tension and conflict between immediate concrete experience and analytical detachment' (Kolb 1984: 9).

His work also emphasised the importance of subjective experience and existential humanistic values as opposed to the dominant behaviourist model that was prevalent during the time these theories were developed. He suggested that individuals should engage with a humanistic scientific process and a spirit of personal enquiry which should allow the expansion of consciousness within authentic relationships. This led to the idea that learning from experience was essential for individual and organisational effectiveness and that experiential learning can occur only in situations where personal values and organisational structures supported actions based on valid information and open and informed choices. These practices have had a profound influence on educational and organisational methods.

Whereas the influences from Dewey and Lewin fit with the empiricist tradition of epistemology, the other major influence on Kolb's ELT theory was the constructivism of Piaget, some of whose ideas have been mentioned previously. From Piaget, Kolb incorporated the idea that intelligence itself is shaped by experience; it is not innate, but arises from the interaction between individuals and their environment. It starts with action but abstract reasoning and symbol manipulation arise later and ultimately derive from interactions with the immediate concrete environment. Piaget asserted that experience, conceptualisation, reflection and action are the basis for the development of adult thought. Thinking develops from concrete to abstract and from active egocentrism to internalised reflection. The process is an interactive cycle between the individual and the environment. There is mutual interaction between accommodation of concepts or mental schemas to experience and the process of assimilation of experiences into existing concepts and schemas. Learning, or 'intelligent adaptation', is the balance between these two processes to maintain cognitive equilibrium.

A number of other psychologists, psychotherapists and educationalists influenced Kolb's ELT, a fact which is often ignored in general descriptions. The work of Carl Rogers in client-centred therapy, and Abraham Maslow in self-actualisation psychology was used to emphasise the importance of adaptation to the affective or emotional aspects of experience. Kolb stressed that healthy adaptation required the integration of cognitive *and* affective processes and that the recognition of the socio-emotional forces influencing development throughout the life cycle of the individual provides a holistic framework for describing adult development. Kolb also saw particular relevance in Jung's theory of psychological types (Jung 1977) to his own development of 'learning styles', as will be described shortly.

Finally, for Kolb ELT was also about the possibility of social action and change and hence he made specific references to Illich's assertion that education is a system of social control in an oppressive capitalist society (Illich 1972) and Paulo Freire's conception that 'knowledge is a process, not a product' and that education should be about developing 'critical consciousness' (Freire 1973).

The structure of the theory

Kolb's theory of experiential learning is introduced as a cyclical process mirroring its origins in the work of both Lewin and Dewey. Indeed, the terms used by Kolb to describe the phases or learning modes of the cycle in Figure 3.2 are taken directly from Lewin's work on action research. However, these modes are interrelated and transformed by the cognitive transactions described originally by Piaget.

Many interpreters of the Kolb cycle (Figure 3.2) concentrate on the four phases of the cycle, seeing them as the components of a continuous process, as did Lewin. Thus 'concrete experience' is often described as the origin of the cycle, where immediate experiences are obtained. This is followed by 'reflective observation', where experiences are transformed by reflection into 'abstract conceptualisations', theoretical knowledge or mental models. Finally, 'active experimentation' is seen as goal-directed activity testing out the consequences of new learning and planning for new experiences. This interpretation of the cycle is a useful heuristic for understanding experiential learning and underpins vocational and professional 'reflective practice' and action planning mediated by the use of portfolios and appraisal.

However, this is a simplified view that ignores much of the richness of Kolb's theory. A deeper approach focuses on the meaning of the two orthogonal axes and the relationships between the dialectically opposed learning modes, as shown in Figure 3.3.

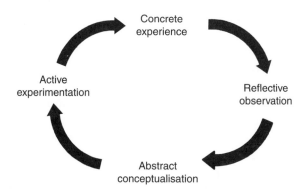

FIGURE 3.2 Kolb's experiential learning cycle.

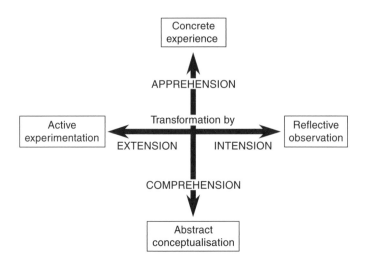

FIGURE 3.3 Prehension and transformation in the Kolb cycle.

The '-prehension' axis represents two opposed processes of how experience is grasped, either through the felt qualities of immediate experience (concrete apprehension) or via conceptual interpretation and symbolic representation (abstract comprehension). Many others have identified these opposed ways of apprehending and comprehending the world, and their interpretations may help to make this distinction more understandable. William James distinguished between 'knowledge of acquaintance'[5] and 'knowledge about'[6] (James 1901), Polanyi between 'tacit knowledge' and 'articulate knowledge' (Polanyi 1958) and Plotkin describes 'knowing by the senses' and 'knowing by the mind' (Plotkin 1994).

For Piaget this opposition between what he described as the 'figurative' aspect of thought can be described by the difference between the 'phenomenalism' of raw experience and the 'constructivism' of mental models and frameworks. In summary, at any moment individuals can focus on either the raw external world of felt perceptions and feelings or the internal world of mental constructions, models and thoughts. Simplistic descriptions of the cycle only seem to acknowledge concrete experience as the source of experience, whereas Kolb clearly explains that the world of abstract conceptualisation is also a source of *inner* experience. We live in the outer world of experience and the inner world of thought simultaneously, and can move between them at will.

Both the inner and outer worlds provide the raw material for cognitive processing by the second axis of 'transformation'. This axis is polarised between action and reflection and represents the transformation of experience by internal reflection ('intention') or by active manipulation and experimentation on the external world ('extension'). The processes on this transformative axis attempt to develop learning and create meaning. Sometimes this involves reflection and analysis, sometimes it involves action and deliberative manipulation of the external world by experimentation.[7] This process of transformation corresponds to Piaget's concept of 'operative' thought where logical, intellectual and sensori-motor processes construct rules to make sense of the world.

Although the relationship of Kolb's theory to some of Piaget's ideas has been presented in this description, it is important to recognise that Kolb's position differs in some important ways from Piaget. Whereas Piaget saw cognitive development as a gradual switch from domination by sensory experience to abstract thought and from egocentric action to internal reflection – in other words, from lower to higher forms of knowing – Kolb sees all four learning modes as equipotent poles in dialectical opposition and transformation: 'The process of learning requires the resolution of conflict between dialectically opposed modes of adaptation to the world' (Kolb 1984: 29). Certainly in the adult all these modes are more or less equally present to the individual; variations might be due to learning styles, as will be discussed later.

This description of the Kolb cycle reveals that it is more than a cycle! Although the dynamic cycle is the one most frequently described, it is important to acknowledge its deeper structure and its relationship to constructivist models of learning and to the scientific process. This more detailed explanation of the cycle reveals that all four learning modes are present to the individual *simultaneously*. The learner can choose to focus on the outer world of raw experience or their inner world of mental representations; they can choose to reflect or act on either of these sources of experience. Thus, according to Kolb, effective learning requires the integration of these four abilities; the learner must constantly move between the concrete or the abstract and between activity or reflection.

Thus Kolb sees learning as an iterative ever-changing process rather than content acquisition and storage. Each act of understanding is a process of continual construction and invention. Nevertheless, during this process experience throws up problems and mis-expectations. According to Dewey it is such problem areas that are the key sources of learning: 'The most powerful learning occurs when the student is dealing with uncertainty' (Dewey 1963: 69). It is precisely when experiences do not fit with inner constructions that the individual has to use their intelligence, their reflections and their actions to find a resolution to the problem. This can take the form of analytical thought, information gathering or active questioning or experimentation. As outlined earlier, this was termed 'cognitive dissonance' by Festinger and goes to the heart of the constructivist process.

Importantly for the aims of this chapter, Kolb asserted that all forms of human adaptation (learning) approximate to scientific enquiry and that the scientific method is the highest philosophical and technological refinement of the basic process of human adaptation. It provides a means for describing the holistic integration of all human functions. Thus there are conceptual analogies between the scientific method and the process of experiential learning, a relationship previously emphasised by Driver for constructivism.

All learning is relearning. How easy and tempting it is in designing a course to think of the learner's mind as being as blank as the paper on which we scratch our outline.... Everyone enters every learning situation with more or less articulate ideas about the topic at hand. We are all psychologists, historians, and atomic physicists. It is just that some of our theories are more crude and incorrect than others. One's job as an educator is not only to implant new ideas but also to dispose of or modify old ones.

(Kolb 1984: 28)

The process of experiential learning can be seen as a mechanism for constructivist cognition and both can be seen to have an underlying connection to the scientific method.

Finally, it should be emphasised that Kolb also stressed the importance of subjective and personal felt experience in addition to objective experience. Learning can be a tension- and conflict-filled process that creates anxiety. In addition he also acknowledged that experience is contextualised and takes place in both an objective and subjective *situation*. Furthermore, there is the recognition that knowledge is mediated by interpersonal and social knowledge (previous human cultural experience) and personal knowledge (individuals' subjective life experiences). It is important to recognise that much of Kolb's theory is derived from work with groups and that it has exerted a significant influence on group organisational theories in business and management. Thus it can be seen that experiential learning leads to connections with theories of situated cognition (Lave and Wenger 1991) and social constructivism (Wertsch 1985). In so far as experiential learning frequently involves observing other people performing specific activities, this framework can easily be related to Bandura's social cognitive theory, where learning from the modelling of others becomes extremely important (Bandura 1977).

Learning styles

From Jung, Kolb took the idea that learning involves holistic integration of thinking, feeling, perceiving and behaving. But the psychotherapeutic work of Jung demonstrated that individuals do not all possess an equal distribution of these learning modalities, a concept developed by Kolb into his own learning styles framework. Some individuals spend their mental energies in active involvement in the outside world (extroverts) whereas others are more introspective and reflective (introverts). Jung developed a theory of psychological types which has been turned into a commonly used psychometric testing framework by Myers-Briggs (Myers-Briggs 1962). Jung's categorisation is more associated with personality types, whereas Kolb has used his framework to develop his Learning Styles Inventory (LSI). Briefly, the LSI uses psychometric analysis to identify four learning styles designated as 'assimilative', 'divergent', 'accommodative' and 'convergent'. A further modification of this framework led Honey and Mumford to develop their own widely used system in which learners are characterised as either activists, reflectors, theorists or pragmatists.[8] There is not space to go into the advantages and disadvantages of learning styles and types, and the reader is referred to a critical study by Coffield *et al.* (2004). Kolb, however, did recognise that they had to be used with caution:

Psychological categorizations of people such as those depicted by psychological 'types' can too easily become stereotypes that tend to trivialize human complexity and thus end up denying human individuality rather than characterizing it. In addition, type theories often have a static and fixed connotation to their descriptions of individuals, lending a fatalistic view of human change and development.

(Kolb 1984: 63)

Educational implications of experiential learning theory

In principle all learning (ignoring any putative 'innate' concepts) is derived from either outer or inner experience transformed by reflection or action, even learning in a classroom. Consequently, experiential learning theory underpins many areas associated with other theoretical frameworks, such as adult learning, social cognitive theory, transformative learning, situated learning and learning in communities of practice. Nevertheless, the practical use of experiential learning theory has been mainly oriented towards individuals in working environments or engaging in vocational work attachments and rotations, field work, work experience, simulations, apprenticeships, internships, projects and self-directed study and research. Learning from experience 'out there' in the world has a primacy that cannot be matched by formal teaching. A number of practical suggestions, oriented towards experiential learners, arise from this framework.

1. Have experiences

Individuals need to ensure they get the experiences they need either individually or as part of communities of practice. There may be educational structures that enable this process or the individual might need to exercise autonomy and assertiveness in ensuring that appropriate experiences are obtained. Useful experiences should be challenging and should generate problems, questions and cognitive dissonance. Experiences could be enhanced by social interaction, activity and discussion. Some experiences are entirely cognitive, but they can also involve practical skills, feelings and emotions. Some experiential learning is collaborative and participative and hence takes place through social interaction, a feature of 'situated' learning

2. Reflect

Possibly one of the most important aspects of ELT is its emphasis on reflection. Experience is transformed into learning by reflection, which may take place by the individual either unconsciously or consciously. This process can be enhanced by interacting with another individual such as a facilitator, teacher, mentor, master or expert. Reflection can also be enhanced by writing, leading to the development of diaries and portfolios. The importance of reflection is further explored by Moon (1999), Kember *et al.* (2001) and Hillier (2002). Encouraging reflection leads to the development of reflective practice, which is an important component of professionalism (Schön 1983). Formal mechanisms, such as regular appraisal or supervisory meetings with a mentor or trainer, where a portfolio or reflective logbook can be discussed and future actions discussed and planned, are a major component of professional development programmes.

3. Feedback

Reflection is fundamentally enhanced by feedback, which can be seen as a type of formative assessment. Ensuring that learners have opportunities to receive constructive feedback from a trained mentor or supervisor is an important feature of experiential learning environments. Feedback can enable the learner to analyse their actions and their understanding and to plan for future learning.

4. Mental models, practical skills and attitudes

It is important to recognise that not only are mental models constructed by reflection on experience, but so are practical skills and attitudes. There should be adequate opportunities for learners to map their experiences onto the experiences of others recorded in textbooks and the 'literature'. Learners should acknowledge that their own mental frameworks are socially connected to the external world of recorded knowledge which they are attempting to internalise.

5. Hypothesis testing and action planning

Learners need opportunities to test out and question their growing body of knowledge, skills and attitudes. They need to talk and debate with facilitators and other learners. They may need to be able to test out their ideas and hypotheses in practical environments. They may need to create action plans for future experiences and may require advice and support from facilitators and mentors.

6. Logbooks and portfolios

Learners can often be 'lost' in experiential learning environments if left to their own devices without supervision. However, they can be supported by having a logbook that defines a core set of experiences or procedures that should be engaged in. Portfolios can be used to record evidence of experience and reflections on those experiences. The contents of a portfolio can be used as a trigger for further discussion and feedback from a mentor or appraiser.

Humanistic theory

The theories described above suggest in broad terms how individuals learn, but do not contain a theory or model of the individual. However, at the heart of learning is a person with a personality, a personal history and hopes and fears. Our understanding of who this person is, where they are coming from and what makes them tick provides the final piece in our theoretical jigsaw. There are many theories of 'human nature' and the more we discover about ourselves through research in the sciences and humanities, the wider these theories grow. In the early part of the twentieth century psychoanalysis and the 'discovery' of the unconscious, through the work of Freud and Jung, was a major development in human understanding which proposed an inner world of motives, desires, repressions, feelings and anxieties.

However, in the United States during the early twentieth century the behaviourist tradition in psychology largely rejected the relevance of these inner states in favour of an empirical exploration of the relationship between stimuli and responses. Into this environment came a number of important psychologists and psychiatrists who adopted a different approach. Eschewing both the psychodynamic theorising of the psychoanalysts and the 'mindless' empiricism of the behaviourists, Abraham Maslow and Carl Rogers developed a 'humanistic' or 'person-centred' approach to the individual which has been found to provide a useful framework for dealing with the individual learner and the educational environment in which they find themselves.

In general terms this psychological approach is characterised by recognising our individuality and our individual needs and by acknowledging that we wish to achieve our full potential. As a theory of the individual it is relatively structureless and value-free, our 'nature' is whoever we are and however we have constructed ourselves with our own personal knowledge and values. As such, it provides a useful model of the individual which is compatible with a constructivist theory of learning.

Maslow emphasised the concept of 'self-actualisation', the idea that we wish to become the best that we can possibly be (Maslow 1968). In this respect, one of his key ideas, which has much practical value in teaching, was to suggest that in order to achieve our full potential, various basic needs must be fulfilled. This is often illustrated using the pyramid shown in Figure 3.4. At the base of the pyramid are various physiological needs such as thirst, hunger and warmth, which must be satisfied before the levels above can be achieved. The second level includes safety needs, such as physical and psychological shelter and security. The following level is concerned with social or interpersonal needs, such as 'belonging' and being part of the group.

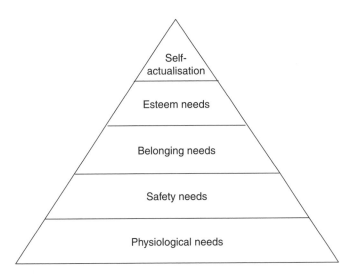

FIGURE 3.4 Maslow's 'hierarchy of needs'.

The next level is concerned with self-esteem and prestige; the top of the pyramid is self-fulfilment and self-actualisation. The implications of this hierarchy are that to achieve the highest levels, the levels below must first be attained. The practical consequences of this theoretical framework can be seen in daily teaching practice. Students will not learn if their physiological and psychological needs have not been satisfactorily dealt with – if they are cold, hungry or anxious, for example. Similarly, if students feel isolated and not part of the group this may inhibit their learning. If they are not given positive feedback, reinforcement and praise they may not learn optimally.

Carl Rogers was a psychologist whose psychotherapeutic work eventually led him in the direction of theories of learning and educational principles. His post-Freudian psychotherapeutic approach was to acknowledge and empathise with the patient's own view of themselves in a 'client-centred' way. Understanding where the patient was coming from in their own terms was a key feature of his method. This therapeutic approach eventually transformed into an educational framework which was very much person- or student-centred (Rogers 1983). Like Maslow, Rogers acknowledged that individuals have a self-actualising tendency towards the achievement of their own potential. In addition, he suggested they have a unique self-concept, need positive self-regard and should be trusted to self-actualise. He stressed the organismic and holistic nature of individuals and emphasised that they had a natural predisposition to learn. Rogers was extremely critical of conventional educational systems: 'Somehow we have managed … to transform one of the most rewarding of all human activities into a painful, boring, dull, fragmenting, mind-shrinking, soul-shrivelling experience' (Rogers 1983: 15).

He advocated self-initiated experiential learning which allowed learners to explore their own ideas and follow their own natural interests. Building on his psychotherapeutic experience he stressed the importance of the teacher–student relationship, arguing that teachers should become 'facilitators' of learning rather than didactic transmitters of information. Facilitators should demonstrate empathy, trust and respect towards their students and be personally genuine. His student-centred theories suggested a number of principles for learning environments. For example, educational organisations should create a climate of trust to allow curiosity and the desire to learn to develop naturally. They should encourage students to take responsibility for their own learning and they should boost students' self-esteem and confidence by providing plenty of positive feedback. Learning environments should be democratic places where learners and facilitators collaborate to promote individual growth and development.

It should be apparent that the humanistic theories of Maslow and Rogers are the foundations for what we now call student-centred or learner-centred approaches to education. Their fundamental starting point is the individual's own place in the world, their own personal frameworks and their own mental models. They stress individual autonomy and encourage learners to take responsibility for their own learning. Hence there is a direct theoretical connection to the constructivist model of learning and to ELT. The constructivist model emphasises that what the student knows is at the heart of learning, it is their starting point for further construction: student centredness is a fundamental principle of constructivist teaching practice. The dynamic of this building process is experiential learning.

Educational implications of humanistic learning theory

1. Respect learners and acknowledge who they are and where they are coming from.
2. Use their knowledge and understanding as a starting point for learning.
3. Ensure physical and psychological conditions for learning are satisfied by paying attention to the learning environment, introductions and group practices.
4. See teaching and learning as a relationship between the learner and teacher/facilitator.
5. Give plenty of praise, support and constructive feedback.
6. Allow learners to explore and follow their own interests as much as possible.
7. Encourage and give time and space for self-directed learning.
8. Trust learners as much as possible to attain their own learning goals.
9. Conduct teaching in a collaborative and democratic way.

Synthesis: constructive experience (with a human touch)

Constructivism, the scientific method, ELT and humanistic learning theory have now been outlined with hints that there may be underlying connections between them, as well as to other learning theories. It is now time to attempt a synthesis to see if a more all-encompassing theoretical framework can be discerned.

Parallels can be drawn between some of the processes identified within experiential and constructivist learning theory and scientific method. For example, the transformation of concrete experience into abstract concepts and mental models by reflective observation is analogous to the process of assimilation in constructivism and to induction in the scientific method. The building up of mental schemas and models by incorporating sensory information provided by experience (assimilation) is equivalent to the process of inductive reasoning in science whereby the accumulation of observed facts leads to the building of theories.

Mental models and theories, however, may not fit or map onto reality, causing cognitive dissonance in the individual and hypothesis testing in the scientific community. By acts of imagination and conceptualisation, deductions from the theoretical framework lead to hypotheses which can be tested by active experimentation resulting in theory modification and hence accommodation via further concrete experiences that feed into the inductive side of the cycle. Thus, ELT and constructivist theory are analogous to the hypothetico-deductive scientific method. In constructivist teaching practice, existing mental models may be created or overthrown by appropriate experiential challenge. Learning in the individual can therefore be seen as an iterative process of theory creation and theory change, of induction followed by deduction, of assimilation followed by accommodation. These parallels are shown in Figure 3.5.

A further analogy between experiential learning and the scientific method is in the nature of the knowledge constructed. In science, theories are tentative; they are models of reality which are capable of being falsified by empirical evidence. In the individual, knowledge is constructed by an iterative process; ideas and concepts are not fixed but are formed and reformed to create provisional knowledge through the cycle of experiential

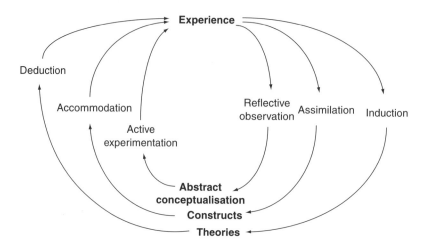

FIGURE 3.5 The parallels between concepts from constructivism, the scientific method and Kolb's experiential learning theory.

learning. This suggests that an appropriate attitude towards learning and knowledge is one of scepticism and open-mindedness. Dogmatism is not a foundation for learning; as Einstein said: 'Blind belief in authority is the greatest enemy of truth' (Einstein 1901).

Thomas Kuhn described how major historical changes in science produce paradigm shifts or 'scientific revolutions' when old frameworks and theories are discarded due to overwhelming negative empirical evidence and new theories are developed (Kuhn 1970). Similar changes can occur to the mental models of individuals and are explained by Kolb's theory of experiential learning and constructivist theory. Mezirov's transformative learning theory (Mezirow 1991) also emphasises changes to personal paradigms via critical reflection and cognitive dissonance and is clearly related to Kolb's framework and constructivist models of learning.

Some may argue that the hypothetico-deductive method of reasoning, which characterises a large proportion of scientific thinking, is not necessarily a model for reasoning and the creation of new knowledge in the arts, humanities and social sciences. It can also be argued that most individuals do not run their lives as if they were 'scientists' despite the claim made here that their knowledge-constructing processes are analogous to the scientific method. Here we must differentiate between content and process. Although the process may be universal individuals and academic and artistic communities construct their own content in terms of their own mental models and their own theories of reality or aesthetics. Children construct a wide variety of theories to explain their experiences which science teachers confront and challenge on a daily basis. Adults construct 'lay theories' by which they make sense of illness, other people's minds, their children's behaviour, money – in fact anything which helps to make sense of life. The content may be wildly different but the process is the same.

On the other hand, the humanistic framework provides a relatively value-free theory of the individual that fits inside either the constructive or experiential learning model. However, the element in the humanistic theory that makes the strongest connection to these latter two theories and makes it the most useful theory for our purposes is the idea that one must begin from where the learner is, one must respect, understand and work with the learner's own constructions.

In conclusion, constructive experience encompasses constructivist theory, ELT and humanistic theory, which together provide a coherent and related framework for understanding the process of learning in children and adults as well as providing recommendations for educational environments. The hypothetico-deductive process of science provides connectivity between constructivist theory and ELT. Humanistic theory provides a relatively value-free theory of the individual learner. A variety of other learning theories can be seen to be derived from or strongly related to these three basic theories.

Constructive experience: implications for teaching

1. Acknowledge and respect the learner and start from where they are.
2. Ascertain, activate and build on their prior knowledge.
3. Provide appropriate learning experiences of an individual and social nature.
4. Facilitate reflection and provide feedback.
5. Recognise the tentative nature of knowledge and encourage enquiry.
6. Encourage individual responsibility for exploration, self-directed learning and action planning.
7. Develop a learning relationship, empathise and show trust.

Notes

1. http://tip.psychology.org lists over 50.
2. http://carbon.cudenver.edu/~mryder/itc_data/constructivism.html presents a comprehensive overview of constructivism.
3. Nevertheless, some radical constructivists, such as von Glasersfeld, acknowledge students' own constructions as valid views of reality and challenge the use of the word 'misconception' (von Glasersfeld 1993).
4. The extreme edge of the constructivist spectrum is, of course, held by the concept of *solipsism*, the idea that there is no external reality (and thus no externally generated experience) and that individual experience is technically a delusion.
5. 'through feelings we become acquainted with things'.
6. 'only by our thoughts do we know about them'.
7. Jarvis (2006) notes that learning need not occur by non-reflection and by acceptance of the status quo.
8. See www.peterhoney.com.

References

Ausubel, D.P. (1968) *Educational Psychology: A Cognitive View.* New York: Holt, Reinhart.
Bandura, A. (1977) *Social Learning Theory.* Englewood Cliffs, NJ: Prentice Hall.
Benton, E. and Craib, I. (2001) *Philosophy of Social Science.* Basingstoke: Palgrave.
Berger, P. and Luckman, T. (1991) *The Social Construction of Reality.* Harmondsworth: Penguin.
Buchler, I. (ed.) (1955). *Philosophical Writings of Peirce.* New York: Dover.

Carruthers, P. and Chamberlain, A. (2000) (eds) *Evolution and the Human Mind: Modularity, Language and Meta-cognition*. Cambridge: Cambridge University Press.

Chalmers, A.F. (1999) *What is This Thing Called Science?* Maidenhead: Open University Press.

Chapman, M. (1988) *Constructive Evolution*. Cambridge: Cambridge University Press.

Chomsky, N. (1988). *Language and Problems of Knowledge*. Cambridge, MA: MIT Press.

Coffield, F., Moseley, D., Hall, E. and Ecclestone, K. (2004) *Should We be Using Learning Styles? What Research has to Say to Practice*. London: LSDA.

Curzon, L.B. (1997) *Teaching in Further Education*. London: Continuum.

Dewey, J. (1938) *Logic: The Theory of Inquiry*. New York: Holt.

Dewey, J. (1963) *Experience and Education*. New York: Collier Books.

Donaldson, M. (1978) *Children's Minds*. London: Fontana.

Driver, R. (1983) *The Pupil as Scientist*. Milton Keynes: Open University Press.

Driver, R. and Oldham, V. (1986). A constructivist approach to curriculum development in science. *Studies in Science Education* 13, 105–122.

Driver, R., Squires, A., Rushworth, P. and Wood-Robinson, V. (1994) *Making Sense of Secondary Science: Research into Children's Ideas*. Oxford: RoutledgeFalmer.

Duit, R. and Treagust, D.F. (1995) Student's conceptions and constructivist teaching approaches. In Fraser, B.J. and Walberg, H.J. (eds), *Improving Science Education* Chicago, IL: University of Chicago Press.

Einstein, A. (1901) *Collected Papers of Albert Einstein*. Vol 1. Doc. 115. Princeton, NJ: Princeton University Press.

Einstein, A. and Infeld, L. (1938) *The Evolution of Physics*. Cambridge: Cambridge University Press.

Fensham, P., Gunstone, R. and White, R. (1994) *The Content of Science: A Constructivist Approach to its Teaching and Learning*. London: The Falmer Press.

Festinger, L. (1957) *A Theory of Cognitive Dissonance*. Stanford, CN: Stanford University Press.

Flavell, J.H. (1963) *The Developmental Psychology of Jean Piaget*. New York: Van Nostrand Reinhold Company.

Fodor, J. (1975) *The Language of Thought*. Cambridge, MA. MIT Press.

Fodor, J. (1983) *The Modularity of Mind: An Essay on Faculty Psychology*. Cambridge, MA: MIT Press.

Freire, P. (1973) *Education for Critical Consciousness*. New York: Continuum.

Furnham, A.F. (1988) *Lay Theories*. London: Pergamon.

Geelan, D.R. (1997) Epistemological anarchy and the many forms of constructivism. *Science & Education* 6, 15–28.

Gergen, K.J. (1995) Social construction and the education process. In Steffe, L.P. and Gale, J. (eds), *Constructivism in Education*. Hillsdale, NJ: Lawrence Erlbaum.

Hillier, Y. (2002) *Reflective Teaching in Further and Adult Education*. London: Continuum.

Illich, I. (1972) *Deschooling Society*. New York: Harrow Books.

James, W. (1901). *The Principles of Psychology*. Vols 1 and 2. London: Macmillan.

Jarvis, P. (2006) *Towards a Comprehensive Theory of Learning*. London: Routledge.

Jarvis, P., Holford, J. and Griffin, C. (1998) *The Theory and Practice of Learning*. London: Kogan Page.

Jung, C. (1977) *Psychological Types: Collected Works*, Vol. 6. Princeton, NJ: Princeton University Press.

Kant, I. (1983). *Critique of Pure Reason*. Translated by Thomas Kingsmith Abbott. London: Longmans, Green.

Karmiloff-Smith, A. (1996) *Beyond Modularity: A Developmental Perspective on Cognitive Science*. Cambridge, MA: MIT Press.

Kelly, A.V. (1986) *Knowledge and Curriculum Planning*. London: Harper & Row.

Kelly, G.A. (1955) *The Psychology of Personal Constructs*. New York: Norton.

Kember, D. (ed.) (2001) *Reflective Teaching and Learning in the Health Professions*. London: Blackwell Science.

Knowles, M.S., Holton, E.F. and Swanson, R.A. (1998) *The Adult Learner* (5th edition). Houston, TX: Gulf Publishing.

Kolb, D.A. (1984) *Experiential Learning*. Englewood Cliffs, NJ: Prentice Hall.

Kuhn, T.S. (1970) *The Structure of Scientific Revolutions*. Chicago, IL: University of Chicago Press.

Lave, J. and Wenger, E. (1991) *Situated Learning: Legitimate Peripheral Participation*. Cambridge: Cambridge University Press.

Marx, K. (1859) *A Contribution to the Critique of Political Economy*. Moscow: Progress Publishers.

Maslow, A.H. (1968) *Toward a Psychology of Being*. New York: Van Nostrand Reinhold.

Matthews, M.R. (1997) Introductory comments on philosophy and constructivism in science education. *Science & Education*, 6, 5–14.

Merriam, S.B., Caffarella, R.S. and Baumgartner, L.M. (2007) *Learning in Adulthood: A Comprehensive Guide* (3rd edition). San Francisco, CA: Jossey-Bass.

Mezirow, J. (1991) *Transformative Dimensions of Adult Learning*. San Francisco, CA: Jossey-Bass.

Millar, R.H. and Driver, R. (1987) Beyond processes. *Studies in Science Education* 14: 388–398.

Mithen, S. (1996) *The Prehistory of the Mind*. London: Thames and Hudson.

Moon, J.A. (1999) *Reflection in Learning and Professional Development*. London: Kogan Page.

Myers-Briggs, I. (1962) *The Myers-Briggs Type Indicator Manual*. Princeton, NJ: Educational Testing Service.

Philips, D.C. (1995) The good, the bad and the ugly: the many faces of constructivism. *Educational Researcher* 24, 5–12.

Piaget, J. (1970a) *Structuralism*. New York: Basic Books.

Piaget, J. (1970b) *Genetic Epistemology*. New York: Norton.

Pinker, S. (1994) *The Language Instinct*. New York: Harper Perennial Modern Classics.

Pinker, S. (2002) *The Blank Slate*. London: Allen Lane.

Plotkin, H. (1994) *Darwin Machines and the Nature of Knowledge*. London: Penguin.

Plotkin, H. (2004) *Evolutionary Thought in Psychology*. Oxford: Blackwell.

Polanyi, M. (1958) *Personal Knowledge*. London: Routledge and Kegan Paul.

Popper, K.R. (1972) *Objective Knowledge*, Oxford: Oxford University Press.

Richardson, K. (1998) *Models of Cognitive Development*. Hove: Psychology Press.

Rogers, C. (1983) *Freedom to Learn for the 80s*. New York: Merrill.

Savin-Baden, M. and Major, C.H. (2004) *Foundations of Problem-based Learning*. Maidenhead: Open University Press.

Schön, D. (1983) *The Reflective Practitioner: How Professionals Think in Practice*. New York: Basic Books.

Solomon, J. (1994) The rise and fall of constructivism. *Studies in Science Education* 23, 1–19.

Steffe, L.P. and Gale J. (eds) (1995) *Constructivism in Education*. Hillsdale, NJ: Lawrence Erlbaum.

Tobin, K. (ed.) (1993) *The Practice of Constructivism in Science Education*. Hillsdale, NJ: Lawrence Erlbaum.

von Glasersfeld, E. (1984) An introduction to radical constructivism. In Waltzlawick, P. (ed.), *The Invented Reality*. New York: Norton.

von Glasersfeld, E. (1993) Questions and answers about radical constructivism. In: Tobin, K. (ed.), *The Practice of Constructivism in Science Education*. Hillsdale, NJ: Lawrence Erlbaum.

Waltzlawick, P. (ed.) (1984) *The Invented Reality*. New York: Norton.

Wenger, E. (1998) *Communities of Practice: Learning, Meaning and Identity*. New York: Cambridge University Press.

Wertsch, J.V. (1985) *Vygotsky and the Social Formation of Mind*. Cambridge, MA: Harvard University Press.

White, R.T. (1988) *Learning Science*. Oxford: Blackwell.

Wood, D. (1998) *How Children Think and Learn*. Oxford: Blackwell.

Thinking philosophically about education; thinking educationally about philosophy

Gert Biesta

It is the mark of an educated mind to be able to entertain a thought without accepting it.

Aristotle

Introduction

In her widely used book *Philosophy of Education,* the American philosopher of education Nel Noddings states that philosophy of education 'is the philosophical study of education and its problems' (Noddings 2012: xiii). Philosophers of education, she writes, 'study the problems of education from a philosophical perspective' (ibid.: xiv). Thus she concludes that the 'subject matter [of philosophy of education] is *education,* and its methods are those of *philosophy*' (ibid.: xiii; emphasis added). While many would agree with this definition – and in a sense philosophy of education can be nothing but the philosophical study of education – it nonetheless raises a number of further questions. One question – a rather big and complicated one – is what philosophy actually is. While some have tried to define the 'essence' of philosophy, others have come to the conclusion that the huge variety of what goes on under the name of philosophy makes it virtually impossible to pin down what philosophy is or what it should be. This is one of the reasons why the American philosopher Richard Rorty has suggested that we should better think of philosophy as a literary genre or 'a kind of writing', as he has put it, held together not by form or matter but by tradition (see Rorty 1978). While it is quite difficult, therefore, to define what philosophy is, it is nonetheless important to gain an understanding of what philosophers have been doing over the centuries in order to get a better sense of what it might mean to study education and its problems in a philosophical manner. In order to understand what philosophy might contribute to the study of education it is, however, also important to take a closer look at its object of study. This brings us to the equally difficult question of what education is or might be – a question already discussed in some detail in the opening chapter of this book. Before I say more, therefore, about the contributions that philosophers have made to the study of education, I will explore in some detail the two constituting parts of philosophy of education. I will do this through a discussion of two challenging but nonetheless crucial questions: 'What is philosophy?' and 'What is education?'

What *is* philosophy?

Our contemporary idea of philosophy emerged in Greek civilisation between about 600 and 150 BC. While the Greek word 'philosophy' originally had a rather broad meaning, referring to a thirst for learning or a thirst for education, over time it came to describe the more specific tradition of thinking and writing and of asking questions and generating answers that we now recognise as philosophy. One common definition of philosophy – and in a sense a literal translation of the word – is that of 'love of wisdom'. In the *Phaedrus*, a dialogue written by Plato (427–347 BC), we can find Socrates (439–399 BC) arguing for a distinction between being wise and having knowledge of the truth on the one hand, and *aspiring to* wisdom, knowledge and truth on the other. Socrates then argues that only a god can be called wise in this sense, that is, as having wisdom and true knowledge, so that human beings who aspire for wisdom, knowledge and truth should more fittingly be called *lovers* of wisdom, that is, philosophers. This line of thought already hints at a prominent characteristic of contemporary philosophy, in that philosophers nowadays would seldom lay claim to having secure or certain knowledge, but rather see it as their task to always ask further critical questions about any particular claim people would make about what they think they know or think is true. In asking such questions, philosophers are particularly interested in exploring the quality and strength of the reasons people have or give for their ideas and beliefs. That is why logic, the study of reasoning and argument, is a prominent branch of philosophy.

The relationship between science and philosophy

The idea that there is a clear division of tasks between science and philosophy, one in which it is the task of science to generate knowledge about the natural and social world and where it is the task of philosophy to raise critical questions about underlying assumptions and the quality of arguments and reasoning, is a relatively modern idea that only emerged with the rise of modern science in the sixteenth and seventeenth centuries. For the Greek philosophers and many of their followers, the distinction between science and philosophy was far less articulate, so that in the writings of philosophers such Plato and Aristotle (384–322 BC) we not only find more familiar philosophical 'themes' such as questions about what we can know and what it means to have knowledge, about what it means to lead a good or virtuous life, about language, about argumentation and logic, about the ultimate nature of reality and about the proper organisation of the state, but also about the origins of the universe, about the substances the universe is made of, about the weather, about animals, about natural processes of growth and decay, and so on. While from a contemporary perspective we might say that thinkers such as Plato and Aristotle *combined* scientific and philosophical work, for them the distinction was actually not really a meaningful one. Their interest was in the broad study of almost anything that could be studied, although the methods and ways of reasoning they used for this were distinctly different from the methods of empirical observation and experimentation that came to characterise modern science.

The rise of modern science thus gradually introduced a division between the empirical – that is, knowledge derived from observation and experiment – and the philosophical – that is, insights based on reasoning and argumentation. As a result of this we can, in our time, make a relatively clear distinction between the domain of empirical knowledge and the domain of philosophy, so that to ask philosophical questions about education or to have a philosophical perspective on education is different from the empirical knowledge we can gain through systematic research of education. On this distinction philosophers would ask critical questions about underlying assumptions, so that if empirical researchers would make claims about, say, students' ability to learn or about their intelligence, philosophers might ask what these notions actually mean and whether they can be researched or measured in the ways researchers claim they can. Or they might raise questions about implicit normative assumptions in such research, such as the implication that some people are by nature more intelligent or more able to learn than others.

The rise of modern science did result in a new division of labour between philosophers and scientists, where the later would focus on doing physics and the former would occupy themselves with metaphysics (roughly to be defined as the exploration of more fundamental questions about being, existence and the world). That this division of labour took some time to crystallise can be seen in the fact that the early scientists would refer to themselves as 'natural philosophers'. (There are actually still professorships of natural philosophy nowadays at the universities of Oxford and Cambridge.) A similar division of labour took place in the late nineteenth and early twentieth centuries between the new disciplines of psychology, sociology and political science, on the one hand, and philosophical anthropology and social and political philosophy, on the other. Other areas of the philosophical tradition, most notably logic (the study of reasoning), ethics (the study of right and wrong action) and aesthetics (the study of beauty and the beautiful) have remained far less affected by such developments.

Questions of knowledge and freedom

The emergence of modern science also gave rise to new fields of philosophical study. Given that modern science not only made strong claims about the natural world – think, for example, of Galileo Galilei's claims about the movement of the earth around the sun, or Isaac Newton's articulation of the laws of motion – but also developed new and effective technologies based on this knowledge – philosophers became interested in questions about the status of scientific knowledge and particularly the question of whether scientific knowledge can claim to provide us with a more accurate and more true account of reality than our everyday knowledge. This became a major theme in the work of modern philosophers such as René Descartes (1596–1650), John Locke (1632–1704), David Hume (1711–1776) and Immanuel Kant (1724–1804), and led to the establishment of the branch of philosophy called *epistemology* or *theory of knowledge*. Epistemology is the branch of philosophy that focuses on questions about what it means to know, how we can know and how we can make any claims about the status, validity and truth of our knowledge claims. One prominent – and ongoing – discussion in this field concerns the question of whether knowledge is something we receive through our senses or whether our mind actively contributes something to what we receive. The latter line of thinking, nowadays known as a constructivist view of knowledge, has become increasingly influential in the second half of the twentieth century as a theory of learning and a theory of pedagogy.

The fact that modern science increasingly depicted the whole of nature, including both animate and inanimate nature, in mechanistic terms, that is, as machines operating according to universal laws of cause and effect, led to a renewed interest in questions about human freedom – particularly the question of whether free will exists – and human responsibility, for example in the writings of such philosophers as Thomas Hobbes (1588–1679), John Locke (1632–1704), Spinoza (1632–1677), Immanuel Kant (1724–1804), Wilhelm Friedrich Hegel (1770–1831) and Arthur Schopenhauer (1788–1860). The question of human freedom also increasingly became a political issue, for example in the American Revolution in the second half of the eighteenth century (resulting in the Declaration of Independence in 1776) and the French Revolution (1789–1799). The writings of Thomas Hobbes and John Locke – often referred to as the 'father of liberalism' – provided important philosophical justifications for the idea of human freedom as the basis for any form of political association.

The Enlightenment

The often violent political struggles for human freedom that took place in the eighteenth century were paired with an intellectual revolution that became known as the Enlightenment. Enlightenment philosophers such as, in Scotland, Adam Smith (1723–1790) and David Hume, in France Voltaire (1694–1778), Montesquieu (1689–1755) and Jean-Jacques Rousseau (1712–1778), and in Prussia Immanuel Kant and Johann Wolfgang von Goethe (1749–1832), all emphasised the human capacity for rational thinking as the basis for freedom and autonomy – an idea that thoroughly influenced modern education (see below). That the struggle for human freedom was not only a matter of overthrowing the power of absolute monarchs but also had to do with overcoming the workings of power within society – for example between the rich and the poor or between the upper classes and the lower classes – became a theme in the writings of social reformers such as the French socialist thinkers Henri de Saint-Simon (1760–1825), Pierre-Joseph Proudhon (1809–1865) and François Fourrier (1772–1837), further developed and radicalised in the work of Karl Marx (1818–1883). Marx thus put questions about the analysis of the dynamics of the economy and the theme of class struggle firmly on the agenda of modern (political) philosophy.

Twentieth-century developments

The twentieth century saw some further innovations and developments in the field of philosophy. One important strand was the transformation of epistemological reflection on the nature of scientific knowledge into the wider (sub-)field of the philosophy of science, initially focusing strongly on the natural sciences and mathematics, but increasingly also paying attention to the human and social sciences. For the natural sciences important work was conducted by the philosophers of the Vienna Circle – including Moritz Schlick (1882–1936) and Rudolf Carnap (1891–1971). A highly influential response to this work was developed by the Austrian philosopher Karl Popper (1902–1994) – whose work became known as critical rationalism and also as falsificationism. In the second half of the twentieth century the philosophical work on scientific knowledge became increasingly connected with and influenced by empirical historical and sociological studies on the development of science and scientific knowledge. In 1962 Thomas Kuhn (1922–1996) published his highly influential book *The Structure of Scientific Revolutions*, in which he depicted the development of the natural sciences as a process of revolution rather than of evolution. Work on the specific nature of the human and social sciences had already started in the late nineteenth century through the writings of Wilhelm Dilthey (1833–1911). Dilthey argued that human phenomena – including education – can only be investigated properly if we approach them as meaningful phenomena. This requires that we try to find out what they mean for those involved. Instead of the methods of the natural sciences, research on human and social phenomena therefore needs to use different methods, particularly methods that aim at a deeper understanding of the meaning of such phenomena. Others who contributed to this discussion were the German philosopher and social theorist Jürgen Habermas (born in 1929) and the French philosopher and historian Michel Foucault (1926–1984) who, according to some statistics, is one of the most cited academic writers of the twentieth century.

A second important development in twentieth-century philosophy – one that, as I will discuss below, has had a profound impact on the philosophy of education – was the emergence of what is known as analytic philosophy. Emerging from the philosophy of logic and the philosophy of mathematics in which significant contributions were made by philosophers such as Gottlob Frege (1848–1925), Bertrand Russell (1872–1970) – a philosopher who also had an explicit interest in education – and Ludwig Wittgenstein (1889–1951), analytic philosophy became increasingly focused on questions of language and meaning. In the second part of his career, Wittgenstein made highly original and influential contributions to the understanding of language and meaning, and thus became important for the development of a strand of analytic philosophy known as 'ordinary language philosophy', where philosophers such as John Austin (1911–1960) and Gilbert Ryle (1900–1976) focused on the critical analysis of everyday language use. In the English-speaking world, analytic philosophy is still the most influential and dominant form of philosophy. For a number of decades after the Second World War it was also the main tradition within philosophy of education in the English-speaking world, particularly through the efforts of such philosophers of education as Israel Scheffler (born in 1923) in the United States and Richard Peters (1919–2011) and Paul Hirst (born in 1927) in the UK (see below).

Contemporary analytic philosophy is often contrasted with 'Continental philosophy', which refers to philosophical traditions and approaches that emerged in countries such as France and Germany from the end of the nineteenth century onwards. One line, emerging in Germany from the work of Edmund Husserl (1859–1953), with further contributions from such philosophers as Max Scheler (1874–1928) and Nicolai Hartman (1882–1950) and the highly original, influential and controversial work of Martin Heidegger (1889–1976), is that of *phenomenology* – a philosophical approach with a strong interest in structures of consciousness and the phenomena that appear in acts of consciousness. This line of work was also developed in France through such philosophers as Gabriel Marcel (1889–1974), Maurice Merleau-Ponty (1908–1961) and Jean-Paul Sartre (1905–1980), whose phenomenologically-inspired philosophy developed into an approach known as *existentialism*.

Another main line of Continental philosophy developed from the work of Marx into what is known as *critical theory*. Important contributions to the development of modern critical theory – which strongly influenced educational thought from the late 1960s onwards, both on the Continent and, about two decades later, in North America – were made by Max Horkheimer (1895–1973), Theodor W. Adorno (1903–1969) and Jürgen Habermas. The 1980s saw the rise of what became known as postmodern or poststructural philosophy. Emanating from France, particularly in the writings of Jean Baudrillard (1929–2007), Jean-Francois Lyotard (1924–1998) and Jacques Derrida (1930–2004), intellectually connected to phenomenology and existentialism, and with a large following in English-speaking countries (albeit more strongly in North America than in the UK), these philosophers rejected the idea that it is possible (for philosophy or science) to identify secure foundations for thought and action. While many perceived this 'anti-foundational' way of philosophising as a form of relativism – in which there are no longer any criteria for truth, justice and beauty so that 'anything goes' – a more careful reading of the work of these philosophers shows a profound engagement with ethical and political questions and a rejection of the idea that such questions can simply be 'solved' by the right knowledge or by scientific truth. Although the Lithuanian-born philosopher Emmanuel Levinas (1906–1995) is not often characterised as a postmodern philosopher, his reflections on the human being and on human existence follow a similar line of thinking, highlighting that our humanity is realised through our responsibility for other human beings.

The final significant development in twentieth-century philosophy is the emergence of an original school of thought in North America known as *pragmatism*. Although the philosophers who inaugurated pragmatism – most notably Charles S. Peirce (1839–1914), William James (1842–1910), John Dewey (1859–1952) and George Herbert Mead (1863–1931) – had a deep knowledge of Continental philosophy (many of them spent several years studying in Germany and France), they developed an approach to philosophy and philosophising that was significantly different from what was happening on the other side of the Atlantic. One distinctive quality of pragmatist philosophy is that it is willing to take insights from modern science into consideration rather than positioning itself as (only) an arbiter of the quality of scientific knowledge claims or as (only) a critic of underlying assumptions. Thus we find, particularly in the work of John Dewey and George Herbert Mead, a strong influence of Darwinist thinking resulting in, among other things, a philosophy that starts from an understanding of human action and interaction rather than one that puts knowledge and knowing at the centre of attention. Pragmatist philosophy is also characterised by a forward-looking orientation. Rather than searching for origins and foundations, it is first and foremost interested in the consequences of thought and action. Although the pragmatists made significant contributions to the study of logic, knowledge and language, their work was not really appreciated by 'mainstream' philosophy of science and analytic philosophy of language. Only in more recent years – particularly as a result of the work of the American 'neo-pragmatist' philosophers such as Richard Rorty (1931–2007) – has pragmatism gained more appreciation within philosophical circles. Within the philosophy of education, pragmatism has always had a strong presence, particularly in North America. This is mainly due to the efforts of John Dewey who, in addition to important contributions to philosophy and sociology, not only wrote extensively about educational matters but was also practically involved in educational reform and renewal, for example through his role in the establishment of the so-called Laboratory School at the University of Chicago in 1896.

Philosophy and education

If we look at this (too) brief history of the development of (Western) philosophy, we can begin to appreciate that behind the simple definition of philosophy of education as 'the philosophical study of education and its problems' (Noddings) we can find a whole universe of philosophical ideas and traditions and of ways and styles of doing philosophy, and this makes it quite difficult if not impossible to reduce this variety to some kind of 'essence' of what philosophy is about. While few, for example, would challenge the suggestion that philosophy is about asking critical questions, it makes all the difference whether in asking such questions one takes inspiration from Socrates, Kant, Marx or Derrida, to name a few (on the particular issue of what it means to be critical, see Biesta and Stams 2001). Or while few would challenge the suggestion that philosophy is about the exploration and exposure of underlying assumptions, it makes all the difference whether in doing so one takes inspiration from Plato, Hume, Hegel or Foucault. While few would challenge the idea that philosophers have important things to say about knowledge, belief and truth, it again makes all the difference whether one does so from the perspective of Aristotle, Descartes, Locke or Dewey. And even while many would insist on the importance of the distinction between philosophical and empirical approaches, there are even those who raise questions about the possibility to keep the two apart and about the desirability of doing so (an idea pursued in the notion of 'empirical philosophy'). Philosophy thus presents us with a vast arsenal of ideas, approaches, traditions and ways of thinking that cover a wide range of areas, including logic, epistemology, ethics, aesthetics, metaphysics, anthropology, social and political philosophy, philosophy of language and philosophy of science. Philosophy thus not only provides a huge resource for the study of education and its problems. Many of the topics that have been explored by philosophers throughout the centuries are actually highly relevant for the study of education. But before we can look into that in more detail we need to pay some attention to the second main question: what is education?

What *is* education?

While many of us would use the word 'education', perhaps on a daily basis, without giving it much thought, on closer inspection 'education' turns out to be a rather messy concept that contains multiple meanings. The word education has Latin roots (a combination of 'ex' and 'ducere') and literally means 'to lead out'. Some have taken this to argue that education not only *is* a process that leads people out of their current beliefs and ways of doing, but also that education *ought to* lead people 'beyond the present and the particular', as Charles Bailey has called it (Bailey 1984). When we look at the word 'education' in more detail, we can distinguish at least five different ways in which it is being used. First, the word is used to refer to *institutions* such as schools, colleges and universities. Hence we talk about primary, secondary, further (or in North America: continuing) and higher education. The latter two are sometimes referred to together as tertiary education. Second, and partly related to this, 'education' is used to refer to *domains of practice*, such as adult education, school education, vocational education, technical education or university education. Third, the word 'education' is used to refer to the *processes* that go on in such institutions and practices – as for example in the title of Jerome Bruner's book *The Process of Education* (Bruner 1960). Fourth, the word 'education' is used to refer to the *activity of educating*. Teaching is one obvious example of this use of the word education – and Richard Peters' analysis of the concept of education as discussed in the opening chapter of this book clearly refers to this use of the word – although parenting is another obvious example of the activity of educating. Fifth, the word 'education' is also used to refer to the *outcomes* of education, such as in the idea of the educated person, a topic extensively discussed in the philosophy of education literature (see, for example, Peters 1970; Martin 1981), but perhaps brought home most poignantly in the quote attributed to Mark Twain – never let schooling interfere with your education.

Some Continental concepts

While the English word 'education' thus contains multiple meanings, other languages are sometimes slightly more helpful in that they use different words for these different meanings (see also Biesta 2011). One such distinction can be found in the German language, where the word *Bildung* is used to refer to processes of education, whereas *Erziehung* is more often used to refer to the activity of educating. *Bildung* (sometimes translated into English as 'formation' or 'edification') refers to the ways in which, through engagement with culture and tradition, we develop our human capacities. It thus comes with an idea of education as cultivation and enculturation and, more importantly, with an explicit idea of what it means to be educated. (In this regard it combines the third and the fifth meaning of education mentioned above.) This obviously means that not *any* engagement with culture and tradition necessarily contributes to the *Bildung* of a human person, so that one important question with regard to *Bildung* concerns the selection of those aspects of culture and tradition that are deemed to be beneficial for one's *Bildung*. The idea of *Erziehung* is less about processes and more about the activity of educating. *Erziehung* therefore implies intention on the side of the educator (an educator has the explicit intention to have some impact on the one to be educated) and the articulation of what the activity of *Erziehung* is supposed to bring about, that is, a sense of the aim or aims of *Erziehung* (see Oelkers 1993; 2001). Most importantly, *Erziehung* implies an orientation towards the education of the person as a free human being. This means that the one being educated is never just seen as an object for influence and manipulation, but always also as a subject (or an emerging subject) in its own right. It is here that we can see a connection between the idea of *Erziehung* and the distinction between education and indoctrination (as discussed in Chapter 1). While, as shown, the distinction is a difficult one to make, one can at least say that if one has the intention to indoctrinate, one denies the subjectivity of the one being educated, whereas if one has the intention to educate, one acts on the assumption that the one being educated is in the process of becoming a subject in his or her own right (see, for example Spiecker and Straughan 1991). In the German context, *Erziehung* is the more encompassing concept and teaching (in German: 'lehren' or 'unterrichten') is mainly seen as a subset of *Erziehung*. While teaching, in this way of thinking, can be understood in a very narrow technical sense – for example, just as the transmission of information or skill – an 'educational' (*Erziehung*) perspective on teaching would always include a wider concern for the formation of the human person (which is not dissimilar from Richard Peters' claim that teaching is about the intentional transmission of something worthwhile *in a morally acceptable manner*; see Peters 1966, and the discussion in Chapter 1 of this book). It is also why the German educationalist Johann Friedrich Herbart (1776–1841) coined the idea of 'educative teaching' ('erziehender unterricht').

Education, values and normativity

The conceptual complexities surrounding the word 'education' have led several authors to claim that 'education' is an 'essentially contested concept' (Gallie 1956). The idea of essentially contested concepts in not so much that they are difficult to define or that people have different opinions about their meaning, but that this difficulty has to do with the fact that such disputes cannot be settled by just referring to 'the facts' or just by means of argument or logic, because the discussion is ultimately not about what the concept means but what it *should* mean. The discussion is, in other words, *normative* and is concerned with people's values and beliefs. We can see this quite clearly in the case of education because on closer inspection many definitions of education are actually statements of what the person defining the concept considers to be *good or worthwhile* education. This is why Richard Peters' definition of teaching as discussion in Chapter 1 of this book is not so much a definition as a statement of his views about *good* teaching, that is, teaching worthy of the name 'teaching'. There is actually nothing wrong with the fact that discussions about what education is or ought to be are thoroughly normative and thus always require engagement with questions of values. After all, if we take education in the sense of educating (the fourth meaning) towards becoming an educated person (the fifth meaning), it is always about deliberate attempts to effect change in someone's knowledge, beliefs, values, attitudes, skills or personhood – which always raises the question of justification, that is, the question to what extent such changes can be considered desirable (which includes the difficult question of who is to make a judgement about the desirability of such change – the educator or the one being educated). This is a complicated discussion with a long history that became even more complicated as a result of the rise of Enlightenment ideas of human self-determination and freedom. If, to put it briefly, before the Enlightenment the educational key-word was that of 'perfection' – that is, making the human being more perfect through its engagement with the best aspects of culture and tradition – from the Enlightenment onwards the educational key-word became that of 'autonomy', that is, using one's rational capacities for responsible self-determined action. This shift has resulted in what has become known in the literature as the 'educational paradox', very aptly summarised by Immanuel Kant in the question 'How do I cultivate freedom through coercion?'

Education and the question of purpose

The normative dimensions of any discussion about education reveal one further characteristic of the concept of 'education' that is important to mention, which is the fact that 'education' is what in the philosophical literature is known as a *teleological* concept, that is, a concept that implies a *telos* – which is the Greek word for aim or purpose. The idea here is that education is not an activity we undertake just for its own sake, but always because we want to achieve something or bring something about. Talking about education, to put it simply, thus always raises the question as to what education is *for*. It will not come as a surprise that people have quite different views about what education should be for, not only depending on their understanding of what education 'is', but also, and more importantly, depending on the values they hold and the views they have about what education ought to achieve. Viewed from this angle it is actually quite difficult if not impossible to make any clear statement about what the purpose or purposes of education should be. This does not mean, however, that it is not possible to bring some more clarity and precision in discussions about the purposes of education. Elsewhere (Biesta 2010) I have suggested that a first step towards such clarification is to acknowledge that educational systems perform a number of different functions. One major function of education – particularly of formal education – is that of *qualification*. It lies in providing children, young people and adults with the knowledge, skills and understandings and often also with the dispositions and forms of judgement that allow them to 'do something' – a 'doing' which can range from the very specific (such as in the case of vocational or professional education) to the much more general (such as the role of education in preparing children and young people for life in highly complex societies). A second major function of education is that of *socialisation*. Socialisation refers to the ways in which, through education, we become initiated into and part of existing social, cultural, political, professional or religious communities, practices and traditions. In some cases socialisation is actively pursued – for example, where the aim is to inculcate the values of democratic citizenship or the ways of doing and being of particular professional communities. But even if socialisation is not an explicit aim of educational programmes and practices, education will still have a socialising 'effect' on those who take part in it (something that has been shown in research on what is known as the 'hidden curriculum'). Through its socialising function education inserts individuals into existing ways of doing and being and thus plays an important role in the continuation of culture and tradition. Education does, however, not only contribute to qualification and socialisation but always also impacts on the human person. While some refer to this as a process of individuation, I prefer to refer to this function as a process of *subjectification* – that is, of becoming a subject of action and responsibility rather than remaining an object of the demands and directions of others. The subjectification functions might perhaps best be understood as the opposite of the socialisation function of education, because subjectification is precisely *not* about the insertion of 'newcomers' into existing ways of doing and being, but is characterised by an orientation towards self-determination and freedom (and in this sense the idea that education contributes to the process of becoming a subject of action and responsibility clearly has its roots in Enlightenment thinking).

The distinction between qualification, socialisation and subjectification is not only useful in order to get a clearer understanding of the different ways in which education *functions*. At the same time, we can consider them as *three different domains of educational purpose*, that is, three domains we can – and in a sense ought to – take into consideration when we try to articulate what education should be for. While some would argue that education should only focus on qualification – this is a rather traditional rationale for the school as an institution that should only focus on knowledge and should shy away from an engagement with values – others would argue that education should also pay explicit attention to socialisation. This has become more prominent in recent years as a result of the introduction of such curricular areas as personal, social and moral education, environmental education and citizenship education. While there is a qualification component to such areas – there are, after all, things to know and to learn about the environment, about morality or about citizenship – there is an explicit ambition to instil particular values and attitudes in children and young people so as to make them into environmentally aware human beings or make them into good democratic citizens. While again some would stop here and argue that schools should only focus on qualification and socialisation, many educators and educationalists would actually agree that any education worthy of the name should also contribute to the formation of the human person and should thus pay explicit attention to the subjectification dimension of education.

Making educational judgements

While the distinction between qualification, socialisation and subjectification leaves many more detailed questions open – and there are many, such as what it would mean to become qualified for a profession or for life in modern society, what it would mean to become part of existing communities and traditions, what it would mean to become a subject of action and responsibility, and so on – it provides at least a framework to engage with more precision with the question as to what education is for, not only in order to analyse different positions and arguments but also in order to develop more explicit and precise justifications for the choices one makes about the purposes of education, from the individual level of the classroom teacher all the way up to the ways in which society justifies its 'stake' in education. One important and difficult question in such discussions has to do with finding the right 'balance' between the three domains. This not only has to do with the fact that the three domains should not be seen as separate but at least as partly overlapping (see Figure 4.1), so that even when one focuses on one domain – say on the transmission and acquisition of a particular body of knowledge – it is likely that this will also have 'effects' in the other domains. More importantly, gains in one domain often lead to losses in another domain. Think, for example, of how an emphasis on exam results might drive up achievements in the domain of qualification but might at the same time 'teach' students that competition is, at the end of the day, preferable over cooperation (a 'message' in the domain of socialisation) and may also contribute to a more self-centred rather than other-centred kind of personality (an 'impact' in the domain of subjectification). There are not only important philosophical questions to be asked here. Making educationally wise judgements about how to deal with such tensions and contradictions is at the very heart of what good teaching is (also) about (see Biesta 2012).

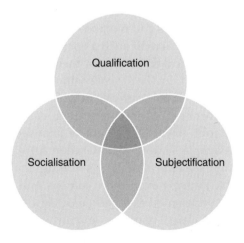

FIGURE 4.1 The three functions of education and the three domains of educational purpose.

The encounter between philosophy and education

Having started from the simple definition of philosophy of education as the philosophical study of education and its problems, and having tried to give an answer both to the question of what philosophy is and to the question of what education is, we can now see that the encounter between philosophy and education contains a vast array of possibilities, not only because of the variety of philosophy positions, traditions and ideas, but also because of the complexity of the very notion of education itself. What makes this encounter even more rich and complex is the fact that, unlike in the domain of science, where new theories and insights tend to replace older ways of thinking, many, if not all, of the ideas generated by philosophers over the centuries remain valid or at least interesting. This is because in philosophy later views tend not so much to *replace* earlier insights and ideas as that they add depth, detail, complexity and controversy to the discussion. The philosopher Alfred North Whitehead (1861–1947) has captured this particular quality of philosophy quite well by suggesting that the whole European philosophical tradition might be seen as a series of footnotes to Plato (Whitehead 1979: 39). While this makes the encounter between philosophy and education both exciting and rewarding, it also makes it quite challenging as there are so many places to start from and so many ideas and insights to work with.

Philosophers writing about education: some 'classics'

When we look at the actual work done in the philosophy of education, two things stand out. One is that throughout the whole history of philosophy, philosophers themselves have been discussing educational issues and in doing so have generated a number of real 'classics'. In Plato's text *The Republic* (see, for example, Plato 1955) we can, for example, find a detailed account of the roles of education in the ideal state, with a clear distinction between the kind of education that the guardians of this state should receive and the kind of education that the rulers of the state, the so-called 'philosopher-kings', should have. Plato not only provides much 'technical' detail but also discusses extensively the aims and methods of such education. Interestingly, Plato connects the education of the rulers of such a society strongly with philosophy – in a sense he proposes a philosophical education for them – highlighting the crucial importance of knowledge of the good. In *The Republic* which, as all of Plato's writings, is written in the form of a dialogue – in this case one in which Socrates is the main protagonist – Plato introduces a number of ideas and metaphors, such as the idea of education as a process of 'turning the soul' towards the light of knowledge, that are still being discussed today (see, for example, Haroutunian-Gordon 2010).

It is, however, not only the *content* of Plato's writings that has made a lasting impact on educational thought. Perhaps even more famous and influential is its dialogical *form*, which itself can be understood as a particular view of education. This often finds Socrates, through a refined play of questions and answers, bringing his interlocutors to insights and understandings including, often, an acknowledgement of the limits and limitations of one's own knowledge on the assumption that the first step to wisdom is recognition of one's own ignorance. Socrates often claimed that he actually knew nothing. This approach has become known in the literature as the Socratic method or Socratic teaching, and often compares teaching to the practice of midwifery, that is, a process of bringing out what is already inside – that is, a process of helping students to come to clearer insights and understanding – rather than as a process where the teacher would transmit something new to the student (on this distinction, see Biesta (2012)). Aspects of the Socratic method can also be found in what is known as *Philosophy for Children*, an approach to engage children in philosophical enquiry developed by the American philosopher Matthew Lipman (1922–2010), that has become a popular programme around the world (see, for example, Lipman *et al.* 1980).

Another important and at the time highly influential text on education written by a philosopher is John Locke's *Some Thoughts Concerning Education*, which was published in 1693 (see, for example, Locke 2008). In this book Locke presents, among other things, his idea of the mind as a 'tabula rasa', that is, as a clean slate upon which experience makes impressions, thus highlighting the crucial important of education on the formation of the human being. Locke also highlighted the importance of instilling good habits in children before embarking on more academic and intellectual forms of education, and discussed extensively the formation of virtue and reason, a process that should focus on treating children as rational beings and on using esteem and disgrace rather than rewards and punishments as the latter would arouse 'passions' rather than reason. That Locke's text was highly popular can be seen from the fact that in the eighteenth century alone it was published in at least 53 editions in English, French, Italian, German, Dutch and Swedish (see Axtell 1968, pp. 100–104).

The third major work to mention here is Jean-Jacques Rousseau's *Émile, or on Education*, which was published in 1762 (see, for example, Rousseau 1979). The book – which contains the famous opening sentence 'Everything is good as it leaves the hands of the author of things, everything degenerates in the hands of man' (*'Tout est bien sortant des mains de l'Auteur des choses, tout dégénère entre les mains de l'homme'*) – uses the device of a story about the education of the child and young man Émile by his tutor and also contains a (shorter) section on the education of Sophie, Émile's wife-to-be. One aspect of what Rousseau puts forward in the book is the question of how to balance what is 'of the child' with what is 'of society'. In the psychological literature this issue is often discussed as the 'nature–nurture' debate and concerns the question of to what extent what we become is the result of internal (nature) factors or the result of external (nurture) factors – nowadays most people would argue that it is an interaction between the two rather than one or the other. The educational question is, however, not about explaining the factors that contribute to what we are or become, but raises the issue of how we can, in terms of Rousseau's argument, maintain the original goodness of the human being while at the same time becoming good and responsible members of society. The educational question here, in other words, is about how to deal with the fact that any engagement with education – either through our own enculturation (*Bildung*) or through the efforts of others to impact upon our growth (*Erziehung*) – is not just a gain but also potentially a loss (for a poignant discussion of this experience, see Kerdeman 1999, and also Mollenhauer 1983).

If I can mention two more classical texts – texts on education written by philosophers which have had an enduring impact on and relevance for contemporary discussions – then the first of these is a short publication attributed to Immanuel Kant (though probably written down by someone else based on notes from a lecture) called *On Education* (*Über Pädagogik*), published in 1803 (see Kant 1803; 1982). In *On Education*, Kant, one of the major Enlightenment philosophers, highlighted the crucial role of education in helping human beings to develop their rational powers in order to achieve rational autonomy – that is, autonomy based on the use of reason. In his short text 'An answer to the question "What is Enlightenment?"' (originally published in 1784; see Kant 1992) Kant had defined the 'motto' of Enlightenment as 'sapere aude', that is, 'dare to think' or have the courage to use your own capacity for reason. What is interesting from an educational perspective is that Kant did not conceive of this capacity as a contingent historical possibility – something that individuals could either acquire or not – but saw it instead as something that was a central part of human nature. He described the 'propensity and vocation to free thinking' as man's 'ultimate destination' and as the 'aim of his existence' (Kant 1982: 701), which meant that to block progress in enlightenment would be 'a crime against human nature' (Kant 1992 [1784]: 93). Interestingly enough, however, Kant also argued that the 'propensity to free thinking' could *only* be brought about through education (see Kant 1982: 710). Kant not only wrote that man 'is the only creature that has to be educated' (Kant 1982: 697); he also argued that the human being can only become human – that is, a rational autonomous being – 'through education' ('*Der Mensch kann nur Mensch werden durch Erziehung*') (ibid.: 699). With Kant the rationale for the educational 'project' became founded on the idea 'of a certain kind of subject who has the inherent potential to become self-motivated and self-directing', while the task of education became one of bringing about or releasing this potential 'so that subjects become fully autonomous and capable of exercising their individual and intentional agency' (Usher and Edwards 1994: 24–25).

The fifth 'classic' to mention here (although this list is far from exhaustive) is John Dewey's *Democracy and Education*, a book that was first published in 1916 (see, for example, Dewey 1966). Although the subtitle of the book was *An Introduction to the Philosophy of Education*, the book does much more than just introduce the philosophy of education. It not only provides a detailed account of Dewey's own theory of education – a theory that, looked at from a Continental perspective, is perhaps more a theory of *Bildung* than a theory of *Erziehung* (see also Siljander *et al.* 2012) – but also includes a statement of his influential ideas about the relationship between education and democracy.

The feminism question in philosophy and philosophy of education

There are of course many more books in which philosophers have engaged with educational questions, and one could argue, looking at the history of such publications, that for a long time major thought about education was indeed generated by philosophers. It is important to mention here – although in a sense it is difficult to have missed this in the discussion so far – that the history of philosophy is entirely dominated by men even if, such as in the case of Rousseau, the discussion is about the education of women. Mary Wollstonecraft (1759–1797), now considered to be one of the early feminist philosophers, actually wrote a strong critique of Rousseau's ideas in her *A Vindication of the Rights of Women* (published in 1792; see, for example, Wollstonecraft 2004). It has only been in recent decades, particularly in North America through the work of such authors as Jane Roland Martin (see, for example, Martin's landmark book *Reclaiming a Conversation: The Ideal of the Educated Woman* from 1985) and Nel Noddings (see, for example, her *Caring: A Feminine Approach to Ethics and Moral Education* from 1984), that feminist thought has begun to influence the philosophical conversation about education (see also Stone 1994; Weiner 1994). While this work draws inspiration from wider developments in feminist philosophy and theory – and while the impact of feminist thought on education has also been achieved through, for example, feminist psychology, sociology and cultural theory – feminist philosophy of education should be understood in the context of an important development in the second half of the twentieth century, that of the establishment of philosophy of education as an own 'field' or specialism more strongly located, institutionally, in university schools and departments of education than emanating from schools and departments of philosophy. (There are ongoing discussions within the field of philosophy of education about its exact status, that is, whether it should be understood as a form of applied philosophy firmly located in the 'mother' discipline of philosophy, or whether it should be understood as a form of educational inquiry which, whilst making use of philosophical resources, has its identity first and foremost as an educational endeavour; see also below.)

Philosophy of education as a 'field'

The major way in which philosophy of education established itself after the Second World War was in the form of *analytic* philosophy of education – sometimes known as 'APE' both by its admirers and its critics. The work of Israel Scheffler in North America and that of Richard Peters and Paul Hirst in the UK played a major role in the development of analytic philosophy of education as the dominant approach in what it meant to do philosophy of education. Many others followed in their footsteps and it can be argued that up to the late 1970s or early 1980s analytic philosophy of education – which took its philosophical inspiration mainly from philosophy of language, logic and epistemology – was the dominant approach in the field. Analytic philosophers of education partly focused their efforts on the analysis and clarification of key educational concepts such as 'teaching' (see, for example, the discussion of Peters' analysis of the concept in Chapter 1; or Macmillan and Nelson 1968) and 'learning' (see, for example, Phillips and Soltis 1985), or of the wider language of education (see, for example, Scheffler 1960; see also Peters 1966; Dearden *et al.* 1972). In addition to the analysis of key educational concepts (see also Soltis 1968), the analytic philosophers of education were also interested in exploring the nature of knowledge, truth and rationality, which resulted in a strong interest within analytic philosophy of education in questions of critical thinking and its education (see, for example, Siegel 1988 and, for a critique and reformulation inspired by feminism and pragmatism, Thayer-Bacon 2000). (For an intriguing and highly readable account of the history of analytic philosophy through a number of intellectual 'self-portraits', see Waks 2008.)

From the 1980s onwards philosophy of education has become increasingly diverse, engaging not only with a much wider array of philosophical ideas and fields – including social and political philosophy, ethics and moral philosophy, and aesthetics – but also with a much wider range of philosophical traditions – including feminist philosophy, postmodern and poststructural philosophy, critical theory and increasingly also with Aristotelian thought. Another important line within philosophy of education was the rediscovery of pragmatism as a philosophy and a philosophy of education (for example, see Garrison 1995).

Concluding comments

The ambition of this chapter has been to provide an introduction into philosophical engagement with educational questions, issues and problems. Rather than presenting philosophy as a particular method – for example, a method of critical inquiry – or a particular body of (philosophical) knowledge, I have taken a more historical approach in order to show the kind of problems and issues that those who call themselves philosophers have been occupied with over the centuries, showing both continuity and change. Given that, unlike in the sciences, new philosophical ideas and approaches do not make older ones invalid, the history of philosophy provides educators and educationalists with a huge resource that can be used in the study of education. Rather than only looking at the philosophy of education through the lens of philosophy I have, in this chapter, also paid explicit attention to questions about how to understand education so as not to make the mistake that philosophy is the complex, difficult and sophisticated part of philosophy of education while education is the obvious, simple and straightforward element. That is why we should think about philosophy of education as an encounter between philosophy *and* education, one in which both have things to contribute – which is why, as I have put it in the title of this chapter, it is not only important to think philosophically about education but also, and perhaps even more, to think educationally about philosophy so as to make sure that the engagement with philosophy ultimately benefits the field of education, both with regard to its theory and its practice. The challenge in the philosophical study of education is to keep educational questions central and use philosophy as a resource to engage with them. For example, the question of whether knowledge should be understood as objective or subjective, as 'given' or as constructed, is in itself an abstract philosophical question about which philosophers have been writing for centuries and are likely to be writing for centuries to come. To just transplant that discussion to the classroom is quite meaningless. But the distinctions made and arguments put forward in the discussion about the nature of knowledge can be helpful when, as educators, we need to make judgements about curriculum and pedagogy – that is, about what knowledge we should make available to our students and about the ways in which we might do this. Here it might indeed be useful to acknowledge that students are less likely to be passive recipients of knowledge but actually actively need to construct their own understandings and insights. But whether this means that knowledge itself is (nothing but) a construction – which is an epistemological rather than an educational question – is quite a different question that, in a certain sense, may well be irrelevant for how we think about the ways in which students acquire and master knowledge and understanding. This is why philosophy of education needs to be a two-way conversation ultimately driven by the things that matter educationally – which is, of course, itself a topic for ongoing discussion.

References

Axtell, J.L. (1968). Introduction. In J.L. Axtell (ed.), *The Educational Writings of John Locke*. Cambridge: Cambridge University Press.

Bailey, C. (1984). *Beyond the Present and the Particular: A Theory of Liberal Education*. London: Routledge and Kegan Paul.

Biesta, G.J.J. (2010). *Good Education in an Age of Measurement: Ethics, Politics, Democracy*. Boulder, CO: Paradigm.

Biesta, G.J.J. (2011). Disciplines and theory in the academic study of education: a comparative analysis of the Anglo-American and Continental construction of the field. *Pedagogy, Culture and Society* 19(2), 175–192.

Biesta, G.J.J. (ed.) (2012). *Making Sense of Education: Fifteen Contemporary Educational Theorists in Their Own Words*. Dordrecht/Heidelberg/New York: Springer.

Biesta, G.J.J. (2012). Receiving the gift of teaching: from 'learning from' to 'being taught by'. *Studies in Philosophy and Education* 32, 449–461.

Biesta, G.J.J. and Stams, G.J.J.M. (2001). Critical thinking and the question of critique. Some lessons from deconstruction. *Studies in Philosophy and Education* 20(1), 57–74.

Bruner, J. (1960). *The Process of Education*. Cambridge, MA: Harvard University Press.

Dearden, R.F., Hirst, P.H. and Peters, R.S. (eds) (1972). *Education and the Development of Reason*. Routledge and Kegan Paul, London.

Dewey, J. (1966). *Democracy and Education: An Introduction to the Philosophy of Education*. New York: Free Press.

Gallie, W.B. (1956). Essentially contested concepts. *Proceedings of the Aristotelian Society* 56, 167–198.

Garrison, J. (1995). *The New Scholarship on John Dewey*. Dordrecht/Boston, MA/London: Kluwer Academic Publishers.

Haroutunian-Gordon, S. (2010). *Learning to Teach Through Discussion: The Art of Turning the Soul*. New Haven, CT: Yale University Press.

Kant, I. (1803). *Über Pädagogik*. Edited by D.F.T. Rink. Koningsberg: Friedrich Nicolovius.

Kant, I. (1982). Über Pädagogik. In I. Kant, *Schiften zur Anthropologie, Geschichtsphilosophie, Politik und Pädagogik* (pp. 695–761). Frankfurt am Main: Insel Verlag.

Kant, I. (1992 [1784]). An answer to the question 'What is Enlightenment?' In P. Waugh (ed.), *Postmodernism: A Reader* (pp. 89–95). London: Edward Arnold.

Kerdeman, D. (1999). Between interlochen and Idaho: hermeneutics and education for understanding. In Steve Tozer (ed.), *Philosophy of Education 1998* (pp. 272–279). Urbana, IL: Philosophy of Education Society.

Lipman, M., Sharp, A.M. and Oscanyan, F.S. (1980). *Philosophy in the Classroom*. Philadelphia, PA: Temple University Press.

Locke, J. (2008). *Some Thoughts Concerning Education*. Charleston, SC: BiblioBazaar.

Macmillan, C.J.B. and Nelson, T. (eds) (1968). *Concepts of Teaching*. Chicago, IL: Rand McNally.

Martin, J.R. (1985). *Reclaiming a Conversation: The Ideal of the Educated Woman*. New Haven, CT: Yale University Press.

Martin, J.W. (1981). The ideal of the educated person. *Educational Theory* 31(2), 97–109.

Mollenhauer, K. (1983). *Vergessene Zusammenhänge*. München: Juventa.

Noddings, N. (1984). *Caring: A Feminine Approach to Ethics and Moral Education*. Berkeley, CA: University of California Press.

Noddings, N. (2012). *Philosophy of Education*. Third edition. Boulder, CO: Westview Press.

Oelkers, J. (1993). Influence and development: two basic paradigms of education. *Studies in Philosophy and Education* 13(2), 91–109.

Oelkers, J. (2001). *Einführung in die Theorie der Erziehung*. Weinheim and Basel: Beltz.

Peters, R.S. (1966). *Ethics and Education*. London: Allen and Unwin.

Peters, R.S. (1970). Education and the educated man. *Journal of Philosophy of Education* 4(1), 5–20.

Phillips, D.C. and Soltis, J. (1985). *Perspectives on Learning*. New York: Teachers College Press.

Plato (1955). *The Republic*. Trans. H.P.D. Lee London: Penguin.

Rorty, R. (1978). Philosophy as a kind of writing: an essay on Derrida. *New Literary History* 10(1), 141–160.

Rousseau, J.-J. (1979). *Emile, or On Education*. Trans. Allan Bloom. New York: Basic Books.

Scheffler, I. (1960). *The Language of Education*. Springfeld, IL: Charles C. Thomas.

Siegel, H. (1988). *Educating Reason: Rationality, Critical Thinking, and Education*. New York: Routledge.

Siljander, P., Kivelä, A. and Sutinen, A. (eds) (2012). *Theories of 'Bildung' and Growth*. Rotterdam/Boston, MA/Taipei: Sense Publishers.

Soltis, J. (1968). *An Introduction to the Analysis of Educational Concepts*. Reading, MA: Addison-Wesley.

Spiecker, B. and Straughan, R. (eds) (1991). *Freedom and Indoctrination*. London/New York: Cassell.

Stone, L. (ed.) (1994). *The Education Feminism Reader*. London/New York: Routledge.

Thayer-Bacon, B. (2000). *Transforming Critical Thinking*. New York: Teachers College Press.

Usher, R. and Edwards, R. (1994). *Postmodernism and Education*. London/New York: Routledge.

Waks, L.J. (ed.) (2008). *Leaders in Philosophy of Education: Intellectual Self-portraits*. Rotterdam/Boston, MA/Taipei: Sense Publishers.

Weiner, G. (1994). *Feminisms in Education*. Buckingham: Open University Press.

Whitehead, A.N. (1979). *Process and Reality*. New York: The Free Press.

Wollstonecraft, M. (2004). *A Vindication of the Rights of Woman*. Harmondsworth: Penguin.

5

Psychology in education

Graham Mitchell

Remember, test scores and measures of achievement tell you where a student is, but they don't tell you where a student could end up.

Carol Dweck (2006: 66)

Introduction

This chapter will examine the significant contribution psychology makes to helping learners end up in a better place. It is about achieving more in education, but it is also about increasing the value and enjoyment of the educational journey along the way. There are six sections that address different themes and topics about psychology in education. The first section introduces the principal perspectives in psychology, and these are then referred to throughout the rest of the chapter. In the following three sections we see psychology's role in measuring traits and abilities, in learning and in motivation. The fifth section looks at developmental disorders, and how psychology can help with diagnosis and remediation. The final section examines more recent work in positive psychology.

Psychological perspectives

Psychology contributes to the study of education through different perspectives or approaches. These include biological, cognitive, behavioural and social approaches. Behaviourism emphasises the role of conditioning in human behaviour. Pavlov's research on salivation in dogs is well known (Toates 2009). By associating a neutral stimulus, like a bell or light, with food, the bell alone eventually becomes sufficient to elicit salivation. This is called classical conditioning. We can see immediate application for this in education. Neutral stimuli like classrooms, books and teachers are commonly associated with pleasurable or unpleasurable experiences. Although the story has become distorted with time (Cornwell *et al.* 1980), two workers, Watson and Raynor, demonstrated how fear could be learnt through classical conditioning with a small boy named Albert (Field 2006). Positive and negative associations in classroom settings may then be responsible for some of our educational likes and dislikes.

Skinner investigated operant conditioning with a box in which rats and pigeons learnt to press a lever repeatedly to receive a food reward. The reward reinforced the lever-pressing behaviour. Skinner also showed how complex behaviours could be taught by reinforcing the behaviour's sub-components separately (Toates 2009). This is called shaping and could be applied to more complex skills like writing. The use of praise and correction in educational settings can be thought about in terms of operant conditioning (Urdan and Schoenfelder 2006). Schools' behaviour management systems tend to follow behavioural principles. We need to question, however, whether simple stimulus–response animal models are sufficient to explain the complexities of classroom behaviour.

Social learning and social cognitive theories propose that we learn by modelling the behaviour of others and noting the consequences of observed behaviour (Mohamadi *et al.* 2011; Woolfolk 2013). Bandura advanced this theory to explain why some behaviours are developed without any apparent reinforcement (Durkin 1995). Social learning is not limited to childhood and can provide a lifelong source of learning experiences.

The cognitive approach is concerned with mental processing (Bruning *et al.* 2004). Miller (2003) argued that a cognitive revolution was necessary to progress psychology beyond the limitations of the observable stimulus–response behaviourist approach. The first cognitive revolution occurred in the 1950s and 1960s. Laboratory experiments, computer modelling and the study of deficits following brain damage are all methods used to examine processes such as attention, perception, learning, memory and language. A second cognitive revolution then followed, and this has focused on self-belief and the implicit theories we hold about ourselves and our world. The social constructionist approach addresses social and cultural influences on development (Vauclair and Perret 2003). This social approach invites us to see that the way we interact with our social world will affect our development and current feelings (Woolfolk 2013). We are embedded in a particular culture, and our sense of self is socially constructed as we engage in social relations and patterns of language. Rather than taking traditional modes of thinking and behaviour for granted, we can adopt a more critical stance when viewing educational institutions and society's educational values.

The psychodynamic approach places an emphasis on unconscious motives and early childhood experiences. Bowlby examined the attachment of young children to their mothers (Hofer 2005). Bowlby's original views have been refined, but the presence of significant others in a child's life is seen to be important for facilitating future social interactions and for providing resources for coping with stressful situations (Durkin 1995). Catch-up effects can occur for children with impoverished attachments, but these will depend on the quality of subsequent relationships with others (Rutter 2000). The study of vulnerable children on the Hawaiian island of Kauai reveals that resilience was associated with the receiving of positive attention from a close attachment figure (Prior 1999; Werner and Smith 1998; Dyer and McGuinness 1966).

The biological approach seeks to explain human behaviour by referring to genetic and physiological mechanisms. Brain functioning and chemical activities are seen to be relevant to an understanding of learning processes (Toates 2011). Brain imaging can be useful when looking at the neural correlates of conditions like dyslexia.

The humanistic perspective became popular in the mid 1950s. Whereas other approaches seem to emphasise determinism by examining environmental, cognitive, psychic and physiological influences on human behaviour, the humanistic approach places an emphasis on free will. Abraham Maslow and Carl Rogers helped to introduce this far more optimistic psychological perspective in which individuals could gain a sense of ownership of processes of growth and development. Maslow proposed a hierarchy of needs (Maslow 1943). Only when basic physiological needs were satisfied would it be possible to meet higher needs, including the experience of self-actualisation. Self-actualisation is related to peak experiences, reaching our potential and gaining self-fulfilment. Student motivation and classroom procedures can be thought about in terms of a hierarchy of needs. It is also worth considering to what extent the pupil or student should experience ownership of the educational process. More recently, Csikszentmihalyi (2002) has extended such ideas with the notion of flow. This is about the enhancement of our current experiences – it is better to travel hopefully than to arrive. Flow is experienced when we are so engrossed in an activity that we lose sense of time; something relevant to student motivation (Ullén *et al.* 2012). This raises the issue of transferring some ownership of the learning process to learners with the intention of gaining more highly motivated behaviour.

Each of the psychological perspectives provides insight into ways of encouraging engagement with educational processes and optimising achievement.

Traits, abilities and attainments

Why is it that some people seem more capable of learning than others, or are more predisposed to study a particular subject? Where do traits and abilities come from? We can frame these questions within a nature–nurture study, and recognise that we result from the dynamic developing interaction between inherited and environmental influences. Monozygotic twins, reared together and reared apart, have been used to examine the role of biological factors in determining intelligence. This is a controversial area where some criticise a general willingness to prioritise inheritance (Rose 1997; Rose *et al.* 1990), and others criticise an overemphasis on environmental influences (Pinker 2002). Genetic and environmental determinism can limit our expectations of others in an educational setting. Early theories of development placed an emphasis on child development and viewed the adult as a stable, fixed consequence of what had occurred in childhood. In lifespan development, we view development as proceeding throughout life. With this view we may be more optimistic about anyone's future progress because development is never finished, and future growth and positive change is always possible (Dweck 2006).

This does not mean that we should never look at a person's past. Recognising developmental correlates of current traits and abilities can be valuable. An awareness of the psychological and social factors that influence development can inform intervention decisions and help to promote optimal development. The child's social, emotional and intellectual worlds will all contain factors that influence development.

Can we, however, measure the consequences of a person's genetic background and past experiences? Psychometric attempts to objectively measure constructs such as intelligence and personality are commonplace. Individuals are scored using questionnaires, inventories and test sheets; but these need to be fit for purpose. A measure is only declared trustworthy when we can demonstrate that it is reliable, valid and standardised (Rust and Golombok 2008).

Reliability refers to the extent to which a measure is capable of delivering consistent findings. There are several different ways to measure reliability. Test–retest reliability involves repeating the test with the same participants and establishing the extent to which there is a correlation between the two sets of test scores.

Validity refers to the extent to which a test measures what it is claimed to. Reliable findings are insufficient if they fail to inform us about the measure we are interested in. A test claiming to measure creativity should be measuring exactly that and not something else. There are several types of validity.

A test needs to be standardised so that the performance of any particular sample of students can be compared to other students of similar age or educational level in the general population. We would therefore be able to judge, for instance, a pupil's intelligence relative to others in their own age group.

We are particularly interested in measuring traits, abilities and attainments, and it is important that we can distinguish between these three categories of measurement.

Traits are the characteristic patterns of behaviour and thinking that we engage in. These are our signature attributes. Personality measurement has received much attention over the past few decades, but perhaps the classification that has received most attention is the five-factor model associated with two researchers, McCrae and Costa (2004). The five factors can be summed up with the acronym OCEAN: Openness to experience, Conscientiousness, Extraversion, Agreeableness and Neuroticism.

Abilities can be thought of as measures of cognitive performance that may facilitate future attainment levels (Cooper 2010). We might be interested, for example, in measuring different facets of intelligence, such as verbal or spatial intelligence. The measurement of intelligence is problematical and efforts are continually being made to devise improved techniques of measurement (Jensen 2011). Intelligence tests may be culturally, racially and gender biased. We are nevertheless able to administer recognised tests in classrooms, record children's scores and then establish where that child is positioned relative to the population the child is drawn from. An intelligence quotient (IQ) is a quantitative judgement based on comparisons with a larger population, and can be the ratio of mental age to chronological age. Popular intelligence tests for assessing ability in schoolchildren have included the Stanford–Binet and the Wechsler Intelligence Scale for Children (WISC). A general intelligence factor or thinking ability factor called g can be measured with psychometric tests, and intelligence differences are claimed to remain relatively stable over a lifetime (Deary 2003). Such differences are associated with later attainment in education and work, and even with health and longevity. Whalley and Deary (2001) provide data indicating that high childhood IQ scores are associated with reduced mortality through to age 76. Intelligence testing has nevertheless been criticised (Gould 1996). Problems with intelligence testing become apparent when we examine the effects of positive and negative labelling. Rosenthal and Jacobson's (1966) work has sensitised us to the limiting and empowering influence of different contexts of expectation. Eighteen schoolteachers were told that particular children in their class had been identified with an unusual potential to make intellectual gains. Even though these children were randomly selected, IQ gains made during the year by the 'bright pupils' were higher than those in the control group. Findings from this study have been used to argue that positive expectations can influence intelligence test results. Chaikin *et al.*'s (1974) work also indicated that positively labelled children received preferential treatment from teachers. Intelligence tests can also be used to determine who is entitled to educational resources. We may decide to assess ability at key stages in a person's life, and allocate educational resources in accordance with test results. This is apparent with the use of the 11+ examination system, which has been used in parts of the UK. Instead of allocating additional resources to children who need them, a common practice has been to make better-resourced grammar schools available to high-scoring children, leaving lower-scoring children with poorer-resourced secondary modern schools.

Gardner popularised the view that intelligence was much broader than previously defined. He proposed eight intelligences, namely verbal/linguistic, logical/mathematical, visual/spatial, bodily/kinaesthetic, musical, interpersonal, intrapersonal and naturalist (Gardner 1998). Gardner's multiple-intelligence approach has proved popular and today provides the basis for many classroom learning style initiatives (Gilbert 2002; Bowkett *et al.* 2007; Delgoshaei and Delavari 2012). Gardner's work nevertheless has received criticism for the marketing of well-established ideas about abilities in the guise of something new (Cooper 2010).

Goleman (1995) questioned whether IQ scores are always associated with later earning power, career advancement or interpersonal aspects of life. Sensitivity to other people's emotions and being in control of one's own emotions were claimed to be far more important qualities. Goleman's work has proved popular, with some academic researchers embracing his notion of emotional intelligence. These more recent concepts of intelligence have served to challenge views that academic success is the only real expression of intellectual worth (Rust and Golombok 2008). Different intelligence measures may nevertheless be useful for monitoring progress and for diagnosing educational problems.

Attainment can be measured through assignments, tests and examinations. Both coursework and end-of-course examinations provide information on individuals' academic attainment. Attainment figures are commonly used to assess individual student progress, identify learning difficulties and evaluate the work of individual teachers and schools. Concern has recently been expressed, however, at the frequent testing of school students, within a culture dominated by performance measures. Performance goal orientation can be seen to contrast with mastery goal orientation (Meece and Daniels 2008). Mastery is about learning for its own sake, the joy of learning and the satisfaction gained from developing worthwhile skills. It may be that a more mastery-oriented culture would provide motivation gains (Reeve 2009) and be of considerable benefit to both teachers and learners.

Ability–achievement discrepancy analyses are conducted to establish whether someone's expected attainment, as measured by an IQ test, is matched by actual attainment. Such tests can be of use when diagnosing conditions such as dyslexia, but inherent in such procedures is the assumption that IQ scores are capable of predicting attainment levels. The beliefs that we hold about intelligence may be important in determining motivation levels and achievement. Carol Dweck (2000; 2006) has conducted research into two mindsets that people hold. The fixed mindset holds that intelligence is stable, lifelong and difficult to change; the growth mindset sees intelligence as dynamic and subject to change. Within a challenging educational setting, those students holding the more optimistic growth mindset performed better. Dweck has also demonstrated that students' mindsets can be changed. We will return to student self-belief later.

Learning

In identifying ways to encourage learning, it is helpful to consider three areas: the processes, the learner and the teacher. Different psychological perspectives can again contribute to our understanding of these areas. We might be interested in the neuronal and chemical changes that occur when we learn something new. This biological approach can help to establish how diet can affect learning, and can investigate how brain changes occur when we learn new things. Colin Blakemore's (2005) work in brain plasticity is of interest. We may be encouraged by the brain's response to environmental enrichment in children (Jenkins 2005) and adults (Baroncelli *et al.* 2010).

The information processing approach of the cognitive perspective permits us to examine learning and memory. Craik and Lockhart (1972) argued that material could be recalled more easily when the original encoding of information took place at a deeper level of processing. A deeper level might involve a more enriching learning experience where additional mental processing of the learnt material takes place. Since memory is so important to processes of learning, full advantage can be taken of this idea in the classroom. It has immediate application because it causes us to think about the nature of the encoding process and the experiences of the student.

If we turn our attention to the student, we can think of learning in terms of units of stimulus–response conditioning, but this may reduce children's learning to a too mechanistic level. Bruner has argued against this approach, maintaining that attention must also be focused on the cognition of the student (Fontana 1995). The student can subjectively interpret stimuli in order to construct internal models and hypotheses, which in turn lead to expectations and predictions about the world.

In the 1960s and into the 1970s Piaget's theory of cognitive development was highly influential in educational studies and in developmental psychology. The *Plowden Report* (1967), a ground-breaking analysis of primary education, was informed by Piagetian theory (Sugrue 2010). Piaget proposed that cognitive development in children proceeds by passing through four qualitatively distinct stages, becoming more abstract and logical as the child develops (Slavin 2006). This theory suggests that children need to interact with their world to advance through the stages and to eventually experience higher-order thinking. Although Piaget is sometimes criticised for providing a too rigid structure of cognitive development, and for not taking sufficient account of environmental and cultural effects, his work has made a huge contribution to an understanding of child development. Classroom arrangements can provide children with the opportunity to actively interact with their surroundings, discovering and reflecting on their findings. The Piagetian account causes us to recognise that thinking skills develop gradually in children and teaching approaches should reflect the stage of development of the child.

Lev Vygotsky provided another account of cognitive development, which placed an emphasis on language and discourse as mediators of the development of cognitive functioning (Lourenço 2012) This approach views knowledge as something that is socially constructed by interactions in society. Learning therefore involves an interaction with others in social groups. The role of the teacher is important in helping the child to learn new tasks that are within their capabilities. This range of attainable but, as yet, unlearned tasks is called the zone of proximal development (ZPD). The zone for each teacher–child interaction shifts, covering different and increasingly demanding tasks and activities. The help that teachers provide in giving cues, prompting action or generally offering support is known as scaffolding. Neither Piaget nor Vygotsky were in favour of IQ tests, preferring less quantitative and more qualitative approaches. The ZPD then becomes a more useful point of focus than the assessment of current IQ scores.

Finally, we will look at the teacher. What is it that makes a teacher effective? Lepper and Woolverton (2002) identified a number of strengths that were effective in bringing about stable positive changes in students' motivation, learning and progress across a variety of situations. The acronym INSPIRE has been used to capture seven common characteristics of effective teachers.

Intelligent: effective teachers are intelligent and knowledgeable about their subject and teaching approaches.

Nurturant: they are nurturant, warm and supportive; attentive to their students' needs and express confidence that they will succeed.

Socratic: a more Socratic and questioning approach is used as opposed to a didactic approach.

Progressive: a progressive approach is used in the way that students are exposed to challenges and problems. Lessons are well structured with regard being paid to student learning pathways.

Indirect: errors are identified, but teacher interventions involve cues and tips, permitting students to recognise and correct their own errors. Recognition of student achievement is made and positive behaviour reinforced without using effusive praise.

Reflective: some priority is given to student understanding rather than just the accumulation of factual knowledge, by encouraging students to reflect on the issues they are studying.

Encouraging: effective teachers help to maintain high motivation levels by encouraging students to feel confident and sense mastery of their developing skills.

Teaching approaches cannot be based on simple formulas, but such findings may help teachers to reflect on their own practices and to consider the adoption of additional strategies, styles and approaches.

Motivation

What are the causes for varying levels of motivation and what can be done to improve pupils' motivation and enjoyment of learning?

Students have their own views about themselves. Some self-beliefs are liberating and empowering, whereas others serve to constrain and limit progress (Ormrod 2006). Often in education we keep our eye on external factors, but there is also the need to focus on internal, cognitive resources. Pajares and Schunk (2002) consider that teachers should pay regard to pupils' self-belief as much as their achievement record, on the grounds that self-belief will influence motivation and, in turn, future academic attainment. Many of the self-belief variables that we measure are reasonably stable and behave like traits. Tests are available for a number of constructs, including self-esteem, self-efficacy, optimism, explanatory style and hope.

Self-esteem refers to our sense of value and worth. It is affected by the way others see us and the way we seem in comparison with others (McMullin and Cairney 2004). High self-esteem is the positive feeling we have about ourselves, despite our shortcomings. It reflects the regard others pay to us and it does not extend to arrogance or conceit.

We can distinguish between global self-esteem, the way people generally view themselves, and specific self-esteem, the way people view themselves in a particular domain of life, such as academic self-esteem. Whereas global self-esteem seems more important when considering overall psychological well-being, academic self-esteem correlates better with academic achievement (Rosenberg *et al.* 1995). Although some significant correlations have been found between self-esteem and academic performance (Skaalvik 1983; Rahmani 2011), this in no way proves that high self-esteem improves achievement or that achievement can be improved by boosting the self-esteem of students (Baumeister *et al.* 2003). It is just as likely that self-esteem is derived from academic performance.

Praise given with the intention of boosting self-esteem can sometimes be counter-productive (McLean 2003). A mastery approach to learning, in which students value effort and personal improvement, seems preferable to a performance approach, in which students wish to gain favourable judgements for their work (Anderman *et al.* 2001). Praising ability rather than effort can encourage students to emphasise performance over mastery. Also, when failure occurs, students may attribute their failure to lack of ability and become less confident as a result. Praise can also be toxic when it is given indiscriminately and for accomplishments requiring little effort. Under such circumstances the teacher's low expectations may well lead to reduced motivation. Dweck (2006) consequently argues that praise for effort is far more effective than praise for ability.

Another related self-belief measure is self-efficacy. This refers to a sense of capability in a specific domain of life (Gaskill and Hoy 2002). In an academic setting, self-efficacy may provide a precursor for self-concept development (Bong and Skaalvik 2003). Self-efficacy can be derived from a sense of competence based on past experience (mastery experiences), seeing how other people perform their tasks (vicarious experiences), noting one's state of anxiety or enthusiasm (emotional and physiological arousal) and from the validation of one's own efforts by significant others (verbal persuasion) (Bandura 1997). Evidence suggests that self-efficacy is associated with task performance (Bandura 1997). Students with high self-efficacy scores are more likely to engage with more demanding tasks, and expend more effort and persist longer with tasks. Such student qualities are welcome in any classroom. Bandura also argues that self-efficacy plays a significant mediation role in academic achievement for factors such as gender, attitudes to school, prior attainment and cognitive ability. He implicates self-efficacy in the development of motivation, intrinsic interest and the resilience needed to buffer the negative effects of academic anxiety. This latter point is relevant since school students face demands to perform well in examinations. Failure can elicit disapproval from those around and block intended career progression routes.

Confidence and higher levels of motivation can seem to grow with the experience of success, but the opposite effect is also at work. Maier and Seligman (1967) conducted behavioural research in which dogs were conditioned to avoid electric shocks. This might represent the way we adopt strategies to avoid unpleasant experiences in life. In a second stage to this work, some of the conditioned dogs were harnessed to prevent them avoiding the shock. The dogs could still put out effort, but it was wasted. The shock avoidance was now no longer contingent on the effort expended. Most dogs gave up, even when the constraint was removed, and developed a state called learned helplessness. Learned helplessness is an effect we are familiar with in educational practice. It affects our confidence, our moods and emotions. It involves the loss of hope and motivation, even in bright, gifted pupils.

Explanatory style has emerged from learned helplessness research and refers to the characteristic way that we explain our failures and successes. The reformulation of the attributional style concept by Abrahamson *et al.* (1978) resulted in three self-belief dimensions (internality/externality, stability/instability and globality/specificity).

With a pessimistic explanatory style, setbacks are explained in terms of internal, stable and global causes. A student attributing an examination failure to lack of intelligence is providing such an explanation. There is something wrong with me (internal), the problem will persist (stable) and it will affect other aspects of life (global). Blaming a hard examiner for failure is an example of an optimistic explanatory style. There is something wrong with the examiner (external), it is unlikely to happen again (unstable) and it will only affect this examination (specific). Peterson and Barrett (1987) looked at the explanatory style of first-year university students and found that an optimistic explanatory style was associated with higher grades. The measure has been refined more recently, but explanatory style remains a useful additional self-belief measure in motivation research.

Self-handicapping strategies are more likely when self-belief resources are limited. Lack of effort can be used as a protective strategy. Trying to succeed may be too risky when failure is attributed to lack of ability. It may be preferable to preserve the belief that 'I could have succeeded had I tried.' Under these circumstances we may feel the safest approach is not to try (Dweck 2000). Self-belief, then, is an important study area when considering motivation in the classroom.

The humanistic approach points to the satisfaction of needs as the basis for motivation. This may provide a helpful perspective for the encouragement and maintenance of motivation in the classroom. Behavioural models suggest that current motivation levels are derived from our past conditioning. Effort is more likely when the association between effort and reward has been learned. We may be concerned, though, that emphasising external rewards will foster an extrinsic performance-oriented educational culture rather than an intrinsic mastery-oriented culture (Alexander 2006).

We can also investigate motivation by examining the social world of the child. The social constructions of gender identities are worth considering with the much-publicised 'under-achievement of boys', particularly at GCSE level. If boys perceive schoolwork to be a feminised activity, they may be less likely to work or to report they are working (Francis 2009; 2010). Together the different psychological approaches provide insights that can serve to improve motivation considerably.

When things 'go wrong'

The area of developmental psychopathology (Kazdin *et al.* 1997; Grant *et al.* 2006) is of interest to us because psychological problems affect educational progress. Development-related disorders include intellectual deficits, social behaviour deficits, learning deficits and attention deficits.

Prompt identification of intellectual deficits with intelligence tests help initiation of remediation procedures. There are, however, some disadvantages as well. Negative labelling can be most unhelpful to children identified as 'slow learners' or 'mentally retarded'. Intelligence test results may not reflect innate learning potential as much as adjustment to the challenges of formal schooling (Peterson 1996). There are many brilliant and well-known individuals who were labelled as being dull while at school. This should tell us something about the problems of classifying someone as dull and limited. Remember that the fixed mindset limits growth in self, and in others too (Dweck 2006). There are likely to be genetic and environmental contributions to mental retardation.

Phenylketonuria is a metabolic disorder that can lead to intellectual impairment. Treatments have to be determined by a consideration of the causes of the condition, and will range from enrichment of the child's environment through to drug treatment and behavioural interventions.

With social behaviour deficits, children may display challenging behaviour that may have arisen through operant conditioning. Such behaviour may permit the child to exercise some control over the environment, by attention-seeking and influencing classroom procedures (Bennett 2011). Behavioural and cognitive-behavioural interventions can be effectively employed to reshape some dysfunctional behaviour.

Autism not only involves social behaviour deficits, but other problems such as those related to communication. Whereas most children will quickly develop non-verbal communication skills, this is not the case with autism, and so social interactions suffer. There are several different types of autism, but it is common for the child to possess a limited understanding of what others might be thinking or feeling. Autism is associated with biological factors such as a higher incidence of seizure disorders by adolescence, and increases in brain cerebral cortex size (Nolen-Hoeksema 2001). Drugs and behavioural therapy are used to reduce the intensity of the symptoms.

Dyslexia is a learning disorder affecting both reading and writing. It is, however, a disorder with very wide-ranging symptoms, including spatial ability problems. Other spatial skills and aspects of creativity may, however, be enhanced by dyslexia. In common with autism, there appears to be a diagnosis bias in the direction of boys. This may be because boys are more active and disruptive in the classroom, and therefore are more likely to be noticed. Dyslexia manifests itself at a behavioural level in the classroom, but cognitive and biological processing are both implicated in its cause. Brain scanning can be helpful in determining whether characteristic brain structure features are present. Remediation strategies include behaviour therapy, drugs and reading strategies.

Attention deficit/hyperactivity disorder (ADHD) is perhaps the most well known of the attention disorders. Children with ADHD are unable to pay attention to instructions and they are also hyperactive. Poor school performance and some degree of social isolation are common consequences. Some children with ADHD grow into normal adults and become symptom-free, whereas others are affected into adulthood (Peterson 1996). Environmental factors, such as family disruption, and biological factors, such as poor frontal lobe development, are linked to this condition. Both drugs and behaviour therapy are used to treat ADHD.

Psychology can make two distinct contributions to developmental psychopathology. The first is concerned with identifying the specific nature of the problem, which makes effective remediation more likely. The second relates to the treatment and monitoring of the condition. Both clinical and educational psychologists may be involved in managing these disorders.

Positive psychology and education

Seligman and Csikszentmihalyi (2000) have argued that psychology has focused on repairing the damage caused by disease, and has neglected the process of building fulfilled individuals. Positive psychology focuses on positive cognitions about the future, such as optimism and hope. It has similar notions to those of the humanistic thinkers several decades ago, debating self-actualisation and peak experiences. Now there are dedicated positive psychology journals, such as *The Journal of Positive Psychology* and *The Journal of Happiness Studies.*

Having examined the problems caused by learned helplessness, we see that more constructive cognitions are likely to pave the way to improved motivation and success in school. Can we help children to develop beliefs that are protective and which increase resilience in the face of the many challenges life provides?

Hope will affect motivation levels and the extent to which educational experiences can be enjoyed. Hope involves two important self-beliefs. One is the belief that pathways can be found to reach an important goal. The second is the belief that one has the will to be sufficiently motivated to reach that goal (Compton and Hoffman 2013). The Children's Hope Scale (CHS) has been developed to measure levels of hope in children (Snyder *et al.* 1997). Hope is associated with improved academic achievement, higher self-esteem, optimism and self-efficacy, better social relationships and lower levels of depression (Ciarrochi *et al.* 2007; Roberts *et al.* 2002; Valle *et al.* 2006). Interventions to build hope have involved activities, ranging from the reading of hopeful stories and subsequent discussions, to the use of a summer day camp for children with psychosocial problems. It has been demonstrated that children's hope scores will tend to rise following these interventions (Roberts *et al.* 2002).

Because positive expectations can be self-fulfilling, there is reason to treat optimism as an asset. Although there are times in life when a more pessimistic approach is called for, optimism is more frequently associated with positive outcomes. Carver *et al.* (2010) and Peterson (2000) have reviewed a number of benefits of optimism, including positive mood, good morale, perseverance, effective problem solving, and academic success. The Life Orientation Test is one measure of optimism for adolescents and adults (Scheier and Carver 1985). This measure provides a score reflecting the overall global optimism of the person. Attributional style questionnaires can be used to establish optimism by measuring the explanatory style of the person. The Children's Attributional Style Questionnaire (CASQ) is one example of this (Seligman 2006).

Based on the notion that pessimism is a predisposing factor for depression, intervention projects have been devised to influence a child's cognitions, particularly with regard to explanatory style and social problem-solving skills. Roberts *et al.* (2002) point out that such interventions are beneficial, and this supports the notion that optimism can be taught.

Although positive psychology has not escaped criticism (Held 2004; Miller 2008), it seems that positive interventions can be made in a child's early life to help develop resilience and coping skills, in preparation for future challenges. Psychology has much to offer education. The reader is now encouraged to select additional study material from the extensive amount of psychological research work related to educational processes.

Carl Jung warns against underestimating psychological factors (Jung 2002). This is certainly true of education, where some insight into psychological factors can result in massive returns for both learner and teacher.

References

Abrahamson, L.Y., Seligman, M.E.P. and Teasdale, J.D. (1978) Learned helplessness in humans: critique and reformulation. *Journal of Abnormal Psychology.* 87, 49–74.

Alexander, P.A. (2006) *Psychology in learning and instruction.* Upper Saddle River, NJ: Pearson.

Anderman, E.M., Austin, C.C. and Johnson, D.M. (2001) The development of goal orientation. In A. Wigfield and J.S. Eccles (eds), *Development of Achievement Motivation* (pp. 197–220). London: Academic Press.

Bandura, A. (1997) *Self-efficacy: The exercise of control.* New York: W.H. Freeman and Company.

Baroncelli, L., Braschi, C., Spolidoro, M., Begenisic, T., Sale, A. and Maffei, L. (2010) Nurturing brain plasticity: impact of environmental enrichment. *Cell Death and Differentiation.* 17, 1092–1103.

Baumeister, R.F., Campbell, J.D., Krueger, J.I. and Vohs, K.D. (2003) Does high self-esteem cause better performance, interpersonal success, happiness, or healthier lifestyles? *Psychological Science in the Public Interest.* 4 (1), 1–44.

Bennett, P. (2011) *Abnormal and clinical psychology.* Maidenhead: Open University Press.

Blakemore, C. (2005) In celebration of cerebration. *The Lancet.* 366, 2035–2057.

Bong, M. and Skaalvik, E.M. (2003) Academic self-concept and self-efficacy: How different are they really? *Educational Psychology Review.* 15 (1), 1–40.

Bowkett, S., Harding, T., Lee, T. and Leighton, R. (2007) *Success in the creative classroom.* London: Network Continuum Education.

Bruning, R.H., Schraw, G.J., Norby, M.M. and Ronning, R.R. (2004) *Cognitive psychology and instruction.* Upper Saddle River, NJ: Pearson.

Carver, C.S., Scheier, M.F. and Segerstrom, S.G. (2010) Optimism. *Clinical Psychology Review.* 30, 879–889.

Chaikin, A., Sigler, E. and Derlega, V. (1974) Non-verbal mediators of teacher expectancy effects. *Journal of Personality and Social Psychology.* 30, 144–149.

Ciarrochi, J., Heaven, P.C.L. and Davies, F. (2007) The impact of hope, self-esteem, and attributional style on adolescents' school grades and emotional well-being: A longitudinal study. *Journal of Research in Personality.* 41, 1161–1178.

Compton, W.C. and Hoffman, E. (2013) *Positive psychology: The science of happiness and flourishing.* Maidenhead: Wadsworth.

Cooper, C. (2010) *Individual differences and personality.* London: Hodder.

Cornwell, D., Hobbs, S. and Prytula, R. (1980) Little Albert rides again. *American Psychologist.* 35(2), 216–217.

Craik, F.I.M. and Lockhart, R.S. (1972) Levels of processing: A framework for memory research. *Journal of Verbal Learning and Verbal Behavior.* 11, 671–684.

Csikszentmihalyi, M. (2002) *Flow: The classic work on how to achieve happiness.* London: Rider.

Deary, I.J. (2003) Ten things I hated about intelligence research. *The Psychologist.* 16, 534–537.

Delgoshaei, Y. and Delavari, N. (2012) Applying multiple-intelligence approach to education and analysing its impact on cognitive development of pre-school children. *Procedia: Social and Behavioral Sciences.* 32, 361–366.

Durkin, K. (1995) *Developmental social psychology: From infancy to old age.* Oxford: Blackwell.

Dweck, C.S. (2000) *Self-theories: Their role in motivation, personality, and development.* Hove: Psychology Press.

Dweck, C.S. (2006) *Mindset.* New York: Random House.

Dyer, J.G. and McGuinness, T.M. (1966) Resilience: analysis of the concept. *Archives of Psychiatric Nursing.* 10 (5), 276–282.

Field, A.P. (2006) Is conditioning a useful framework for understanding the development and treatment of phobias? *Clinical Psychology Review.* 26, 857–875.

Fontana, D. (1995) *Psychology for teachers.* London: Palgrave/BPS.

Francis, B. (2009) The role of The Boffin as abject Other in gendered performances of school achievement. *The Sociological Review.* 57 (4), 645–669.

Francis, B. (2010) Re/theorising gender: female masculinity and male femininity in the classroom? *Gender and Education*. 22 (5), 477–490.

Gardner, H. (1998) A multiplicity of intelligences. *Scientific American Presents*. 9 (4), 18–23.

Gaskill, P.J. and Hoy, A.W. (2002) Self-efficacy and self-regulated learning: The dynamic duo in school performance. In J. Aronson (ed.), *Improving academic achievement: Impact of psychological factors on education* (pp. 185–208). London: Academic Press.

Gilbert, I. (2002) *Essential motivation in the classroom*. London: RoutledgeFalmer.

Goleman, D. (1995) *Emotional intelligence: Why it can matter more than IQ*. London: Bantam Books.

Gould, S.J. (1996) *The mismeasure of man*. London: Norton.

Grant, K.E., Compas, B.E., Thurm, A.E., McMahon, S.D., Gipson, P.Y., Campbell, A.J., Krochock, K. and Westerholm, R.J. (2006) Stressors and child and adolescent psychopathology: evidence of moderating and mediating effects. *Clinical Psychology Review*. 26, 257–283.

Held, B.S. (2004) The negative side of positive psychology. *Journal of Humanistic Psychology*. 44 (1), 9–46.

Hofer, M.A. (2005) The psychobiology of early attachment. *Clinical Neuroscience Research*. 4, 291–300.

Jenkins, J.S. (2005) Prodigies of nature. *Journal of the Royal Society of Medicine*. 98, 277–280.

Jensen, A.R. (2011) The theory of intelligence and its measurement. *Intelligence*. 39, 171–177.

Jung, C.G. (2002) *The undiscovered self*. London: Routledge.

Kazdin, A.E., Kraemer, H.C., Kessler, R.C., Kupfer, D.J. and Offord, D.R. (1997) Contributions of risk-factor research to developmental psychopathology. *Clinical Psychology Review*. 17 (4), 375–406.

Lepper, M.R. and Woolverton, M. (2002) The wisdom of practice: lessons learned from the study of highly effective tutors. In J. Aronson (ed.), *Improving academic achievement: impact of psychological factors on education* (pp. 135–158). London: Academic Press.

Lourenço, O. (2012) Piaget and Vygotsky: many resemblances, and a crucial difference. *New Ideas in Psychology*. 30, 281–295.

McCrae, R.R. and Costa, P.T. (2004). A contemplated revision of the NEO five-factor inventory. *Personality and Individual Differences*. 36, 587–596.

McLean, A. (2003) *The motivated school*. London: Paul Chapman Publishing.

McMullin, J.A. and Cairney, J. (2004). Self-esteem and the intersection of age, class, and gender. *Journal of Aging Studies*. 18, 75–90.

Maier, S.F. and Seligman, M.E.P. (1967) Learned helplessness: theory and evidence. *Journal of Experimental Psychology: General*. 105, 3–46.

Maslow, A.H. (1943) A theory of human motivation. *Psychological Review*. 50 (4): 370–396.

Meece, J.L. and Daniels, D.H. (2008) *Child and adolescent development for educators*. London: McGraw-Hill.

Miller, A. (2008) A critique of positive psychology: or 'The new science of happiness'. *Journal of Philosophy of Education*. 42 (3–4), 591–608.

Miller, G.A. (2003) The cognitive revolution: a historical perspective. *Trends in Cognitive Sciences*. 7 (3), 141–144.

Mohamadi, F.S., Asadzadeh, H., Ahadi, H. and Jomehri, F. (2011) Testing Bandura's theory in school. *Procedia Social and Behavioral Sciences*. 12, 426–435.

Nolen-Hoeksema, S. (2001) *Abnormal psychology*. London: McGraw-Hill.

Ormrod, J.E. (2006) *Essentials of educational psychology*. Upper Saddle River, NJ: Pearson.

Pajares, F. and Schunk, D.H. (2002) Self and self-belief in psychology and education: a historical perspective. In J. Aronson (ed.), *Improving academic achievement: Impact of psychological factors on education*. (pp. 3–21). London: Academic Press.

Peterson, C. (1996) *The psychology of abnormality*. London: Harcourt Brace & Company.

Peterson, C. (2000) The future of optimism. *American Psychologist*. 55, 44–55.

Peterson, C. and Barrett, L.C. (1987) Explanatory style and academic performance among university freshmen. *Journal of Personality and Social Psychology*. 53, 603–607.

Pinker, S. (2002) *The blank slate*. London: Penguin Books.

Plowden Report (1967) *Children and their primary schools: A report of the Central Advisory Council for Education (England)*. London: HMSO.

Prior, M. (1999) Resilience and coping: The role of individual temperament. In E. Frydenberg (ed.), *Learning to cope: Developing as a person in complex societies* (pp. 33–52). Oxford: Oxford University Press.

Rahmani, P. (2011) The relationship between self-esteem, achievement goals and academic achievement among the primary school students. *Procedia: Social and Behavioral Sciences.* 29, 803–808.

Reeve, J. (2009). *Understanding motivation and emotion.* Hoboken, NJ: John Wiley and Sons.

Roberts, M.C., Brown, K.J., Johnson, R.J. and Reinke, J. (2002) Positive psychology for children. In C.R. Snyder and S.J. Lopez (eds), *Handbook of positive psychology* (pp. 663–675). New York: Oxford University Press.

Rose, S. (1997) *Lifelines: Biology, freedom, determinism.* London: Penguin Press.

Rose, S., Lewontin, R.C. and Kamin, L.J. (1990) *Not in our genes: Biology, ideology and human nature.* London: Penguin.

Rosenberg, M., Schoenbach, C., Schooler, C. and Rosenberg, F. (1995) Global self-esteem and specific self-esteem: Different concepts, different outcomes. *American Sociological Review.* 60, 141–156.

Rosenthal, R. and Jacobson, L. (1966) Teachers' expectancies: Determinants of pupils' I.Q. gains. *Psychological Reports.* 19, 115–118.

Rust, J. and Golombok, S. (2008) *Modern psychometrics: The science of psychological assessment.* London: Routledge.

Rutter, M. (2000) Children in substitute care: Some conceptual considerations and research implications. *Children and Youth Services Review.* 22 (9–10), 685–703.

Scheier, M.F. and Carver, C.S. (1985) The Self-Consciousness Scale: A revised version for use with general populations. *Journal of Applied Social Psychology.* 15, 687–699.

Seligman, M.E.P. (2006) *Learned optimism.* London: Vintage Books.

Seligman, M.E.P. and Csikszentmihalyi, M. (2000) Positive psychology: an introduction. *American Psychologist.* 55, 5–14.

Skaalvik, E.M. (1983) Academic achievement, self-esteem and valuing of the school: some sex differences. *British Journal of Educational Psychology.* 53, 299–306.

Slavin, R.E. (2006) *Educational psychology: Theory and practice.* London: Pearson.

Snyder, C.R., Hoza, B., Pelham, W.E., Rapoff, M., Ware, L., Danovsky, M., Highberger, L., Rubinstein, H. and Stahl, K.J. (1997) The development and validation of an individual-differences measure of hope. *Journal of Pediatric Psychology.* 22, 399–421.

Sugrue, C. (2010) Progressive education: a 4-decade odyssey? *Curriculum Inquiry.* 40 (1), 105–124.

Toates, F. (2009) *Skinner: The shaping of behaviour.* Basingstoke: Palgrave Macmillan.

Toates, F. (2011) *Biological psychology.* Harlow: Pearson.

Ullén, F., de Manzano, Ö., Almeida, R., Magnusson, P.K.E., Pedersen, N.L., Nakamura, J., Csíkszentmihályi, M. and Madison, G. (2012) Proneness for psychological flow in everyday life: associations with personality and intelligence. *Personality and Individual Differences.* 52, 167–172.

Urdan, T. and Schoenfelder, E. (2006) Classroom effects on student motivation: goal structures, social relationships, and competence beliefs. *Journal of School Psychology.* 44, 331–349.

Valle, M.F., Huebner, E.S. and Suldo, S.M. (2006) An analysis of hope as a psychological strength. *Journal of School Psychology.* 44, 393–406.

Vauclair, J. and Perret, P. (2003) The cognitive revolution in Europe: taking the developmental perspective seriously. *Trends in Cognitive Science.* 7 (7), 284–285.

Werner, E.E. and Smith, R.S. (1998) *Vulnerable but invincible: A longitudinal study of resilient children and youth.* New York: Adams, Bannister, Cox.

Whalley, L.J. and Deary, I.J. (2001) Longitudinal cohort study of childhood IQ and survival up to age 76. *British Medical Journal.* 322, 819–822.

Woolfolk, A. (2013) *Educational psychology.* London: Pearson

6

Learning styles

Implications for teaching and learning

John Pelley

The purpose of an educational institution is to lead the students, who initially believe the educational institution is there to educate them, to the realization that they must educate themselves.
  They must ... learn how to learn [integratively]...
  Willis Hurst (2001) [*Emphasis and word added by Pelley and Dalley, 2008*]

Introduction

Learning style is a preference, not a limitation. It becomes a limitation, however, when it is used to design instruction. This limits instruction by taking attention away from important outcomes-based learning objectives that should be achieved regardless of the student's learning preferences. It also limits learning by appealing only to what the learner already does well, thus taking attention away from what the learner needs to develop. If, instead, learning style is used to help identify underused learning skills, the learner can develop the skills needed to learn how to learn at any level of complexity.

The goal of education is the development of the whole brain, and learning style should be used as a tool to achieve this end. This chapter is designed to address how and why learning style can be employed as part of a deliberate whole-brain method for achieving 'educational self-actualization' (see *self-actualization* in Maslow 1954). The primary message of this chapter is that learning style is only useful as a means for developing whole-brain thinking – and for that, it is essential.

The literature abounds with commentary, pro and con, concerning the concept of learning style (Felder and Brent 2005; Pashler *et al.* 2008) and it is also addressed in Chapter 3 of this volume. In order that the frame of reference for this chapter is clear, the terminology and/or semantics related to learning style need to be defined. An interesting example of the need for semantic clarification is the distinction between learning style and cognitive style (Cuthbert 2005). Cognitive style, as first proposed by Riding (1997), is considered as an inborn preference for how a learner responds to new information. This definition can be usefully compared to a definition of learning style as originally proposed by Kolb (1984) in that it is also preference for responding to new information. However, Kolb more thoroughly extends the definition to include a preference for the way new information is 'transformed through whole brain learning' from experience into knowledge. Further review of the literature on the learning style concept will reveal mental models that involve either a reductionistic or a holistic construct based on the basic psychological concepts of: (1) perception, (2) cognitive controls and processes, (3) mental imagery and (4) personality. The primary error made in many studies of learning style is to define it as different ways that people learn. As this chapter will clarify, it is different ways that people 'prefer' to learn and that all learning occurs through precisely the same steps.

The extensive variety of semantic interpretations of 'learning style' has led to the inevitable debate over the utility of the concept. One argument that continues to emerge in the educational research literature, and also continues to be rejected by the evidence, is that learning style can be used to design instruction in order to enhance learning (Pashler 2008; Coffield *et al.* 2004). Kolb has also additionally posed a caution concerning the adoption of stereotypes that trivialise human complexity (see Chapter 3, pages 54–55). Kolb did not have access to the *MBTI Manual* (Myers *et al.* 1998) at the time he authored his book on learning styles, or he would have been aware of the extensive caution given regarding the interpretation of Jung's psychological type theory. The view of learning style in this chapter supports the arguments that instructional design, and even curriculum design, should not be based on learning preferences of the learners. Instead, it will be shown here that the learning style concept is highly relevant when used for self-assessment to develop additional learning skills in the learner. Both the constructivist model (see Chapter 3) and the transformative model (Mezirow 1997) will be used to illustrate how both teaching and learning are enhanced when the metacognitive perspective is used to teach learners about their learning.

We will first establish a functional correlation between the Kolb experiential learning cycle (ELC, see Chapter 3) and the Jungian mental functions (JMF) that are identified by the Myers-Briggs Type Indicator (Myers, *et al.* 1998). This correlation between the ELC and JMF provides a basis for understanding whole-brain thinking because it shows how every learner processes information through the same process (ELC) while placing different emphasis (JMF) on the individual ELC steps. The process of whole-brain thinking will then be described in the context of the ELC to provide a way to visualise experiential learning occurring within the brain (Figure 6.1). The connection between the ELC, JMF and whole-brain thinking will then be used to help understand how higher order thinking skills (HOTS) are achieved.[1] When the teacher obtains a complete grasp of the correlations between learning style, the ELC and regional specialisation of the brain, the phrase 'sense–integrate–act' will serve as a reliable reminder of the self-directed learner. The theoretical groundwork will be balanced by a discussion of practical recommendations that can be broadly applied. As a final introductory note, this chapter was not conceived as a review or a critique of existing learning style theories, each of which has endured due to their utility in various venues. Instead, the broad goal is to help develop an appreciation of how learning style as a concept can be applied to an understanding of how the brain learns.

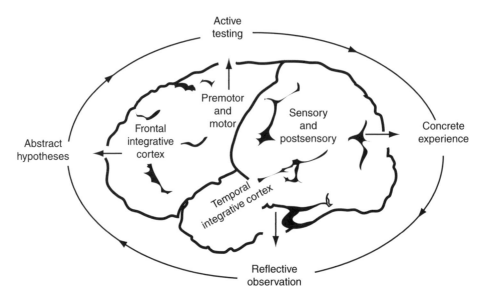

FIGURE 6.1 The link between functional areas of the brain and Kolb's experiential learning cycle (source: Zull, 2002, *The Art of Changing the Brain*, used with permission).

Learning style relationship to the experiential learning cycle

Learning style models attempt to identify observed learning behaviours that are habitual due to preferences held by the learner. The learning behaviours described by the ELC were proposed by Kolb to represent a sequence of four characteristic learning behaviours: (1) involvement in the experience (concrete experience); (2) reflection about the experience (reflective observation); (3) using analytical skills to conceptualise the experience (abstract generalisation); and (4) using decision-making and problem-solving skills in order to act on the new ideas gained from the experience (active testing). These individual behaviours had already been recognised as important in learning theory, but Kolb arranged them in a specific order to comprise a cycle whose output became fresh input for the cycle to continue (see Figure 3.2). As will be shown here, the ELC sequence is fundamental to all learning – even rote learning – and thus constitutes a universal truth.

As a constructivist model, the ELC is a complete description of the steps that show how the human brain uses prior experience to transform new experience into knowledge (Figure 6.1). But, the ELC does not provide the critically important insight concerning the efficiency with which each of the four steps is performed by different learners. For example, if the abstract conceptualisation step is performed less efficiently than the reflective observation step, it will impair the learning cycle in a characteristic way. In this case we would expect a strong command of factual information (reflective observation) but a sense of uncertainty in posing possible predictions from those facts (abstract conceptualisation). Reciprocally, if the reflective observation step is performed less efficiently than the abstract generalisation step, we would expect skilful formation of alternative possibilities, but without the complete use of the facts. Thus, the same sequence of information processing in different brains would lead to different learning outcomes. This emphasis of one step over another is precisely how the JMF work.

In Jungian personality type, the mental functions also have a functional sequence of information processing (Figure 6.2), but it is not considered to proceed as a cycle, nor does it need to be.[2] This insight is readily provided by the four Jungian personality preferences: Sensing, Intuition, Thinking and Feeling, referred to as the 'mental functions' (Myers *et al.* 1998). For the Jungian *Sensing* type, facts and concepts receive most of the thinking time compared to an emphasis on alternatives and possibilities in the thinking time spent by the *Intuitive* type. Just as all learners use the complete ELC, they also use both sensing and intuition in the sequence of mental functions. The differences in the final outcome of thinking are due to the relative amounts of time spent with facts and concepts compared to time spent with possibilities and 'big picture' thinking. The consistent unequal use of time for the steps in both the ELC and the Jungian sequence helps us to see that learning style is both unconscious and habitual.

The habitual use of one part of our thinking more than another is supported by other mental models such as Gardner's multiple intelligences (Gardner 1993). It is not difficult to see that if any particular activity is easier to perform, it will be preferred. If an individual is clumsy at catching and throwing a ball but facile in pressing keys on a piano, their favourite pastime is not going to be baseball. The likelihood of a genetic basis for using different areas of the brain differently is well established and will be

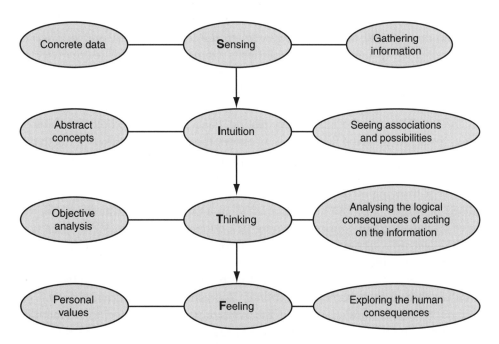

FIGURE 6.2 The Jungian mental functions: sensing, intuition, thinking and feeling – an information processing model.

addressed shortly, but at this point the primary emphasis is simply that different people use their brains differently. This different use of the brain produces different responses to experience, thus producing different behavioural outcomes. The external evidence of these responses is identifiable as a personality type, or when thinking of a learner, a learning style.

If we try to match steps in the ELC with steps in the JMF, we will not find a complete overlap. The first step in the ELC, concrete experience, does have a partial match with the Sensing preference in the JMF because Sensing types are identified by their preference for giving attention to facts and details. This is the basis for Jung's choice of terms, i.e. Sensing types paid most attention to that which is immediately observed by the senses. The second step in the ELC, reflective observation, also has a partial match with the Sensing type because this step in the ELC is concerned with whether the learner recognises elements in the concrete experience from previous learning. Recognition from previous learning can introduce a bias in what the learner thinks they are perceiving with their senses.

The third step in the ELC, abstract conceptualisation, compares well with the Jungian Intuitive preference because the thinking is about the future instead of the past. The ELC describes how the learner seeks to understand through generation of hypotheses or alternative possibilities – educated guesses, if you will. The learner is proposing what the new experience might mean. The Intuitive type likewise pays more attention to alternatives and possibilities about what the new experience means. They are seeking to understand the experience instead of simply making a record of it. Both of these mental models make active use of the imagination to create the alternatives that they must choose for active testing. The creation and testing of alternatives provides an opportunity to distinguish between the terms *creativity* and *intelligence*. The process of creating alternative possibilities is a simple way to define creativity and the ability to test and choose the best possibility is a simple definition for intelligence. The latter is evident on intelligence tests when learners are asked to choose the most correct answer.

The fourth step in the ELC, active testing, has a similarity to both the thinking and feeling preferences in the JMF. The ELC allows the choice of methods for active testing to be chosen by the learner, but does not specify whether the outcome criteria are logical or emotional, or both. Active testing can be as simple as paraphrasing (written or spoken) or drawing a concept map (both require action). If an alternative can be verbalised intelligently or can be diagrammed in a clear, meaningful structure, then the active testing step can confirm meaning or understanding. The JMF tells us what criteria the learner might use as a basis for accepting the outcome of active testing. The Jungian thinking type will trust more the use of logic in assessing outcomes compared to the Jungian feeling type, who will trust more the use of emotive or subjective values. In either case, the assessment is rational. The remaining preferences in the Jungian personality types, extraversion and introversion (not considered to be mental functions), might be thought to relate to active testing, but that would be too restrictive. These preferences relate to the inherent level of arousal in the learner's brain (Ornstein 1995) and only indicate how the learner prefers to conduct the learning sequence. The extravert will attempt to increase the level of arousal through active processing, e.g. speaking, in order to provide immediate sensory feedback, while the introvert will attempt to decrease the level of arousal through more subdued outward behaviour, e.g. quiet contemplation, in order to reduce excessive arousal.

Of primary importance in using either mental model, the ELC or the JMF, is the capacity for free will in the learner to compensate for their preferences when the circumstances demand. These demands can be teacher directed or learner (self) directed. Fundamental to the intelligent use of the learning style concept is the awareness that preferences only tell us how information is learned under conditions that permit freedom of choice. However, learning objectives often require the Sensing type to develop alternative possibilities (an Intuitive preference) and often require the Intuitive type to memorise details (a Sensing preference). Because every learner uses both mental functions in everyday life, they can shift their learning emphasis to fit the objectives. The only difference in learning when using the non-preferred functions is that it takes more mental energy and is not trusted as much. The basis for preferences in individuals is more easily understood from an explanation of how they relate to the functional areas of the brain during learning.

Experiential learning cycle relationship to whole-brain thinking

What is whole-brain thinking? Is it using 'all' of the brain instead of only part of it? Is it just being able to use selected parts of the brain depending on the nature of the learning? An overview analysis of the functional specialisation of the major areas of the brain will help us see that we always use all of our brain during the ELC, but that we each use these major areas slightly differently. These differences help us to understand learning style. A correlation between the major functional areas of the brain and the four steps in the ELC has been described by Zull (2002; Figure 6.1). The areas involved in the ELC are part of the cerebrum, also called the neocortex, the area of the brain responsible for thinking and learning. The areas of the cerebrum that we will consider are the occipital/parietal (sensory) cortex, temporal (long-term memory) cortex, prefrontal (decision-making) cortex and frontal/motor (voluntary action) cortex. A correlation can also be made between the major areas of the brain and the JMF if we include an older area of the brain, the limbic system (emotion, feeling), which is not part of the cerebrum. Before describing the comparison of how the ELC and the JMF use these areas of the brain to produce learning, it is important to explain how and when the brain changes during learning.

The brain changes its structure during the learning process (see Zull 2002 for more detailed explanation). The change would not be visible to the naked eye, but rather occurs at the level of the nerve cells, called neurons. The permanent formation of a new pattern of connections between the neurons during learning is called consolidation. If we are referring to memory then the term is 'consolidation of memory'. However, other functions of the brain will also undergo change when they are used and so decision making will lead to 'consolidation of decision making skills'. Learning also involves a temporary storage of information referred to as short-term memory, which is like the RAM memory in a computer. As soon as attention is shifted to a new 'concrete experience', the information in short-term memory is lost. The consolidation of memory is more analogous to storage on the hard drive of a computer. It will remain there until it is erased. Interestingly, the brain has a counterpart to erasing, termed 'pruning'. At the level of the neuron, consolidation happens when networks of connections are formed (learning) and pruning occurs when these connections are later removed (forgetting). This explains why learning a new concept may also require unlearning, i.e. pruning, a conflicting and incorrect concept.

These connections between neurons can be seen as a form of 'computing power' for each nerve cell. It is known that in order to bring about consolidation, the repeated transmission of new learning patterns is necessary. However, it is not generally known that these changes occur only during sleep. Specifically, during non-dreaming deep sleep the hippocampus, an area of the limbic system, rehearses (replays) and records the activities from the previous day through the process of consolidation (Stickgold and Ellenbogen 2008). If the active testing stage of the ELC is not done, then the hippocampus has nothing to rehearse and no consolidation takes place. This cannot be overcome by simply taking in information through reading or listening, even with repetition. Repetition can only reinforce what has already been learned. Furthermore, because the hippocampus represents the emotional brain, it will only record learning that has an emotional connection. Such connections can be realised through the feeling of closure in completion of concept maps or skilfully written organisation of notes, or especially through interpersonal dialogue. To summarise, the brain learns during sleep through rehearsal of activity that it cares about. With this in mind, we can now correlate the ELC with the functional areas of the brain and emphasise how consolidation of learning can be purposely stimulated in each of the four stages.

The ELC begins with concrete experience transmitted through the sensory pathways, where it is organised by the sensory areas of the brain (Figure 6.1). This activity has prompted many neuroscientists to claim that we see with our brain, not our eyes. However, more than vision is sensed. Smell, touch, sound and taste provide sensory information that the brain can process during learning. As an activity, sensing the environment is a process that can undergo development through directed training. This is especially evident when one of the senses, such as vision, is lost and others, such as hearing and touch, develop to compensate.

Sensory information is interpreted by the nearby area called the temporal cortex, which engages in the second step, reflective observation. The temporal cortex processes long-term memory and thus is responsible for recognition of sensory information. Since long-term memory is connected through neural networks with other memories during integrative learning, sensory information can trigger recall of patterns as well as facts. If a learner has incorrect or incomplete memory, the temporal cortex can readily misinterpret what is being learned during reflective observation. This is emphasised by the report by Bransford *et al.* (2000), where they recommend that teachers draw out pre-existing understandings that learners bring with them. Thus, the sensory cortex that processes concrete experience influences the temporal cortex that processes recognition of the concrete experience, and that influence is reciprocal.

It is the neurons in the temporal cortex that grow network connections while facts and concepts are consolidated during sleep. When experiments are conducted that block the growth of connections, memory is blocked. Individuals who have easier consolidation in the temporal cortex compared to other areas will have a learning style that prefers the use of facts and specifics, such as the Sensing type in the JMF.

Whenever one area increases its connections, another unused area undergoes pruning to compensate for the physical space required. This does not mean that other learning is lost, since pruning only occurs in areas that do not contain emotionally important, or meaningful, information. As more and more patterns are stored, the capacity to attach meaning to what is observed is increased. The consolidation of meaning is not the same, however, as the creation of meaning.

Meaning is created for the learner during the third step of the ELC, abstract conceptualisation. The area that engages in this activity is the prefrontal cortex. It is distinguished from the more general term, frontal cortex, in that the latter also includes the motor area that is involved in the last step of the ELC, active testing. Experience can be conceptualised as 'a problem requiring a decision'. Whether we are engaged in formal learning or in the normal everyday activities of living, our behaviour is made up of decisions. Writing a thought a certain way or speaking a thought a certain way requires a decision among the words chosen. This is evident when different learners express the same thought uniquely. In order to come to a decision, the prefrontal cortex must create options, each of which has meaning. Each option must project an outcome into a future scenario: 'If I do this, then this will happen.' The greater development of the prefrontal cortex in humans helps to explain why we are able to conceive of a future, an ability not present in lower animals. These future scenarios that form a basis for active testing are a result of the act of creation – creating possibilities and attaching meaning to each.

The prefrontal cortex has two sources of information that can be used to create meaningful possibilities: the sensory cortex and the temporal cortex. The sensory cortex provides new information for creative thinking and the temporal cortex provides remembered information. The prefrontal cortex is able to create new pattern arrangements with the information provided; these new pattern arrangements are called generalisations. Thus, the ELC abstract conceptualisation step amounts to a 'guess' about future knowledge. A learning style that prefers to see possibilities, such as the Intuitive type in the JMF, may be explained by easier consolidation in the prefrontal cortex compared to other areas.

Creativity, the creation of alternative meanings, is only one of the processes necessary for a decision. The other process is the use of intelligence to select the alternative or possibility that makes the most sense, both logically and emotionally. This process is also mediated by the prefrontal cortex. The selection of an alternative possibility constitutes a decision. This is the point in learning where new knowledge is created – and it is created by the learner, not by the teacher. The knowledge provided by a teacher is simply another sensory resource that the learner uses to create meaning in the new experience.[3] The prefrontal cortex, with its short-term memory, is not designed to remember a decision, and it would be a disadvantage to do so. How do we know if it is a good decision unless we test it?

The motor cortex is responsible for carrying out the active testing of the decisions made by the prefrontal cortex. The motor cortex has the capacity to physically act on decisions by using tools for writing, by keyboarding, by speaking to others and by any combination of these and other actions. Like the other areas of the brain, the motor cortex can also acquire a memory of how to communicate thinking and how to carry out physical tasks. The results from active testing constitute new concrete experience for the ELC to continue through its stages. Thus, learning 'from' experience is not complete until learning decisions 'are' experienced.

Learning style is more readily understood as a preference by considering that different individuals carry out each activity in the ELC in its respective area of the brain with different degrees of ease. One learner might use their temporal cortex with greater ease than the prefrontal cortex and thus have a greater ability with memory for facts and details and an avoidance of finding meaning. The important educational principle revealed here is that all of the activities in the ELC are critical to higher-order thinking. We must teach to all of the cerebral cortex, the whole brain, if we are to develop HOTS.

Importance of whole-brain thinking

Whole brain thinking produces the maximum possible transformation of experience into knowledge by the cerebral cortex and the limbic system. We can evaluate this more easily by reviewing the ELC in reverse order (see Figure 6.1). If active testing by the motor cortex is to be most effective, it must act on highly creative and intelligent decisions in the prefrontal cortex. If the prefrontal cortex is to make highly intelligent decisions, it must be supplied with high-quality information available from the temporal cortex and sensory cortex. If the temporal cortex is to retain the high-quality information that is needed by the prefrontal cortex, the sensory cortex must convey accurate information from the environment, including outcomes of active testing. This reverse order review illustrates that each of the mental activities in the ELC are critically dependent on those that precede them.

A similar dependence is seen for the JMF (see Figure 6.2). Similar to the sequence above, reversing the order will consider first the feeling function, then the thinking function, the Intuitive function and finally the Sensing function. If subjective values (feeling function) in the form of emotions are to be used by the limbic system to evaluate a decision, they will be of little value if the decision is not logical. How can one feel good about a decision that makes no sense, i.e. a decision that is unworkable? If the most logical decision (thinking function) is to be determined by the prefrontal cortex, it will be dependent on having all of the alternative possibilities to choose from. If the prefrontal cortex is to determine a complete list of alternative possibilities (Intuitive function), then it will be important to have all of the high-quality information available. If there is to be a reliable and sufficient amount of information available (Sensing function) from the temporal cortex, then a well-developed ability to create a present moment awareness of experience by the sensory cortex as well as an ability to remember enough information will be necessary. Thus, the Jungian sequence uses all of the brain, just as the ELC sequence.

If learning style informs us about the part of the brain that the learner uses most readily, it can also inform us about what is being neglected. Neglect is not caused by inability, but rather by unequal time sharing. We spend more time with the abilities that we trust the most, those that are more comfortable. We give our preferences more of our thinking time, but the other steps in the ELC, and also the JMF sequence, are also accessible and responsive to a knowledgeable teacher. This ability of each student to utilise their whole brain forms the basis of the growth mindset (GM) postulated by Dweck (2006). GM theory states that learners who understand how their brains learn will demonstrate higher achievement than those who don't. GM learners understand that there are some aspects of learning that are more difficult (their learning style opposite), and they take steps to compensate during their learning activities. Again, high academic achievement can only come from mastery of each of the steps in learning, that is, from balanced use of all of the areas of the cerebral cortex.

The GM works because the brain can grow neural networks (i.e. consolidate) in any area that is specifically used. GM learners deliberately practise with their learning style opposite (non-preferred) to produce neural network branching in that area. The mastery of long-term memory in the temporal cortex in Jungian Sensing types must be balanced by development neural networks used for creative activity in the prefrontal cortex, the learning style opposite of the Sensing type. Similarly, active testing is a motor skill that can be developed through construction of concept maps or through clear verbal arguments – or both! Sensory input can be improved by developing the brain through appropriate exercises that help focus and attention in the present moment.

The most effective method for development in GM learners is that of deliberate practice (DP). This approach to learning has emerged from human performance studies that have examined the development of expert skills (Ericsson *et al.* 1993). DP has been applied to thinking skills in chess players as well as physical skills in jet pilots. In general, DP focuses attention on areas of limitation with immediate feedback. With teacher support, the learning skill in the area of limitation is brought into balance with other skill strengths. The identification of learning style helps to determine not only the learning skills that are used with greater ease, but to also identify areas of skill limitation. Non-preferred steps in either the ELC or the JMF are an indication of potential underuse and underdevelopment.

If instruction were designed to conform to a learner's learning style, it would retard their learning by neglecting the very areas that need attention. The neglect of any part of the cerebral cortex will result in minimal neuron growth and consolidation in that area. Thus, a critical part of instruction is in metacognition, that is, in teaching 'how people learn' (Bransford *et al.* 2000).

Since the function of the brain during learning can be understood by both the teacher and the learner, we can identify their respective responsibilities in the educational process. Fulfilment of these responsibilities is the only sure route to producing lifelong learning, as discussed in Chapter 15.

Teacher responsibilities for whole-brain learning

In the report of their key findings, a select committee of the National Research Council (United States) provided three overall recommendations to be addressed in education (Bransford *et al.* 2000) and these form a basis for addressing teacher responsibilities for whole-brain learning. The Council recommendations are summarised as:

1. Adopt a metacognitive approach to instruction to help learners become self-directed.
2. Engage learners at their pre-existing level of understanding to help them grasp new concepts in order to prevent preparing only for the test and then reverting to preconceptions.
3. Teach selected high-impact topics in greater depth to provide a contextual framework for organising knowledge and solving problems.

Integration of metacognition

Learners can't develop whole-brain thinking until they know what it is. A stage- and age-appropriate introduction to how we think and learn can be integrated into other existing topics in the curriculum. For example, it has been demonstrated that an inquiry-based approach to physics that allowed students to compare reflective assessments with other students, the *Thinker Tools Curriculum*, produced higher achievement in sixth grade than those taught by conventional methods in grades 11 and 12[4] (White and Frederickson 1997). Information on teaching the GM is available (Dweck 2006) and an introduction to the concepts and application of DP are explained by Ericsson *et al.* (1993) and Colvin (2008). One of the key advantages to inclusion of principles of DP is that it teaches self-monitoring. Also, the focus on expert skill development is more favourable for producing high achievement than a focus on minimum adequate standards.

Pre-existing level of understanding

The constructivist model of learning prescribes that we design curriculum and instruction to build upon prior learning. However, prior learning from prerequisite courses or topics can be difficult to interpret from records alone. If learners have not learned through whole-brain thinking, the likelihood of long-term memory or of problem-solving skills that match the course grades is unlikely. Many learners are capable of preparing for and performing on examinations and forgetting all of the knowledge tested within weeks, if not days. Thus, an understanding of how the learners have been assessed is important in determining their pre-existing level of understanding. Assessment has no meaning without clear learning goals and objectives, and goals and objectives have no purpose without skilful assessment. Goals and objectives acquire a consistent meaning and are useful for planning lessons when they are classified within a taxonomy of learning complexity. A simple taxonomy has been proposed by Quellmalz

(Stiggins *et al.* 1988).[5] The five levels in increasing complexity are: (1) recall (facts, details), (2) analysis (grouping), (3) comparison (similarities, differences), (4) inference (generating possibilities) and (5) evaluation (prediction). Each level uses the thinking skills of the levels below it and, likewise, each level engages the prefrontal cortex to a greater extent than the levels below it. The same topic can be taught and learned at any one of these levels of complexity, so when determining the pre-existing level of understanding it is important to know the level in the taxonomy.

Regardless of the level of complexity in either objectives or examinations, each learner's learning style will have influenced their performance and their current level of understanding. By inclusion of instruments such as the Myers-Briggs Type Indicator to identify the learners' learning preferences, the teacher can individualise the application of DP to achieve whole-brain learning. Examinations and other forms of assessment are much easier to compose when clear objectives have been written. Every objective, like every examination question, can then be classified within the learning taxonomy. An example of one of the useful reference guides for writing learning objectives is Gronlund and Brookhart (2009).

Teaching topics in greater depth

Teaching in greater depth equates to whole-brain thinking. It provides more factual knowledge needed for more thorough abstract conceptualisation. More thorough conceptualisation creates deeper understanding through more sophisticated active testing. Since time for teaching is limited, this approach cannot be comprehensive, nor does it need to be. The ability of the brain to transfer learning by generalisation will extend the value of each in-depth teaching lesson.

The importance of dialogue during whole-brain teaching cannot be overstated. Dialogue amplifies the entire ELC and the JMF sequence by engaging the whole brain. As learners speak to each other (frontal cortex), they are involved in active testing, because composing and expressing a thought can be successful, or a failure to communicate. Without a partner or team members, there would be no measure of sensibility or clarity. Learners will express their thinking primarily through their learning style, so an Intuitive-type learner will use language that poses possibilities and alternatives, also matching the abstract conceptualisation of the ELC. Those learners with the Sensing-type learning style will benefit by hearing this expression and acquire this skill through transfer of learning. Equally important, however, the Sensing learner will also contribute facts and concepts that are missing and in doing so they fill in concrete experience and reflective observation (ELC) for the Intuitive learner. Dialogue that concerns problem solving always engages the whole brain for any learning style preference. It also engages the limbic system, not because all dialogue is emotional but because it involves people. There is an inherent satisfaction in reaching agreement or in debating the choice between alternatives.

Like interpersonal dialogue, internal dialogue can also be encouraged as a part of the process of DP. Speaking to oneself can be audible or silent, but an advantage is gained if it is made audible since the area of the brain responsible for speech (Broca's area) is in the frontal cortex. The development of self-assessment skills through self-talk is fundamental to DP. The research in DP shows that the moment self-assessment diminishes, skill performance becomes automated and deteriorates (Ericsson *et al.* 1993).

Learner responsibilities for whole-brain learning

Transformative learning theory (Mezirow 1997) encourages a change, or transformation, in the learner from a receiver of information to a producer of knowledge. The 'receiver' approach best describes assimilative learning where learners simply acquire new information that fits into their pre-existing knowledge. Assimilative learning does not require whole-brain learning and as a result does not produce HOTS.

It is not surprising that the term 'transformation' has multiple uses in educational thought. Education is permeated with transformational events. Information is transformed into knowledge, the brain is transformed into new physical arrangements, teachers are transformed through their own experience and learners are transformed into self-directed producers of their own understanding. Whole-brain learning requires all of these forms of transformation.

There are two primary areas of responsibility for each learner that are essential to achieve their transformation into a producer of their own understanding. These are summarised as:

1. responsibility for conscious application of the ELC;
2. responsibility for seeking assistance in DP.

Conscious application of the ELC by the student

The ELC can be consciously applied in a stepwise protocol. Each step can be a major focus and can be a task undertaken by either an individual learner or a group of learners. Such a stepwise protocol is only appropriate as an initial focus for developing thinking. The actual process of learning will involve a progressive blending of the ELC steps as the learner produces their own understanding of the concepts. A four-stage learning model called the conscious competence sequence illustrates this (Howell 1982; Figure 6.3). The first stage, unconscious incompetence, represents the inexperienced learner. At this stage the dependence on a step-by-step ELC protocol is useful and helpful for organising thinking. The second stage, conscious incompetence, represents the learner's first attempts at learning from new concrete experience. As progress is made in skilful use of the ELC, the learner is able to process the results of active testing in the ELC to produce self-directed learning and proceed to the third stage, conscious competence. Repeated use of the ELC produces meaning by refining the results of active testing for each experience. As the learner further associates these new meanings with new concrete experience through reflective observation, they freely employ any step in the ELC in any order that is appropriate – and they are unaware of it. This final stage of unawareness in thinking is called unconscious competence. Thus, as the

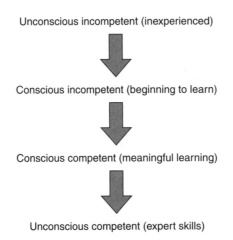

Unconscious incompetent (inexperienced)

Conscious incompetent (beginning to learn)

Conscious competent (meaningful learning)

Unconscious competent (expert skills)

FIGURE 6.3 The conscious competence cycle.

learner progresses through the conscious competence sequence to reach unconscious competence, they become less linear in their use of the ELC.

The conscious application of the ELC will prompt the learner to work first on establishing that all of the facts and concepts provided by the teacher are available for reflective observation. The learner has the benefit of teacher-generated learning objectives and teacher-provided instruction for this stage. The learner then employs reflective observation to find and verify definitions for new terminology. Other activities such as reviewing examples that have been taught as well as use of additional learning organisers provided by the teacher also facilitate reflective observation. The learner or group of learners then pose possibilities concerning the meaning of the new experience (abstract conceptualisation). This can be a list of predictions of cause and effect, a reorganisation of the material or the construction of similarities or differences. It is worth emphasising the advantage held by group dialogue at this stage since each learner will increase the total learning perspective from their own unique thinking. Finally, the different conceptualisations are tested through various activities that produce new concrete experience. Learners can explain their preference for one possibility compared to others, they can reorganise the material in a concept map or they can predict the outcome of acting on a possibility.

If such a learning approach is habitual, it will become a skill that is used with increasing facility. Such a self-directed learner will automatically assume the responsibility for making certain that all the information from the experience is available, that the information has been recognised, that the experience has meaning and that the meaning can be tested in order to generate new experience. At that point, the learner will produce their own knowledge.

Seeking assistance in DP by the student

Learners with the GM experience high achievement through DP through an understanding of how their brain learns. Learners will demonstrate different preferences in learning and those preferences can extend to the psychomotor domain as well as the cognitive domain. The learner cannot make use of DP without both an awareness of their preferences and an awareness of how these preferences can be balanced. When the student is aware that their preferences are not limits on their learning, it permits a focus on developing non-preferred learning skills. The awareness of the ELC steps that they prefer and awareness of their Myers-Briggs personality type (JMF preferences) will be sufficient for any student to achieve this development. An understanding and acceptance of the GM can only be accomplished by the learner. Without this mindset, DP will be ineffective.

The teacher's finest moment may well be in the assistance of the learner through DP. The learner is at their most vulnerable because they are getting feedback on the thinking that is least comfortable for them. The ability to support and guide the learner to persist in this development is one measure of a master teacher. Because DP is not fun, it may well produce results that are less dependent on intelligence and more dependent on motivation. Motivation, like self-awareness, is not in the teacher, it is in the learner.

Selected teaching and learning strategies

Examples are always helpful in illustrating the application of theory. There are many publications, such as Harmin (1995), that describe teaching strategies for application in the classroom. These learning strategies can be used to produce whole-brain learning. The following additional selected strategies help to illustrate how teachers can help learners fulfil their responsibilities:

1. flipped classroom
2. prefrontal pause
3. concept mapping
4. question analysis

Flipped classroom

A flipped classroom[6] delivers instruction online outside of the classroom so that homework can be completed in the classroom. This recent innovation was made possible by the ability to record lectures and other instruction and make it available on the internet. Thus, learners work on the ELC concrete experience and reflective observation steps at home. During class time, the learners are able to clarify misunderstandings to complete the reflective observation step and then to complete the remaining ELC steps under the teacher's supervision. This facilitates the use of DP by supporting the needed individual development of learning skills for them to master whole-brain thinking. The Intuitive-type learners will have a greater ease with this process than the Sensing types. The primary concern of the Sensing type is that they need the certainty that they are coming up with the most correct possibility. The flaw here is clear. The most correct possibility isn't determined until the active testing step, but the Sensing learner is attempting to determine it from recognition (reflective observation). This is where the teacher can provide support by simply offering reassurance that it is natural for a brief period to not know something with certainty. The Sensing-type learner will want the correct possibility to already be known. However, with regular support, the Sensing-type learner will adapt and perform this ELC step with greater skill. Thus, this type of learner will become a more skilled learner through DP. The Intuitive-type learner will experience difficulty with using all of the facts that are needed during the concrete experience and reflective observation steps of the ELC. Again, the teacher can provide support through exercises that facilitate present moment awareness and that temporarily discourage distraction from the 'interesting' material. This illustrates the nature of a big picture learner. They become uninterested in details once they have formed their big picture.

Prefrontal pause

A prefrontal pause is a brief interruption at a suitable break point in the concrete experience step of the ELC – during a lecture for example – to allow the learners an opportunity to turn to a neighbour and discuss the answer to a question. The question is framed to use concepts just taught in the previous 10–15 minutes and it is a higher-order question, not a recall question. The task could be to list the similarities between two concepts (Quellmalz – comparison level) or to list other components that would be part of a grouping (Quellmalz – analysis level). Because the question requires more than recall, it pushes the learner to think at the abstract conceptualisation step of the ELC, or in other words, to use the front of their brain to make some decisions. Hence, the term 'prefrontal pause'. If the teacher labels the exercise consistently as a prefrontal pause, it will reinforce the learner's awareness of how they are using their brain and facilitate both the GM and the application of DP.

Concept mapping

Concept mapping is a method of recording information that is otherwise contained in text or outline form by representing it as a series of bubbles, called nodes, containing one or more terms that name a concept and are connected by lines, called links (Figure 6.4). The links can have additional terms, such as verbs, that are drawn on the line to clarify the nature of the link. A simple link represents a single fact. If a node is a grouping term then several links will branch from it. A branch point, then, becomes a level of hierarchy. When one branch is compared to another, a special type of link, called a cross-link, is created.

There are numerous definitions of a concept map. One definition refers to concept maps as 'living documents'. Since concept maps are hierarchical, they can continually be linked or networked by connecting new information, hence they 'grow'. The significance to this definition is that it relates directly to the constructivist view that new knowledge is based on existing knowledge. Another definition for concept mapping is that it is a reading method (Pelley and Dalley 2008). There is no other method that

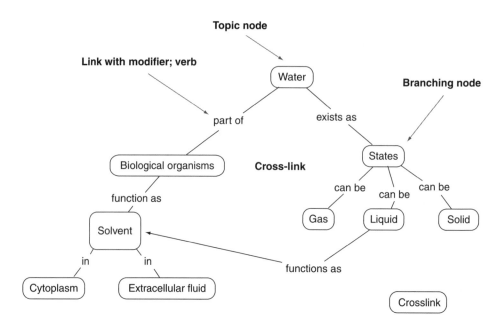

FIGURE 6.4 Concept map of water.

exceeds the depth of reading produced by the construction of a concept map. The only document that is read more thoroughly is a love letter:

> they read for all they are worth. They read every word three ways; they read between the lines and in the margins; they read the whole in terms of the parts, and each part in terms of the whole; they grow sensitive to context and ambiguity, to insinuation and implication; they perceive the color of words, the odor of phrases, and the weight of sentences. They may even take the punctuation into account. Then, if never before or after, they read.
>
> (Adler 1972)

If a learner wants to consciously apply the full ELC to their learning, they can accomplish the task by constructing a concept map of the material that they want to learn. The first step in map construction involves the inspection of the material at hand for concepts that rank highest in the hierarchy, i.e. the grouping terms. Immediately, they are using concrete experience skills (the factual content), reflective observation skills (definitions, examples) and abstract conceptualisation skills (determination of likely possibilities) to make a short list from which to begin the concept map. The actual construction of the map constitutes the active testing step as each concept is added. Evaluation of the map is achieved by verbalisation of every concept relationship. If the map can guide dialogue that is understandable to both the learner and the teacher, it becomes a new concrete experience. Since each link placed in a map is a decision, it represents active testing skills in creating a logical hierarchy. The activity of recursively adding concepts to the map requires inspectional reading and analysis of options for representing them in the map.

Since the construction of a concept map involves every step in the ELC, it is an ideal tool for the development of learning skills through DP. Every learner will encounter greater ease with some of the steps in map construction and greater difficulty with others. A teacher working with a learner's concept map in a flipped classroom is in a position to help with the areas of greater difficulty to strengthen whole-brain learning.

Question analysis

Since they are so amenable to machine scoring and analysis, multiple choice questions dominate learning assessment. A test preparation industry has emerged in response to their importance in standardised testing, entrance examinations and certification examinations. Among the services provided by this industry is the provision of item banks of sample or representative questions. There are two main methods for using such questions: diagnostic and analytic. The diagnostic approach uses sample questions to identify areas of deficiency that are then reviewed by standard methods of study. This is inefficient and counterproductive for two reasons. First, the learner is attempting to refine learning in a general topic identified by the incorrectly answered question without establishing a concrete issue to learn. Second, the question itself contains needed information that can guide learning.

Question analysis follows four main steps (Pelley and Dalley 2008): (1) concept identification, (2) verification of the correct answer, (3) verification of the incorrect answers and (4) rephrasing to make some answer choices correct. Because the process requires research concerning all of the answer choices, it is less effective with questions requiring only simple recall. Question analysis can take the reader outside of assigned reading materials to additional resources when needed. All steps in question analysis require inspectional reading. While a learner might read passively in preparation for an examination, it is impossible to read passively while engaged in question analysis.

Concept identification requires the learner to verify that definitions are known and understood. Because all of the terms in the question are related concepts, there is a strengthening of the reflective observation step through pattern recognition and association. Verification of the correct answer requires that the learner determine a verbal rationale for justifying the correct answer. This requires a decision to include only the information necessary to make logical sense and excluding information that does not contribute to the rationale. This process seems subtle, but it trains the learner to give attention only to the subset of information relevant to the rationale. This involves the abstract conceptualisation step by deciding between relevant and irrelevant information and active testing by verbalising the rationale. Similarly, verbalisation of the incorrect answers requires seeking out specific information that is relevant to the decision to rule out the incorrect answer. Again, decision making in the prefrontal cortex is selecting from all of the available information only that information needed to know that the incorrect answer is wrong. Verbalising the rationale is the active testing that completes the ELC.

The question analysis is finalised by an attempt (not always possible) to rephrase the question to make other answer choices correct. This deepens understanding by strengthening associations which, in turn, strengthen reflective observation. The overall process has the benefit of causing the learner to review analytically an entire topic from the outcomes point of view. A test question can serve as a learning objective in this way and thus drive reading that covers the topic by using the entire ELC. An additional benefit is obtained since each incorrect answer in a proper test question is a rational alternative. That means that each can be a correct answer in a related question. Analysis of one question can prepare a learner for five or more questions on the examination.

Further study by those learning to be teachers will reveal similar use of the ELC in other active learning methods. Engaging all of the steps in the ELC to produce whole-brain thinking will transform learners from receivers of information to producers of their own knowledge.

Epilogue

Educating a robot or any other machine only requires devising an algorithm to be programmed into the machine's memory, and it only requires this to be done once. Machines provided with search/select algorithms can have a well-developed capacity for searching stored information and selecting that which is needed, but they lack the creative ability to determine what alternatives to apply this searching and selecting to. Machines don't create alternatives to choose from, but people do.

Educating a learner requires that the instruction causes them to make decisions. They must make decisions that they can act on, that is, decisions they can experience. Ideally they must learn how to do this through deliberate practice using their own awareness of their learning style and its application in the experiential learning cycle. Decision-making learners are self-actualising problem solvers that take their learning style into account.

Notes

1. The concept of HOTS is functionally equivalent to critical thinking and/or analytical thinking skills.
2. Each mental model provides a different window for looking into the mind. Each reveals its own metaphor of the working of the mind.
3. Thus, the ELC helps us to delineate the responsibilities of the teacher and the responsibilities of the learner, a topic that will be discussed later in this chapter.
4. Grades 11 and 12 are usually the last two years of high school in the USA (ages 17 and 18, respectively).
5. A similar learning taxonomy, that of Bloom, is referred to in Chapter 1.
6. www.knewton.com/flipped-classroom

References

Adler, M. and Van Doren, C. (1972) *How to Read a Book*. New York: Touchstone
Bransford, J.D., Brown, A.L. and Cocking, R.R. (2000) *How People Learn: Brain, Mind, Experience, and School*. Washington, DC: National Research Council.

Coffield, F., Moseley, D., Hall, E. and Ecclestone, K. (2004) *Should We be Using Learning Styles? What Research has to Say About the Practice.* London: LSDA.

Colvin, G. (2008) *Talent is Overrated: What Really Separates World-class Performers From Everybody Else.* New York: Penguin Group.

Cuthbert, P.F. (2005) The student learning process: learning styles or learning approaches?, *Teaching in Higher Education*, 10, 235–249.

Dweck, C. (2006) *Mindset: The New Psychology of Success.* New York: Random House.

Ericsson, K.A., Krampe, R. and Tesch-Römer, C. (1993) The role of deliberate practice in the acquisition of expert performance, *Psychological Review*, 100, 363–406.

Felder, R.M. and Brent, R. (2005) Understanding student differences, *Journal of Engineering Education*, 94, 57–72.

Gardner, H. (1993) *Frames of Mind: The Theory of Multiple Intelligences.* 2nd edn. New York: Basic Books.

Gronlund, N.E. and Brookhart, S.M. (2009) *Gronlund's Writing Instructional Objectives.* 8th edn. Upper Saddle River, NJ: Prentice Hall

Harmin, M. (1995) *Strategies to Inspire Active Learning.* Edwardsville, IL: Inspiring Strategy Institute.

Howell, W.S. (1982) *The Empathic Communicator.* Belmont, CA: Wadsworth.

Kolb, D.A. (1984) *Experiential Learning.* Englewood Cliffs, NJ: Prentice Hall.

Maslow, A. (1954) *Motivation and Personality.* 3rd edn, New York: Harper and Row.

Mezirow, J. (1997) Transformative learning: theory to practice, *New Directions for Adult and Continuing Education*, 74, 5–12.

Myers, I.B., McCaulley, M.H., Quenk, N.L. and Hammer, A.L. (1998) *MBTI Manual: A Guide to the Development and Use of the Myers-Briggs Type Indicator.* 3rd edn. Palo Alto, CA: Consulting Psychologists Press.

Ornstein, R. (1995) *The Roots of the Self: Unraveling the Mystery of Who We Are.* New York: HarperCollins.

Pashler, H., McDaniel, M., Rohrer, D. and Bjork, R. (2008) Learning styles: concepts and evidence, *Psychological Science in the Public Interest*, 9, 106–119.

Pelley, J.W. and Dalley, B.K. (2008) *Success Types in Medical Education*, www.ttuhsc.edu/SOM/success, accessed 22 April 2014.

Riding, R.J. (1997) On the nature of cognitive style, *Educational Psychology*, 17, 29–49.

Stickgold, R. and Ellenbogen, J.M. (2008) Sleep on it: how snoozing makes you smarter, *Scientific American Mind*, August.

Stiggins, R.J., Rubel, E. and Quellmalz, E. (1988) *Measuring Thinking Skills in the Classroom*, Alphareta, GA: National Education Association.

White, B.Y. and Frederickson, J.R. (1997) *The ThinkerTools Inquiry Project: Making Scientific Inquiry Accessible to Students.* Princeton, NJ: Center for Performance Assessment, Educational Testing Service.

Zull, J.E. (2002) *The Art of Changing the Brain.* Sterling, VA: Stylus.

7

Assessment

Tim Heywood

To measure is to know.

William Thomson (Lord Kelvin)

What is assessment?

Any attempt to define a word in this way will be fraught with difficulties. This is a strange phenomenon; we have all, usually many times, been the subject of an assessment and so we have an idea of what our own definition of the word should be, based on our own experiences. However, to create an all-encompassing definition immediately hits the problem that anyone who attempts to define a word on the basis of their own experience with it will necessarily create a definition which is unique to their perspective, and so which stands a good chance of sounding foreign to anyone else.

Perhaps the most obvious form of assessment is the type which certifies us in some way to progress in life: a driving test; an A-level; a degree; an entrance examination; an interview. All these share one important common feature: they measure our performance in some way. Sometimes the measurement relates to how we performed against a group of others (e.g. in an interview), and sometimes there is a set standard against which we are measured, regardless of the performance of others in our group (e.g. a driving test). Sometimes there are only two possible outcomes – pass or fail – each with very different and clear-cut implications for our immediate future. Others stratify us into grades – A, B, C, D or E – placing us in a pecking order, the results of which are not immediately clear. Notwithstanding these variations, they are all still ways of measuring us. They are familiar, challenging and usually frightening. They are called 'tests', 'exams', 'interviews', 'dissertations', 'theses' and other adrenaline-inducing phrases, and we need to fear them. Don't we?

Well, not always. Not by any means. Is it not a form of assessment if a tutor says at the start of a seminar, 'Tell me everything you already know about this subject'? For sure your knowledge is being assessed – measured, even – but to define you as capable or otherwise of continuing with the seminar, but with the intention of making the seminar relevant to you and your needs at the time. What about a seven-year-old reading aloud to a teaching assistant in class? This can't be just for reading practice, for if it were what role is the teaching assistant playing? What about the chat about how your

driving is going with the instructor after only your second lesson? A letter of com,
or praise a doctor receives from a patient? A spouse or partner commenting about your
skills (or lack of them) in maintaining the tidiness of the house?

All these situations are just as much measuring devices as the more familiar list.
They vary in how trustworthy they are measures of genuine performance – i.e. they
are not necessarily *very good* measuring devices. They vary in both the intended and
actual outcomes they achieve – i.e. they are measuring performance for different reasons. They vary in how thoughtfully they have been designed to fulfil their purpose –
i.e. they can be ad hoc or highly planned. But they all share the common process: they
all measure performance to achieve a desired outcome. If we are to understand assessment, then we must seek to understand how these two sides of the assessment equation interact – how the desired outcome of any measurement affects the way we design
and then make the measurement.

Classification of assessment

Before we embark on a classification it is wise to remind ourselves that any classification is a simplification of a complex reality, whose purpose is to help us understand
such a reality better. Seen in this way, classification is a useful tool. However, all too
often we are seduced by the artifice of simplicity that is created and start to see the
simplification – the model – as the reality, and start to twist the complexities of the
reality which are unexplained by our model instead of the more logical approach,
which would be to recognise the limitations of the model. This is a problem we will
come across more than once in thinking about assessment, and often in other aspects of
life.

Notwithstanding this limitation, there are several ways in which we will often see
assessments classified. Rarely will any individual assessment be the pure form
described at one end of each of the spectra described below; it is much more common
to find that real assessments are some combination of both ends.

Formative vs summative

This classification is based on the primary purpose of the assessment, and the way in
which it will influence the learner's life. *Formative assessment* has a primary purpose of
discovering the extent to which a student's knowledge and/or skills are developed
(Black and Wiliam 1998). While many curricula have a requirement that students
should *take* a formative assessment, one of the hallmarks of formative assessments is
that the result doesn't affect the student's progression through the curriculum – there
is no pass mark. Such an assessment is designed to give the student (and her teachers)
information about how much of the curriculum is already known and understood,
how much work there is to do to reach a certain standard and what sort of work that
should be.

Formative assessments are sometimes obviously assessments, and sometimes more
covertly so. They can be done by others or by ourselves. They can be formal or

informal. Examples include a mock driving test, the questions at the end of a chapter in an A-level physics textbook and playing a piano piece to our teacher in preparation for a music exam. The unifying factor in these tests is that the outcome is not a grade, not a percentage or a numerical mark (although these methods may be used to deliver the outcome). The outcome is information about how close we are to achieving a goal, whatever that goal may be. The only person who will really judge and interpret the outcome is the student himself.

In contrast, *summative assessments* generate outcomes which are judged by others (Harlen and James 1997). They do not tell us how we are doing, but how we have done. There is usually a concept of success (Heubert and Hauser 1999) and failure attached to them, and they are almost invariably formally delivered. These are assessments that we recognise as assessments – driving tests, A-levels, job interviews, university selection procedures – and they are usually somewhat daunting.

As hinted at above, in reality it is rare that any assessment is purely formative or purely summative. Many formative assessments have a degree of summation about them – for instance, performance at the piano may be so bad that the teacher gets up and refuses to teach the pupil again – and many (high-quality) summative assessments will also give feedback to candidates on why they achieved the mark they did. When delivering any assessment we should ask ourselves 'What are the formative elements in this assessment? What are the summative elements?' and use them accordingly.

Continuous vs terminal

Terminal assessment merely means assessment that occurs at the end of a course or module. It is usual, given this, that a terminal assessment is also a summative one, as the purpose is to measure the effect of the learning that has occurred during the course.

Continuous assessment is exactly what is says it is and is perhaps best described as 'the opposite of terminal assessment'. It goes on throughout the course or module, and may be formative or summative. In reality, assessment is never actually continuous; the term usually describes any assessment which is non-terminal and occurs several times at discrete intervals throughout a course. Continuous assessment is very commonly used in a formative fashion, sometimes formally (e.g. weekly spelling tests in primary schools) and sometimes informally (e.g. discussions with a tutor during an undergraduate degree course).

High-stakes vs low-stakes (Heubert and Hauser 1999)

This classification generally relates to summative assessments and describes the consequences of failure. If ever stakes were applied to formative assessments, the application of them would automatically change the nature of the assessment to summative, and, as we shall see, this change may render a high-quality formative assessment into a poor-quality summative one.

The division between high and low stakes can be somewhat subjective, dependent on the point of view of the candidate. Most medical students, for instance, regard their finals as higher stakes than their first-year assessments, as they are the assessment which certifies them fit to practise as a junior doctor. In fact, in many medical schools the consequences of failure are identical (typically one resit opportunity and, if that is failed, exclusion from the course unless the student is allowed to repeat the year), which has an identical effect on the candidate's future (loss of one year's salary or a change of career).

However, if the stakes are genuinely low (e.g. in a driving test, which can be taken any number of times and only risks losing the entry fee and perhaps some social credibility) then the design of the test may be different, with different tolerance for measurement error.

Knowledge vs skills assessment

The body of what should be learned has been divided several ways, but one of the most pervasive is into knowledge, skills and attitudes (Bloom 1956). To visualise this model, think of the process by which ice-cream is made. I know the recipe and can tell you it. You may then be able to describe how it is made, but were you to actually attempt to make it, the outcome could be disastrous. This would mean you have the knowledge, but not the skill. In fact, the distinction is not necessarily so clear cut – how could one have the skill of making ice-cream without the knowledge to support it? – but in terms of assessment design it is easy to see that a valuable method for assessing at the knowledge level could be woefully inadequate at the skills level.

Classification based on method of delivery

Assessments can be delivered by multiple means and it is sometimes useful to think of the classification of them based on these methods. They can be written or practical. Written ones can be computer-based or paper-based. They can be short or long answers, multiple choice, single best answer, essay, dissertation or thesis, structured or unstructured. Computer-based assessments can include media clips. Practical assessments can be an observation of performance of a skill either directly or remotely (in space or time) or oral questioning (the *'viva voce'*).

What is a good assessment?

An easy method of manoeuvring any debate so that it is fought on your own terms is to answer a question such as this with another question, namely, 'What do you mean by "good"?' Before we embark on designing any assessment, or involving ourselves in a curriculum which utilises an assessment designed by someone else, we should have a clear idea of what that assessment is designed to achieve. There are certain aspects of assessment which would help us decide at which end of the various classification spectra described above an assessment should be placed. However, there are also some features of quality in assessment which are common to all assessments.

When we stop to think what the desirable qualities in an assessment are, it is easy to generate a list of the obvious. Let's do it anyway. A good assessment must:

1. measure something
2. measure something relevant
3. measure something relevant that we are interested in knowing
4. measure that something accurately
5. give similar results if repeated in similar situations
6. avoid accidentally measuring other things that might confuse the outcome.

This wish list represents the qualities that are described as *validity* and *reliability*; these two qualities are the methods by which we can really understand the quality of an assessment. They are most easily described by considering the familiar measuring tool many of us may find ourselves on each morning in our bathrooms – the scales.

Imagine you are keen to become healthier. We know that excess body fat is associated with being unhealthy, so knowing how much body fat you have is a useful thing to know. It is not the only aspect of being healthy, however, but it is easy to measure. But how good an assessment is it of our increased health when we are on a diet?

Validity

Validity is a measure of the extent to which the assessment measures the concepts that we want to measure (Carmines and Zeller 1979). People on a diet will commonly step on the bathroom scales at intervals and have significant emotional involvement in the outcome. But how valid is that emotional reaction? When we step on the scales, we measure not just body fat, but muscle, bone, bowel contents, bladder contents, clothing, hydration status and other indices. Some of these are easy to control for – we can stand on the scale knowing we are naked and that our bladder is empty, for instance. However, as we look at total body weight we can't calculate easily what proportion of the change relates to fat loss and what proportion relates to an increase in muscle mass caused by our increased level of exercise. It is easy to see how we may become distressed by a slow rate of weight loss despite significant efforts, when in fact we are getting much healthier as our body loses fat and gains muscle at the same time. Our concern is inappropriate because of a low validity of using total body weight as a sole marker of health. We have ignored the fact that we are seeking to measure health by using the surrogate endpoint, total body weight, and failing to recognise the validity limitations of doing so.

Validity has been further subdivided by many authors and it can be useful to think of validity by considering such subdivisions as long as the *caveats* relating to categorisation of anything are borne in mind.

Face validity (Nevo 1985) is the extent to which the assessment appears, at a gut-feeling level, to assess what it is supposed to assess. The practical section of the UK driving test has high face validity, because it is an assessment of how well a candidate can drive, which is done by watching them drive. It would have lower face validity if the candidate had to describe how to drive by writing an essay, for instance, and very low face validity if the candidates were asked to demonstrate their skills by riding a bicycle. Face validity is important for public examinations and for certification examinations for professions such as airline pilots and doctors, because the public must trust the rigour of the assessment while not understanding either the profession being assessed nor the science of assessment. However, it is possible for an excellent assessment to have relatively low face validity, as well as for quite poor assessments to have excellent face validity.

Similar to face validity are *content validity* and *construct validity*. Like face validity, these relate to the assessment measuring what it purports to measure, but they involve a more rigorous analysis of the assessment than the 'gut feeling' of face validity. Content validity relates to how well the assessment tests the material the curriculum has planned to deliver. Therefore an assessment of content validity requires an analysis of the desired learning outcomes for the course being assessed, and an estimation of what proportion of those outcomes have been assessed, and if anything that is assessed is not in the outcomes of the course. The method by which assessments are checked in this way is referred to as *blueprinting*.[1] This is a formalised process in which each aspect of the assessment is mapped to the learning outcomes of the course so that it is possible to look at the outcomes and know where they are to be assessed, and look at the assessments and see which aspects of the course are being assessed, and which are not. It is not necessary to assess every learning outcome of a course. Consequential validity (described below) tells us that if there is a reasonable expectation that a particular outcome will be assessed, the students will be motivated to learn about it. Obviously the greater the proportion of the outcomes that are assessed in any given sitting, the greater the certainty students will learn the whole curriculum. The spread of outcomes assessed can be numerated, and this process is called *sampling*.

Blueprinting is important for teachers, as they can be confident that the assessment will not cover items which are not on the syllabus. It is important for students, for the same reason. It is important for assessors as a way of addressing quality control to supervising bodies that will hold assessors accountable for the validity and reliability of the assessments.

Construct validity is similar to content validity, but held at a more abstract level, and to understand it, we must first understand what is meant by 'construct'. Certain aspects of life are easy to measure to acceptable levels of accuracy. Most of us know how tall we are to within an inch or a centimetre or so. We all know our shoe size. We all understand what the Met Office mean when they say the daytime maximum temperature will be 21 degrees Celsius (although some of us will need that information converted to Fahrenheit first!). It is often useful to measure these easily measurable values, but often it is not enough. When thinking about assessing students at any level of education, it is not long before we come across a concept or an idea which is not easily measurable. Examples include problem-solving skills, communication skills and even intelligence itself. There is no direct way of measuring these abstract entities, and yet it is not difficult to see how desirable it could be to measure them. As with the example of using body weight as a predictor of health, the underlying unmeasurable (in this case, health) can be broken down into one or a series of measurable surrogates (in this case, body weight). For the same reasons described above, however, we can see that measuring body weight alone is not a perfect indicator of the construct 'health', and it would be likely that if we added 'blood pressure' as another surrogate and looked at the result of both weight and blood pressure, we might have a better estimate of the construct 'health'. But what about two people with normal blood pressure and a healthy weight, one of whom has, say, diabetes? If we only measure the two surrogates, we would assess them as equally healthy. Are we tempted to add a third surrogate then? And a fourth? What about an eleventh?

This is the sort of dilemma that tells us we are thinking well about construct validity. How good a test of our desired construct is the series of surrogates we have selected? Do they test a broad enough range of the construct to mean that we have captured enough data? On the other hand, what if they test surrogates that are *not* part of 'health'? In this case the construct validity might be low because there is variation in marks achieved related to matters which have no impact on health, and so we end up labelling certain subjects as more healthy than others when in reality their health status might be the same (or even worse).

Testing construct validity is a difficult task, and the mathematics of it are beyond the scope of this chapter (and, if I'm honest, probably this author). However, it cannot be assessed without such calculation, because to do so would mean that the results were based on gut feeling, albeit the gut feeling of an expert, and that, by definition, is a form of face validity.

Consequential validity relates to how the assessment affects the learning process of the students on the course. Most of us will recognise from personal experience of certification assessments how easy it is for students to become assessment focused. How many of us learned to 'turn the car in the road using the forward and reverse gears' because we anticipated safer driving, lower insurance premiums and a greater internal sense of fulfilling our responsibilities to society by being able to perform this task safely and efficiently? And how many of us learned it because it was in the driving test? There may be a few wonderful individuals who fall into the former category, but most, I suspect, are with me in the latter. Any assessment, with the exception of perhaps the genuine 'surprise test' will affect students' engagement in the course and teachers' delivery of it. Even the surprise test is not a surprise to the teacher, who may have consciously or otherwise prepared his class for it. And if a teacher has a reputation for delivering surprise tests, the class may well prepare for them just in case.

If, then, a given test encourages students to develop knowledge, skills or attitudes which are not part of the desirable course outcomes, then these aspects of the test have low consequential validity. Sometimes it is even possible that the assessment encourages students or teachers to develop characteristics that are positively *un*desirable for the outcome of the course.

Predictive validity relates to how well a test predicts performance after the test is complete. This requires long-term follow-up of candidates, but can be a very powerful vindication of a particular testing strategy. One defence of A-levels as an assessment strategy to inform admission criteria for medical schools relates to evidence that they predict future academic performance in higher education in the medical sector (McManus *et al.* 2003). One problem of predictive validity is deciding what point in the future you wish to predict. Imagine that a particular test was found to be very good at predicting which students at A-level would perform best in the first-year undergraduate assessments on an education course. Such data may be used to inform the admissions tutors for that course. But what if further follow up showed that, of those who went on to teach, the assessment negatively predicted ability to interact with a class (i.e. a higher test score led to better first-year performance, but poorer performance in the classroom)? Perhaps the tutors would consider a different admissions strategy.

Academics debate the value of subdividing validity into these (and sometimes other) categories (Andreatta and Gruppen 2009). Readers should remember that the categorisation is to aid understanding of the complex reality, rather than vice versa. The categories are not distinct entities without overlap.

A final point about validity is that it is context dependent. An assessment which is highly valid for one purpose may be valid or invalid for another. For instance, the practical section of the UK driving test may be a very valid way of dividing candidates into two categories – (a) safe enough to be able to drive unaccompanied or (b) not safe enough to be able to drive unaccompanied – but may be very poor at ranking the driving schools of the candidates into quality categories. Despite this, driving schools have in the past used the pass rate of their candidates as a selling point.[2]

Reliability (Carmines and Zeller 1979)

The reliability of an assessment is the extent to which the measurement achieved is repeatable, and the same result is achieved. Thinking about the weight loss example again, validity is the construct that tells us weight is worth measuring to help us determine health status. Reliability, on the other hand, is what tell us how likely the tool we use to measure our weight is to give us the same result every time.

Imagine I weigh 70.64823 kg (I wish!). I don't know this yet, because I haven't stood on the scales. However, I obviously *have* a weight before I stand on the scales, and that it what it is. To make it easy, say I'm about to buy a new hang-glider, and so I'm not interested in my weight as a surrogate of the construct 'health', but as a surrogate for the construct 'how likely I am to drop out of the sky if the wind drops a bit'. (Okay, so this might be a little bit tied up with 'health status' after all but…. No. Leave that there.) As the construct is a serious one, I end up weighing myself each morning over a week to make sure I really know how big a hang-glider to buy. Table 7.1 shows the results I may get from two different sets of scales.

What can we say about the readings that these sets of scales give? First, with respect to validity, we don't yet have enough information to tell. Face validity is good – these are weights, not numbers of fish. Content validity is good, too – again, weight is what is required. The construct validity is likely to be good, assuming that the manufacturer of the hang-glider has shown that weight is the primary issue which determines which size glider you need to reduce the chances of it dropping out of the sky. The predictive validity is also likely to be good, but depends on the manufacturer having modelled

TABLE 7. 1 Daily weight readings from two sets of scales

Day	Reading from Scale 1 (kg)	Reading from Scale 2 (kg)
Monday	70.0	72.3
Tuesday	70.1	68.8
Wednesday	70.1	70.6
Thursday	70.0	67.2
Friday	70.1	74.8
Saturday	70.0	70.5
Sunday	70.1	69.9

and tested the various wing designs effectively. But remember that validity is context-dependent, so we would need to ask the hang-glider manufacturer which weights are safe for which size of glider. Imagine that there were two sizes of glider, and that those weighing more than 100 kg needed the larger size. In this case the readings of both scales provide valid and reliable readings because the mean of both scales is similar and below 100 kg. But what if the manufacturer states that you need the larger size if your weight is above 70 kg? In this situation the results from Scale 2 vary too much to be able to predict from a single reading which glider to buy. This is summarised by the statement 'Scale 1 is more reliable than Scale 2.'

Here we can also see some of the interdependence between reliability and validity. While most of the aspects of validity are unchanged by the results in this table, the predictive validity of Scale 1's readings are higher than those of Scale 2 when the manufacturer's cut-off is 70 kg, as it is possible that if I weigh myself only on Thursday, the weight does not predict longevity as well as using Scale 1.

So it seems reliability is superior to validity, but this is not the whole story. Let us now imagine that a third scale is used and returns the results in Table 7.2.

We can see that Scale 3 is even more reliable that Scale 1 – every reading is the same. The problem is that the readings are consistently very wrong. They are highly reliable, but the predictive validity is, for the context of the hang-glider decision, fatally low.

TABLE 7.2 Daily weight readings from three sets of scales

Day	Reading from Scale 1 (kg)	Reading from Scale 2 (kg)	Reading from Scale 3 (kg)
Monday	70.0	72.3	55.0
Tuesday	70.1	68.8	55.0
Wednesday	70.1	70.6	55.0
Thursday	70.0	67.2	55.0
Friday	70.1	74.8	55.0
Saturday	70.0	70.5	55.0
Sunday	70.1	69.9	55.0

So we should aim for high validity *and* high reliability in every assessment. Shouldn't we? Not necessarily. The reason is that the ideal world can be a very difficult and expensive place to build, and there are usually compromises to make to allow an assessment to be delivered feasibly. To understand those compromises, we should first understand the factors that affect reliability.

Factors affecting reliability

In order to consider this, it is first important to bring into our collective consciousness that there is an assumption that almost everyone makes about learning. This assumption, on first verbalisation, seems too obvious to waste the ink on, but it is, in fact, very important to realise it is just an assumption. It is one of the assumptions of the model of assessments called classical test theory (CTT) (Traub 1997) and it states that whatever the construct that is being assessed, the individual we are assessing possesses a certain quantity of that construct, and if we can apply a valid and reliable measuring tool to that individual, we can quantify that construct in that individual. As an example, think about the assessment of height. It is a natural assumption to think that each individual has a particular true height, and as long as we have an accurate enough ruler we can discover that height. However, we know we live in the real world and that rulers have limitations: they have broader or narrower gradations; they have greater or lesser dead-space at the ends before the zero point; they change their size slightly depending on temperature, etc. However, despite this, we can control even for such limitations and make our measurement more and more accurate, i.e. closer and closer to the true height. This leads to the equation:

$$\text{True score} = \text{Observed score} + \text{measurement error} \tag{1}$$

While validity is related to how large the difference between the observed score and the true score is, we can see from this equation that reliability is more about consistency of scoring and consistency of error, keeping the right-hand side of the equation as constant as possible. Therefore, when seeking sources of variation in reliability, we are really seeking sources of inconsistency in either observed score, or in error.

Inter-rater reliability refers to the extent to which two rating instruments (usually human examiners, but the term can also apply to other measuring devices) give similar values when assessing the same thing. Sources of variability between human examiners are numerous and are as diverse as they are numerous. Any factor which leads one examiner to mark consistently differently to another falls into this category. For instance, it may be a set of scales that consistently reads the true weight +5 per cent compared to other scales. It may be a driving examiner who has high standards and so is less likely to pass any learner in their driving test than average. It may relate to a misinterpretation of a question by a lead examiner in one of several groups, who ends up briefing the examiners in his team differently, causing them all to deliver fewer marks than the question writer had intended. In short, the term relates to any behaviour in which the marks awarded vary because of factors other than those relating to the construct being tested, but those factors make individual examiners behave consistently.

On the other hand there are issues which will cause individual examiners to behave differently with different students. This creates problems with intra-rater reliability. Variation may also occur for a wide variety and number of reasons, for instance ambiguous mark schemes, gender or racial prejudice in the examiner, variation in examiner performance with tiredness through a long day of assessments, examiner distraction with non-work matters which may affect ability to concentrate. Paradoxically, it can even occur when an examiner who is keen to act reliably realises they have been too harsh in the morning and so they change their style of examining in the afternoon.

Not all sources of variation relate to the examiner. The design of the test itself can mean that examiners behaving completely predictably and logically may award a different mark to two students of the same ability in the contrast being measured. This is called test–retest reliability, which is not a perfect name; it suggests that a student performing the same test twice should achieve the same mark on both occasions. However, the very act of sitting the test will alter the student's expectations of the test, and their readiness for it, so making it likely that a second sitting of an identical paper would score higher than the first sitting. When defined like this, test–retest reliability would require some magical device which erased the student's memory of the first sitting (but only of the first sitting) before they undertook the second sitting. Of course, this can't happen, but thinking of a test in this way can help examiners discover reliability limitations in this category. There can be several reasons why students may score differently on different sittings. For instance, a question that is designed as a single-best-answer question may have two answers which are partially correct, even though the question writer has only allowed the marking scheme to give credit for one of them. It may be that the assessment involves a piece of equipment which measures differently under different conditions. Imagine measuring something wooden with a ruler made of metal in different seasons. The ruler will contract more than the wood in the cold winter and expand more than it in the warm summer, meaning that the actual result reflects both the desired construct (length) and an undesired one (ambient temperature) at the same time.

Sometimes it is desirable to test the same constructs with different tools. This can easily be understood, for instance, if one considers a mathematics paper run each year for ten years. In the first year the paper may have very high validity and be delivered to all students across the country with very high inter-rater and intra-rater reliability. Excellent job, exam board. But in the second year, the board have to set different questions, or run the same paper again. If they know the past papers are in circulation among the students, though, setting the same paper reduces validity (as it may become more a measurement of how much emphasis is placed on past papers in the teaching method rather than student ability) and so it becomes desirable to set a different paper. If the questions are different, though, it is almost impossible to ensure that the levels of difficulty are identical in both papers. Despite methods of setting a pass mark which takes this into account, there may still be error, which means that marks vary for reasons other than student ability. This is termed inter-method reliability or parallel forms reliability.

Increasing reliability

If we think further about these potential threats to reliability, we will see that there are several strategies for increasing it (Norman and Eva 2010). The first is to increase the number of items in the test. From Equation 1 we can see that the observed score differs from the true score by the measurement error. Each time any item is delivered, the error is likely to differ slightly, but after a lot of items the probability rises that all sources of error which artificially inflate the observed score are balanced by errors which artificially deflate the observed score. This means that the average score more closely represents the true score, and so the more items we have, the more reliable the test is.

Similarly, we can see that if some examiners tend to be harsh and give low marks (the 'hawks') and others tend to be lenient and give high marks (the 'doves'), then exposing any candidate to more examiners will mean that the inflations of the doves are more likely to be cancelled out by deflations of the hawks, meaning that the observed score more reliably represents the true score.

Ensuring the questions are of high quality is one of the key aspects of reliability. Each should only test one construct[3] and this is very difficult to achieve, especially if you want to test a broad area of the curriculum. Each question should be unambiguous, with the answer deemed as correct on the marking scheme being the only correct answer. Each question should be of known difficulty. These three stipulations of high quality usually mean that each question must be written by a team of people who are expert in both the subject area and assessment design, piloted on a cohort of students, analysed by statistical experts, revised and re-piloted before being used.

There are other ways in which reliability can be increased – thorough examiner training, robust moderation procedures, having scripts marked by more than one examiner, feedback to examiners (which only improves reliability for subsequent iterations of the assessment) and others – and the uniting issue of them all is that they are resource-intensive. As well as that, because a reliable question tends to ask about a small part of the curriculum, it can be difficult to blueprint the assessment to cover a wide enough part of the curriculum for content validity to be high. In other words, reliability comes at a cost.

The cost is not always financial, although that is a huge factor in designing and using assessments. But what is implied by cost in a resource-limited arena is that trade-offs must be made depending on the purpose of the test.

Feasibility

Remember those calculations in GSCE physics experiments in which Newton's laws were exerted in an ideal world without friction, air resistance or the bending of space-time by mass? The physical world at GCSE was easy to explain, easy to calculate with and, well, wrong. So it is with assessments. It would be possible to design an assessment with high estimated validity in all the various subdivisions of validity, with questions piloted to within an inch of their life, standard set and checked and quality assured to perfection. It would be possible to set as many of these as required to achieve a Cronbach's alpha[4] of 0.85 and deliver it in a way that fully assesses every aspect of the curriculum without error. However, it would take so long and cost so much to do this that no student would ever get to take the assessment, let alone pass it.

Assessments are delivered in the real world, with real financial constraints, by people with lots of other things to do on their to-do lists, and in rooms that have an annoying hum that distracts students who wear hearing aids more than those that don't. These factors must be addressed. They may affect the reliability or the validity of the assessment, or both, but that doesn't mean that the assessment is fatally flawed.

As well as such factors external to the assessment, there are factors within it that may generate the need for compromise. For instance, a reliable knowledge question tends to have a definite answer, and so covers only a small slice of the curriculum. When the stakes are high, for instance in a final exam at medical school, the cost of generating a lot of highly reliable questions is justified. But in a formative assessment at the beginning of a course to find out what students already know, it is well worth sacrificing reliability for the ability to give some information about the current state of knowledge a student has for the entire curriculum. This could be done with a few very broad questions that would never be reliable enough to say if someone was good enough to proceed, but whose ability to discover holes in knowledge is excellent.

Anyone involved in writing assessments must embrace these compromises and be able to defend the decisions made as a consequence in the light of the purpose of the assessment. Anyone involved in the delivery of an assessment should be aware of the compromises that have been made (and the reason for them) before using the results of the assessment for any purpose other than that for which the assessment writer has designed it.

Standard setting

Determining how valid and how reliable an assessment is does not necessarily tell you how hard it is for students to complete. Formative assessments usually do not require a robust method of knowing precisely how well students have done in comparison to others, but in summative assessments this knowledge is often vital. Even for this there is no single method that works in all cases, but the gist of them all stems from the same question – who has passed, and who has failed?

There are two broad methodological categories (again bearing in mind the dangers of categorisation) of determining the answer to this most abrupt of questions relating to assessment. These are norm referencing and criterion referencing. Norm referencing occurs when a predetermined number or proportion of students will pass the assessment, regardless of performance of the cohort as a whole. The simplest version of norm referencing is the job interview,[5] in which only the candidate judged to be the best ('the top one') will get the job. Other manifestations of norm referencing occur when papers are marked 'on the curve', in which it is pre-determined that the top, say, 10 per cent of candidates will be given an A grade, the next 16 per cent a B grade, and so on. This type of referencing is common when there is limited capacity to accommodate successful candidates (the job interview) or if the cohort size is so large that it is likely to be a representative sample of the population as a whole. This means that if the paper is harder than usual, the top 10 per cent score less than the top 10 per cent did last year or before, but they are still the top 10 per cent, and the variation in marks is likely to be due to variation in the paper.

But what if the cohort is relatively small? If the marks achieved one year are lower than usual, how can we be sure that this is not because the paper was harder, but that the cohort of candidates were not as capable as in previous years? Or what if we want all those who meet a certain standard to pass, or are happy for all those who fail to meet a certain standard to fail? The answer here is to generate a criterion-referenced assessment. In this methodology, the pass mark (or cut score, as it is often known) is set by some process without reference to the performance of the cohort. The hallmark of criterion referencing is that all students can pass and all can fail, although in reality this seldom happens.

There are various ways to set the pass mark in a criterion-referenced way, and the details of these is beyond the scope of this chapter. It is worth knowing that they vary depending on the type of assessment being delivered, that they sometimes are performed before the students take the assessment and sometimes during and afterwards, and that they usually have either eponymous titles (e.g. Ebel, Anghoff, Hofstee) or titles describing the mathematical functions behind them (e.g. the borderline median method). Readers who go on to be the setters of assessment in future, particularly in settings where results may be challenged in law, will need to become very familiar with these methods. Other readers should only trust assessments that have used a validated method, but need not know how the methods actually work in practice.

Conclusion

Anyone setting out on a career in education will come across assessment on a very regular basis, first as the subject of it, later as the deliverer and, maybe, finally as the writer. At each stage it is important to understand the concepts that have led to the particular design chosen, the compromises that have had to be made to get to that point and the limitations inherent in the assessment as a result of these compromises.

Educators need to know that an assessment they are delivering is trustworthy or they will have no confidence in preparing students for it, and their students' preparation will lack direction. Curriculum planners need to know how they are to assess the learning outcomes that they plan their course to deliver, and they need to design adequate assessment into the process at the start, not as an afterthought.

Finally, students (and their future employers and teachers) need to at least trust that their assessment is useful and valuable to them, or the basis of selection of future study of employment will begin to collapse. Even better, they should go beyond trust, and actually understand the principles themselves. By sharing this understanding, learning will be of higher quality, better, directed to the outcomes of the course and, ultimately, more effective and satisfying.

Notes

1. A similar process can happen with respect to the delivery of the teaching on a course, such that it is possible to show at what point in the course each of the learning outcomes are covered for students. The nomenclature gets a little muddy here, though, as when the process is applied to teaching delivery, it is sometimes referred to as 'blueprinting' and sometimes as 'mapping'. 'Blueprinting' appears to be becoming the accepted version for the process applied to assessments, but even this is not yet fully standardised.
2. This is not to say that candidates' pass rates are not indicators of the quality of a driving school. It is merely a point to note that a test designed to assess a candidate's driving ability does not automatically also assess the quality of teaching; the two outcome measures should be evaluated separately. Another example of this are the English National Curriculum Assessments (colloquially known as Standard Assessment Tests or SATs), which are used variously to compare individual students to their age-matched peers, to generate leagues tables of teaching quality in entire schools and to stream children into secondary schools when the intake is from more than one primary school. These assessment goals may be possible in a single assessment, but it is not safe to assume that any assessment can achieve all these goals unless they have been specifically designed to do so.
3. Imagine you wished to know both the speed of a car and its weight. These are unrelated constructs, except in the special case that you wished to know its momentum. Ignoring this special case, it is necessary to have a separate test for each, and to report each separately. A car doing 20 metres per second (45 mph) and weighing 1,750 kg, if measured on a single additional scale, would have the value 1,770 units, and be indistinguishable on the same scale from a vehicle weighing 1,000 kg and travelling at 770 metres per second (1,720 mph). The traffic authorities are likely, however, to have very different levels of interest in these two vehicles were they proceeding along a road in a built-up area in rush-hour. This apparently trite example is of interest every time any assessment which tests more than a single construct is reported with a single final mark.
4. Cronbach's alpha is one of the statistical methods of stating reliability numerically. Its values range from 0.0 to 1.0. The exact value aimed for depends on the type of assessment, but it is generally held that a value of >0.8 is excellent. I once was involved in an assessment with Cronbach's alpha of 0.93 and went to the statistician as pleased as punch. His face fell. It was so reliable that there must have been an error, he said. There was, of course. It is therefore apparently possible to have an assessment that is *too* reliable, but this is only possible once the GCSE physicists' idea of an ideal world is abandoned.
5. Editor's note: the selection for interview should, in order to be fair, be criterion-referenced to the person specification for the post. The interview itself will also have criteria to be met and hence one could find oneself as the only interviewee for a job and not get it. If you are in such a situation, you could justifiably say that no-one is better than you since no-one got the job!

References

Andreatta, P.B. and L.D. Gruppen (2009). 'Conceptualising and classifying validity evidence for simulation'. *Medical Education* 43(11): 1028–1035.

Black, P. and D. Wiliam (1998). 'Inside the black box: raising the standards through classroom assessment'. Retrieved 14 May 2012, from http://floridafastpacks.com/PrincipalConference/BlackBox.pdf.

Bloom, B.S. (1956). *Taxonomy of educational objectives: the classification of educational goals*, Longmans, Green.

Carmines, E.G. and R.A. Zeller (1979). *Reliability and validity assessment*, Sage.

Harlen, W. and M. James (1997). 'Assessment and learning: differences and relationships between formative and summative assessment'. *Assessment in Education* 4(3): 365–379.

Heubert, J.P. and R.M. Hauser (1999). *High stakes: Testing for tracking, promotion, and graduation*, National Academies Press.

McManus, I., E. Smithers, P. Partridge, A. Keeling and P.R. Flemming (2003). 'A levels and intelligence as predictors of medical careers in UK doctors: 20 year prospective study'. *BMJ* 327(7407): 139–142.

Nevo, B. (1985). 'Face validity revisited'. *Journal of Educational Measurement* 22(4): 287–293.

Norman, G. and K. Eva (2010). 'Quantitative research methods in medical education'. In *Understanding medical education: Evidence, theory and practice*. Ed. T. Swanwick. Wiley-Blackwell: 301–322.

Traub, R.E. (1997). 'Classical test theory in historical perspective'. *Educational Measurement: Issues and Practice* 16(4): 8–14.

8

Social and spatial disparity in the history of school provision in England from the 1750s to the 1950s

Colin Brock

The task of the modern educator is not to cut down jungles, but to irrigate deserts.

C.S. Lewis

Introduction

A relatively neglected dimension of the study of education is the issue of scale: temporal and spatial. Simplistic blocks of time are sometimes employed, such as 'the eighteenth century'. Centennial boundaries are usually meaningless. Likewise, in comparative education national units are often adopted. This overlooks the geography of educational reality on the ground, with its myriad spatial disparities.

Education, in all its forms, is culturally based and as far as the formal and non-formal modes are concerned, politically delivered. The political factor is not only a matter of formal territorial control. It also operates through cultural and societal forces such as religion, language, gender, class and ethnicity.

With England being by far the slowest of the early-industrialised nations to establish a complete national system of formal schooling, control of organised learning has been akin to a battlefield. For many centuries control over such formal and institutionalised learning as existed had much to do with organised religion, language and gender: Christianity, Latin and male, respectively. Faith had little to do with it. From its inception, the Anglican Church fought successfully to contain the curricula of the expanding number of locally founded schools from elementary schools in villages where the priest was amenable to being a teacher, to endowed grammar schools in towns, mostly intended for the poor but often appropriated. The distribution of both was disparate and incomplete.

Spatial and locational analysis is what geography is about. Here we are concerned with the historical geography of education (Brock 2010). Human geography has to do with: (a) precise locations (points); (b) areas (spaces); and (c) flows (along lines) (Walford 1973: 105). When applied to education this means, for example: (a) locations of learning; (b) controlled territories of learning; and (c) networks of organisation and information flow. Within human geography, it is the cultural dimension that relates closely to education in spatial terms. Sack (1984), on societal conception of space, argued that societies tend to create organisations that serve to develop their influence over spatial aspects of their identity. This could be at particular locations such as towns, over areas such as a parish or through networks such as a range of related institutions. All are spatial, and lead to a territorial definition of society overtaking a social definition of territory. The story of formal and non-formal education in England is largely the gradual emergence of a national system of control over a plethora of initiatives at local or regional level.

Dodgshon (1987), with relation to Europe, charts the change from (a) control of territory through rule over people to (b) control over people through rule over territory, through horizontally oriented functional systems, including educational. Some nation-states such as France and Prussia were quick to see the role of a system of education to help effect that control. In England it didn't happen like that. Perhaps the growing maritime empire, with its economic relationship to industrial and commercial expansion, was the scale of paradigm that obtained. Another factor may have been the lack of concern to secure any land-based boundaries. A third was social class: the control of artisans from an early age onwards who needed only instrumental skills to play their part. The corrupt Church was happy to control the learning of the diminishing number of pupils of endowed and local grammar schools, as well as the discredited and largely irrelevant universities of which there were still only two in England by the turn of the nineteenth century.

It is with the seeds of agitation for non-denominational educational opportunity and reform from around the 1850s that we shall begin. These were nurtured and germinated differentially by the working classes and expanding middle classes from their respective perspectives, and differentially in many locations. This is a story that takes about 200 years of socio-political struggle to finally achieve a national system of schooling of sorts up to the age of 15 through the *Education Act of 1944*. It will draw on innovations in specific locations, networks of radical action and the tortuous process of contested territorial control of education from dioceses and school boards to local authorities and a national ministry of education. The issue of selection as a prime function of any education system is fundamental (Timmons 1988). It still dominates in the early twenty-first century, though we will follow the story only to the 1950s.

Dissention and disparity from the 1750s to 1868

It would be tempting to begin with the *Reform Act of 1832*, but the seeds of dissention were sown nearly a century earlier. The upper class had previously dominated both education and national politics. They schooled at home, or through a few so-called 'great schools' such as Eton and Winchester, then Oxford and Cambridge. A largely localised and small middle class had begun to benefit from the numerous endowed grammar schools, but acquired no significant power largely due to the wealth of the Anglican Church and its appropriation by the upper classes.

The industrial revolution provided for the dislocation of this cartel, and although by no means the only seed of disruption, was certainly a major influence (Timmons 1988). Through a combination of wealth creation and non-conformist dissent, significant elements of educational influence developed, mainly in some areas of the north of England. Dissenting academies were founded to provide educational opportunity to those denied access to the two universities by virtue of their non-conformism (Reid 2010). Although just one of several, the Unitarian academy at Warrington (O'Brien 1989) found itself in the vanguard partly through its association with Joseph Priestley, the discoverer of 'dephlogisticated air' – oxygen. He was a Unitarian priest with a distinctly instrumental philosophy of education, and his life span (1733–1804) covers a significant period of socio-economic upheaval that enabled reformers in the early nineteenth century such as Bentham to have a significant effect. Preistley was mainly concerned with the advance of the middle class, as Fowler (1963) indicates by quoting him thus:

> The lowest of the vulgar will not easily be brought to think on subjects that are wholly new to them.... As to persons in the highest classes of life, they are chiefly swayed by their connections and very seldom have the courage to think and act for themselves.
>
> (p. 393)

Priestley and other non-conformist reformers became the subject of violent attack by mobs organised by the Anglican-related establishment. His home, goods, papers and apparatus were all destroyed, and even King George III stated that Priestley 'should now feel the wickedness of the doctrines of democracy he was propagating' (O'Brien 1989: 133). One of the bones of contention was the liberal nature of the curriculum Priestley was advocating, comprising: religion, ecclesiastical history, civil history (i.e. laws and government), manufacture, commerce, foreign travel (for people in their twenties), mathematics, science (including natural history, geology, biology) and modern languages (especially French). This was the kind of pedagogical vision that alarmed the establishment and fuelled their opposition to taking the grammar school curriculum beyond classics and Christianity. As Elliott and Daniels (2010) record, some Georgian grammar schools had been promoting geography!

Although the ideas of Priestley and fellow dissenters survived, their academies were forced to move from place to place, or even close. The late eighteenth century saw what Simon (1974: 62–71) termed 'the eclipse of the reformers'. Nonetheless, he recognised the momentum created by the emergent middle classes:

> The class which had created Warrington Academy, Manchester Academy and New College Hackney, though temporarily on the defensive at the close of the eighteenth century was to emerge later and carry all before it. But it was to emerge as a class whose characteristics had changed, whose purposes were narrower, and

who were engaged in a sharp struggle on two main fronts – against the landed aristocracy on the one hand, and against the emerging proletariat on the other.

(p. 70)

There had been educational opportunities for some in the form of apprenticeships both in traditional trades and in new manufacturing skills associated with industrialisation. Stephens (1998) goes further, suggesting that as early as 1750 'schools of some kind were within geographical reach of all but comparatively few children' (p. 1). This begs the question of what proportion of children actually attended, even though some types of school were set up by the working class for the working class. These were still the days of child labour, much valued by many parents as well as by factory and land owners. There seems by the late eighteenth century to have been marked regional disparities in terms of an evident 'education culture'. By the time of the first central government legislation relating to education – the *Factory Act of 1802* that applied only to working children – dynamic networks of local schooling were growing, albeit sporadically and spatially disparate. In response, religious bodies were able to gain control of the growing voluntary school movement through the offices of the British and Foreign Schools Society (BFSS), established by non-conformists in 1808 as the 'Lancastrian Society' and the 'National Society for Promoting the Education of the Poor in the Principles of the Established Church', founded in 1811. The importance of territorial control became readily apparent as the Anglicans benefited from existing parishes and dioceses, whereas the BFSS 'lacked the underpinning of an established territorial administrative structure. Its supporters belonged to different denominations, unevenly distributed geographically' (Stevens 1998: 6). Even after the *Reform Act of 1832* and the grant for school buildings to these two bodies the following year, the first Boundaries Commission of 1837 merely rationalised ward boundaries in towns, with no connection to the provision of schooling (Freeman 1968).

This was a period of massive industrialisation and urbanisation and although the Catholic Church was by now establishing elementary schools, the combined efforts of the religious bodies were unable to keep up with such a scale of demographic change. This was also associated with the concentration of poverty on a scale hitherto unheard of except in London. As Wardle (1970) indicates, 'the new urban proletariat lay quite outside the existing social and political organisation' (p. 23). Many of the skills and occupations rapidly developing in new industrial processes had no relationship at all to the apprenticeships of traditional crafts. In any case, as he observes, 'the organisation of gilds, companies and corporations had shared in the general decline of administrative energy which characterised the eighteenth century' (p. 29). That no significant form of technical education emerged at this time was a function of the simplicity of tasks required of mass production in the factory context. The inventors of these new processes and the machinery behind them were few, usually self-made and self-educated members of the middle class. Though such employers became wealthy, there were few opportunities open to them to become part of the governing class. Some, however, did engage in the governing of local endowed grammar schools (Hull Grammar School 1979) or the founding of new proprietary secondary schools which rapidly came and went.

Lawson (1952) describes two examples from Hull, where, in 1830, there was 'just a decaying grammar school and a number of small profit-making private concerns of dubious efficiency' (p. 14). In 1836 a meeting was held to discuss establishing a Hull and East Riding Proprietary School. It was modelled on University College School in London and opened in a splendid new building as 'Hull College' in 1837. The headmaster had to be an Oxbridge graduate (i.e. Church of England). Nonetheless, an explicitly Anglican school was opened in the same year, named Kingston College, also in a splendid new building. Both schools had shareholders who were local merchants and bankers and offered liberal curricula, but neither could be sustained on that basis. One became private in 1846 and the other in 1848, there being no functional administration in the city to maintain them once the initial interest group moved on. Such short-lived proprietary school initiatives were common in the expanding cities of the day, as the nouveau riche attempted to provide for their male offspring. In other, commonly smaller towns they attempted to gain control of the usually declining endowed grammar school. Once on the local corporation and/or the governing body they worked to reform the statutes to accommodate more liberal curricula, despite the stifling of the Leeds Grammar School initiative, in effect by the government, in 1805. But the outcome of that case, having as it did such strong backing from both the Church and state, continued to frustrate senior members of the middle classes up and down the country. Even the establishment of the Central Society for Education, 'an influential organisation set up to promote educational reform' (Simon 1974: 109), proved unable to combat the vested interests of the upper classes and the Church. Consequently, the even more rapidly growing and wealthy upper middle class turned to the private sector for the schooling of their male offspring. This was not a sector in the modern sense. Such elite schools were a class of their own, presenting a profile unattractive to the worthy middle class. With their large bodies of boarders they were, as Simon (1974) put it, 'something in the nature of schoolboy republics, with their own morality and law' (p. 99). Violent rebellions were not uncommon. They remained both socially and geographically discrete from the mass of the working class and the emergent middle classes.

The period from the mid eighteenth century up to the more rapid mass urbanisation of the railway age from the mid 1840s was one of marked differentiation between various types of urban and rural economies. Neither urban nor rural communities in general represented a type with regard to levels of literacy or nature of schooling. Differences in occupational structure and economic well-being multiplied, but one feature arising from increasing migration was that: 'The greater the proportion of the resident population to have been born locally, the lower the literacy level' (Brock 1992: 145). As Gratton (1982) discovered in his study of the literacy patterns in the periphery of Liverpool, those communities distant from the main arteries of communication, turnpike roads, navigable rivers, canals and railways, exhibited the lowest levels of literacy in the first half of the nineteenth century. Figure 8.1 provides a generalised profile of 'Peaks and Troughs in Literacy and Schooling in the Major Ecological Zones of Mid-Nineteenth Century England' (Brock 1992: 150).

The railways were a major influence on increased disparity and diversification of education in spatial terms well before any attempt to put a national system of schooling

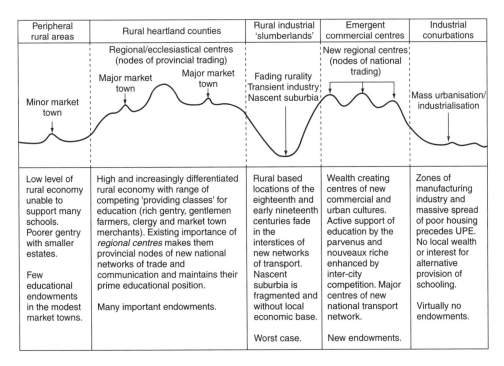

Peripheral rural areas	Rural heartland counties		Rural industrial 'slumberlands'	Emergent commercial centres	Industrial conurbations
Low level of rural economy unable to support many schools. Poorer gentry with smaller estates. Few educational endowments in the modest market towns.	High and increasingly differentiated rural economy with range of competing 'providing classes' for education (rich gentry, gentlemen farmers, clergy and market town merchants). Existing importance of *regional centres* makes them provincial nodes of new national networks of trade and communication and maintains their prime educational position. Many important endowments.		Rural based locations of the eighteenth and early nineteenth centuries fade in the interstices of new networks of transport. Nascent suburbia is fragmented and without local economic base. Worst case.	Wealth creating centres of new commercial and urban cultures. Active support of education by the parvenus and nouveaux riche enhanced by inter-city competition. Major centres of new national transport network. New endowments.	Zones of manufacturing industry and massive spread of poor housing precedes UPE. No local wealth or interest for alternative provision of schooling. Virtually no endowments.

FIGURE 8.1 Peaks and troughs in literacy and schooling in the major ecological zones of mid nineteenth-century England.

in place. For the upper classes they merely enabled easier journeys to their already exclusive 'great schools'. For the growing middle classes, and especially the more affluent, the railways enabled access to the new public schools and the further development of that sector. Bamford (1974) includes information on parental home location of entrants to Rugby School in terms of distance from Rugby. In 1750 there were 22 entrants of whom only four came from more than 50 miles distant, while in 1850 there were 148 entrants of whom 112 came from more than 50 miles. Such was the benefit of the railways for the mainly upper middle social class. The further acceleration of urbanisation occasioned by the proliferation of railways in the 1840s was also selective and differential. Some of the well located established boroughs became nodes in the new network, but many, such as Stamford, were overtaken by other sometimes nearby rivals, in this case Peterborough.

Although some initiatives relevant to education followed the *Reform Act of 1832*, such as the establishment of the Committee in Council in 1839, they had no territorial relationship to the highly disparate incidence of urbanisation. Extraordinarily rapid growth together with new modes of manufacture combined to bring about a decline in educational levels, even of literacy. However:

> while the predominantly rural counties continued to exhibit relatively good profiles in terms of levels of literacy and incidence of voluntary elementary school foundations, and were further boosted by the long standing educational activity of

their market and county towns, they contained not only areas of decline proximate to the expanding manufacturing centres but also considerable internal disparity due to the variable activities of their 'providing classes'.

(Brock 1992: 148)

Gillett (1952) paints a dismal picture at this time of reform and change for predominantly rural Lincolnshire. In 1832 there were 11 small endowed grammar schools in towns and 46 village schools in parishes.

A further 26 parishes were permitted to send children to schools in their neighbours. All were Anglican controlled, but:

> There was, in consequence, great administrative diversity and a marked variation in efficiency. Some schools were good, some very bad. In some the master really taught the children. In others he merely drew his income and gave but small service in return.
>
> He might be ignorant, dissolute or senile, but once he was appointed he could rest in reasonable certainty that the law would treat his office as his freehold and that the chance that he would ever be dismissed was infinitely small.

(p. 27)

Virtually no funding or administrative support was forthcoming from the Lincoln diocese. The 1841 census for the area indicated that there was only one school place available for every 30, and that attendance was poor and mainly in winter. Most of those who attended only did so, on average, for a year. There were some private schools, including village night schools that could be attended by boys in winter. These were at the bottom of a jumbled hierarchy, while only a few of the grammar schools proved to be assets for the small clusters of middle classes, the best being in Louth.

In the absence of any central planning and administration of schooling throughout England, the census every ten years did at least provide information for those who were working towards the improvement of schooling as well as those, especially in Church and state, who wished to contain it. According to Freeman (1968) the 1851 census introduced significant changes, 'producing something simpler and more practical than the division into liberties, hundreds, wards or wapentakes that had existed and developed for centuries' (p. 59). He continues:

> In some ways the 1851 Census commissioners were cavalier-minded in their treatment of administrative districts, and readers of their fascinating report will realise that they would have liked to discard the existing structure and to construct a new one more appropriate to the Britain of 1850 than to that of 1650 or even 1450.

(p. 60)

Coming as it did a year after a bill sponsored by the National Public Schools Association, itself founded in the same year, the 1851 census could have provided a framework for a proposed national education administration with invaluable data for the territorial planning of school provision. In the event, the bill was killed by the opposition of the denominationalists in parliament, but according to Barnard (1971) it foreshadowed the first national *Education Act* in 1870. In the interim a proto 'ministry' had been created in the form of the Education Department in 1856.

Disparity and regulation from 1868 to the 1950s

As Marsden (1987) has graphically illustrated, 'The territorial mobility of nineteenth century people was remarkable' (p. 62), enabled by the ever evolving railway network and even some of the roads. The phenomenon of the exploding middle class was a significant factor in the establishing of the Royal Commission known as the Schools Enquiry Commission that produced the Taunton Report of 1868 (Maclure 1973). This was one of a succession of enquiries into aspects of popular education that emerged after 1856 and the first to propose a degree of territorial regulation. It did so not in the form of an innovation in political geography, but more in relation to social class. This it did through the formalisation of a hierarchy of secondary provision based on its contention that: 'The wishes of the parents can best be defined in the first instance by the length of time during which they are willing to keep their children under instruction' (Maclure 1973: 92). Thus it proposed three grades of school. The first grade schools would accommodate those who remained in school until the age of 18 or beyond (the upper and upper middle classes); the second grade was for those who would leave at 16 (the middle classes) and the third for those who would leave at 14 (the lower classes). The text of the report spelt out clearly how the Commissioners saw and defined these social classes.

The operation of the Taunton Commission engendered a number of interesting attempts at the spatial organisation of schooling. Brereton (1874) proposed a structure along the lines of the French pyramidal system with provinces, departments, counties and communes. In England this was unworkable partly because such functional territorial units did not already exist, and partly due to the long distances that would have to be covered by first- and second-grade school students outside of the major conurbations. There were existing counties, but they were rendered unfit for purpose due to the transgression of their boundaries by massive and ongoing urbanisation. Nonetheless, the rapidly developing rail network did, in some areas, enable the logistics of the Taunton scheme to be operated, thus cementing existing disparities in provision. This was especially so in relation to the endowed schools located as they were in established nodes in the settlement hierarchy. This also enabled upper middle class boys to commute daily to first-grade schools whether in rural or market town locations or from affluent suburbs of conurbations, especially London, to the inner city. Marsden (1987) illustrates this cartographically in relation to 'Endowed School Gradings and the Railways in Lincolnshire 1868' (p. 122) and 'Endowed Middle Schools in London in 1860 in Relation to Railways' (p. 123).

The proposed rationalisation of territorial units by the 1851 census commission having been discarded, the first stage of the creation of a fully national system of elementary education, namely the *Elementary Education Act of 1870*, was implemented without any adjustment of regulated space, save the creation of School Board areas themselves. Rather than leading to a greater conformity or equity in elementary schooling, the boards tended to add to the spatial disparity. In terms of the geography of education, especially in cities, each board tended to be idiosyncratic. While spatial patterns of schooling varied within the larger board areas, there were irregular tracts, even complete towns, without even the degree of regulated space provided for in the administration itself. This was partly due to the class-based micro-politics at work. Even within the 'progressive' boards of major cities, the acute status consciousness and related hierarchies of the upper working and lower middle classes led to excluding children from 'inferior social strata'. Indeed, it was the stated view of the government that fees should be differentially applied 'so as to suit the particular class of children for which a particular school had been erected' (Marsden 1987, p. 10). Voluntary schools took full advantage of this as they sought to relieve the tension between their obligation to cater for the masses, and the need to attract the fiercely competitive lower middle class.

The politics of individual boards from elections to administration were intensely idiosyncratic and volatile, as Ratcliffe (1970) describes with respect to Tees-side. After the initial excitement illustrated by a 90 per cent turnout of the electorate in 1871, by 1877 it had dropped to 48 per cent. There were attempts to avoid contests altogether by 'fixing' between interest groups and their candidates, and other forms of skulduggery. With respect to the Darlington Board, Ratcliffe reports:

> A month before Darlington's first elections, the parties met and agreed to share out the board places: 3 to the Anglicans, 2 to the Quakers, 2 to the Free Churches, 1 to the Roman Catholics and 1 to a representative of the working class. However, the Anglicans failed to keep to their side of the bargain: they had four parishes with much jealousy between them, and attempts to get them to agree on the three candidates broke down amid much bickering and mudslinging. The Unsectarians, for their part, had managed to agree on their official candidates, but when it became obvious that more than three Anglicans would stand and so a contest was unavoidable, minority interests which had felt underrepresented, decided to put up Unsectarian candidates of their own. The number of candidates soon reached 23, and the election was fast degenerating into a sectarian squabble. To avoid this, the mayor called a public meeting to elect 9 candidates and so avoid a contest. Several candidates agreed to abide by the vote of the meeting, and after the 9 had been elected, Quaker Arthur Pease gave up his place to a Roman Catholic, in order to make the proposed board more representative. But three of the unsuccessful candidates refused to abide by the vote, and forced a contest.

(pp. 31–32)

And so it went on through the elections of 1874, 1877 and 1883. Only two undisputed elections occurred in Darlington throughout the three decades of the Board's brief existence. Very few male working class candidates came forward; likewise female candidates from any class.

This experience was not untypical, and meant that most boards were the preserve of the vested interest of the male middle/business class and the Churches: a reactionary partnership likely to preserve disparity and inequality, spatially as well as socially. The role of the Church is neatly encapsulated in the title of an article by John T. Smith (2009): 'The enemy within? The clergymen and the English school boards, 1870–1902'. As a result of deep-rooted antagonisms, practical issues were neglected. School buildings were neglected and deteriorated differentially. Sometimes this was as a result of the dissolutions of boards altogether. Everything became chaotic, including rapid changes in land values.

Inevitably such disparities and uncertainties were most marked in the metropolis, under the vigorous policy of the London School Board to transform the manners and morals of the manual working class. According to Rubinstein (1977) 500 elementary schools were built, occupying 500 acres of valuable land, while the voluntary sector stagnated. The London Board was fired by the evidence of acute poverty and educational neglect contained within the surveys of Charles Booth, but in carrying out its regeneration it demolished the houses of the poor as well, in order that elementary schools be made available and accessible to all children. Booth was distraught at this outcome from one perspective, but Rubinstein records that he proclaimed that: 'Each school stands up from its playground like a Church in God's acre ringing its bell' (Rubinstein 1977: 237).

Between the foundation of the Science and Art Department in 1853, as a nascent proto ministry, and the 1899 *Education Act* in effect creating that ministry in the form of the Board of Education, there were a number of innovations relevant to the ongoing struggle between radical and reactionary interests. For example, in 1872 the Science and Art Department decided to propose the establishment of 'Organised Science Schools' by approved local committees. By the time the first national public education system for England and Wales had been created by the Education Act of 1902, local initiatives had founded about 150 such secondary schools. One example was Rutlish School in Merton, South London (Brock 1995).

> It was up to local groups, usually with some funds of their own, to put proposals to the Department if they wished to establish such a school, and for Rutlish the 16th January 1894 saw the conversion of local aspiration into an instrument of legal empowerment. On that day the Charity Commissioners ordered a 'Supplemental Scheme' to that already in place for the administration of the Charity of William Rutlish thereby enabling the establishment of a Rutlish Science School in the parish of Merton that would qualify for grants from the Department.
>
> (p. 1)

This in itself would not have been sufficient to create such a school, but the support of county councils, created by the *Local Government Act of 1888*, could be crucial. Despite such councils having no formal responsibility for secondary schools they were empowered by virtue of the Report of a Royal Commission on Technical Instruction (The Samuelson Report) in 1884, followed by the *Technical Instruction Act of 1889*, to spend up to the product of a penny rate on technical and manual instruction. And so it was that Surrey County Council voted to contribute at least £500 per annum towards the maintenance costs of the new Rutlish School, which enabled it to open in 1895.

The creation of such schools from 1872 to 1902 helped to meet part of the increasing demand for secondary education, but by the nature of their mode of foundation their distribution throughout the country was erratic, as was the effect of the Taunton Commission's hierarchical scheme from 1868. Neither was sufficient to meet the increased demand for secondary schooling fuelled by the creation of a universal elementary sector in 1870. Many school boards attempted to meet the growing demand by establishing 'higher grade schools', whereby some pupils could stay on and study beyond the age of about 12. This alarmed the vested interest of the Churches and the central government as it challenged their control of organised learning through the middle and upper classes. The London School Board was very strong on this issue.

Its achievements were monumental, not least in the nature of cultural geography, as communities were often transformed by the establishment and/or extension of a school into the higher grade. Such schools in the London Board area were pioneers of 'one of the most relevant and forward-looking developments in English educational history' (Marsden 1987: 118), and in some degree a parallel to the German *realschulen*. But whereas the *realschulen* formed part of an officially accepted hierarchy in an organised system, the higher grade schools represented a more organic response to educational evolution in the urban jungle where, in the case of England, socio-political forces prevailed over economic. In Marsden's view (1987), in eliminating the school boards the 1902 *Education Act*:

> gave a new lease of life to the educationally relatively obsolete but socially reputable voluntary elementary sector; a sector that had proved itself intrinsically incapable of keeping pace with the wide-ranging and intensifying social demands both for a more comprehensive and for a more finely-tuned provision of schooling in increasingly complex urban environments.
>
> (p. 18)

While this Act gave powers to the county councils, which as shown with reference to Surrey above, did not have any previous territorial role in respect of education, it broadly followed the lead of the Bryce Commission of 1895 for: (a) the creation of a central authority for education; (b) an Educational Council to assist the minister; (c) the right of county councils to establish local authorities for secondary education. The central authority was created by the Act of 1899 as the Board of Education, but the 1902 Act, following the Cockerton Judgement of 1899, prevented the new local authorities from continuing the development of higher grade schools. Instead, a selective system was set up to enable a limited number of boys, and by now girls as well, to proceed to academic secondary schools called grammar schools. The existing endowed grammar schools and the aforementioned science schools initially formed this new sector to which local authorities could add new grammar schools, though these mostly came after the 1914–1918 war.

The *Local Government Act of 1888* had finally taken on board the spirit of the 1851 census and created both counties and county boroughs, to reflect the realities of urbanisation in England. There were 120 in all, including 61 new territorial units. As Freeman (1968: 98) describes: 'The new county boroughs had all the powers of counties and their creation marked the culmination of a process by which rural areas were separated from urban areas as local government units. County boroughs were supposed to have a maximum population of 50,000, but could accommodate additions or reductions. As suburbs grew, many soon exceeded this limit. The mantra of 'a national system of school provision locally delivered' gave the impression of real decentralisation, but the institution of a highly selective secondary sector in fact legitimised the hold of the upper and middle classes over the formal learning horizons of the majority of children.

The 1902 Act created a new hierarchy, Part II authorities, that is to say counties and county boroughs, that were authorised to provide both elementary and secondary provision; and Part III authorities, smaller units, such as urban districts, medium-sized towns (e.g. Maidstone) and even small cities with sufficient demographic and historical clout that enabled them to make their case (e.g. the City of Peterborough). Altogether some 180 such authorities came into being (Barnard 1971: 209). Part III authorities were a concession by the government, politically motivated, and had the inevitable effect of introducing even greater disparity into the emergent system, largely for the benefit of the Church authorities, with their own diocesan boards of education. As Chambers (2006) describes, with Peterborough being a cathedral city the established Church was strong, and 'Non-conformist Peterborough citizens were as hostile towards the proposal as anywhere in the country' (p. 63). Non-payment of rates was proposed and other forms of non-cooperation. As the local education committee was formed, local electoral disputes reminiscent of those in the old school boards occurred. In Peterborough the issue of competence also came into question when, unlike in most such cases, the town clerk (experienced in local educational issues) was not appointed clerk to the new authority. Instead, a political appointment was made, a certain Henry Wilson of a conservative persuasion. As Chambers continues:

> A prerequisite of successful local government has been described as a mixture of 'professional and amateurs, and local authorities where an experienced education officer was appointed were the areas of most educational progress'. Maidstone, a Part III Authority comparable to Peterborough appointed Edgar Abbot, a visionary with exceptional skills of producing plans to fit situations, and he succeeded in widening the educational horizons of the borough.
>
> (p. 67)

As it happened, Henry Wilson in Peterborough was an honourable man, but the issue was one of competence. Such disparities in leadership and management skills abounded throughout England, especially in the smaller authorities, making the emergent system something of an educational lottery in respect of quality as well as accessibility. Under the cover of this patchwork quilt the local middle classes were able to cement their hold on formal educational opportunity, while the upper middle and upper classes floated above it on the magic carpet of the ever growing and prestigious 'public school' network, itself reinforced by the increasing influence of the Headmasters Conference.

Pressure to accommodate high-achieving students from poorer classes in the grammar schools led to the formulation of a scholarship scheme, as MacClure (1973) relates:

> New secondary school regulations published in 1907 laid down that all secondary schools receiving grants from the Board of Education should provide free places for 25 per cent of their annual entry. This, formally was the beginning of the scholarship ladder leading from elementary school to university.
>
> (p. 162)

At the same time the foundation of new grammar schools by Part II local authorities gathered pace, with lost ground being made up especially for girls. This increase was related to the growth of middle class suburbia in the major cities and especially London. This was served by the railways, new bus services and, in London, the underground. Such transport networks, plus new affordable housing backed by mortgages provided by building societies generated by the wealth of the industrial north, enhanced the mobility of the aspirant lower middle classes. They desired to see their children benefit from a grammar school education. Inter-census population increase in the area of South London from which boys travelled to the aforementioned Rutlish School was phenomenal in an area that covers 12 of the pre-1964 boroughs of the old London County Council founded in 1888. In the then borough of Merton and Morden alone, where the school is located, the increase in population over 1911–1921 was 24 per cent, and in 1921–1931 it was 135 per cent, the Northern Line of the London Underground having been extended to terminate in Morden (Brock 1992). Since there were several other such schools in the area the aggregate diurnal migrations of their students was phenomenal.

Another aspect of significant change in the first three decades of the twentieth century was an increased awareness of the rights of education due to the working classes with regard to both schooling and adult education. The nature of working class relationships to education in England is complex and contested (Woodin 2007), but pressure had been gathering pace even in the late nineteenth century through such movements as the Mechanics Institutes (Hemming 1977) and the Yorkshire Miners' Association (Neville 1976). Although not strictly speaking schooling initiatives, the activities of these occupation-related innovations did include opportunities for the acquisition of basic literacy and numeracy by children of school age as well as adults. They shared certain characteristics with the schools of the day in that their distribution and outreach was extremely disparate, highly concentrated in some locations and totally absent in others. The Mechanics Institutes shared a political characteristic with the schools in that they were manipulated by the rising middle class for a mixture of altruistic and self-interested motives: more the latter than the former. Nonetheless, as Hemming (1977) indicates:

The relatively progressive programmes of the day schools at Leeds and Manchester, including commercial and physical training, workshop practice and the aforementioned natural science classes for girls, together with some notable academic successes, constituted an academically attractive package which progressed and contributed to the modern and technical school traditions.

(p. 24)

In the case of the Yorkshire Miners' Association, support was boosted by the provision of education for their children as a result of the 1870 *Education Act* and educational facilities provided specifically for the Yorkshire miners by the West Riding County Council, the universities of Leeds and Sheffield and the Workers Educational Association (WEA) (Neville 1976).

Some miners who had gained a basic education through these means sat on school boards and later the education committees of the county and county borough councils formed after the 1902 *Education Act*. Even colliery owners supported educational initiatives for working children and their mothers (Benson 1980). Initially the motives were to do with safety and increased productivity, but they filled some of the geographical gaps in provision:

It was in the coalfields where large-scale mining operations combined with widespread immigration had thrown up new communities with inadequate educational facilities, that colliery undertakings made their greatest contribution. Thus, although extensive mining organisations tended to produce settlements in which unsatisfactory social conditions prevailed, they were able, because of their very size, to attempt to alleviate these evils. Colliery communities were generally both working-class preserves and isolated from the rest of society so that the mine owner himself was almost the only member of the middle-class whose social conscience was available to be awakened and turned towards educational ends.

(p. 17)

The momentum created by the networks of movements such as these contributed to the involvement of the nascent labour movement in the cause of education for all beyond the elementary school. In response to the rebuff of the 1902 *Education Act*, the Labour Party and the Trades Union Congress sponsored Education Bills in 1906 concerning 'the improvement of education and the physique of children attending elementary schools. Simon (1974: 257–258) lists the main provisions called for, including that: all elementary schools receiving government grants be under the control of the elected local education authorities; that such authorities be able to purchase denominational and private schools in their areas; that the curriculum should comprise secular subjects only; that local authorities should be empowered to provide secondary and technical schooling to those who wanted it; that one free meal be provided at school by the local authority; that each authority appoint a medical officer to record the height and weight of all children in school and maintain a longitudinal record. The new Liberal government attempted to fudge the secular issue with its own proposals, and this heralded a phase of growing popular working class dissent central to which was the issue of secondary schooling for all. Positions became polarised and remained so, with the 1914–1918 war inevitably curtailing a resolution.

The contribution of R.H. Tawney (1922) to the cause of 'secondary education for all' is well known. Although a committed Anglican with a privileged Rugby School and Oxford education – a profile similar to that of Michael Sadler, 20 years his elder – Tawney despaired of the position of his own Church on state education. Like Sadler he initially promoted the cause of adult education and was aware of the spatial disparities in provision for young adults highlighted in Sadler's book of 1890, co-authored with the pioneer Oxford geographer Halford Mackinder. As a young man Tawney worked for the Workers Educational Association. His appreciation of the injustice of denial of post-elementary education to the working class majority was, like other liberal-minded members of the middle and even upper classes, sharpened by the contribution of millions of ordinary men and women to the national cause during the Great War. The qualities exhibited by the masses were not lost on the majority reactionary members of the establishment either, but rather invoked feelings of insecurity. Socialist revolutions in Mexico and Russia did not help calm such fears.

Despite the TUC having produced the 'Bradford Charter' in 1916, calling for 'universal free compulsory secondary education', Simon (1974) records that 'The Labour Movement receives no mention in *The Times Educational Supplement* (of the 4th July 1917) among those contributing to "schemes of educational reform amounting in fact to educational revolution" pouring into the press in the spring of 1917' (p. 346). At that very time a new bill was being formulated by the government which was presented a few months later, and then became the *Education Act of 1918*. Even though it contained some progressive elements that were to provide limited opportunities for the majority to enjoy through some new forms of post-elementary provision at the discretion of individual local authorities, it was condescending, grudging and paternalistic. This was clearly evident in the address to the House of Commons by the President of the Board of Education, H.A.L. Fisher (Maclure 1973) when, after acknowledging the 'increased feeling of social solidarity which has been created by the War' (p. 173), he continued:

> I notice also that a new way of thinking about education has sprung up among many of the more reflecting members of our industrial army. They do not want education only in order that they may become better technical workmen and earn higher wages. They do not want it in order that they may rise out of their own class, always a vulgar ambition, they want it because they know that in the treasures of the mind they can find an aid to good citizenship, a source of pure enjoyment and a refuge from the hardships of a life spent in the midst of clanging machinery in our hideous cities of toil.
>
> (p. 174)

In the event some local authorities took up the option of continuing educational provision to the age of 14 for those not selected for places in grammar schools by creating 'central schools' or 'technical schools'. But the fact that these were not mandatory added considerably to the disparities of provision and access that already existed. Inter-war suburban 'seas of bricks and mortar' as they became known grew all round the capital as well as in every major town and city in the country. With the provision of grammar school education for the selected few being a national regulation incumbent on local authorities, additional selective schools for boys and girls were founded in the expanded suburbs. The aforementioned Rutlish School, having originated as a science school in 1895 and redesignated a grammar school after 1902, was joined by a number of new grammar schools within the area from which it drew its selected intake, such as Raynes Park Grammar school and Surbiton Grammar School. This proliferation of grammar schools created its own spatial disparities as parents opted for the grammar school of their choice should their offspring be successful in the 11-plus process. This was never an examination in the true sense because the number selected for any grammar school had to be equivalent to the physical capacity (i.e. number of desks) of that school. Further disparity occurred due to the then mandatory provision for single-sex as well as co-educational forms of grammar school. Consequently, in areas well endowed with grammar schools such as South London there was a one in three chance of selection, while in parts of East Yorkshire it was more like one in ten.

The provisions of the *Fisher Act* remained, with minor adjustments, in force until the passing of the 1944 *Education Act*, despite the efforts of Tawney and others to promote secondary education for all. The economic depression and political machinations of the 'long weekend' followed by the 1939–1945 war prevented the recommendations of the Hadow Report of 1926 and the Spens Report of 1938 from progressing the cause. Indeed, because of the inevitable delays of post-war reconstruction, implementation of the first ever form of secondary education for all was not fully realised until the late 1940s.

Because the outcome of the 1944 Act was a tripartite system of grammar, secondary modern and technical schools, even further spatial disparity of provision emerged. Not all authorities provided much in the way of the technical option, some bilateral schools were created, and in a few rural areas non-selective secondary schools were necessarily the option. These became known as comprehensive schools (Pedley 1963). They inevitably challenged the long-standing notion, and in most areas reality, of a grammar school opportunity being mainly the preserve of the middle classes. The first London-based comprehensive school was opened in 1954 amid much publicity, and set in motion the near national creation of a unified secondary sector for all through the Labour government's circular 10/65. But even then some local authorities did not fall in line. In any case, the majority that did created a kaleidoscope of different non-selective schemes that meant that innumerable disparities of school provision and operation remained the characteristic of the compulsory stage in England. The Churches were, and are, still involved, with the Church of England and the Roman Catholic Church providing from one-quarter to one-third of maintained schools. That is our legacy, and causes further disparities of access due to the very uneven distribution of Church schools in general and as between denominations (Gay and Greenough 2000).

Dissonance between the socio-cultural and political bases of schooling provision remain. The *Education Reform Act of 1988*, and many radical adjustments in the first decade of the twentieth century, have taken this beyond disparity to fragmentation, but that is another story (Pring 2012).

References

Bamford, T.W. (1974) *Public School Data*, Hull, University of Hull Institute of Education.

Barnard, H.C. (1971) *A History of English Education from 1760*, London, University of London Press.

Benson, J. (1980) *British Coalminers in the Nineteenth Century: A Social History*, Dublin, Gill and Macmillan.

Brereton, J.L. (1874) *County Education: A Contribution to Experiments, Estimates and Suggestions*, London, Bickers and Son.

Brock, C. (1992) The Case for a Geography of Education, Unpublished PhD thesis, University of Hull.

Brock, C. (1995) *Rutlish School: The First Hundred Years*, Merton, The Rutlish Foundation.

Brock, C. (2010) Spatial Dimensions of Christianity and Education in Western European History, with Legacies for the Present, *Comparative Education*, 46:3, pp. 289–306.

Chambers, B. (2006) The Education Act 1902: The Making of a Part III Authority, *History of Education Researcher*, 78, pp. 61–71.

Dodgshon, R.A. (1987) *The European Past: Social Evolution and Spatial Order*, Basingstoke, Macmillan.

Elliott, P. and Daniels, S. (2010) 'No Study so Agreeable to the Youthful Mind': Geographical Education in the Georgian Grammar School, *History of Education*, 39:1, pp. 15–34.

Fowler, M. (1963) The Educational Ideas of Joseph Priestley (1733–1804), *Studies in Education (University of Hull)*, July, pp. 390–402.

Freeman, T.W. (1968) *Geography and Regional Administration: England and Wales 1830–1968*, London, Hutchinson.

Gay, J. and Greenough, J. (2000) *The Geographical Distribution of Church Schools in England*, Abingdon, Culham College Institute.

Gillett, E. (1952) Some Lincolnshire Schools in the Age of Reform, *Studies in Education (University of Hull)*, May, pp. 27–38.

Gratton, J.M. (1982) Literacy, Educational Provision and Social Structure in the First Half of the Nineteenth Century: The Case of Liverpool's Suburban Periphery, Unpublished MEd Thesis, University of Liverpool.

Hemming, J.P. (1977) The Mechanics Institutes in the Lancashire and Yorkshire Textile Districts from 1850, *Journal of Educational Administration and History*, 9:1, pp. 18–31.

Hull Grammar School (1979) *The City and the School: Commemorating the 500th Anniversary of the Endowment of the Grammar School of Kingston Upon Hull*, Hull, Hull Grammar School Anniversary Committee.

Lawson, J. (1952) Two Forgotten Hull Schools: The Foundation of Hull College and Kingston College, 1836, *Studies in Education (University of Hull)*, May, pp. 7–26.

Maclure, J.S. (1973) *Educational Documents England and Wales: 1816 to the Present Day*, London, Methuen.

Marsden, W.E. (1987) *Unequal Educational Provision in England and Wales: The Nineteenth Century Roots*, London, The Woburn Press.

Neville, R.G. (1976) The Yorkshire Miners and Education 1881–1930, *Journal of Educational Administration and History*, 8:2, pp. 30–37.

O'Brien, P. (1989) *Warrington Academy 1757–86: Its Predecessors and Successors*, Wigan, Owl Books.

Pedley, R. (1963) *The Comprehensive School*, London, Penguin.

Pring, R. (2012) *The Life and Death of Secondary Education for All: Dream or Reality?*, London, Routledge.

Ratcliffe, K.G.M. (1970) Elections and the School Boards: Tees-side 1870–1902, *Journal of Educational Administration and History*, 2:2, pp. 30–38.

Reid, D.A. (2010) Education as a Philanthropic Enterprise: The Dissenting Academies of Eighteenth-Century England, *History of Education*, 39:3, pp. 299–318.

Rubinstein, D. (1977) Socialisation and the London School Board 1870–1904: Aims, Methods and Public Opinion, in McCann, P. (ed.) *Popular Education and Socialisation in the Nineteenth Century*, London, Methuen, pp. 231–264.

Sack, R.D. (1984) The Societal Conception of Space, in Massey, D. and Allen, J. (eds) *Geography Matters: A Reader*, Cambridge, Cambridge University Press, pp. 34–47.

Simon, B. (1974) *The Two Nations and the Educational Structure 1780–1870*, London, Lawrence and Wishart.

Smith, J.T. (2009) The Enemy Within? The Clergymen and the English School Boards, 1870–1902, *History of Education*, 38:1, pp. 133–150.

Stephens, W.B. (1998) *Education in Britain 1750–1914*, Basingstoke, Macmillan.

Tawney, R.H. (1922) *Secondary Education for All: A Policy for Labour?*, London, The Labour Party.

Timmons, G. (1988) *Education, Industrialisation and Education*, London, Routledge.

Walford, R. (1973) *New Directions in Geography Teaching*, London, Longman.

Wardle, D. (1970) *English Popular Education 1780–1970*, Cambridge, Cambridge University Press.

Woodin, T. (2007), Working Class Education and Social Change in Nineteenth and Twentieth Century Britain, *History of Education*, 36:4/5, pp. 483–496.

Schooling in Ireland

Policy and practice from penal times to the present day

Deirdre Raftery and Martina Relihan

Education is not the filling of a pail, but the lighting of a fire.

W.B. Yeats

Introduction

The history of education in Ireland is characterised by periods of change, during which control of the provision of schooling was contested by the Roman Catholic and the Protestant Churches, and policy on education was variously the concern of the British and Irish governments. The management of some systems was highly efficient while that of others was ad hoc, and there was a strong relationship between education policies and political developments. This chapter provides an overview of that history up to, and beyond, Ireland's attainment of independence from Britain. The chapter indicates some of the important policies that changed the face of Irish education, and describes education practices over several hundred years. The bibliography to this chapter provides the interested reader with additional sources, through which greater insight into Irish education may be pursued.

The early period: education and cultural development

In Ireland between the first and the fifteenth centuries, education was closely linked to the development of skills and the sharing of cultural practices. Celtic peoples with some social status, in Ireland and elsewhere, used a system called 'fosterage', whereby they sent their children away from home to be raised by foster parents, who would teach the children skills. Boys learned horsemanship, shooting and swimming, while girls were taught to do fine needlework. The contractual arrangement whereby children were fostered was laid down in the Brehon Law,[1] and this law established the kind of education suited to the different social ranks.

Fosterage continued in Ireland until Tudor times, and is an example of a native initiative, through which learning and cultural development were passed from generation to generation. Another initiative which emerged was the monastic schools, through which the Church gave formal education to the sons of landowners, and to men who would become clerics. Boys were taught Latin and studied the Psalms, and Irish monks were central to the spread of Christianity in Europe, earning the country the title 'Island of Saints' (*Insula sanctorum*).[2] In addition to monasteries, convents also provided education, while some craft guilds made provision for the education of members.

By the sixteenth century, Tudor policy on schooling was that it should spread the influence of the Reformation in Ireland, promoting Protestantism and the English language.[3] In 1537, legislation was introduced to support this, and in the seventeenth century further legislation severely curtailed educational provision for Catholics.

Education for social control: the penal period

The seventeenth century was a period during which sustained attempts were made to secure British dominance in Ireland by limiting the power of the Catholic Church. A series of penal laws was passed, which directly affected education, preventing Catholics from sending their children abroad to be educated at Catholic seminaries and convents, and equally prevented them from conducting Catholic education at home. Persons found in breach of *An Act to Restrain Foreign Education* (1695), and *An Act to Prevent the Further Growth of Popery* (1703) were severely punished, and some were deported to British colonies. By way of providing an alternative to Catholic schooling, different forms of Protestant educational provision flourished in parts of Ireland by the eighteenth century. The 'charity schools', which were very much a part of schooling in England, were promoted in large towns such as Dublin and Cork, while the 'charter schools' were founded to provide a system for the education of the poor and the promotion of the Established Church of Ireland.

The charter schools comprised a network of residential schools throughout Ireland, that were founded by the Incorporated Society for Promoting English Protestant Schools in Ireland. This society, founded in 1737, articulated its aims as follows:

> First, to promote the glory of God, and the salvation of souls, by rescuing the children of the poor natives ... and train[ing] them up in the pure Protestant faith.... Secondly ... to strengthen His Majesty's government, by increasing the number of Protestants. ... Thirdly ... to cure, by degrees, that habit of idleness, which is too prevalent among the poor of this kingdom.
>
> (An abstract of the proceedings of the Incorporated Society 1733)

A substantial study of the Irish charter schools reveals that while the aim was to provide poor children with some form of vocational preparation, such as farming or weaving skills, the schools failed to provide adequate literary instruction and many charter schools were characterised by environments of cruelty and brutality towards children

(Milne 1997). Pupils recruited to these schools were raised as Protestants, and were 'transplanted' to areas far from their homes in order to lessen the possibility that their Catholic families would maintain contact with them. When a commission to enquire into Irish education was appointed in the early nineteenth century (Commission of Irish Education Enquiry 1825), it was damning of the charter schools, and it demonstrated how the practice of transplanting erased the personal memories of many children who, after years of schooling, could not remember their age or how long they had been institutionalised.[4]

The most successful Catholic response to the limits on educational provision in this period was the development of illegal 'hedge schools' (McManus 2002). These were small schools conducted subversively, in barns and ditches, with lessons provided by peripatetic masters who moved regularly from town to town to avoid apprehension by the authorities. Hedge school masters taught Latin, Greek, English, mathematics and astronomy, and were held in high regard. By the end of the eighteenth century, about 9,000 of these illegal schools were in existence, providing education to the Catholic poor.[5]

Mass education: towards a national system of elementary schooling

Both the British government and the hierarchy of the Established Church were, unsurprisingly, concerned at the popularity of the hedge schools. One response was to channel state funding through the Society for Promoting the Education of the Poor in Ireland, also known as the Kildare Place Society (KPS), from 1811, to support a new system of elementary schools for the poor, with a view to spreading mass literacy. The supporters of this society were mainly Quaker and Protestant businessmen, interested in a range of philanthropic endeavours, and the development of the KPS paralleled that of similar initiatives in Britain, such as the National Society for Promoting the Education of the Poor (the National Society), and the Royal Lancasterian Institution for the Education of the Poor of Every Religious Profession (later the British and Foreign Schools Society) founded by Joseph Lancaster.

The KPS, influenced by the educational theories of Lancaster, founded and developed schools in which the monitorial system of instruction was included. They also supported the founding of a teacher training college for men and women, and produced teaching materials and textbooks for use in their schools. While the KPS schools enjoyed some success during the period 1811–1831, the society fell into disrepute. Its original aim to afford the 'same facilities to all professing Christians without any attempt to interfere with the peculiar religious opinions of any' was criticised when it was found that the KPS allowed the Bible to be read in classrooms 'without note or comment'. This was a practice not acceptable to the Catholic Church, which thus condemned the Society. As noted elsewhere, 'the image of the society was further tarnished when it emerged that this non-denominational society was paying grants to schools supported by Protestant evangelical societies' (Raftery and Relihan 2012: 73).

By the early nineteenth century there was increasing pressure by the Catholic hierarchy to have an acceptable form of education for its flock, which comprised over

6.5 million Irish Catholics out of a total population of some eight million. The last decades of the eighteenth century had seen the repeal of relevant Penal Laws, and Catholic children were being educated by religious orders such as the Presentation Sisters and the Christian Brothers. By 1824, a campaign for reform, led by Archbishop John McHale of Tuam and Bishop James Warren of Kildare and Leighlin, resulted in a petition to parliament, and the subsequent Commission of Irish Education Inquiry (1825), which recommended that public funding should be withdrawn from Protestant education societies. What was proposed instead was that a government board of education should be established for building and maintaining 'national schools' in which Catholic and Protestant children would be educated together for secular instruction and separately for religious instruction (Raftery 2012).

The 'Stanley Letter' and national education

It was not until 1831 that a successful blueprint for a national system of education was drawn up. Known as the 'Stanley Letter', this document, drafted by the Chief Secretary of Ireland, Lord E.G. Stanley, described a system of 'combined literary and a separate religious education'.[6] State funding was granted to support a National Board of Commissioners, and to provide teacher training, schools, and the production of textbooks. The Board also supported some existing schools, such as those managed by the Presentation Sisters. Within ten years, the National Board had 1,978 schools operating under its control. Although Stanley's aim had been to provide a non-denominational education system, the majority catered to Catholic families, with the number of denominational schools reaching over 8,000 by the end the century. In addition to these schools, three model schools and a teacher training college were established, and a model farm school was opened on the outskirts of Dublin city. The National Board provided two-thirds of the cost of building new schools, and they also supplied classroom equipment and books.[7]

While the national system was not without critics, it grew significantly and was central to the provision of mass literacy in Ireland. As noted elsewhere, it determined the future education policy of the country, and it reflected wider social and political changes. Carefully selected reading materials and curricular content, and the erasure of Irish history, language and culture from the classroom at that time, ensured that the national schools had a political function (Raftery and Relihan 2012: 75). The five 'graded reading books' produced by the National Board are a useful source for scholars interested in developing insight into the school as an agent of social control, and they are also useful for giving some sense of what children experienced at school. Strongly moralistic in tone, the reading books reminded children that they should demonstrate self-control, and obedience to their elders and betters, while special reading books for girls taught its young readers that 'a practical knowledge of plain needlework is probably the most important acquirement for females, especially for those attending the National Schools of Ireland' (Commissioners of National Education in Ireland 1869). The strong messages about subservience which permeated the National School reading books, along with the absence of the Irish language and culture, have led some scholars to argue that the schools facilitated the British cultural assimilation policy for Ireland.[8]

The 'results' era: balancing failures and successes

Scholars who are interested in determining the relative 'successes' and 'failures' of the Irish education system find the later decades of the nineteenth century compelling for a number of reasons. On the one hand, efforts to 'assimilate' Irish children seemed to be succeeding, in as much as they were increasingly becoming English-speaking; on the other hand, progress at schools was poor, there were high levels of absenteeism around the country and many school buildings were in poor repair.[9] The country had suffered famine, with the attendant spread of contagious diseases, and mass emigration, and it was unclear how schooling was faring. A Commission was appointed in 1868, under the chairmanship of Lord Powis, to examine the state of national education and determine whether or not the system represented value for money.

One of the recommendations of the Powis Commission was the introduction of 'payment by results': teachers would henceforth be paid a 'results fee', in addition to a basic salary, depending on the performance of their pupils in examinations. A scale of payments was devised, and assessments were undertaken within the schools by a visiting examiner each year. Among the 'successes' of the payment-by-results era was the significant increase in literacy by the end of the century, with the reading and writing proficiency of pupils showing marked improvement; another positive outcome was an improvement in school attendance. On the other hand, the system was examination-driven, and encouraged rote learning; it also favoured bright children over those who struggled, and there was little incentive to teachers to persist with children who could not attain a good result and the accompanying payment. However, the rising educational standards indicated the need for an additional second-level system as the century drew to a close.

Second-level schooling: the growth of the intermediate system

As already noted, a consequence of the gradual repeal of the penal laws that had affected Catholic education was that religious orders of nuns, priests and brothers could found schools and teach. Many orders established schools throughout the nineteenth century, and they soon dominated education at secondary level, which had traditionally been the preserve of a small minority of Protestant families. Large diocesan boarding schools were founded by the bishops for the education of Catholic boys and also to facilitate recruitment of future members of the clergy. St Patrick's College, Carlow (1793), St Jarlath's, Tuam (1800), St Finian's, Navan (1802), St John's, Waterford (1807) and St Peter's, Wexford (1819) all offered a classical education for Catholic boys, while also functioning as minor seminaries to prepare some of them to become secular priests. In addition to the colleges founded by the bishops, religious orders (priests) also grew their network of schools and, by 1867, there were 47 Catholic colleges for boys under the direction of the Dominicans, Jesuits, Holy Ghosts, Vincentians and others. For girls, convent schools run by various orders developed: the Loreto, Sacred Heart, Ursuline and Dominican orders are just a few of the continental groups of sisters who founded many schools in Ireland, while two Irish congregations, the Presentation Sisters and the Sisters of Mercy, also grew large networks of schools (Raftery and Relihan 2012: 77).[10]

In 1878 the *Intermediate Education (Ireland) Act* was passed, legislating for a system of examinations that carried prizes, scholarships and exhibitions. The Act did not provide for the establishing or funding of schools, nor did it interfere in the training or paying of teachers at that time. Instead, schools that were able to provide the kind of 'superior' education assessed by the intermediate examinations would benefit from 'results fees' that were paid to school managers in respect of successful examination candidates. The examinations were not unlike the Cambridge and Oxford 'Local' Examinations in England, and schools had to provide teaching in classical and modern languages, mathematics, English language and literature, history and geography. Within a short space of time, the intermediate examinations (or the Inter Cert, as it became known) became the route to civil service jobs and university education. This allowed Catholics access to managerial and professional jobs that had traditionally been denied to them. The Catholic Church retained an almost vice-like grip on what was a largely single-sex second-level system, into the early twentieth century. While opinion is divided on the legacy of such control, it is generally agreed that the Church made a sustained contribution to the spread of literacy and numeracy, thereby improving the prospects of the Irish population.

The national school system, 1900–1922

The beginning of the new century saw the publication, under the auspices of the National Board of Education, of *The Revised Programme of Instruction in National Schools*. The programme was based on the recommendations of the Commission on Manual Instruction, popularly known as The Belmore Commission. The introduction of this new curriculum for schools constituted 'a key policy initiative that had significant implications for primary education in Ireland' (O'Connor 2010: 145). It marked the formal abandonment of the payments-by-results system as instituted by the Powis Commission of 1870. The influence of the ideas of educationalists such as Froebel and Rousseau on the document was discernible. The curriculum was predicated on a 'child-centred' approach with a radically expanded range of subjects which included drawing, singing, elementary science and physical education. The programme proved difficult to implement without significant attendant improvements in teacher training and funding, which were not forthcoming. Nonetheless, many children benefited from a more attractive school day with 'less of the drudgery accompanying the older programme and new coloured teaching charts of fauna and flora and of societies in faraway places brighten[ing] the school walls' (Coolahan 1981: 36).

The national school system that had been introduced in 1831 had an appreciable effect on both literacy rates and school attendance. By the turn of the century the proportion of those who could both read and write rose from 33 per cent in 1851 to 84 per cent by 1911. One historian contends that 'without this revolution the foundations of a modern Irish state could not have been laid' (Lyons 1971: 88).

The early years of the new century witnessed a burgeoning interest in the revival of the Irish language as the spoken language of the people, with the language revival organisation, the Gaelic League, garnering wide support for its programme of Irish language classes and related cultural activities throughout the country. The organisation also functioned as an effective pressure group for the improvement of the status of the language in the school curriculum. During the nineteenth century the study of the language received no more than a perfunctory acknowledgement in the curriculum. It could be taught as an 'extra' subject outside school hours, for which the teacher was paid a fee. With the introduction of the new programme in 1900 'Irish could now be taught as an optional subject during school hours or as an extra subject for fees outside ordinary school hours' (Kelly 2002: 6–7). In 1904, the National Board of Education introduced the Bi-Lingual Programme for schools located in Irish-speaking districts of the west of Ireland. These 'Gaeltacht' areas were henceforth permitted to teach the school programme through the medium of Irish. In spite of these concessions, native Irish administrations after 1922 fostered the view that the National Board was unremittingly hostile towards the language (Relihan 2005).

The national school system and the Free State era

The Irish Free State was established early in 1922 following the signing of the Anglo-Irish Treaty in December of the previous year. It consisted of 26 of Ireland's 32 counties, which were mainly located in the predominantly Catholic south and west of the country. The remaining six counties of the north-eastern corner of Ireland, where most of the Protestant population resided, were to form a separate state within the United Kingdom which had its own parliament in Belfast.

The formation of the Irish Free State within the context of an Ireland which had been partitioned along ethno-religious lines dramatically altered the dynamic of the education system. The changes which the new native administration immediately initiated were felt most acutely in the country's national schools. Several ministers of the new government had been prominent members of the Irish language organisation, the Gaelic League. It was, therefore, unsurprising when the newly appointed Chief Executive of Irish Education, Bradley, promptly disbanded the National Board of Education in 1922 while informing its members that it was 'the intention of the new Government to work with all its might for the strengthening of the national fibre by giving the language, history, music and traditions of Ireland their natural place in the life of Irish schools' (*The Irish Times* 1 February 1922, in Coolahan 1981: 41). Thus 'energies were harnessed for a cultural revolution based on the schools' (Coolahan 1981: 38). A Department of Education was established in 1924 to administer the system at both primary and secondary levels. This body, which operated under a Minister for Education, replaced the National and Intermediate Boards of Education of the British era. Apart from this modest measure and a *School Attendance Act* of 1926, which made schooling compulsory for pupils between six and 14 years of age, 'the inherited pattern of administration, financing and control remained very much as it had been under the British regime', with no attempt being made to institute a thorough reform of the system (Coolahan 1981: 38).

The government promptly issued a public notice in February 1922 that Irish was to be taught for at least one full hour per day in all schools where there was a teacher competent to teach it. This notice reinforced the status which had been granted to the language in the constitution of the Irish Free State, Article 4 of which stipulated that the Irish language was to be recognised as the national language while it simultaneously recognised English as an 'official' language (Relihan 2008: 74). Henceforth the national schools were to be utilised as the means by which the State could revive the Irish language as the spoken language of the people. This was a daunting task. In spite of the success of the Gaelic League, the Irish language was spoken fluently only by isolated pockets of people located mainly along the western seaboard or Gaeltacht areas. It was estimated that some two-thirds of teachers had no qualification whatever to teach Irish (Lyons 1971: 638).

In spite of these considerable logistical difficulties the government was determined to pursue its aim of 'Gaelicising' the nation and utilising the schools as the means of doing so. The effect of this was deleterious from an educational point of view. Pedagogical considerations were abandoned and the school curriculum was reconfigured to serve a political agenda. Many of the subjects, such as drawing and nature study, which had been included in the curriculum introduced in 1900, were dropped from the new programme of instruction in order to devote maximum time to the study of Irish. Teachers were also obliged to use Irish as a medium of instruction for other school subjects as far as possible. Infant classes were to be taught virtually entirely through the Irish language. A high standard of Irish was demanded of students on entrance to the teacher training colleges and the study of the language was to have a prominent place in the training courses. School textbooks, sanctioned by the government, frequently reflected the political and cultural ideology of the state.

Some stakeholders in the education system expressed serious misgivings about aspects of the language policy, especially the emphasis on the use of Irish as a teaching medium for other school subjects and its exclusive use during the infant school day. The main Protestant denomination, the Church of Ireland, frequently expressed its unease at the 'compulsory Irish policy' especially during the 1930s and 1940s (Lyons 1971: 128–193). The most powerful interest group to express its concerns vis-à-vis the policy was the Irish National Teachers' Organisation (INTO). It published a report based on the findings of a survey of teachers on the Irish policy in 1942 (INTO 1942). The report, while maintaining support for the overall aim of the language revival, was severely critical of the aspects of the policy which caused such disquiet to the Church of Ireland authorities. It was also especially uneasy about the effects of the teaching of mathematics through the medium of the language (Kelly 2002: 49–54).

The government remained impervious to such protests, regardless of their provenance, and doggedly persisted with the policy. A Council for Education was established by the government in 1950 to review education policy, but its findings were broadly supportive of the status quo. The use of Irish as a medium of instruction in schools was finally ended in 1960. A new curriculum was introduced into the national schools in 1971. This was 'in its ideology, content and format' a 'radical contrast' to its predecessor, offering as it did 'a wide subject range' based on 'teaching methods with pupil interest and involvement as the prime objectives' (Coolahan 1981: 135).

Second-level education in the early twentieth century: 'dark and confused'

In contrast to the reforms which had been instituted at elementary level, second-level education continued to be narrowly focused on the results of examinations. Twenty years after the passing of the *Intermediate Education Ireland Act* (1878), the government published a report on the findings of The Commission on Intermediate Education (Pallas Commission). This was followed in 1904 by the report on the system by two English inspectors, Dale and Stephens. Both reports were critical of the relatively small proportion of pupils progressing beyond the preparatory grades to the senior levels. The reports were also critical of the uneven provision of second-level schooling throughout the country, with schools in the west of Ireland especially badly served. Dale and Stephens criticised the poor physical condition of many of the schools. The lack of formal teacher training courses and the small proportion of teachers who were graduates were other issues requiring attention (Hyland and Milne 1987: 220). The report recommended 'that a central authority should be set up to co-ordinate education at different levels and that payment by results should be abolished in intermediate schools' (Hyland and Milne 1987: 220). Notwithstanding the difficulties, pupil numbers at second-level schools increased from some 22,000 in 1871 to 35,000 in 1901, while those presenting for the Board's examinations rose from 4,000 to 9,000 during the same period (Coolahan 1981: 65). However, the system proved highly resistant to reform during the remainder of the pre-independence period up to 1922. The schools continued to operate as independent fiefdoms under the management of the individual churches.

The approach of the new state towards second-level education in the early decades of its existence was considerably less intrusive than in the national schools. The tiny number of pupils attending the secondary schools was just under 23,000 in 1924, scarcely 5 per cent for the almost half a million pupils attending the national schools (Coolahan 1981: 47). One historian has described second-level education of this era as inhabiting a world which was 'dark and confused', constituting a plethora of privately owned schools typically under the control of a religious order or board of governors (Lyons 1971: 649).

The Department of Education did exert considerable control in the area of state examinations. The *Intermediate Education (Amendment) Act* of 1924 established two examinations, the Intermediate and Leaving Certificates. These replaced the old Junior, Middle and Senior Grade examinations. The government's concentration on the revival of the Irish language was also reflected in the secondary schools. In 1928 it was made compulsory for students to pass Irish in order to obtain the Intermediate Certificate. This provision was extended to the Leaving Certificate in 1934. From 1932 onwards, all recognised secondary schools were obliged to study Irish. Schools were no longer to be funded on the basis of their examination results but on a capitation fee for each recognised pupil and the payment of the greater portion of teachers' salaries. A pupil was required to study Irish if he/she was to be recognised for the purposes of funding. State grants for secondary schools were increased if the school taught some subjects through the medium of Irish and were further increased if it taught all subjects through the language (Relihan 2008).

Coming out of the darkness

Arguably the 'dark and confused' era drew to an end in the middle of the twentieth century, with the dramatic expansion of second-level education in Ireland. As Coolahan (1981) has noted, 'the number of secondary schools nearly doubled and the enrolled pupils more than trebled from 1924 to 1960' (see Table 9.1). Most schools charged a fee, and were single-sex institutions managed by Catholic religious orders (priests, nuns and brothers), although there were also vocational schools run by local statutory committees. While vocational schools aimed at providing an education that would prepare pupils to work in trades, the predominant model of Irish second-level schooling at the time was the secondary school, which favoured the kind of education given in English grammar schools. As the *Report of the Council of Education* (1962) confirmed, the primary purpose of secondary schooling was the inculcation of religious faith. Although the report did not make recommendations to develop free secondary education provision, this major innovation was to come about in 1967.

By the time the 'free-education scheme' was introduced, education was increasingly seen as an economic investment, which would benefit long-term growth in the country. Secondary schools could opt to enter the scheme, whereby the state provided capital grants to run the schools and fees were abolished. Most secondary schools joined the scheme. The 1960s also saw scholarship schemes, travel grants and the removal of many barriers to education. By 1972, the school-leaving age was raised to 15, and there was a conscious effort to provide alternatives to traditionally academic schooling, thereby encouraging more children to remain at school long enough to be able to pursue skilled work.

As the numbers of people entering religious life declined rapidly in the second half of the twentieth century, and particularly in the decades following the Second Vatican

TABLE 9.1 Expansion of secondary education in Ireland, 1924–1960

Year	No. of secondary schools	No. of pupils in attendance
1924–1925	278	22,897
1930–1931	300	28,994
1940–1941	352	38,713
1950–1951	424	48,559
1960–1961	526	76,843

Source: Annual Reports of Department of Education, cited in Coolahan (1981: 79).

Council, the traditional 'teaching orders' could no longer supply staff for their schools. There was a significant increase in the number of lay or secular teachers working in secondary schools, and there were gradual changes in the management of these schools, many of which retained their denominational ethos.

A handful of comprehensive schools was introduced in Ireland from 1966, and community schools were introduced in 1970. Community schools are fully financed by the state and are mixed-sex. They provide both academic and vocational subjects under one roof, and are managed by a Board which represents local interests. Many were formed following the amalgamation of smaller secondary schools and vocational schools, while some were newly built in areas of population growth. There are now 85 community and comprehensive schools, which provide for a little over 15 per cent of all second-level pupils, while 247 vocational schools, which are state-established and managed by Vocational Education Committees, provide for approximately 30 per cent of pupils. The secondary school remains the type of school attended by the majority of Irish pupils. Ireland has 419 secondary schools, and 91 per cent of these do not charge fees. Privately owned and managed, they are mostly single-sex, and while they all provide 'traditional' academic subjects, increasingly they also make some provision for technical and practical subjects.

Schooling in Ireland today

The historical influences on Irish education can, despite many changes, still be seen today. Most primary schools are state-aided parish schools, with a religious ethos – and for demographic reasons this religious ethos is almost always Catholic. There are also some non-denominational schools, multi-denominational schools and Irish-medium schools (Gaelscoileanna). The state pays the building and running costs of these national schools, and there is also a small number of fee-paying primary schools.

The post-primary sector, comprising vocational, community, comprehensive and secondary schools, provides for a three-year Junior Cycle programme, followed by a two-year Senior Cycle programme, although schools may offer an additional optional Transition Year between the Junior and Senior Cycles. Like primary schools in Ireland, most second-level schools have a denominational ethos. While the school-leaving age is now 16, over 90 per cent of pupils complete senior cycle education through to the Leaving Certificate examination, and therefore remain in school until at least 17 years of age. The Junior Cycle ends with an examination for the Junior Certificate, while the Senior Cycle terminates with the Leaving Certificate, the Leaving Certificate Applied (LCA) or the Leaving Certificate Vocational Programme (LCVP). Syllabuses are available in over 30 subjects, and pupils are required to take at least five, one of which must be Irish.[11]

Concluding comments

Schooling in Ireland has experienced periods of dramatic change, with the question of Church–state control of education often to the fore. The nineteenth century saw the development of 'official' state-funded systems, and the passing of legislation which supported mass education and which eventually led to a climate of accountability, examinations and even performance-related payments to teachers. The twentieth century saw great political change in the country, with the establishment of the Free State in 1922; among the changes of that era was the re-instating of the Irish language in a prominent position in formal schooling. Second-level education developed in the late nineteenth century, and by the early twentieth century it was largely provided by the Catholic religious orders. It was to remain the preserve of those who could afford to pay for it until the 1960s.

While the education system has undergone remarkable change, it has retained some distinctive characteristics: the Irish language has retained a special position, and the denominational character of education is still imprinted – albeit faintly – on schooling. Education in Ireland is highly centralised. The Department of Education and Skills, situated in Marlborogh Street, Dublin for almost 100 years, generates and manages state policy on education, including school inspection, curriculum and assessment, school governance and building and planning. It also responds to the changing needs of the population, engaging with contemporary issues such as the growing demand for non-denominational schooling and schooling for pupils of diverse ethnicities.

Notes

1. This was the system of law in Ireland when it was finally supplanted by the English common law. See www.courts.ie/Courts.ie/library3.nsf/pagecurrent/3CBAE4FE856E917B80256DF800494ED9 for details.
2. For a discussion of this, see McGrath (1979).
3. An *Act for the English Order, Habit and Language*, 1537 (28 Henry VIII, c. 15).
4. For a discussion of the charter schools, see Raftery (2009).
5. For a discussion of the hedge schools, see Raftery and Relihan (2012).
6. Letter from the Secretary for Ireland to his Grace the Duke of Leinster on the formation of a Board of Education. 1837 (485) ix 585, in Hyland and Milne (1987: 100).
7. While the Board supplied two-thirds of the cost of building a new school, the remaining cost was to be supplied by local communities. For a discussion of this, see Raftery and Relihan (2012: 74).
8. See, for example, Coolahan (1981) and Raftery (2011). See also Goldstrom (1972).
9. For an overview, see Raftery (2010).
10. For a discussion of the Catholic Church and schooling in Ireland, see Raftery (2012).
11. See www.education.ie/en/The-Education-System/Post-Primary.

References

'Abstract of the proceedings of the Incorporated Society (1733)', in Áine Hyland and Kenneth Milne (1987) *Irish Educational Documents*, Vol. I, Dublin: CICE.

Commission of Irish Education Enquiry (1825) *First Report of the Commission of Irish education Inquiry*, 1825 (400) XII.

Commissioners of National Education in Ireland, *Manual for Needlework* (1869).

Coolahan John (1981) *Irish Education, History and Structure*, Dublin: IPA.

Goldstrom, J.M. (1972) *The Social Content of Education, 1808–1870: A Study of the Working Class School Reader in England and Ireland*, Shannon: Irish University Press.

Hyland, Áine and Kenneth Milne (1987) *Irish Educational Documents*, Vol. I, Dublin: CICE.

INTO (Irish National Teachers Organisation) (1942) *Report of Committee of Inquiry into Use of Irish as a Teaching Medium to Children whose Home Language is English*, Dublin: INTO.

Kelly, Adrian (2002) *Compulsory Irish: Language and Education in Ireland, 1870s–1970s*, Dublin: Irish Academic Press.

Lyons, F.S.L. (1971) *Ireland Since the Famine*, London: Fontana/Collins.

McGrath, Feargal (1979) *Education in Ancient and Medieval Ireland*, Dublin: Studies Special Publications.

McManus, Antonia (2002) *The Irish Hedge School and its Books, 1695–1831*, Dublin: Four Courts Press.

Milne, Kenneth (1997) *The Irish Charter Schools*, Dublin: Four Courts Press.

O'Connor, Maura (2010) *The Development of Infant Education in Ireland, 1838–1948*, Oxford: Peter Lang.

Raftery, Deirdre (2009) 'The legacy of legislation and the pragmatics of policy: historical perspectives on schooling for Irish children', in Sheelgh Drudy (ed.), *Education in Ireland: Challenge and Change*, Dublin: Gill and Macmillan.

Raftery, Deirdre (2010) 'The pragmatics of policy and the legacy of legislation', in: Sheelgh Drudy (ed.), *Education in Ireland: Challenge and Change*, Dublin: Gill and Macmillan.

Raftery, Deirdre (2011) 'Colonising the mind: the use of English writers in the education of the Irish poor, c. 1750–1850', in Mary Hilton and Jill Shefrin (eds), *Educating the Child in Enlightenment Britain: Beliefs, Cultures, Practices*, Farnham: Ashgate.

Raftery, Deirdre (2012) '"Among school children": the churches, politics, and Irish schooling, 1830–1930', *Studies: An Irish Quarterly Review* 100: 433–440.

Raftery, Deirdre and Martina Relihan (2012) 'Faith and nationhood: church, state and the provision of schooling in Ireland, 1870–1930', in Laurence Brockliss and Nicola Sheldon (eds), *Mass Education and the Limits of State Building, c. 1870–1930*, Basingstoke: Palgrave Macmillan.

Relihan, Martina (2005) 'A retrospective and prospective look at the "happy English child": the applicability of postcolonial theory to the British government's education policy in Ireland in the late nineteenth and early twentieth centuries', *Irish Educational Studies* 24, 2–3: 123–131.

Relihan, Martina (2008) 'The Church of Ireland and its relationship with the irish education system 1922–1950 with particular reference to the Irish language and Gaelic culture'. Unpublished PhD thesis, University College Dublin.

Report of the Council of Education (1962) in Áine Hyland and Kenneth Milne (1992) *Irish Educational Documents*, Vol. II, Dublin: CICE.

10

Education in Scotland

David Matheson

The Scottish Parliament, which adjourned on March 25, 1707, is hereby reconvened.
Winifred Ewing MSP on the occasion of the first meeting of the devolved Scottish Parliament,
12 May 1999

The Scottish idea of education

Clearly there is more to education than school and more to school than simply attending lessons. In Scotland, as everywhere else, the educational experience at whatever level and in whatever circumstances is bound up in history and culture. Questions may arise as to *whose* history and *whose* culture, but these become absorbed into popular mythology and give basis to rationalisations. It's not my intention here to do more than present some of the bases of the Scottish idea of education. Analysis of the possible roots of these bases may be found in Matheson (2000), who discerns three major myths in Scottish education:

1. that the Scottish curriculum, at whatever level, is wider than anyone else's;
2. that Scottish education is better than anyone else's;
3. that Scottish education is more egalitarian than anyone else's and that every learner can go as far as his/her talents permit.

These are myths which the Scots universalise but, in truth, 'anyone else' usually means England and the English who have traditionally been the 'Other' against whom the Scots have defined themselves, though there is increasing evidence that this is decreasingly the case (Matheson and Matheson 2000a). The myths may or may not be true, but the essential is that they are believed. However, as Mark Twain is reputed to have said, we should never let truth get in the way of a good story. Myths whereby the Scots learn more, learn it better and have it learned by a wider sector of the population help to sustain a 'feel good factor' in Scottish education which is not quite so noticeable, for example, in England. This surrounds education, however construed, with a sense that it is positive and it is this positiveness which has acquired a mythical status of its own. As Paterson (1998b) tells us,

> There [has] continued to exist a belief in public education as a public good.... Scottish research has actually influenced Government action through the Scottish Office, though keeping a critical distance from it. That basis of publicly shared knowledge is one reason why faith in the education system remains strong.
>
> (n.p.)

The positive view of Scottish education extends also to the parents. As Munn (1995: 213) puts it: 'There is a considerable body of evidence which indicates that parents have a good deal of trust in the professional expertise of teachers and that trust has so far not been radically shaken.' As we shall see later, this trust has had major ramifications in the governance of schools and in the reaction in Scotland to initiatives imposed by the Westminster government.

The origins of modern Scottish education

The question of when to place the origins of any educational institution or establishment is akin to asking the length of a piece of string. As regards the Scots, they are no different from any other group and will attach as much longevity as necessary to any educational project. However, some traditions have been around longer than others, so let us begin with an old one.

Despite claims that Gaelic is the third oldest written language in Europe (after Latin and Greek) (McClure 1988; Matheson and Matheson 1998), there is little evidence that reading and writing Gaelic was being taught in any systematic manner in the Dark Ages. Nonetheless, the fact that literature in Gaelic does date back so far indicates that there must have been learning of reading and writing in the language. However, this was never developed in any systematic manner and by the beginning of the nineteenth century illiteracy was widespread in the Highlands and Islands of Scotland. Pole ([1814] 1968) cites figures showing that 86 per cent of the Highlands and Islands' population were illiterate in either Gaelic or English. This may have been a reflection of the declining social conditions of the Highlanders in the face of the continuing *mi-rùn mòr nan Gall*, the Great Malice of the Lowlander, which extended to England in the light of the 1715 and 1745 Rebellions. The Great Malice, however, reached its apotheosis in the Highland Clearances, the systematic depopulation of the Highlands to make way first for sheep and then for deer. The prime movers behind the Clearances were the Highland chiefs themselves, who had become more English than the English and needed money to remain so.

It is perhaps a reflection of the internal dominant hegemony in Scotland that most of the older history of education in the country is in fact a history of education in the Lowlands. Nonetheless, 'the landing of Columba in 563 [on Iona in the Inner Hebrides] may be taken as the beginning of effective Scottish education' (Scotland 1970: 3). This monastic base grew into a de facto international study centre, attracting scholars from throughout Europe, while from the thirteenth century the Dominican friars in particular, together with other teaching orders (Scotland 1970), established convent schools, abbey schools and cathedral schools and some *studia generalia* – 'the embryo of later universities' (Findlay 1973: 10).

The part of the population that these initiatives reached was almost certainly very small, but it is significant that records remain of schools for lay persons (rather than just for youth destined for Holy Orders) throughout much of the Lowlands. However, until the end of the Wars of Independence (at the Treaty of Edinburgh-Northampton in 1328 (Lynch 1992)) the Scottish nobility had more need of the arts of war than the science of reading. Simple survival has, as always, to take priority over refinement (Scotland 1970).

Once out of a near permanent state of war with its larger southern neighbour, Scotland was able to develop in other areas and with time the *studia generalia* were able to grow. This was assisted by the Schism in the Church, which resulted in the papacy of Avignon, a rival to Rome, and it was to Avignon that the Scottish Episcopacy long remained loyal. When the Avignon Pope Benedict XIII was expelled from France in 1408, 'a number of masters who had formerly taught in French universities' (Lynch 1992: 102) returned to Scotland. By 1412 they had founded a school at St Andrews which received within a year the 'six bulls of protection and privilege according it university status and the right to confer degrees' (ibid.). This establishment was followed in 1450–1451[1] by that of the University of Glasgow, Aberdeen (King's College) in 1495 (and later Marischal College, which merged with King's in 1860 (Bell 2000)) and then Edinburgh in 1583. Edinburgh was arguably the first civic university, founded as it was by the Town Council and not by Papal Bull (Osborne 1968). These were all the universities in Scotland until the middle of the twentieth century, but there were also other colleges, many of which eventually became universities in their own right. One such was in Dundee, originally a college of St Andrews University: 'In 1883 when a further new university college was opened in Dundee ... its Principal felt able to claim that the availability of university places per head of population in Scotland at that time was exceeded only in Switzerland' (Bell 2000: 166).

Scotland's higher education experienced significant growth even before the creation of University College Dundee. In the eighteenth century the 'total student population tripled ... with student numbers at Edinburgh University alone increasing from 400 in 1700 to 2,300 in 1824' (Smith 2000: 311), though few bothered to graduate. As Smith (2000) makes clear, the current divide between education and entertainment simply did not exist as we know it now. Indeed, she argues that amusement *and* instruction were a major feature of at least some Scottish higher education and that the instruction was indeed *higher* education. In this way, this eighteenth- and early nineteenth-century idea of *infotainment* was not a dumbing down of higher education in order for it to appeal to a wider public.[2] As importantly, if not more so, Smith demonstrates that until the full force of the Victorian cult of domesticity began to be felt by Scottish women there was a major and continued growth in the opportunities afforded to wealthier Scottish women to attend courses of higher education, estimating that 'there were over 5,000 class enrolments by women at the Andersonian alone, between 1796 and 1845' (Smith 2000: 326). The Andersonian would eventually become a College of Advanced Technology and then finally the University of Strathclyde in 1964.

This 'storming of the citadel' was severely hampered by the growing link from the mid nineteenth century between university *qualification* and professional employment.

Men, it seems, did not mind women educating themselves in the same manner that they minded women seeking prestigious employment. It was only from 1889[3] that legislation enabled Scottish universities to confer degrees on women, though it took until the last quarter of the twentieth century for women (in Scotland as in the rest of the British Isles) to achieve overall parity of numbers with men in higher education.

In social class terms, higher education in Scotland has long had a reputation for being more open than that of England. Simply having more higher education places for a much smaller population would, of course, help greatly. As important, if not more so, is the notion that, as a Scots saying puts it, 'we're aw Jock Tamson's bairns' (McCrone 1996: 102).[4] In other words, we are all from the same basic roots and have all the opportunity to get on in the world. This meant, for example, that:

> Aberdeen took in large proportions of students from agricultural backgrounds (16 per cent in 1860 and 20 per cent in 1910) [while] Glasgow had a higher percentage from manual working-class backgrounds (19 per cent in 1860 and 24 per cent in 1910).
>
> (McCrone 1992: 101)

This greater availability of higher education has entered popular mythology and, while there is still a long way to go before all social classes have their proportionate representation in Scottish higher education, it is highly significant that 'When social class is taken into account, 37% more Scots enter university education than would be expected on the basis of what happens in England and Wales' (Matheson 1999: 148). Part of this expectation arguably comes from the notion of the Godly Commonwealth promoted by the Scottish Reformers and a literal interpretation of the Biblical parables focused on making the best of what talents one has.[5]

Scotland was greatly influenced by the Reformation, especially in the Lowlands[6] and among the gentry throughout the country. The Reformation brought with it the demand that people learn to read in order to read the Bible and hence be saved. With this in mind, John Knox and his fellow Reformers in their 1560 *First Book of Discipline* 'sketched out an articulated system, from parish school to university, and aimed at providing basic religious instruction and literacy in each parish' (Anderson 1999: 215). Knox's school system was to be paid for by local taxes and took a long time to develop, but develop it did. It is, however, questionable to what extent the Reformers created their education system *ex nihilo* (as they very much pretended) and to what extent they built upon what was already there:

> There were certainly far more pre-Reformation schools than the strictures of the *First Book of Discipline* of 1560 suggest, and the same is true of the two Education Acts of 1633 and 1696.... There were probably at least 700 schools in early seventeenth-century Scotland, spread unevenly over the country's 1,000-odd parishes.
>
> (Lynch 1992: 259)

Regardless of the truth of the situation prior to the Reformation, as Scotland moved into the eighteenth century, at least as far as the Lowlands were concerned, it was one of the very few parts of the Western world that could lay claim to having an actual system of education which extended to all parts of the community. In this respect, the story of Robert Burns, who was born into a ploughman's family in 1759 and yet became fully literate, was far from unique in the Lowlands. Burns, of course, was somewhat unique in becoming such a celebrated poet, but his actual level of literacy was not.[7]

One experience that Burns and his contemporaries were almost certainly without was any form of preschool. However, the 'very first nursery, reputedly in the world' (Wilkinson 1999: 42) was established in Scotland by Robert Owen in 1816 (Mackintosh 1962) as part of the New Lanark village. It was a fairly short-lived venture since, as Wilkinson (1999) tells us, 'after Owen left, in 1825, to establish New Harmony in America, the nursery was discontinued' (p. 42).

The man who gave shape to Owen's ideas on nursery education was James Buchanan, who left New Lanark in 1819 to take charge of an infant school in London. Buchanan influenced Wilderspin, as did the ideas of Froebel, and this combination was then re-imported to Scotland by David Stow. Stow opened his first infant school in Glasgow in 1827 and by 1831 there were five in the city (Mackintosh 1962). It is worth mentioning that not all writers agree that these institutions were in fact nursery schools at all. As James Scotland (1969) puts it: 'there was a tendency to absorb [infants] early into ordinary teaching; the nursery school as we know it did not exist' (p. 46).

Preschool education's development in Scotland 'has ... been spasmodic, diverse, and variable' (Watt 1999: 307). The laws such as the 1945 *Education (Scotland) Act* 'laid a duty on education authorities to establish nursery schools wherever there was enough parental demand' (Scotland 1969: 174) but this was not for a long time given any noticeable priority. Such was the case until the demographic decline at the end of the Baby Boom.

When I was growing up in Glasgow in the 1960s and 1970s, I knew no one at all who had been to nursery school.[8] In contrast, by the time I returned to Glasgow in 1986, nursery education was commonplace and it seemed a rare child who started primary school without having had at least one year of preschool of some sort or another.

Adult and vocational education

It would be impossible in the space available to give any real history of adult and vocational education in Scotland. It is self-evident that since people were people (and perhaps even before) there have been concerted efforts to pass on skills and knowledge necessary for earning one's living. As elsewhere in Europe, much of the history of vocational education[9] in Scotland from the Middle Ages to the Industrial Revolution was the history of the guilds, with their concomitant secrecy and rituals.

The development of industrialisation almost inevitably raises the value of literacy and in this light a demand for literacy acquisition became apparent across the UK.

Thus, Kelly (1962) informs us that in 1851, of Scotland's 438 evening schools (with their 15,071 pupils), 403 gave writing as their most popular subject.[10]

Vocational and adult education as presently constituted can be said to be descended from the Mechanics Institutes of the nineteenth century, the first of which was formally established in Edinburgh in 1821 (Hall 1994), though Kelly (1962) puts the first foundation in Glasgow in 1800 and attributes it to George Birbeck. In Mechanics Institutes, 'workers could improve their basic skills, learn new scientific and technological knowledge and broaden their minds' (Hall 1994: 3), initial job training being done on the job.

Concomitant with the Mechanics Institutes was the growth and development of the public libraries such as that founded in 1821 by J.B. Neilson under the title of the *Glasgow Gas Workmen's Library*, which developed 'into a mutual improvement society, with library, laboratory and workshop' (Kelly 1962: 118). Mechanics Institutes frequently held their own libraries, though these were of very variable size.

Much more significant in this area of non-formal education was the public library movement, whose most noted benefactor was Andrew Carnegie, whose largesse was assisted by the passing of the various *Library Acts* in the latter part of the nineteenth century. These enabled local authorities to establish public lending libraries without having to go through cumbersome procedures (Kelly 1962).

It is well documented that Mechanics Institutes did not survive the century and there are arguments that by the mid-century they were dying on their feet. Nonetheless, what is important in the Mechanics Institutes, the other organisations which tread a similar path (such as the Scottish Chartists and the Scottish Co-operative Movement) and the growth of the public libraries is that they brought sophisticated knowledge within the reach of the masses. That the masses may have been slow to make full use of them is another matter, but at least they were afforded the opportunity to do so.

Adult education in Scotland waxed and waned over the course of the twentieth century. The Workers' Educational Association (WEA) was never able to develop to quite the same extent as in England since, among other things, it was denied *Responsible Body Status* as a provider of adult education and this made its 'development heavily dependent on collaboration with the universities, local authorities[11] and trade unions' (Duncan 1999: 106). In the cities and in some rural areas (notably the Grampians and Ross and Cromarty), university extra-mural classes saw considerable success in attracting students. This was, however, dealt a heavy blow with the slow but steady reduction in subsidies provided by local authorities and the application of market forces from 1979 onwards. In this way, an evening language class like the Danish one I undertook at Glasgow University in 1977 at a cost of £2.50 cost £200 in 2013.

Vocational education for its part became increasingly separated from its adult education cousin and moved, until the massive expansion of private providers of training, almost entirely into colleges of further education. However, as Scotland (1969) makes clear, even in the late 1960s the situation was never very satisfactory, with employers not always very willing to allow apprentices to attend day-release classes, and employees not always very willing to attend them either. In the 1970s the plethora of awarding bodies did not lend itself to a simplification of the situation. The creation of two main awarding bodies, the Scottish Business Education Council (SCOTBEC) and the Scottish Technician Education Council (SCOTEC) eventually resolved this, at least partially. These in turn were amalgamated in 1985 to form the Scottish Vocational Education Council (SCOTVEC), which assumed the main responsibility for 'designing, awarding and accrediting vocational qualification' (Hall 1994: 58) and was held to liaise closely with industry, its lead bodies and vocational education providers. In 1997 SCOTVEC and the Scottish Examinations Board joined forces to create a unitary organisation, the Scottish Qualifications Authority (SQA), responsible for virtually all sub-degree formal education.

Development of school structures

At the time of the Union of the Parliaments in 1707, 'educational provision … and the Church of Scotland [the Established Church] were specifically exempted from the … Act' (Grant 1985: 19). This provision, together with the maintenance of a separate Scots Law, meant that when education came under secular control it continued to maintain a basis for its distinctiveness from that of England. Mind you, the fact that until Devolution in 1999 Scottish education laws were passed by a parliament dominated by English MPs always had the potential for some inappropriate legislation. However, historically, circumspection (or apathy?) tended to win the day and it was remarkable just how few English MPs would remain in the House of Commons to debate bills on Scottish education. This is not to say that they did not return for the voting and much legislation on Scottish education was passed in the teeth of opposition from Scottish MPs.

While the rest of the British Isles had to wait until the nineteenth century for the state to take an interest in schooling, in Scotland in the seventeenth century there was a virtual national curriculum for the grammar schools.

> This was partly due to the use of standard textbooks, but it was also the result of the interest taken by both [the] General Assembly[12] [of the Church of Scotland] and parliament in what was taught in the grammar schools.
>
> (Lynch 1992: 259)

This interest from parliament effectively fell into abeyance at the Union of the Parliaments and it was not until 1834 that the UK government showed an interest in education in Scotland. At this point, some financial assistance was extended to Scottish schools but on the same terms as for those in England. 'National differences were at best regarded as regional peculiarities' (Osborne 1968: 1). However, when it came time in 1840 to establish Her Majesty's Inspectorate of Schools (HMI) in Scotland, it had its base in Edinburgh and has remained there ever since.

The particular case of Scotland was given account in the preparation and enactment of the 1872 *Education (Scotland) Act* and, as well as making formal education compulsory for all of Scotland's children (ages 5–13), set up the Scotch Education Department[13] which nonetheless remained in London until 1922 (Osborne 1968). The Act transferred the administration of schools from the 'church to secular authorities' (Scottish Education

Department 1972: 2) and established School Boards to carry out this administration. 'Church' in this case meant the Free Church of Scotland and Church of Scotland. The Scottish Episcopalians and the Catholic Church, wary of the dominance of the Presbyterians on the School Boards, declined the offer of joining the state system until the 1918 *Education Act*, which put in place enough safeguards to alleviate their fears of proselytism. The Catholics and Episcopalian schools did, however, continue to receive state grants to help with running costs but not capital expenditure (Anderson 1999).

A further effect of the 1872 Act was the expansion of the provision of secondary education, the term 'secondary' having appeared only in the 1860s (Anderson 1999). While this affected only a very small part of the cohort, it is significant in that it set the tone for the development not only of the secondary sector, which would be universalised after the Second World War, but also for the impact on university admissions procedures – an impact which endures to the present day.

In 1888, the Scotch Education Department established the Leaving Certificate, an examination at three levels – Honours, Higher and Lower. The universities quickly began to recognise passes at the Higher level as exempting students from the universities' own Preliminary Examination (Dobie 1967). Such exemption permitted students to undertake an Ordinary MA in three years instead of four. From being an examination in separate subjects, the Leaving Certificate became a group examination early in the twentieth century and remained thus until 1951, when it was once again available as separate subjects. The Honours level was dropped in 1907 and the Lower level was effectively separated from the Higher from 1951 onwards (Osborne 1968). To the present day, the Higher is the principal entrance qualification for higher education in Scotland.

At the outset, the Leaving Certificate was examined by HMI and this remained so until 1962 when the new Ordinary Grade replaced the Lower (and was always to be taken in the fourth year of secondary school). Growing numbers of candidates also meant that the burden of setting and marking the examinations became too much for the HMI and the Scottish Certificate of Education Examinations Board was established (Findlay 1973). Henceforth the examinations would be known as SCE Higher Grade and SCE Ordinary Grade.[14] Anderson (1999) makes the point that the 'new' Higher Grade 'was less university-orientated than the old Leaving Certificate' (p. 222). The extent to which this is true is debatable as regards most subjects. Where there is no argument concerns certain subjects which were traditionally more popular with females than with males. While technical subjects were always recognised for university entrance (and were dominated by males), secretarial studies and home economics (and their antecedents) (dominated by females) were not. This distinctly sexist discrimination was long justified on the basis of academic content but personally, despite close examination of the 1980s and 1990s syllabuses of the subjects concerned, I have never found any basis for it other than sexism. The technical aspects of secretarial studies and the scientific basis of home economics were simply ignored.

To end this section, let us note that the Higher is never referred to as the *Gold Standard* in the manner than many English commentators refer to the A-level. Rarely is the Higher referred to as 'traditional', again unlike the A-level. And yet the Higher (or at least its name) has been around for more than 60 years longer than the A-level.

Cultural hegemonies

Language and culture

'Cultural domination is a fact of life for millions of students throughout the world' (Apple 1993: 51). Students in Scotland experience daily such domination. Indeed, it would not be an exaggeration to suggest that the mass of Scottish people, even those belonging to the dominant hegemony, are subject to one or more forms of cultural domination.

Scotland has never quite figured out how to be a country. Prior to the unions (of crowns and parliaments) with England, it was never a united kingdom as the clans in the north basically did what they liked and were tolerated to do so as long as they supplied soldiers when required and kept the Lowlands supplied with meat. The Highlands and Islands did not speak the same language as the Lowlands. When the Reformation came, it was embraced by the Lowlands but long shunned by the mass of ordinary people in the Highlands and Islands. The Reformation also brought the Bible in English into the homes of Scots speakers, the two languages being sufficiently close together that no translation was thought necessary. The Royal Court decamped to London in 1603 and with it went a major source of the continuing credibility of Scots. The end result was a long and continuing disparagement of the various dialects of Scots while the Gaelic of the Highlands and Islands shrank under the continued onslaught of the 'civilising' influence of English.[15] Ironically, it was frequently Scots that the linguistic missionaries propagated – a point lost on many Scots speakers, even today, being that the language they are speaking is not some sort of 'bad' English but rather Scots of one dialect or another (Matheson and Matheson 2000b).

The problem of the status of the Scots language is one major ingredient in the inferiorist attitude of the Scots. Even its bourgeoisie feel insecure. As Young puts it, Scotland in much its modern history was: 'a total culture in which an insecure and authoritarian elite articulated an obsessive awareness of its own provincial inferiority and backwardness' (Young 1979: 21). This self-deprecation created what has been termed *Anglo-Britishness*, with its emphasis on England as civilised and its marginalisation of 'the Scottish past by rewriting Scottish history to downplay the way in which the Scots had preserved freedoms against external enemies and tyrannical kings' (Goodman 1999: 292). 'England represented modernity rather than a dominant core, and the peripheries were seen less as threatened pluralisms than as areas of backwardness, fortunate enough to be undergoing assimilation and accelerated progress' (Kidd 1993: 214 in Goodman 1999: 292)

This Anglicising hegemony was (and frequently still is) a total package. Scottish history has long been viewed as quaint and parochial, while Scots languages have been deemed, at best, unworthy of comment, if not downright barbaric. It is worth bearing in mind that to be English was an aspiration of much of the Scottish intelligentsia in the years following the Union of the Parliaments (Gikandi 1996) and this had a continued effect in the centuries that followed.

A consequence of the growth of the Anglocentric hegemony was that Scots effect-ively ceased to exist as a dynamic written language except as regards some poetry and as a device used by writers such as Walter Scott to demonstrate that their characters were native Scots people. Gaelic was assailed on all sides even to the extent of the Scot-tish Society for the Propagation of Christian Knowledge (SSPCK) encouraging teaching in Gaelic in order to get children in a position to learn English and thus (it was hoped) forget the Gaelic (Grant 1984).

The situation of Gaelic declined even more with the 1872 Act:

> The 1872 Education Act bringing education to all the children of Scotland seems to have served some of them ill, since it provided school education only through the medium of English. While the 1918 Education Act did state the duty of local authorities to provide for the teaching of Gaelic in Gaelic-speaking areas, little action seems to have followed.
>
> (Sutherland 2000: 203)

The latter quarter of the twentieth century did bring a change of heart on the part of the authorities and in the overall perception of Gaelic, at least by those with the funds to do something about it. Scots, for its part, is not *quite* so disparaged as previously but all depends on the dialect of Scots in question.

Gaelic is no longer castigated, children no longer disparaged for speaking this lan-guage. Rather, it is seen as an asset to be encouraged. This is despite the very small minority of Scots with any Gaelic at all. Indeed, it would not be wide of the mark to sug-gest that only a very small proportion of Scots can even say 'hello' in Gaelic. Gaelic is not and never has been a national language of Scotland. Only with devolution did Gaelic (and Scots) become an official language. Catherine Matheson and I have argued elsewhere that Gaelic will probably always remain on the linguistic periphery (Matheson and Matheson 2000b), but at least we were able to take heart from the growing notice being given to Gaelic as an important part of Scotland's heritage, and this especially through the medium of informal education which is television. Children's programmes in Gaelic appear in the daytime, while there are regular current affairs programmes on the BBC such as *Eòrpa* (on other linguistic minorities in Europe) and there was the launch in 2008 of the Gaelic-language television station *BBC Alba*. The profile of Gaelic has been successfully raised and indeed it was my experience as a Glasgow schoolteacher that few children reached secondary without having at least seen *Pàidrig Post* (Postman Pat) or one of the home-grown Gaelic programmes such as *Dòtaman*, whose silliness and visual humour is such that actually understanding what the characters are saying is almost secondary.

More substantively, there are now Gaelic-medium primary and secondary schools across most of Scotland, other than in the Borders and Dumfries and Galloway, neither of which have a historical connection with Gaelic, whether indigenous or via immigra-tion, unless one goes back several centuries to the days when Galloway was *Gall-Ghaidhealaibh*, or *land of the foreign Gaels*.

The SQA permits pupils to take Higher and other examinations in geography, history and mathematics in Gaelic and also offers both levels in separate examinations for native speakers and learners. The big, unsolved problem, however, lies in finding the teachers who can teach in Gaelic – this alone may well stifle any further major expansion of provision, despite the Scottish Executive awarding grants to encourage the training of teachers in Gaelic.

Scots, on the other hand, has only a few embers of hope glowing in the educational darkness. Under the *Higher Still* scheme, with its multiple levels of course and examination,[16] which students undertake in their fifth and sixth years of secondary school, candidates may present their oral work in English using the Scots language. This may sound a bit oxymoronic, but it is symptomatic of the bane of the Scots language: it has no real status whatsoever as a language.[17] Accounts abound of young Scots, myself included, being told to speak properly (i.e. speak Standard English with the closest approximations to so-called Received Pronunciation (RP) being the most highly regarded). I personally saw, as late as the 1990s, children in schools in Glasgow being punished for saying *aye*. I even witnessed a plaintiff in Glasgow Sheriff Court (in 1990 or thereabouts) being fined for contempt of court for speaking his own language of Glaswegian Scots. He had committed no other crime but to drop his *t*s and slur some words together. Crowther and Tett (1997) recount a similar tale, this time in Edinburgh, where a young man was jailed for contempt of court in 1993 for saying *aye* instead of *yes.*

Scots has been seen as corrupted English for a very long time. Its death has been 'asserted since the eighteenth century and yet the language refuses to die' (Macafee 1988: 9). Even in its most prestigious forms it is not a language of power. Scots, especially in its urban forms, is the language of the poor. It suffers from a long history of prejudice and elitism which has led 'to speakers being ashamed of their mother tongue' (MacLeod 1989: 41). This leads inevitably to speakers of Scots being all too frequently ashamed to open their mouths when in the presence of speakers of 'powerful' dialects of what they perceive as English. This pervades the whole of the educational system from preschool to postgraduate. Fundamentally, if your language is of low status, associated as, for example, is Glaswegian with thuggery and low-life pursuits, then in order to enhance your cultural capital you will get rid of it. Unfortunately, in doing so, you may be throwing away your very national identity. At the very least, you are divorcing yourself from your roots. As Menzies (1991) puts it

> Even if the English dialect speaker takes lessons to perfect an RP accent, he will still be English. If the Scot does this, he may throw away more in the loss of an outward, recognisable identity. If the two hypothetical speakers are to talk together, both may disguise their regional origins but only one belies his national identity.
>
> (p. 3)

The Scottish educational system has long set its sights on destroying the Scots language in all its forms. That is, except when Burns' Night hoves into view and children might receive prizes for the very language for which they were punished for using the previous day. This negative attitude towards the *Mither tongue* has immense ramifications for Scottish education and the Scottish psyche. It means, for example, speaking one language while writing another. It means adopting an inferiorist attitude to one's native culture and changing one's perceptions to see the stereotype as defined by the dominant linguistic discourse. It means seeing one's native language as 'slang' and hearing one's teachers dishing out exhortations to 'speak properly'. This is in true ignorance of the fact that, as Macafee (1988) puts it, 'slang terms are usually transient' (p. 40). Scots words, even in Glaswegian, have for the most part a long history behind them. There is certainly slang in Scots, but the existence of some slang does not make slang of the whole language in its multiple dialects.

Scots has had a number of revivalist movements and one problem that each of these has suffered is in its disparagement of the urban varieties of Scots, especially that of Glasgow, as not being authentic Scots at all. This lays before us the scenario of some future date at which the Glaswegians are no longer put down for speaking 'bad' English but are put down for speaking 'bad' Scots instead. As it is, for the moment, Scots is slowly becoming acceptable, at least in theory, in oral work in school. The problem is that there is no agreement as to what constitutes Scots and this in itself risks perpetuating the age-old attacks on the language of the urban working class but under another name.[18]

Religion

'Religion is everywhere in Scotland' (O'Hagan 2000: 25). This was certainly the case when I grew up in Glasgow in the 1960s and 1970s. Football was suffused with religion. Politics ran through it. Names were identified as 'good Protestant' or 'fine Fenian'. Depending of who one bumped into, being a Billy or a Dan[19] could easily be the cause of a thumping. Things were made worse by Catholicism being associated with Irishness and being frequently seen, by Catholics and non-Catholics alike, as not Scottish. The Irish (or more correctly those of Irish descent) dominated the Catholic population of Scotland and this led to a generalised (though far from universal) conflation of these two markers of identity. It also led to complications in the lives of Catholic lads and lassies who, like myself, had little or no Irish in their origins. In my own case, having a surname which is closely associated with the Isle of Lewis, a bastion of the Free Church of Scotland (an organisation not generally noted for positive views of anything Catholic[20]), just complicated life further. This even went to the extent of several of my primary school teachers telling me that I was not a 'real' Catholic since I did not have an Irish [sic] name.

It also meant regular and systematised discrimination on the basis of religion, one's Catholicism (or lack of it) being usually evident from the name of one's 'last school attended'. In the 1960s, it was also common in Glasgow newspapers to see situations vacant which sought a 'Protestant man'.

Unlike Switzerland, which managed to reach a geographical compromise over the matter of the Reformed and unreformed churches,[21] Scotland declared itself Protestant in 1560 by Act of Parliament (Skinnider 1967: 13). This meant that penal laws outlawed Catholicism and it vanished (at least from public view) from all the towns and cities, surviving in any strength only in areas remote from the gaze of the enforcers of the law. This was a situation that was only markedly changed by the Irish immigration of the nineteenth century, when people left Ireland in their millions to escape famine and poverty. The penal laws were repealed with the *Catholic Emancipation Act* of 1829.

In 1831 there were '35,554 Irish in Glasgow, the majority of whom were Catholic' (Skinnider 1967: 14). In the last 30 years of the nineteenth century, the Catholic population of Glasgow 'rose by over 100,000' (Devine 1999: 379), the majority of whom were Irish or of Irish descent.[22]

Despite the dramatic growth in numbers of Catholics in Scotland over this period and the absence of any religious test in Scottish universities, their presence in higher education was negligible. 'Only two could be found in a sample of 1,779 students between 1860 and 1900, although in 1891 Catholics numbered about 8.5 per cent of the Scottish population' (Brown 1987 in McCrone 1992: 101). 'As the Irish presence grew, the small Scottish Catholic minority feared that the majority Protestant population would equate Irish with Catholic, and their own improving situation would deteriorate' (Finn 1999: 872). This indeed proved to be the case, but the road towards de-Scottifying the Catholics was neither direct nor simple. Nor was it marked by consistent prejudice or bigotry. A few examples suffice to demonstrate this.

> Scottish [Protestant] businessmen and churchmen came together with Roman Catholics to found the Glasgow Catholic Schools Society in 1817. Under a committee composed half of Protestants and half of Catholics, subscriptions were raised and eventually five schools were established by the 1840s. The denominational difficulty was solved by having Catholics appointed as teachers while the Protestant version of the Scriptures was used without comment.
>
> (McCaffrey 1997: 57)

Skinnider (1967) puts the establishment of the five schools as having happened by 1831 (p. 15) but, regardless of the date, the important point is that at this moment in time, parts of the Protestant majority were actively working to help their Catholic brethren. Even Dr Thomas Chalmers, 'the leading Scottish churchman later founder of the Free Church, preached to raise funds for Catholic schools' (Aspinwall 2000: 106). Precisely why these Protestants should have wanted to help the Catholics is open to conjecture. A spirit of charity may well have moved them. They may have, as Hickman (1997) suggests was the case in Liverpool, been moved by a desire to keep the Catholics separate from the Protestants for fear of contamination of the latter by the former and thus been inspired by a sense of anti-Catholicism. The weight of the evidence points to the former: that a spirit of charity moved certain important individuals. In any case, regardless of the subtext, the result was that sufficient funds were raised from Catholics and non-Catholics to establish and maintain a separate Catholic school system until such times as the state assumed funding.

The 1872 *Education Act* made attendance at school compulsory for children aged 5–13 but, unfortunately from the point of view of the Catholics and other non-Presbyterians, 'it required that all religious education given within public schools was according to the reformed faith' (Devine 2000: 101). Devine, Catholic Bishop of

Motherwell and one-time Catholic Chaplain to the University of Glasgow, insists that, far from this being a sectarian provision, it was contrived to 'avoid schools being deprived of all religious education and being overrun by the French rationalism of the time' (ibid.).

The net result was that, as noted earlier, the Catholics and Episcopalians kept their schools out of the public system and, at great sacrifice to themselves, continued to build, maintain and run their separate schools until the 1918 *Education Act* brought the safeguards they required.

In the meantime,

> A separate Catholic Education Committee for Scotland was established by the Church in 1906.... The issue was primarily about equity in the financing of Catholic schools; this would become a struggle about the control of the schools in return for public finance.
>
> (Hickman 1997: 49)

Ten days after the end of the First World War, 'the Education (Scotland) Act 1918 was passed' (Fitzpatrick 1999: 256). That this was passed by a coalition government neatly avoided any one party having to answer to the cries from certain Protestant quarters about this 'Rome on the Rates' (Bruce 2000: 139). Demands by Orangemen in the 1920s that the Act be revised went unheeded even though the Scottish Secretary of State from 1924 to 1929 was the Orangeman Sir John Gilmour (Walker 2000: 127):

> The system established in Scotland in 1918 has been generally deemed successful by the Catholic Church and the State. This is due to the fact that the national education system was structured and organized on the assumption that the preference of the body politic was for segregation. Inevitably, separate schools result in differentiation of the population and this has had repercussions for identity formation.
>
> (Hickman 1997: 51)

Whether Catholic schools should remain in existence has been a subject for political and popular debate ever since these schools entered the public school system. The Labour Party has at times openly advocated their closure; the Scottish National Party has waxed and waned over the issue, moving in its history from being very anti-Catholic to openly courting the Catholic vote. The Conservatives have never been quite sure, despite their one-time links with aspects of Orangism. As for the Liberals, they too have been largely non-committal. Nonetheless, the association which exists between Catholicism and the working class vote is such that any party which attacks Catholic schools per se does so at its peril since not only do Catholics form a substantial minority in the working class but, as McCaffrey (1997: 67) puts it: 'A long history of discrimination, at a popular and institutional level, has made Scottish Catholics (the bulk of them Scoto-Irish) very defensive as regards their separate place within the country's public school system since 1918.'

It is worth mentioning that much of the phlegm expended around Catholic schools has been, and continues to be, done in the Central Lowlands of Scotland. The Highlands and Islands have their Catholic enclaves (such as the Islands of Barra and South Uist), but there was never, it seems, the level of anti-Catholic bitterness which infected parts of the Central Belt. Similar has been said of the north-east of Scotland, where, as Styles (2000) makes very clear, those few Orange marches that have ever taken place have been seen as an invasion by an alien culture. Additionally, in Aberdeen, there is no separate Catholic secondary-school system, the one Catholic secondary having closed in the 1970s with no rumpus at all.

A common point between the areas spared sectarianism is that there was never an influx of Irish immigrants to them. This point alone might make one wonder whether the anti-Catholicism of bodies such as the Loyal Orange Order (or at least of a number of its members) or the 1930s Scottish Protestant League (Bruce 2000) was not in fact a cover for actual anti-Irish feeling, a point underlined by the Northern Irish Protestants who also settled in the Central Belt and pointedly avoided referring to themselves as Irish, preferring British or, at a pinch, Ulstermen (and women).[23]

Centres of power

Central and local government

Until Devolution the ultimate responsibility for education in Scotland lay with the UK Parliament in Westminster. This went as far as the original Scotch Education Department having no statutory Scottish representation and sharing its 'President, Vice-President and Permanent Secretary with the Department of Education for England and Wales' (Skinnider 1967: 87). However, as McPherson and Raab (1988) make clear, until at least the advent of Thatcherism in 1979 it was a partnership, not a dictatorship. Real power was vested in the local authorities (LAs). This meant that in 1965, when the government produced Circular 600, asking LAs to submit plans for the comprehensivisation of their secondary schools, there could only be suggestions of negative consequences for those LAs which resisted (Bell and Grant 1977). In the event, Scotland took to comprehensive schooling in a manner rarely repeated in England (Benn and Chitty 1997).[24] It is, however, arguable the extent to which these 1960s comprehensives were indeed comprehensive or whether they merely operated a form of internal, as opposed to external, selection (Matheson 2000). This is not to say that there was unbridled enthusiasm for comprehensive schools throughout Scotland. Comprehensivisation meant a stark choice for two small but significant groups of schools: selective LA schools which charged nominal fees; and schools which had been funded to 50 per cent of their costs via direct grants from the Scottish Education Department. This meant that these schools had to either enter the public sector entirely and become comprehensive or become independent and seek their own funding. Such was the depth of feeling that in 1967 the issue of comprehensive schools 'almost cost the Labour party its majority in Glasgow for the first time in decades' (Scotland 1969: 212).

The arrival of the Conservative government in 1979 heralded another era of potential clashes between central and local government. In the 1988 *Education Reform Act*, the Conservatives introduced mechanisms in England and Wales whereby the financial and administrative decisions were devolved from local education authorities to schools and their lay governors. It was a virtual certainty that the Scottish Office would quickly follow suit and this it duly did, but not before Strathclyde Regional Council's Director of Education, Frank Pignatelli, had devised his own scheme and convinced teachers, their unions and the headteachers that it was the road to follow. Pignatelli's scheme 'avoided many of the problems south of the border, where funding formulas proved too rigid and encouraged school governors, for example, to remove experienced teachers and replace them with cheap young ones' (Pickard 1999: 230). This left the Scottish Office unable to promote its own scheme since that of Strathclyde was manifestly better. The Pignatelli scheme was not so much greeted by teachers with enthusiasm as seen as a lucky escape. So it is that Scottish headteachers, unlike their English counterparts, did not control the teachers' salaries budget and thus a major area of potential conflict between management and staff was avoided. As far as the Scottish School Boards were concerned, these had very little say over the budget and none at all over discipline in their school as it affects individual staff or pupils. School Boards were abolished by the Scottish Parliament in 2006 and replaced with a two-tier system of Parent Forums and Parent Councils.

However, revenge that arrives late is still revenge and in 1996 the Conservatives enacted legislation which dissolved the Regions. Strathclyde, which contained 40 per cent of Scotland's population, organised a referendum under the auspices of the Electoral Reform Society in which the overwhelming mass of the electorate voted in favour of keeping the Region. The Conservative government, which contained insufficient Scottish MPs in Westminster to fill all the ministerial posts in the Scottish Office, rejected the referendum result as 'invalid'. So much for subsidiarity.

Until 1993, when the *Further and Higher Education Act* came into force, Scotland's universities were the responsibility of the Department of Education[25] in London and not the Scottish Education Department:

> Until the 1990s the universities of Great Britain (but not those of Northern Ireland) were under the oversight of what was essentially an *English* ministry of schooling … while most non-university higher education was handled … in Scotland by the central Scottish Office.
>
> (Bell 2000: 163; original emphasis)

The same Act, applicable in its various ways throughout the UK, removed further education colleges from local authority control and allowed central institutions (a variety of higher education institutions some of which had been created by local authorities) to seek university status. The Act established the Scottish Higher Education Funding Council (SHEFC) for all higher education, while the 'incorporated' further education colleges were funded directly from the Scottish Office. At a stroke, the 1992 Act naturalised the funding of Scottish higher education while breaking the bond that had held further education colleges to their local authorities. Other than the enormous loss of assets which this entailed for the local authorities, it meant that until funding mechanisms were worked out, schools had much less opportunity to collaborate with the colleges. Seeking funding from wherever it could be had added impetus to moves by further education colleges to offer higher education. This had long been done to some extent in the form of Higher National Diplomas. Incorporation meant the possibility of seeking funding from SHEFC for degree courses validated by a cooperative university. The result was that 'in 1998–99, 28% of higher education students attended courses in further education institutions' (Scottish Executive 2000a: n.p.).

In 1999, the first Scottish parliament since 1707 opened for business. As such, responsibility for education in all forms and at all levels passed to the Scottish Executive Education Department.

The new parliament found itself, unlike its Westminster parent, with a coalition government, the Liberal Democrat part of which was vowed to remove all student fees. Indeed, only the Labour Party seemed in favour of the fees. The Liberal Democrats made an investigation into the financing of Scottish students a condition for remaining in the coalition with Labour. This immediately created problems in the Scottish Executive's relationship with Westminster and could easily have led to a constitutional crisis. Nonetheless, a review of student finance was established under the chairmanship of Andrew Cubie (Scottish Office 1999a). Cubie's report recommended the abolition of student fees and a revamp of the basis of student funding. The Scottish Executive, for its part, announced in January 2000 that tuition fees would be abolished from August 2000 for eligible Scottish and EU students. Scottish students studying outwith Scotland would still have to pay fees on the same basis as other UK students. Fees for further education in Scotland were also abolished, though again only for Scottish resident students and those from non-UK EU countries. The only concession made to non-Scottish UK students was that they would no longer have to pay for the final year of a four-year degree. The future financing of these initiatives was to be through *The Graduate Endowment Scheme for Higher Education* (Scottish Executive 2000b), but this was abolished in 2008 and replaced by a system of loans and bursaries. Notable is the fact that the maximum fees which a student ordinarily resident in Scotland (or the EU or Switzerland but not other parts of the UK) can be charged are significantly lower than the maximum fees allowed in England.

The General Teaching Council for Scotland

In addition to comprehensivisation, 1965 was also notable for the creation of the General Teaching Council for Scotland (GTC), modelled on the General Medical Council and with very similar powers and responsibilities.

> The General Teaching Council for Scotland is a statutory body whose functions include reviewing the standards of education, training and fitness to teach of entrants to the teaching profession; advising the Secretary of State for Scotland on teacher supply; accrediting courses of education and training of teachers in

relevant institutions; keeping a register of teachers; deciding whether to use its disciplinary powers to withdraw or refuse registration.

(Smith 1997: 42)

Despite the GTC's range of powers, Smith (1997) asserts that 'it is not an exaggeration to suggest that most Scottish teachers know little and care less about the GTC' (p. 42). While this may be true on a day-to-day basis, when push comes to shove, Scottish teachers are not only aware of the GTC but are often very happy that it exists. It is, for example, largely due to the GTC that Scotland does not have a national curriculum *à l'anglaise*, or that other English notion *School Centred Initial Teacher Training*, despite government attempts in both cases to impose these initiatives on an unwilling Scottish school system.

The GTC, of course, builds on the traditions surrounding the Scottish teacher and Scottish education. 'Because education is generally seen as lying at the heart of the Scottish educational culture, the teacher has long been seen as a cultural leader' (Paterson 1998a: 282). Part of this involves the trust that the Scottish public has long shown in its teachers.

Empowering parents

That trust was evident when School Boards (a form of Board of Governors nominally based on a Danish model with an in-built majority of parents) came into existence in 1989. The Boards had the possibility of organising a referendum of parents with a view to leaving the control of the LA and becoming self-governing and hence answerable only to the Scottish Office Education Department. In the event, only two schools, one primary and one secondary, succeeded in becoming self-governing. One then voted in 1999 to discontinue itself (there being no mechanism until 2000 to allow a school to return to LA control) and the LA (Highland Council) opened a notionally new school on the same site (Scottish Office 1999b). As regards the other, the *Standards in Scotland's Schools etc. Act* (2000: paras 14–20) allowed its self-governing status to be ended without the Board and parents having to vote to discontinue the school. In 2001 the school in question, St Mary's Episcopal Primary School in Dunblane, was forcibly returned to LA control.

Boards were required to maintain the parent majority and, if a School Board failed to fill sufficient parent places as they fell vacant, it had to fold (although the *Standards in Scotland's Schools etc. Act* (2000) allowed some vacancies to be filled by co-option of parent members). Such was the case of the Board of which I was Chairman[26] from 1989 to 1991. After two years, half the parent members were due to stand for re-election. In the event, there were no candidates and so the Board folded. This need to establish and maintain the parent majority initially caused many schools to fail to form a board. However, after nine years 'Of the eligible schools at May 1998, School Boards were formed in 82 per cent of primary, 97 per cent of secondary and 61 per cent of special education [local] authority schools' (Scottish Office 1998).

It remains unknown whether those schools without a Board remained so as witness to the trust in teachers or to the apathy of the parents. In any case, the *Scottish Schools*

(Parental Involvement) Act 2006 abolished School Boards and replaced them with Parent Councils, which appear much more organic to the school concerned and to its particular circumstances than did the School Boards which were felt by many of those I encountered in my time on School Boards (both as a parent member and as a staff member) to be an alien imposition.

By way of a conclusion

With the advent of the Scottish Parliament, Scotland, its people and their education system entered a phase unknown for nearly three centuries. For the first time since the Union of the Parliaments, it was representatives of Scottish constituencies and they alone who legislated on the country's education and how it would shape up to the always uncertain future. It was in Scotland's parliament that the débâcle of the 2000 SQA examination results, whereby several thousand candidates received incorrect certificates, was discussed and re-discussed. It was for the Scottish Parliament to find solutions to avoid this occurring again in the future.

It was Scotland which signed up to instruments such as the *European Charter on Minority Languages* and it was Scotland which enacted at least some of the provisions of this Charter. This was the same Scotland which has lived through most, I would say, of its sectarian past. It began to define itself without reference to that customary 'Other', the English, and to look to its own past with a view to making better sense of the present. In many respects, it was living through what Fanon (1963) sees as a precursor for independence. It was using its past as a positive attribute, rather than as a millstone, and moving towards defining, in so far as any of us can, its future.

In short, Scottish education was having its agenda set by Scots. The apron-strings were stretching and have since stretched further. How much longer until they break? Perhaps we shall know the answer in the light of the Referendum on Scottish independence, whatever the outcome.

Notes

1. Nigel Grant (1998) points out that 'as the year then began in March and the University was officially founded in January, it was 1450 by the old calendar, 1451 by the new' (p. 1).
2. Anyone who tries to make a distinction between education and entertainment doesn't know the first thing about either – Marshall McLuhan (1911–1980).
3. The corresponding Act for England was passed in 1875 but, as in Scotland, did not prevent overt discrimination continuing against women for many years.
4. What or who is or was Jock Tamson is rarely tackled. I have come across writings in which this was a folk name for God. In others, the name belonged to Satan. In yet others it was a term for a penis.
5. Such as in Luke 19: 11–27.
6. The Lowlands are not just the Central Belt. They extend from Ayrshire (at least) in the south-west through the Central Belt and up the east coast to Aberdeen.
7. Notably, Burns was never quite able to keep Scots separate from English in his writings. He drifts from one to the other, and in attempting to write Scots makes liberal use of apostrophes to show where letters have been glottalised from English.
8. Stanley Nisbett's 1958 report for the Scottish Council for Research in Education on nursery education (quoted in Scotland 1969: 198) states that 'the demand far exceeds the supply, which at present provides nursery education for only one child in twenty'.

9. For simplicity's sake, I will refer to vocational education, rather than try to distinguish between education and training. In any case, the philosophical arguments that distinguish the two are often exercises in the splitting of very fine hairs. See, for example, Winch (2000).

10. Oddly enough, reading is seldom mentioned even though this is arguably a more important skill than is writing. Even in older texts, these two, quite different skills are frequently conflated.

11. Scotland has never had Local Education Authorities in the manner of England and Wales. Following the 1872 Act, there were ad hoc School Boards established and these gave way to Local Authority Education Departments in 1918.

12. The General Assembly is in effect the parliament of the Church of Scotland. It meets once a year (usually) for a few weeks at a time and will debate any and all issues on which the Church wishes to comment.

13. Having started as the Scotch Education Department in 1872 (Bell and Grant 1977), it was variously known as the Scottish Education Department, the Scottish Office Education Department, the Scottish Office Education and Industry Department. Under the devolved Scottish Parliament, it is now Education Scotland.

14. Such was the theory. The Scots, however, were so imbued with English nomenclature that right up until the demise of O-Grades in the late 1980s, they were regularly referred to as O-Levels.

15. Both my paternal grandparents were native speakers of Gaelic – one being from the village of Gravir on the Isle of Lewis and the other being from the village of Applecross in Wester Ross. Their six children, all but the eldest born in Glasgow, grew up hearing Gaelic spoken in the family home although my grandparents were regularly reminded (by teachers *inter alia*) that teaching children Gaelic would retard their acquisition of English. The end result was that the grandparents eventually stopped addressing their children in Gaelic and their last two children, although they understood the language, never learned to speak it as children. Neither grandparent ever learned to read Gaelic.

16. *Higher Still* replaces the previous regime for fifth- and sixth-year pupils with an attempt at a coherent course framework. Students can undertake the programme at any of five levels, depending on their previous attainment, and also progress between levels.

17. For Montgomery (1995), 'a language is a dialect with an army and a navy' (p. 186).

18. The interested reader is directed to the various websites dedicated to Scots, most notably that of the Scottish Language Resource Centre at http://www/pkc.gov.uk/slrc. See also Matheson and Matheson (1998, 2000a, 2000b).

19. Protestant or Catholic. Catholics might also be termed Tims. Tim and Dan were judged 'typical' Irish names while Billy refers to William of Orange.

20. The Free Church has tended over recent years to see Catholics more as misguided than as evil. The Free Presbyterians, for their part, are known to refer to the Pope as the Anti-Christ and to consign all dead Catholics directly to Hell, 'not out of any especial dislike, but simply because that's where all Catholics automatically go' (Reilly 2000: 30).

21. Towards the end of the Reformation, Cantons and Communes declared themselves Catholic or Protestant and agreed not to seek to convert each other. See Matheson (1992).

22. For detailed discussion of the Irish in Scotland, see Connell (2000).

23. The various protests under the banners of *Ulster is British* serve to underline this point. However, Northern Ireland is only part of Ulster. Ulster consists of Counties Cavan, Donegal and Monaghan in the Republic of Ireland and Counties Antrim, Armagh, Down, Fermanagh, Derry and Tyrone in Northern Ireland.

24. Duffield (1998) insists that 'the more complete comprehensive reorganisation of secondary schools in Scotland prevented some of the excesses of market competition between schools for a favourable pupil intake which emerged in England' (p. 2).

25. Like its Scottish counterpart, this Westminster department has been through a multitude of names.

26. While Chairman is not exactly politically correct, this was the term that the *School Boards (Scotland) Act 1988* employed.

References

Anderson, R. (1999) The history of Scottish education, pre-1980, in T. Bryce and W. Humes (eds) *Scottish Education*. Edinburgh: Edinburgh University Press.

Apple, M.W. (1993) *Official Knowledge*. London and New York: Routledge.

Aspinwall, B. (2000) Faith of our Fathers living still … the time warp or Woof! Woof!, in T.M. Devine (ed.) *Scotland's Shame? Bigotry and Sectarianism in Modern Scotland*. Edinburgh: Mainstream.

Bell, R. (2000) Scotland's universities, *Comparative Education* 36 (2): 163–175.

Bell, R. and Grant, N. (1977) *Patterns of Education in the British Isles*. London: Unwin Education Books.

Benn, C. and Chitty, C. (1997) *Thirty Years On: Is Comprehensive School Alive and Well or Struggling to Survive?* Harmondsworth: Penguin.

Bruce, S. (2000) Comparing Scotland and Northern Ireland, in T.M. Devine (ed.) *Scotland's Shame? Bigotry and Sectarianism in Modern Scotland*. Edinburgh: Mainstream.

Connell, L. (2000) The Irish in Scotland and the construction of Scottish national identity. Unpublished PhD thesis, University of Sussex.

Crowther, J. and Tett, L. (1997) Inferiorism in Scotland: the politics of literacy north of the border. Paper presented to the 27th annual SCUTREA conference.

Devine, J. (2000) A Lanarkshire perspective on bigotry in Scottish society, in T.M. Devine (ed.) *Scotland's Shame? Bigotry and Sectarianism in Modern Scotland*. Edinburgh: Mainstream.

Devine, T.M. (1999) *The Scottish Nation 1700–2000*. London: Penguin.

Dobie, T. (1967) The Scottish Leaving Certificate, 1888–1908, in T.R. Bone (ed.) *Studies in the History of Scottish Education 1872–1939*. London: University of London Press.

Duffield, J. (1998) Unequal opportunities, or don't mention the (class) war. Paper presented to the Scottish Educational Research Association Conference, Dundee, 24–26 September.

Duncan, R. (1999) A critical history of the Workers' Educational Association in Scotland 1903–1993, in J. Crowther, I. Martin and M. Shaw (eds), *Popular Education and Social Movements in Scotland Today*. Leicester: NIACE.

Fanon, F. (1963) *The Wretched of the Earth*. Harmondsworth: Penguin.

Findlay, I. (1973) *Education in Scotland*. Newton Abbot: David & Charles.

Finn, G. (1999) 'Sectarianism' and Scottish education, in T. Bryce and W. Humes (eds), *Scottish Education*. Edinburgh: Edinburgh University Press.

Fitzpatrick, T. (1999) Catholic education in Scotland, in T. Bryce and W. Humes (eds), *Scottish Education*. Edinburgh: Edinburgh University Press.

Gikandi, S. (1996) *Maps of Englishness*. New York: Columbia.

Goodman, J. (1999) Undermining or building up the nation? Elizabeth Hamilton (1758–1816), national identities and an authoritative role for women educationists. *History of Education* 28 (3): 279–296.

Grant, N. (1984) Education for multicultural societies, in T. Corner (ed.), *Education in Multicultural Societies*. Beckenham: Croom Helm.

Grant, N. (1985) Education in Great Britain: a Scottish viewpoint. *Education Today* 35 (2): 17–27.

Grant, N. (1998) Universities in Scotland in the era of late modernity. Unpublished paper.

Hall, V. (1994) *Further Education in the United Kingdom*. 2nd edn. London: Collins Educational/Staff College.

Hickman, M. (1997) Constructing the nation, segregating the Irish: the education of Irish Catholics in nineteenth-century Britain. *Aspects of Education* 54: 33–54.

Kelly, T. (1962) *A History of Adult Education in Great Britain*. Liverpool: Liverpool University Press.

Kidd, C. (1993) *Subverting Scotland's Past: Scottish Whig Historians and the Creation of an Anglo-British Identity: 1689–1830*. Cambridge: Cambridge University Press.

Lynch, M. (1992) *Scotland: A New History*. London: Pimlico.

Macafee, C. (1988) Some studies in the Glasgow vernacular. Unpublished PhD thesis, Glasgow University.

McCaffrey, J. (1997) Education and national identity: the Scoto-Irish experiences and aspirations. *Aspects of Education* 54: 55–71.

McClure, J.D. (1988) *Why Scots matters*. Edinburgh: The Saltire Society.

McCrone, D. (1992) *Understanding Scotland: The Sociology of a Stateless Nation*. London: Routledge.

Mackintosh, M. (1962) *Education in Scotland: Yesterday and Today*. Glasgow: Robert Gibson.

MacLeod, S. (1989) *Language death in Scotland*. Unpublished PhD thesis, University of Aberdeen.

McPherson, A. and Raab, C. (1988) *Governing Education: A Sociology of Policy Since 1945.* Edinburgh: Edinburgh University Press.

Matheson, C. (1999) Access to education, in D. Matheson and I. Grosvenor (eds), *An Introduction to the Study of Education.* London: David Fulton.

Matheson, C. and Matheson, D. (2000a) Education and cultural identity, in C. Matheson and D. Matheson (eds), *Educational Issues in the Learning Age.* London: Continuum.

Matheson, C. and Matheson, D. (2000b) Languages of Scotland: culture and the classroom. *Comparative Education* 36 (2): 211–221.

Matheson, D. (1992) Post-compulsory Education in Suisse romande. Unpublished PhD thesis, University of Glasgow.

Matheson, D. (2000) Scottish education: myths and mists. *Oxford Studies in Comparative Education* 9 (2): 63–84.

Matheson, D. and Matheson, C. (1998) Problématique régionale et questions linguistiques en Ecosse, in S. Perez (ed.), *La Mosaïque linguistique: regards éducatifs sur les pays industrialisés.* Paris: L'Harmattan.

Menzies, J. (1991) An investigation of attitudes to Scots and Glasgow dialect among secondary school pupils, in J.D. McClure *Scottish Language* 10 (Aberdeen) available at www.ndirect.co.uk/~love/menzie1.htm, accessed 24 Janaury 2000.

Montgomery, M. (1995) *An Introduction to Language and Society.* London: Routledge.

Munn, P. (1995) Teacher involvement in curriculum policy in Scotland. *Educational Review* 47 (2): 209–217.

O'Hagan, A. (2000) Into the ferment, in T.M. Devine (ed.), *Scotland's Shame? Bigotry and Sectarianism in Modern Scotland.* Edinburgh: Mainstream.

Osborne, G. (1968) *Change in Scottish Education.* London: Longman.

Paterson, L. (1998a) The civic activisms of Scottish teachers: explanations and consequences. *Oxford Review of Education* 24 (3): 279–302.

Paterson, L. (1998b) You take the Higher road. *Times Education Supplement Scotland,* 9 October.

Pickard, W. (1999) The history of Scottish education, 1980 to the present day, in T. Bryce and W. Humes (eds), *Scottish Education.* Edinburgh: Edinburgh University Press.

Pole, T. ([1814] 1968) *A History of the Origin and Progress of Adult Schools.* London: Woburn Press.

Reilly, P. (2000) Kicking with the left foot: being Catholic in Scotland, in T.M. Devine (ed.), *Scotland's Shame? Bigotry and Sectarianism in Modern Scotland.* Edinburgh: Mainstream.

Scotland, J. (1969) *The History of Scottish Education, vol. 2.* London: University of London Press.

Scotland, J. (1970) *The History of Scottish Education, vol 1.* London: University of London Press.

Scottish Education Department (1972) *Public Education in Scotland.* Edinburgh: HMSO.

Scottish Executive (2000a) *Students in Higher Education in Scotland: 1998–99,* Press release SE 2087/00, 27 July.

Scottish Executive (2000b) *Scotland the Learning Nation: Helping Students,* available at www.scotland.gov.uk/consultations/lifelonglearning/stln-00.asp, accessed 22 April 2014.

Scottish Office (n.d.) *Gaelic in Scotland Factsheet,* available at www.scotland.gov.uk/library/documents6/eid_ach_gisf_index.htm, accessed 24 January 2009.

Scottish Office (1998) *School Boards in Scottish Schools: May 1998,* Press Release 2505/98, 30 November, available at www.scotland.gov.uk/news/releas98_3/pr2505.htm, accessed 22 April 2014.

Scottish Office (1999a) *Andrew Cubie Nominated as Chair of Student Finance Review,* News Release 1338/99, 28 June, available at www.scotland.gov.uk/news/releas99_6/pr1338.htm, accessed 22 April 2014.

Scottish Office (1999b) *Minister Welcomes Return of 'Opted Out' School,* Press Release SE0192/99, 30 July, available at www.scotland.gov.uk/news/releas99_7/se0192.htm, accessed 22 April 2014.

Skinnider, M. (1967) Catholic elementary education in Glasgow 1818–1918, in T.R. Bone (ed.), *Studies in the History of Scottish Education 1872–1939.* London: University of London Press.

Smith, R. (1997) The General Teaching Council: the Scottish experience. *Education Review* 11 (1): 42–45.

Smith, S.J. (2000) Retaking the register: women's higher education in Glasgow and beyond, c. 1796–1845. *Gender and History* 12 (2): 310–335.

Styles, S. (2000) The non-sectarian culture of north-east Scotland, in T.M. Devine (ed.), *Scotland's Shame? Bigotry and Sectarianism in Modern Scotland.* Edinburgh: Mainstream.

Sutherland, M. (2000) Problems of diversity in policy and practice: Celtic languages in the United Kingdom. *Comparative Education* 36 (2): 199–209.

Walker, G. (2000) Sectarian tensions in Scotland: social and cultural dynamics and the politics of perception, in T.M. Devine (ed.), *Scotland's Shame? Bigotry and Sectarianism in Modern Scotland.* Edinburgh: Mainstream.

Watt, J. (1999) Pre-five education, in T. Bryce and W. Humes (eds), *Scottish Education.* Edinburgh: Edinburgh University Press.

Wilkinson, J.E. (1999) Pre-school education in the UK, in D. Matheson and I. Grosvenor (eds), *An Introduction to the Study of Education.* London: David Fulton.

Winch, C. (2000) Education and training, in C. Matheson and D. Matheson (eds), *Educational Issues in the Learning Age.* London: Continuum.

Young, J. (1979) *The Rousing of the Scottish Working Class 1770–1933.* London: Croom Helm.

Education in Wales

Alison Murphy

For England, see Wales.

Stephen Gorard (2000)

Introduction

In recent years with the advent of devolution, the education systems in Wales and England have become increasingly divergent in terms of curricula policy and practice. Assessment, particularly the abolition of SATs in Wales, represents further contrasts with the English system. Wales is a bilingual country which has over the past 60 years witnessed a renaissance in Welsh and Welsh-medium education (Lewis 2006) and the promotion of the Welsh language currently has a prominent role in educational policy. Therefore this chapter aims to explore education in Wales historically from the sixteenth century onwards, as well as current educational provision including Welsh-medium education.

The early foundations of education in Wales

Prior to the sixteenth century, there was little or no access to schooling in Wales. Only the landowning classes had the means to afford to send their children to schools such as Oxford and Cambridge across the border in England, or to fund their entry into the Church or legal profession. However, during the sixteenth century there was a significant development in the education system in Wales in the form of 'the creation of a network of grammar schools' (Jones and Roderick 2003: 12). The establishment of these schools was in response to the emerging middle classes of merchants and professional people who wanted their children to become educated. According to Jones and Roderick (2003), the development of these schools in Wales was delayed compared to their English counterparts. These grammar schools only catered for boys; they relied on teaching by rote and learning was regimented, teaching the classical languages such as Latin, seen as a prerequisite for becoming an educated gentleman.

Cromwell's government came to power in 1649 and around this time, concern was expressed regarding the education system in Wales in comparison to England. At this time 60 'free' schools were established. These schools followed a similar curriculum to that of the grammar schools and there was no provision for education via the medium of Welsh. Unfortunately, 'free' schools had a very short life span and there were only 21 left by 1660 (Jones and Roderick 2003).

In the eighteenth century, as part of the charity schools movement, Thomas Gouge was instrumental in setting up the Welsh Trust. This initiative provided a fund to set up Welsh-language schools across Wales using the Bible and other religious texts to teach literacy skills. The Bible had been translated into Welsh in 1588, which was a landmark for education through the medium of Welsh. With similar aims to the Welsh Trust, the Society for the Promotion of Christian Knowledge was created and this generated a system of charity schools throughout Wales. The curriculum consisted of literacy skills, and boys were taught arithmetic and girls were taught needlework, spinning and weaving. Schools were inspected on an annual basis.

Another significant character in the development of education in Wales was Griffith Jones. He set up a series of small village schools run by teachers who were itinerant. These were known as Circulating Schools. These schools were similar to those set up via the Society for the Promotion of Christian Knowledge and used similar texts. Funding was the primary factor in the dissolution of these schools; however, the result of this expansion of schooling was to inspire a desire for learning. Thomas Charles is also seen as a heroic figure in the history of Welsh schooling, 'whose name has always been associated with the Sunday school movement in Wales' (Jones and Roderick 2003: 43), and also in terms of the dissemination of the Welsh Bible in the eighteenth century. Sunday schools offered basic tuition around the scriptures; this again fuelled the appetite for learning and was also significant in supporting the Welsh language.

In 1811, the National Society was set up; this organisation had similar ideals to that of the Society for the Promotion of Christian Knowledge. The main ethos was the promotion of education through the scriptures of the Anglican Church. As in the schools funded by the Society for the Promotion of Christian Knowledge, reading, writing and simple arithmetic were taught as well as some craft. Discipline was also a fundamental element of these schools. By 1833 there were 146 National Society schools in Wales. Alongside this there were 15 schools that were funded via the British and Foreign Society, which promoted non-sectarian education; this organisation did not have the benefits of the established Anglican dioceses and the landowner support for this type of religious-based education.

State intervention in the school system

In 1833 the government began to provide funding for the erection of schools. This funding was shared between the National Society and the British and Foreign Society. Again the National Society, with its diocesan system, was able to take advantage of this influx of money and set up a further 231 schools in Wales. Non-conformist schools also began to develop, with approximately 107 in existence by 1847.

The year 1847 was a landmark one for education in Wales. In 1846, William Williams tabled a measure before the House of Commons calling for an investigation into the education system in Wales. This came about after a period of social unrest, and the government appointed three commissioners to visit the length and breadth of Wales to explore Welsh education. The appointed commissioners were non-Welsh speaking and Anglican. They completed their review and the subsequent reports were printed in three volumes commonly referred to as the Blue Books. These documents were translated into Welsh and, according to Jones and Roderick (2003: 60), were viewed by Non-conformists as 'an English and Church inspired attack on the Welsh, and it was soon to be known as *Brad y Lyfrau Gleision* (The Treason of the Blue Books)'. This report was damning not only about the state of education in Wales, but in addition to this, commented on the religious and moral standing of the Welsh nation as well as viewing the Welsh language as a drawback. Subsequently, this affected the consciousness of the nation and 'ordinary Welsh people began to believe that they could only improve themselves socially through education and the ability to speak and communicate in English' (The National Library of Wales 2014) The Welsh Not was associated with this period in Welsh history. This practice was to give a stick or a plaque to any child heard speaking Welsh in school. When school was finished the child left holding the Welsh Not was punished. According to Davies (2007) this was not an actual government policy and not as widespread as first thought. It was used in National and British schools, but attendance at these schools was voluntary and therefore if the headmaster was implementing the policy of the Welsh Not, it was with parental approval.

The next milestone was the *Education Act* of 1870. At this time there were 300 Non-conformist schools in Wales and over 1,000 Anglican schools. The Act provided education for all children up to the age of 13. The National Society (Anglican) schools and the British Society Non-conformist schools would continue to have funding from the government. The School Board system was set up and Board schools were established in areas where provision was inadequate. School Boards had to pay the fees of poor children attending denominational establishments. British schools became incorporated into the Board system, but Anglican and Roman Catholic schools chose to remain separate from this system, which resulted in a decrease in their funding.

In 1876, the next *Education Act* reinforced the principle of regular attendance and by the Education Act 1880 confirmed that school attendance was compulsory up to the age of ten. County joint education committees were established via the *Welsh Intermediate Education Act* of 1889. According to Jones (2006: 268), this was 'the first significant Act of Parliament to apply to Wales alone since the seventeenth century'. This created an education system that was unique to Wales. Education was now funded in Wales via public money, something which occurred in Wales sooner than in England. The county schools (later called grammar schools) were funded by a combination of rates, grants from the treasury, fees and endowments. However, in 1891, elementary education became free of charge and by 1899 the school leaving age had increased to 12. In 1902 Local Education Authorities (LEAs) were created and these organisations adopted responsibility for both elementary and intermediate schooling. Church schools were now termed as non-provided schools and Board schools were provided schools, according to their funding mechanisms. Jones (2006: 269) terms the events of 1904–1905 as the 'Welsh Revolt'. Again, the issue here was funding, when most of the LEAs in

Wales refused to implement the 1902 *Education Act*, which called for increased funds for denominational schools (non-provided schools). The government response to this Welsh insurgence was to introduce a further *Education Act* in 1905, which compelled the Welsh LEAs to come into line. This became known as the 'Coercion of Wales Act', but the subsequent political regime withdrew this Act when they came to power.

The school leaving age was raised to 14 in 1918, and by 1944 the *Education Act* steered through Parliament by R.A. Butler saw the introduction of free secondary education for all. As a result of this Act, the school leaving age was again raised, this time to 15, and the 11-plus examination was maintained. This effectively created a two-tier system of grammar schools and secondary modern schools. The former accommodated those who had succeeded in passing the 11-plus, and the latter providing a more technical education for secondary-age pupils. Prior to the 1944 Act, pupils who were unsuccessful at the 11-plus had to stay at junior school.

Finally, in 1972, the school leaving age was raised to 16, concurrent to today's practice. During the 1960s many LEAs abandoned the two-tier system of secondary education in favour of comprehensive schools, which were intended to cater for all abilities. By the end of the 1970s the 11-plus was almost obsolete in Wales. The 1944 Act remained the main framework for state education until the *Education Reform Act 1988*. Schools in both the primary and secondary sectors were given the opportunity to opt out of LEA control and to receive their funding from central government.

In 1997 a referendum on devolution in Wales was held and, subsequently, the people of Wales chose by a narrow majority to opt for separation from the UK Parliament in key areas such as education and health. In 1998 the *Government Act of Wales* established the National Assembly in Wales and thus the power to create a separate education system in Wales. According to the National Assembly for Wales (2012) this was in contrast to the primary law-making powers given to the Scottish Parliament. However, in 2011, following a further referendum, the people of Wales voted in favour of a further extension of law-making powers

Education in Wales post-1998

As a result of devolution and the establishment of the Welsh Assembly Government in 1999, there has been a continuous divergence in educational policy between England and Wales. Prior to this time, education in the twentieth century was very much an England and Wales affair, with Scotland and Northern Ireland already having different systems. According to the Welsh government (2011) only 2 per cent of children in Wales attend independent schools, which is much lower than the percentage in England. Therefore the provision in Wales at secondary level does not reflect the same diversity as in England. The Education (Wales) Measure 2011 has prevented the further development of foundation schools in Wales. Foundation schools are run by the governing body and they own the land and buildings and subsequently employ staff. Foundations schools set their own admissions criteria. Currently the policy of school academies in England is not being considered as a model for Wales, according to the *Times Educational Supplement* (2013).

Curricula and testing, in particular, have reflected the most significant departure from the 'English' model, especially in the primary sector with the initial abolition of SAT testing in Wales and then the introduction of the Foundation Phase curriculum in 2008. In Wales SATs were replaced by internal teacher assessments between 2002 and 2004. There is some debate regarding the consistency of these teacher assessments at a national level compared to the more standardised measures at the end of secondary school, i.e. GCSE grades. More recently, however, there has been somewhat of a U-turn on this non-testing policy, with the introduction of reading and numeracy tests for children aged 6–14 years. There is also the current debate regarding GCSE provision. In September 2012, Michael Gove, the Education Secretary for the UK government announced the intention to introduce the English Baccalaureate Certificate, which will initially replace GCSEs in English, Maths and Science. This will then later be extended to other subject areas such as history, geography and languages. The new system will revert to a more exam-based system as characterised by the previous O-level provision, whereby assessment consisted of one examination at the end of the course. Leighton Andrew, the current Education Minister in Wales, called these plans a 'backward step', although GCSE provision in Wales is also under review.

Primary curriculum

Up until 2008 the primary curriculum in Wales was concurrent with the English counterpart with the exception of the *Curriculum Cymreig*. The Curriculum Cymreig was introduced in 1989 in order to reflect the various linguistic, cultural, social, historical and geographical contexts in Wales. The Welsh Assembly Government introduced updated guidance in 2003 to identify ways in which schools could promote the Welsh dimension throughout all subject areas and 'develop whole school approaches so that the Curriculum Cymreig is an essential part of the school's ethos' (ACCAC 2003: 3). ESTYN (2005) produced an evaluation of the progress made by schools in implementing the ACCAC guidance on the Curriculum Cymreig from the Early Years to Key Stage 3. This report states that 'Pupils are developing a good knowledge, skill and understanding of the way in which historical events, people and landscapes have influenced artists, poets and authors in various parts of Wales' (ESTYN 2005: 5). The Curriculum Cymreig aims to foster a sense of belonging, place and heritage in pupils being educated in Wales, and therefore may be a contributory factor in the development of their national identity.

In 2008 an even greater departure was seen in the form of the Foundation Phase Curriculum (Welsh Assembly Government 2008). This particular curriculum initiative was set out in the Welsh Assembly Government document *The Learning Country* (2001). This new, often seen by some as radical, introduction of a play-based curriculum for children aged 3–7 years would signal the move away from the more formal structure of the National Curriculum towards a more creative, discovery-based learning approach.

The Foundation Phase Curriculum (Welsh Assembly Government 2008) is underpinned by experiential learning and active involvement. Findings from the EPPE project (Sylva *et al.* 2003), which focused on preschool education, revealed the need for provision in the early years to focus on informal learning coupled with meaningful interactions with practitioners. Based on this approach and with influences from Scandinavian curricula, the Welsh Assembly Government proposed a curriculum whereby well-being coupled with personal and social development formed the core of early years provision. Wyn Siencyn and Thomas (2007: 149) state that this new play-based model of learning can 'help children learn how to learn; develop thinking skills; and acquire positive attitudes to lifelong learning'. However, Aasen and Waters (2006) argue that the term well-being is not clearly defined within curriculum documentation and the methods to be used in the classroom to promote well-being in the classroom are not obvious. This could therefore lead to ambiguity and individual interpretations of the curriculum.

Outdoor play and learning was another key feature of the Foundation Phase Curriculum (2008). The outdoors is seen as an integral part of the learning environment so children in Wales would experience a range of cross-curricular learning opportunities. Indoor and outdoor learning would combine to create a homogenous learning experience. Waller (2007), like Aasen and Waters (2006), questions the indistinct nature of the curriculum guidance. He maintains that 'There is no clear guidance on outdoor pedagogy' (Waller 2007: 4) and that practitioners may have different perceptions of outdoor spaces and may not understand their role in facilitating meaningful play in these spaces. Overall, the adoption of a play-based curriculum with well-being and learning outdoors identified as key themes has required practitioners to assess and reflect on the way they interact with children and initiate learning encounters in the early years.

Initially the curriculum was introduced following a pilot study which was conducted in 41 statutory and non-statutory settings throughout Wales in 2004. A review of the pilot study was carried out in 2006 by Siraj-Blatchford *et al.* Key recommendations included making sure there was adult-guided learning to offer appropriate challenge as well as prioritising language and literacy experiences. Eventually, the curriculum rolled out to a further 42 schools in 2007 and was fully introduced in 2008.

There are eight areas of learning:

1. personal and social development
2. well-being and cultural diversity
3. language, literacy and communication skills
4. mathematical development
5. Welsh language development
6. knowledge and understanding of the world
7. physical development
8. creative development.

Assessment in the Foundation Phase is primarily through observational methods either on an individual basis or as part of a group. Initial assessments are carried out within a six-week time frame, i.e. within six weeks of their entry into the Foundation Phase. This will form a baseline assessment and will then be followed by ongoing formative assessment.

A review of the Foundation Phase is currently being carried out by a team of academics from various organisations in conjunction with WISERD (Wales Institute of Social & Economic Research). This study will take into account the views of practitioners, parents and children. It will focus primarily on the implementation of the Foundation Phase, the impact of the Foundation Phase and create an evaluation framework for the future tracking of outputs and outcomes of the Foundation Phase. It remains to be seen whether the innovative play-based learning agenda is meeting the needs of all concerned in early childhood education in Wales.

Welsh-medium education in the twentieth and twenty-first centuries

Historically in Wales children have been taught through the medium of Welsh since the translation of the Bible into the Welsh language in 1588. However, during the nineteenth century children in some schools were punished for speaking Welsh as a result of government policy which deemed speaking Welsh to be disadvantageous. In the first part of the twentieth century Welsh-medium schools were predominantly set up in areas where Welsh was the first language, mainly in the north and west of the country. The first state Welsh-medium primary was established in 1947 in Llanelli and the first Welsh-medium secondary school opened in 1956. However, from the 1960s there was a demand for Welsh-medium education in traditionally non-Welsh-speaking areas. Jones (1997: 393) describes the second half of the century as witnessing 'an unprecedented expansion of bilingual education in Wales'. Schools where education was taught via the medium of Welsh were often termed as *Ysgolion Cymraeg* (Welsh schools).

In 1988 Welsh became a core subject of the National Curriculum in Welsh-medium schools and a foundation subject in schools where children were taught in English. This raised the status of the language and enshrined it into the compulsory education framework. Devolution in 1999 signified a new direction for Wales, in that education now came under the remit of the newly formed Welsh Assembly Government. In 2003, recognising the need to boost the proportion of Welsh speakers, the Welsh Assembly Government set targets for a 5 per cent increase by 2011. Iaith Pawb (Welsh Assembly Government 2003: 3) affirms the Welsh language as 'an integral part of our national identity … and an essential and enduring component in the history, culture and social fabric of our nation. We must respect that inheritance and work to ensure that it is not lost for future generations'. The Welsh language, according to data collected in the 2001 census, is witnessing resurgence in the numbers of Welsh speakers. The census reported an increase from 18.5 per cent in 1991 to 20 per cent in 2001. Aitchison and Carter (2004) attribute the increase of Welsh speakers to numbers of school age pupils now identified as competent Welsh speakers. Thus educational policy has had and continues to have a key role in the revival of the Welsh language.

According to Redknap (2006) the substantial rise in pupils educated via the medium of Welsh can be attributed to those children entering Welsh-medium education from homes where Welsh is not the first language. These children are taught using the immersion model, whereby the children are immersed in the language. Most pupils coming from English-speaking homes generally enter Welsh-medium education in the early years. Johnson and Swain (1997) define the immersion method as consisting of several core features including instruction through the medium of the second language and that the curriculum taught parallels the local first-language curriculum. Teachers within this system are generally bilingual and second-language exposure is generally confined to the classroom. Immersion has been used in other regions around the world to develop bilingualism, such as in Canada, where children who are not native French speakers are taught via the medium of French. In Wales, children from non-Welsh speaking backgrounds usually enter Welsh-medium education at the beginning of their educational career.

In order to develop further models of immersion, the Welsh government has also looked at introducing intensive teaching at Key Stage 2 based on the immersion method. In 2006, following a pilot study into the development of immersion projects from Key Stage 2 onwards, ESTYN (Inspectorate for Education and Training in Wales) reported that such initiatives are impacting on Welsh as a second language as a whole. However, for such projects to be successful pupils would need access to Welsh-medium education at secondary level. Some secondary schools in Wales now offer dual-language delivery, whereby the pupils have the choice of being taught via the medium of Welsh or English. These schools were originally English-medium secondary schools but have now adapted to meet the Welsh government's drive to promote bilingualism in Wales.

In 2010 the Welsh Assembly Government produced a further Welsh-Medium Education Strategy in order to respond to the continuing demand for Welsh-medium education. In 2009, 438 primary schools were regarded as being Welsh-medium (Welsh Assembly Government 2010). The rise in Welsh-medium provision at secondary level has been slower, with 55 schools now providing Welsh-medium lessons in more than half the curriculum subjects (Welsh Assembly Government 2010). There is a maintained commitment from policy makers in Wales to consolidate and expand Welsh-medium provision in Wales as a priority at national, regional and local level.

Language and national identity have been linked in a number of studies. As stated above, the introduction of the Curriculum Cymreig in 1989 was designed to develop children's knowledge and understanding of the various linguistic, cultural, social, historical and geographical contexts in Wales. A study by Scourfield *et al.* (2006) carried out an exploration of children's national identity in Wales. The project looked at middle-school pupils aged 8–11 and their perceptions of place and nation. The primary schools participating in the project represented a diverse cross-section of the Welsh population, i.e. the study chose Welsh-medium and English-medium schools in both rural and urban locations. Results of this qualitative study displayed 'an inclusive notion of what it is to be Welsh' (Scourfield *et al.* 2006: 152) and linked this to Welsh-sounding names or the ability to speak Welsh. Thus language was defined as a key feature in the primary-school-age children's perception of national identity and Welshness.

At secondary level, Coupland *et al.* (2005) looked at the attitudes of sixteen-year-olds in Wales to Welsh and Welshness in order to establish whether there were clear links between the ability to speak and interact in Welsh and affiliation to the Welsh nation. Their study revealed 'Quite high affiliative identity to Wales exists across the sample in most subgroups (including some with low competence in Welsh)' (Coupland *et al.* 2005: 18). The researchers assert that the idea that the Welsh language is valued as a tool to display a group's distinctiveness or in-group affiliation applies 'only in a very muted way' (Coupland *et al.* 2005: 17). Ability to speak Welsh in this study with secondary-age pupils does not appear to strongly affect affiliation to Wales and Welshness. In summary, the importance of the Welsh language in children's perceptions of national identity is disputed by various research projects discussed. However, bilingualism is a primary objective of the Welsh Assembly Government coupled with the development of a sense of belonging and heritage through Curriculum Cymreig. Both of these educational policies could be seen as having an influence on children's ideas of national identity in Wales.

Conclusions

Historically and via contemporary policy and practice, issues of education and language in Wales cannot be separated. Welsh-medium education in Wales is clearly effective. There have been substantial increases recorded in the numbers of English-speaking parents wanting to send their children into Welsh-medium education. Language is a key component of the curriculum in Wales, but this alone does not separate it from the English system. Since devolution Wales has begun to forge a separate and distinct education system which has sought inspiration from other international models, such as the immersion system in Canada and the Scandinavian early years ethos, which is reflected in the Foundation Phase curriculum. Recent signals such as the decisions about GCSE provision have shown no desire to emulate changes to the English system. Going it alone has been challenging for Welsh policy makers in recent years; however, new practices and innovative directions such as the play-based Foundation Phase curriculum have allowed Wales to develop a distinct model of education which may contribute to other educational systems, both in the UK and further afield.

References

Aasen, W. and Waters, J. (2006) The new curriculum in Wales: a new view of the child?, *Education, 3–13*, 34: 2, 123–129.

ACCAC (2003) *Developing the Curriculum Cymreig*. Surrey: ACCAC.

Aitchison, J. and Carter, H. (2004) *Spreading the Word: The Welsh Language 2001*. Y Lolfa York: Cambridge University Press.

Coupland, N., Bishop, H., Evans, B. and Garrett, P. (2005) Imagining Wales and the Welsh language: ethnolinguistic subjectivities and demographic flow. *Journal of Language and Social Psychology*, 25: 4, 351–376.

Davies, J. (2007) *A History of Wales*. Harmondsworth: Penguin.

ESTYN (2005) *Y Cwricwlwm Cymreig: Progress Made by Schools in Implementation of ACCAC Guidance Issued in 2003*. Cardiff: ESTYN.

Gorard, S. (2000) For England, see Wales. *Oxford Studies in Comparative Education*, 9: 2, 29–44.

Johnson, R.K. and Swain, M. (eds) (1997) *Immersion Education: International Perspectives.* Cambridge: Cambridge University Press.

Jones, D.V. (1997) Bilingual mathematics: development and practice in Wales. *Curriculum Journal*, 8: 3, 393–410.

Jones, G.E. (2006) Education and nationhood in Wales: an historiographical analysis. *Journal of Educational Administration and History*, 38: 3, 263–277.

Jones, G.E. and Roderick, G.W. (2003) *A History of Education in Wales.* Cardiff: University of Wales Press.

Lewis, G.W. (2006) *Welsh-medium Primary Education: The Challenges and Opportunities of the Twenty-first Century. Welsh Medium and Bilingual Education.* Bangor: School of Education, University of Wales.

National Assembly for Wales (2012) *The History of Welsh Devolution*, available at http://www.assemblywales.org/abthome/role-of-assembly-how-it-works/history-welsh-devolution.htm, accessed 24 April 2014.

National Library of Wales (2014) *The Blue Books of 1847.* Aberystwyth: National Library of Wales, available at http://www.llgc.org.uk/collections/digital-gallery/printedmaterial/thebluebooks/, accessed 27 May 2014.

Redknap, C. (2006) *Welsh-medium and Bilingual Education and Training: Steps Towards a Holistic Strategy. Welsh Medium and Bilingual Education.* Bangor: School of Education, University of Wales.

Scourfield, J., Dicks, B., Drakeford, M. and Davies, A. (2006) *Children, Place and Identity: Nation and Locality in Middle Childhood.* London: Routledge.

Siraj-Blatchford, I., Sylva, K., Laugharne, J. and Milton, E. (2006) *Monitoring and Evaluation of the Effective Implementation of the Foundation Phase (MEEIFP) Project across Wales.* Cardiff: Welsh Assembly Government, available at http://wales.gov.uk/docs/dcells/publications/120419fppiloten.pdf, accessed 24 April 2014.

Sylva, K., Melhuish, E., Sammons, P., Siraj-Blatchford, I., Taggart, B. and Elliot, K. (2003) *The Effective Provision of Pre-school Education (EPPE) Project: Findings from the Pre-school Period.* London: Institute of Education, University of London.

Times Educational Supplement (TES) (2013) 'The differences between teaching in England and Wales', 23 July, available at http://www.tes.co.uk/article.aspx?storyCode=6344294, accessed 24 April 2014.

Waller, T. (2007) 'The Trampoline Tree and the Swamp Monster with 18 heads': outdoor play in the Foundation Stage and Foundation Phase. *Education 3–13*, 35: 4, 393–407.

Welsh Assembly Government (2003) *Iaith Pawb: A National Action Plan for a Bilingual Wales.* WAG: Cardiff.

Welsh Government (2011) *Independent Schools Census*, available at http://wales.gov.uk/statistics-and-research/independent-schools-census/?lang=en, accessed 24 April 2014.

Welsh Assembly Government (2001) *The Learning Country.* Cardiff: Welsh Assembly Government.

Welsh Assembly Government (2010) *Welsh-Medium Education Strategy*, Cardiff: Welsh Assembly Government, available at http://wales.gov.uk/docs/dcells/publications/100420welshmediumstrategy en.pdf, accessed 24 April 2014.

Wyn Siencyn, S. and Thomas, S. (2007) Wales, in: M.M. Clark and T. Waller (eds), *Early Childhood Education and Care: Policy and Practice.* London: Sage.

12

Early childhood education and care in the UK

Alice Mongiello

Play is the highest expression of human development in childhood, for it alone is the free expression of what is in a child's soul.

Friedrich Froebel (1887)

Introduction

The origins of early childhood education and care in Britain can be dated back nearly 200 years to the time of the social reformer Robert Owen. As part of his model village based in New Lanark, Scotland, Owen established a nursery, arguably the first in the world, for young children whose parents worked in his mill. Practice within the nursery was based on stimulating a child-centred environment incorporating play, exploration, singing and dancing. Some would argue that the true founder of the child-centred philosophy in early childhood education and care today was Fredrick Froebel (1792–1852).[1] Influenced by the Swiss educator Pestalozzi, Froebel proposed a more natural, livelier, child-like way of teaching that would liberate the young child's mind. Froebel set himself apart from the then established view of how children learn with his outspoken condemnation of 'rote-learning', which he felt closed a child's mind to understanding. His belief that nature's laws were a child's best teachers eventually led him to create the first 'child's garden of learning' or 'Kindergarten' in Prussia in 1837. He was convinced that children learned by interacting with their environment both indoors and outdoors through symbolic play and creative activities. To help children experience and understand basic concepts he introduced play materials which he called 'gifts and occupations', such as soft and hard balls as well as wooden blocks, prisms and cylinders. He believed that, given the right environment and stimulus, children will learn for themselves. Much of Froebel's philosophy can be seen in early childhood and care settings today.

Recently we have witnessed a significant interest in early childhood education and care in most Western countries. While there are many reasons for this current interest, three can be identified as having most significance. First, research has demonstrated the all-round psychological and social benefits to young children that high-quality early childhood education and care offers. Second, it has been shown that a good early years experience has positive effects on subsequent educational achievement. Third, early childhood and care services contribute to meeting the objectives of a healthy and prosperous society by promoting a more effective labour force and a more supportive family environment. As noted by the then Scottish Minister for Children and Early Years, Adam Ingram, at the launch of the *Standard for Childhood Practice*:

> I believe the support we give to children in the early years can make an important contribution to the kind of country we want Scotland to be: one which is smarter, wealthier and fairer, healthier, safer and stronger and greener.
>
> (Ingram 2008: 1)

The structure and benefits of early childhood education and care have been prominent features in both policy and research over the years. Dating back to 1967, the *Plowden Report* concluded that each child must be treated as an individual and emphasised that there was clear evidence that young children learn best through play rather than formal teaching: 'finding out' is better than 'being told'. More recently, *The Early Years Framework* (Scottish Government 2008a: 4) outlined a new conceptualisation of early childhood education and care, one which recognised that children should be valued and provided for within communities; that children have the right to a high quality of life and access to play; and that children need to be put at the centre of early childhood and care provision. The findings of seminal research (McCartney 1984; Philips *et al.* 1987) on the lasting effects of early childhood education on children's psychological and social development are now well established. Research has also demonstrated that high-quality early childhood education and care for young children living in poverty contributes to their intellectual and social development in childhood and their school success and economic performance and reduced commission of crime as adults (Schweinhart *et al.* 2005). This longitudinal *High/Scope Perry Preschool* research study confirms that the positive effects of high-quality early childhood education and care are not just long term, but lifetime effects (the study spans four decades and still continues). In a review of relevant literature the following was concluded:

> When pre-school education is of high quality it leads to lasting enhancement of educational performance and later employment. It does this through encouraging high aspirations, motivation to learn and feelings of task efficacy, especially for children from disadvantaged backgrounds.
>
> (Sylva and Wiltshire 1994: 47)

This finding was further echoed by Ball (1994) in the report for the Royal Society of Arts: *Start Right: The Importance of Early Learning*. A more recent review of the literature also concluded the lasting effects of early childhood education and care (Melhiush 2004). This view is shared in many countries such as the United States, Scandinavian countries and New Zealand.

The most significant UK-based study to demonstrate the positive effects of early childhood education and care was the longitudinal study undertaken by Sylva *et al.*

from 1997 to 2004. The Effective Provision of Pre-school Education (EPPE) project compared and contrasted the developmental progress of over 3,000 children selected from a wide range of social and cultural backgrounds in six local authorities in England that offer differing preschool experiences (Sylva *et al.* 2004). At the heart of the project was an investigation into the effects of preschool education and care on development and attainment for children aged 3–7 years old. Five central questions were explored during the project:

1. What is the impact of preschool on children's intellectual and social/behaviour development?
2. Are some preschools more effective than others in promoting children's development?
3. What are the characteristics of an effective preschool setting?
4. What is the impact of the home and childcare history on children's development?
5. Do the effects of preschool continue through to Key Stage 1 at age 6/7 years? (Key Stage 1 refers to the first two years of schooling in maintained schools in England and Wales).

The key findings were:

Impact of attending a pre-school centre
- Pre-school experience, compared to none, enhances children's development.
- The duration of attendance is important with an earlier start being related to better intellectual development and improved independence, concentration and sociability.
- Full time provision led to no better gains for children than part time provision.
- Disadvantaged children in particular can benefit significantly from good quality pre-school experiences, especially if they attend centres that cater for a mixture of children from different social backgrounds.

The quality of practices within pre-school centres
- The quality of pre-school centres is directly related to better intellectual and social/behaviour development in children.
- Good quality can be found across all types of early years settings. However quality was higher overall in settings integrating care and education and in nursery schools/classes.
- Settings which have staff with higher qualifications, show higher quality and their children make more progress.
- Where settings viewed educational and social development as complementary and equal in importance, children make better all-round progress.

(Sylva *et al.* 2003: 1–2)

These findings clearly demonstrate how attending good-quality early childhood education and care can benefit children's all-round development. In support of these findings, all managers/lead practitioners in Scotland employed within a private/voluntary early childhood setting are now legally required to be qualified to degree level. This further supports the view that having a highly qualified and high-quality workforce will make a real difference to the outcomes for Scotland's children and their families.

While the impact of good-quality early childhood education and care on children's all-round development is well established, we must also reflect upon the positive effects on wider social issues. It is now recognised that early childhood provision counteracts poverty by facilitating parental economic activity; it provides the main caregiver with temporary relief from constant vigilance; and it can provide employers with continuity in valued personnel if provision for young children is readily accessible. The introduction of flexible working patterns and increased parental leave further supports these wider social issues and reflects a positive shift in relation to the value of early childhood experiences in Britain today.

While parents are now more economically active than at any time since the Second World War, is the trend for more working parents good for young children? In countries where it is the cultural norm for parents to work (for example, Denmark) the state provides extensive early childhood services and there is no evidence to suggest that children are disadvantaged in such circumstances. However, there is contradictory research. Over the past ten years, sensationalised BBC News articles have fuelled this debate: *Working mums harm child's progress* and *Working mothers' link to school failure*. Although the research (Ermisch and Francesconi 2001) supporting these articles has been heavily criticised and viewed as exaggerating the effects of the working pattern of mothers, it does put parents, in particular mothers, in a very invidious position. What is clear is that the issue about whether working mothers can have a detrimental impact on their children's well-being remains unresolved. Indeed, more recent research (Brown *et al.* 2010) suggests that the children of mothers who work part-time are healthier than those of their full-time or stay-at-home counterparts and further shows that mothers who work part-time went to considerable lengths to ensure the time they did spend with their children was high quality. This debate is likely to continue for the foreseeable future as more mothers continue to enter the labour market; at present in the UK some 60 per cent of women with children under five work.

Mothers with young children returning to work is a more recent occurrence in the UK, and this has been particularly pronounced in families with children under the age of three. There is a commonly held view that children under three are better off with their mother rather than in nursery or with a child-minder. While dated, the work of Bowlby (1952) on the psychological impairment of children as a consequence of maternal deprivation is still influential despite contradictory research that demonstrates that young children are quite capable of appropriate bonding with a range of adults (Schaffer 1977). The work of Belsky (2001) supports the view that, if a child is placed in childcare outside the home for more than 20 hours per week when the child is under one year of age, there may be some detrimental effects when the child is slightly older if the childcare is not of the highest quality. In contrast, more recent research (Brooks-Gunn *et al.* 2010) found no negative effects of first-year maternal employment, although children did fare better if their mothers worked part-time (fewer than 30 hours per week). While recognising the significance of Bowlby's work on attachment, Brooks-Gunn *et al.* (2010) found little or no evidence that first-year maternal employment affected child attachment. More important factors were identified relating to the quality of parenting and children's experiences of childcare.

While we continue to debate the impact of working parents, in particular working mothers, on children's development, a significant factor is the accessibility of affordable, good-quality early childhood provision. We have already established convincing evidence in support of early childhood education and care. Writers such as Moss and Penn (1996) have consistently argued that quality early childhood education and care should be made universally available by the state to families with young children. In response to these arguments the government introduced a policy of free pre-school places, albeit part-time, for all four-year-olds whose parents wish it from 1999 and for all three-year-olds whose parents wish it from 2001 (DfEE 1998a; Scottish Office 1998). In 1998 the government's policy for the early years entitled *Meeting the Childcare Challenge*, now referred to as the *Childcare Strategy*, represented a sea change in the relationship between the state and the family with young children. The state was now set to take a much more proactive role in the provision of early childhood services.

The National Childcare Strategy

Prior to the 1998 UK National Childcare Strategy, childcare was largely viewed as a private matter. During this time childcare provision was limited and restricted employment among low-income families, especially lone parent families. The National Childcare Strategy's aim was to improve the availability, affordability and quality of childcare and also formed part of the government's strategy to lower child poverty through expanding childcare to assist more parents into employment. By 2005 582,000 new early childcare places in the UK had been created (HM Treasury 2005: 15). Today, while there are 650 fewer nurseries and childminders, the number of childcare places has risen slightly during December 2011 and March 2012. In total, there are now 82,282 childcare providers in England, offering 1,310,738 places (OfSTED 2012). However, across the UK families can still be faced with variation in the quality of provision, high costs and difficulty in finding childcare places. Still relevant today, at the heart of the National Childcare Strategy for all parts of the UK, is the aim of providing good-quality, affordable and accessible childcare. As already highlighted, early childhood education and care has social and economic benefits for both parents and children; parents are able to access employment and/or further training and children are offered play, social and educational opportunities (Scottish Government 2008).

As a result of Childcare Strategy funding, across the UK Childcare Partnerships (Scotland) or Early Years Development and Childcare Partnerships (England) have developed between local authorities and the different childcare providers, e.g. private and voluntary sectors. The Childcare Partnerships were deemed responsible for meeting the local childcare needs in their area. As outlined by the Department for

Education and Employment (1999), any new childcare partnership should be considered in relation to several factors:

- diversity: voluntary, private and public sector involvement;
- accessibility to rural and disadvantaged families;
- inclusion of special needs and children with disabilities where possible and appropriate;
- equal opportunities for different cultural, ethnic and religious backgrounds;
- quality, stimulating care with staff who aim to continuously improve their services;
- affordability;
- accessibility to where the children live and the parents work;
- integration of early years education with childcare;
- access to accurate local information for parents, carers, children, employers and providers.

In Orkney, the Childcare Partnership's vision statement, *'Working together to make life better for the children of Orkney'*, reflects the 'joined up' thinking promoted in present-day childcare provision. The aim for Moray Childcare Partnership is to bring together the private and voluntary sectors, parents and the community; indeed all those with a key interest in childcare locally. In partnership with the private and voluntary sectors, Aberdeenshire Childcare Partnership aims to create new childcare provision, expand existing childcare provision and promote childcare training. In England and Wales, local authorities developed Early Years Development and Childcare Partnerships (EYDCP). In Ealing the EYDCP's main purpose is to ensure that every child gets the best possible start in life by the provision of high-quality, integrated, early education and childcare services for children aged from birth to 14, or 16 for children with special needs.

Partnership with parents

Promoting partnerships between different childcare providers is at the heart of the National Childcare Strategy, as is the partnership individual providers have with parents. For many children, attending a childcare setting is often the first step to independence, and as such can be an exciting yet anxious time for all involved: children, parents and professionals. Working in partnership with parents is not a new concept. We could argue the origins date back to the early 1900s when Margaret McMillan (1860–1931) opened an 'open air' nursery in Deptford. McMillan believed in the importance of good-quality early childhood education and care based on play and the positive impact it could have on the future lives of children and their parents. She emphasised the importance of a close partnership with parents and actively encouraged parents to develop alongside their children. There was and still is a belief that working in partnership with parents ensures children thrive and achieve their potential.

A successful partnership is based on mutual trust and respect; all involved must feel safe, which encourages effective communication and a balance of power and agreement. We must not forget that the home environment in general is richly educative (Tizard and Hughes 1984). Parents are children's first and most enduring educators. In a review of the literature, Desforges (2003) highlighted that young children receive not just skills, knowledge and intellectual stimulation at home; they also absorb a positive attitude towards learning and a strong self-image as a successful learner. It is therefore important to view parents as equal partners whereby 'Parents have rights and responsibilities in relation to the development and care of their child. Professionals have a duty to acknowledge and understand the unique role and relationship each parent has with their child' (DfES 2003a: 12).

Childcare providers that achieve the best social and educational outcomes for their children are those that openly share their educational aims clearly with their parents and actively encourage high levels of parental engagement. They work on building parent confidence in what they already do at home and they offer ideas to further support this. Most importantly, they regularly exchange information with parents on a weekly or monthly basis and provide complimentary activities suitable for parents to undertake in the home environment (Sylva et al. 2004).

Early childhood services in the UK

There are three main categories of early childhood provision for children under five years of age in the UK: local authority, voluntary and private services. This arrangement, unique to the UK, is often referred to as the 'mixed-economy model' of early childhood services.

While it was Robert Owen's intention to integrate the function of 'care' and 'education', in the years following the opening of his first nursery in 1816, 'care' and 'education' of young children developed along separate lines. Until fairly recently, local authority provision consisted of two subdivisions – education-based services and social work (care) services. Of the education-based provision there are three types: nursery schools, nursery classes attached to primary schools and (with the exception of Scotland) reception classes in primary schools. These types of provision are primarily staffed by nursery teachers and nursery nurses. However, since the repeal of the Schools (Scotland) Code in 2003, the role of the nursery teacher has undergone considerable change. Of significance is the removal of the statutory requirement for a qualified headteacher of a nursery school or teacher of a nursery class. This has led local authorities across Scotland to review their services for children; teacher deployment in nursery education now varies across local authorities and within Childcare Partnership providers (private and voluntary). Nursery nurses now have a much more active role in the day-to-day running and managing of the provision. Of the social work (care) services there are day nurseries, family centres and children's centres staffed largely by nursery nurses. With the exception of reception classes, the differentiation between education-based and care-based services is being eroded. It has long been known that for young children 'care' and 'education' are interdependent and inseparable: they need both (Sylva and Moss 1992). The pioneering work on integration in Strathclyde Region in Scotland in the late 1980s (Penn 1992; Wilkinson 1995) further supported this view; quality services for young children must integrate both 'care' and 'education', thus providing an all-embracing approach to children's needs (Moss 1991). Many local authorities have now established 'integrated' provision where 'education' and 'care' are fully integrated. An integrated philosophy has been more recently supported in Scotland with the implementation of *Getting It Right For Every Child* (GIRFEC) (Scottish Government 2008b) and the equivalent in England, *Every Child Matters* (DCSF 2003).

In the voluntary sector, playgroups are predominantly run by local mothers, assisted in the main by a playgroup leader. Most places in playgroups are one or two sessions each week with a small fee being charged for each session. In Scotland, Childcare Partnership Playgroups offer a standard of education and care at least on a par with local authority nurseries. The main difference is that these are charities which are community owned and managed, and as a result there is usually a greater level of parental involvement. There are ongoing funding and sustainability issues facing many playgroups in Scotland today. This has led some playgroup providers to consider caring for rising threes, as well as offering 'wraparound' provision, e.g. breakfast clubs and after-school clubs. Less prevalent are mother and toddler groups and crèches.

In the private sector, provision varies widely from childminders (who look after children in their own homes) through private nurseries (very similar to local authority nursery schools) to nursery classes in fully independent schools. Childminders and private nurseries meet the ever-increasing demand of working parents who are willing or, more importantly, able to meet the cost of these services. Findings of the Daycare Trust (2011) indicate that childcare costs have typically increased by more than the average wage, placing parents under further financial strain in the face of rising living costs. The cost of a childminder for a child aged two and over in Scotland has increased by 8.3 per cent – almost four times as much as the average wage. The average yearly expenditure for 25 hours of nursery provision per week for a child under two is £5,028 in England, £5,178 in Scotland and £4,723 in Wales. While the introduction of means-tested Working Tax Credits reduces the overall cost of childcare, availability is still a significant issue. In 2011, 60 per cent of Family Information Services across the UK said that parents had reported a lack of childcare provision in their area during the past 12 months (Daycare Trust 2011). Interestingly, a recent large-scale survey found that nearly half (47%) of all parents in the UK use informal childcare; grandparents are cited as the most likely to provide this (Daycare Trust 2012). Indeed over one-third of parents interviewed who use childcare used grandparents as their main form of childcare when formal childcare was not available (Daycare Trust 2012). Parents in Scotland are the most likely to use grandparents as the main form of childcare; over half of parents interviewed using childcare utilised this option (Daycare Trust 2012).

Despite investing heavily in the National Childcare Strategy to improve services for young children and families, important challenges remain, including that many families still have difficulty finding childcare provision that meet their needs, and the quality of provision varies. However, in 2009 the government reported significant progress:

Thanks to the hard work across the sector, early learning and childcare is more flexible, affordable and better quality than ever before. Many more families are benefiting from new rights and services – such as extended paid maternity and paternity leave, new Sure Start Children's Centres and better financial support.

(DCSF 2009: 5)

The *Childcare Act* (2006), which regulates childcare in England, passed into law in July 2006. This Act gives local authorities responsibility for ensuring there is enough childcare provision available to meet the needs of parents locally. While the National Childcare Strategy and resulting policy and legislation has resulted in significant improvement in access to early childhood services, there are still concerns about whether these are meeting the diversity of family needs; there is still variation in cost, staffing and opening times of early childhood services in the UK. The vast majority of early childhood places are part-time, attendance being for half a day, either mornings or afternoons. Although the proportion of children accessing early childhood services has virtually doubled since the mid 1990s, over 80 per cent is on a part-time basis. In addition, local authority nursery schools and classes close for the summer holidays. Furthermore, there is a professional distinction between nursery nurses and nursery teachers, resulting in differentiation of status, remuneration and promotion prospects.

As previously outlined there is an on-going debate on the effects of placing very young children (i.e. children under three) in early childhood provision outside the family home. Although disputed, there is still a widespread view that very young children will be seriously impaired developmentally unless they are cared for by their mothers. This has resulted in little local authority early childhood provision for under-threes, despite comparative evidence that many European countries provide extensive and successful facilities for under-threes. However, this view is currently being challenged and as a result provision for under-threes is being taken seriously by respective government departments in order to meet the continuing demand of working parents, in particular working mothers. For example, in Scotland, originally published in 2003 and revised in 2010, national guidelines have been issued to those professionals working with very young children: *Pre-Birth to Three: Positive Outcomes for Scotland's Children and Families* (LTS 2010). In England and Wales, the equivalent *Birth to Three Matters* framework was published in 2002 (DfEE 2002). While neither of these documents should be viewed as a 'curriculum', they do highlight new thinking about the importance of children under three years and indicate a shift in the ways this age group should be viewed; historically young children's welfare has been viewed as a private rather than public concern (Abbot and Langston 2005). As a result, provision for under-threes is improving, though largely confined to the private and voluntary sectors. In addition, the government's Sure Start programme aimed at improving the health and well-being of families and children before and from birth up to the age of four is also having a positive effect on children under three years deemed to be in disadvantaged circumstances.

An emerging early childhood and care profession

Changing national policy has placed early childhood education and care (ECEC) at the core of strategic developments, with the agreement that the Scottish Social Services Council (SSSC) will register the workforce. This has created a context in which advanced graduate-level training for ECEC staff will be increasingly recognised. The intention is to develop graduate leadership in the ECEC workforce by ensuring appropriate professionals, those with leadership and supervisory responsibilities will be qualified to or working towards graduate-level qualifications to be eligible to register with the SSSC. All managers working in ECEC services in Scotland are now legally required to be qualified to graduate-level to be eligible to register with the SSSC. Similarly, south of the border, in 2007 the government introduced the graduate Early Years Professional Status (EYPS) for staff working in ECEC; the only government-endorsed graduate-level professional accreditation. By 2015, the government aims to have at least one Early Years Professional in every daycare setting. The introduction of 'graduate leaders' in ECEC settings is aimed at equipping the ECEC profession with the skills and knowledge to make a real difference to the outcomes of children and families across the UK and is supported by research which shows staff in ECEC settings with higher qualifications show higher quality and their children make more progress (Sylva *et al.* 2003).

Historically, the ECEC workforce has been under-valued, often being viewed as 'women's work' (Moss 2003); an easy job that could be done by anyone. Gender is inextricably linked with the ECEC sector; in 2010 95 per cent of the total ECEC workforce were female (Scottish Government 2010). Dalli (2001) argues that there is a traditional alignment of ECEC work with the role of mothering and that this acts to disempower the ECEC sector from claiming professional status. The development of graduate-level training offers the ECEC sector an opportunity to improve their career prospects and earning potential and gain recognition as a degree-led profession.

In Scotland, all graduate-level training is based on the *Standard for Childhood Practice* (QAA 2007), which supports the establishment and recognition of the professional status of the ECEC workforce. It also informs an integrated qualifications and professional development framework. Menmuir and Hughes (2004) note that for too long the skills of ECEC workers and their career development needs have gone largely unrecognised and undervalued. The *Standard for Childhood Practice*, resulting in childhood practice graduate-level qualifications along with SSSC registration requirements in Scotland, have laid the foundation for developing an ECEC profession in line with other established professions (e.g. teaching, social work and health). To what extent this will be achieved is yet to be fully realised, but without appropriate pay and conditions put in place to support this emerging profession newly qualified staff armed with graduate-level qualifications may leave the ECEC sector to gain employment in more lucrative careers.

The early childhood curriculum

Since Owen's first nursery in New Lanark, play has been a central feature of early childhood care and education. As noted by Froebel (1887), 'Play is the highest expression of human development in childhood, for it alone is the free expression of what is in a child's soul.' However, it was not until after the Second World War that governments began to take an interest in early childhood care and education provision. In Scotland, the 1950 Primary Memorandum published by the then Scottish Education Department defined the aim of early childhood education: 'The aim of nursery school education is to provide the right conditions for growth, and so ensure the harmonising of the whole personality of the child' (Scottish Education Department 1950: 127). The Memorandum went on to state: 'The value of the physical aspect is perhaps the most obvious. In general, the term covers medical care, adequate rest and sleep, balanced diet, play within doors and in the open air, suitable clothing, and training in hygienic habits' (Scottish Education Department 1950: 127).

As can be seen, it was the healthcare aspect of early childhood education that was emphasised by central government in the post-war period. The focus on health was the dominant influence in early childhood education for some 30 years, with many early childhood education settings being under direct supervision of the Ministry of Health. In social work day nurseries, healthcare was viewed as paramount; children had to be protected from disease and squalor. During this period, early childhood education was often viewed as a form of compensatory education:

> Providing an environment in which the small child from a poor or deprived home can flourish; and in so far as the child flourishes he acquires benefits which place him at less of a disadvantage in relation to his privileged peer.
>
> (Lodge and Blackstone 1982: 122)

During the 1970s a change began to take place as we shifted our focus more to children's intellectual needs. In *Before Five* (Scottish Education Department 1971) the focus of early childhood education was broadened into activities aimed at child development: 'The ideal educational environment in these years will afford opportunities for the child to develop his physical, intellectual, social and emotional capacities' (Scottish Education Department 1971: 1).

At the heart of early childhood education and care is a child-centred pedagogy based on play. This was most clearly outlined in separate reports on primary and nursery education published in 1965 and 1971, respectively (Scottish Education Department 1965; 1971). As noted by Watt (1990: 79), a child-centred early childhood curriculum stresses:

> Children's all-round development: their social relationships as well as their mathematical and scientific understanding; their feelings and emotions as well as their communicative skills; their creativity and imagination as well as their physical well-being. It is an integrated curriculum which starts with children themselves.

During the 1980s there was a reluctance to develop a national early childhood curriculum in the UK despite the general acceptance of a child-centred pedagogy. In fact, one of the main reasons for this reluctance was its child-centred nature. As highlighted by Moyles (1989: 92): 'It is evident in committing anything to paper ... connotes an unacceptable didacticism.'

Despite reservations, throughout the 1990s local authorities across Scotland produced their own version of an early childhood curriculum (e.g. *A Curriculum for the Early Years*, Lothian Region Council Education Department 1992; *Early Years (3–8) Guideline*, Central Region Council 1991; *Education Three to Five: Nursery Education Guidelines*, Dumfries and Galloway Regional Council 1992). In England *The Education of Children Under Five* (DfES 1992) was published. All documents advocated a child-centred pedagogy based on a sound understanding of child development and how children learn. Play was also viewed as the most important vehicle for learning.

In 2000 England established the 'Foundation Stage' as a distinct period in the English education system. The Foundation Stage is defined as that period in a child's life from age three to the end of reception year at age five. At this time the Qualifications and Curriculum Authority (QCA) issued a set of curriculum guidelines for professionals, outlining appropriate learning experiences for children at this stage (DfEE 2000). The guidance outlined six areas of development:

1. personal, social and emotional development;
2. communication, language and literacy;
3. mathematical development;
4. knowledge and understanding of the world;
5. physical development;
6. creative development.

Within each area learning outcomes referred to as learning goals were identified. To assist practitioners in planning appropriate activities, the guidelines introduced the concept of 'stepping stones'. These 'stepping stones' outlined the knowledge, skills, understanding and attitudes that children needed to experience during the Foundation Stage in order to successfully achieve the desired learning goals. It was the process of learning rather than the outcome that was significant.

More recently, a *Statutory Framework for the Foundation Stage in England* (DfES 2007) has been introduced. The Early Years Foundation Stage (EYFS) framework builds on the previous guidance by integrating the care and education of young children into a single document and reinforces a more child-centred pedagogy. Its aim is to achieve the five outcomes as outlined in *Every Child Matters* (DCSF 2003) of staying safe, being healthy, enjoying and achieving, making a positive contribution and achieving economic well-being. Since 2006 the EYFS has been given legal force through the Order and Regulations made under the *Children Act 2006*. As a result, from September 2008 all schools and early childhood settings registered by OfSTED have been legally required to implement the EYFS.

In Scotland the early childhood curriculum has witnessed several developments. In 1997 *A Curriculum Framework for Children in their Pre-school Year* (Scottish Office 1997) was published. Following the expansion of nursery provision to include three-year-olds, this framework was replaced by *A Curriculum Framework for Children 3 to 5* (LTS 1999). At the heart of this framework is the belief that high-quality early childhood education and care is based on the following:

- the best interest of the child whereby professionals work in partnership with parents and recognise children as unique individuals;
- the central importance of relationships which form the basis on which all learning takes place;
- the need for children to feel included, encouraging them to actively take part from the earliest years;
- an understanding of the ways in which children learn, the need to build on what the child already knows and the recognition that learning is a complex process.

(LTS 1999: 2)

Following the publication of *The Education (Scotland) Act 2000* the Scottish Executive launched the National Debate on Education in 2002. This wide-ranging consultation enabled the Executive to find out what features of the present curriculum were valued and what aspects of the curriculum it was felt needed to be changed. The views from this debate were then considered by a 'Review Group' set up in 2003. Their task was to consider the comments made in the context of recent research in 'learning theory and styles' as well national and global issues which may affect the purpose and content of the school curriculum, such as the increasing use of technology in the workplace. The resulting document produced by the Review Group was *A Curriculum for Excellence 3–18* (Scottish Executive 2004). One of the key design principles of the *Curriculum for Excellence* (CfE) is to remove the artificial barriers that children meet when moving from early childhood education and care to primary education and from primary to secondary education. The new curriculum provides a seamless transition whereby at each stage children have the opportunity to build on previous knowledge and experience. In 2009 the CfE was rolled out across both early childhood settings and statutory schools across Scotland.

The purposes of the CfE are defined as four capacities. These are that children and young people should have the opportunity to become:

1. successful learners
2. confident individuals
3. responsible citizens
4. effective contributors.

These purposes represent a very broad range of outcomes, including learning how to learn and the promotion of positive attitudes and attributes. The opportunity for children to develop the four capacities strongly depends upon:

- the environment for learning;
- the choice of teaching and learning approaches;
- the ways in which learning is organised.

Respectful and constructive relationships are the starting point for successful learning. By having high aspirations for each child, early childhood settings are able to support children in developing confidence and ambition throughout the Early Years Level as defined by the CfE (the Early Years Level covers children aged three to approximately six years old). At the heart of the Early Years Level is the process of active learning (Scottish Executive 2007); an active learning approach adopts the stance that 'work' and 'play' are inseparable in early childhood education and care. It encourages children to immerse themselves in meaningful and challenging activities that encourage divergent and imaginative thinking.

Thus, for the first time in the 200-year history of early childhood education in the UK, governments have specified parameters of young children's learning. The drivers for this policy are based on raising standards of educational achievement in the compulsory school years and facilitating parents to be more economically active. The significant difference between the English Early Years Framework and the Scottish CfE is that the CfE remains as guidance to early childhood settings and is not enshrined in legislation, although the CfE does play a crucial role in the inspection of settings by Her Majesty's Inspectorate of Education (HMIE).

Assessment for Learning

Assessment for Learning (AfL) means children and early childhood practitioners work alongside each other to determine where children are in their learning and where they need to go and how best to get there (Assessment Reform Group 2002). It is founded on the idea of collaborative working and active learning (Blandford and Knowles 2011). Without children's active involvement, assessment becomes a judgemental activity, resulting in a one-sided view of a child's achievement. AfL is more likely to result in raising standards, because children are more focused, motivated and aware of their own capabilities and potential. Sharing learning goals with children helps them to become more reflective and aware of what they may be learning; it also enables children to evaluate what they are doing for themselves (Lewis 1987). For many young children, education is viewed as a series of unrelated tasks where the purpose is unclear and even what counts as success is mysterious (Wiliam 2006). Therefore AfL promotes learning by helping children to understand the learning outcomes and what counts as success.

Dialogue is at the heart of the AfL process as it shows children that their views are valued and encourages them to become more reflective learners. While it could be argued that young children lack the cognitive skills to actively engage with the AfL process (Ross 2006), Whitebread *et al.* (2005) suggests that early childhood practitioners can provide young children with metacognitive experiences and model the processes of learning for children. This approach is referred to as 'cognitive apprenticeship'

(Collins *et al.* 1989). Black and Wiliam (1998) highlighted the benefits for children in terms of improved knowledge and understanding when they have the opportunity to discuss their work with early childhood practitioners. This is further supported by findings from the EPPE study (Sylva *et al.* 2004), which suggested that discussion is most effective when it involves some aspect of sustained shared thinking.

The introduction of the Foundation Stage Profile (DfES 2003b) at the end of the Foundation Stage has brought greater focus to assessment for learning in early childhood education. Since 2008 all early childhood education and care settings in England are required to draw up a profile on each child's achievements based on the six areas of learning and development outlined in the Early Years Foundation Stage. Testing children in early childhood education is not encouraged. The profile is based on early childhood practitioners' ongoing observations and assessments.

In Scotland, the principles of assessment for learning have been actively embraced throughout all stages of education since 2002. In 2002 Assessment is for Learning (AifL) was introduced, which consisted of three main strands: assessment *FOR* learning, assessment *AS* learning and assessment *OF* learning. An AifL early childhood setting recognises that children learn best when they:

- understand clearly what they are trying to learn, and what is expected of them;
- are given feedback about the quality of their work, and what they can do to make it better;
- are given advice about how to go about making improvements;
- are fully involved in deciding what needs to be done next, and who can give them help if they need it.

(Scottish Government 2005)

Conclusion

Early childhood education and care has come a long way since the days of Froebel and Robert Owen. Although much of the original informality has been retained, early childhood education and care are now more formally defined. Rapid expansion of provision, in particular for under-threes, has thrown into sharp focus the ongoing debate about the nature of early childhood experiences most beneficial to young children. It is now accepted that exposure to a formal early childhood education can have detrimental effects on children's subsequent educational experiences. In many European countries (particularly in Scandinavia) formal schooling does not begin until children are over seven years old. Prior to this, young children's experiences are firmly rooted in experiential learning which consists of exploration, play, music and social activities. In Scotland much of this spontaneity forms part of the CfE Early Years Level. With the introduction of the Foundation Stage in England there is now less emphasis on formal learning that was apparent during the 1980s and early 1990s.

Accessible, affordable and high-quality early childhood education and care has untold benefits for children, parents, professionals and the wider society. It forms the foundation not only for subsequent school experiences, but also promotes a more tolerant and understanding society. What happens to children in their earliest years says much about our society and is key to outcomes in adult life (Scottish Government 2008a). We owe it to our children to offer them the best possible start in life and early childhood education and care plays a key role in achieving this.

Note

1. Other influential historical pioneers were Rudolph Steiner (1861–1925), Margaret McMillan (1860–1931), Maria Montessori (1870–1952) and Susan Isaacs (1885–1948).

References

Abbott, L. and Langston, A. (eds) (2005) *Birth to Three Matters: Supporting the Framework of Effective Practice*, Maidenhead: Open University Press.

Assessment Reform Group (2002). *Assessment for Learning: 10 Principles*, Cambridge: ARG.

Ball, C. (1994) *Start Right: The Importance of Early Learning*, London: Royal Society of Arts.

Belsky, J. (2001) Developmental Risks (Still) Associated with Early Childcare, *Journal of Child Psychology and Psychiatry*, 42(7), 845–859.

Black, P. and Wiliam, D. (2006) *Inside the Black Box*, London: Nelson.

Blandford, S. and Knowles, C. (2011) Assessment for Learning: A Model for the Development of a Child's Self-competence in the Early Years of Education, *Education 3–13: International Journal of Primary, Elementary and Early Years Education*, 40, 487–499.

Bowlby, J. (1952) *Maternal Care and Mental Health*, Geneva: World Health Organization.

Brooks-Gunn, J., Han, W.-J. and Waldfogel, J. (2010) *First-Year Maternal Employment and Child Development in the First 7 Years*, Boston, MA: Wiley-Blackwell.

Brown, J.E., Broom, D.H., Nicholson, J.M. and Bittmand, M. (2010) Do Working Mothers Raise Couch Potato Kids? Maternal Employment and Children's Lifestyle Behaviours and Weight in Early Childhood, *International Journal of Social Science and Medicine*, 70(11), 1816–1824.

Central Regional Council (1991) *Early Years (3–8) Guideline*, Falkirk: CRC.

Collins, A., Seely Brown, J. and Newman, S.E. (1989) Cognitive Apprenticeship: Teaching the Crafts of Reading, Writing and Mathematics. In Resnick, L.B. (ed.), *Knowing, Learning and Instruction*, London: Lawrence Erlbaum.

Dalli, C. (2001) Being an Early Childhood Teacher: Images of Professional Practice and Professional Identity During the Experience of Starting Childcare. Paper presented at the NZARE Annual Conference, 6–9 December, Christchurch.

Daycare Trust (2011) *Summary of the Childcare Costs Survey 2011*. Available at www.daycaretrust.org.uk/pages/summary-of-the-childcare-costs-survey-2011.html, accessed 24 April 2014.

Daycare Trust (2012) *Improving Our Understanding of Informal Childcare in the UK*. Available at www.daycaretrust.org.uk/data/files/Interim_report_executive_summary_5.pdf, accessed 24 April 2014.

Department for Children, Schools and Families (DCSF) (2003) *Every Child Matters*, London: The Stationery Office.

Department for Children, Schools and Families (DCSF) (2009) *Next Steps for Early Learning and Childcare Building on the 10-Year Strategy*, London: DCSF Publications.

Department for Education and Employment (DfEE) (1998a) *Meeting the Childcare Challenge*, London: HMSO.

Department for Education and Employment (DfEE) (1998b) *Early Years Development and Childcare Partnership: Planning Guidance 1999–2000*, London: DfEE Publications.

Department for Education and Employment (DfEE) (1999) *Good Practice for EYDC Partnerships: Developing and Supporting High Quality, Sustainable Childcare*, London: DfEE Publications.

Department for Education and Employment (DfEE) (2000) *Curriculum Guidance for the Foundation Stage*, London: QCA.

Department for Education and Science (DfES) (1992) *Aspects of Primary Education: The Education of Children Under Five*, London: HMSO.

Department for Education and Skills (DfES) (2002) *Birth to Three Matters*, London: QCA.

Department for Education and Skills (DfES) (2003a) *Together from the Start: Practical Guidance for Professionals Working with Disabled Children (Birth to Third Birthday) and Their Families*, London: DfES.

Department for Education and Skills (DfES) (2003b) *Foundation Stage Profile Handbook*, London: QCA.

Department for Education and Skills (DfES) (2007) *Statutory Framework for the Early Years Foundation Stage*, London: DfES.

Desforges, C. (2003) *The Impact of Parental Involvement, Parental Support and Family Education on Pupil Achievements and Adjustment: A Literature Review*, London: DfES Publications.

Dumfries and Galloway Regional Council (1992) *Education Three to Five: Nursery Education Guidelines*, Dumfries: DGRC.

Ermisch, J. and Francesconi, M. (2001) *The Effects of Parents' Employment on Children's Lives*, London: Family Policy Studies Centre.

Froebel, F. (1887) *Education of Man*, London: D. Appleton and Company.

HM Treasury (2005) *Support for Parents, the Best Start for Children*, London: The Stationery Office.

Ingram, A. (2008) Investing in Children's Futures: The New Childhood Practice Awards, *SSSC*, 1.

Learning and Teaching Scotland (LTS) (1999) *A Curriculum Framework for Children 3 to 5*, Dundee: LTS.

Learning and Teaching Scotland (LTS) (2010) *Pre-Birth to Three: Positive Outcomes for Scotland's Children and Families*, Dundee: LTS.

Lewis, R. (1987) *How to Help Learners Assess Their Progress*. London: Council for Educational Technology.

Lodge, P. and Blackstone, T. (1982) *Educational Policy and Educational Inequality*, London: Martin Robertson.

Lothian Regional Council Education Department (1992) *A Curriculum for the Early Years*, Edinburgh: LRC.

McCartney, K. (1984) Effect of Quality Day Care Environment on Children's Language Development, *Developmental Psychology*, 20(2), 244–260.

Melhuish, E.C. (2004) *A Literature Review of the Impact of Early Years Provision on Young Children, with Emphasis Given to Children from Disadvantaged Backgrounds*, London: National Audit Office.

Menmuir, J. and Hughes, A. (2004) Early Education and Childcare: The Developing Profession, *European Early Childhood Education Research Journal*, 12(2), 33–41.

Moss, P. (1991) Policy Issues in Day Care. In Moss, P. and Melhuish, E., *Current Issues in Day Care for Young Children*, London: HMSO.

Moss, P. (2003) Who is the worker in services for young children? *Children in Europe*, 5: 2–5.

Moss, P. and Penn, H. (1996) *Transforming Nursery Education*, London: Paul Chapman.

Moyles, J. (1989) *Just Playing*, Maidenhead: Open University Press.

OfSTED (2012) *Registered Childcare Providers and Places in England March 2012: Key Findings*. Available at www.ofsted.gov.uk/resources/registered-childcare-providers-and-places-england-december-2008-onwards, accessed 24 April 2014.

Penn, H. (1992) *Under-Fives: The View from Strathclyde*, Edinburgh: Scottish Academic Press.

Philips. D., McCartney, K. and Scarr, S. (1987) Child Care Quality and Children's Social Development, *Developmental Psychology*, 23(4), 537–543.

Quality Assurance Agency (QAA) (2007) *The Standard for Childhood Practice*. Available at www.qaa.ac.uk/Publications/InformationAndGuidance/Documents/earlyYears.pdf, accessed 24 April 2014.

Ross, J. (2006) The Reliability, Validity and Utility of Self-Assessment, *Practical Assessment Research and Evaluation*, 11(10), 1–13.

Schaffer, H.R. (1977) *Mothering*, London: Fontana.

Schweinhart, L.J., Montie, J., Xiang, Z., Barnett, W.S., Belfield, C.R. and Nores, M. (2005) *Lifetime Effects: The High/Scope Perry Preschool Study Through Age 40*, Ypsilanti, MI: High/Scope Press.

Scottish Education Department (1950) *The Primary School in Scotland*, Edinburgh: HMSO.

Scottish Education Department (1965) *Primary Education in Scotland*, Edinburgh: HMSO.

Scottish Education Department (1971) *Before Five*, Edinburgh: HMSO.

Scottish Executive (2004) *A Curriculum for Excellence 3–18*, Crown Copyright.

Scottish Executive (2007) *A Curriculum for Excellence: Building the Curriculum 3–18 (2) Active Learning in the Early Years*, Crown Copyright.

Scottish Government (2005) *Assessment is for Learning*. Information Sheet.

Scottish Government (2008a) *The Early Years Framework*, Edinburgh: Scottish Government.

Scottish Government (2008b) *A Guide to Getting it Right for Every Child*. Edinburgh: Scottish Government.

Scottish Government (2010) *Pre-school and Childcare Statistics 2010*. Available at www.scotland.gov.uk/Resource/Doc/326162/0105080.pdf, accessed 24 April 2014.

Scottish Office (1997) *A Curriculum Framework for Children in their Pre-school Year*, Edinburgh: Scottish Office.

Scottish Office (1998) *Meeting the Childcare Challenge: A Childcare Strategy for Scotland*, London: The Stationery Office.

Sylva, K. and Moss, P. (1992) *Learning Before School*, London: National Commission on Education.

Sylva, K. and Wiltshire, J.E. (1994) The Impact of Early Learning on Children's Later Development, *Education Section Review*, 18(2), 47.

Sylva, K., Melhuish, E., Sammons, P., Siraj-Blatchford, I., Taggart, B. and Elliot, K. (2003) *The Effective Provision of Pre-School Education (EPPE) Project: The Pre-school Period*, Nottingham: DfES.

Sylva, K., Melhuish, E., Sammons, P., Siraj-Blatchford, I. and Taggart, B. (2004) *The Effective Provision of Pre-School Education (EPPE) Project: Final Report*, DfES and Institute of Education, University of London.

Tizard, B. and Hughes, M. (1984) *Young Children Learning*, London: Fontana.

Watt, J. (1990) *Early Education: The Current Debate*, Edinburgh: Scottish Academic Press.

Whitebread, D., Anderson, H., Coltman, P., Page, C., Pino Pasternak, D. and Mehta, S. (2005) Developing Independent learning in the Early Years, *Education 3–13*, 33(1), 40–50.

Wiliam, D. (2006). Does Assessment Hinder Learning? *S*peech delivered at the ETS Europe breakfast seminar (11 July). Available at www.dylanwiliam.net, accessed 24 April 2014.

Wilkinson, E.J. (1995) Community Nurseries: Integrated Provision for Pre-Fives, *Early Childhood Development and Care*, 108, 1–106.

13

Compulsory education in the United Kingdom

Ian Menter, Carmel Gallagher, Louise Hayward and Dominic Wyse[1]

My mother wanted me have an education, that's why she kept me out of school.

Margaret Mead

Introduction

Compulsory education – a simple phrase, but what does it mean? For a child born 1,000 years ago, it would have meant very little. The emergence of education as a social system only started – and then only in Western Europe and for a small proportion of children – during the Middle Ages. Few children born in England or Scotland in 1600 would have received 'an education'. In the eighteenth century, registers show that proportionately more people in Scotland signed their name on parish registers than in most countries in Europe. By 1800, a boy born to the landed classes or into a clerical family might well have been compelled to attend school; a girl of the same background might have received an education from a private governess. In addition, middle-class boys in towns in Scotland often had the opportunity in new academies to develop the skills needed to grow businesses. However, by 1901, every child born in Britain was required by law to attend school to the age of 14. Exemptions from this rule were possible in England only where the child possessed a certificate indicating that they had reached the educational standard required by the local by-laws (DfES 2003).

By the 1990s, not only was attendance at school compulsory for the majority of children from the age of five until the age of 16, but for much of the time spent there, the content of the curriculum had also become statutory, at least in England, Wales and Northern Ireland, with non-statutory guidelines in Scotland. By 2000, the majority of children in England aged 5–11 were compelled to attend school, compelled to follow a defined curriculum and compelled to be taught for part of the day through a centrally determined method – the literacy and numeracy national strategies. Those who were not compelled to attend school were nevertheless to be educated 'otherwise' (see below) and those attending private schools were not required to follow the National Curriculum or the national strategies.

In this chapter we trace the apparent steady encroachment of the state, through its education system, on the 'freedom of the child', from the nineteenth century through to the present. The first half of the chapter examines these historical developments in more detail and seeks to explore the intentions and motivations behind each element of compulsion. In the later part of the chapter we describe and critically examine the current situation across the four countries that make up the UK. There is a sense in which it is helpful to judge developments in other parts of the UK as responses to English developments – sometimes accepting and adopting similar policies and sometimes reacting against and developing alternative policies.

The development of compulsory education in the UK

The emergence of state education

Green (1997) has noted that the education systems developed after the formation of the British state. Therefore, by contrast with several other European countries, the education system played a less significant part in the formation of national identity, except in Scotland where education, church and law remained as distinctive markers of Scottish identity. Rather, the way in which the education system developed may be seen as a reflection of the existing 'settlement' of national identity. As we shall see, the notion of national identity in the context of Great Britain or of the United Kingdom is far from settled. 'British' has often been confused with 'English' – particularly by the English and by people from outside the UK.

In tracing the emergence of state education systems we can see the strong influence of a 'voluntary' sector. Green (1997) goes so far as to suggest that:

> Both in the eighteenth and nineteenth centuries this voluntary approach was held to be morally, and educationally, superior to compulsory schooling schemes in continental Europe. These were associated with despotism and subservience, in contrast to the freedoms enjoyed by British citizens, which were seen as being essential to British character. Voluntarism ... meant freedom for pupils from compulsory attendance, and freedom for schools from state interference.
>
> (p. 94)

Towards the end of the nineteenth century this voluntaristic ideology came into considerable tension with some other strong emergent beliefs. There was a powerful belief in the rights of all children to be educated to a basic level of literacy in order to engage with the modern world. There was also a separate, but often related, belief in the development of society through education. But third, and most powerfully of all, was the belief that in the interest of maintaining morality in society, all people should be able to read – in order to have personal access to the messages contained in the Bible.

Thus it was from the outset that the churches played a major role in the provision of schooling. Even before elementary schooling was made compulsory in the 1870s, a very large majority of children were attending some form of schooling for at least a year or two, with a strongly Christian dimension. The quality of provision was very variable and few stayed beyond the age of 11. In Scotland the leaving age was 13 from 1872 and in England it was set at 11 in 1893; by 1901 it had been raised to 14 in both countries.[2]

Driving the development of schooling and its emergence as a state system was the motor of the Industrial Revolution. The nineteenth century saw both an enormous expansion of the population in Britain (almost doubling in 50 years from 1821 to 1871, to an estimated 26 million), but also very large increases in the proportion of that population who were children and of the proportion who were living in urban settlements.

Provision of secondary education during the nineteenth century was even more uneven than that of elementary schooling. Secondary schools existed largely as foundations established to provide entry into the higher professions, often via one of the universities, and the pupils were largely children from middle and upper social classes, although even at this time it was possible for a small number of pupils from poor backgrounds to gain admission. It was not until 1902, with the creation of Local Education Authorities in England and Wales, that a national system of secondary education began to emerge. The Board of Education had been established in 1899 and by 1904 it had defined a four-year secondary programme leading to a certificate.

In Scotland, School Boards continued to be responsible for school education until the establishment of elected Education Authorities in 1918; the territories of these corresponded to the 35 counties and cities which took over educational responsibilities in the 1930s. The 1918 Act also transferred all Catholic schools to these Education Authorities.

School Boards were not intended to provide secondary education. The long-established secondary schools continued in existence; however, School Boards in urban areas began to find ways of establishing higher grade schools – secondary schools in all but name. The Higher examination was established in 1888 by the four ancient universities.[3] Responsibility for this later passed to Her Majesty's Inspectorate; a number of other certificates, some of which were short-lived, were created for pupils who left school before the age of 16.

These developments of elementary and secondary education, together with major developments in university education, effectively established – by the end of the nineteenth century – the framework for education in Britain that still exists today.

It is possible to understand the way in which state education developed in its compulsory form as a continuing struggle between different interest groups in society. Raymond Williams (1961) offered a very interesting account along these lines in his influential book *The Long Revolution*. The revolution of Williams' title was the gradual emergence by the second half of the twentieth century of social democracy in Britain. He examines the way in which transformations in a number of social and cultural institutions – including the press, broadcasting, fiction and drama – have played a part in the creation of this society.

In his account of the development of education, Williams identifies three groups who each played a part in the way in which state education was constructed in the late nineteenth century, but who, he also argues, could still be identified at the time he was writing, in the second half of the twentieth century. The three groups he identified were:

1. the public educators – who argued that 'men had a natural human right to be educated, and that any good society depended on governments accepting this principle as their duty';
2. the industrial trainers – who 'promoted education in terms of training and disciplining the poor, as workers and citizens';
3. the old humanists – who promoted 'a liberal education, in relation to man's health as a spiritual being' (Williams 1961: 162–163).

As we trace compulsory education through the twentieth century, it is not difficult to see these three groups continuing to argue their cases, sometimes in cooperation with each other and sometimes in opposition.

The development of state education in the twentieth century

The legacy of the nineteenth century for elementary schools was a tightly defined and – in the light of subsequent developments – narrow, knowledge-based curriculum. This was broadened, at least in theory, when the Revised Code was published in 1904. The purposes of elementary schools was 'to form and strengthen the character and develop the intelligence of children, and ... assist both girls and boys, according to their different needs, to fit themselves, practically as well as intellectually, for the work of life' (quoted by Ross 2000: 21). As secondary schools developed in the early part of the twentieth century, however, their curriculum was based very much on subjects, including English, Latin, geography, history, mathematics and science, drawing, manual work, physical exercises and housewifery (in girls' schools) (see Ross 2000).

So both in the emerging primary and in the secondary curriculum we can see the influence of Williams' industrial trainer strand and of the public educator strand. The old humanist strand is there too, in the commitment to particular forms of intellectual knowledge, but this came increasingly to the fore as the century progressed, through the development of a child-centred philosophy which emphasised the individualism of each human being and, drawing on ideas from the burgeoning discipline of psychology, as well as some traditional philosophical strands, educationists argued for an approach which was based on the individual needs of the child. This way of thinking was especially prevalent in relation to younger children and was clearly articulated in the Hadow Reports of 1926, 1931 and 1933.

The Second World War had a major impact on the development of the 'welfare state'. It was recognised that families whose young people had served the country so bravely in wartime deserved the kind of social support that should now be affordable, at least once post-war reconstruction was fully underway. So it was that the National Health Service and the social security system both emerged at this time. In education in England, Wales and Northern Ireland, the coalition government of the day supported the development of the 1944 *Education Act*, under the leadership of the Secretary of the Board of Education, R.A. Butler. The parallel legislation in Scotland was the 1945 *Education (Scotland) Act*. The significant achievement of these pieces of legislation was the establishment of the provision of universal secondary education for the first time. This was achieved through creating a two-stage approach to compulsory education, bringing in a transfer from primary to secondary education at the age of 11.

A further 'achievement' of the act was to legitimate differentiation in secondary schooling, a feature that was the subject of considerable contestation throughout the rest of the twentieth century and indeed continues in different forms to this day. The idea which underpinned this policy was that children could be classified by their ability to benefit from different forms of education. It was believed that some children were capable of greater intellectual development than others, according to their supposedly innate – and therefore fixed – level of intelligence. So it was that children could legitimately be channelled into a grammar school or a secondary modern school or a technical school. The channelling (actually selection) was largely achieved through the administration of a public examination, the '11-plus',[4] as it became known. Sociological studies carried out during the 1950s and 1960s claimed to show how this system severely curtailed opportunity for many children from working-class backgrounds, which led the Labour Party to commit itself to the provision of 'comprehensive education' in 1965, a universalist approach to compulsory schooling which aimed to see all children attending their local neighbourhood school. In England this goal was only partially achieved during the later part of the century and, under 'New Labour', around the recent turn of the century, we saw the emergence of a new discourse of specialisation, through which secondary schools are encouraged to develop a profile in a particular area of the curriculum and pupils can be selected, in part, through their aptitude in this field, whether it be the arts, sport, languages or whatever other field the school claims strength in. In Scotland all publicly funded schools are comprehensive.

The private schooling sector (of which some schools are in England confusingly described as 'public schools') has continued its parallel existence throughout the whole historical period, effectively ensuring that a sector of society, mostly those with sufficient wealth to have the choice, is removed from the state school population. Schools in the private sector are not required to offer the National Curriculum, or to administer national tests. There is a further group of students who are not educated in school at all but may be taught at home, often by one or both of their parents. For those parents who are against schooling as a form of education or who believe their children will not benefit from institutional provision, it remains possible to opt out. However, both the private sector and home schooling are subject to legal requirements, designed to ensure that the education, health and welfare needs of children are met.

The legal dimension to the compulsion in school attendance – or 'education otherwise' – has been given added significance over recent years because of two factors. The first has been the increased emphasis on 'parental choice' of the school their children will attend. The discourse of choice was very much a part of the Conservative government's approach to the marketisation of education from the 1980s onwards. 'Open enrolment' was a phrase derived from their 1988 *Education Reform Act*, which imposed on schools the requirement to admit children who wished to attend. This requirement could not be entirely open-ended, however, for very practical reasons, including the physical size of a school and the need to organise pupils into viable class units. So what was the parent who could not secure a place for their child at their chosen school meant to do? Although there were appeal procedures and parents were often offered a range of alternatives, in the end the law required them to ensure their child was educated. As Harris (1993) says:

> The basic legal duty on a parent to ensure that his or her child receives an efficient full-time education suitable to his or her age, ability and aptitude, 'either by regular attendance at school or otherwise', has not changed since the Education Act 1944.
>
> (p. 43)

The second factor that has increased the significance of compulsion is the increased attention which has been paid to truancy. This has been a high priority under all recent governments. Truancy rates (actually more positively described as attendance rates) have been a key performance indicator for schools since the development of published profiles and performance tables during the 1980s. It was the Labour government, however, which strengthened new legislation in England aimed at bringing the parents of frequent truants to court.

In the development of compulsory education in the UK over the past 100 years or so, England can be seen as having been the main driving force – because of its size and the locus of power in Westminster – at least until devolution in the late 1990s. However, it is often said that education is more highly valued in each of the three smaller parts of the UK than it is England. Certainly, Scottish identity has a strong element of pride in its education provision. This stems in part from the success of the Scottish ancient universities in the stimulation of the 'invention of the modern world' (see Herman 2001). Since the creation of the uneasy union between England and Scotland in 1707, education, together with the Church and the legal system, have been seen as the triumvirate of Scottish distinctiveness. Among those who have written about the separate development of the Scottish education system, Humes and Bryce (2003) have described its distinctiveness in terms not only of organisational differences (which are described below) but also in terms of national culture and identity, including a particular set of values (see also Paterson 2003).

The particular distinctive elements of the provision of compulsory education in Wales and Northern Ireland are discussed in the next section of this chapter.

Compulsory education in the twenty-first century UK

Organisation

As noted in the first section of this chapter, currently all pupils aged between five (or four in Northern Ireland) and 16 must receive full-time education either at school or through alternative arrangements approved by the state. Education is free at the point of delivery in each of the more than 22,000 primary schools and the 4,300 secondary schools of the UK, and statutory education is organised as a continuous progression between primary and secondary education with very slight variations in the age of transfer to secondary education between the four countries (Figure 13.1).

It can be argued that, over the last 50 years, compulsory education in the UK, and in England more particularly, has been characterised by the two seemingly conflicting trends of *rationalisation* and *diversification* of its provision. Table 13.1 presents a complex system of state-maintained, selective and independent schools together with more recently introduced schemes in England such as 'academies' and 'free schools'. There have also been several distinctive national initiatives, such as *Integrated Schools* in Northern Ireland and the introduction of *New Community Schools*, *Learning Communities* and *Schools of Ambition* in Scotland. Furthermore, the existence of *Welsh-medium*, *Gaelic-medium* and *Irish-medium* schools in Wales, Scotland and Northern Ireland, respectively, is an indication of the ongoing debate, fuelled by devolution, around issues of national identity, the place of indigenous languages in the education system and that of education generally in the process of nation building.

The first rationalisation move was a result of the 1944 *Education Act* in England and Wales and the 1947 *Education Act* in Northern Ireland, which abolished the former division between elementary and higher education and established three phases of education with the first two – primary (5–11) and secondary (11–15, and later 16) – being compulsory. This generally resulted in the construction of new schools as well as the progressive reorganisation of primary and secondary schools in accordance with the new pattern.

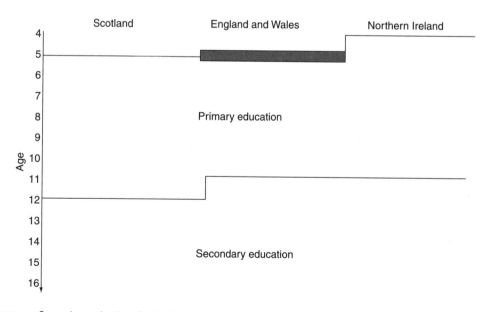

FIGURE 13.1 General organisation of schooling.

TABLE 13.1 Primary and secondary schools in the UK

	Wales	England	Northern Ireland	Scotland
Primary schools	Public sector: (1,624) ■ *Infant (4–7)* ■ *Junior (7–11)* ■ *Infant/junior (5–11) 27%* *Welsh-medium schools* **In some parts:** *Preparatory schools (5–12/13)*	Public Sector: (16,814) ■ *Infant (4–7)* ■ *Junior (7–11)* ■ *Combined infant and junior (5–11)* **In some parts:** First schools (5–8) Middle schools (9–14) Academies: 561 Free schools: 17	Public sector: (854) Irish-medium 27 *Grammar school Prep departments* 15	Public sector: (2,271) ■ *Gaelic-medium schools (58)*
Secondary schools	**Comprehensive and non-selective** Public sector: (227) Of which Welsh-medium schools (14) <u>Non-maintained (56)</u>	**Mostly comprehensive, some selection** Public sector: (3,226) ■ *LA maintained: (1,891)* Academies (1,331) Free schools (4) <u>Independent schools – primary and secondary phases (1,918)</u>	**Selective** Public sector: (235) Grammar schools (68) Secondary (148) Irish-medium (1) Integrated (20) Special schools (41) Hospital schools (2) Independent (15)	**Comprehensive and non-selective** Public sector: (387) ■ *Gaelic-medium schools (19)* <u>Non-maintained (122)</u>

In England, at least until recently, most primary schools have been maintained by local authorities, and are divided into infant schools (5–7), junior schools (7–11) and combined infant and junior schools, which cater for both age groups. In some parts of England a three-tier system still exists which can consist of first (5–8), middle (9–14) and then high or upper schools. There are more than 19,000 schools, early years and other settings in England that are maintained fully or in part by local authorities compared to just over 1,900 independent schools and settings (www.education.gov.uk/edubase) that, as their name suggests, are independent of government funding. There were four main types of state schools: community schools; foundation and trust schools; voluntary-aided schools; voluntary-controlled schools. Community schools aim to develop strong links with the local community and are run by local authorities who decide on the admission criteria. Foundation and trust schools are run by their own governing body, as are voluntary-aided schools, which are mainly religious schools. Voluntary-controlled schools are also mainly religious schools but are run by local authorities. The range of types of formal educational settings in England increased significantly as a result of the policies of the New Labour government of 1997 and the Conservative-Liberal Democrat coalition government of 2010. The types of schools includes: free schools; academies; university training schools; university technical colleges (UTCs) and studio schools; faith schools; and trust schools (www.education.gov.uk/schools/leadership/typesofschools). Perhaps the most controversial of these types are the *free schools*. The first free school opened in September 2011. According to the government, the key feature of free schools is that they are set up to respond to local demand. They are non-profit-making, independent state-funded schools (to add further confusion to the public–private, independent–state divisions) that can be located in any suitable premises and can be set up by a wide range of proposers. Free schools do not have to follow the national curriculum but are inspected by the national inspection organisation, OfSTED.[5]

Funding for schools in Wales still comes from the UK government as part of the Barnett formula, a non-statutory mechanism based on population, which is used to decide funding to the different countries.[6] In Wales each county and county borough council is responsible for the funding and organisation of schools in its area.[7] This applies across the two main types of schools in Wales that are either fully maintained by the local authority or voluntary-aided schools. The general statistics about schools in Wales in 2012 included the following break down: nursery schools 23; primary schools 1,435; secondary schools 222; special schools 43; and independent schools 66.[8] Wales has also seen significant changes to its national curriculum leading to a Foundation Stage for children from birth to age eight, followed by a primary phase and a secondary phase. The other key difference about Wales is the ways in which Welsh bilingualism has influenced the system (see Wyse *et al.* 2013).

In Scotland and Northern Ireland, primary schools cover the whole seven years of primary education from Primary 1 to Primary 7 and are funded by the Local Authority Education Departments in Scotland (now with a range of titles, e.g. Children's Services) and the Education and Library Boards in Northern Ireland. Some children are educated in the preparatory department of grammar schools in Northern Ireland.

Despite the establishment of national schools in the nineteenth century on the principle of non-denomination, in Northern Ireland schools have historically become segregated along religious lines. At primary level, there are four main categories of schools: (1) controlled primary schools, which are attended mainly by children from a Protestant background; (2) voluntary maintained primary schools, which are attended mainly by children from a Catholic background; (3) integrated schools, which are attended by children from both denominations; and (4) grammar preparatory schools.

At secondary level, a second rationalisation occurred in 1965 with the generalisation of comprehensive schooling mentioned earlier that would cater for all children regardless of their ability. Within just over a decade there were no selective secondary schools in Scotland. In England, the number of grammar schools and secondary modern schools declined rapidly in the 1970s and 1980s. In Wales, as in Scotland, there are now only comprehensive schools. Grammar schools remain in Northern Ireland and some in certain parts of England. Whether at primary or secondary level, the majority of Welsh pupils (97 per cent) attend comprehensive schools. In Scotland and England the figures are 95 per cent and 89 per cent, respectively (Croxford 2000). The remaining pupils attend selective schools in the public sector or fee-paying independent schools.

In Northern Ireland, state-sponsored selection by ability ceased in 2009 but was quickly replaced by unregulated selection through two types of selection tests operated by private companies, on behalf of the maintained, largely Catholic, grammar school system and the controlled, largely Protestant, grammar school sector. Around 70 per cent of children aged 11 take either or both tests to gain entry to one of the 68 grammar and some integrated schools. The results show that while some schools, mainly in Belfast, only accept students with top grades, other schools accept students with much lower scores. This trend has led to more pupils attending grammar schools than was the case under the regulated system. In 2011–2012 grammar school intake had risen to 63,000. Those who do not sit the test or cannot gain entry to oversubscribed grammar schools (around 84,000 pupils in 2011–2012) attend one of the 148 secondary intermediate schools. Again both grammar and secondary schools are divided between controlled and voluntary maintained schools, segregated along religious lines, except for 20 schools which are officially designated as integrated.

Croxford (2001) has investigated the implementation and impact of compulsory schooling in the UK. She reports that in Scotland 'the change from selective to comprehensive schooling between 1965 and 1975 led to an increase in the average attainment of all pupils but especially those with low prior attainment and girls' (p. 1). Talking to the Northern Ireland Association for Headteachers in secondary schools, Croxford argued that because Scotland has embraced a comprehensive system more wholeheartedly than England and Northern Ireland, comprehensive education has been more successful in Scotland in reducing social inequality. It has also resulted in a reduction in extremes of low and high pupil attainment which, she argues, are reinforced by less uniform or more selective schooling provision, such as that currently existing in England and Northern Ireland, respectively. She points out, however, that through parents' choice of school or use of subject specialism, hidden forms of selection can be found in both Scotland and England.

Since the late 1980s, compulsory education in the UK has been characterised by an increasing diversity of provision between its four components. In Northern Ireland, the creation of mixed-faith schools by parents, known as *integrated schools,* many of which are now grant-aided, has resulted in 7 per cent of students now attending one of 60 integrated primary schools and 20 integrated secondary schools. The opening of new integrated schools has slowed down as a result of declining demographics and financial constraints. However, some schools with a mixed religious intake have chosen to 'transform' to integrated status. The most recent initiative to try to address the segregated nature of schooling, entitled 'Sharing Education', encourages schools to cooperate across sectors and share classrooms, courses and resources across neighbouring schools. Against the backdrop of the ongoing financial crisis and demographic downturn there is currently a major move towards strategic planning on an area basis to reshape the structure and pattern of education provision. Viability audits are being undertaken to inform the creation of an effectively planned, sustainable and affordable pattern of schools to ensure the delivery of financially viable quality education.

In Scotland there has been a range of initiatives that seek to encourage the integration of the provision of school education with social work and health education. The most high-profile of these was the New Community Schools (NCS) initiative (SCRE 2001). The aim was to raise children's educational achievement through the improvement of the child's wider social, physical and familial condition. In the case of the NCS, extra funding was provided to either single schools or clusters of schools to allow the integration and expansion of the range of services offered to young people in disadvantaged areas (SEED 2003). More recently, all schools in Scotland were organised into clusters, most commonly centred around a secondary school and its associated primary schools.

Diversity of provision in the UK is nowhere more marked than in England, where a concern for diversity and parental choice emerged strongly in the 1980s under the then Conservative government (see Clough *et al.* 1991; Docking 2000a). The changes made to the schooling provision in England differ in their nature from those implemented in the Scottish system, whose 'strong egalitarian and universalistic tenor … has proven resistant to attempts to devolve governance to institutions and to use competition to improve performance' (Ozga and Lawn 1999: 228). From the mid 1990s in England, the New Labour government took up the Conservative commitment to diversity while reasserting at the same time a somewhat conflicting rationalisation agenda thereby seeking to introduce 'co-operation within a system designed for competitiveness' (Jackson 2000: 178).

The election of the Conservative–Liberal Democrat coalition government in 2010 brought a mixture of radical change and the reassertion of historically recurring ideas to educational policy. Much New Labour thinking was swept away, in most cases literally removed from government websites and archived (e.g. the National Curriculum, see below). The government White Paper *The Importance of Teaching* (DfE 2010) clearly set out the new agendas. The most important of these agendas is the perceived need to compete with international competitors, as David Cameron, the prime minister, and Nick Clegg the deputy prime minister, make clear in their introductory remarks.

Although the explicit emphasis on measurement by international surveys of achievement such as PISA (the Programme for International Student Assessment) by Cameron and Clegg was new, the comparison with other countries was also clearly seen in New Labour policy, e.g. the comparisons with Taiwan in 1997. Building on the City Technology Colleges idea of the government of Margaret Thatcher, and the Academies programme of New Labour, the coalition government intensified its support for academies. The government's claim was that schools performing well in statutory assessments of pupil progress would be able to convert to academy status provided they worked with other schools to help them improve, or if they become part of a federation of schools, but our conversations with headteachers suggest that such collaboration is not always necessary. The status and quality of teachers is also high on the government's agenda, with high praise for *Teach First* (the import from the United States that recruits high-achieving students from the country's best universities into the teaching profession) and an intensification of school-based teacher training. A key paragraph in the White Paper links teacher status with high standards and, somewhat paradoxically, freedom from external control:

> In England, what is needed most of all is decisive action to free our teachers from constraint and improve their professional status and authority, raise the standards set by our curriculum and qualifications to match the best in the world and, having freed schools from external control, hold them effectively to account for the results they achieve. Government should make sure that school funding is fair, with more money for the most disadvantaged, but should then support the efforts of teachers, helping them to learn from one another and from proven best practice, *rather than ceaselessly directing them to follow centralised Government initiatives*.
>
> (DfE 2010: 8; emphasis added)

The paradox is that high-profile initiatives such as the *phonics screening check* for all six-year-old children in England, and the initiatives linked to this in teaching, teacher training and associated areas aiming to ensure compliance, shows much increased government control even when compared to New Labour. One of the main features of the ideological shift in policy is a tension between offering more freedoms to professionals including teachers while at the same time assuming even greater control than New Labour of key areas of schooling.

Curriculum

The system of compulsory education in England, Wales and Northern Ireland as we know it today is the result of the state's unprecedented intervention in education from the late 1980s. Through the 1988 *Education Reform Act* and the introduction of a National Curriculum the Conservative government effectively took away from the teaching profession their responsibility for deciding what should be taught to pupils of compulsory school age in all state schools in England and Wales. The new statutory document also set out attainment targets for learning and provided a specific framework for the assessment, monitoring and reporting of pupils' learning (see *Assessment*, below). Similar curricula already existed in other European countries such as France or Germany, where education historically played a much more prominent role in the construction of the state, but in England and Wales this initiative was perceived as having 'fundamentally and probably irreversibly transformed the nature of state education' (Bash and Coulby 1989: 1). The curriculum was implemented between 1989 and 1996 in England and Wales and a number of changes were introduced during that time by the Secretary of State in each country.

The *Education Reform Act* of 1988 did not apply to Northern Ireland and Scotland, both of which had their own separate curriculum arrangements (see Table 13.2). However, until 2006 it could be said that in all four countries 'curricula are formulated in terms of aims and objectives, including 'general teaching requirements' or 'common requirements' and educational cross-curricular themes, programmes of study, targets of attainment and exemplary schemes of work' (Le Metais *et al.* 2001: 9).

In Northern Ireland, a compulsory 'common' curriculum was established by the *Northern Ireland Order 1989* and was introduced into schools in 1990. The curriculum underwent significant review between 2000 and 2007 to increase curriculum *relevance* and to move towards the *development of important life skills* (Smith 2003: 4). The content of the 14–16 curriculum was particularly criticised by the CCEA Chief Executive, Gavin Boyd, in 2001 as being 'too rigid, too narrow and too academic, with vocational and technical qualifications often seen as second best' and therefore failing to prepare pupils for the challenge of the twenty-first century (CCEA 2001a). The revised Northern Ireland Curriculum, implemented since September 2007, moved away from a heavily content-led curriculum towards a more flexible framework which allowed for increased teacher agency and a more explicit emphasis on skills and capabilities at all key stages.[9] The aim of the revised curriculum is to enable young people to achieve their potential and to make informed and responsible choices and decisions throughout their lives as individuals, and as contributors to society, the economy and the environment. Provision at all Key Stages is enhanced by nine (cross-curricular) key elements and by a framework for thinking skills and personal capabilities. Each element of the revised curriculum is explained and justified in a detailed 18-page rationale.

At Key Stages 1 and 2 pupils have access to seven areas of learning including: language and literacy; maths and numeracy; the arts; the world around us; personal development and mutual understanding; physical development/education; and religious education (Figure 13.2).

At Key Stage 3 pupils have access to nine areas of study, similar to those for the primary curriculum but with the additional provision for modern languages and learning for life and work (Figure 13.3).

In a similar way to England and Wales, where *citizenship* was introduced in September 2002, in Northern Ireland the new area of *learning for life and work* makes modular provision for *local and global citizenship*, and also for *personal development*, *employability* and *home economics*.

Following the enactment of the *Standards in Scotland's Schools Act* (2002), incorporating ideas from the UN Declaration on the Rights of the Child (2001), a national debate

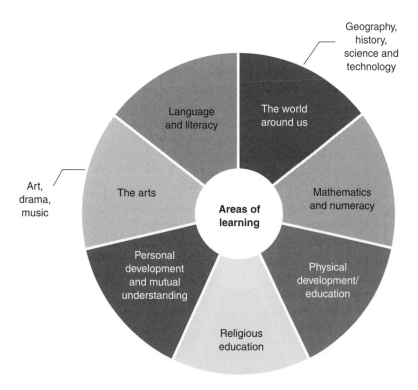

Geography,
history,
science and
technology

Language
and literacy

The world
around us

Art,
drama,
music

The arts

**Areas of
learning**

Mathematics
and numeracy

Personal
development
and mutual
understanding

Physical
development/
education

Religious
education

FIGURE 13.2 Subjects at Key Stages 1 and 2 (source: www.nicurriculum.org.uk/parents_site/primary/subjects/index.asp).

on the future of education in Scotland was initiated. A view had emerged that the 5–14 curriculum, described earlier, had become cluttered, fragmented and over-assessed. Further, there was a view that teachers' practices were being overly constrained by the 5–14 guidelines that had been implemented in ways described as being similar to tramlines. A new curriculum, entitled *Curriculum for Excellence* (CfE), was introduced in 2004 as an attempt to address a number of issues of such concerns. For the first time, there was to be a single curriculum 3–18, to be supported by 'a simple and effective structure of assessment and qualifications' (SEED 2004b: Foreword). CfE made explicit the values on which it was based, those engraved on the Scottish Mace (wisdom, justice, integrity and compassion). Like all previous curricula in Scotland, although CfE is in essence advisory, not statutory, it is the basis of education in every local authority in the country. The framework comprises a broad general education (ages 3–15) with greater specialisation in the senior phase (ages 16–18) when young people are working towards National Qualifications. CfE in Scotland aims to focus on making learning more engaging and relevant to the real world, increase personalisation and learners' choice, raise standards, enable young people to improve their confidence, skills, achievement and attainment and introduce more flexibility, giving teachers greater professional freedom.

Literacy, numeracy and health and well-being are cross-curricular elements in CfE. This curriculum emphasises the important contribution to learning of the ethos and life

FIGURE 13.3 Subjects at Key Stages 3 and 4 (source: www.nicurriculum.org.uk/parents_site/post_primary/subjects/index.asp).

of the school as a community, of the ways in which learning is organised and of inter-disciplinary work. One of the innovative features of CfE lies in its concern to recognise young people's personal achievements within and beyond school, through partner-ships with, e.g. business, arts and community organisations, in addition to school-based learning.

In attempting to make explicit what it is to be an educated Scot in twenty-first-century society, CfE identifies four 'capacities' all young people should become: successful learners; confident individuals; responsible citizens; and effective contributors.

The curriculum identifies experiences and outcomes, identified as 'I can' statements in eight curriculum areas (Scottish Government 2009):

- expressive arts
- languages and literacy
- religious and moral education
- social studies

- mathematics and numeracy
- sciences
- technologies
- health and well-being.

The experiences and outcomes are presented within a framework of levels for ages 3–15:

- *Early*, in preschool and in Primary 1 (age ~3–6).
- *First* by end of Primary 4 (age 7–8), but earlier or later for some.
- *Second* by end of Primary 7 (age 10–11), but earlier or later for some.
- *Third* and *fourth* in Secondary 1–3 (age 12–15), but earlier for some.

The fourth-level experiences and outcomes are intended to provide possibilities for choice: an individual young person's programme will not include all of the experiences and outcomes at this level.

The CfE policy entitles all young people to a senior phase of education, which takes place broadly between the ages of 15 and 18. The senior phase is intended to build on the broad general education to age 15. This phase offers young people the opportunity to build a portfolio of qualifications which recognises their learning, enables them to continue to develop their skills and offers pathways to the next stage.

Contrastingly, the National Curriculum for England and Wales is divided into Key Stages 1 and 2 (for primary) and Key Stages 3 and 4 (for secondary). In 2010 the government initiated another review of the national curriculum in England (immediately after the review that the New Labour government had commissioned which had published a new national curriculum for primary schools online). The review was led by the DfE and supported by an expert group chaired by Tim Oates from Cambridge Assessment. In 2012 the government's response to the expert group's final report was controversial as it caused three members of the expert group, Andrew Pollard, Mary James and Dylan Wiliam, to publicly distance themselves from the outcome and publicise their previous attempt to resign from the group due to unhappiness with the direction that the government seemed to be taking. In his response to the expert group recommendations, the Secretary of State for Education, Michael Gove, announced that detailed draft programmes of study for only maths, English and science would be consulted on. Other subjects – art and design, design and technology, geography, history, ICT, music and physical education – would have much less detail in their programmes of study, the detail of which would be announced later. The teaching of a modern foreign language in each year group of Key Stage 2 from ages 7–11 became compulsory for the first time.

A summary of curriculum arrangements across the four nations is provided in Table 13.2.

The most recent reviews of school curricula in the various parts of the UK all appear to have been an opportunity for the curriculum authorities to articulate what the purpose of education should be for their society. Smith (2003) points out that 'the

TABLE 13.2 Curriculum arrangements in the UK

Curriculum	England	Wales	Scotland	Northern Ireland
Name and nature	National Curriculum (statutory)	National Curriculum (statutory)	5–14 Guidelines 14–16 Standard Grade Curriculum (advisory)	Northern Ireland Curriculum (compulsory)
Time span	5–16 4 Key Stages KS1: 5–7 KS2: 7–11 KS3: 11–14 KS4: 14–15	5–16 4 Key Stages KS1: 5–7 KS2: 7–11 KS3: 11–14 KS4: 14–15	5–14 No Key Stages 14–16	4–16 4 Key Stages Foundation Stage 4–6 KS1: 6–8 KS2: 8–11 KS3: 11–14 KS4: 14–16
Subjects and/or curricular areas/ themes	*Subjects with detailed government programmes of study* Maths, English, science *Subjects with shorter government programmes of study* Art and design, design and technology, geography, history, ICT, music and physical education. Foreign language begins at KS2. Fewer compulsory subjects at KS4 *Other legal requirements* Religious education Sex education	*Core subjects* Maths, English, ICT, science, Welsh Fewer compulsory subjects at KS4 *Foundation subjects* Technology, history, geography, music, art, physical education, Welsh (in schools where it is not a core subject) and from KS3, a modern foreign language	*Curricular Areas (5–12)* ▪ Language ▪ Mathematics ▪ Environmental studies ▪ Expressive arts and physical education ▪ Religious and moral education with personal and social development and health education. *14–16 subjects (12–14)* English, mathematics, history, geography, modern studies, science, modern foreign language, art and design, PE, technology, RME, music, drama, and social and personal development, computing	*Curricular Areas 4–11* The arts Language and literacy Mathematics Numeracy Personal development and mutual understanding Physical development Religious education The world around us *Curricular areas 11–14* The arts Environment and society Language and literacy Learning for life and work Modern languages Mathematics and financial capability Physical development Religious education Science and technology

curriculum can still be regarded as the clearest statement by any society on the purpose of education, the values it holds most dear and an expression of what the society strives to be' (p. 2). Yet, such a statement was not necessarily made explicit in the earlier curricular documents mentioned previously which set out a framework for compulsory education in the four countries.

In 2000 the revised National Curriculum for England and Wales set out the aims and values of the school curriculum (DfEE and QCA 2000). It also laid down what the purpose of this national framework was:

- To establish a learning entitlement for all pupils, regardless of their socio-economic background, culture, race and gender and ability.
- To establish standards for the performance of pupils.
- To promote continuity and coherence of pupils' learning experience.
- To promote public understanding of the work of schools and teachers.

These aims, and the aims for the new secondary curriculum 2007 that had been developed through extensive consultation led by the then Qualifications and Curriculum Authority (QCA), were rejected as part of the government's review of the National Curriculum in England from 2010 onwards. One of the most significant outcomes was the government decision to not adopt the aims suggested by the expert group and instead re-open a national consultation on aims. However, it looked likely that the Secretary of State Michael Gove had a very clear idea of the kinds of aims he expected as the following quotation from his letter to the chair of the expert group made clear:

> I agree with your clear recommendation that we should define the aims of the curriculum. We need to set ambitious goals for our progress as a nation. And we need clear expectations for each subject. *I expect those aims to embody our sense of ambition, a love of education for its own sake, respect for the best that has been thought and written, appreciation of human creativity and a determination to democratise knowledge by ensuring that as many children as possible can lay claim to a rich intellectual inheritance.*
> (Letter from Secretary of State for Education Michael Gove to Tim Oates, Chair of the Expert Group on the National Curriculum in England, responding to the report from the expert group; emphasis added)

In Williams' terms what we read here is the prioritisation of the old humanist and public educator perspectives and the omission of the industrial trainer view.

Assessment

With the National Curriculum, the 1988 *Education Reform Act* also introduced a specific framework for assessment of all pupils aged 5–16 in all state schools in England and Wales. Each subject had its own set of attainment targets and pupils' progression towards the targets was assessed as part of a national programme of assessment through Standard Assessment Tasks (SATs), which take place at ages 7, 11 and 14 in England and Wales, as well as through teacher assessment. Pupils in England are assessed in all core subjects by teacher assessment *only* at the end of Key Stage 1. At the end of Key Stage 2, however, they are assessed by teacher assessment and are also required to sit SATs in core subjects only. In Welsh-medium schools, Welsh language replaces English as a core subject. At the end of Key Stage 3 all pupils are assessed in both core and foundations subjects by their teacher and also through SATs.

A new statutory assessment known as *baseline assessment* was introduced in the late 1990s in all four parts of the UK, albeit in different ways. It refers to the assessment of four- and five-year-old pupils in all or one or two of the following: reading, writing and personal and social skills. *Baseline assessment* has been mandatory in England and Wales since 1997, but a new scheme of teacher observation has been introduced to replace formal testing from August 2002. In Scotland, as for 5–14 assessment generally, it remains at the discretion of the local authority, and can take the form of external tests or teacher assessment (Croxford 2003: 740–741).

Proposals for revised statutory assessment arrangements for Northern Ireland, due to come into effect in 2012–2013, require that teachers must assess and report (using levels of progression) on achievement in communication, using mathematics (from 2012/2013) and using ICT (from 2013/2014) at the end of Key Stage 1 (age 8), Key Stage 2 (age 11) and Key Stage 3 (age 14). Responsibility for assessing and reporting on subject strands/areas of learning and what are reductively referred to as the 'other' skills (thinking skills and personal capabilities) has been delegated to schools. At the end of Key Stage 4 (age 16) a number of National Qualifications are offered by a range of awarding bodies[10] to pupils in England and Wales and Northern Ireland. Most of them take the General Certificate in Secondary Education (GCSE) in which they can choose a range of single general or vocational subjects. The number of subjects to be taken by pupils is not regulated. Short GCSE courses and alternative specialist or vocational qualifications as well as Entry Level qualifications for pupils who are performing below GCSE level are now available at the end of Key Stage 4 in England and Wales and, with some restrictions, in Northern Ireland.[11]

In Scotland CfE is supported by a new assessment framework including qualifications. Assessment within CfE advocates that learners and learning should be at the centre of the assessment process. The aim is to ensure that assessment and qualifications policy and practice is fully aligned with the intentions of the curriculum.

'Building the Curriculum 5: A Framework for Assessment' (Scottish Government 2010) sets out guidance on assessment to support learning at ages 3–18. This guidance makes links to previous work in Scotland, *Assessment is for Learning* and *National Qualifications*. Within the new system, quality assurance and moderation approaches are intended to build expertise in sharing, understanding and applying standards and expectations and to build trust and confidence in teachers' judgements. An online National Assessment Resource (NAR) has been developed, intended to support teachers and build expertise and capacity in the education system. NAR provides quality-assured materials exemplifying a range of assessment approaches.

Assessment information will be used to report on learners' progress and achievement against standards and expectations, based on the experiences and outcomes. Described from the learner's point of view, using terms like 'how well...' and 'how much...', this approach aims to promote greater breadth, depth and application of learning. In 2012, support structures at national level were developed to support quality assurance and moderation processes. The framework of curriculum levels for children and young people has been designed to provide a basis for tracking progression within the new curriculum. A series of national guidance documents on assessment (Scottish Government 2010a, 2010b, 2010c) provide advice on recognising young people's achievements beyond curricular learning, both within and beyond the school, and on profiling. Profiles should provide a snapshot of a learner's best achievements and should be produced at the key points of transition in Primary 7 and Secondary 3.

Standards over time are monitored nationally through the Scottish Survey of Literacy and Numeracy, a national sample-based survey. Data are collected in alternate years at Primary 4, Primary 7 and Secondary 2. The survey also aims to provide information for teaching staff to inform improvements in learning and teaching and assessment.

After the end of the broad general education (3–15) pupils will take national qualifications, which replace the previous system of Standard Grade/Intermediate and Higher examinations. These are called National 1–5, Higher (new) and Advanced Higher (new). The National 1–5 qualifications were introduced in 2013/2014 followed by the new Higher in 2014/2015; the new Advanced Higher will follow in 2015/2016.

Practice may vary across schools, but a possible pattern is that National 1–5 will be taken by pupils in the fourth or fifth year of secondary school (aged 15–17), according to the stage of progress they have reached in each curricular area. Again according to their stage of progress, pupils will take the Higher qualification in the fifth or sixth year and the Advanced Higher in the sixth.

Pedagogy

'The cultures of teaching are shaped by the contexts of teaching' (Feiman-Nemser and Floden 1986: 515); that is, what is understood as the role of the teacher and the activity of teaching is highly context-dependent. Williams' old humanist strand, such an important part of the early development of schooling in England, is associated with principles of *individualism, morality* and *specialism* (McLean 1990). A key characteristic of such *humanism* is that it is anti-rational, and hence it has been suggested that little weight is given in England to 'rational, methodical and systematic knowledge objectives' (Holmes and McLean cited in McLean 1990: 126). With the principles of *individualism* and *morality* the emphasis in English education is on the whole child and the development of the individual. Traditionally, Scottish secondary education has evolved differently from its English counterpart, with rational-encyclopaedic elements and less emphasis on specialism and experience in the learning process (McLean 1995). In his famous book, *The History of Scottish Education*, James Scotland had argued that 'the training of the intellect' was of paramount importance in Scotland and education in the classroom was definitely more teacher-centred than child-centred (in Humes and Bryce 2003). For a long time in Scotland it was thought that strong discipline and, if required, corporal punishment, were *sine qua non* for effective and productive learning to take place. The 1965 report *Primary Education in Scotland* brought about more child-centred approaches to teaching and learning and eventually led to the abolition of corporal punishment in 1981 in Scotland, later than many Western European countries but earlier than England and Wales, which waited until 1986. Harrison (1997: 164) points out that in Scotland, 'child-centred educational philosophy was adopted more cautiously although perhaps more thoroughly than in England'. If the primary classroom in Scotland aspires to be a more and more 'child-centred, caring place', until recently teaching and learning in the secondary schools remained strongly subject-oriented and examination-oriented, especially so for pupils aged 14–16. With the introduction of 'health and well-being', and literacy and numeracy across the new curriculum this may be changing.

The introduction of a National Curriculum in 1988 in England and Wales, and of national frameworks to raise the standards of numeracy and literacy in the primary school in England and also in Scotland have had a significant impact on teachers' work in the classroom, as has the setting of performance targets for schools in all four parts of the UK in the late 1990s.

The impact of the National Curriculum on teaching and learning in the primary classroom in Wales has been investigated by Cox and Sanders (1994) and in England by Pollard *et al.* (1994) and Croll (1996). The findings for both countries were remarkably similar: teachers and headteachers in both countries were generally positive about the National Curriculum, which, they claimed, provided a useful framework for planning and progression (especially throughout Key Stages 1 and 2) and some clarifications of teaching and learning aims (Cox 2000). Furthermore, it resulted in an increase in collaboration on curriculum planning within schools and therefore more coherence in pupil entitlement. Data collection for these studies took place before the first review of the National Curriculum in 1993, which slimmed down its content, and teachers expressed serious misgivings about the overloaded content and the demands placed on them by what they perceived as burdensome procedures for assessment and recording of pupils' learning. The English report stressed the predominance of work in core subjects (particularly English and mathematics) and the lack of flexibility of the framework which made it difficult for them to adapt their teaching to the children's needs (Cox 2000). Likewise, Le Metais *et al.* (2001: 22) report that 'the high profile given to English/Welsh and mathematics through the frameworks in Wales have temporarily reduced the amount of time devoted to [the foundation subjects]'. Finally, the Welsh study reported evidence that the organisation of the National Curriculum in a great number of core and non-core separate subjects made it hard for teachers to retain cross-curricular activities in their teaching (Cox and Sanders 1994, quoted in Cox 2000).

With the arrival of New Labour in government in 1997, teaching methods in the primary school were to undergo yet more changes in England, with the introduction of methods for teaching literacy and numeracy in primary schools. The National Strategies for Literacy and Numeracy were originally conceived by the Conservatives, who piloted them shortly before they left office (Docking 2000b). As with several Conservative initiatives, these were taken up and implemented by the Labour government in 1998 and 1999, respectively, as a result of a controversial OfSTED report on the teaching of reading in London Boroughs (HMI 1996) and in light of evidence from international studies of pupils' achievements in English and Maths, where English pupils appeared to perform less well than many of their foreign counterparts (Docking 2000b).

Primary teachers' teaching of literacy and numeracy were blamed and this justified an unprecedented central intervention into teaching methods. Both strategies aimed to set high expectations and challenging targets for pupils, promote active participation and engaging activities, and support teaching and learning.

The literacy and numeracy strategies in England provide teachers with what can be seen as a rather prescriptive (although non-statutory) approach for the teaching of reading and writing, as well as for mathematics. The 'Literacy Hour' effectively provides the teacher with a set teaching plan for reading and writing, in which the lesson is divided into four parts of 10–20 minutes each and which combines whole-class teaching and group work. Likewise, teachers are encouraged to allocate 45–60 minutes to mathematics teaching everyday using a three-part lesson which consists of an *oral mental starter*, a *main activity* and a *plenary*. The strategies strongly recommend that teachers spend more time on core subjects and that they use more whole-class teaching and questioning and engage the class in interaction.

In contrast with the English initiative, a major characteristic of the Scottish Early Intervention Programme (EIP) was its flexibility and lack of prescriptiveness, with education authorities being expected to 'consider the needs of their area and devise programmes to suit' (SOEID 1999, quoted in Fraser *et al.* 2001: 18). Yet, the national evaluation of EIP in Scotland reported a 'remarkable similarity in the teaching methodologies being adopted across the 32 authorities' (Fraser *et al.* 2001: 24). The document reports evidence of significant changes to classroom practice following the implementation of the programme, with an emphasis on phonic-based approaches to reading, more direct teaching of mental arithmetic involving high levels of pupil–teacher interaction, and an increased reliance on whole-class teaching generally (Fraser *et al.* 2001).

A number of evaluations of the literacy and numeracy strategies in England have been conducted, some of which are by Her Majesty's Inspectorate of Schools (OfSTED 2002a, 2002b) and others by an independent team of Canadian researchers (Earl *et al.* 2000, 2001, 2003). The OISE/UT evaluation (Ontario) reports that most of the teachers and headteachers interviewed felt that classroom teaching had improved considerably as a result of the strategies, with greater use of whole-class teaching, more structured lessons and improved planning. Opinions vary, however, as to the extent to which pupil learning has improved. In any case, all appear to value the numeracy strategy more than its literacy counterpart in terms of pupil learning and simplicity of implementation.

Following what they considered to be the successes of the National Literacy and Numeracy Strategies in primary schools, non-statutory frameworks for the teaching of English and mathematics at Key Stage 3 were introduced in the 2001/2002 academic year (Key Stage 3 Strategy), followed in 2002/2003 by similar frameworks for the teaching of science, ICT and the foundation subjects at the same level. The answer to the question of whether the National Literacy Strategy Framework for Teaching and its pedagogy was effective is made difficult to answer because it was not subject to rigorous large-scale experimental trials. However, there is now a significant amount of evidence in general about the effectiveness of the National Literacy Strategy, particularly in primary schools. Wyse *et al.* (2010) and Wyse and Torrance (2009) summarised this in their research for the *Cambridge Primary Review* by analysing studies of primary class-rooms and trends in national test outcomes. Although reading showed slightly better gains than writing according to some sources, the overall trend in national test scores can be explained as modest gains from a low base as teachers learned to prepare pupils for statutory tests, then a plateau in scores as no further gains could be achieved by test coaching. Overall, the intense focus on testing and test results in the period of the National Literacy Strategy resulted in a narrowing of the curriculum, driving teaching in the opposite direction to that which research indicates will improve learning and attainment.

In Northern Ireland similar emphasis has been placed on the improvement of literacy and numeracy, but with much less prescription than in England. 'Count, Read: Succeed' (DENI 2011) places a renewed focus on the centrality of teachers to the improvement of literacy and numeracy and seeks to clarify the role of teachers and others who support them. The emphasis within the Northern Ireland Curriculum is more strongly focused than elsewhere on literacy and numeracy as cross-curricular responsibilities, with the result that the traditional focus on English and maths as key carriers has been replaced by the cross-curricular skills of communication, using maths and using ICT.

At the heart of the Revised Northern Ireland Curriculum there is also an explicit pedagogical emphasis on the development of pupils' skills and capabilities for lifelong learning and for operating effectively in society. Teachers are encouraged to engage in enquiry-based learning and to provide interactive opportunities for pupils to develop explicit thinking skills and capabilities, including: managing information, solving problems, making decisions, being creative, managing their own learning and working effectively with others (CCEA 2007b). Significant guidance has been developed to promote these approaches.[12]

Another initiative which was introduced throughout the UK and had a noticeable impact on teachers' work and pedagogy is the introduction of performance targets for schools, otherwise known as target setting. Since 1998, in England, benchmarking information based on public examination results and SATs is provided to schools and local authorities by the Department for Education to enable them to set their own targets for improvement, mainly in relation to pupil performance. As with the national frameworks for literacy and numeracy in England and Scotland, mentioned earlier, the driver behind target setting is governments' concern with raising standards. Yet, while the National Literacy Strategy and National Numeracy Strategy focus on processes and transaction, the driver behind the introduction of target settings is more a concern with measurable outcomes. Measurable outcomes are linked to discourses of school *effectiveness*, which are in sharp contrast with initiatives such as EIP, for instance, where the emphasis is more on school *improvement* through 'achieving changes in practice at both management and classroom level' (Fraser *et al.* 2001: 8). Currently, a main concern with target settings is that pressure on schools to achieve targets can result in assessment-driven curriculum and pedagogy and that the way teachers teach becomes increasingly determined by these initiatives (MacGilchrist 2003).

What is clear is that in England, and increasingly in Northern Ireland also, 'policies still seem to be based on the belief that standards will not be raised without targets being set and monitored and that teachers, teacher-trainers and education authorities need to be told how to do their work' (Bines 1998). Brown (2001) has argued, however, that the same comment can increasingly be made in relation to Scottish policies. The particularly prescriptive approach to the Literacy and Numeracy Strategies, and the Key Stage 3 Strategy was not implemented outside England. In fact, as Cox (2000) noted, in the very year that the Literacy Strategy was introduced in England, the Welsh Office published its own vision of a much more collaborative approach to raising standards in literacy in its report *National Year of Reading: Getting Ready*, which argues that teachers and policy makers should work together at improving teaching and learning strategies. Like Wales, Northern Ireland adopted a more collaborative approach to promoting literacy and numeracy improvement and has recently published a revised Literacy and Numeracy Strategy, 'Count, Read: Succeed' (DENI, 2011), which emphasises similar collaboration but without specific resources to support it. Despite some of the improvements which the national strategies and the centrally manufactured local education authorities and schools collaboration may result in, in light of more genuinely collaborative developments in other parts of the UK, one could argue with Croll (1996) that 'the government may find a partnership model more effective in getting educational change to happen than a model based upon the view of teachers as implementers' (in Cox 2000: 80).

Compulsory education post-devolution

The educational and legislative traditions of England, Wales and Northern Ireland mean that they share many similarities in terms of educational and curricular structure and terminology. This convergence is reinforced by the fact that pupils from the three nations traditionally take GCSE and GCE Advanced Level examinations at ages 15–16 and 17–18, respectively. However, the devolution of responsibility for education to the Assemblies, and the emergence of alternative forms of external accreditation of learning, may result in greater divergence over time (Le Metais *et al.* 2001: 5). Recent suggestions in England of a return to two-tier examining involving a return to traditional O-levels and CSE-style syllabi and to linear rather than modular examining is likely to drive national systems further apart. For example, in England the English Baccalaureate was introduced as a performance measure in the 2010 performance tables, not as a qualification in itself but as a measure which recognises pupils who have secured a grade C or better across a core of academic subjects – English, mathematics, history or geography, the sciences and a language. In 2012 the Secretary of State ruled that modular examining should be phased out and that students should take all exams at the end of a course, rather than sit a series of bite-sized modular exams throughout the course. The thinking informing this move is to end what was described as a culture of 'resits'. It seems likely that Northern Ireland for one will not follow suit in reintroducing the linear exams or a baccalaureate performance measure.

We have also seen some of this diversity in our description of provision for curriculum, assessment and pedagogy. We may also be starting to see some evidence of the smaller parts of the UK leading the way for England. Northern Ireland has developed a much more flexible framework-style curriculum, specifying only a minimum entitlement at Key Stage 3, and has led the way on the explicit development of a thinking skills and personal capabilities framework, as well as a foundation stage curriculum for 4–6-year-olds, covering the first two years of the former Key Stage 1. The relaxation of the curriculum in the early years is well underway in Wales and in Scotland also. A major review of the secondary curriculum has led to attempts to develop a less subject-based framework. In England, where teachers and some parents have been calling for such moves, we may yet see similar policy developments.

Changes such as these do nothing to reduce the compulsion of attendance at school, but they may reduce the compulsion on schools and teachers to teach particular content in particular ways. Education is likely to remain high on the political agenda, not least because of the increased perception of the linkage between economic success and education. With this being the case, we are likely to see continuing debates about the purposes of education, reflecting the continuing struggles between industrial trainers, public educators and old humanists. Indeed, there may well be a fourth key grouping now, which is a global rather than a national force. These might be called the global networkers, who believe that electronic communication is creating a global information society, where national boundaries are becoming increasingly irrelevant. Certainly, there are many aspects of learning and teaching which now make use of the World Wide Web. With economic activity increasingly being organised at transnational level, it would seem essential that future citizens have access to an understanding of these networks and can make full use of them in their learning.

Indeed, the very real possibility is raised that for many young people, more learning will be available through their privately owned technology than is available through formal schooling. Such a scenario could give rise to a very different view of compulsory schooling, where it is seen less as an entitlement and more as an imposition. Of course, such a scenario is also dependent on young people having access to the necessary technology and there must be very real fears that a 'digital divide' will open up between those in the UK who own the technology and those who do not. On the other hand, with careful investment, these new technologies have the potential to expand basic educational provision in a way which could not have been foreseen by those who originally argued for compulsory education.

The other developing agenda which must call into question a simple view of compulsory education covering only the early phase of life is that of lifelong learning. If we are, as is argued, living and working in a society where change is continuing to accelerate, then the idea that compulsory schooling between the ages of five and 16 can equip individuals for all of life's needs is highly dubious. If, on the other hand, the implication of these changes is indeed that individuals will require learning opportunities throughout their lives, then why should these early years receive such priority? Certainly, we may still argue for the acquisition of a range of essential skills during one's childhood, but the promotion of particular forms of knowledge may be far less important than in the past.

Notes

1. The previous versions of this chapter were written by the late Estelle Brisard and Ian Menter. The chapter has been updated for this edition by some of the members of 'CAPeR-UK', a research group looking at curriculum, assessment and pedagogy reform across the UK.
2. This was the theory at least. The present editors' two grandfathers – one in Glasgow and the other in Garvir on the Isle of Lewis – both left school at age 13.
3. St Andrews, Aberdeen, Glasgow and Edinburgh.
4. The Scottish equivalent was the Qualifier (or Qually as it was popularly termed) which was taken at 12+ to reflect the fact that the Scots had seven years of primary school before transferring to secondary around age 12, while the rest of the UK had six years of primary with the transfer to secondary taking place around age 11.
5. See: www.education.gov.uk/schools/leadership/typesofschools/b0061428/free-schools/what.
6. See: http://wales.gov.uk/topics/educationandskills/schoolshome/fundingschools/schoolfunding/fundingfromukgov.
7. See http://wales.gov.uk/topics/educationandskills/schoolshome/fundingschools/schoolfunding.
8. See http://wales.gov.uk/docs/statistics/2012/120529keyeducation12en.pdf.
9. www.nicurriculum.org.uk.
10. There are three unitary awarding bodies in England (AQA, EDEXCEL and OCR) one awarding body in Northern Ireland (CCEA) and one in Wales (WJEC).
11. www.ucas.ac.uk/candq/ukquals/eng/quals.html; www.deni.gov.uk/teachers/circulars/latest/dc2003-06.pdf.
12. See www.nicurriculum.org.uk/TSPC/the_think_pack/index.asp#top.

References

Bash, L. and Coulby, D. (1989) The Education Reform Act: Competition and Control. London: Continuum

Bash, L. and Coulby, D. (1991) *Contradiction and Conflict: The 1988 Education Act in Action.* London: Cassell.

Bines, H. (1998) Hail zero intolerance? Opinion. *Times Educational Supplement*, 22 May, p. 15.

Brown, S. (2001) *What is Teaching for?* The General Teaching Council (Scotland) Annual Lecture, 8 May.

CCEA (2001a) *Replacing Selection Means Creating Real Choice.* Press release. Available at http://www.rewardinglearning.org.uk/newsroom/press/2001/nr05.01.asp, accessed 24 April 2014.

CCEA (2007a) *The Statutory Curriculum at Key Stage 3: Rationale and Detail.* Belfast: CCEA. Available at www.nicurriculum.org.uk/docs/key_stage_3/statutory_curriculum_ks3.pdf, accessed September 2008.

CCEA (2007b) *Thinking Skills and Personal Capabilities for Key Stage 3*, Belfast: Northern Ireland Council for the Curriculum, Examinations and Assessment.

Clough, N., Lee, V., Menter, I., Trodd, T. and Whitty, G. (1991) 'Restructuring the education system?', in Bash, L. and Coulby, D. (eds), *The Education Reform Act.* London: Cassell.

Cox, T. (2000) 'The impact of the National Curriculum upon primary education in Wales', in Daugherty, R., Phillips, R. and Rees, G. (eds), *Education Policy-making in Wales: Explorations in Devolved Governance.* Cardiff: University of Wales Press.

Cox, T. and Sanders, S. (1994) *The Impact of the National Curriculum on the Teaching of 5 Year-Olds.* London: Falmer Press.

Croll, P. (1996) 'Practitioners or policy makers? Models of teachers and educational change', in Croll, P. (ed.), *Teachers, Pupils and Primary Schooling.* London: Cassell.

Croxford, L. (2000) *Inequality in Attainment at Age 16: A "Home International" Comparison.* Edinburgh: Centre for Educational Sociology.

Croxford, L. (2001) *Comprehensive Schools in Great Britain: Evidence from Research. A Report to the Northern Ireland Association of Headteachers in Secondary Schools.* Edinburgh: Centre for Educational Sociology.

Croxford, L. (2003) 'Baseline assessment in Scotland', in Bryce, T.G.K. and Humes, W.M. (eds), *Scottish Education*, 2nd edition. Edinburgh: Edinburgh University Press.

DENI (2011), *Count, Read: Succeed. A Strategy to Improve Outcomes in Literacy and Numeracy*. Bangor: Department of Education.

Department for Education (DfE). (2010). *The Importance of Teaching: The Schools White Paper 2010*. Norwich: The Stationery Office.

Department for Education and Skills (2003) *School Attendance: Frequently Asked Questions*. Available at www.dfes.gov.uk/schoolattendance/faq, accessed 6 January 2003.

DfEE and QCA (2000) *The National Curriculum: Handbook for Primary Teachers in England: Key Stages 1 and 2*. London: DfEE and QCA. Available at http://webarchive.nationalarchives.gov.uk/20130401151715/https://www.education. gov.uk/publications/standard/publicationDetail/Page1/QCA/99/457, accessed 24 April 2014.

Docking, J. (ed.) (2000a) *New Labour's Policies for Schools*. London: David Fulton.

Docking, J. (2000b) 'Curriculum initiatives', in Docking, J. (ed.), *New Labour's Policies for Schools*. London: David Fulton.

Earl, L., Department for Education and Skills, Ontario Institute for Studies in Education of the University of Toronto (2000) *Watching and Learning: OISE/UT Evaluation of the National Literacy and Numeracy strategies*. London: DfEE.

Earl, L., Department for Education and Skills, Ontario Institute for Studies in Education of the University of Toronto (2001) *Watching and Learning 2: OISE/UT Evaluation of the National Literacy and Numeracy Strategies*. London: DfEE.

Earl, L., Department for Education and Skills, Ontario Institute for Studies in Education of the University of Toronto (2003) *Watching and Learning 3: Final Report of the External Evaluation of England's National Literacy and Numeracy Strategies*. London: DfEE.

Feiman-Nemser, S. and Floden, R.E. (1986) 'The cultures of teaching' in Wittrock, M.C. (ed.), *Handbook of Research on Teaching*, 3rd edition. New York: Macmillan.

Fraser, H., MacDougall, A., Pirne, A. and Croxford, A. (2001) *National Evaluation of the Early Intervention Programme*, Final Report. Glasgow: SCRE.

Green, A. (1997) *Education, Globalization and the State*. London: Macmillan.

Harris, N. (1993) *Law and Education: Regulations, Consumerism and the Education System*. London: Sweet and Maxwell.

Harrison, C. (1997) 'How Scottish is the Scottish curriculum: and does it matter?' in Clark, M.M. and Munn, P. (eds), *Education in Scotland*. London: Routledge.

Her Majesty's Inspectorate of Schools (HMI) (1996) *The Teaching of Reading in 45 Inner London Primary Schools*. London: OfSTED.

Herman, A. (2001) *The Scottish Enlightenment: The Scots' Invention of the Modern World*. London: Forth Estate.

Humes, W. and Bryce, T. (2003) 'The distinctiveness of Scottish education', in Bryce, T.G.K. and Humes, W.M. (eds), *Scottish Education*. 2nd edition. Edinburgh: Edinburgh University Press.

Jackson, P. (2000) 'Choice, diversity and partnerships', in Docking, J. (ed.), *New Labour's Policies for Schools*. London: David Fulton.

Le Metais, J., Andrews, R., Johnson, R. and Spielhofer, T. (2001) *School Curriculum Differences across the UK*. Slough: National Foundation for Educational Research.

MacGilchrist, B. (2003) 'Has school improvement passed its sell-by date?' Professorial lecture delivered at the Institute of Education, University of London, 14 May.

McLean, M. (1990) *Britain and a Single Market Europe*. London: Kogan Page.

McLean, M. (1995) *Educational Traditions Compared: Content, Teaching and Learning in Industrialised Countries*. London: David Fulton.

Office for Standards in Education (OfSTED) (2002a) *The National Numeracy Strategy, the First Three Years, 1999–2002*. London: OfSTED.

Office for Standards in Education (2002b) *The National Literacy Strategy, the First Four Years, 1998–2002*. London: OfSTED.

Ozga, J. and Lawn, M. (1999) 'The cases of England and Scotland within the United Kingdom', in Lindblad, S. and Popkewitz, T. (eds), *Educational Governance and Social Integration and Exclusion*. Uppsala: Uppsala University Press.

Paterson, L. (2003) *Scottish Education in the Twentieth Century*. Edinburgh: Edinburgh University Press.

Pollard, A., Broadfoot, P., Croll, P., Osborn, M. and Abbot, D. (1994) *Changing English Primary Schools? The Impact of the ERA at Key Stage One*. London: Cassell.

Ross, A. (2000) *Curriculum: Construction and Critique*. London: Falmer.

Scottish Council for Research in Education (SCRE) (2001) 'Glasgow's learning communities', *SCRE Newsletter* 69.

Scottish Executive Education Department (SEED) (2003) *Key Findings from the National Evaluation of the New Community Schools Pilot Programme in Scotland*. Edinburgh: SEED.

Scottish Government (2009) *Curriculum for Excellence*. Edinburgh: Scottish Government. Available at www.educationscotland.gov.uk/Images/all_experiences_outcomes_tcm4-539562.pdf, accessed 24 April 2004.

Scottish Government (2010a) *Building the Curriculum 5: A Framework for Assessment*. Available at www.ltscotland.org.uk/Images/Building the Curriculum5_assess_ tcm4-582215.pdf, accessed 29 June 2012.

Scottish Government (2010b) *Building the Curriculum 5: Quality Assurance and Moderation*. Edinburgh: Scottish Government. Available at http://www.educationscotland.gov.uk/publications/b/publication_tcm4617374.asp?strReferringChannel=search&strReferringPageID=tcm:4-615801-64, accessed 24 April 2014.

Scottish Government (2010c) *Building the Curriculum 5: A Framework for Assessment: Understanding, Applying and Sharing Standards in Assessment for Curriculum for Excellence: Quality Assurance and Moderation*. Edinburgh: Scottish Government. Available at http://www.educationscotland.gov.uk/publications/b/publication_tcm4630061.asp?strReferringChannel=search&strReferringPageID=tcm:4-615801-64, accessed 24 April 2014.

SEED (2004a) *A Curriculum for Excellence*. Edinburgh: Scottish Government. Available at www.scotland.gov.uk/Publications/2004/11/20178/45862, accessed 24 April 2014.

Smith, A. (2003) 'Teacher education and the Northern Ireland Curriculum review'. Paper presented at a conference on Teacher Education in a Climate of Change, organised by the Department of Education for Northern Ireland and the Department for Employment and Learning, Limavady, 28–29 April.

Williams, R. (1961) *The Long Revolution*, Harmondsworth: Penguin.

Wyse, D. and Torrance, H. (2009). 'The development and consequences of national curriculum assessment for primary education in England'. *Educational Research* 51 (2), 213–228.

Wyse, D., McCreery, E. and Torrance, H. (2010). 'The trajectory and impact of national reform: curriculum and assessment in English primary schools', in Alexander, R., Doddington, C., Gray, J., Hargreaves, L. and Kershner, R. (eds), *The Cambridge Primary Review Research Surveys*. London: Routledge.

Wyse, D., Baumfield, V., Egan, D., Gallagher, C., Hayward, L., Hulme, M., Leitch, R., Livingston, K., Menter, I. and Lingard, B. (2013). *Creating the Curriculum*. London: Routledge.

14

Post-compulsory education (further and higher education)

Catherine Matheson and Philip Woodward

Next in importance to freedom and justice is popular education, without which neither freedom nor justice can be permanently maintained.

James Garfield

Introduction

Until the Kennedy Report the term 'further education' (FE) seldom seemed to cross politicians' lips, except in so far as when mentioned as part of the seamless boundary between further and higher education (Kennedy 1997). Higher education, on the other hand, has increasingly become a major policy issue (Dearing 1997; DfES 2004a; HEFCE 2005).This chapter gives a brief overview of post-school and further education before focusing mainly on issues related to higher education.

Post-school and further education

This section will briefly examine the historical background to post-school and further education before examining the 14–19 qualifications framework and discussing current issues and future challenges.

Historical overview

In the Victorian era the British ruling class valued individualism, enterprise and *laissez-faire* liberalism and hence saw centralisation and state control as having a corroding influence on the dynamics of individual entrepreneurship. Hence, industrialisation was able to progress rapidly despite a lack of state control over vocational and technical education (Green 1990). However, the need for a more skilled workforce to meet economic challenges led to several Royal Commissions into technical education in the nineteenth century. In the 1880s the independent City and Guilds London Institute for the Advancement of Technical Education and the new polytechnics were established. The Samuelson Commission on Technical Instruction (1884) praised the well-organised continental trade schools that were well integrated within a secondary education system that offered a superior type of secondary education for those with limited means as opposed to the overlapping and muddled British apprenticeship system (Green 1990). Samuelson paved the way for some important developments that took place as a consequence of the *Technical Instruction Act* (1889) that 'allowed now local councils to set up technical education committees that could be financed by a one penny rate and the 1890 Local Taxation (Whiskey Money) Act provided public funds that could be spent on technical education' (Green 1990: 299).

Just over a decade later, the *Education Act* (1902) established local education authorities (LEAs) in England and Wales, among the duties of which was the organisation of technical and vocational education. The *Education Act* (1902) also enabled LEAs to establish grammar and junior technical schools, giving pupils the choice of an academic or vocational route after leaving compulsory school at 13. In Scotland the 1918 *Education (Scotland) Act* created local authority education departments (rather than LEAs), among whose duties was the organisation of the provision of technical and vocational education.

Higher National Certificates (HNCs) and Diplomas (HNDs) were developed in the 1920s to try to address the skills shortage after the First World War.[1] The 1944 *Education Act* and the 1945 *Education (Scotland) Act* raised the school leaving age to 15, made provision for technical and other further education and introduced the Ordinary and Higher National Certificates. The Percy Report (1945) set out a radical policy aimed at raising both the provision and status of a small number of technical colleges that should develop degree-level courses. It also first proposed the creation of a new degree status and practical orientation diploma in technology to equip students for working in industry. The White Paper *Technical Education* (DES 1956) identified a large and rising demand for scientists and engineers, as well as technicians and craftsmen. Consequently, it recommended that regional colleges of advanced technology should be created and that the new degree-level Diploma in Technology should be offered as a new alternative route to higher education as university places were limited.[2] The initiative was successful as the greatest higher education expansion was in advanced technology colleges (Simon 1991: 119–203). However, the Crowther Report (1959) also highlighted a poor uptake of places in FE by school leavers as more pupils than expected stayed at school beyond the school leaving age of 15. The involvement of employers in technical education was increased with the *Industrial Training Act* (1964), which led to the formation of the Industrial Training Boards (Central Training Council 1965). These were the forerunners of a series of employer-led organisations including the Manpower Services Commission, the Training Agency and, more recently, Training and Enterprise Councils (Jessup 1991; Keep 1996).

In 2001 new regulations for the inspection of FE provision and the training of FE teachers came into effect in England and Wales (DfES 2001a). The Office for Standards in Education (OfSTED) assumed responsibility together with the Adult Learning Inspectorate (ALI) for the inspection of FE provision which had previously been undertaken by the funding body Further Education Funding Council (FEFC) (replaced as a funding body by the Learning and Skills Council in 2001). In Scotland, inspection of FE remained in the hands of Her Majesty's Inspectorate of Education (HMI).

Qualifications framework 14–19

England

With roots in technical and vocal education the FE sector has a very wide-ranging curriculum: from academic qualifications in the form of GCSEs, A- and AS-levels to a range of ever-expanding vocational courses, especially so since the introduction of National Vocational Qualifications (NVQs) in 1986 and General National Vocational Qualifications (GNVQs) in 1996. Vocational courses are available in general FE colleges and specialist colleges, as well as in partnership with many employers. These courses include subjects as diverse as science and technology, art and design, business, travel and tourism, catering, construction trades and hairdressing and beauty. Regulated by the Qualifications and Curriculum Authority (QCA) established in 1997, a National Qualifications Framework (NQF) was established to more easily compare academic and vocational qualifications (Coles 2004).

In December 1997, following the *Review of Qualifications for 16–19 Year Olds* (Dearing 1996) and the subsequent consultation on its recommendations, the government decided that the post-16 curriculum in England was too narrow and lacked flexibility. Curriculum 2000 is outlined in *Qualifying for Success* (DfEE 1997). The reforms introduced in September 2000 sought to broaden the curriculum and achieve parity of esteem between academic and vocational qualifications, that is, to encourage young people to study more subjects over two years than had been the case previously, while also helping them to combine academic and vocational study (OfSTED 2001). The Curriculum 2000 reforms fully modularised all A-level programmes and split the qualification into Advanced Subsidiary (AS) and A-level (A2), which carried increased coursework weighting while academic and vocational subjects could be combined. The modular approach is deemed to increase the motivation of learners and to provide regular progress checks, but as modules are assessed twice a year in January and June, there is much more time spent on preparation for assessment than previously. The Curriculum 2000 reforms also included a change in the title of Advanced GNVQs to 'Vocational A-levels'[3] and, more importantly, the introduction of Key Skills. Since many employers thought that young people lacked skills such as ICT, communication, teamwork, self-confidence and willingness to learn, a solution to this problem was to suggest adding Key Skills to the curriculum at age 14 as part of Key Stage 4, in line with recommendations of *14–19 Opportunity and Excellence* (DfES 2002b) that work-related learning should contribute to the curriculum of all Key Stage 4 pupils. Following the *Learning and Skills Act* in 2001, the FEFC and Technology Education Councils were replaced by the Learning and Skills Council (LSC), which assumed responsibility for the planning and funding of FE and government-funded training. The LSC works through a regional network of 47 Local Learning and Skills Councils (Evans 2006).

The problems arising from the implementation of Curriculum 2000 prompted the government to commission a wide-ranging review of the whole 14–19 qualifications structure, chaired by Mike Tomlinson. The report concluded that the changes had been implemented too quickly with inadequate piloting and unrealistic demands on candidates and inadequate training of examiners and officers. The report focused on the development of a coherent range of 14–19 learning programmes and on assessment methods and qualification structures (Tomlinson 2002).

Although there have been efforts to harmonise academic and vocational qualifications in terms of parity of esteem and assessment methodology, many of which have been described above, the need for younger pupils to experience vocational subjects has only been addressed relatively recently. A variety of new initiatives have had an impact on the curriculum in FE and schools. Vocational GCSEs became available in 2002 in a range of subjects, including business, engineering, health and social care and travel and tourism. Each vocational GCSE consists of three units and is the equivalent of two non-vocational GCSEs and carries a double grade. Assessment is by internally marked and externally moderated tests and assignments. Other available qualifications include BTEC First Diploma and NVQs, which were not previously available to those aged under 16. Progression to Foundation and Advanced Modern Apprenticeships is also possible in a scheme that includes an extended period of work placement. The Green Paper *14–19: Extending Opportunities, Raising Standards* (DfES 2002c) proposed to formalise the stages at which vocational training enters the curriculum. This means a much more proactive role for the careers service, a modified Key Stage 4 curriculum with a core of English, maths, ICT, citizenship, religious education, careers and physical education and finally the award of a 'Matriculation Diploma' covering Key Skills, vocational and academic qualifications and work-based learning at three levels, depending on the qualifications achieved. *Success for All* (DfES 2002a) was the long-term reform programme launched by the government in 2002 to transform the quality and responsiveness of the learning and skills sector in England. The programme recognised the diversity of the FE sector in terms of the learners, learning providers and models of delivery. *Success for All* recommended the need for FE provision to meet national and local skills needs, broaden the curriculum and improve collaboration between schools, colleges, private training providers and employers (DfES 2002a). *Success for All* also set an agenda to improve literacy and numeracy according to recommendations made in *Skills for Life* (DfES 2001b).

In 2003 the White Paper *21st Century Skills: Realising our Potential* (DfES 2003a) set an agenda for the development of Key Skills, particularly in relation to work-based learning and especially to the Modern Apprenticeship scheme established in 1993. *Principles for Reform of 14–19 Learning Programmes and Qualifications* (DfES 2003b) proposed the incorporation of skills such as numeracy, communication and IT skills, problem solving, working with others, the ability to respond to change, entrepreneurship, facilitation, ethical competencies, leadership, cultural awareness, customer handling and meta-competencies, including instinct and judgement. However, concerns remain about whether Key Skills will fully meet employers' requirements. More recently, in September 2013, and in response to Wolf's review in 2011 (Wolf 2011), concerns over numeracy and literacy have prompted the introduction of compulsory maths and English in post-16 education for those who do not achieve a good GCSE pass grade (A*–C) at school (DfE 2013).

An Education Maintenance Allowance (EMA) scheme was introduced in September 2004. The EMA scheme involved paying young people entering Year 12 to remain in FE and to improve their attendance and coursework by means-tested payments of up to £30 per week for up to three years, plus a bonus of £100 for remaining on the course and making good progress. Payments were dependent on satisfactory attendance and progress. Piloting the EMA scheme for two years led to significant improvements in achievement, particularly on vocational courses, and confirmed the effectiveness of the scheme (DfES 2002d). However in 2011 the EMA scheme was discontinued and replaced by the 16–19 bursary fund. The fund is distributed through education providers and seeks to target vulnerable young people (DfE 2011).

Scotland

Scotland has its own schools examination system which comes under the management of the Scottish Qualifications Authority (SQA), which replaced both the Scottish Examination Board (SEB) and the Scottish Vocational Education Council (SCOTVEC) in 1997. The SQA is now the single body responsible for all Scottish qualifications other than those offered by universities and professional bodies (i.e. schools, FE colleges, workplaces and education centres). In the summer of 1999 the SQA introduced the system of National Qualifications (also known as the Higher Still development programme) which brought together academic and more vocational and work-related subjects.

Higher Grades had been introduced in 1888 as a university entry qualification six decades before A-levels, which were introduced in 1951. Standard Grades replaced O-Grades in 1988. Since 1999 Scottish qualifications 16–19 have been completely restructured with the introduction of the *Higher Still* programme. Previously some pupils aged 16–17 did up to five Highers in the fifth year while other pupils did Highers in some subjects and various National Certificate modules in others and the remaining pupils did only National Certificate modules in fifth year. Now, all pupils entering the fifth year enrol on National Qualifications. Those with Standard Grade 1 and 2 do up to five Highers, which will enable them to take Advanced Highers in the sixth year. Those with Standard Grades 3 or 4, and 5 or 6, and no grade do an Intermediate 1, Intermediate 2 or Access Level (1, 2, 3) programme, respectively. Successfully completing courses at Intermediate allows access to the relevant Higher. The new system allows the more academic pupils a progression route to enter higher education while others can climb the qualifications ladder in the way that best suits them.[4] In terms of equivalency with England, the Universities and Colleges Admission Service (UCAS) considers Highers to be worth slightly more than AS-level and Advanced Highers to be equivalent to A-levels.[5]

The new system operates under the Scottish Credit and Qualifications Framework (SCQF), which is a partnership between the Scottish Qualifications Authority (SQA), the Quality Assurance Agency (QAA) for Higher Education and Universities UK, which is supported through the Scottish Department for Enterprise, Transport and Lifelong Learning. Unlike in England, Scotland has a single awarding body for both vocational and academic education 14–19. Working in partnership with the SQA, Scottish higher education institutions (HEIs) have driven the creation of the SCQF. What distinguishes the Scottish SCQF from the English NQF is that it includes all levels of education and training (from Access 1 at SCQG level 1 to Highers at SCQF level 6 to Honours degree at SCQF level 10 and PhD at SCQF level 12).[6] In contrast, the English National Qualifications Framework is separate from the Framework for Higher Education Qualifications.

The Group Award (SGA) consists of a number of courses and units which fit together to make a coherent programme of study. Group Awards are available at six levels of study within the Higher Still programme (from Access Level 2 to Advanced Higher). A group award can be gained in one year of full-time study or built up over a longer period of time. Awards are made up of courses, units and external assessments combined to form a group which is recognised by employers, colleges, universities and other providers of education and/or training. It is a benchmark of a student's level of attainment (examples are: science, art and design and travel and tourism. Not everyone needs to take a Group Award. Programmes of study can involve free-standing courses and units; some students may study for four subjects at Higher level that are not inter-related, and do not constitute a sufficiently coherent group to be described as a Group Award.[7]

Current debates and issues

Work-based training and the skills deficit

The current model of work-based training has its roots in a series of initiatives resulting from a response to high youth unemployment in the late 1970s. However, the main criticism of NVQs and SVQs relates to their narrow focus on a range of highly job-specific tasks to the extent that the skills accredited are deemed to be very low and not easily transferred to other occupations (Keep 1996). Having FE and work-based education as separate entities, with the government being responsible for the organisation and funding of the former and employers the latter, has led to the UK faring much less well when compared with other countries (Keep 1996). The proportion of young people remaining in education after the school-leaving age has been lower than other European countries and UK employers have been willing to employ school-leavers with minimal qualifications (OECD 2001). Half the number of UK workers have vocational qualifications when compared with Germany and only 5 per cent of pupils aged 15 are enrolled on vocational programmes compared with 9 per cent in France, 20 per cent in the Netherlands and 30 per cent in Germany (OECD 2002).

Overall, one in four of those who are economically active lacks a qualification, or has qualifications below the equivalent of NVQ Level 4 (Campbell 2001). Vocational qualifications overall are in the minority of all qualifications taken in the UK, with half of the economically active population holding academic qualifications (including GCSE, Standard Grade, Higher Grade, O-, AS- and A-level and degree), while only a quarter of the population of England hold vocation qualifications (Hodgson and Spours 2000). A key problem in the UK is that the vocational education system is not proactive in response to trends and predictions and tends to react to crises as a result of skills shortages rather than be able to respond to changes in the labour market (Campbell 2001).

Access and widening participation

Inclusiveness and participation have been major themes in FE over the last 15 years. The Kennedy Report (1997) *Learning Works: Widening Participation in Further Education* is the report of a committee established in 1994 by the FEFC to identify under-represented groups and advise how funding should be arranged to increase participation in post-compulsory education generally and especially in FE. The Kennedy Report (1997) drew attention to the disadvantages of institutions applying marketplace criteria to decisions on their curriculum offer. The report emphasised that non-traditional students were likely to require more support and that additional costs were needed to recruit them and to support them effectively. Strategies were proposed such as frameworks for credit transfer and accumulation, entitlement to support and guidance, universal access to qualifications to NQF Level 3 (SCQF Level 7), embedding widening participation in quality-assurance systems and the development of value-added measures in FE (Coles 2004). Although well received by the government, the more radical recommendation of changing the governance of FE institutions in favour of a greater representation from the community was not addressed and not implemented (Parry and Fry 1999).

Looking towards the future

Despite many initiatives designed to provide coherent pathways for young people, whether their strengths lay in academic or vocational subjects, there still remain significant skills shortages and a widely held perception that the current system still favours those with academic strengths and that a significant proportion of the population took part neither in vocational nor academic education and that their inclusion held the key to social and economic prosperity (Coles 2004). The difficulty of having a coherent post-16 curriculum providing equality of opportunity for those having diverse career aspirations was acknowledged in the introduction to the Kennedy Report (1997):

> Further education suffers because of prevailing British attitudes. Not only does there remain a very carefully calibrated hierarchy of worthwhile achievement, which has clearly established routes and which privileges academic success well above any other accomplishment, but there is also an appalling ignorance amongst decision-makers and opinion-formers about what goes on in further education.
>
> (Kennedy 1997: 1)

There is a long history of the academic/vocational divide, but so far, largely due to a fear of tarnishing the A-level 'gold standard', there has been relatively little success in achieving parity of esteem between the two routes However, recently various initiatives have been introduced to provide greater integration and greater parity to esteem between academic and vocational qualifications and sufficient flexibility to respond to future economic and social challenges (Coles 2004).

In October 2004 the *14–19 Curriculum and Qualifications Reform* final report of the Working Group on 14–19 Reform led by former Chief Inspector of Schools Mike Tomlinson was published (Tomlinson 2004). The report advised greater inclusion of vocational learning into the current education system. The proposals recommend the development of a diploma that would, over time, bring all existing academic and vocational qualifications within a diploma framework. Under the proposals, young people would study a range of academic and vocational subjects, and would have to satisfy clear national standards in basic skills (written and oral communication, numeracy and ICT). They would also complete an extended project (Tomlinson 2004).

In February 2005 the response to Tomlinson (2004) was formalised in the new *14–19 Education and Skills* White Paper, the key points of which were: new functional skills content or acquiring a mastery of functional English and mathematics at the heart of new general (GCSE) Diplomas and specialised Diplomas before leaving education; improving vocational education; stretching all young people and helping universities to differentiate between the best candidates; re-motivating disengaged learners; and ensuring quality assurance in the delivery of vocational and academic education (DfES 2005a). The White Paper proposed the introduction of new specialised diplomas in 14 broad sector areas. Employers, through Sector Skills Councils, will lead in their design, and HEIs will also have an important role to play. The specialised Diplomas will replace the current system of around 3,500 separate qualifications and will provide an alternative gateway to higher education and skilled employment. In December 2005 the government published the *14–19 Implementation Plan* to set out how the White Paper was going to be implemented (DfES 2005b). The main points included: a duty on the local authority and the LSC to ensure that there was sufficient provision at local level to meet the needs of 14–19-year-olds; a duty on schools to ensure that young people on their roll would have access to all the Diplomas available locally; and every area to establish a 14–19 partnership, led by the LA and the LSC and a prospectus drawn up during 2006, which would set out the full range of learning opportunities available to young people locally. The first five specialised diplomas were introduced in September 2008 (DfES 2005b).

In March 2005 the government published the White Paper *Skills: Getting on in Business, Getting on at Work*, which builds on the government's first national Skills Strategy published in July 2003 and sets out proposals and reforms designed to place the employers' needs at the centre of the design and delivery of training (DfES 2005c). In November 2005 *Realising the Potential: A Review of the Future Role of Further Education Colleges* was published (Foster 2005). Key findings include a focus on supplying economically valuable skills and responding to specific local and regional employers' needs and strengthening the voice of the learner. Measures to boost the skills of

Britain's workforce were set out in the FE White Paper in March 2006, *Further Education: Raising Skills, Improving Life Chances* (DfES 2006). Proposals included giving greater freedom to colleges that are performing well and taking tougher action on poor quality and on institutions that are classed as failing. A greater role for business, with experts being encouraged to teach, and more partnerships with local industry were among the measures which seek to remedy the skill shortage. FE colleges in England would be able to waive their tuition fees to give young adults between the ages of 19 and 25 a second chance to study for qualifications equivalent to two A-levels. New Adult Learning Grants would also be available to help students with living costs. Funding would furthermore be redirected from failing college courses to those in demand from students and employers, giving top-performing colleges the chance to expand while putting poorer performers under threat of closure. New providers could also be brought in to widen the availability of popular courses. The FE White Paper also revealed plans to attract high-fliers into working in FE (DfES 2006).

In a government-commissioned investigation into the UK skills deficit led by Lord Sandy Leitch, which began in 2004 and covered the period up to 2020, it was underlined that the UK lagged behind competitors and ranked 24th out of 29 developed nations. The Leitch review of skills, the final report of which was published in December 2006 after an interim report in 2005, called for better-skilled workers to ensure the UK remained competitive (Leitch 2005, 2006). Key recommendations included an emphasis on the need for the UK to develop a world-class skills system by setting higher targets; routing public adult education funding through the 'train to gain' scheme and learner accounts; transferring responsibility for qualifications to Sector Skills Councils and creating a single information, advice and guidance service covering young people and adults (Leitch 2005, 2006).

Hopefully, these reforms will provide sufficient flexibility to respond to future economic and social challenges by providing greater integration and greater parity to esteem between academic and vocational qualifications in order to improve the economic prosperity for this country. However, in their White Paper *14–19 Education and Skills* (DfES 2005a) the government ignored one of Tomlinson's (2004) key recommendations for parity of esteem, which was the introduction of one overarching qualification 14–19 (at four levels: entry, foundation, intermediate and advanced, building in progression) whereby, as is the case in Scotland, both vocational and academic subjects would be covered within the qualification framework, using A-levels and GCSEs as building blocks for a unified diploma, blending core subjects such as English with specialist learning. Instead, the *14–19 Education and Skills* White Paper proposed the retention of GCSEs and A-levels and the introduction of separate vocational diplomas at three levels (with universities involved in the design of those at level 3), as well as more A-level grades to assist universities to differentiate between students (DfES 2005a). In 2008 the A* A-level grade was introduced to stretch and challenge candidates who achieve in excess of 90 per cent in their qualification.[8]

Higher education

While FE in the UK has a long history of greater or lesser marginalisation, higher education (HE), on the other hand, and especially in the last 40 years, has increasingly moved to centre stage. If HE has been firmly at the centre of the political agenda since the 1990s, at the time of writing (July 2007) this is due in no small part to the controversy over the introduction in 2005 of variable student tuition fees in England, better known as top-up fees, whereby the government had legislated that HEIs could impose up to a maximum fee of £3,000 (Baty 2003) (Tuition fees of £1,000 were first introduced in the UK in 1998, while means-tested maintenance grants were abolished in 1999.) Subsequently, from 2012 the government raised the maximum tuition fee that HEIs could impose to £9,000.

The present discussion will focus on a historical overview of HE from the nineteenth century, followed by examination of the evolution of patterns of participation by key variables (ethnicity, sex, age, geography and social class) and the changes in external structures and in the nature and scope of HE, focusing on access and widening participation policies, entry requirement and qualifications, changes in the nature of acceptable knowledge, and key differences between the English and Scottish policy contexts.

The nineteenth century

At the beginning of the nineteenth century the British universities were unevenly distributed. England had only two universities, Oxford and Cambridge, while Scotland, with only one-tenth of the population, had four: St Andrews, Glasgow, Edinburgh and Aberdeen. The Scottish universities had seen their student numbers rise sharply in the latter part of the eighteenth century and offered large lectures and a less developed tutorial system than did Oxford and Cambridge (Stephens 1998). The two English universities were far more aristocratic and elitist than their Scottish counterparts and concentrated in the liberal education in the arts and humanities, providing mainly non-vocational courses for residential, as opposed to predominantly local, students. Although the University of Durham, founded in 1832, was based on the Oxford and Cambridge 'aristocratic' model of a collegiate university, University College London, established in 1827, was based on the Scottish model (Bell 2000).

In the second half of the nineteenth century several of the industrial English cities established civic or 'bourgeois' universities, which were locally supported, vocationally oriented and closely related and dependent upon local business and industry, with middle-class students living largely at home. Whether aristocratic or bourgeois, university education in the nineteenth and early twentieth century was largely a privilege for the fortunate and wealthy, especially in England (Bligh 1990). A notable exception was the University of London, created in 1836, a purely examining body and offering only external degrees until the end of the nineteenth century for courses in technical colleges and other institutions, as well as correspondence courses and which thus provided an alternative route of part-time study, distance learning and franchised degrees for non-traditional entrants such as women, mature and working-class students (Stephens 1998). A relatively unknown aspect of HE is that in the late nineteenth century part-time students constituted the majority outside Oxford, Cambridge and Durham, while residence did not become a dominant feature until the early twentieth century, when the provincial colleges obtained university charters and more especially after the expansion of HE in the 1960s (Wright 1989).

> In 1883 when a further new university college was opened in Dundee ... its Principal felt able to claim that the availability of university places per head of population in Scotland at that time was exceeded only in Switzerland.
>
> (Bell 2000: 166)

Scotland's HE experienced significant growth even before the creation of University College Dundee. In the eighteenth century the 'total student population tripled ... with student numbers at Edinburgh University alone increasing from 400 in 1700 to 2,300 in 1824' (Smith 2000: 311), though few bothered to graduate. As Smith (2000) makes clear, the current divide between education and entertainment simply did not exist as we know it now. Indeed, she argues that amusement *and* instruction were major features of at least some Scottish HE and that the instruction was indeed *higher* education. In this way, this eighteenth- and early nineteenth-century idea of *infotainment* was not a dumbing down of HE in order for it to appeal to a wider public. As importantly, if not more so, Smith demonstrates that until the full force of the Victorian cult of domesticity began to be felt by Scottish women there was a major and continued growth in the opportunities afforded to wealthier Scottish women to attend HE courses, estimating that 'there were over 5,000 class enrolments by women at the Andersonian [Institution in Glasgow] alone, between 1796 and 1845' (Smith 2000: 326). The Andersonian would eventually become a College of Advanced Technology and then finally the University of Strathclyde in 1964 (Smith 2000).

This 'storming of the citadel' was severely hampered by the growing link from the mid nineteenth century between university *qualification* and professional employment. Men, it seems, did not mind women educating themselves in the same manner that they minded women seeking prestigious employment. It was only from 1875 in England and 1889 in Scotland that legislation enabled universities to confer degrees on women, though it took until the last quarter of the twentieth century for women in Great Britain to achieve overall parity of numbers with men in HE (McDermid 2000).

The twentieth century

Evolution of structural and funding changes until Robbins (1963)

In the UK before 1889 the universities were autonomous[9] and relied entirely on student fees, endowments and the support of local communities.[10] In 1889 the government offered £15,000 to help universities and from then on contributions escalated (Bell 2000). A British system of HE was established in 1916 when the Universities Grants

Committee (UGC) was created to channel centrally provided public funds to help finance universities. The UGC provided grants rather than payment for services and was only marginally accountable to the state (Smith 1999). In 1988 the UGC was replaced by the Universities Funding Council (UFC), which exerted tighter control on universities, but gave them better incentives to respond to student demand (Booth 1999). In 1966 the public sector institutions that offered degrees and higher national diplomas outside the university sector became autonomous corporate bodies (Pratt 1997) under the control of LEAs in England and local authorities in Scotland and funded by the National Advisory Body for public sector HE (NAB), before being financed from 1988 to 1992 by central government through the Polytechnics and Colleges Funding Council (PCFC) in England and the Scottish Education Department (SED) in Scotland (Jackson 1999). In 1992 the *Further and Higher Education Act 1992* removed the binary divide between universities and public sector institutions. Consequently, the number of universities more than doubled when the public sector institutions became new universities and different national funding councils for HE were established for each of the UK countries (Mackinnon and Statham 1999).

From the Renaissance until the Modern Age the most insurmountable barriers to HE had been on the grounds of sex and also very often of religious discrimination, especially in England when the only universities were Oxford and Cambridge. In the latter half of the nineteenth century the barriers of religion and sex were legally removed, but the financial and hence social class barrier to university education was slower to disappear. At the institutional level the idea of providing scholarships to ease the way for students of limited means developed at a snail's pace. In any case, few scholarships were sufficient to allow a student without other support to attend university, although various discretionary local grants had been available for teacher training since the nineteenth century and especially more so since the *Education Act 1902* that established LEAs (Schuller *et al.* 1999). Age, whether for men or for women, was not a barrier to higher education in so far as mature students were not excluded from it and had been catered for in considerable numbers by franchised degrees from the University of London and at the provincial colleges which gained university charters in the early twentieth century (Wright 1989).

Another barrier was arguably the consequence of the number of HEIs. By way of comparison, let us note that in 1900 there were seven universities for an English and Welsh population of 23 million, five for a Scottish population nearly ten times smaller, while the US state of Ohio with the same population as Scotland (three million) boasted 37 HEIs (Miliband 1992). Throughout the twentieth century new HEIs were established to cater for the continual acceleration of full-time undergraduate student numbers. Table 14.1 shows the evolution of full-time student numbers in the UK, as well as the evolution of the Age Participation Index (API).[11]

In 1987 the API reached 15 per cent, which signalled the passage from elite to a mass HE system (Trow 1973). The API more than doubled in 1994 when it reached 32 per cent (Smith 1999: 153). From 1994 to 2000 the growth remained static and started to increase again in 2001, when the participation rate reached 35 per cent (HEFCE 2005); to be more precise 52 per cent for Scotland and 32 per cent for England

TABLE 14.1 Age participation index (API) and number of students in the UK, 1900–2006

Year	API in %	Undergraduate students in HEIs (rounded up)
1900	0.7	35,000
1950	3.0	140,000
1960	5.0	180,000
1980	12.0	400,000
2001	35.0	1,610,000
2011	49.0	2,496,645

Sources: derived from Edwards 1982; HESA 2002, 2013; Carpentier 2004; DfES 2004b.

(Scottish Executive 2004). In 2001/2002 there were 2,086,080 students (of whom 1,610,000 were undergraduate) in 168 British HEIs (Ramsden 2004: 11, 28). If the number of students doing HE courses in FE is taken into account (7 per cent of the total number in England and 25 per cent in Scotland) the total number of higher education students was 2,294,165 (Ramsden 2004: 10). The Higher Education Initial Participation Rate (HEIPR) has now superseded the API. This measures initial HE participation by 17–30-year-olds (DfB 2012[12]; UK Statistics Authority 2010). In overall terms participation in HE in the UK at undergraduate level now accounts for approximately 1.8 million students, with 1,108,685 undertaking full-time undergraduate degrees (HEFCE 2010: 19) across a range of 165 HEIs including 131 in England (HEFCE 2010: 8).

The Robbins Report (1963)

Broadly speaking, before the Second World War, university education in the UK had the function of supporting and reproducing a socio-professional elite, and universities were attended and staffed mainly by people drawn from the upper middle class. As a consequence of the White Paper *Technical Education* (DES 1956), Diplomas in Technology (HNDs) were introduced in some technical colleges to remedy the shortage of both HE places and shortage of scientific and technical skills. Most of the expansion in HE students in the 1950s was in the technical colleges (Simon 1991). A seemingly inevitable consequence of the expansion or universalisation of secondary education would be the growing pressures for HE places.

In the case of HE the simple question of reducing disparities in participation was for a long time clouded by the substitution of the question of equality of opportunity, a very elastic term and as elusive a philosophical concept as it is a practical target, which has been taken to apply to those able and willing to make use of HE. The concern for equality of opportunity to enter HE began in earnest with the Anderson Report (Ministry of Education/Scottish Education Department 1960) that recommended the introduction of means-tested mandatory rather than discretionary grants for all full-time students of HE to cover maintenance and fees (Schuller *et al.* 1999). The students received maintenance grants and the HEIs received fees directly from the LEAs in

England and local authorities in Scotland (Longden 2002). The discourse of equality of opportunity culminated with the so-called Robbins meritocratic principle that anyone able to get the necessary qualifications and willing to go should find a place in HE. Having highlighted that the proportion of middle-class children who reach degree-level courses was 'eight times as high as the proportion from working class homes' (Robbins 1963: 46) and had remained unchanged since the 1920s, the Robbins Committee Report, a sociological analysis of the influence of class on access to HE, argued for a massive expansion in the provision of university places within the discourse of equality of opportunity in terms of extending educational opportunity to all those qualified and willing to participate.

While the Robbins Report (1963) recommended a massive expansion of HE on the grounds of equality of opportunity, the exponential growth (which has so often in Britain been attributed to the Robbins Report) actually started in 1956 and was almost exactly duplicated throughout the individual countries in Europe (Edwards 1982). The API showed a more significant increase *before* the Robbins Report than *after*, as the rate went from 3 per cent in 1950 to 8.5 per cent in 1962, only to reach 12.7 per cent in 1977, 14 per cent in 1987, 20 per cent in 1992 and 34 per cent in 1998. In other words, the age participation rate nearly tripled in the 12 years before Robbins, and rose by only about one-third in the course of the following 14 years; 24 years after Robbins it had not even doubled (Edwards 1982).

The 'sharp and internationally synchronous and uniform escalation of higher education post-1955 indicated that a sufficiently powerful change in the international climate of economic and social thinking could trigger off a rapid change in the demand for higher education' (Edwards 1982: 67), especially if the ground had been prepared by raising the school-leaving age in the previous decade. Robbins had recommended an expansion of the university sector. However, the creation of new HE provision and the sharp escalation in student numbers from 1956 to 1970 took place in the public sector institutions (polytechnics and technical colleges) that offered degrees and HNDs rather than universities. Between 1965 and 1991 higher education in the public sector grew five-fold. This was about twice the rate of expansion in the universities. By 1992 the public sector awarded more degrees than all the universities together (Jackson 1999).[13] In 1966 the White Paper *A Plan for Polytechnics and Other Colleges* (DES 1966) had introduced two parallel forms of HE: the binary system of universities and public sector institutions. The public sector institutions were not new. LEAs had long funded technical colleges that offered HE courses. 'What was new was the idea that the public sector should be one of two large pillars supporting higher education' (Jackson 1999: 111).

Evolution of patterns of participation by key variables

The participation of women saw a steady increase from 1971 to 1981, reflecting a trend in the school system, with more girls gaining qualifications to enter HE. The percentage of full-time students in the UK universities was seven men to three women in 1971–1972, and six men to four women ten years later (Williamson 1986). The number of full-time mature students increased slowly but fairly steadily from 8,500 in 1971–1972 to 10,200 in 1979–1980; the proportion of mature students, however, fell marginally, although there was a sharp rise in the number of women over 25 and a fall in the proportion of men, especially those aged 21–24 (Squires 1981). Regional participation rate when known variations in social class composition were taken into account showed that Scotland, Wales and the North-west of England were doing better than expected on the basis of social class trends, while Northern England and East Anglia were doing rather worse (Williamson 1986).

After the Anderson Report (Ministry of Education/Scottish Education Department 1960) discretionary grants awarded by local authorities were replaced by mandatory income-related grants to full-time students accepted for first-degrees. Despite Anderson, the implementation of the Robbins recommendations failed to significantly increase the relative participation of working-class students. Hence the removal of the financial barrier did not remove the more entrenched social class divide, perhaps because of the increasing emphasis on residence ever since the early twentieth century, and more especially since the early 1960s, or perhaps simply because, although the cost of the post-Robbins expansion was borne by all the taxpayers, the balance of reward favoured those who were already better-off (Williamson 1986). Overall, the expansion in student numbers favoured most those from affluent backgrounds (Edwards and Roberts 1980) while in the decade 1968–1978 the proportion of students from professional and managerial classes expanded even more rapidly (Edwards 1982). However, the public sector accounted for slightly more students from skilled manual, semi-skilled and unskilled backgrounds, but more especially more mature students, and above all more students from ethnic minorities. In 1991 students from ethnic minorities represented 14 per cent of the intake, while they represented 8 per cent of the intake in the universities (Jackson 1999).

Changes in the nature and scope of higher education

From 1960 onwards the nature and scope of HE changed substantially. Since maintenance grants were only available for full-time courses, many students who did not manage to secure a university place went to the polytechnics (Booth 1999). Consequently, polytechnics became more like universities because the student demand was for degrees in liberal humanities and social sciences (Pratt 1997). At the same time new subjects such as media studies, film and television studies, business studies, sport science and technology management and new ways of learning (group work, peer tutoring, projects) emerged from the polytechnics and conventional subject materials were restructured by the creation of modular courses (Booth 1999). By the 1980s media studies, film and television studies, and more generally cultural studies, were on offer in universities as well as in the polytechnics (Jackson 1999). Modular courses are now the norm in HE, which no longer means only a full-time, 3–4-year residential, narrowly focused learning experience, at the expense of the state and with socially advantaged elites (Finegold et al. 1992: 24). After 1992 the inclusion of professional training courses such as chiropody, nursing, occupational therapy and radiography, previously undertaken as work-based learning and offered at diploma level, further modified the nature and scope of HE (Thomas 2001).

'Equality of opportunity' is replaced by 'access and widening participation'

After entitlement to secondary schooling became universal[14] the educational discourse shifted from a focus on equality of opportunity for entry to secondary education to a focus on equality of opportunity for entry to HE. The latter discourse was in turn superseded in the late 1970s by the discourse of 'access and widening participation' to HE, which took place against a background of rapidly expanding student numbers and has now become a major policy issue in post-school education in the British context (Fulton 1981, 1989; Parry and Wake 1990; Williams 1997a; Robertson 1997; Dearing 1997; CVCP 1998; DfEE 1998a; DfES 2004a; Scottish Executive 2004; HEFCE 2005) and worldwide (Halsey 1992, 1993; Davies 1995; Lynch and O'Riordan 1998; Skilbeck and Connell 2000). In the UK and in many industrialised countries

> the impact of the idea of access has arguably been felt most keenly in the last decade or so [since the mid-1980s] and then in the sectors of, first higher education and then, more recently higher education and training.
>
> (Tight 1996: 131)

Since the early 1990s 'access and widening participation' has thus increasingly become 'the mission for institutions of higher education, defining the character of courses and academic structures, pervading the values of institutions and transforming historic patterns of organisations' (Robertson 1997: 31).

As the concept of access to HE has undeniable political resonances and has to do with who gets educational opportunities and who does not, it is worth bearing in mind that the question as to who should have access depends on what HE is for and on the advantages it brings, both for the individual and for society. In the UK the discourse of access and widening participation raises fears about lowering of standards and credential inflation, as well as fears that a graduated system of institutions and courses would still privilege an elite (Scott 1995; Williams 1997b).

Because the motivations behind the major policy issue of widening access and increasing participation were the uncertainty caused by the demographic decline and fluctuations of the traditional entry cohort of the 16–19-year-olds and a desire to open up opportunities for more and different people, it is useful to examine how the government and funding bodies have approached the issue of access since the mid-1970s.

Two Labour government documents at the end of the 1970s, a 1978 Green Paper *Higher Education into the 1990s: A Discussion Document* (DES/SED 1978) and a 1979 report (DES 1979) *Future Trends in Higher Education*, looked at the impact of the projections of an increasing 18-year-old population in the early 1980s followed by a rapid decline in the second half of the decade, which would leave the system with considerable spare capacity. The immediate concern was to prevent a too-rapid expansion in the early 1980s while attempting longer-term planning by suggesting measures against a severe pruning of HE because of a projected demographic fall in the traditional entry cohort. Because of predictions that between 1981 and 1996 the number of people aged between 30 and 44 would increase by about 1.6 million, the number aged over 44 by about 0.3 million, and the number aged between 16 and 29 would decrease by about 0.6 million, the effect of these two government papers was to make many academics and institutions much more aware of the potential of mature student entry because they suggested ways of avoiding the impending fall in student numbers, and this for the best of reasons: expansion and equalisation of educational opportunities (Squires 1981).

Indeed, for many, mature students were beginning to be seen as the way to save HE from decline in the 1990s. Although the 1978 Green Paper had suggested that a way of coping with the demographic fall was to increase the number of mature students, especially those from a working-class background and to further increase the participation of women, there were many obstacles to the effective implementation of these ideas, not least of which was the arrival of a Conservative government in May 1979 led by Prime Minister Margaret Thatcher (Wagner 1989). In the summer of 1981 the Conservative government announced a programme of cuts in public expenditure in the universities which was to reduce their income by about 20 per cent in real terms in the next two years. The government let it be known that the major objective of the squeeze was to reduce the number of students entering HE. The financial disincentive for not meeting target numbers had a rapid effect on institutional behaviour of the universities (Wagner 1989). Because the polytechnics were funded within a local authority system, the impact of reduced unit costs on their institutional finances was not as immediate as it was with the universities. The polytechnics consequently expanded as fast as possible, reasoning that their unit costs would have been even further reduced if other HE institutions had expanded and they had not (Pratt 1997).

The attempted squeeze of HE provision in the first half of the decade was therefore marked by an unprecedented expansion in student numbers (30 per cent increase) along with reduced unit costs (25 per cent decrease) in the polytechnics and colleges which saw students denied university places flocking to them (Wagner 1989). In 1984 the funding bodies (UGC and NAB) each produced two strategy documents as well as a joint statement which, by stressing 'ability to benefit' from HE, raised awareness and changed forever the climate for access and continuing education (UGC 1984a, 1984b; NAB 1984a, 1984b). The following year came the government's response in the form of a Green Paper *The Development of Higher Education into the 1990s* (DES 1985) which accepted the 'ability to benefit' as long as it was greater than the costs and not at the expense of standards. Efficiency and a rather elitist concept of quality were underlined (Wagner 1989). The 1987 White Paper *Higher Education: Meeting the Challenge* (DES 1987) nevertheless widened the criteria for entry even further by saying that 'places should be available for all with the necessary qualities [and not qualifications] to benefit from higher education' (DES 1987: 7). In 1989, in a speech at Lancaster University, the Secretary of State for Education and Science urged that the participation rate among the 18-year-olds should double from 15 per cent to reach 30 per cent within the next 25 years and that in the latter part of the 1990s the expansion of HE should see an increase in participation from the conventional student age group and from the 'new patterns of recruitment among non-conventional students' (Wagner 1989: 156).

Access courses and alternative routes to higher education

The broad idea of wider access has different ideological roots and is not to be confused with the narrower concept of Access courses designed for mature students without formal qualifications to gain specific entry to FE and HE and which offer an alternative to established examination systems designed for adolescents, whether A-levels, Highers or vocational qualifications. While some mature students follow the traditional route and return to college or school to study A-levels or Highers, a steadily growing minority of students now enter university via the above-mentioned alternative routes.

Although there have always been older people studying for degrees, the admission of mature students without the conventional entry qualifications was given a boost in the mid 1970s when the grant regulations were changed to make such students, if they were studying full-time, eligible to receive mandatory awards as opposed to awards at the discretion of LEAs. In 1978 the first government recognition of Access courses occurred when the Department of Education and Science asked seven selected local authorities to provide special courses for people who had 'special needs which cannot be met by existing educational arrangements' and who possessed 'valuable experience but lacked the qualifications required' (DES 1978). The 1985 Green Paper had welcomed Access courses provided that the challenge of non-standard entry is to maintain a reasonable degree of openness while ensuring that academic rigour and standards are maintained (DES 1985). The 1987 White Paper and subsequent government pronouncements have placed increasing emphasis on extending access and have seen Access courses as playing an important role in it by recognising them as one of three entry routes, the other two being A-levels or Highers and vocational qualifications (DES 1987). Although the number and range of Access courses has grown exponentially since 1978, they are only one of the recognised routes of access to FE and HE for mature students over the age of 21. Access to HE by other alternative routes does also exist and includes long-standing diverse and flexible methods such as examination or assessment, through liberal adult education provision, through assessment of prior (experiential) learning, through probationary enrolment and through open entry schemes (Tight 1996).

Over the years Access courses have gained increasing recognition among politicians and others as providing an answer to problems of participation in HE in the 1990s. Arguably, the more broad-based Access courses which offer a closer matching of requirements than A-levels or Highers because they tend to be linked to a particular institution and which emphasise continuous assessment rather than final examinations, provide an alternative, more flexible route while emphasising equality of opportunity (Stowell 1992). Access courses are often perceived by providers and recipients as a form of positive action targeting disadvantaged minority groups and seeking to increase their representation in HE, despite which 'access courses have yet to make a major impact upon the social make-up or the assumptions of higher education' (Tight

1996: 132). This particular criticism of Access courses perhaps explains, or is perhaps explained by, the fact that they tend to overemphasise HE as a destination and thus help sustain traditional perceptions rather than seek to change them (Tight 1996).

The Dearing Report 1997

From 1964 the history of HE has been, along with the discourse of widening access and increasing participation which followed that of equality of opportunity, one of decreased financial commitment and increased control. This is further illustrated by the fact that the whole system of mandatory grants was gradually replaced from 1990 by a part-grant, part-loan scheme (DES 1987).

From 1997 the Labour government has commissioned reports, responded to and produced reports that emphasised the importance of access and widening participation. The Dearing Report (1997) recommended reducing the disparities in participation for those with the potential to benefit from higher education and also to provide the support necessary to maximise their chances of success. The government responded positively to Dearing in *Higher Education for the New Century: A Response to the Dearing Report* (DfEE 1998a) and also in *The Learning Age: A Renaissance for a New Britain* (DfEE 1998b) in which the government announced it aimed 'to widen access to learning in further, higher and adult education' and 'expand further and higher education to provide for an extra 500,000 young people and adults by 2002' (DfEE 1998b: 5, 9). The government also set a target of 50 per cent participation for those aged 18–30 by 2010, as well as a target to increase participation among traditionally under-represented socio-economic groups (DfEE 1998b). There is an apparent paradox in the government's attitude to access. On the one hand, the government accepted Dearing's (1997) recommendation that increasing participation 'must be accompanied by the objective of reducing the disparities in participation in higher education between groups' (Dearing 1997: 101) and admitted that the student support arrangements had not encouraged students from lower socio-economic groups to enter HE, whether on full-time or part-time courses (DfEE 1998a). On the other hand, Tony Blair's Labour government took things even further in terms of decreased financial commitment by introducing tuition fees in 1998 and in removing maintenance grants in 1999 when loans became available to part-time students for the first time (Woodrow 2001).

The twenty-first century

Balance of relative participation between socio-economic groups still unchanged

Paradoxically, one benefit of the funding squeeze in the 1980s and the shift in funding towards a focus on student numbers has been a greater openness on the part of many institutions to mature, part-time and other 'non-traditional students'. In 1991 a quarter of university entrants were classified as entering via 'non-traditional' routes and in 1995 one-third of undergraduate entrants were over 21 (HEFCE 1996). This has in some way reflected the desire of HEIs to maintain numbers during a demographic decline of the traditional cohort, but also reflects some determination to offer new opportunities to previously under-represented groups (Miliband 1992). Although the White Papers of 1987 and l991 (DES l987, 1991) talked less about qualifications and more about 'qualities' required to enter HE and stressed flexibility and accessibility, they did not outline specific measures for coherent reform.

Hence, the unprecedented expansion of HE in the late 1980s and early 1990s most benefited the professional and managerial social classes, women, mature students and some ethnic minorities (Dearing 1997; CVCP 1998). However, neither the expansion nor access and widening participation policies were able to shift the balance of opportunities between most social groups (Dearing 1997; Robertson 1997). Young people from very high-income professional neighbourhoods in exclusive areas have a 75 per cent chance of getting to university, those from middle-class families in owner-occupied suburban semi-detached houses 35 per cent; and those from low-income semi-skilled and unskilled families living in areas of high unemployment 7 per cent (Carvel 1997; HEFCE 1997a). In 1998 Baroness Blackstone, the HE minister, even suggested that A-levels were 'too narrow and elitist' and prevented too many young people, especially those from working-class backgrounds, from going on to HE (Clare 1998: 1).

According to the Higher Education Funding Council for England (HEFCE) the young participation rate, which approximately corresponds to those eligible to progress to HE typically at age 18, increased to 36 per cent by the late 2000s (HEFCE 2010: 1). Also, in 2007 overall participation for all 18–30-year-olds, ran at 39 per cent (Chitty 2009: 213). In a recent report the Office for Fair Access (OFA) established that in overall terms HE has been successful in widening participation, claiming that the most under-privileged socio-economic groups have increased participation and higher groups have, for the first time, increased at a lower rate (OFA 2010: 6). Their findings are partly based on a recent HEFCE report (2010) that found that: 'The proportion of young people living in the most disadvantaged areas who enter higher education has increased by around +30 per cent over the last five years, and by +50 per cent over the last 15 years' (p. 2).

However, increasing participation has not removed inequalities in access. Participation can be linked to factors such as social class, gender, ethnicity and age. The HE landscape in contemporary Britain sees improved participation rates for many groups. In terms of gender, women have higher levels of participation than men, with women accounting for 56.4 per cent of all HE students in 2010/2011 (HESA 2012). Ethnic minority participation is also increasing with 18.1 per cent of new entrants to HE in 2009/2010 being recruited from ethnic minorities (HESA 2012). Older students also increasingly participate, with 56 per cent of part-time degree students aged over 30 years (HESA 2012). However, the same trends cannot be identified in relation to social class. While expansion and participation have increased, the more traditionally advantaged groups predominate in elite HEIs. In contemporary research by Smithers and Robinson (2010), compiled on the basis of data from the Department for Education, UCAS and Oxbridge, applicants from the independent sector maintain a significant advantage as they are twice as likely to be accepted from the most prestigious HEIs,

'48.2 per cent of independent school pupils in England were accepted … compared with 18 per cent of pupils in non selective state schools' (Smithers and Robinson 2010: 2). They also point to the top 100 elite schools, which represent 3 per cent of all schools with sixth form provision. These schools account 'for just under a third (31.9%) of admissions to Oxbridge during three years. These schools are composed of 84 independent schools and 16 grammar schools' (Smithers and Robinson 2010: 3). Similar patterns are also revealed in research conducted by the OFA. They confirm that, in terms of the most prestigious and most selective universities, participation is not widening: 'currently talented young women and men from disadvantaged backgrounds who could apply to selective universities, are disproportionately not doing so, so reducing their chances of upward social mobility' (OFA 2010: 7). Further analysis of data derived from the HEFCE (2010) points to no increase in participation for lower socio-economic groups at the top third of HEIs, with the 'the most advantaged 20 per cent … six times more likely to attend in the mid-1990s … [increasing to] seven times more likely by the mid-2000s' (OFA 2010: 17).

Looking towards the future

At the end of the twentieth century the issue of access to HE had clearly become a topic at the very core of the government's agenda, especially in so far as the provision of non-standard modes of entry is concerned (Open University, Access courses, Accreditation of Prior Experiential Learning and now two-year Foundation degrees). New ways of funding students and institutions as well as performance indicators have been recently introduced to support not only access and expanding participation, but more specifically widening participation or reducing disparities by attempting to overcome the far wider pattern of social exclusion of less well-off and disadvantaged groups in HE, especially students from skilled manual, semi-skilled and unskilled social class background, those from deprived geo-demographic areas, from under-represented ethnic minority groups, those with learning difficulties and disabled students (Woodrow 2001).

FOUNDATION DEGREES

The closing years of the twentieth century were marked by the development of yet another route into HE, the Foundation degree, a vocationally focused HE qualification which was introduced in September 2001 (DfES 2003c). Foundation degrees were designed for persons with professional experience wishing to develop their knowledge further. Indeed, in many cases, professional experience and not qualification was the deciding factor in permitting entrance to the course, whose length ranged from two to three years part-time. The aim of the Foundation degree is to increase the number of people qualified at higher technician and associate professional level (DfES 2003c). Possession of the Foundation degree permits the holder to either enter the final year of an existing undergraduate course or to enter a specially created 'top-up' degree. In the case of learning support assistants or teaching assistants it was commonly intended that the 'top-up' degree be with Qualified Teacher Status. However, at the time of writing the existing one-year top-up degrees do not yet give QTS and a PGCE has to be undertaken afterwards in order for the students to gain QTS status, although there do exist some *two-year* top-up degrees with QTS.[15]

It is too early to say what market value Foundation degrees will acquire. Neither can we be sure whether holders of 'top-up' degrees will be treated on par with holders of traditional degrees, but we need only look to the experience of holders of degrees of the Open University to see what might well occur. It is well documented that for many years following the creation of the Open University in 1970 that holders of its degrees were frequently viewed with more than a little suspicion. That they had entered their course with no qualifications was frequently justification enough for this attitude; that they had done the course part-time simply added fuel to the fire. Time will tell if the Foundation degree follows a similar path. Foundation degrees are offered in a range of forms and formats by a wide range of institutions. It is too early to evaluate and comment on the influence of Foundation degrees in the HE landscape.

PERFORMANCE INDICATORS AND NEW STATUTORY DEVELOPMENTS

The first set of Performance Indicators (PIs) was published in December 1999 by the HEFCE on behalf of all four funding councils in the UK. Performance indicators were access and widening participation, especially from socio-economically underrepresented groups,[16] non-continuation rates after first year, projected outcomes and efficiencies and research output. However, PIs differed according to the profile of the institution so that institutions could only be compared with institutions of a similar profile (Thomas 2001). Since 2000 significant statutory developments have required HEIs to adopt more proactive methods to work towards reducing disparities in access and widening participation. These were the *Human Rights Act 1998*, which came into force in October 2000, the *Race Relations (Amendment) Act 2000* and the *Special Educational Needs and Disability Act 2001* (SENDA), which came into force in May and September 2002, respectively, and the Equality Act 2010.

THE *HIGHER EDUCATION ACT 2004*

In addition to performance indicators and the above statutory developments, the White Paper *The Future of Higher Education*, published in January 2003, set out the government's plans for radical reform in higher education (DfES 2004d). The key proposals were: raising the aspirations of young people through the *Aim Higher* programme; good-quality accessible 'second-chance' routes into HE; fairer admissions procedures; better benchmarks for institutions to monitor widening participation; reintroducing grants for those from the poorest families, abolishing up-front tuition fees; and allowing universities to set their own fees which could range from £0 pa to £3,000 pa if they fulfilled the requirements on access (DfES 2004a).

No acknowledgement was given to the fact that debts running to thousands of pounds may act as a disincentive and, as above, this could be exacerbated by the increased £9,000 fee threshold. However, the introduction of bursaries and the removal of up-front tuition fees will go some way towards reducing barriers to participation. As is the way of many White Papers, much was left unsaid. Hence in April 2004, the DfES published *Widening Participation in Higher Education* (DfES 2004b). This set out the government's proposals for the creation and remit of the OFA and its vision for widening participation (DfES 2004c). Attainment is to be raised primarily through the various initiatives aimed at secondary school and at FE:

> There are still significant barriers of aspiration facing young people from non-traditional backgrounds, as well as disabled students and those from some ethnic minority groups. 59 per cent of a sample of 16–30 year olds from social classes C1, C2, D and E[17] did not plan ever to go to university, and almost half of the sample had never thought about doing a degree. 45 per cent of the sample agreed that 'the student image is not for me'. And aspirations are often set at an early age – one study found that the decision to participate in higher education was made by the age of 14 by the majority of pupils, and some made the decision even earlier.
>
> (DfES 2004a: para. 6.6)

Consequently, the White Paper stated that as the top-up fees were introduced the government was determined to ensure that access to HE was broadened, not narrowed (DfES 2004b: 2). However, widening access and tuition fees are more likely to be mutually exclusive rather than compatible. Keep and Mayhew (2004: 298) suggest that, given the current social class composition of HE entry, 'there are significant risks that yet greater expansion, unless it is attended by fundamental redistribution of access opportunities, will lead to further declines in social mobility'. Parsons and Bynner (2005) claim that social mobility was greater in 1958 than at the start of the twenty-first century. To safeguard against potential further decline in social mobility, the government has placed on any university in England that wishes to apply fees higher than the basic level (£1,250 in 2006/2007, £6,000 in 2013/2014) the obligation to enter into an Access Agreement with the OFA whereby the university will undertake to produce a plan for access, admissions and student support by means of bursaries.

In July 2004, the *Higher Education Bill* received Royal Assent and entered the statute books and became the *Higher Education Act 2004*. The new grants were offered for the first time in October 2004 and the 'top-up' fees introduced in 2005. Since universities like Bristol and Cambridge are not going to be launching two-year vocational degree programmes, the significant increase in numbers attending university may not, in itself, do much to widen the overall socio-cultural profile. Meanwhile, the government made clear that the bulk of the expected increase in student numbers would come through the provision of extra places on two-year Foundation degree courses. There is a good economic argument for this. Britain needs more skilled technicians (Hindmore 2004).

Despite the new access and widening participation legislation, some socio-economic groups remain under-represented: skilled manual and more especially semi-skilled and unskilled socio-economic groups; men; some ethnic minorities such as Afro-Caribbean; and disabled students (HEFCE 2005). Although participation of women equalised in 1994 and now women represent nearly 60 per cent of full-time undergraduate students, some previous disparities between men and women nevertheless remain. Men are more attracted to computer sciences, engineering and technology, physical and mathematical sciences, architecture, building and planning and less pulled towards education, languages and paramedical subjects (Jary 2001). Mature students are more likely to enter newer universities than traditional universities, especially elite universities. Geographical inequalities are changing and growing. In 2000 the highest young participation rates by real cohorts were found in Scotland with 38.7 per cent, London with 36.4 per cent and the South-east of England with 33.3 per cent. Regional comparisons can be misleading, because participation differentials are sharpest when looking at small areas such as parliamentary constituencies and wards rather than larger geographical areas (HEFCE 2005).

Key differences between higher education in England and in Scotland

Since 1992 HE has been funded along national lines with separate funding councils for England, Wales, Scotland and Northern Ireland. As a consequence there is the likelihood that the already diverse patterns of provision and participation will increase. Unlike the Robbins Report (1963), the Dearing Report (1997) had the advantage of having a separate Scottish Committee (Garrick) to take account of the distinctiveness of Scottish HE. The creation of the Scottish parliament further shaped the nature, size and direction of Scottish HE in ways that were different from England.

The Scottish HE system contains many features which distinguish it from that of England and the rest of the UK: the main differences between the English and Scottish HE systems are as follows:

- The four ancient universities[18] developed as community resources and never acquired the social remoteness of Oxford and Cambridge and of those English universities strongly influenced by Oxbridge, which means that localism continues to be important for nearly all Scottish HEIs except Stirling and St Andrews (Bell 2000).
- There are a large number of English academics in Scottish HE since the 1960s (Paterson 1997) and in some institutions such as Edinburgh and St Andrews nearly one-third of students are English, with English 'top-up' fees serving to increase numbers even further (Schofield 2006).
- Scotland has a more uniform and universal system of comprehensive education,[19] later transfer to secondary education and only one year of post-compulsory education before entry to HE is possible (McPherson et al. 1972).
- Scotland has a broader upper secondary curriculum and a broad generalist tradition in HE derived from a distinctive educational tradition and four-year Honours degree courses and a three-year ordinary degree course[20] (McPherson et al. 1972).
- The binary divide was less evident than in England since non-university institutions had a distinct purpose in science and technology rather than humanities and social sciences (Bell 2000).

- The SCQF was established as a consequence of partnership between the SQA and Scottish HEIs and includes all levels of education and training, including degrees and higher degrees (in contrast, the English NQF is separate from the Framework for Higher Education Qualifications).[21]
- Foundation degrees do not exist in Scotland and there are no plans for them, but there are clearer progression routes and a better articulation between FE and HE (it possible to do an HND at an FE college and then move straight into year two or three of a degree at an HEI) and a larger standardised provision at sub-degree level with a national framework of HNCs and HNDs and a correspondingly large involvement of FE colleges in HE (Scottish Executive 2001).[22]
- The participation rate is higher in Scotland at 52 per cent in 2001 against 35 per cent for England, due to the fact that the proportion of HE courses in FE was around 30 per cent for Scotland but only 8 per cent for England (Scottish Executive 2001), which is the consequence of a more seamless transition from school to HE because of a close articulation between FE and HE,[23] but 41.5 per cent of Scottish students in HEIs are over 25 compared with 44.8 per cent in England (Schuller and Bamford 1999)
- Finally, and more importantly, a separate funding council has operated in Scotland since 1992, and there are no fees.[24]

To expand on the final point, from 1998 Scottish HEIs have been able to waive tuition fees for part-time undergraduate students who are unemployed or on low incomes and to develop more courses tailored to their needs (SHEFC 1998). Indeed, tuition fees became a key issue for the Scottish Parliament and this coincided with the (re)creation of this Parliament in 1999. Interestingly, because of intense political pressure by the Liberal Democrats, the Cubie Committee was set up in 1999 not by the Scottish Executive Education Department (SEED), but by the Scottish Parliament itself, thus making the enterprise a more significant one (Mackie 2001). The SEED accepted Cubie's recommendations that bursaries for low-income independent students and for those with additional support needs should be reintroduced. The SEED also accepted that every student would be entitled to student loans, even those from high-income families. Finally, the FE system was restructured along Cubie's lines and anomalies between the sectors removed, thus reinforcing the notion of a seamless robe between FE and HE (Mackie 2001).

In practice all the above means that for students domiciled in Scotland, HE costs less than for students domiciled in England, around £6,000 for a four-year Honours degree course instead of an average of £10,000 for a three-year Honours degree course. The support for students in part-time employment is also better and student retention higher (Mackie 2001). In 2001 the up-front tuition fees of £1,000 per year were replaced by a graduate endowment of £2,000 to be repaid once a graduate earned a salary of around £16,000.

However, in June 2007 the Scottish Education Secretary Fiona Hyslop told the Scottish Parliament that current and subsequent students would not have to pay the endowment. Scrapping the current £2,289 endowment gained just enough parliamentary backing to go through. UK students from outside Scotland but who study there pay up to £9,000 per year.

Conclusion

Higher education no longer means only a full-time 3–4-year residential engagement with a narrowly focused learning experience, at the expense of the state. HE has opened new opportunities and diversified its provision and hence arguably met the challenge of the twenty-first century, whereby the right of access to HE should be available to potential learners throughout their lives. However, many believe that HE itself needs to provide more support for under-represented groups, facilitate a mix-and-match approach and transfer from one institution to another, take courses outside its walls and to the people, use more Accreditation of Prior Experiential Learning (APEL) to select students, offer courses for professional groups and activities and learning methods for mature students (Thomas 2001). The advent of Massive Open Online Courses (MOOCs) might achieve some of this,[25] but time will tell whether they overcome the challenges faced by other attempts at online learning, such as learner isolation and high drop-out rates.

Much has been done and still has to be done to stimulate demand for HE from under-represented groups through raising expectations and improving attainment by measures such as community outreach and promotion, information, advice and guidance and development of progression routes. But more needs to be done to change the internal barriers that are personal inhibitions (linked to social class, gender, ethnicity, age) and the public barriers to graduate employment that are sex, ethnicity, age and disability discrimination (Thomas 2001).

Although the changes in HE since the 1960s, and especially since the late 1980s, were embedded in a discourse, espoused by the access movement, underpinned by an ideology of social justice and equity (Williams 1997b), national policies have nevertheless seemingly tended to be driven by a preference for numerical growth and not by a concern for social justice and equity. In particular, expansion and structural changes, and even the recognition of alternative routes, have failed to a significant extent to challenge the culture of elitism and consequently how HE is perceived among the under-represented groups. If the balance of opportunities between most social groups has not markedly changed since Robbins (1963) despite the changes in policy context, this is perhaps because of the inherent tensions and contradictions between the theory and practice of access and widening participation. The key to the contradictions is that, more so in England and less so in Scotland, HE is 'a mass system in its public structures but still an elite system in its private instincts' as many of its practices 'remain rooted in an elite past' (Scott 1995: 2, 23). Thus, a hierarchy of prestige survives within the HE system in both England and Scotland in terms of institutions and subjects (Jary 2001). This hierarchy of prestige is at its most evident in the persistent socially biased pattern of Oxbridge admissions. In 2000, according to a post code analysis, 80 per cent of applicants to Cambridge came from the professional and managerial classes, some 46 per cent of entrants were state school applicants and 45 per cent came from the independent sector (Lampl 2000).

Despite wider access to HE, and despite the focus of Parliament in widening access to HE, UK productivity lags behind other industrialised countries. American and

French workers produced 26 per cent and 21 per cent, respectively, more for every hour worked than British workers (Brennan 2003). Since FE has a greater impact on the whole UK workforce than HE, this means that learners in FE deserve as much support as undergraduates, and since a better-skilled workforce is a more productive workforce, this means providing learners and employers with courses that meet their needs. Until now, FE colleges faced many bureaucratic difficulties in offering flexible training and qualifications and especially in gaining funding for them (Brennan 2003), but the *Education Act 2004* and various FE-related White Papers have aimed to allow greater flexibility within the FE sector to help increase the skills levels and remedy skills shortages, an outcome that has been desperately needed in the UK for a long time (Hodgson and Spours 1999).

Meanwhile HE in the UK has had to prepare for the outcome of the Bologna Declaration (1999) and ensuing process. The Bologna Declaration is an intergovernmental initiative that aimed to create a European Higher Education Area (EHEA) by 2010 and to promote the European system of HE worldwide. The Bologna Declaration now has 45 signatory countries (29 in 1999) and is conducted outside the formal decision-making framework of the European Union. Decision making needs the consent of all the participating countries. The broad objectives of the Bologna Process are: to remove the obstacles to student mobility across Europe; to enhance the attractiveness of European HE worldwide; to establish a common structure of HE systems across Europe; and for this common structure to be based on two main cycles, undergraduate and graduate. In its drive to improve the quality of HE and, in turn, human resources across Europe, the Bologna Process aims to play a key role in delivering stronger, lasting growth and to create more and better employment.[26]

Notes

1. Ordinary Certificates (ONCs) were awarded after a three-year part-time course at a technical college while Higher Certificates (HNCs) were awarded after a further two years. Ordinary and Higher Diplomas (O/HNDs) required two and three years of full-time study, respectively, and were sub-degree qualifications (Evans 2006).
2. In 1956 the National Council for Technical Awards and the National Council for Diplomas in Art and Design were established. They eventually became the Council for National Academic Awards (CNAA) in 1964, which validated most degrees in the public sector until 1991 (Evans 2006).
3. These became available as six-unit (Single Award) and 12-unit (Double Award) qualifications and could be taken at AS- and A-level (A2).
4. All levels consist of three units, each of which counts as a qualification in its own right and all units beyond Access level have a terminal examination. See www.sqa.org.uk for more details.
5. See www.ucas.ac.uk/candq/tariff/tariff0403.doc for more details.
6. See www.sqa.org.uk for more details.
7. See www.ceg.org.uk/nq/access2/frm-000a.htm for more details.
8. See www.ucas.com/how-it-all-works/explore-your-options/entry-requirements/tariff-tables/gce-a.
9. In continental Europe universities became completely state controlled with staff having the status of civil servants and ministries of education being closely involved in determining curriculum content. The norm is that students go as a right to the university of their choice rather than being selected by them.
10. In the case of Edinburgh, the very first civic university, the town council had a say in its financial and curricular policies. English civic universities followed a similar model since they were established at the initiative of local business and industry elites (Bell 2000).

11. The Age Participation Index (API) for the UK measured the number of home-domiciled young (aged under 21) initial entrants to full-time and sandwich undergraduate courses expressed as a proportion of the average number of 18–19-year-olds in the UK for that given year (DfES 2004b).

12. See also www.gov.uk/government/uploads/system/uploads/attachment_data/file/16203/12-p140-participation-rates-in-he-2010-11.pdf.

13. From 1964 to 1991 public sector degrees were validated and awarded by the CNAA so they would be comparable to university degrees.

14. The Norwood Report of 1943 led to the 1944 *Education Act* for England and Wales and the broadly similar 1945 *Education (Scotland) Act*. These parallel acts gave full and unequivocal access to secondary education for all, free at the point of delivery.

15. See, for example, www.leedstrinity.ac.uk/dev/registration/chooselevel.asp?route=6.

16. Access performance indicators were: the percentage of students who attended a school or college in the state sector; the percentage whose parents' occupation is classed as skilled manual, semiskilled or unskilled; and the percentage whose home area, as denoted by its post code, is known to have a low proportion of 18–19-year-olds in HE (HEFCE 1999).

17. Skilled non-manual, skilled manual, semi-skilled and unskilled.

18. St Andrews, Edinburgh, Glasgow and Aberdeen.

19. Scottish state education is less diversified than in England due to the historical uniformity of the system and early re-organisation to a more completely comprehensive system. Schools are less autonomous, but the headteacher has gained in decision-making power. Schools were encouraged, rather than required, to implement the 5–14 guidelines which were introduced gradually and with extensive consultation.

20. The Ordinary degree is the traditional broad general Scottish degree where, in the Faculty of Arts of traditional universities, students had to take a first-year philosophy course as a compulsory subject as well as a modern language or English language or mathematics. Honours were introduced in 1889 but only after 1918 did the number of students taking Honours significantly increase. Now very few students take Ordinary degrees in Scotland. In the 1960s, however, many people still took Ordinary degrees and there was a strong correlation between sex and degree taken, with 70 per cent of women in the humanities taking Ordinary degrees, and 60 per cent in the sciences (McPherson *et al.* 1972).

21. See www.sqa.org.uk for more details.

22. See also www.foundationdegree.org.uk/institutions/faqs_5.shtml.

23. The high participation rate is largely attributed to the funding model which existed already before the (re)creation of the Scottish Parliament (when the Scottish Office Education (and Industry) Department funded HE courses instead of the Scottish Higher Education Funding Council, as was the case for the HEFC in England) (Smith and Bocock 1999).

24. Students from elsewhere in the UK still have to pay fees in Scottish universities, as do Scottish students in English, Welsh and Northern Irish universities, but students from elsewhere in the EU are treated on the same terms as Scottish students (as EU law requires).

25. See http://en.wikipedia.org/wiki/Massive_open_online_course for a useful discussion of MOOCs and how they can be used.

26. See www.ond.vlaanderen.be/hogeronderwijs/bologna for more information.

References

Baty, P. (2003) 'TUC backlash over fees hike', *Times Higher Education Supplement*, 12 September, 2.

Bell, R. (2000) 'Scotland's universities', *Comparative Education* 36 (2), 163–175.

Bligh, D. (1990) *Higher Education*. London: Cassell.

Booth, C. (1999) 'The rise of the new universities in Britain', in D. Smith and A.K. Langslow (eds), *The Idea of a University*. London: Jessica Kingsley.

Brennan, J. (2003) 'Now is the time to help people top up their skills', *The Independent*, 6 November.

Campbell, M. (2001) *Skills in England 2001: The Research Report*. Leeds: Policy Research Institute.

Carpentier, V. (2004) *Historical Statistics on the Funding and Development of the UK University System, 1920–2002*. Data Archives UK, available at www.data-archive.ac.uk, accessed 7 February 2007.

Carvel, J. (1997) 'University intake startlingly biased towards the rich', *The Guardian*, 19 April.

Central Training Council (1965) *Central Training Council: Report to the Minister*. London: HMSO.

Chitty, C. (2009) *Education Policy in Britain*, 2nd edition. Basingstoke: Palgrave Macmillan.

Clare, J. (1998) 'Universities told to make entry easier', *Daily Telegraph*, 18 September, 1.

Coles, A. (2004) 'Post-compulsory education 14–19', in D. Matheson (ed.), *An Introduction to the Study of Education*. 2nd edition. London: David Fulton.

Committee of Vice-Chancellors and Principals (CVCP) (1998) *From Élitism to Inclusion: Good Practice in Widening Access to Higher Education*. London: CVCP.

Crowther, G. (1959) *15 to 18: A Report of the Central Advisory Council (England)*. London: HMSO.

Davies, P. (ed.) (1995) *Adults in Higher Education: International Experiences in Access and Participation*. London: Jessica Kingsley.

Davies, P. (1997) 'Number crunching: the discourse of statistics', in Williams, J. (ed.) *Negotiating Access to Higher Education: the Discourse of Selectivity and Equity*. Buckingham: SRHE and Open University Press.

Davies, P., Williams, J. and Osborne, R. (2002) *Mature Students Recruitment to Higher Education*. London: DfES.

Dearing, R. (1996) *Review of Qualifications for 16 to 19 Year Olds*. London: School Curriculum and Assessment Authority.

Dearing, R. (1997) *Higher Education in the Learning Society. Report of the National Committee of Inquiry into Higher Education*. London: HMSO.

Department for Business, Innovation and Skills (DfB) (2012). *Participation Rates in Higher Education; Academic Years 2006/2007–2010/2011*. London: DfB.

Department for Education (DfE) (2011) 'EMA Replacement Scheme; 16–19 bursaries and associated transitional arrangements – equality impact assessment'. Available at www.gov.uk/government/uploads/system/uploads/attachment_data/file/180808/ema_replacement_scheme___equality_impact_assessment.pdf, accessed 17 December 2013.

Department for Education (2013) 'Major reform will help hundreds of thousands of young people get good jobs'. Available at: www.gov.uk/government/news/major-reform-will-help-hundreds-of-thousands-of-young-people-get-good-jobs, accessed 17 December 2013.

Department for Education and Employment (1997) *Qualifying for Success: A Consultation Paper on the Future of Post-16 Qualifications*. London: DfEE.

Department for Education and Employment (1998a) *The Learning Age: A Renaissance for a New Britain*. London: The Stationery Office.

Department for Education and Employment (1998b) *Higher Education for the 21st Century: Response to the Dearing Report*. London: DfEE.

Department for Education and Skills (2001a) *The Post-16 Education and Training and Inspection regulations 2001*. London: DfES.

Department for Education and Skills (2001b) *Skills for Life; The National Strategy for Improving Adult Literacy and Numeracy Skills*. London: DfEE.

Department for Education and Skills (2002a) *Success for All*. London: DfES.

Department for Education and Skills (2002b) *14–19 Opportunity and Excellence*. London: DfES.

Department for Education and Skills (2002c) *14–19: Extending Opportunities, Raising Standards*. London: DfES.

Department for Education and Skills (2002d) *Implementation of the Education Maintenance Allowance Pilots: The Second Year*. London: DfES.

Department for Education and Skills (2003a) *21st Century Skills: Realising our Potential*. London: DfES.

Department for Education and Skills (2003b) *Principles for Reform of 14–19 Learning Programmes and Qualifications: Working Group on 14–19 Reform*. London: DfES.

Department for Education and Skills (2003c) *An Introduction to the Foundation Degree*. London: DfES. Available at www.foundationdegree.org.uk, accessed 5 May 2005.

Department for Education and Skills (2004a) *The Future of Higher Education*. London: The Stationery Office.

Department for Education and Skills (2004b) *Widening Participation*. London: The Stationery Office.

Department for Education and Skills (2004c) *White Paper and the Higher Education Act.* London: The Stationery Office. Available at www.dfes.gov.uk/hegateway/hereform/whitepaperconsultation/index.cfm, accessed 3 March 2005.

Department for Education and Skills (2004d) *Higher Education Reform.* London: The Stationery Office. Available at www.dfes.gov.uk/hegateway/hereform/index.cfm, accessed 3 March 2005.

Department for Education and Skills (2005a) *14–19 Education and Skills.* London: DfES.

Department for Education and Skills (2005b) *14–19 Education and Skills Implementation Plan.* London: DfES.

Department for Education and Skills (2005c) *Skills: Getting On in Business, Getting On at Work.* London: DfES, DfES, DTI, HM Treasury, DWP.

Department for Education and Skills (2006) *Further Education: Raising Skills, Improving Life Chances.* London: DfES.

Department of Education and Science (DES) (1956) *Technical Education.* London: HMSO.

Department of Education and Science (1966) *A Plan for Polytechnics and Other Colleges.* London: HMSO.

Department of Education and Science (1977) *Young People and Work.* London: HMSO.

Department of Education and Science (1978) *Letter of Invitation to Chief Education Officers.* London: DES.

Department of Education and Science (1979) *Future Trends in Higher Education.* London: HMSO.

Department of Education and Science (1985) *The Development of Higher Education into the 1990s.* London: HMSO.

Department of Education and Science (1987) *Higher Education: Meeting the Challenge.* London: HMSO.

Department of Education and Science (1991) *Higher Education: A New Framework.* London: HMSO.

Department of Education and Science and the Scottish Education Department (DES/SED) (1978) *Higher Education into the 1990s: A Discussion Document.* London: HMSO.

Edwards, E.G. and Roberts, I.J. (1980) 'British higher education: long-term trends in student enrolment', *Higher Education Review* 12 (2), 7–43.

Edwards, E.G. (1982) *Higher Education for Everyone.* Nottingham: Spokesman.

Evans, R. (2006) *The History of Technical Education: a Short Introduction.* Cambridge: T Magazine Ltd. Available at www.tmag.co.uk/extras/history_of_Technical_Education.pdf, accessed 07 July 2007.

Fieldhouse, R. and associates (1996) *A Modern History of British Adult Education.* Leicester: NIACE.

Finegold, D. *et al.* (eds) (1992) *Higher Education: Expansion and Reform.* London: Institute for Public Policy Research.

Foster, A. (2005) *Realising the Potential: A Review of the Future Role of Further Education Colleges.* London: DfES.

Fulton, O. (ed.) (1981) *Access to Higher Education.* Guildford: SRHE.

Fulton, O. (ed.) (1989) *Access and Institutional Change.* Milton Keynes: SRHE and Open University Press.

Green, A. (1990) *Education and State Formation: The Rise of Education Systems in England, France and the USA.* Basingstoke: Macmillan Press.

Halsey, A.H. (1992) 'An international comparison of access to higher education', *Oxford Studies in Comparative Education* 1 (1), 11–36.

Halsey, A.H. (1993) 'Trends in access and equity in higher education: Britain in international perspective', *Oxford Review of Education* 19 (2), 129–140.

Higher Education Funding Council for England (HEFCE) (1996) *Widening Access to Higher Education: A Report by the HEFCE's Advisory Group on Access and Participation.* Bristol: HEFCE.

Higher Education Funding Council for England (1997a) *The Participation of Non-traditional Students in Higher Education.* Bristol: HEFCE.

Higher Education Funding Council for England (1999) *Performance Indicators in Higher Education.* Bristol: HEFCE.

Higher Education Funding Council for England (2005) *January 2005/03 Research Report: Young Participation in Higher Education.* Bristol: HEFCE. Available at www.hefce.ac.uk/pubs/hefce/2005/05_03/05_03c.pdf, accessed 5 May 2005.

Higher Education Funding Council for England. (2010). *A Guide to UK Higher Education*. Bristol: HEFCE.

Higher Education Statistical Agency (2002) *Students in Higher Education Institutions 2000/2001*. Cheltenham: Higher Education Statistics Agency.

Higher Education Statistical Agency (2012) *Statistics: Students and Qualifiers at UK HE Institutions*. Bristol: Higher Education Statistics Agency.

Higher Education Statistical Agency (2013) *Students in Higher Education Institutions 2011/2012*. Cheltenham: Higher Education Statistics Agency.

Hindmore, A. (2004) 'Public policy, but domestic policy didn't stop', *Parliamentary Affairs* 57 (2), 315–328.

Hodgson, A. and Spours, K. (1999) *New Labour? Educational Agenda: Issues and Policies for Education and Training from 14 Plus*. London: Kogan Page.

Hodgson, A. and Spours, K. (2000) *Qualifying for Success: Towards a Framework of Understanding*. London: IOE.

Jackson, R. (1999) 'The universities, government and society', in D. Smith and A.K. Langslow (eds), *The Idea of a University*. London: Jessica Kingsley.

Jary, D. (2001) 'Access and widening participation', *Higher Education Digest Supplement* 40 (1), 5.

Jessup, G. (1991) *Outcomes: NVQs and the Emerging Model of Education and Training*, London: Falmer Press.

Keep, E. (1996) 'Missing presumed skilled: training policy in the UK', in R. Edwards, S. Sieminski and D. Zeldin (eds), *Adult Learners, Education and Training*. London: Routledge.

Keep, E. and Mayhew, K. (2004) 'The economic and distributional implications of current policies in higher education', *Oxford Review of Economic Policy* 20 (2), 298–314.

Kennedy, H. (1997) *Learning Works: Widening Participation in Further Education*. Coventry: FEFC.

Lampl, P. (2000) 'The scandal of bright children turned away by our top universities', *The Times*, 10 April.

Leitch, S. (2005) *Skills in the UK: The Long Term Challenge*. London: The Stationery Office.

Leitch, S. (2006) *Prosperity for All in the Global Economy: World Class Skills*. London: The Stationery Office.

Longden, B. (2002) 'Funding policy in higher education: contested terrain', *Research Papers in Education* 16 (2), 161–182.

Lynch, K.L. and O'Riordan. C. (1998) 'Inequality in higher education: a study of class barriers', *British Journal of Sociology* 19 (4), 445–478.

McDermid, J. (2000) 'Women and education', in J. Purvis (ed.) *Women's History: Britain 1850–1945*. London and New York: Routledge.

Mackie, D. (2001) 'How do access policies compare? England, Northern Ireland, Scotland and Wales'. Paper presented to the CHERI Conference Access and Retention in Higher Education, City University Conference Centre, 18 May.

Mackinnon, D. and Statham, J. (1999) *Education in the UK: Facts and Figures*. London: Hodder & Stoughton with Open University Press.

McPherson, A., Swift, D. and Bernstein, B. (1972) *Eighteen Plus: The Final Selection*. Milton Keynes: Open University Press.

Miliband, D. (1992) 'Introduction: expansion and reform', in Finegold, D. *et al.* (eds) *Higher Education, Expansion and Reform*. London: Institute for Public Policy Research.

Ministry of Education/Scottish Education Department (1960) *Report on University Student Awards: Effects on the General Grant of Decisions on Awards Policy* (The Anderson Report). London: HMSO.

National Advisory Body (NAB) (1984a) *Report of Continuing Education Group*. London: NAB.

National Advisory Body (1984b) *A Strategy for Higher Education in the Late 1980s and Beyond*. London: NAB.

Office for Fair Access (2010) *What More Can be Done to Widen Access to Highly Selective Universities*. Bristol: OFA.

OfSTED (2001) *Curriculum 2000: The First Year of Implementation – September 2000 to July 2001*. London: HMI.

Organisation for Economic Co-operation and Development (OECD) (2001) *Education policy Analysis*. Paris: OECD.

Organisation for Economic Co-operation and Development (2002) *Education Policy Analysis*. Paris: OECD.

Parry, G. and Fry, H. (1999) 'Widening participation in pursuit of the learning society: Kennedy, Dearing and "The Learning Age" ', in A. Hayton (ed.), *Tackling Disaffection and Social Exclusion: Education Perspectives and Policies*. London: Kogan Page.

Parry, G. and Wake, C. (1990) *Access and Alternative Futures for Higher Education*. London: Hodder & Stoughton.

Parsons, S. and Bynner, J. (2005) *Does Numeracy Matter More?* London: NRDC.

Paterson, L. (1997) 'Trends in participation in higher education in Scotland', *Higher Education Quarterly* 51 (1), 29–48.

Percy, E. (1945) *Higher Technological Education*. London: HMSO.

Pratt, J. (1997) *The Polytechnic Experiment 1965–1992*. Buckingham: SRHE and Open University Press.

Ramsden, B. (2004) *Patterns of Higher Education Institutions in the United Kingdom*. London: Universities UK.

Robbins, L.C. (1963) *Higher Education*. London: HMSO.

Robertson, D. (1997) 'Growth without equity? Reflections on the consequences for social cohesion of faltering progress on access to higher education', *Journal of Access Studies* 12 (1), 9–31.

Samuelson Royal Commission (1884) *Technical Instruction*. London: HMSO.

Schofield, K. (2006) 'Fee refugees "squeezing out" Scots students', *The Scotsman*, 26 January.

Schuller, T. and Bamford, C. (1999) *Initial and Continuing Education in Scotland: Divergence, Convergence and Learning Relationships*. Edinburgh: SCRE.

Schuller, T., Raffe, D., Morgan-Klein, B. and Clark, I. (1999) *Part-time Higher Education: Policy, Practice and Experience*. London: Jessica Kingsley.

Scott, P. (1995) *The Meaning of Mass Higher Education*. Buckingham: SRHE and Open University Press.

Scottish Executive (2001) *Participation in Higher Education in Scotland*. Available at www.scotland.gov.uk/stats/educ.htm, accessed 5 May 2005.

Scottish Executive (2004) *Students in Higher Education in Scotland 2002/03*. Edinburgh: Scottish Executive.

Scottish Higher Education Funding Council (SHEFC) (1998) *More Opportunities for Part-Time Students in Higher Education*. Edinburgh: SHEFC.

Simon, B. (1991) *Education and the Social Order: British Education since 1944*. London: Lawrence and Wishart.

Skilbeck, M. and Connell, H. (2000) *Access and Equity in Higher Education: An International Perspective on Issues and Strategies*. Dublin: HEA.

Smith, D. (1999) 'The changing idea of a university', in D. Smith and A.K. Langslow (eds), *The Idea of a University*. London: Jessica Kingsley.

Smith, D. and Bocock, J. (1999) 'Participation and progression in mass higher education: policy and FHE interface', *Journal of Education Policy* 14 (3), 283–299.

Smith, S.J. (2000) 'Retaking the register: women's higher education in Glasgow and beyond, c. 1796–1845', *Gender and History* 12 (2), 310–335.

Smithers, A. and Robinson, P. (2010) *Choice and Selection in School Admissions: The Experience of Other Countries*. The Sutton Trust.

Squires, G. (1981) 'Mature entry', in O. Fulton (ed.) *Access to Higher Education*. Guildford: Society for the Research into Higher Education.

Stephens, W.B. (1998) *Education in Britain 1750–1914*. London: Palgrave Macmillan.

Stowell, M. (1992) 'Equal opportunities, access and admissions: tensions and issues for institutional policy', *Journal of Access Studies* 7 (2), 164–179.

Thomas, E. (2001) *Widening Participation in Post-compulsory Education*. London: Continuum.

Tight, M. (1996) *Key Concepts in Adult Education and Training*. London: Routledge.

Tomlinson, M. (2002) *Inquiry into A Level Standards: Final Report*. London: DfES.

Tomlinson, M. (2004) *14–19 Curriculum and Qualifications Reform*. London: DfES.

Trow, M. (1973) *Problems in the Transition from Elite to Mass Higher Education*. Berkeley, CA: Carnegie Commission on Higher Education.

UK Statistics Authority. (2010). *Assessment of Compliance with the Code of Practice for Official Statistics*. UK Statistics Authority.

University Grants Committee (UGC) (1984a) *Report of the Continuing Education Working Party*. London: HMSO.

University Grants Committee (1984b) *A Strategy for Higher Education into the 1990s*. London: HMSO.

Wagner, L. (1989) 'National policy and institutional development', in O. Fulton (ed.), *Access and Institutional Change*. Milton Keynes: SRHE and Open University Press.

Williams, J. (ed.) (1997a) *Negotiating Access to Higher Education: The Discourse of Selectivity and Equity*. Buckingham: SRHE and Open University Press.

Williams, J. (1997b) 'The discourse of access: the legitimation of selectivity statistics', in J. Williams (ed.), *Negotiating Access to Higher Education: The Discourse of Selectivity and Equity*. Buckingham: SRHE and Open University Press.

Williamson, B. (1986) 'Who has access?', in J. Finch and M. Rustin (eds), *A Degree of Choice? Higher Education and the Right to Learn*. Harmondsworth: Penguin.

Wolf, A. (2011) *Review of Vocational Education: The Wolf Report*. Available at: www.gov.uk/government/publications/review-of-vocational-education-the-wolf-report, accessed 17 December 2013.

Woodrow, M. (2001) 'Are access policies and current funding arrangements compatible?'. Paper presented to the CHERI Conference Access and Retention in Higher Education, City Conference Centre, 18 May.

Wright, P. (1989) 'Access or exclusion: some comments and future prospects of continuing education in England', *Studies in Higher Education* 14 (1), 23–40.

15

Lifelong learning

Catherine Matheson and David Matheson

When planning for a year – sow corn.
When planning for a decade – plant trees.
When planning for a lifetime – train and educate people.

Kuan Tsu, third century BCE

Introduction

'Learning, like breathing, is something everyone does all of the time' (Tight 1996: 21). It is an inevitable part of life that humans learn continuously unless some major physical or psychological trauma interrupts the process. Even when we are asleep, we learn. Indeed, it is increasingly believed that some aspects of learning can even take place in the womb. Babies learn to associate certain rhythmic sounds with a calm, soothing environment and, once born, will respond positively to such sounds being played to them. From cradle to grave, we are acquiring knowledge, skills and attitudes. We pick up incidental bits of information; we are influenced in manners sometimes subtle, sometimes evident. From this it becomes clear that the concept of lifelong learning must concern itself with something more than simply learning throughout life. Otherwise it is a mere tautology and is hence beyond elaboration. Instead it must concern itself with purposeful learning, be this formal, non-formal or informal. We might want to term this *education* but then there is the other problem of deciding when learning constitutes education and when it does not.

Historical overview

Although there are references in Plato to lifelong education and Comenius certainly advocated learning throughout the lifespan, adult and lifelong education as we know it in the UK has its likeliest ancestor in the Mechanics' Institutes of the nineteenth century. In the Mechanics Institutes, 'workers could improve their basic skills, learn new scientific and technological knowledge and broaden their minds' (Hall 1994: 3), initial job training being done on the job. The notion of broadening the mind is crucial and ties in directly with the goal of the University Extension classes, born as a direct consequence of the growth in the railway system and the postal service. Tutors would tour the country armed with cases of books, lodging in cheap hotels, teaching evening classes in just about every university subject imaginable (except the 'professions') to workers who had spent their day toiling in the mines or in factories. The correspondence course, for its part, had been launched in the immediate wake of the introduction of the postage stamp in 1840. Thus, in the course of the eighteenth century we see two distinct forms of learning distant from the institution concerned: on the one hand there is the correspondence course where the learner's only contact with the centre is by post – together with the occasional trip to the centre for examinations; on the other there is the Extension class, with the tutor travelling sometimes great distances to reach the learners. Interestingly enough, we see both in modern forms in that most hi-tech of establishments, the Open University.

The literary aspect of the Extension classes is underlined in the report of the Committee on Distribution of Science and Art Grants (1896), which advised the allocation of additional grants to enable students attending evening science and art classes to gain further literary instruction through University Extension classes. As we shall see shortly, it was through the University Extension classes that one of the mainstays of adult education in the UK, the Workers' Educational Association (WEA), was born.

The late eighteenth and early nineteenth century also saw the creation of the model village. Devised by industrialists ostensibly to house the workers and their families, these were constructed at some distance from any centre of population and so quite effectively allowed the owner control over multiple aspects of the inhabitants' lives. We shall briefly discuss two such model villages, New Lanark, near the Falls of the Clyde and Bourneville (now part of Birmingham). There were many more, but not all shared the idea of the benevolent, paternalistic employer.

In 1800 Robert Owen, a Welsh entrepreneur who had made his money in the Manchester cotton trade, arrived in New Lanark to take over management of the cotton mill from his father-in-law, the social reformer David Dale. Owen realised that he could increase productivity by improving on the already high-quality housing (Kreis 2000) and by educating not just the children of the workers but also the workers themselves (Donnachie 2003). We can speculate as to the true motives for this venture but the upshot is clear, as Owen (1835) claims in his *A New View of Society* that by education one can give any character one wants to a community. As we saw in Chapter 10 of this volume, Owen established the first nursery school; he also set up his *Institute for the Formation of Character* which was in effect a school and a community centre.

> The three lower rooms (in the Institute) will be thrown open for the use of the adult part of the population, who are to be provided with every accommodation requisite to enable them to read, write, account, sew or play, converse or walk about. Two evenings in the week will be appropriated to dancing and music, but on these occasions, every accommodation will be prepared for those who prefer to study or to follow any of the occupations pursued on the other evenings.
>
> (Owen 1816: n.p.)

Following in many respects the social reform trends set by Owen, George Cadbury and his brother Richard constructed Bourneville in 1879, initially for key workers in their chocolate factory, only later expanding it to admit other workers. Like Owen before them, they included a school in the village but George, unlike Robert Owen, was a committed teacher who spent Sunday mornings teaching in the Quaker-run (though secular in its curriculum) Birmingham Adult School. Within the village, the Cadburys operated what might now be termed community education by organising leisure activities for the inhabitants. They were incidentally among the first employers to give their workers free time on Bank Holidays and reputedly the first to make Saturday a half-day, instead of the usual full-day, in order to give their workers more time for other activities (Spartacus Educational 2002).

Following its creation by the Rochdale Pioneers in 1844 (Holyoake 1907), the Co-operative Movement formally took education as one of its aims in 1882: 'Technical correspondence courses and junior classes were developed during the 1890s and by 1900 over 1,000 students were enrolled for courses, over 500 adults had already taken exams in industrial history, bookkeeping and citizenship and over 900 juniors' (Co-operative College 2003).

Although the educational mission of the Co-op has waxed and waned over the years it has left a lasting legacy on at least two fronts. One is the continuing existence of the Co-operative College, which 'aims to provide adult and lifelong learning programmes that emphasise co-operative values and principles and be a centre of excellence in training, learning, consultancy and research for the co-operative and mutual sector in the UK and internationally' (Co-operative College 2003). Another is the WEA.

Marsh (2002) tells us how the founder of the WEA, Albert Mansbridge, had effectively grown up in the Co-operative Movement. Mansbridge then moved on to University Extension classes where, between 1891 and 1901, he studied a wide range of subjects and later became an evening class teacher. However, Mansfield recognised that the University Extension classes had become a haven for the middle classes. His solution was to found an organisation for the workers, run by the workers. His initial title for the organisation, reflecting the sexism of his age, was the *Association to Promote the Higher Education of Working Men*. This was quickly changed to the *Workers' Educational Association*.

The fortunes of the WEA in England and Wales are somewhat more positive than in Scotland. The WEA became a major provider of adult education in the former, while in the latter it was denied *Responsible Body Status* as a provider of adult education and this made its 'development heavily dependent on collaboration with the universities, local authorities and trade unions' (Duncan 1999: 106).

The University Extension classes, for their part, grew, developed and changed into a plethora of extra-mural courses, covering almost every subject imaginable until, in the 1990s, much of the subsidy provided to them by local government was withdrawn (Vorhaus 2002). Indeed, from 1979 onwards, market forces had been steadily applied and course fees steadily increased. This is aptly illustrated by the example of a class in Danish language which in 1977 cost £2.50; by 2013 it cost £200.[1]

Nonetheless, the twentieth century saw the development and perhaps the apotheosis of the notion of lifelong learning. Especially in the period after 1972 (the year that *Learning To Be* – the Faure report – was published by UNESCO), lifelong learning became increasingly a positive term, first among academics and social activists and then among politicians. The problem was that they did not generally mean the same thing. Lifelong learning quickly became an elastic concept, one which basically meant whatever the person using it wanted it to mean, just as long as there was some notion of lifelong and some notion of learning. Lifelong education came into fashion as did terms such as *learning society* and *learning age.* However, while the advocates of the concept from the 1970s until the mid 1990s concerned themselves principally with improving quality of life, the political advocates from the mid 1990s onwards seemed more concerned with the economic aspects of lifelong learning. The government Green Paper *The Learning Age: A Renaissance for a New Britain* (DfEE 1998) emphasised above all else that by continuing to seek qualifications – and not merely learning or even education – one increased one's chances of improving one's economic situation. We continue to be forever reminded of the pace of technological change, and it would not take a great cynic to believe that there are conscious attempts to make workers feel threatened, and this goes beyond the notion of simply avoiding or removing complacency.

Despite all this, at ground level a locally spawned initiative appeared in a few areas which directly presented active learning as a lifelong activity. This was the admission of adult learners into secondary schools. While adults were admitted to a rare few secondary schools in England (such as the community schools in Sutton in Ashfield and Milton Keynes), in Scottish urban areas in particular, as a direct response to falling school rolls, adults were actively sought, first for leisure classes and later to study for O-grades and Highers. This meant adolescents learning alongside adults, while in the school's crèche some of those same pupils might be learning childcare with the children of some of the adults (Matheson 2000). Active learning was thus presented as something which one can do for the full length of one's life.

Before we move on to look at the concept of lifelong learning, we need to spend a moment considering the main target of lifelong learning initiatives, the adult, and examine a few ideas around adults as learners.

A few myths surrounding teachers and learners

Like many other human activities, education in all its various forms has developed its own myths and mythology. Sometimes these have a basis in truth, sometimes not. By way of reorientation, if needs be, let us look at a few educational myths and check their validity.

Teachers are old and learners are young is perhaps a view which we maintain from those days in which we were young and our teachers were not so young as us. In other words, we were at school. We were most likely segregated from the rest of the learning population. We learned from our teachers and were blissfully unaware of any learning we might be giving them. Learning was seen as a one-way street, a unilateral process. Concomitant with this notion are the ideas that *teachers teach children* and *education equals school.* The latter notion clearly denies the educational validity (or even existence) of non-school education, but we dealt in Chapter 1 with some of the difficulties in the use of *school* and *education* as interchangeable terms. The former notion is p̲ently ridiculous unless the sharing of knowledge, understanding, skills and attitudes which teachers outwith school engage in is somehow not really teaching. The notion that teachers teach children is further undermined when one considers famous teachers from history. An initial list might well include the following: Confucius, Lao-Tse, Moses, Jesus, Mohammed, Buddha, Plato, Socrates. Every one of them was a teacher of adults and none taught in a school as we know it.

It is commonly believed that *learning gets harder as you get older*. But what evidence is there for this? Anecdotes? Common sense? Or is this just another manifestation of the pro-school bias in the widely held view of what education is? One thing is clear: adults have generally greater demands on their time and energies than do young people. Adults often have higher levels of responsibility. In these senses, there are potentially more distractions for the adult than for the young person. But what do these hurdles tell us about the capacity of an adult to learn? Precisely nothing. At best we can say that adults are better at making excuses, *in believing them* and *in getting them believed* than are young people. Educators with experience of both older and younger learners may like to consider here their own attitudes towards the excuses given by learners for work not being done, and more importantly the different attitudes they manifest towards the older and younger learners who are making the excuses. Perhaps because people view adults and their learning differently from younger people and their learning, they are, we would contend, more likely to accept the excuse of the adult who claims simply to have been 'too busy' than they are to accept, say, an adolescent saying the same. Yet, what evidence do we have for adults actually being more busy than adolescents? This is not to say that there are not busy adults or indolent adolescents, but rather to underline the anticipation that adults are, per se, busy and more importantly that their excuses are valid since they emanate from an adult.[2]

The making of excuses to one's self and others – and the believing of them by self and others – arguably presents one of the biggest challenges for any so-called learning society – to get potential learners over the hurdle so eloquently put by Homer Simpson when his daughter Lisa was starting to learn the saxophone:

Don't try, Lisa. Trying is the first step to failure.

Certainly there are some mechanical tasks for which a younger person might well have greater suppleness in, for example, the fingers, but beyond these there does not seem to be much of a case for not being able to *teach an old dog new tricks*. Besides, one thing which adults have in greater measure than young people is life experience. Consequently they have a greater context within which to situate their learning. This unfortunately includes negative experiences as well as positive ones and account has to be taken of the baggage the learner, whether adult or younger, brings to the learning experience. In other words, one has to ascertain what the learner knows and teach accordingly (Ausubel *et al.* 1978).

The concept of lifelong education

The movement towards mass education has gained much momentum over the last 200 years – to attend school as a child for example is now considered the international norm. So much so that Faure felt inclined to write that, between 1960 and 1968, by not being able to attend school 'every year some 2 million or more children (aged between 5 and 14) were denied the right to an education' (Faure *et al.* 1972: 38).

Of course, other than those missed entirely by schooling one must also consider the drop-outs, the school failures (although whether a child fails school or is failed by it is open to conjecture), the unemployed, the misoriented, etc. The list is vast of those categories of people for whom the skills and knowledge acquirable at school might be of use. To this must be added the skills and knowledge acquirable outside of school which might help an individual to be educated. The result is certainly an enormous mass of people who could benefit physically, mentally or financially from furthering their education and widening their knowledge and understanding.

The background notions in lifelong education as defined by UNESCO are a mixture of old and new. A basis for the idea comes from Erasmus, who wrote: 'We are not born human, we become human or rather ... we make ourselves human' (Margolin 1981: 172). Compare this with the following quotes used by Faure as 'the major argument in favour of lifelong education'; Lapasade: 'One never ceases to enter life'; and Fromm: 'The individual's entire life is nothing but a process of giving birth to [her/]himself; in truth we are only fully born when we die' (Faure *et al.* 1972: 158).

Despite the span of several centuries the ideas are shades of the same thing. However, there remain problems in defining the concept of lifelong education. For example, according to Dave 'the learning process is the key to all education' (Dave 1972: Concept Characteristic 10) while for Faure education is conceived of as a vector: 'the path to learning is irrelevant; only what is learnt or acquired has any importance' (Faure *et al.* 1972: 185). The contradiction between these standpoints is clear but there is also a major contradiction within Faure; in lifelong education the end is, by definition, death. Therefore, unless the path to learning is seen as part of the learning there is little point in learning at all as the path to learning begins at birth and ends at death. Besides, there is a distinct lack of logic in viewing final products of an educative process (short of death) as identical on the basis only of what has been learned or acquired. If the experience has been different then the product must be also. Faure, however, characteristically hedges his bets by employing the word 'acquire' instead of some stronger term.

According to Gelpi: 'the hypothesis of lifelong education [is] that the educators need not necessarily be professionals' (Gelpi 1979: 19). This is essential for Dave for whom: 'Lifelong education seeks to view education in its totality. It covers formal, non-formal and informal patterns of education and attempts to articulate all structures and stages of education' (Dave 1972: 35). For Skäger 'lifelong education is not a concept or a thing but a set of basic principles' (Griffin 1983: 156). This effectively says nothing and may even contradict itself, depending on how strong a meaning is taken of concept or principle. Besides, is not a true concept in fact a set of basic principles? Cropley takes an almost equally spurious tack when he writes that 'lifelong education is an orientation, concept or principle, not a tangible thing' (Cropley 1979: 113). Unfortunately, Cropley does not define his meaning for tangible upon which his argument hinges. The *Shorter Oxford Dictionary* admits three meanings that encompass both the concrete and the abstract. *Assuming* that Cropley means that lifelong education is not concrete then he agrees with Lengrand, who insists on the indefinable nature of lifelong education remaining forever so: 'Lifelong education is still at the conceptual stage. As with other principles such as freedom, justice and equality, it will doubtless retain indefinitely that certain distance in relation to concrete achievements which is in the nature of concepts' (Lengrand 1978: 98). Thus Lengrand places the question of 'what is lifelong education?' on almost the same footing as a moral philosopher might put the question 'what is good?'. This doubtless raises the philosophical status of lifelong education but does nothing to expedite its implementation, unless of course it can be argued that there is a moral imperative to lifelong education as might be claimed for 'good'.

For De'Ath, lifelong education is of anthropological importance in that it 'could be instrumental in not only preserving all kinds of cultural diversity but also in placing a positive value on individual and collective difference' (De'Ath 1972: 247).

All these writers demonstrate the lack of rigour that Lengrand warns of when he writes: 'the term lifelong education is used haphazardly and loosely in a variety of situations and realities' (Lengrand 1979: 29).

Conceptually there is very little to grasp in the lifelong education debate that consists of anything more than very fine straws or collections of undefined terms and hurrah words such as those used by Cropley and De'Ath above. What there is consists of:

1. an attempt to view education as not confined to school but as consisting of purposeful and process learning undertaken wherever and whenever;
2. a view of education as a whole-life activity which ought to be facilitated by the state and in which some may take longer than others to achieve their goals but no-one is deemed a failure.

There are immediate problems with this facilitation, especially when one sees lifelong education as an activity driven by economic need. At this point, and especially where the long-term unemployed are concerned, facilitation may easily turn into compulsion as we see in some of the Welfare to Work programmes in the United States, which have been considered for adoption in various European countries.

Lifelong learning at the dawn of the twenty-first century

We live in the era of perhaps the most rapid change known to humanity. The paradigms our parents knew (and that perhaps we ourselves grew up with) are being steadily swept away. Notions such as a job for life are all too clearly obsolete except perhaps for an elite cadre of highly skilled, highly paid workers (Longworth and Davies 1996), while the rest are left with the realisation that in our possibly postmodern world there is a dearth of permanent, decent jobs (Aronowitz and Giroux 1993).

Politicians talk about educating the workforce, by which they generally mean training them while training itself is held up as the great panacea. As an editorial in the *Observer* of 21 July 1996 commented, training is:

> The great palliative of our time. All parties support it and none asks what work there is for the trainees when the training ends. As a policy, it has the immense advantage of being far cheaper than building homes or creating jobs.

Mixed in with this rhetoric is increasing talk about lifelong learning from politicians. The Labour opposition in the UK promised before the 1997 General Election that lifelong learning would be the subject of a White Paper (Labour Party 1994) (while the then-Conservative government (DfEE 1996) contributed to the debate which led to the publication in 1996 of *Learning: The Treasure Within* Delors *et al.* 1996), this being a consultative document leading to a bill before Parliament. Less than one year into office and the promised White Paper had appeared as a Green Paper (DfEE 1998)) – in other words, merely a consultation document which need not lead to anything else. The debate goes on but where it will lead remains to be seen. There persist, however, the conceptual problems with lifelong learning which show no sign of resolution, except in so far as the liberal aspects of lifelong learning are vanishing from view.

Lifelong learning is what Knapper and Cropley (1985: 20) term 'a utopian idea – an elastic concept which means whatever the person using the term wants it to mean'. As Lengrand (1986: 10) reminds us: 'There is no single centre of thought from which this idea has been disseminated, nor is there a code of propositions that would enable the faithful to be distinguished from the heretics.' Nonetheless, it is a powerful idea which captures the public imagination and makes it sound as though the interlocutor wants to actually do something positive.

Lifelong learning and school

Strictly speaking, any account of lifelong learning ought to contain a consideration, if not of the first learning experiences that a person has, then at least of the first formal learning experiences, such as those that occur in preschool and in school itself. We have seen earlier some of the influences and effects that can occur in preschool and school that affect self-esteem and growing self-concept. Influences such as whether one attends preschool at all, the effect of social class or of one's gender, 'race' and racialisation, the younger learner's needs and the adult's responsibilities in satisfying those needs. School is an undeniably formative influence on a learner's perception of him/herself and also on his/her perception of him/herself as a learner.

It is in school that learners generally have their first introduction to formalised learning strategies. School introduces to learners the essential skills without which all further attempts at purposeful learning are impeded. These basic essential skills are generally held to include, for example, reading, listening and sifting information. It is worth mentioning in passing, however, that both Freire and Illich[3] question whether reading is such a basic skill as we in the industrialised countries claim it to be. Nonetheless,

> Schools ... have to start a dynamic process through which pupils are progressively weaned of their dependence on teachers and institutions and given the confidence to manage their own learning, co-operating with colleagues, and using a range of resources and learning situations.
>
> (Abbott 1994: 108)

The extent to which schools succeed in this 'weaning' is very much open to debate. In this respect it is worth reflecting on one's own learning from school and judging how much of one's autonomy as a learner is due to influences from school and conversely how much of one's dependency is due to influence from the same source.

Lifelong learning implies by its very nature that learners have become equipped with basic learning skills, that they know how to learn, that they have gained the equipment, the skills and the attitudes needed to pursue their own learning. Learners have to have moved from a dependency stance to one of autonomy, to have developed a sense of self-direction, to have, in the terms of Malcolm Knowles, moved from needing pedagogy to demanding andragogy; in other words, they have to have moved from needing the security which comes from being told what to do, when to do and how to do it to being able to define their own educational goals and the pathways to them (Knowles 1998). The question arises as to when the learners assume this level of autonomy. One might also ask whether all learners *should* assume such a level and consider some possible ramifications. Let us keep these thoughts at the back of our minds as we continue.

As Howe puts it: 'A person who leaves school ill equipped with the competencies required for learning independently throughout the remainder of a life is at a severe disadvantage' (Howe in Claxton 1990: 165). Much of the literature which appeared in the wake of *Learning To Be* (Faure *et al.* 1972) assumed tacitly or overtly that being properly equipped with learning tools was a necessary condition for lifelong learning. Its starting point is generally that: 'Today no one can hope to amass during his or her youth an initial fund of knowledge which will serve a lifetime. The swift changes taking place in the world call for knowledge to be continuously updated' (Delors *et al.* 1996: 99).

We witness daily the truth of this statement as we rush forward in technology (and leave many old certainties behind) and in itself it implies a need for schools to instil lifelong learning skills in their pupils. Examples of how dismally schools fail in this task are not hard to find. It is unfortunately true, for example, that the rate of borrowing books from public libraries is in constant decline; employers everywhere complain about how difficult their recruits find mastering new skills; teachers in higher education complain about the declining levels of autonomy they see among their students. We should perhaps take some of these complaints with a small pinch of salt but not dismiss them entirely. Nostalgia is not what it used to be, but nonetheless perceptions breed perceptions on the part of both the observer and the observed, roles which interchange constantly.

Despite this, however, anyone who enters a job has to assume that the skills they begin with are almost guaranteed to become outmoded and will require updating or even replacement. Even the most apparently unchanging of occupations are altered by technology and countless others have changed beyond all recognition in the last 20 years, while a multitude of other, new professions, particularly relating to information technology, have come into existence.[4]

However, as Stoikov (1975: 114) (and many other writers besides) points out, 'it is usually those who already have a good educational and training background who volunteer for additional education and training'. In *Learning: The Treasure Within* (Delors *et al.* 1996) we find the same message: 'Adults' further participation in educational and cultural activities is related to the level of schooling already received: [so] the more education you have then the more education you want' (Delors *et al.* 1996: 101). In other words, it is no new phenomenon that the educated educate themselves the most. If ever there was an argument for wider initial education then this is it. It is also worth noting that Blackledge and Hunt (1985: 170) remind us: 'Educated parents equip their children for a successful career in education.' So if we want formal education to be a real agent for social mobility then we ought to be pressing for adults to increase their level of education in order to encourage their children to increase theirs. In this respect, we find echoes of Paolo Freire and his attempts at teaching literacy. It is well known that Freire despaired of teaching children to read when their parents were illiterate and so he set about teaching their parents, but using materials and learning circumstances which were of relevance to them. As Furter (1999) puts it, he tried to move people from mere literacy to cultural development.

Lifelong learning and economics

In an ideal world, in a true learning society, any person would be free at any time to learn anything that lay within their intellectual capabilities and would feel supported and nurtured in taking such initiatives. Unfortunately, simple economics removes this option immediately. All activities, be they formal or non-formal, must be paid for. Each subsidy must be argued for and the formal, initial domain of education clearly and indisputably has first priority. In most countries it would be unthinkable to levy general charges on primary school children, although this is increasingly demanded for some artistic activities; similarly, in lower secondary, although paying some fees for upper secondary school is quite common across Europe. Education beyond upper secondary has to play second fiddle: after all, it applies to a smaller and smaller proportion of the population. Indeed as we move up the age range of the target population, the greater the likelihood of fees being applied in one way or another. There are, however, exceptions such as courses aimed at the long-term unemployed which might be funded at 100 per cent by central government or via unemployment insurance. In this last respect, the challenges laid by the economy are performing exactly as d'Hainaut and Lawton (1981: 37) predict when they say that 'the economy serves as a powerful stimulus to education in general and to lifelong education in particular'. A cynic might say that it gives the government and its agencies something to do with the unemployed. In this light, we might think back to training and the palliative effect that it has.

It is worth bearing in mind that 'by its very nature, lifelong learning involves a change in the distribution of activities over time and among members of the population, and such a redistribution has implications for the future social structure' (Stoikov 1975: 7). This obliges us to ask the extent to which we, as a society, want to maintain the status quo or whether we want to encourage social development.

If lifelong learning is to become the perceived norm then there is clearly an essential need for major subsidy of those who cannot pay the fees. Otherwise it will serve as further reinforcement of economic stratification as equivalent to cultural stratification. The 'better-off' have access to most culture (by dint of having more cash to pay for it, by generally having more education with which to appreciate it), but should this necessarily be so? Is there not a role for lifelong learning in offering cultural openings to those whose purse strings cannot usually stretch that far?

However, fine as this is in theory, in practice it means the poorer student having to submit to some kind of means test to decide the fee to be paid. There is also the concomitant problem of over-subsidising learning experiences, since it is all too often the case that when something is perceived (by the consumer) as costing nothing, it may be seen as being worth nothing.

For those who can afford courses there are the dire warnings of Ohliger and Dauber that: 'concomitant to lifelong education is lifelong students, condemned to perpetual inadequacy' (Cropley 1977: 156). This is a certain problem: how can learners be encouraged to seek purposeful lifelong learning without feeling that their need for learning (for there must be such if they are to seek learning) is witness to a deeper feeling of inadequacy? This is unless a different view of learning need is promoted. One that we might term an ameliorative view of learning whereby the learning is sought to improve an already 'good' (by whatever terms) situation. This stands in contrast to the deficit model so promoted by governments and training providers where the message is one of 'train or get left behind' rather than 'learn in order to add to your life'.

However, there is always 'the spectre of uselessness' (Ranson 1998: 255) which hangs over workers feeling insecure in their employment.

Lifelong learning: leisure or education?

This brings us to our next point: is lifelong learning to be a leisure activity or an educational activity? If the former, then she/he who cannot partake of it for whatever reason may not perceive the loss or lack as so great as if it is the latter. The danger is that in attempting to raise the value of lifelong learning its providers, especially to secure funding, may downplay the leisure side with the concomitant risk of creating a sort of education addict, forever driven from course to course by an insatiable appetite whetted and fuelled by inadequacy. If this became generalised through lifelong learning becoming the perceived norm, then how much more inadequate will be those denied access?

On the other hand, if lifelong learning is perceived as leisure then not only is its social value decreased but it is also seen as nothing more than an optional extra, as a luxury to which only some may be expected to aspire. As a leisure activity, it loses any moral *right* to funding which an educational activity may claim. In this light, we must consider blurring boundaries.

We are used to a society which separates work from play, 'non-work' from 'work' (which often means that activities which do not lead to a wage are diminished in social status terms), and which separates learning from work (although the one may impinge on the other). We are also, perhaps most importantly, used to defining ourselves by our work. If you answer the question as to what you 'do' by describing yourself as 'student in education' then this would probably be considered quite normal. Were you to respond by saying that you enjoy cooking and baking and trying to play jigs and reels on the fiddle, then the one who has asked the question might well look askance. To define oneself by one's work (or pursuits equivalent to work) is acceptable and may even be perceived as being somewhat hedonistic. To define oneself by non-salaried work or by leisure pursuits is not so readily acceptable. This apparent digression reveals its importance when we consider the lack of permanency in many, if not most, jobs. As John White (1997: 71) puts it, 'Education for unemployment may become a fixed part of the vocational landscape.' In other words, instead of education being conceived as a precursor to work, it may be construed as equally a precursor to non-work, or to leisure, to meaningfully filling one's days.

It is well documented that 'working class' persons tend to eschew education and training which does not immediately impinge on work or the possibility of obtaining work. Education and training are seen as purely, or at least largely, instrumental. What is most easily qualified as intrinsic learning, adult education classes, are dominated by 'middle class' persons. We have different cultures perceiving education and training according to different terms. This would suggest that, unless lifelong learning is just going to reinforce existing social divisions, it will have to cross the divide between work and leisure. It will have to bridge the cultural and perceptual gaps which exist. How it does so is another question, but it is arguable that a change in attitude at the level of the school might help if it abolished the arbitrary divide between work and play, the former being currently seen as serious, the latter frivolous and often confused with fun; in this respect the quote from Froebel, with which Chapter 12 in the present volume opens, is most appropriate. Our postmodern world seems to strive to break down boundaries. The gaps between education and leisure, work and play, and work and non-work are just a few more to be tackled.

Conclusion

Lifelong learning, lifelong education, the learning society and the learning age have been high on the political agenda for over 30 years. They have built on a long heritage and an ever-increasing literature. Each of the terms can be best construed as a hurrah word. However, each can also mean whatever the interlocutor wishes it to mean. For the present UK government and its immediate predecessors, it means lifelong training. Quality of life, previously a key feature in lifelong learning, now seems to have faded from the discussion. 'Workers require lifelong learning' (*Times Higher Education Supplement*, 19 December 1997), 'Lifelong learning: they're making it work' (*The Independent*, 21 May 1998) and the whole thrust of *The Learning Age: A Renaissance for a New Britain* (DfEE 1998) demonstrate the direction that the rhetoric has taken. However, even in the versions from the 1970s, a number of potentially important elements were missing, namely: emotion, moral development and spirituality. These are vaguely subsumed under quality of life, but are never actually highlighted. It is almost as if humans were seen as not needing those very parts which are arguably those that make them human.

Yet we stand at a moment in time when Western society has lost its old paradigms and, most importantly, lost a large measure of its faith in the future. In this respect, we have an occasion to define the goal of lifelong education in a manner not evident in the 1970s. We have the possibility of moving beyond the present confusion of the hurrah word and the insecurity which is its undertone, towards placing humans and their feelings at the centre. Let us propose that the aim of lifelong education be to restore and to maintain hope. We can term this *consciencisation* if we wish, but with this simple goal in mind we have at our disposal the means of developing a concept which not only hangs together but which we can explain to our political masters and to the public at large in terms which are meaningful to them and which stand some chance of loosening purse strings. Failure to do so will result in lifelong education continuing to be a political buzzword destined to mean whatever an orator wishes it to mean. Failure to actualise lifelong education will mean even more social stratification, more situations where those who have shall receive (in this case education and wealth), while those who have not must content themselves with the droppings from the rich man's table. Otherwise, the last words on lifelong learning will be those of Frank Coffield, who claims that lifelong learning died in 2003:

> She was all things to all people. The politicians loved her because in their hands she was so flexible, the practitioners loved her because they could do anything they liked in her name, and the researchers loved her because they made money recording her every twist and turn.
>
> (Coffield 2003: 5)

Notes

1. See www.gla.ac.uk:443/departments/adulteducation/index.php?SelectedSubject=Languages&SelectedSubheading=Danish.
2. One of the present writers recalls on one occasion asking an adolescent where his homework was and getting as the reply: 'I'm sorry I wasn't able to do it but I had to sit up all night with my dad.' The dad was later revealed to be a heroin addict and the boy (who was very big and strong) would sit up with his stoned father until the latter fell asleep. The son would then carry him to bed and lay him in the recovery position. This could take all night. How many adults could beat that for an excuse? And how many adults would believe this for an excuse?
3. Both Illich and Freire began to question the intrinsic value of literacy when they observed in their work in Latin America that the rural poor may have nothing to read and yet their cultures have evident value (Pierre Furter, personal communication).
4. As time goes on, it will be interesting to observe the effect that computer-based communications have on spelling. As anyone who habitually uses e-mail can testify, the smallest mistake in the address and the communication does not go where it is supposed to go. At this point, immense care must be taken. On the other hand, the actual message is often marked by a complete insouciance for grammar, spelling and syntax.

References

Abbott, J. (1994) *Learning Makes Sense*. Letchworth: Education 2000.

Aronowitz, S. and Giroux, H. (1993) *Postmodern Education*. Minneapolis, MN: University of Minnesota Press.

Ausubel, D.P. Novak, J.D. and Hanesian, H. (1978) *Educational Psychology: A Cognitive View*. New York: Holt, Reinhart and Wilson.

Blackledge, D. and Hunt, B. (1985) *Sociological Interpretations of Education*. London: Routledge.

Claxton, G. (1990) *Teaching to Learn*. London: Cassell.

Coffield, F. (2003) 'Epitaph for the Big L', *Times Education Supplement*, 5 September, p. 5.

Committee on Distribution of Science and Art Grants (1896) *Report of the Committee Appointed to Inquire Into the Distribution of Science and Art Grants*. London: HMSO.

Co-operative College (2003) available at www.co-op.ac.uk, accessed 24 April 2014.

Cropley, A.J. (1977) *Lifelong Education: A Psychological Analysis*. Oxford: Pergamon.

Cropley, A.J. (1979) 'Lifelong learning: issues and questions', in Cropley, A.J. (ed.) *Lifelong Education: A Stocktaking*. Hamburg: UNESCO Institute of Education.

d'Hainaut, L. and Lawton, D. (1981) 'The sources of content reform geared to lifelong education', in d'Hainaut, L. (coordinator) *Curricula and Lifelong Education: Education on the Move*. Paris: UNESCO.

Dave, R.H. (1972) 'Foundations of lifelong education: some methodological aspects', in Dave, R.H. (ed.), *Foundations of Lifelong Education*. Oxford: Pergamon.

De'Ath, C. (1972) 'Anthropological and ecological foundations of lifelong learning', in Dave, R.H. (ed.), *Foundations of Lifelong Education*. Oxford: Pergamon.

Delors, J., Al Mufti, I., Amagi, I., *et al.* (1996) *Education: The Treasure Within*. Paris: UNESCO/HMSO.

DfEE (1996) *Lifetime Learning*. London: HMSO.

DfEE (1998) *The Learning Age: A Renaissance for a New Britain*. London: The Stationery Office.

Donnachie, I. (2003) 'Education in Robert Owen's New Society: The New Lanark Institute and Schools', *The Encyclopedia of Informal Education*. Available at www.infed.org/thinkers/et-owen.htm, last updated 24 May 2003.

Faure, E., Herrera, F., Kaddoura, A.-R., *et al.* (1972) *Learning To Be*. Paris: UNESCO.

Furter, P. (1999) *From Literacy to Cultural Development*. Northampton: Nene-University College School of Education Occasional Paper.

Gelpi, E. (1979) *A Future for Lifelong Education*. Manchester: Manchester Monographs.

Griffin, C. (1983) *Curriculum Theory in Adult and Lifelong Education*. Beckenham: Croom Helm.

Hall, V. (1994) *Further Education in the United Kingdom*. London: Collins Educational/Staff College.

Holyoake, G.J. (1907) *Self-Help by the People: The History of the Rochdale Pioneers*. London: Swan Sonnenschein.

Knapper, C.J. and Cropley, A.J. (1985) *Lifelong Learning and Higher Education*. London: Croom Helm.

Knowles, M. (1998) *The Adult Learner*. Houston, TX: Gulf Publishing.

Kreis, S. (2002) *Robert Owen 1771–1858*. Available at www.historyguide.org/intellect/owen.html, accessed 24 April 2014.

Labour Party (1994) *Opening Doors to a Learning Society: A Policy Statement on Education*. London: Labour Party.

Lengrand, P. (1978) *An Introduction to Lifelong Education*. Paris: UNESCO.

Lengrand, P. (1979) 'Prospects of lifelong education', in Cropley, A.J. (ed.) *Lifelong Education: A Stocktaking*. Hamburg: UNESCO Institute of Education.

Lengrand, P. (1986) 'Introduction', in Lengrand, P. (ed.) *Areas of Learning Basic to Lifelong Learning*. Oxford: UNESCO/Pergamon.

Longworth, N. and Davies, W.K. (1996) *Lifelong Learning*. London: Kogan Page.

Margolin, J.-C. (1981) 'L'éducation au temps de la Contre-Réforme', in Vial, J. and Mialaret, G. (eds) *Histoire Mondiale de l'Education*. Paris: Presses Universitaires de France.

Marsh, G. (2002) *Mansbridge: A Life*. Available at www.wea.org.uk/pdf/Mansbridge.pdf, accessed 24 January 2004.

Matheson, C. (2000) 'Education in non-traditional spaces', in Matheson, C. and Matheson, D. (eds), *Educational Issues in the Learning Age*. London: Continuum.

Owen, R. (1816) *Address to the Inhabitants of New Lanark*. Available at www.robert-owen.com/quotes.htm, accessed 24 January 2004.

Owen, R. ([1835] 1965) *A New View of Society and Report to the County of Lanark* (Gatrell, V.A.C. (ed.)). Harmondsworth: Pelican.

Ranson, S. (ed.) (1998) *Inside the Learning*. London: Cassell.

Spartacus Educational (2002) *George Cadbury*. Available at www.spartacus.schoolnet.co.uk/REcadbury.htm., accessed 23 September 2007.

Stoikov, V. (1975) *The Economics of Recurrent Education and Training*. Geneva: International Labour Office.

Tight, M. (1996) *Key Concepts in Adult Education and Training*. London: Routledge.

Vorhaus, J. (2002) Lifelong learning and new educational order? A review article, *Journal of Philosophy of Education* 36 (1) 119–129.

White, J. (1997) *Education and the End of Work*. London: Cassell.

16

Comparing educational systems

Trevor Corner and Nigel Grant

Let us give our attention to the learning of culture in face-to-face situations, since it is in these intimate contacts that our most vivid experience of culture takes place, and other forms of communication gain their grip on us mainly by feeding face-to-face communication.

Lawrence Stenhouse (1967)

Introduction

The first problem that needs to be dealt with in comparative education is in deciding what it is for, both generally and in terms of the individual considering making use of it. It is an inherent part of the work of government bodies, national and international agencies and senior managers in education to take evidence of the relevant experience of others to illuminate their own problems.

Comparative studies in education are based on a body of methodological research work which has enabled it to evolve over the past 100 years (Holmes 1981; King 1979; Watson 2001). Most students who study comparative or international education (or both) are not specialists in the field themselves. Quite properly, they are looking to the study to give them comparative insights into some other field, whether it be a teaching subject, the curriculum, educational policy and management. This is just as well, for the capacity to provide this perspective is one of the strengths of the subject's appeal, namely its value to the non-specialist.

This raises fundamental questions about approaches to the subject. Methodological discussions are concerned with finding the most effective ways of explaining the behaviour of educational systems, and it is in this light that the relative merits of the various approaches – national case-studies, cross-cultural thematic studies, the construction of models and typologies and the search for valid generalisations – have to be considered. For the purposes of research, there is general agreement that the study of comparative education has to progress from accurate *description* to *analysis*, and from that to the forming of *generalisations* about the working of educational systems. There are strong disagreements about the best ways of achieving this (Crossley 2001), and different methodologies are continuously being proposed (Leibman and Poulson 1994;

Thomas 2012), but little dispute about the broad aims themselves. But when one considers the position of the non-specialist student, other criteria must be thought of as well; and these will influence the way in which the subject is presented.

Comparative perspectives

What, then, can non-specialist students gain from the study of comparative education? To say that they can develop a 'comparative perspective' on their own special fields, while true enough, needs further elaboration. Leaving aside particular interests, one might suggest that a comparative perspective can offer the following elements at least:

1. Awareness of the differences between systems and their policies and practices in various countries

Whether these are more important than the similarities is arguable; but the point needs to be made that educational problems, and the ways of tackling them, can differ considerably from those with which we are familiar.

2. Similarities between systems also have to be made clear

If only the differences are dealt with, the impression may be conveyed that the experience of other countries is irrelevant to one's own, and the main point of pursuing such study at all is lost.

3. The relevance of other countries' experiences to one's own follows logically from this

It is crucial to realise that education does not work in a vacuum, but is profoundly influenced by the geographical, demographic, historical, economic, cultural and political aspects of the society which it serves. At the same time, lest the impression be conveyed that the relationship between education and society – any society – purely reflects the context, the influence of the system *on* its context also has to be examined. It has to be understood that no educational system operates in isolation, but has a complex and dynamic relationship with its natural and social environment.

4. The relevance of other countries' experiences to one's own follows logically from this

Otherwise it may be felt that, fascinating though it may be for the specialist, comparative study has little to offer anyone else. Not that one would argue for the direct *application* of other systems' practices to one's own country; this may be feasible sometimes, but involves serious dangers. The experience of other systems can contribute to an understanding of one's own; indeed, it can be argued that this is the most valuable contribution of comparative education to the non-specialist.

Strategies in comparative education

If, then, these are acceptable as learning objectives, we can go on to consider various approaches as *strategies of* study. One popular method is the 'themes' approach, which starts by taking particular topics such as the curriculum, primary schools, vocational training, educational planning and so forth, and comparing them across a number of selected systems, with the aim of formulating valid generalisations about the behaviour of educational systems in particular circumstances. An important alternative, the 'systems' approach, examines complete educational systems as functioning units in their particular societies. These are not really disagreements about where the study should be going, but about the most effective starting point.

The *themes approach* has the advantage of coming to grips with the real stuff of comparative education – comparison and analysis – right from the start. But it presents great difficulties for those without much knowledge of other educational systems, for there are many temptations to make comparisons out of context and thus fall into some serious errors. The possibility of such error is large, but a few examples will serve.

1. Education does not necessarily mean the same thing in all societies

It may have quite different aims, operate under different conditions and be assessed by different criteria. The differences are not absolute, or comparative study would lose much of its point. But there is much to be said for emphasising the differences, as these are likely to be overlooked or misunderstood if we go directly into cross-cultural comparison. For example: politicians and even senior managers in education are fond of reinforcing their arguments with assorted pieces of evidence from the experience of other countries. Many advocates of comprehensive schooling in the UK seek comfort in vague statements about European reforms and higher financial investment in schools; their opponents were equally fond of dire warnings of what they thought had been happening in the Soviet Union or, perversely, what continues to happen in the United States. Such arguments often ignore the constant American debates on school choice, charter schools, private religious schools and the merits or otherwise of restructuring one or other of the state systems (Good and Braden 2000; Payne and Knowles 2009). That much of this 'evidence' may be wrong is not really the point; even when the information was accurate, it could easily be used with little appreciation of the differences between the other systems and one's own (Grant 1968).

Advocates of greater emphasis on lifelong learning in the UK make use of the Scandinavian countries, the United States or France as models or as inspiration; supporters of bilingualism in Scottish, Welsh, Irish or English schools point to Canada, Catalonia, Israel, Finland and the Faeroes (Haugen *et al.* 1980; Baker 2001). Again, this is not to say that the comparisons are invalid, let alone the causes. The situation in the Faeroes or Catalonia, where there has been a strong numerical base for the language and vigorous institutional support, has sustained a continuing interest for younger genera-tions in these languages despite pressures from the mass media and global social net-works. This situation does not easily transfer to the circumstances of the Gaels of the Western Isles or the Punjabi-speakers of Glasgow, Birmingham or London, where the languages are penetrated to some degree by the use of English. The purpose, expecta-tions and effectiveness of using the language may not be only through education: 'The ownership of two languages has increasingly become seen as an asset as the "commu-nication world" gets smaller. As swift communication has become possible in recent decades ... so the importance of bilingualism has been highlighted' (Baker 2001: 417). This applies to some extent to all countries that now have to deal with the implications of the internet and its role in promoting or, in the view of some, demoting the use of languages (Naughton 1999). In this post-colonial age the sense of *loss* of language is widespread, extending from nationalist sensitivities in the older colonies of England – Scotland, Wales, Ireland – to ethnic minority migrants such as Sikhs, Kurds and Ber-bers being as it is a choice they have to make when facing the daily imperative of mastering the host language, English, French or Arabic (Davies 2003; Busch 2011).

The differences between systems can be quite profound. The very word 'education' can have different connotations in different societies. Indeed, some languages are unable to make the distinctions which others find essential. In English, for example, the single word 'education', although constantly doing battle with 'training', 'peda-gogy' or 'lifelong education', normally has to fulfil all the functions of *Bildung*, *Ausbil-dung* and *Erziehung* in German, *éducation*, *instruction* and *enseignement* in French, while Russian has a whole battery of words. But even when the same word is used, the asso-ciations that go with it may be different. A good example of this may be seen in com-parisons between the United States and the United Kingdom; these were particularly common during discussions in the 1960s on the comprehensive reorganisation of schools in the UK, and especially in England, where the issue can still arouse more controversy than in Scotland or Wales. The Scottish Parliament was opened in June 1999 followed by the Welsh Assembly in 2006; during the ten years to 2008 the North-ern Ireland Assembly was often in abeyance but completed a full third term in 2011 and is now into its fourth. This process of political devolution has led to the British educational systems growing more distinct in their evolution of educational legislation and practice.

It is more difficult to generalise about school standards (or anything else) in the United States than in England. American education is more decentralised, and its financing is much more dependent on the resources of the particular areas in which the schools are located. Standards in American schools therefore vary greatly from state to state, and within each state, and *any* generalisation thus has to be hedged about with qualifications.

But just suppose, for the sake of argument, that even broadly equivalent groups – those following academic courses to proceed to higher education – do show a marked disparity in standards (as many American educationists would readily concede). What exactly are we comparing? Debates on the range of scholastic attainment as measured by examinations are common on both sides of the Atlantic, though few American teachers, parents or students would accept this as the only criterion of what the school is trying to do. American schools devote a great deal of time to socialisation, to the preparation of the student for life in American society, stressing the development of social and communication skills. It may be that the outward manifestations of this – the patriotic rituals, the varied social events, the morale-boosting sessions for the school football team and so on – would strike English teachers as faintly comical. But the same could be said of a German *Gymnasium* teacher's impression of the games and character-building by which some remaining grammar schools still set such store. The German final school certificate, the *Abitur* or *Reifeprüfung* (test of maturity), the Danish *Studenterexamen* and *Højere Forberedelsereksamen* and many of the European final school certificates taken mostly between 18–20 years of age are both broader and academically ahead of the English A-level. Interest in a broader and deeper version of the A-level has actually been helped by comparisons with the American Students Aptitude Tests (SAT) and the International Baccalaureate, which is now offered in an increasing number of schools and further education (FE) colleges across Britain, Europe and America.

These are examples of how even the meaning of 'education' can be affected by different sets of priorities. But many other factors determine what education is, what it can do and how its aims are defined; these have to be considered if any useful comparisons are to be made. In countries like America, France, Spain or Britain, for example, it is at least *possible* to consider leaving the choice of textbooks to the schools and the open market; the *actual* decision can be taken on a variety of grounds. But in the Baltic States, the Faeroes or Iceland, decisions are severely constrained by the small numbers speaking the national languages, whatever policy the authorities might prefer.

Again, the existence of substantial linguistic minorities in Russia, India, Belgium, Spain and a host of other countries raises problems that now have to be considered by the relatively homogeneous countries like England or Denmark, where the settlement of immigrants and their descendants had confirmed their development into multicultural societies too. As for matters like distance and difficulties in communication, these are not *major* factors in Denmark, Ireland, the Netherlands or most of the UK, but they are in a huge country like Russia and they were in the United States when the pattern of educational organisation was taking shape, and are in India and China. The increased power of international agencies over education policy and practice worldwide has increased cross-cultural transfers, shown by the impact on the post-Soviet Union countries in Europe or Asia where curricula, policies and the very purpose of education have been through considerable transformation (Crossley and Watson 2003).

Climate, demographic patterns and economic circumstances raise needs or impose severe constraints that do not occur in the developed world. UNESCO highlights those situations in developing countries where there are insufficient means to guarantee even universal primary education and where population growth or war can nullify every hard-won advance. These background conditions are so important for the functioning of education – and even for defining it – that they must be taken into account if we are to make any sense of the systems themselves.

2. The parts of any educational system are interdependent, and have to be examined in relation to the whole

Many attempts to make international comparisons across several countries fall into the trap of assuming that things with the same name must have the same function. They may, but there can also be substantial differences. 'Primary school', for example, means in England and Wales a school for children between the ages of 5 and 11 (although it is now common for there to be an optional Reception Class which takes children aged 4); but in Scotland it is from 5 to 12, and in the Republic of Ireland usually from 4 to 12. This is within an area, the British Isles, with close past or present political links; elsewhere, the difference can be greater. What is usually translated as 'primary school' or 'école primaire' or 'Grundschule' can cover the ages of 7–16 in Denmark and in Sweden. Rapid change in developed countries in preschool education has, in practice, led to most children having some form of schooling experience from three years of age and often earlier. Various systems organise their structures differently, preferring in some cases to make the main division of primary/secondary at mid-adolescence, the end of compulsory schooling, and in others at the point of transition from undifferentiated to subject-specialised teaching.

Similarly, the term 'secondary school' may mean the entire stage from pre-adolescence onwards (as in the systems of the British Isles or the United States), or it may be only the stage entered *after* compulsory school, as in Scandinavia. But this does not apply everywhere; in some countries, only *certain* post-compulsory schools – generally those leading to higher education – are designated as 'secondary', thus distinguishing them from vocational or trade schools (Bell and Grant 1977).

Many common schools in Central and Eastern Europe provide the whole course from 6 to 17; and when this happens, the term 'secondary' is applied to the *entire* school, *including its primary section.* There were, and still remain in some of these countries, 'secondary specialised schools' which can be entered after completion of the *general* secondary school. Further, changes may take place but old titles may remain in use. Even on official notices, they use the formal title, with the informal and old-fashioned title, which is what everyone says and had a different structure, in brackets, as in Germany where unification of East and West has fundamentally affected the direction of reforms after 1990 (Wilde 2000). It is a dangerous business, especially when translation is involved, to pull institutions with similar-sounding titles out of context for separate examination.

Opportunities for misunderstanding do not end there. Schools and students in England, Wales and Scotland are often compared unfavourably with those elsewhere. School effectiveness and outcomes have been used, often in official publications, to suggest a crisis of falling standards, especially in English schools, with a perceived inability to stand up to global competition. Where evidence of widening participation and increasing pass rates of school-leaving examination is discussed this is countered by suggestions of lowering standards. The Third International Mathematics and Science Study (TIMMS) has done an extensive comparison of pupil achievements in maths and science, while the Programme for International Student Assessment (PISA) is an ongoing triennial worldwide evaluation in 62 OECD member countries of 15-year-old school pupils' scholastic performance, which also includes a reading evaluation. Both of these international studies are regarded as providing convincing evidence for the *relative* failures of schools in England, Wales, Scotland, Germany, the United States and the generally good performances of some Asian countries, Scandinavia and Finland, as evaluated across the curriculum areas of mathematics, science and reading. However, various reasons, such as different response rates and the over-emphasis on accountability and performance measures, make these comparisons seem somewhat flawed. A common view of education during the twentieth century, and up to the present time, has focused on its under-achievement, inequality and a perceived fall in standards, perhaps because more is expected from education by each succeeding generation. (Peyreyra *et al.* 2011; OECD 2010)

In England (as in most European countries) the end of secondary schooling is still quite a reasonable point at which to consider what standards have been achieved. Enough of the age group stay on to make the judgement worthwhile, but with widening access to higher education there is increasing differentiation of standards for entrance. But this is even more so in the United States, where something like four-fifths of the age cohort proceeds to tertiary education. Some take only short-cycle courses, some of these transfer to full higher courses, others enter longer ones from the start but drop out, and some of these drop back in again, making it difficult to keep track of any particular age group, but a reasonable estimate would be that about half eventually complete first degrees.

Admittedly, the standard of American degrees varies considerably, and with the advent of league tables for UK universities disparity of degree standards are increasingly questioned. Some American universities and colleges (public and private) can easily stand comparison academically with any higher educational institutions in the world, while others award degrees too mediocre to be recognised in other countries (or in the United States itself); and in between can be found almost every imaginable variety, from the admirable to the abysmal. But, with very few exceptions, even the worst could be reckoned to come up at least to English A-level standard and, of course, most go well beyond that. It follows, therefore, that in the United States a higher proportion of the population reaches at least A-level standard than was ever admitted to grammar schools in England in the heyday of selective schooling. Even by the narrowest scholastic criteria more get there in the end; and unless we postulate some mystic law whereby certain standards must be attained by a fixed age, American education appears to perform more creditably than its detractors (on both sides of the Atlantic) would allow. To attempt an adequate assessment of a system, we have to look at all of it, not just a part. A similar point could be made about the age of starting primary school and the relevance of preschool provision.

Nor need such considerations be confined to the formal school system, for other organisations can attend to 'curricular enrichment', as the Pioneers did in the former Soviet Union. That is all gone now, but there are some parallels in China and Cuba, and of course the *efterskoler* and *folkehøjskoler* in Denmark and the various Church organisations in some countries, particularly in Latin America, fulfil some needs for 'public enlightenment', especially for young adults. Many countries have youth and adult organisations in the cultural, linguistic, nature and athletic areas. There are real limitations nowadays on most of these as they often lack adequate support and finance; they also tend to be fragmented so that they touch few of the young people or children they are aimed at. But they are there, and sometimes function as a vital adjunct to the normal experience of formal schooling (Webber and Liikanen 2001).

There other examples, but these should make the general point – *educational systems have to be examined as wholes, and in their contexts*, before cross-cultural studies can be expected to yield much benefit. Objective data on particular institutions can seem quite precise; but unless they are seen in relation to other institutions in the same system, and unless that system is examined in the light of the factors that make it what it is, we are in danger of misunderstanding how it works. Further, since the most common use of evidence out of context is to back up educational arguments at home, there is the additional danger that such misunderstandings may simply reinforce misunderstanding of one's own system. This is not what comparative education is for.

What, then, is it for? What, particularly after all these warnings about the importance of context, is the relevance of education in other countries to our own problems? And what is its usefulness for teachers?

Part of the answer has to do with *informing educational policy*. Individual teachers rarely feel they have much of a role to play here, but they often have more influence on the success or failure of policies than they may be aware of. In some countries they have considerable discretion in the choice of subject matter, method and even organisation, and therefore have an obligation to make thoughtful and informed choices rather than fall back on precedent or hunch. They are also involved in the larger issues in their capacity as citizens. Unless teachers are to be reduced to functionaries, the uncritical executors (however efficient) of decisions taken by someone else, wider understanding of the options available in the educational process is not only desirable but, at a time of constant educational change, necessary.

This could be said for educational theory in general, or any of its contributory disciplines. What benefits, then, can be expected for the thoughtful teacher from this particular kind of educational study?

Borrowing ideas

The possibility of borrowing ideas is usually the first that comes to mind and is often held to be the main purpose of comparative education. Governments are all too often limited in their view of its possibilities to seeing it (if at all) as a method of identifying practices that could be transplanted to their own country. But great care is needed here. Quite apart from the risk that the other countries' practices may be misinterpreted anyway, they may be too closely bound up with their specific contexts to be applicable anywhere else.

Certainly, the exportation of practices has often had unfortunate effects. After the Second World War, for example, the new communist governments in Eastern Europe drew heavily on Soviet models. This was hardly surprising, in view of the political hegemony of the USSR; the newly established regimes were not only inclined to display political loyalty, but were also trying to reform their traditional systems along Marxist–Leninist lines, and at that time the USSR was the only country with experience of this.

Unfortunately – but, given the political atmosphere of the time, unsurprisingly – the remodelling on Soviet lines was quite uncritical. History was taught from a Russo-centric viewpoint, textbooks were modelled on their Soviet counterparts (and sometimes were straight translations), even degrees were often re-named to correspond to Soviet practice, and of course policy was modelled on that of the USSR, sometimes even to the wording, whether appropriate to local conditions or not (Grant 1982, 2000).

The former British and French colonial empires are clearer illustrations of the effects of uncritical borrowing. Most ex-colonial countries still retain their inheritance of British- or French-style school systems, with examinations linked to assumptions about the relationship between paper qualifications and job expectations that are wildly out of keeping with these countries' needs and conditions. The damage caused is not so much by the persistence of inappropriately Europeanised curricula, which are changing anyway; it is rather caused by the expectation that going to school will provide certificates leading to white-collar jobs in the city, when the vast majority are certain to be disappointed at some stage. Large numbers of young Africans thus receive just enough schooling to make village life unacceptable, but not enough to equip them for anything else – an explosive situation due in part to an educational system devised in London or Paris that makes little allowance for conditions in Lagos or Bamako, let alone a tribal village (MacIntosh 1971).

We continue to see the adoption of European and American models over much of the developing world. These systems differ greatly, of course, but they have all been devised to meet the needs of relatively affluent and highly industrialised societies, quite different from the low-income agrarian countries to which they have been exported. We have seen something of this in post-colonial Africa, but it is not just from former colonial powers that inappropriate models are received, but from the industrial world in general. It has become increasingly obvious that these models do not serve the needs of the 'Third World' countries, even if they could afford them; but as long as they offer such great advantages to those lucky enough to go through the whole process successfully, they make it difficult to devise other and more suitable models.

This is not to say that importation can never be valuable. For all the uncritical borrowing from the USSR in Eastern Europe, there were *some* valuable innovations, such as the development of systems of adult education and the breaking down of some of the more rigid class barriers between different kinds of schools. On a more limited scale, there is the spread of folk high schools across the Scandinavian countries, and even some influence on adult education in Germany and Great Britain (Korsgaard 2000).

Again, for all the unfortunate effects of over-hasty and uncritical adoption of American progressive methods, their positive contribution has to be recognised as well. 'Progressivism' may have run its course by now, but it has left its mark on practice.

Whenever a primary teacher teaches capacity by getting children to pour water into cans rather than recite tables, she/he is using what at first were American 'progressive' methods. That this is rarely apparent is an indication of how far these methods have been naturalised. The adoption by the Open University and the modern universities in the UK of a credit system owes much to American practice,[1] and has created a degree of flexibility hitherto lacking in British higher education. But this has not been a straight copy, but an adaptation of an American procedure to the rather different needs of part-time students in the UK, which still managed to avoid some of the problems in the US system. It could be added that the Open University in its turn has had a considerable impact on higher education in many other countries, especially the United States.

There are many other examples of effective borrowing, with one thing in common: they were taken from systems sufficiently like the importing ones to fit in, or were adapted to do so. This, possibly, is one of the most valuable contributions of comparative studies: not only can they set forth a range of alternative ideas and practices but, intelligently applied, they can help distinguish what can reasonably be imported from what can not; and by examining educational practices in context can help indicate the kind of adaptation needed to fit them into another system.

Educational policy and analysis

Comparative education can render a particularly valuable service by providing a background of contrasts against which to examine our own problems. If our horizons are bounded by our own system, many of its practices may seem natural or inevitable; yet they may have arisen in circumstances that no longer obtain, and may now be unnecessary, arbitrary or even harmful. It is not impossible to examine one's own system critically from the inside, but it is more difficult without a comparative perspective. The very existence of other assumptions and practices can provide a necessary challenge to some of our own. It does not automatically follow that we *have* to change; even if we are alone in this practice or that, it may still fit our own circumstances. But the existence of alternatives obliges us to justify rather than assume, so that if we do adhere to something, there is a chance of knowing why we do it.

An example can be seen in the horizontal and vertical divisions within the school system. In most of the UK it is taken for granted that the division between primary and secondary school at 11 or 12 reflects a qualitative and necessary change in pedagogical styles, and even that it has some natural sanction. Sensible and convenient it *may* be, but it is not inevitable. The break at this point is also found in the United States, Italy, France and some German states; but in Denmark, Sweden, Spain and some countries of Eastern Europe (and was in all of them before the Soviet system collapsed) the main division, and the main point of differentiation, is at 15 or 16.

The same variation applies to *vertical* division into parallel schools for the same age group, as was common throughout Great Britain before comprehensive reorganisation. Segregation of this kind was regarded as quite unacceptable in the former USSR but as absolutely essential in most German states, where nearly two-thirds of young people receive their post-secondary education in vocational institutions covering over 350 state-regulated and recognised occupations (Idriss 2002). In the United States the common school is taken for granted, but so is *internal* division (known as 'tracking'). In every case, the matter is open to argument; and here the existence of alternatives can be a useful corrective to the widespread habit of taking one's own practice as the norm.

Comparative studies can also clarify our ideas of what is possible, a useful step before deciding whether something is *desirable*. International practice is frequently evoked over some of the more emotive issues, like school uniforms or sexual differentiation, but they are often not the best examples, as they are closely bound up with a broader complex of social expectations and pressures. It would be rash, for instance, to attribute too much of the disorder in many American schools to the schools themselves; there are too many other forces in operation. But curriculum policies, for example, can profitably be looked at with an eye to what is being done elsewhere, as in the debate in the UK on specialisation versus generalisation, or the relation between school and work.

To take one example, little is expected in the English-speaking countries of average or below-average pupils in the learning of foreign languages. In the British systems, languages were formerly largely confined to the 'academic' schools or streams, and although there are an increasing number of language secondary schools, many teachers are still convinced that trying to teach languages to any but the top third of the ability range is a waste of time. Whether it is desirable that they should do so is, of course, another argument; but international evidence does not support the idea that the average child has some inherent linguistic incapacity. Bilingual and multilingual communities are common throughout the world; and even school-based learning can be extremely effective. In Scandinavia, for instance, all children learn at least one foreign language (usually English), and many learn at least one more besides; the levels of competence vary, but are generally high. Unless we believe in some kind of inborn incapacity among the Americans and British, we have to reject the idea that 'languages for all' is *impossible*. Discussions of the *desirability* of such a policy has a chance of being considered on its own merits, then, without unnecessary presuppositions.

But an international perspective can also provoke re-examination of some of our educational concepts (or slogans) like 'standards', 'discipline', 'indoctrination', 'excellence', 'leadership', 'freedom of choice', 'general culture' and so on. We are not always clear, however, just what we mean by them; and one incentive to clarify our definitions is seeing how different they are elsewhere. For example, 'democratic education' would mean maximum curricular choice and grass-roots control to most Americans, but would suggest a centrally determined uniform curriculum to the French, on the grounds that the child must be free of the chances of local circumstance. 'Leadership' has positive connotations in England, but in Scandinavia is still regarded with suspicion outside the business schools.

Teachers and academics in most countries have a fairly clear notion about what is meant by, say, 'university standard', but usually have difficulty in defining this. 'Indoctrination', in the sense of a deliberate inculcation of values, may be more obvious to someone looking at a system from outside than to someone actually in it; 'indoctrination' may turn out to be something that *other* people do, but which we prefer to call something else – 'moral education', perhaps, or 'citizenship'. Unless we are prepared simply to dismiss other interpretations as 'wrong' just because they are different, their very existence requires us to attempt a definition of *our* terms. We may, once again, decide that they are valid and useful, but at least we should have a better idea of what we are talking about.

Conclusion

Comparative education thus has the capacity to do in space what educational history does in time; it can provide the opportunity to understand better the workings of the educational process by giving us a wider view than the here and now. At a time when everyone in contemporary educational systems is faced with unprecedented challenges, as crises of resource and direction loom ever larger, and as the need to educate for future uncertainty becomes more urgent, the importance of clear and radical thinking could hardly be more obvious. This is not to say that *everything* is on the agenda for change; tribal customs may after all have their place, but it does not help to confuse them with laws of nature.

Comparative education cannot, of course, pretend to offer any uniquely valid set of answers, but can claim to be one useful tool for the better understanding of the educational process in general and one's own system in particular. While it uses big ideas over the global scale, it is rooted in precise observation of the particular. It will continue to have a role in informing government policy just as governments will continue to have a vital interest in their educational systems. Some new tasks are providing practical and purposeful goals for advising governmental educational reforms, investigating the role of public and private agencies in education and analysing changing structures and forces such as private education, partnerships, e-learning and the internet (Corner 2000).

Note

1. A practice which is now widespread across the higher education sector in the UK at both undergraduate and postgraduate levels.

References

Baker, C. (2001) *Foundations of Bilingual Education and Bilingualism*. 3rd edition. Clevedon: Multilingual Matters.

Bell, R.E. and Grant, N. (1977) *Patterns of Education in the British Isles*. London: Allen and Unwin.

Busch, B. (2011) 'Trends and innovation practices in multilingual education in Europe: an overview'. *International Review of Education* 57: 541–549.

Corner, T. (2000) 'Education and the third wave', in Matheson, C. and Matheson, D. (eds), *Educational Issues in the Learning Age*. London: Continuum.

Crossley, M. (ed.) (2001) 'Comparative education for the 21st century: an international response'. *Comparative Education* 37 (4).

Crossley, M. and Watson, K. (2003) *Comparative and International Research in Education: Globalisation, Context and Difference.* London: RoutledgeFalmer.

Davies, A. (2003) *The Native Speaker: Myth and Reality.* Clevedon: Multilingual Matters.

Good, T. and Braden, J. (2000) *The Great School Debate.* London: LEA Publishers.

Grant, N. (1968) 'Comparative education and the comprehensive schools', *Scottish Educational Studies* 1 (2): 16–23.

Grant, N. (1982) 'Work experience in Soviet and East European schools', in Eggleston, J. (ed.), *Work Experience in Secondary Schools.* London: Routledge and Kegan Paul.

Grant, N. (2000) 'Tasks for comparative education in the new millennium', *Comparative Education* 36 (3): 309–317.

Haugen, E., McClure, V. and Thomson, D.S. (eds) (1980) *Minority Languages Today.* Edinburgh: Edinburgh University Press.

Holmes, B. (1981) *Comparative Education: Some Considerations of Method.* London: Allen and Unwin.

Idriss, C. (2002) 'Challenge and change in the German vocational system since 1990', *Oxford Review of Education* 28 (4): 473–490.

King, E. (1979) *Other schools and Ours.* 3rd edition. New York: Holt Rinehart and Winston.

Korsgaard, O. (2000) 'Learning and the changing concept of enlightenment: Danish adult education over five centuries', *International Review of Education* 46 (3/4): 305–325.

Leibman, M. and Paulston, R. (1994) 'Social cartography: a new method for comparative studies'. *Compare* 24 (3): 233–245.

MacIntosh, J. (1971) 'Politics and citizenship', in Lowe, J., Grant, N. and Williams, T.D. (eds), *Education and Nation-Building in the Third World.* Edinburgh: Scottish Academic Press.

Naughton, J. (1999) *A Brief History of the Future: The Origins of the Internet.* London: Weidenfeld and Nicolson.

OECD (2010) *PISA 2009 Results: Executive Summary.* Paris: OECD.

Payne, C. and Knowles, T. (2009) 'Promise and peril: charter schools, urban school reform, and the Obama Administration'. *Harvard Educational Review* 79 (2): 227–239.

Pereyra, M., Kotthoff, H. and Cowen, R. (eds) (2011) *PISA Under Examination: Changing Knowledge, Changing Tests and Changing Schools.* Rotterdam: Comparative Education Society in Europe/Sense Publications.

Stenhouse, L. (1967) *Education and Culture.* London: Nelson Thornes.

Thomas, G. (2012) 'Changing the landscape of inquiry for a new science of education'. *Harvard Educational Review* 82 (1): 26–51.

Watson, K. (ed.) (2001) *Doing Comparative Education Research: Issues and Problems.* London: Symposium Books.

Webber, S. and Liikanen, I. (eds) (2001) *Education and Civic Culture in the Post-Communist Countries.* London: Palgrave.

Wilde, S. (2002) 'Secondary education in Germany 1990–2000: one decade of non-reform in unified German education?' *Oxford Review of Education* 28 (1): 39–51.

17

Education and development

The contribution of comparative education

Dominique Groux

The object of education is not perfection in the accomplishments of the school, but fitness for life; not the acquirement of habits of blind obedience and of prescribed diligence, but a preparation for interdependent action

Johannes Pestalozzi (1830)

Learning may be defined as a laying down of concentric and intertwining ideas and identities. The child, who is already the result of the mixing of their parents' genes, develops only by admixtures. All teaching and learning sees the child reconceived and reborn: born left-handed one learns to use the right, remains left-handed or is reborn right-handed. One is born to a local identity but learns a national one. If one travels, one assumes more identities, more cultures. One takes on the culture and language of his/her significant other. The circles of identity and culture subdivide and mix and become like a patchwork of intertwining and overlapping segments. (Serres 1991: 86–87)

All learning, whether in school or otherwise, transforms the individual and adds to their patchwork of culture and identity. In discussing how an individual moves across cultures, Serres (1991) uses the term *renaissance* or *rebirth* to describe how they are transformed by being subject to multiple cultural influences and by learning how to live with otherness and diversity.

This means that through their contact with education, every person, from their most tender years, progressively forges a multi-stranded identity; in effect a web of identities, by which she/he becomes pluricultural and acquires pluricultural skills. One's identity becomes a patchwork with multiple affiliations perfectly integrated and inseparable. These constitute the person's identity. A subsequent phase in education would certainly consist in recognising in oneself the diverse components of one's identity and to recognise how human nature is founded on diversity. In order to be in a position to help a pupil carry out this analysis, the teacher needs to have done it for him/herself. It is only after having understood and accepted one's own internal diversity that one can really accept the diversity of the other; the otherness of the other, so to speak.

School: a key player in development

It is a well-worn saw to say that school is an essential player in development. It is in school that the early learning takes place and it is in school that children learn to reflect and to begin to do so critically. It is in school that children develop intellectual curiosity and the thirst for learning – key elements which if acquired will permit the individual to engage in lifelong learning

It is also at school where the child begins to develop the four basic skills described by Jacques Delors *et al.* (1996). These are 'learning to know, learning to do, learning to be, learning to live together' (p. 37). It is school which lays the bases for the individual's future development, for what might be termed their lifelong education. It is in this sense that I will be using the concept of *development* in the course of this chapter. It is the development of the individual and I shall be looking at how comparative education can help in this lifelong development.

Access to complete and universal knowledge: myth or reality?

Since the dawn of time, people have dreamed of acquiring complete and universal knowledge. This even found its way into one of the earliest European satirical novels, Rabelais' sixteenth-century series *The Life of Gargantua and Pantagruel*[1] in which the father (the giant Gargantua) writes to his son (the giant Pantagruel) to set him the goal that he must learn all that there is to know, a task which seemed quite possible, if somewhat challenging, in the sixteenth century:

> I expect and I demand that you will memorise all history…. Of the liberal arts of geometry, arithmetic and music, I gave you a taste of them when you were still quite little, maybe about five or six. As for the rest, and as for astronomy, make sure you know the key works. As for civil law, I want you to know by heart all the fine texts and to discuss them with me philosophically.
>
> And as for natural history, I want you to give your curiosity full vent so that there is not a sea or river or fountain where you don't know all the fish; make sure you know all the birds of the air, all the trees, bushes and shrubs of the forest, all the herbs of the earth, all the metals hidden in the deepest abyss, all the jewels of the Orient and the Middle East.
>
> Make sure you revisit carefully the books of the Greek, Arab and Latin doctors, without ignoring the Talmudists and Cabbalists, and by careful study you will acquire a perfect knowledge of the other world which is man….

And all this while following a moral education since, as Rabelais tells us, 'knowledge without conscience is but the ruin of the soul' (Pantagruel, ch. 8).

This somewhat ambitious programme for the acquisition of knowledge sits very far from the objectives given nowadays to schools for the very good reason that we can no longer envisage mastering the totality of knowledge.[2]

Universal knowledge may be beyond any of us, but nonetheless, teachers have as their central mission to help children develop from the outset intellectual curiosity and a thirst for knowledge.

Developing intellectual curiosity and the thirst for learning

We need to lead the learner to discover the joy of culture which ought to be within the grasp of everyone and not just those who inherit the cultural capital from their families which allows them make culture their own and hence to live comfortably with it.

Let us now consider the question of what constitutes worthwhile knowledge.

School and knowledge

What counts as worthwhile knowledge? Is it fixed or does this change with the times? This is a legitimate question to pose in this chapter as we try to establish the correlation, if any, between school and development. Numerous polemics accuse school teaching in France today of seriously lowering the demands made on pupils and of neglecting the transmission of the canon of knowledge; this, they say, is most true of children from the working class. They seem to predict the school of tomorrow as one devoid of knowledge. A major challenge to this perspective came in a study conducted in 1983, which studied 300 educational priority zones (EPZs) in France, two years after these came into existence. Eighty per cent of respondents reported that they prioritised classical methods of transmitting knowledge, rather than more facilitative approaches.

This study is clearly somewhat dated and it would be hard to believe that the demands put on children are the same in the EPZ as in the primary and secondary schools frequented by the middle classes. School may continue to be recognisable as school and to act to ensure the transmission of knowledge, but it nonetheless varies according to the public concerned.

This said, disquiet over teachers deemed too lax in the demands they make on their pupils is nothing new. In 1899, for example, there was much debate over the unequal standing of different subjects. Some commentators leaned towards the sciences and other towards classical languages – Latin and Greek – and both argued that their stance was the hallmark of a modern education. In the 1930s the argument was over the opening of the curriculum to the modern world, with its rapid scientific and technical developments and whether as a result there should be more emphasis on science and technology and consequently less on classics, humanities, aesthetics and general culture.

At this point, let us leave the question of worthwhile knowledge but not without mentioning the pleasure, and indeed happiness, to be had in acquiring such knowledge – but in order to do so one needs to have well-developed reading skills and this serves to underline the central importance in the primary school of the acquisition of sound reading skills.

The pleasure of reading

It is tautological that reading allows one to access knowledge. It is generally at school that one learns to read and it is at school that one acquires – or not – the taste for reading. This means that the child who is happy to read has more chance of accessing knowledge and of developing their general culture than has the child who reads reluctantly. While there are certainly other ways of accessing knowledge, be this by radio, TV, or internet, or by travelling and other kinds of cultural exchanges, reading is one of the means of acquiring knowledge which allows a systematic, rigorous, measured and profound entry into the world of knowledge.

Books discovered in childhood help forge one's identity and often leave a lasting impression. Porcher (1994) writes

> I am always amazed that, when biographers are recreating a person's intellectual (and also emotional) journey, they don't pay more attention to the first books their subject read, the ones from their childhood, as these constitute the very ground in which their individual cultural capital takes root and grows.
>
> (p. 9)

And when one has been able to develop with books a passionate relationship, they accompany use throughout our lives:

> A taste for reading lands on you and, like the hand of God, pins you to the wall. There is no escape, short of losing your soul.... The book or the reader, none can say which one holds the other. Suffice to say that they are inseparable to the end.
>
> (Porcher 1994: 13)

From this it follows that the teacher of the first years in primary school needs always to take the greatest care to allow the child to enter the world of the book with curiosity, passion and enthusiasm. The book needs to become for the child the means of discovering the joy of learning.

School holds out to the child knowledge which is simple and knowledge which is complex. And in the best of circumstances that, thanks to the intellectual curiosity which has been regularly stoked in the class, thanks to the pleasure being had from reading, thanks to the feeling of well-being the child experiences in the class, they move with pleasure into diverse realms of knowledge.

Ensuring the child is happy at school

In what kind of school can one be happy? Happiness is, after all, such an indispensible part of life that one easily forgets to speak of it. It is necessary in life but also, and especially, in school. Until one reaches the end of compulsory schooling (at age 16 in most industrialised countries), one spends around 11,700 hours at school. It would clearly be better to spend these 11,700 hours in happiness and even joy than in rejection, refusal or failure.

In what kind of school can one be happy to learn? In paraphrasing Verlaine, we could write: 'I often have a strange and haunting dream of a school such as I have never known and which I love and which loves me.' Is the idea of happiness at school an illusion or a dream? Is it simply utopian? Why couldn't we be happy to learn in a school built for us, adapted to our needs and careful to sustain our motivation in our incessant quest for knowledge?

Finally, in what kind of school can one be happy in going towards others? Humans are social animals and cannot be happy alone. In the microcosm which is the school, as in life itself, we need to bear in mind the essential otherness, the indispensable opening towards the Other which one acquires through education. Happiness attains depth and intensity when one takes account of the other, whether this be the classmate or those outside the school. The challenge is therefore to find happiness in one's contact with others, to have the school open to the world and to share with the Other not just in terms of knowledge but also globally, to get in touch with their being and to share their humanity.

After I began to think about the relationship between school and development, I came up with a trinity: for the child to develop intellectually and humanely, she/he needs to be happy in class, happy with the teachers and happy with his/her class-mates. This state of mind has every chance of leading the child to knowledge and understanding. Undoubtedly subjective, this trinity is the product of my experience but perhaps a consensus can be reached around the importance for the child of three notions: happiness, knowledge and respect for others – happiness through knowledge and by encountering other people.

The mission of school could be to achieve this triple objective and hence to put in place the means of achieving it. However, before turning to consider possible means for achieving this goal, let us examine the question of consensus around the triple proposal of happiness, knowledge and respect for others.

We can start by turning to Epictetus,[3] the Stoic thinker of the first century CE, who tells us that the knowledge which it is essential that the school transmit is detachment (Epictetus). This is not an indifference but rather an acceptance that there are things we can change and things we cannot. By disengaging emotionality then we can come to tell these apart.

Each of us needs to first of all distinguish between those things that depend on us and those things that do not.

> Wretch, are you not content with what you see daily? Have you anything better or greater to see than the sun, the moon, the stars, the whole earth, the sea?... When, then, you are going to leave the sun itself and the moon, what will you do? Will you sit and weep like children? Well, what have you been doing in the school? What did you hear, what did you learn?
>
> (Epictetus, *Discourses*, book 2, ch. 16)

The main purpose of the school would therefore be to give the child the means to con-struct his/her own happiness. But this is an exercise that demands training, here and now: one needs to cultivate happiness on a daily basis. And what does a child have on a daily basis? School. The child needs to feel well in school, knowing that it is going to help him/her to develop into an adult and that it is there that she/he will learn happiness.

When Georges Snyders entitled his 1991 book *Happy Children … Reflexions on Joy in School*, he advocated 'reconciling school and joy' (Snyders 1991: 29) and made the following remark:

> Young people are showing an increasing impatience with a school that offers them so little joy and finally they are challenging it more and more. At stake is the role that school plays and perhaps even its very existence. We need to finally admit that young people only find joy outside of school and that school should be reduced to the minimum of basic skills.
>
> (Snyders 1991: 29)

I am increasingly astounded by the way in which children suffer at school. Assessment is everywhere in our classrooms. It manifests itself in the regular tests that mark out the rhythm of the week, the month, the year. Children work towards tests. They strive to pass, to have good grades. When they fail, they are heartbroken or disillusioned. Most of the time they seem to have forgotten why they are at school: to learn how to know the world, to know themselves, to know others, to reflect on what they expect from life, to construct a value system to orient their life and to reflect on the meaning of life.

Meanwhile teachers don't question the purpose of the assessments they impose on their pupils and the perverse effects these are having on them. They fail to see that assessment emphasises failure and not success. They don't see that if they were relying on the pupil's successes, they would be practising that famous pedagogy of success, often invoked but rarely put in place. Pedagogy of success gives confidence to the pupil, gives him/her courage, built on true success, to go further and further. Instead of this, teachers practise an assessment based on sanctions which lock the pupil into a cycle of failure, destroys his/her self-confidence and prevents the realisation of his/her potential. The PISA inquiries (see Chapters 13, 16) have this clearly as regards French pupils: they are continuously afraid, if not anxious. I have personally seen primary school children going to school with fear in their bellies and all because they are going to be examined in a test. So many traumatisms could have been avoided if we rethought our culture of assessment, if we inspired ourselves from what goes on in some Scandinavian countries.

There is a tendency to accept this dichotomy, this split between difficulty and sufferance at school on the one hand and happiness outside of school on the other hand. And yet, as Snyder reminds us, cultural joy is a verifiable fact. The challenge is to get this cultural joy into the school system. Having now touched – and barely touched at that – the question of happiness in the classroom, let us now consider the question of how one learns to relate to others.

What comparative education can tell us about learning to live with others

We have seen how important it is to develop intellectual curiosity and the thirst for learning. We then saw how happiness at school is essential if the aim is to engender a child fulfilled and well balanced, always wanting to acquire knowledge. It is well known that happiness makes learning easier and that a happy person simply learns better. Let us now consider the third element in our triptych: knowledge, happiness, respect for others.

At this point we need to say a few words on comparative education and what one expect from it. Through the need to take into account what happens in education elsewhere (and the developments which led to this), comparative education allows us to benefit from the experiences of others, to share knowledge and know-how in education, and to enrich educational research. It is clear, from this perspective, that educational exchanges have an important role to play. Exchanges allow a better understanding of the 'Other' with all the distinguishing characteristics, and to benefit from his/her pedagogical capital (knowledge of school), cultural capital (knowledge of culture), linguistic culture (knowledge of language[s]) and human culture (knowledge of one's fellow humans). Comparative education is thus intrinsically linked to education for the respect of others.

One cannot think of school without giving an important place to respect for others, to education for respect for others, to know how to take account of others, other their differences, of respect for differences and of taking an interest in these differences. But how can one educate a child for respect for others from the earliest age? I can see several ways to do this but for the moment I am going to discuss just two: learning foreign languages and undertaking intranational and international exchanges.

Learning foreign languages

Already in the sixteenth century Rabelais and Montaigne appealed to their contemporaries to learn foreign languages. Montaigne is well known for having received a bilingual education since his father insisted on him having a foreign tutor (in this case a German) to teach him Latin. The tutor had to be foreign and not Francophone so that Montaigne was forced to learn a third language from a teacher who did not speak his first language! As for Rabelais, in that famous letter from Gargantua to Pantagruel that we mentioned before, he affirms the importance of foreign languages:

> I expect and I require that you learn certain languages perfectly: firstly Greek, as Quintilian requires, secondly Latin, then Hebrew for the sacred writings, and Chaldean and Arabic and that you develop a style in Greek like that of Plato and in Latin like that of Cicero.
>
> (Rabelais 1532)

In the twenty-first century it is more necessary than ever to master languages and to have access to several cultures as we are confronted every day with cultural *habitus*, as we regularly cross national borders, and as the mass media send us everyday images of the entire world. Our reference points in every domain, whether political, economic, commercial, social, artistic or gastronomic, etc., are becoming more and more transnational. This means economic, commercial, touristic, educational and other exchanges are going to increasingly develop and it is important to play a part in this, to understand what is at stake, to appreciate the benefits, the limitations and even the side-effects.

In this context, foreign languages represent an important asset, as much in the professional context as in the human. We know from Bourdieu's (1982) essay *Ce que parler veut dire: L'économie des échanges linguistiques* (*What speaking means: the economics of linguistic exchanges*) that competence in foreign languages gives the speaker linguistic capital which leads to an incontestable social capital, social recognition and a strong symbolic power. This is something the privileged social classes have always understood and have invested vast sums in sending their children to other countries to learn foreign languages.

So what can we do to establish some measure of social equality as far as languages are concerned? In 1989 the project EILE (*l'enseignement d'initiation aux langues étrangères* = introduction to learning foreign languages) was launched France to respond to the demands of parents. The project gradually spread throughout French primary schools. The project had various failings: teachers were not trained for the teaching; there was no follow-up from primary school to lower secondary (collège); the methods and teaching materials had not been thought through. This makes quite a list and the experiment took place in conditions that were sometimes chaotic. At the present time (25 years later) the conditions around this initiation to foreign language learning and the chances of success are hardly any better. Basically this exposure to a foreign language at near-homeopathic levels (around 15 minutes per day in the first year of primary school) does not bring very much to the acquisition of linguistic competencies. Clearly this way of teaching is not up to the task. Let us look therefore at what a properly bilingual school is like.

The bilingual school teaches some subjects (say, history, geography, science and music) directly in the foreign language; the mother tongue and the foreign language are taught in parallel from the very start of the programme and by different teachers. This is exactly the form taken by numerous bilingual schools throughout the world and whose results are incontestable (Groux 1996). In France, a particular school merits our attention: a state French–Arabic primary school, to be found on the Rue de Tanger (Paris 19ème) and which welcomes children from very modest backgrounds. Other than the fact that the children acquire solid competencies in a foreign language, the results achieved by the children in the bilingual section of this school are superior in French and mathematics to those achieved by children in the monolingual section of the same school.

As for the language to choose for the bilingual school, one might choose the language of a neighbouring country in order to reinforce regional exchanges, or perhaps a language of immigrant groups, or a language to which one is emotionally attached.

Let us now show, in the perspective of education for respect of others, the way in which educational exchanges are important because they can contribute to the pupil acquiring an understanding of the Other and developing that essential virtue which is respect.

Education without borders

Educational exchanges have existed since the dawn of history: in Ancient Greece, Xenophon attributed the greatness of Sparta to the education it gave its children. He compared Sparta with Athens and asked:

> I leave it to the judgment of him whom it may concern, which of the two has produced the finer type of men. And by finer I mean the better disciplined, the more modest and reverential, and, in matters where self-restraint is a virtue, the more continent.
>
> (Xenophon, ch. 2 para. 15)

This interest in education elsewhere has continued throughout history, with the most notable resurgence in Marc-Antoine Jullien de Paris in 1817 and the Special Reports on Educational Subjects under the direction of Michael Sadler (1897–1902) setting the scene for the modern resurgence in comparative education. In other words, the interest we have today for educational exchanges is not new. However, the context is different as we can no longer escape globalisation and we need to know how to control its effects on us.

What is at stake in educational exchanges?

Educational exchanges allow us to struggle against ethnocentrism, which needs to be one of the aims of school. In effect, children need to know that there exist multiple ways of thinking, of acting and also that what constitutes normal behaviour for them is not a universal norm. Adolescents and adults needs also to struggle against their own egocentrism and acknowledge that their point of view is not necessarily the best and that there are other ways to see the world. When people work with a foreigner, they uncover other cultural identities, other *habitus* and other affiliations. They notice that they themselves are the foreigners with respect to the other. Every relation one has with the world is necessarily biased and educational exchanges allow us to uncover by which bias we perceive the world. This consists of a decentring, of allowing the individual to grow their capacity to understand and comprehend that which is not of oneself, to open up to the world and to abandon one's ethnocentrism, in a generous move towards respect for other people.

Developing educational exchanges

At the present time, pupil exchanges can be funded in full or in part through schemes and organisations such as Comenius, the European Commission, the British Council, the French–American Commission, the *Office franco-québecois* and so on. Despite this, let us note that pupil mobility only concerns 3.5 per cent of the European pupil population. For these exchanges to develop, it would certainly help if the costs were covered by the institutions concerned and the exchange programme built into the curriculum. This would go in the direction of greater social justice, as it would allow children, regardless of their social origin, to benefit from such mobility, such as open-mindedness, intercultural and linguistic competencies, psychological maturity, thus enriching not only their knowledge but also their personality.

The benefits of exchanges are just as important when they are intranational. Of course, in the heart of a multi-ethnic class there are also very rich exchanges which occur.

Unfortunately, teachers are not always adept at managing the intercultural relations within a class, as they may not themselves have received adequate training. Intercultural education is one of the components of education for inclusion of Otherness and it is clearly necessary to integrate this into curricula, not only in primary and secondary schools but also into teacher training as this is not always the case across Europe. Teachers need to be trained in how to go about preparing and organising exchanges, in carrying them out and in following them up afterwards.

Here is how I see the class of tomorrow: happiness in the classroom, thirst for learning and intellectual curiosity, generous and welcoming to outsiders, accepting that perceived differences are an enrichment of the tapestry of life and not a burden to be borne, together with a sense of solidarity between pupils.

Rabelais signed Gargantua's letter to Pantagruel from Utopia. I too have developed a great dream, but we all need to dream and it is dreams, accompanied by militant action, which pushes society forward and advances humanity.

Training teachers in comparative education, in the service of development

To accompany this reflection on the importance of happiness at school, which permits a better acquisition of knowledge, the development of solidarity among pupils and the putting in place of clear and effective assessment strategies, we need to consider the training of teachers.

If trained in comparative education, teachers would be able not only to compare pedagogical practices, but also to consider other educational systems, other educational policies and other ways of dealing with the issues and problems that schools encounter. In this way, school failure, violence at school, the teaching of languages and so on could be considered from a variety of viewpoints emanating from different countries, different systems and different ways of understanding.

Such a decentring would permit teachers to appreciate the diverse standpoints which are taken over education and, by comparison and contrast, to be able to understand better their own system and how it functions.

When you speak to students on teaching placements and you ask them which subjects they would like to see included in their programme of study, they never mention anything to do with international education, whether this be comparing education systems, educational exchanges or even intercultural education. Their priorities concern mainly how to maintain order in the class with all the concomitant issues around authority and the ways to eradicate violence. We need to appreciate the fears of students on placement who are confronted for the first time by pupils for whom they are to be responsible, even if overseen by a teacher, and who fear that they might be overwhelmed when they themselves are in charge of their own class. They therefore seek pedagogical recipes and quick fixes which will permit them to immediately face up to every difficult situation they might encounter. The result is that when it is suggested that they might reflect on the relationship in schools between religion and the state, or on comparative education, or even on the history or philosophy of education, they turn away as they do not see the immediate need.

Learning for educational exchanges

When one has only ever encountered an educational system as either a student or teacher, one's only reference point is one's 'home' system. It can be hard to imagine that there might be other ways to organise teaching and learning, other systems of discipline, other ways of organising the school year or other ways of assessing learning. It is precisely for this reason that teachers need to discover other educational systems and that they need to live through the decentring that is entailed in entering into the logic of the Other.

This decentring is also needed when one approaches another culture. In effect, the realisation that one's cultural references points are not unique happens naturally in foreign countries and so we can learn for educational exchanges by actually doing educational exchanges. However, some theory is necessary as the teacher needs to know clearly the reason for having the exchange and to have a clear idea of the skills that she/he wishes to see develop in the learners. The teacher also has to have some idea how to assess the impact of the exchange on the learners.

All too often, school exchanges and trips abroad are organised by language teachers as special occasion to improve the pupils' language skills or as occasions to make the pupils visit a country in order to learn the language. And the teachers content themselves with these modest objectives with a clear conscience. To go beyond this, teachers need to realise that there are numerous benefits to be gained from educational exchanges in terms of:

- culture
- personal development
- education for Otherness.

In brief, every exchange programme should be built around these three objectives. Once the objectives have been defined, we need to move to the conceptual phase of the project and to do so in close collaboration with the partner institution. This does not mean to present to the partner a project with every *i* dotted and every *t* crossed, but rather to discuss together what each partner seeks to get out of the exchange and how to achieve this. Each partner has to know how to listen to the other and how to cooperate and collaborate in order to develop the project and bring it to fruition.

Each partner has to be able to understand and appreciate the cultural particularities of the other and to work together in a spirit of patience and understanding to avoid problems of misunderstanding and to overcome those that occur.[4] All this work is necessary if we want to achieve all the benefits that can be had from exchanges and avoid the negative effects which can occur from poorly organised exchanges which can simply reinforce stereotypes and even encourage xenophobia (Groux and Porcher 2000).

Learning for understanding the Other and for pluricultural skills

When we put the emphasis on cultural differences we run the risk of creating oppositions. On the other hand, when we seek similarities, we have more chance of finding the common ground of humanity, that common ground that gives humanity to people; in this we will find that we all look somewhat alike.

Let us now consider both the challenge of learning for understanding the Other and let us see what is possible to achieve and what is not.

The concept of culture

Before going on, we need to make clear how we are using the concept of culture. Bourdieu proposes a generic definition which is transferable between all sorts of different kinds of culture:

- culture one cultivates
- anthropological culture
- media culture
- popular culture[5]
- commercial culture
- managerial culture
- technical culture
- technological culture
- generational culture
- regional culture
- professional culture
- national culture
- and so on…

According to Bourdieu, 'culture is the ability to work out the differences between things'. To be cultivated, whether a little or a lot, is to avoid mixing things up or inappropriately joining them up. In other words, to be able to distinguish between things and to be able sort them with some rigour (Groux and Porcher 2003: 69–70).

Approaches to the literature of other cultures

It can be suggested to teachers to consider various kinds of literature:

- tales from different countries;
- travellers' tales;
- texts written by writers who are working in a language other than their mother tongue;
- works of theory.

Baraona (2009) analysed the different sorts of exile lived by four writers who adopted French as the language of their writings: Nancy Huston, Vassilis Alexakis, Ying Chen and Agota Kristof. Huston's mother tongue is English but she writes almost exclusively in French and has translated many of her works into English. Alexakis established himself in Paris at the time of the Greek dictatorship (1967–1974) and never wanted to renounce one or other of his two cultures. Ying Chen feels herself liberated in Montreal, where she was 'reborn'. For Kristof, the exile is forced.

We might consider the extent to which these different sorts of exile impact on the relationship between the writer and the language of the country that has welcomed them and which they have chosen as the language of their writings. Baraona (2009) argues that for Kristof writing was a condition of her very survival. For her to write in French was to distance herself from the country (Hungary) which had forced her to flee. For the others, writing in a second language, which they had learned later in life, gave them the freedom to express themselves in ways that would not have been possible in their native tongue.

Reflecting on the issues around exile, literature can allow teachers to think about the notion of otherness and on the idea that literature exists to open the mind to new ideas. It can do this by leaning on theoreticians such as Bakhtin (1984), who leads the reader to adopt what he terms a polyphonic approach to works of literature whereby there are many ways of reading the same text. We might turn to Umberto Eco, whose *Lector in fabula* (1985) shows brilliantly that there are multiple ways to read the same text and who arrives at the conclusion that there are as many ways of reading a text as there are readers. We could look to Campagnon (1998), who asserts that 'Literary value cannot have a theoretical basis; this is a limitation of theory, not of literature'; he concludes that 'perplexity is the only basis for literature' (p. 283).

Reflecting on the issues around exile literature is pertinent in the multicultural perspective in which we live. To nourish and sustain perplexity ought to be one of the major preoccupations of teachers and one which can bring them to consider with the learner the ways in which their own culture and its biases affect the manner in which they read and understand a text. Through such an understanding the learner might come to understand better their own interpretation of the world and hence better understand how others understand it for themselves.

Developing the ethical dimension

According to Groux *et al.* (2003: 272), 'ethics is the branch of philosophy whose aim is to judge the difference between good and bad.... It distinguishes itself from morality in that the latter is context-dependent, varies according culture and is individual.'

Aristotle's *Nicomachean Ethics* (1869 translation) leans on the common experience of the most diverse people in order to establish ethical principles transcending individual differences. For Kant, ethics is tied to metaphysical research and is placed above morality (Groux *et al.* 2003: 272). For Spinoza, good is nothing other than the means by which we get closer to the ideal model of humanity (Groux *et al.* 2003: 272). In this way, ethics can be seen as a universal value system for 'good' and 'well-being'. However, there are differences in emphasis between occidental and oriental viewpoints. Occidental philosophers agree over a number of values, such as justice, temperance and compassion. Oriental philosophers tend to agree with them over the values of humanity, righteousness, equity and equality, and justice in human relations, but they agree less over the idea of liberty in particular.

As for the values which are affirmed clearly in education systems in Europe, these are very much the values of democracy and the values which feature in the *Universal Declaration of Human Rights*, and yet these same values are not always internalised and acted upon at the level of the individual. Although these values are held up as values to which we should all subscribe, they do not always find a place in the morality lived by each individual. Despite the fact that these values come up again and again in citizenship education, multicultural education and in learning about democracy, a gulf remains between the theory and the practice and all this theorising does not suffice to bridge it. To bridge the gap, this type of education needs to be undertaken very early on in the curriculum and it needs to be applied in a practical sense, and not just theoretically. Each child needs to be able to live ethics in a concrete manner and teachers need to help the child develop their moral judgement in order for them to reflect on their value system and beliefs, and the teacher needs to give the child the space and possibility for this to happen. Teachers need to be invited to reflect on the importance of philosophy in the school (see, for example, *Philosophy with Children* 2013).

Conclusion

I have tried here to show that we cannot think of school as a part of the lifelong development of the individual without having their teachers properly educated in comparative education. This education requires reflexion on the mobility of persons and starts with the establishment of educational exchanges which, in turn, facilitate the struggle against ethnocentrism, encourage the development of the generosity of spirit which leads to an acceptance of perceived difference as an asset and develops solidarity between pupils.

This education demands reflexion on foreign literature(s), such as the literature on exile, on foreign languages and cultures and on the diverse conceptions of culture, whether these be generational, professional, sexual, ethnic, social or otherwise.[6] It shows an interest in developing cultural and intercultural knowledge and familiarity in order to refuse to succumb to dogmatism and to establish a basis for critical thinking. It puts in place a capacity to reflect on the education's problematic and to do so from a comparative perspective.

It is only through working on these essential aspects of teacher training that we can put in place a school which will actively encourage intellectual curiosity and a thirst for knowledge, engendering knowledge which is at one and the same time global, cultural and intercultural, all the while developing critical and ethical thinking.

Notes

1. For an introduction to Gargantua and Pantagruel, see the Wikipedia entry. Wikisource contains an entire English translation.
2. And for the fact that Rabelais aimed his programme at the aristocracy of whom he wrote:

   In their rulebook, there is only one clause:

   DO WHAT YOU LIKE

   Because free people, well born, well instructed, conversant in honest company, have by the very nature an instinct and a bent which always pushes them towards virtuous acts and away from vice; this they name honour.

3. See www.philosophos.com/philosophy_article_20.html.
4. Editor's note: even when countries share a language they can be culturally poles apart. Misunderstandings can come from the simplest of things, such as the way in which dates are written. This is exemplified by British and American date systems which have led to innumerable misunderstandings. As G.B. Shaw said of the UK and United States, they are two countries separated by a common language.
5. Cf. Hoggart (1957).
6. Cf. Labov (1972).

References

Aristotle (1869) *Nicomachean Ethics*, trans R. Williams. London: Longmans, Green and Co.

Bakhtin, M.M. (1984) *Problems of Dostoevsky's Poetics*. Edited and translated by Caryl Emerson. Minneapolis: University of Minnesota Press.

Baraona, G. (2009) Littérature d'écrivains d'expression française (quatre études de cas): des clés pour une éducation à l'interculturel? Nanterre, unpublished PhD thesis.

Bourdieu, P. (1982) *Ce que parler veut dire, L'économie des échanges linguistiques*. Paris: Fayard, available at http://asso.univ-lyon2.fr/masai/IMG/pdf/BOURDIEU_Ce_que_parler_veut_dire_FICHE_DE_LECTURE.pdf, accessed 24 April 2014.

Campagnon, A. (1998) *Le Démon de la théorie*. Paris: Seuil.

Delors, J. (chair) (1996) *Learning: The Treasure Within*. Paris: UNESCO.

Eco, U. (1985) *Lector in Fabula*. Paris: Grasset.

Epictetus (n.d. a) *Discourses*. Available at http://classics.mit.edu/Epictetus/discourses.mb.txt, accessed 24 April 2014.

Epictetus (n.d. b) *The Art of Living: The Classic Manual on Virtue, Happiness, and Effectiveness*. Available at: Available at http://webcache.googleusercontent.com/search?q=cache:http://www.gobookee.org/art-of-living-sharon-lebell, accessed 24 April 2014.

Groux, D. (1996) *L'enseignement précoce des langues*. Paris: Chronique sociale.

Groux, D. and Porcher, L. (2000) *Les échanges éducatifs*. Paris: L'Harmattan.

Groux, D. and Porcher, L. (2003) *L'altérité*. Paris: L'Harmattan.

Groux, D., Perez, S., Porcher, L., Rust V. and Tasaki, N. (2003) *Dictionnaire de l'Education compare*. Paris: l'Harmattan.

Hoggart, R. (1957) *La culture du pauvre*, Paris: Les éditions de minuit.

Isambert-Jamati, V. (1990) *Les savoirs scolaires*, Paris: Editions universitaires.

Jullien de Paris, M.A. (1817) *Esquisse et vues préliminaires d'un ouvrage sur l'éducation comparée, et séries de questions sur l'éducation*, Paris: L Colas.

Labov, W. (1972) *Language in the Inner City*. Philadelphia, PA: University of Pennsylvania Press.

Lipovetsky, G. and Serroy, J. (2008) *La culture-monde, Réponse à une société désorientée*, Paris: Odile Jacob.

Pestalozzi, Johann Heinrich (1830) *Education of Infancy*. Boston: Carter and Bender.

Philosophy with Children (2013) Available at www.thephilosophyshop.co.uk/about-us/philosophy-with-children/our-phie-method, accessed 24 April 2014.

Porcher, L. (1994) Les Compagnons de la lecture, *Perspectives documentaires en éducation*, 33.

Porcher, L. and Abdallah-Pretceille, M.(1996) *Ethique de la diversité et éducation*. Paris: PUF.

Rabelais, F. (1532) *Gargantua's Advice to Pantagruel*. Available at http://faculty.txwes.edu/csmeller/human-experience/ExpData09/03Biee/BIEE-RDs/5-dEurRDs/dEurR_Rab-GarPantSEL.htm, accessed 24 April 2014.

Serres, M. (1991) *Le Tiers Instruit*. Paris: Editions Folio.

Snyders, G. (1991) *Des élèves heureux*. Paris: EAP.

Special Reports on Educational Subjects Vol. I (1897) *Education in England, Wales, Ireland, France, Germany, Denmark, Belgium*, under the direction of M.E. Sadler. London: HMSO.

Special Reports on Educational Subjects Vol. II (1898) *Education in England and Wales; Physical Education; The Heuristic Method of Teaching; University Education in France*, under the direction of M.E. Sadler. London: HMSO.

Special Reports on Educational Subjects Vol. III (1898) *National Organisation of Education in Switzerland; Secondary Education in Prussia, Baden and Sweden; Teaching of Modern Languages; Higher Commercial Education in France, Germany and Belgium*, under the direction of M.E. Sadler. London: HMSO.

Special Reports on Educational Subjects Vol. IV (1901) *Educational Systems of the Dominion of Canada, Newfoundland and the West*, under the direction of M.E. Sadler. London: HMSO.

Special Reports on Educational Subjects Vol. V (1901) *Educational Systems of Cape Colony, Natal, Commonwealth of Australia, New Zealand, Ceylon and Malta*, under the direction of M.E. Sadler. London: HMSO.

Special Reports on Educational Subjects Vol. VI (1900) *Preparatory Schools for Boys: Their Place in British Secondary Education*, under the direction of M.E. Sadler. London: HMSO.

Special Reports on Educational Subjects Vol. VII (1902) *Rural Education in France*, under the direction of M.E. Sadler. London: HMSO.

Special Reports on Educational Subjects Vol. VIII (1902) *Education in Scandinavia, Switzerland, Holland, Hungary*, under the direction of M.E. Sadler. London: HMSO.

Special Reports on Educational Subjects Vol. IX (1902) *Education in Germany*, under the direction of M.E. Sadler. London: HMSO.

Special Reports on Educational Subjects Vol. X (1902) *Education in the U.S.A. Part I*, under the direction of M.E. Sadler. London: HMSO.

Special Reports on Educational Subjects Vol. XI (1902) *Education in the U.S.A. Part II*, under the direction of M.E. Sadler. London: HMSO.

Xenophon (n.d.) *The Polity of the Lacedaemonians*. Public domain translation. Available at http://ancienthistory.about.com/library/bl/bl_text_xenophon_lacedaemonians.htm, accessed 24 April 2014.

18

Special educational needs in context

A historical overview

Mary Kellett

Education is a political activity and educational change is a political process.

Reid (2010: 133)

Introduction

This chapter provides an overview of special educational needs (SEN) from first inception to contemporary practice. It is a journey characterised by philosophical and ideological shifts reflected in the buffeting of SEN policies on the sea of government change. An understanding of SEN today can only be understood in the context of its historical evolution and the charting of the principal ideological and pedagogical debates that have shaped it. The chapter summarises important legislation that has influenced the course of special education over time and discusses the development of various pedagogical approaches to enhance SEN practice. The final part of the chapter brings the debate to contemporary classrooms and the critical issues and challenges facing present-day teachers.

The origins of special educational needs

We pick up the historical trail in the nineteenth century, when discourses on education produced the 'medical' and 'charitable' models of disability. The medical (sometimes known as 'deficit') model viewed children's behaviour in terms of *internal* biological differences, categorising 'syndromes' and 'conditions' as defects within the child. This perspective disregarded any *external* factors such as poverty, health or life experience as having any bearing on the nature of the disability. The charitable model personified disable children as tragic figures, deserving of pity. This was a disempowering perspective that categorised them as passive recipients of philanthropy. The fault was seen to lie within the child – disability was a personal defect. Because of the dominance of these discourses, when basic education for most children was established (Forster's 1870 *Education Act* and the 1872 *Education (Scotland) Act*), no provision was made in these Acts for disabled children or children with learning difficulties.

Doctors could diagnose four levels of special 'condition': *idiot, imbecile, feeble-minded* and *moral-defective.* The Departmental Committee on Defective and Epileptic Children (1898) investigated whether the education system could be adapted for any of these children. The committee concluded that *imbeciles* were best placed in an asylum, the *feeble-minded* and *moral-defectives* could attend special schools but *idiots* were deemed ineducable and excluded from the education system altogether. The differentiation of these categories was not clearly defined and school boards were required to appoint a medical officer to decide a child's 'condition' and educational placement (1913 *Mental Deficiency Act*). In Scotland, the *Education of Defective Children (Scotland) Act 1906* gave school boards the ability to cater for defective children in special schools or classes. Those incapable of learning were, as in England, assigned to institutions by their local parish councils.

The 1921 *Education Act* required that numbers of 'feeble-minded' and 'backward' children within each local authority be recorded so that separate education could be provided for them. This maintained a powerful link between the diagnosis of a category and the allocation of a particular type of education. It was this impetus that led to the development and rapid adoption of the intelligence test (Burt 1937) as a diagnostic tool to determine degrees of SEN.

The 1944 *Butler Act* heralded a radical reappraisal of the education system (Stakes and Hornby 1997). The terms 'subnormal', 'remedial' and 'maladjusted' came into common usage. Educationally subnormal children were identified as those retarded by more than 20 per cent for their age but who were not so low grade as to be ineducable. This accounted for approximately 10 per cent of the child population, 1 per cent of whom attended special schools or hospitals, the remainder being taught in small groups within the umbrella of a school. An increasing number of special schools were opened between the 1950s and 1970s and the number of hospital special schools also grew.

Behaviourist teaching

The 1970 *Education (Handicapped Children) Act* and the 1974 *Education (Mentally Handicapped Children) (Scotland) Act* finally brought all children into the framework of education irrespective of their disability or degree of learning difficulty. The absolute right to a full education for all children without exception was established and the 'ineducable' category abolished. As a consequence of this, educators began to turn their attention to a better understanding of ways in which children with severe and complex learning difficulties could be taught (Rose 2001). Many of the approaches adopted were based on behaviourist methods. This model assumed that most behaviours are learned, including, for example, challenging or difficult behaviour. Rather than diagnosing a deficit, the behaviourist model begins by identifying what the child needs to learn and then constructs a way of teaching this behaviour. These techniques were adapted to teach a whole range of skills in a behaviourist-based curriculum. The Skills Analysis Model (Gardner *et al.* 1983) is one such example. It advocated breaking the teaching process down into six small steps:

1. identify core areas of the curriculum;
2. subdivide these areas into their component parts;
3. write targets for each identified component;
4. prioritise the targets;
5. write a programme to teach each target;
6. assess and record whether the target has been achieved.

Although these methods achieved some modification in undesirable behaviour and acquisition of certain discrete skills, the approach was heavily criticised because it promoted learning without understanding and skills acquired in this way could not be transferred to other situations (McConkey 1981; Collis and Lacey 1996).

This new interest in special education was reflected in the setting up of the Warnock Committee in 1974 to review provision in the UK. The Warnock Report (1978), and the resulting 1981 *Education Act* that it informed, was a watershed in the history of special education. For the first time it created the concept of a special educational 'need' and appropriate *provision* rather than a 'condition' and *treatment*. The committee regarded the terms 'educationally sub-normal' (England and Wales) and 'mentally handicapped' (Scotland) as causing unnecessary stigmatisation, particularly in later life. It was decided that these would be replaced by a single term: 'children with learning difficulties'.

What is a special educational need?

As described above, the idea of a special educational 'need' was first coined in the Warnock Report, along with the term 'children with learning difficulties'. But what exactly do we mean by these terms? Pupils are deemed to have a special educational need when they are unable to reach their learning potential without either additional support or adaptations to their learning environment. This can be for a variety of global and/or specific reasons. There could be global cognitive delay when pupils may experience difficulty learning at the same level or pace as their typically developing peers. There may be a specific learning difficulty with e.g. reading or writing (sometimes known as dyslexia, although dyslexia is itself a large umbrella term for many specific learning difficulties) or numeracy. Equally there may be a specific difficulty related to e.g. attention span or memory. Emotional and behavioural difficulties can also interfere with the learning process and require special support. Correspondingly, there are children who are very able (the current educational term for this is 'gifted and talented') and not able to reach their learning potential without adaptations to their learning environment and additional resources. It should be clear from these examples that provision for a special educational need is all about accommodating the individual learner through provisions and adaptations that *enable* rather than *disable*.

The Warnock recommendations

The Warnock Committee recommended that special educational need be seen as a continuum. A five-stage assessment procedure was established with progressively greater input from professionals at each stage along the continuum, culminating in a 'statement'. This Statement of Educational Need (Record of Need in Scotland) was to be produced when a child required extra educational provision. The document legally committed the local education authority (LEA) to meet the child's identified SEN. Parents were involved in the process and a 'named person' acted as a key contact for them.

The Warnock Report judged that one in five children were likely to require special educational provision at some time during their school career. Therefore a more flexible approach was proposed where the majority of children with SEN could be identified and helped within the ordinary school. Adaptations to the school building, the curriculum and teaching techniques were to be considered where this would help meet a child's 'special educational need'.

Integration (not to be confused with inclusion, which is discussed later) was encouraged by the Warnock Report (1978) and was described as a way of bringing children with SEN into the community of mainstream schools. This could be achieved in three different ways.

1. locational integration – special units or classes set up within an ordinary school;
2. social integration – children attending a special class or unit but eating, playing and socialising with other children;
3. functional integration – children with special needs joining a mainstream class either on a part-time or full-time basis.

Interactive approaches

A backlash from behaviourist teaching resulted in the promotion of interactive teaching approaches (Collis and Lacey 1996; Nind 2000) and an emphasis on person-to-person interaction as a basis for learning. More attention was given to creating a responsive learning environment (Ware 1996). For pupils with severe and complex learning difficulties some of these approaches, such as *intensive interaction* (Nind and Hewett 1994) were developed from a theoretical basis of caregiver–infant interaction, with an emphasis on contingent responding and working from a child's strengths – in other words, building on what a child could do rather than concentrating on what a child could not do.

The labelling culture

However laudable the abolition of inappropriate labels such as idiot or imbecile is, if one label is simply replaced by a different one the potential for denigration and ridicule is not necessarily removed. The substitution of these terms by categories such as 'mentally retarded', 'educationally subnormal' and 'maladjusted' led to abusive taunts of 'retards' and 'subnormals'. It has taken a long time to learn from these early blunders and even in the 1980s and 1990s we were compounding, not lessening the problem. One of the consequences of Warnock's 'continuum' of SEN was that it reinforced categorisation. Along this continuum children could have a range of learning difficulties categorised as mild, or moderate (ESN), severe and complex (SLD), profound and multiple (PMLD) or emotional and behavioural (EBD). Inevitably this led to increased use of the abbreviated terminology and terms such as 'EBDs', 'SLDs' and 'PMLDs' were soon in common use among professionals. The problem with this is that the word 'child' or 'pupil' does not appear anywhere, suggesting that the category relates to something other than human. Even when the odd child acknowledgement tag was thrown in for good measure (e.g. 'our EBD kids' rather than 'our EBDs'), the child part always came after the label. Child activists felt that this put the spotlight on the disability rather than the child. A child is a child first and foremost; some children also happen to have learning difficulties. Hence, in the first decade of the twenty-first century it became common practice to refer to children who have special needs as e.g. a child *with* severe and complex learning difficulties rather than an SLD child. This applied equally to adults, the value of the human individual being always prized above the learning difficulty.

Curricular initiatives

The *Education Reform Act 1988* introduced the National Curriculum in England and Wales and gave an impetus to considering how the whole curriculum could be made accessible for children with SEN. The relevance and importance of the National Curriculum for children with SEN was controversial. Some writers have argued that it brought new opportunities to previously excluded children (Carpenter *et al.* 1996). Others saw significant parts of it as inappropriate or limiting (Fletcher-Campbell 1994). There was criticism that the prescriptive nature of the National Curriculum placed too much emphasis on product not process. National Curriculum 2000, one of a series of revisions to the original National Curriculum, went some way to redressing this and offered guidance on meeting pupils' diverse learning needs.

Another concern was that the first level of attainment was so far beyond the reach of some pupils that they would have no realistic opportunity of achieving at anything (Tilstone 1991). In 1998 the Qualifications and Curriculum Association (QCA) introduced eight 'P' levels – preparatory levels of attainment leading up to level 1 – but there was criticism that even these were too widely spaced to be meaningful for many pupils with profound learning difficulties. Assessment by level of attainment was also viewed by some as anti-inclusionary because it leads to grouping of children by ability.

Other statutory curricular initiatives including the national numeracy and literacy strategies (1998 onwards) widened the gap further when whole-class, prescriptive teaching aimed at middle-ability children largely replaced literacy and numeracy small-group work in primary schools. Five years later, this approach was modified (*Excellence and Enjoyment* paper, 2003) giving schools greater control of the way they implemented the curriculum. It cleared the way for schools to develop more innovative and individual approaches to literacy and numeracy and encouraged the involvement of parents in learning partnerships. These were positive steps towards better provision for children with SEN. However, there is still widespread debate about whether any adapted 'National Curriculum' can be appropriate for all pupils, particularly those with profound and complex learning difficulties. On the one hand it is a powerful enactment of the common humanity of all children and their rightful entitlement to the same curriculum. On the other hand, a 'one-curriculum approach' may be inhibiting for some groups of children if it prevents time being spent on training for essential life skills or complementary teaching approaches and therapies that are known to be beneficial for a child's specific need. Ultimately, the onus is on teachers to use the National Curriculum in ways they judge to be relevant. There are many fine examples of teachers successfully including pupils, even those with very profound learning difficulties, in a meaningful way. One such example was documented by Tilstone *et al.* (2000: 14):

> It is hard for her teachers and caregivers to know when Manjula is learning because she does not use speech or any kind of sign language. However, by including her in the visit to the cathedral they are providing her with important experiences, shared with other children. In fact, these experiences give Manjula the opportunity to show that she is aware of important things during the visit. Sitting in her wheelchair, beneath the cathedral's Rose Window, Manjula is left for a few minutes to look, listen, and feel where she is. As the sun shines through the window, Manjula smiles and wrings her hands with pleasure. Back in school, Manjula's teacher and learning support assistant help her to make a 'sensory' picture book as part of a topic on the cathedral. They make her a personal tape of the kind of organ music heard during the visit. This brings learning to life for Manjula, and brings other real benefits. Some of her classmates also enjoy the organ music and the class teacher organises a small 'listening group'. Manjula's mother and father when they hear about this successful activity, decide to make her a tape of Buddhist chants used in their community temple. Thereafter, whenever the family visits the temple, they play the tape in the car and Manjula gets very excited with anticipation. The curriculum experience described here has been well matched to Manjula's needs, and importantly, this has been 'negotiated' on the basis of her response to an activity. She might have been left out of the visit, but instead she was included and showed her educators, friends and family that she was developing a seemingly new awareness that could help her develop valuable choice making skills.

The government introduced a new strategy in 2004, 'Removing Barriers to Achievement', for children with SEN which focused on early intervention and support and placed greater emphasis on personalised learning. It advocated more children being taught in mainstream schools, with special schools becoming centres of excellence – working closely with mainstream schools to share expertise. Special schools continued to educate children with the most severe and complex needs. The Education and Skills Committee report on Special Educational Needs (2006) called for a major review of SEN provision and stressed the importance of local flexibility within any nationally proposed framework. The policy initiatives that emanated from the *Every Child Matters* (2003) and *Children's Act* (2004) agendas broadened the face of SEN provision to take account of wider life skills. This was encapsulated in the five aims of *Every Child Matters* – be healthy; stay safe; enjoy and achieve; make a positive contribution; achieve economic well-being – which require a collaborative inter-agency approach to SEN. Closer partnerships between education, health and social services and the voluntary sector were recommended and momentum gathered around the Extended Schools and Children's Centres programme (DfES 2007) as their potential to enhance special educational provision for all children was identified.

Resourcing special educational needs

The *Education Act* 1993 placed a duty on the Secretary of State to issue a Code of Practice for SEN and the power to revise it at will. The first Code of Practice came into effect in 1994 and was updated in 2001. It provided practical advice to LEAs, maintained schools, early education settings and others on carrying out their statutory duties to identify, assess and make provision for children's SEN. In this respect it maintained an approach which looked for individual difficulties rather than developing a whole-school approach, but the involvement of pupils themselves in this process was at least one step towards empowerment and a wider emphasis on children's rights.

In the past, SEN were entirely funded from LEAs. The introduction of the local management of schools brought devolved funding directly to schools. The *Standards and Frameworks Act* (1998) required local authorities in England and Wales to delegate at least 80 per cent of their overall education budget directly to schools. The remaining 20 per cent was used to support advisory services and fund provision for pupils with statements of SEN. With a large portion of direct funding coming to individual schools, headteachers were able to appoint more special educational needs coordinators (SENCOs) to oversee the organisation and management of SEN. This role quickly became pivotal and is generally regarded as a senior role in school leadership and management teams. The majority of devolved funds are spent on teaching assistant support staff to work directly with children who have learning difficulties in the classroom.

Inclusion

The drive towards inclusion emanated from what is referred to as the social model of disability. This perspective views society as disabling rather than condition(s) associated with any individual. Here it is society's failure to adapt the environment to accommodate an individual's condition that becomes the disabling factor. In education, mainstream schools are required to adapt their physical environment, teaching styles and curricular provision where necessary to meet the diverse needs of all pupils. The context for inclusion is situated within a human rights discourse predicated on the

United Nations *Convention on the Rights of the Child* (1989). Segregation of children from their peers is seen as a denial of those human rights. Inclusion and participation are essential to human dignity and to the enjoyment and exercise of human rights. The UNESCO Salamanca Statement (1994) called on the international community to endorse the approach of inclusive schools by implementing practical and strategic changes. The Centre for Studies on Inclusive Education (2002) emphasised that this statement was a clear commitment to 'education for all' within the mainstream system. The concept of inclusion extends beyond SEN and disabilities to the wider embracement of human diversity; of gender, ethnicity, sexuality, cultural heritage and religion.

In 1997 the UK's commitment to inclusion was underlined by the Green Paper *Excellence for All*. The paper supported the move from segregated to mainstream education for more children. Special schools were to have a more flexible role, part of which would be to provide active support for children moving to mainstream schools and act as a source of training and information for mainstream staff.

If schools are to educate a diverse range of learners in one and the same classroom, then a variety of different teaching approaches need to be considered. This may involve physical changes to the learning environment, sometimes additional adult support and invariably adaptations to the curriculum. The emphasis on 'diversity' steers thinking towards the total learning environment rather than individual 'need' or 'difficulty'. Some argue that inclusion involves accessing specialist teaching skills (e.g. Hornby and Kidd 2001), whereas others claim that no special set of methods or pedagogies are needed to teach children with diverse learning experiences (e.g. Thomas and Loxley 2001). These opposing viewpoints illustrate deep-rooted tensions that exist among professionals in their different approaches to inclusion.

The inclusion debate

While there have been few ideological objections to inclusion, there have been many concerns raised about the feasibility of its implementation. There is evidence of resistance from teachers who worry that they do not have the skills to teach children with specific learning difficulties and/or children with emotional and behavioural difficulties. Other camps of opinion congregate around the impact inclusion will have on typically developing pupils in their classes (Florian 1998). Others argue that inclusion sells some children short, especially those with severe and complex learning difficulties, since they can no longer access specialist teaching in small purpose-built classrooms that typically populate special schools. One of the difficulties appears to be that inclusion moved too quickly, before mainstream schools and mainstream teachers had enough time to adapt. Pupils began to move out of special schools and into mainstream ones, but the specialist teaching skills did not follow them. Specialist teachers stayed with the remainder of the pupils left in special schools and the government's aim for this expertise to be used to support children in mainstream schools and provide training for mainstream staff did not wholly materialise. There are, of course, many inclusion success stories such as the Barnado's special school that successfully transformed itself into an inclusion advisory service (Bannister *et al.* 2003).

A major concern for teachers is that inclusion only works when properly resourced and many maintain it is under-resourcing, not flawed ideology, that fuels disillusion. Children with diverse and multiple disabilities need more staff to be able to accommodate their needs – sometimes on a one-to-one full-time basis. Despite increased recruitment of assistants to support classroom teachers, insufficient numbers and insufficient training remain major obstacles. Clough and Nutbrown (2002), in their exploration of early years educators' attitudes to inclusion, found mixed responses:

> A lovely idea – inclusion – and when it's good, it's great! I have been able to have children in the nursery with Down's Syndrome and children with various emotional difficulties – abused children – but when they (the LEA) asked us to take in a child with autism, well, we had to say 'no'. Too risky – I was frightened that if we did – something terrible would happen and it would be my responsibility. So yes, lovely idea – but it really is an ideal that will never be achieved – total inclusion is impossible.
>
> (Janie, nursery teacher, 3–10 years; cited in Clough and Nutbrown 2002)

It is noteworthy that this early years teacher thinks in terms of being asked to *take in* a child with autism, as if the child is somehow 'outside' the frame. There is no apparent conception of the child's entitlement to be included as a right, or of the nursery's obligation to adapt its provision in order to accommodate all children, whether autistic or not.

The *Special Education Needs and Disability Act* (2001) caused many schools to reconsider their attitude to inclusion. Schools can only refuse to take a child if they can demonstrate that the admission would harm the education of other pupils in the school. The Act places education within the remit of the *Disability Discrimination Act*, rendering it illegal to discriminate against a pupil because of his or her disability.

Some schools encountered difficulties in the transition towards greater inclusion and one of the initiatives that served as a self-help tool was *The Index for Inclusion* (Booth *et al.* 2000). The *Index* provided a set of materials to guide schools through the inclusion process promoting the building of supportive communities to foster high achievement for all pupils.

> The *Index* involves a process of school self-review on three dimensions concerned with inclusive school cultures, policies and practices. The process entails a progression through a series of school development phases. These start with the establishing of a coordinating group. This group works with staff, governors, students and parents/carers to examine all aspects of the school, identifying barriers to learning and sustaining and reviewing progress. The investigation is supported by a detailed set of indicators and questions which require schools to engage in a deep and challenging exploration of their present position and the possibilities for moving towards greater inclusion.
>
> (Booth *et al.* 2000: 2)

Most support for pupils who have learning difficulties is provided by teaching assistants and a primary pedagogical concern is whether this support should be provided 'in' or 'out' of the classroom. In the past it was common practice for pupils to be taken out of their classrooms and supported on a one-to-one or small-group basis. From an inclusive perspective this is problematic since an inclusive ideology adapts the learning environment to the pupil's needs rather than creating a separate 'exclusive' learning environment. Moreover, there are consequences for the social and cultural dimensions of learning if support is provided outside the classroom.

Inclusion has not evolved without its critics. Such criticisms (e.g. Farrell 1997; Wilson 1999) focused on the tension that exists between the philosophical principle of inclusion and a continuing level of support for specialist segregation (Croll and Moses 2000). Although critics embrace inclusion as an educational ideal, they discuss the need for a pragmatic response. They suggest that special schools still have a role to play with regard to children with severe learning difficulties and emotional and behavioural difficulties, question the capacity of mainstream schools to meet their needs and highlight the problem of inadequate resources and funding. Many of these issues were also raised by the Education and Skills Committee report (2006). In its response, the then government affirmed its commitment to retaining special schools both as centres of excellence and as a choice provision for children with the most severe and complex needs.

Exclusion

Despite the laudable ideology of inclusion there are still a great many pupils who are excluded from schools, not because they are deemed 'ineducable' in the historical sense but because they are judged to be 'too difficult'. Most of these pupils fall into the special need category known as emotional and behavioural difficulties. In such cases, pupils are passed out to special schools or pupil referral units (PRUs), some of which are residential. In principle these 'referrals' are for an agreed fixed term with the aim being to re-integrate pupils back into mainstream schools. In practice this rarely happens and the placement becomes all but permanent. Visser *et al.*'s (2002) research on pupils with emotional and behavioural difficulties concluded that not enough was being done to encourage schools to become more open, positive, diverse communities that are 'barrier-free' to pupils with emotional and behavioural difficulties. Again, this was something that was picked up on by the Education and Skills Committee report (2006), which succeeded in pressing for action over children with SEN in PRUs, noting the need to plan and act much earlier if children with emotional and behavioural difficulties are to avoid long stays in PRUs.

The coalition government

The advent of the coalition government in 2010 heralded an unprecedented pace of change in education. The new government moved swiftly to distance itself from many New Labour flagship initiatives. The Department for Children, Schools and Families was absorbed into a new Department for Education and, while the coalition did not turn away from the principles of *Every Child Matters*, it hurriedly discarded the branding. It proposed ambitious and sweeping changes for SEN in its 2011 Green Paper *Support and Aspiration: A New Approach to Special Educational Needs*. Frustration with the inadequate and overly complex systems supporting SEN had been voiced towards the end of New Labour's term of office (Bercow 2008; Lamb 2009; Rix *et al.* 2010). The 2010 OfSTED SEN and disability review identified early identification of needs as being crucial, quality training for professionals, more involvement of parents and greater equity. These themes were echoed in four key indicators from the consultation period for the Green Paper (DfE 2011: 26)

1. The system for supporting children, young people and families is overly complex, bureaucratic and adversarial.
2. Parents want better information on the services available and the choice of schools.
3. Better training is needed for school staff to recognise children's needs and work better with children and their parents.
4. Education, health and social care services need to work better together to identify and deliver on children's needs.

Building on this, coalition policies are moving away from complex and prescriptive, centralised control to a simplified single assessment in the form of an 'education, health and care plan' with more freedom and accountability at local levels. Two key drivers underpin this: one is to increase the number of academies and free schools; and the second is the devolving of greater power and choice to parents through personalised SEN and disability support budgets. This has widened the inclusion debate even further and kept the door open for the retention of special schools. Indeed, the coalition is actively encouraging greater diversity of provision and the involvement of voluntary organisations. This could see the conversion of PRUs into specialist academies and the setting up of free schools that specialise in SEN and/or disability. At the time of writing, it is too early to judge how these policies will fair and whether the rhetoric will match the practice.

Conclusion

When we consider SEN in the context of history, we understand better how the thinking behind present policies has evolved. One of the aims of this chapter has been to explore where different arguments about special education and inclusion are mutually supportive and where there is tension and conceptual confusion. There is general agreement at the moral stage of defining inclusive education, but the ideological unity becomes more fragmented when enacted in practice (Clough 2000). Valuing diversity underpins the centrality of the philosophical platform that explores differences between 'special education' and 'inclusive education'. 'Special education' might be defined in terms of 'separate but equal', whereas 'different but equal' more aptly describes 'inclusive education'. Reflecting on the historical journey of special education, it becomes apparent that the newest actor to emerge onto the contemporary SEN stage is likely to be the parent. However, it is the ability to adapt to change, embrace flexibility and champion diversity that will secure the brightest future for the two million UK children identified as having a special educational need.

References

Bannister, C., Sharland, V., Thomas, G., Upton, V. and Walker, D. (2003) 'Changing from a special school to an inclusion service', in Nind, M., Sheehy, K. and Simmons, K. (eds), *Inclusive Education: Learners and Learning Contexts*. London: David Fulton.

Bercow, J. (2008) *The Bercow Review: A Review of Services for Children and Young People (0–19) with Speech, Language and Communication Needs*. London: DCSF.

Booth, T., Ainscow, M., Black-Hawkins, K., Vaughan, M. and Shaw, L. (2000) *Index for Inclusion: Developing Learning and Participation in Schools*. Bristol: CSIE.

Burt, C. (1937) *The Backward Child*. London and Aylesbury: University of London Press Ltd.

Carpenter, B., Ashdown, R. and Bovair, K. (1996) *Enabling Access*. London: David Fulton.

Centre for Studies on Inclusive Education (2002) *The Inclusion Charter*. Bristol: Centre for Studies on Inclusive Education. Available at http://www.csie.org.uk/resources/inclusion-charter.pdf, accessed 24 April 2014.

Children's Act (2004) London: HMSO.

Clough, P. (2000) 'Routes to inclusion', in Clough, P. and Corbett, J. (eds), *Theories of Inclusive Education: A Students' Guide*. London: Paul Chapman.

Clough, P. and Nutbrown, C. (2002) The index for inclusion: personal perspectives from early years educators', *Early Education*, spring.

Collis, M. and Lacey, P. (1996) *Interactive Approaches to Teaching*. London: David Fulton.

Croll, P. and Moses, D. (2000) 'Ideologies and utopias: education professionals' views of inclusion', *European Journal of Special Needs Education* 15 (1), 1–12.

DfE (2011) *Support and Aspiration: A New Approach to Special Educational Needs and Disability – A Consultation*. Norwich: The Stationery Office.

Department for Education and Employment (1994) *The Code of Practice on the Identification and Assessment of Children and Special Educational Needs*. London: DfEE.

Department for Education and Employment (1997) *Excellence for All Children: Meeting Special Educational Needs*. London: DfEE.

Department for Education and Skills (DfES) (2001) *Code of Practice on the Identification and Assessment of Children and Special Educational Needs*. London: DfES.

Department for Education and Skills (2007) *Every Child Matters: Change for Children*. London: HMSO.

Department for Education and Skills (2003) *Excellence and Enjoyment: A Strategy for Primary Schools*. London: DfES.

Education Act (1870) London: HMSO.

Education Act (1921) London: HMSO.

Education Act (1944) London: HMSO.

Education Act (1981) London: HMSO.

Education Act (1993) London: HMSO.

Education Act (Handicapped Children) (1970) London: HMSO.

Education and Skills Committee (2006) Third Report of Session 2005–06, Special Educational Needs, HC 478–I.

Education Reform Act (1988) London: HMSO.

Every Child Matters (2003) London: HMSO.

Farrell, P. (1997) The integration of children with severe learning difficulties: a review of the recent literature, *Journal of Applied Research in Intellectual Disabilities* 10 (1), 1–14.

Fletcher-Campbell, F. (1994) *Still Joining Forces? A Follow Up Study of Links Between Ordinary and Special Schools*. Slough: NFER.

Florian, L. (1998) 'An examination of the practical problems associated with the implementation of inclusive education policies', *Support for Learning* 13 (3), 105–108.

Gardner, J., Murphy, J. and Crawford, N. (1983) *The Skills Analysis Model*. Kidderminster: BIMH Publications.

Hornby, G. and Kidd, R. (2001) 'Transfer from special to mainstream – ten years later', *British Journal of Special Education* 28 (1), 10–17.

Lamb, B. (2009) *SEN and Parental Confidence*. London: Crown Copyright.

McConkey, R. (1981) 'Education without understanding', *Special Education: Forward Trends* 8 (3), 8–11.

Mental Deficiency Act (1913) London: HMSO.

National Curriculum (2000) http://curriculum2000.co.uk/new_curriculum.htm.

Nind, M. (2000) 'Teachers' understanding of interactive approaches in special education', *International Journal of Disability and Education* 47 (2), 183–199.

Nind, M. and Hewett, D. (1994) *Access to Communication: Developing the Basics of Communication in People with Severe Learning Difficulties Through Intensive Interaction*. London: David Fulton.

Report of the Departmental Committee on Defective & Epileptic Children. Vol II. Minutes of Evidence, Appendices etc. (1898) London: HMSO.

Reid, A. (2010) 'The politics of educational change', in Arthur, J. and Davies, I. (eds), *Education Studies Textbook*, Abingdon: Routledge.

Rix, J., Walsh, C., Parry, J. and Kumrai, R. (2010) 'Introduction: another point of view' in Rix, J., Nind, M., Sheehy, K., Simmons, K., Parry, J. and Kumrai, R. (eds), *Equality, Participation and Inclusion: Diverse Perspectives*, Abingdon: Routledge.

Rose, L. (2001) 'Primary school teacher perceptions of the conditions required to include pupils with special educational needs', *Educational Review* 53 (2), 147–156.

Special Education Needs and Disability Act (2001) London: The Stationery Office.

Stakes, R. and Hornby, G. (1997) *Change in Special Education Provision: What Brings It About?* London: Continuum.

Thomas, G. and Loxley, A. (2001) *Deconstructing Special Education and Constructing Inclusion*. Buckingham: Open University Press.

Tilstone, C. (1991) (ed.) *Teaching Pupils with Severe Learning Difficulties*. London: David Fulton.

Tilstone, C., Lacey, P., Porter, J. and Robertson, C. (2000) *Pupils with Learning Difficulties in Mainstream Schools*. London: David Fulton.

UNESCO (1994) 'Salamanca Statement', World Conference on Special Educational Needs: Access and quality, Paris.

United Nations (1989) *Convention on the Rights of the Child*, New York: United Nations.

Visser, J., Cole, T. and Daniels, H. (2002) 'Inclusion for the difficult to include', *Support for Learning* 17 (1), 23–26.

Ware, J. (1996) *Creating a Responsive Environment*, London: David Fulton.

Warnock, M. (1978) *Special Educational Needs: Report of the Committee of Enquiry into the Education of Handicapped Children and Young People*. London: HMSO.

Wilson, J. (1999) 'Some conceptual difficulties about inclusion', *Support for Learning* 14 (3), 110–112.

19

'Race', ethnicity and education

The English experience

John Stanley

'Please. Do me this one great favour, Jones. If ever you hear anyone, when you are back home … speak of the East', and here his voice plummeted a register, and the tone was full and sad, 'hold your judgment. If you are told "they are all this" or "they do this" or "their opinions are these", withhold your judgment until all the facts are upon you. Because that land they call "India" goes by a thousand names and is populated by millions, and if you think you have found two men the same among that multitude, then you are mistaken. It is merely a trick of the moonlight.'

Zadie Smith (2000)

Introduction to race

Although ideas about race can be traced back through ancient history, the categorisation of people based on the modern idea of race became common in the late eighteenth and early nineteenth centuries. The events which created awareness of race came in the enslavement of millions of African peoples who were transported as slave labour to the Americas. Equally, the European exploration, colonisation and imperial domination of much of the world stimulated racial ideas about the inferiority of black Africans and the association of certain forms of behaviour with particular racial groups. Hence the idea that different groups of people have different natures, and that there is a clear line of distinction between them, became generally accepted in those parts of the world which experienced colonisation.

What are often called scare quotes are generally used with the word 'race'; this indicates that there are some conceptual problems connected with this use of the word. However, since in the following discussion we shall be coming to terms with its usage and meaning, we shall proceed from now on without the scare quotes. The term has been used to categorise different groups of people across the globe using physical/ genetic features such as skin, hair, physique and facial features, and subsequently to make assumptions about their characteristics and behaviour. Such a connection is a false one, although a case has been made by some commentators who claim that intelligence is determined by genetics and that the low overall educational achievement of black pupils is due to a lower, inherited intelligence. The assertions of Jensen (1969, 1973) in the United States and Eysenck (1971) in Britain were subjected to intense criticism, and the myth was exploded when the unreliability of the data was established. Kamin (1977) and Mabey (1981) have convincingly repudiated the work on the genetic influence. A more recently argued case supporting Eysenck and Jensen is found in Herrnstein and Murray's (1994) book *The Bell Curve*, which claims that black people are genetically inferior to white people because of their lower IQs. A consequence of such ill-founded beliefs was the resurrection of the genetic account of why West Indian children generally had been under-performing in state schooling. There clearly was support in favour of the claims that the inferiority of educational performance among black pupils was a result of inherited, inferior intelligence. Despite the fact that there was considerable research evidence to discredit and combat the genetic explanation of black under-achievement (Montagu 1999; Miles and Brown 2003). Herrnstein and Murray (1994) had much later recharged the claim that an inferior intelligence in the black population did indeed support the notion of the black underclass. The misjudgement about the educational potential of sections of society was further exaggerated by a group of right-wing academics and their political connections (Cox and Boyson 1977). The working class were defined as being lazy, with children low in intelligence which saw the poor and under-achieving where they were expected to be in terms of attainment and behaviour in schools.

Together, the weakness of the research procedures and processes, to say nothing of the inadequacy of the conceptualisation problem and the ultimate interpretation of findings, meant the case for nature rather than nurture fell apart. Science suggests that there is not a species-type difference between peoples. Race is not a social category that can identify groups of people, relying on their physical appearance to predict characteristics, behaviour and educational achievement (see Nei and Roychoudhury 1983). Indeed, there are strong and reliable claims that genetic variability is found between individuals generally, and not between the so-called different races. Classifying people into races is a social product rather than a biological reality. The continuing development of the science of genetics seems likely further to confirm the unreliability of the ideas associated with the word race:

> Here we have a concept which refers to a false perception: that the only legitimate use of the term race is as a device for recognizing that people categorise and behave differently towards one another on the basis of and significance attached to physiological differences, not the physiological differences themselves.
>
> (Foster *et al.* 1996: 51–52)

Even after establishing that the category of race is invalid, that it has no scientific base, the problem that it engenders does not disappear. The designation of inferiority that goes with the term race serves to rationalise people's social position, achievements and treatment. Denying its validity will not remove it from the discourse of people and institutions. Even where it is denied, it has tended to be replaced by an equally difficult concept – namely ethnicity. Steve Fenton (2010: 3) suggests that ethnicity is a word referring to social identities – typically about 'descent' and 'cultural difference'. The contemporary tendency has been to refer to a person's ethnicity rather than race; this can produce similar results in the production of cultural stereotypes which mislead, oversimplify, categorise and, again, result in injustice. Reference to the ethnic origins of people from minority groups can lead to a reification of ethnic categories, and promote an ethnic absolutism that often refers to extended kinship groups residing in another part of the worlds, or else to static cultures. The emphasis is still on the difference between groups of people and the danger is that connotations about specificity of human groups carried in the notion of race are reconfigured under the label of ethnicity. There must be some degree of consciousness about how fixed ethnic categories can be, and how significant they are for children in the context of formal education.

The word race does get used regularly to distinguish between pupils in schools in Britain. The outcome is that a distinction is made between those pupils who come from a range of ethnic backgrounds, and those coming from white indigenous families. Since the *Education Act* of 1944, the relative life chances available to pupils have been evident in studies on inequalities in educational outcome at all levels of the education system. The desired improvements and achievements in educational outcomes have not been distributed evenly and fairly, with one influence on children's educational achievements being their social class origins. Another is race, which is also seen as a very significant factor in the background of many pupils and one which influences their educational achievements. To understand the phenomenon of race requires an examination of its meaning in the discourse of social relations. For example, race is accepted as a means of categorising pupils in schools, and a simple reference to skin colour is often taken to confirm a child's race. Race presents an important social and political issue across the modern, globalised world: that does not mean that it carries the same meaning, or results in the same response. There are no basic genetic differences between different ethnic groups of the human race. In fact, the existence of broad genetic features in humans is of greater significance than differences. In considering the meaning of race in common usage and acknowledging its significance in relation to pupils' backgrounds, we must confront its position as an ideology based on false knowledge and prejudice. This ideological explanation allows for an assumption of differences in ethnic origins, that is, a myth of racial difference is used to explain differences in pupils' achievements when it would have been more relevant to provide differences based on social status, culture and descent, or family origins, as factors providing a more valid explanation of the educational performance of children. Scientific evidence does make the case for there being no such thing as race in the sense that humans come from different racial species. The case we are making here is that race is used to promote differences is cultural stereotypes that are simplistic, malevolent and inaccurate. We must then be aware of the significance of this and take up a more valid explanation:

> There are a quite small number of 'stocks' of the human race who share physical features and unequal abilities, are genuinely members of an ancestral 'family'

grouping and, in race theory, are predicted to have common, non physical characteristics such as temperament and ability. Five landmarks may be discerned in the
demise of this idea ... first ... Darwinian ideas of evolutionary change ... put paid
to the idea of 'fixed types' ... second is Durkheim's argument that 'races' ... was
not a meaningful sociological category and could not be the basis of the explanation of social difference. The third was the attack on social determinism ... that
racial characteristics were the basis of social difference ... social anthropologists
argued that social difference was explainable by the environment and culture.
Fourth ... concerted attack on the use of the word 'race' (and) its replacement by
... 'ethnic groups'. Fifth came the ... UNESCO-organised group ... decided the use
of races was imprecise ... the problem to be studied was not 'races' but racism.

(from Rex in Fenton 2010: 53)

Fenton is explaining that the old idea that there are stocks of the human race, that is
people who share physical features and have non-physical common characteristics like
temperament and intelligence, must be dropped. However, when we turn to examine
and describe the achievements of pupils of various ethnic groups in present-day
schooling, there is a long way to go in our understanding of differing levels of achievement by pupils. The differences in pupils' performance often carries elements of
culture, biology, religion and nation and makes the explanation of differences part of
everyday discourse. Nonetheless, as Tomlinson (2008) points out, set against the efforts
of other European countries, English schools have made tangible attempts to focus on
their responsibility to cope with the needs of pupils of different ethnic/cultural and
religious groups. At least, that commitment to the needs of pupils from different ethnic
groups is seen to have been taking place in most state schools, with primary phase
schools making a significant contribution. The issues to be confronted have been those
of national identity, cultural heritage, multiculturalism and anti-racism. Unfortunately,
the provision of the multicultural education was piecemeal, and by no means compre-
hensively provided in schools around the country. In the early days of OfSTED, little
attention was paid to a school's multicultural commitment when the report was written, and its omission seemed not to influence the final report. As a consequence 'several generations of young people have emerged from schools, many still ignorant of
the multi-ethnic society and world they live in, and many imbued with hostility to
other groups' (Tomlinson 2008: 2).

Differing performances

It appears that there are shortcomings in the response of schools to the needs of the
multicultural society. The first is facing up to the needs of pupils from a range of ethnic
minority groups in our schools because although children from a range of multi-ethnic
groups have shown some success by gaining recognisably good educational qualifications, others have not. Children of Ugandan Asian descent have been getting far better
results than those of West Indian origin, who have significantly lower achievements. It
is clear that accepting and implementing multiculturalism and integration in schools is

experiencing conflicting arguments and varied support, and so schooling is provided which can be inappropriate to the needs of many pupils from a range of ethnic minority backgrounds. Although going back to the 1970s, there is evidence of some concern for the multicultural society in schools, nonetheless there is a strong case for Gillborn's (2008) reference to 'whiteness ... absolutely natural norm' in present-day schooling.

The allocation of pupils to schools prior to the late 1940s was taken for granted. In the main the selective system allocating places to secondary modern, technical and grammar school was accepted by all, since, although in the main the intake into grammar schools was of mainly children from middle-class families, a significant number of working-class pupils made it too. Often the locality in which children lived had a significant effect on chances of entry in grammar school since percentages of entry varied from 10 per cent to 15 per cent. The majority of working-class pupils ended up in secondary modern schools. From the 1960s to the present day ethnic minority children have been entering the English education system. At this time there was considerable support for the possibility of the socially inclusive society, where social mobility is available to all citizens to pursue their potential. The 1960s aspirations were made to provide a universal form of education inspired by the idea of equality of opportunity. However, a fair and socially integrative system was a long way off. In the early days the inflow was from the old British colonies of India, Pakistan, parts of Africa and the Caribbean; others came from the Far East, Hong Kong and Vietnam. In the main the attraction was the work to rebuild Britain after the Second World War. Those immigrants worked and lived mainly in the industrial towns and cities of the Midlands and the North and some London boroughs. By the 1990s the children of the early migrants were British citizens and also by the 1990s, migrants from European countries were adding to the workforce and schools. The education authorities in the regions of settlement were reasonably successful in accommodating in schools a diverse cultural and religious group of children.

The approach used to meet the needs of immigrant pupils in English schools was much like that emerging from numerous other countries experiencing a good deal of migration, that is, by means of assimilation. The idea is that there is one dominant culture in a country/nation, a majority culture which all must aspire to and become effective citizens. Minority cultures would be required to at least play down their original cultures as they became efficient citizens in the major culture. The needs of many black and Asian group pupils whose first language was not English were initially seen to require more attention, and to be threatening the time available for teaching local, white pupils. Section 11 of the *Local Government Act 1966* gave a local authority permission to recruit extra teachers to cope with the needs of pupils from the ethnic minorities. The problem with the assimilation ideology was that it denied access to equal opportunities, and so the deeply rooted cultures of black and Asian pupils brought about injustice in education and ultimately injustice in employment. By the middle of the 1960s the policy of assimilation was in decline (Mason 2000). In response to the clear shortcomings of the education service, the minority groups' parents brought into being a Black People's Alliance (Sivanandan 1982) to promote their concerns for the education of their children.

In the 1960s and 1970s the different education authorities in the English education system had almost total control of the working of their schools. Naturally, they worked in different ways to accommodate immigrant children who came to their schools. The DES Circular 7/65, *The Education of Immigrants*, had a section entitled 'Spreading the Children'. Therein was a recommendation that no more than one-third of a class should consist of immigrant children; this was accompanied by a proposal that local authorities should arrange for dispersals between schools. A good deal of research was carried out in schools with substantial numbers of ethnic minority pupils, and not all research could be regarded as valid and helpful. Sally Tomlinson cites the example of studies from the 1960s where clearly unfair testing was undertaken

> Assumptions that the experiences of the children were roughly similar, and fair comparisons could be made, were dubious in the extreme. Given that debate on the racial politics, educational value and morality of IQ and other forms of psycho-metric testing had been in progress both in the US and Europe for some decades, and test results had been used consistently in the USA to denigrate immigrant and black groups, much of the 1960s research can be regarded as politically naïve and damaging to the education of the immigrant children in Britain.
>
> (Tomlinson 2008: 34)

Although at the end of the 1970s much had been learned about the education system and its ability to cope with immigrant children, and some local education authorities (LEAs), schools and teachers treated immigrant children with fairness and respect. There was, however, as Tomlinson goes on to observe, 'the belief that their presence (immigrant children) constituted a problem, and the lingering pseudo-scientific beliefs in the intellectual inferiority of black children also marked the decade' (Tomlinson 2008: 40).

Multicultural education and anti-racist education

The performances of ethnic minority groups in Britain revealed overall a picture of under-achievement. The roots of these inequalities were confronted by two important policy developments: one was *multicultural education* and the other *anti-racist education*. Multicultural education promoted an interest in ethnic, religious and cultural back-grounds of pupils of different heritages. The idea was that it would produce an environment more conducive to learning in schools and bring significant benefits to the whole of society since it would provide a basis for a better understanding of the cultural background of, in particular, Asian and West Indian people. A significant weakness in multicultural education was that it did little more than produce examples of cultural differences involving food, music and dress. Troyna and Ball (1985) charac-terised multicultural education as the three Ss – saris, samosas and steel bands. The radical Left saw the promotion of the intentions of multicultural education as being little more than an exercise in social control (Carby 1982). Minority group children were seen to be contributing to their own exploitation as they engaged in activities and displays which claimed to be serving their needs as ethnic minority group members. Other attacks on multicultural education claimed that ethnic minorities were getting some preferential treatment as the classroom work and environment promoted minority interests.

The main commitment to multicultural education came in the primary schools where children would be located in the same classroom, with the same teacher, for most of the school day. Displays could be arranged and left for use and reflection over a period of time. Secondary schools found such arrangements were not possible and where displays were available they were small in number and generally only available as pupils visited the specialist rooms of subject teachers. In the broader scheme of things there were many schools in the UK who saw themselves as being located in the 'white highlands' and thus far away from the 'problem' areas where children of ethnic minority background lived. The suggestion that all children should be versed in multi-culturalism in preparation for life in the multicultural society was never going to be persuasive, and the absence of any effective lead by the government confirmed that multicultural education was not being taken seriously enough to encourage any thoughts of success.

A few education authorities took up the cause of ethnic minority pupils' education by subscribing to a more direct and radical approach to their needs. Brent, an education authority in London, got rid of what remained of multicultural education and with it suspended a well-liked headteacher, Maureen McGoldrick, apparently on the grounds of a 'racist' remark she had made to a council official. The next stage for the Brent authority was to recruit teachers committed to anti-racist education. The approach was so radical that it attracted substantial media attention and incurred opposition from many Asian and African-Caribbean parents. The Brent education authority was subjected to some fierce criticism for allowing its school system to be subverted by people with a strong left-wing, anti-racist ideology which meant that 'Brent undertook a root and branch re-appraisal of the education delivered to local children' (Ratcliffe 2009: 78). Other local authorities which felt that multicultural education lacked a sharp edge to its policy supported anti-racist education by adapting its pedagogic and management styles (Troyna and Carrington 1990).

An apparent indictment of the anti-racist education programme came in 1986 at the all-boys Burnage High School in Manchester, where an Asian boy, Ahmed Iqbal Ullah, received fatal stab wounds inflicted by a disturbed 13-year-old white boy. Here was a desperate and violent situation at a school which had an anti-racist policy. The anti-racist policy was blamed in sensationalist media accounts of the incident and gave the impression that the anti-racist policy was to blame. Ian MacDonald QC chaired a committee which produced a report in 1988. There was criticism of senior management for insufficient consultation with teachers, parents and pupils on the anti-racist policy, together with the all-male culture of Burnage school which fostered a machismo style in the school. There was also reference by MacDonald to the influence of racism prevalent in wider society. The publication of the entire report was not undertaken by the Manchester LEA because they feared the possibility of libel. Instead the MacDonald Committee published its report (MacDonald *et al.* 1989). The murder of the Asian boy had fuelled a sustained criticism of anti-racist policies, and those councils with such policies came in for a media assault as 'looney-left' councils. LEAs that had held off involvement in anti-racist education felt justified for their avoidance of the intervention in what they regarded as a controversial subject. However, David Gillborn (1995) reflects the view of many commentators that the Burnage Inquiry had been misinterpreted by many as meaning an end of anti-racism, when instead the report was 'a brave attempt to move beyond simple binary oppositions and push antiracists to confront the complexity of life in school, where issues of social class, sexism and able-ism interact in an unpredictable and sometimes deadly combination of oppressions' (Gillborn 1995: 3). Gillborn then goes on to Sivanandan's observation of the biased response from the media

> still the voices of those, like myself, who tried to say that there was no body of thought called antiracism, no orthodoxy or dogma, no manual of strategy and tactics, no demonology. What there was in our society was racism in every walk of life, and it had to be combated – in every conceivable way.
>
> (Sivanandan 1988: 147)

The media's interest in what was happening in the education service was decidedly selective and some important developments to do with exclusion and achievement of black pupils seemed to escape their interest. In the two large conurbations in England, Inner London and Birmingham, a high percentage of black pupils being suspended from schooling was causing concern among parents of black pupils. Although the category of 'educationally subnormal' had been abolished by the 1981 *Special Education Act*, there was still much concern about the suspension of black children from mainstream schools. The policies designed to produce race equality in schools were in evidence, but little seemed to be done to the structure and organisation of schools to promote developments which might offer a reconstruction of existing inequalities. In the teacher training institutions students were being made aware of the consistent under-achievement of certain ethnic minority pupils, but that knowledge was likely to be interpreted as a self-fulfilling prophecy rather than a challenge to find ways of solving the problem of minority group under-achievement. The race relations legislations of the 1970s made some impact at the institutional level in that it called for some official response, but it made little impact on the educational experiences of children, and so the 1980s produced numerous interpretive studies on schooling and 'race'/ethnicity; these studied a range of responses by pupils and teachers in multiracial and all-white schools.

Some comparisons made

Early research on educational achievement and minority ethnic group pupils is summarised in a review by Tomlinson (1980) of 33 studies of educational attainment of ethnic groups in schools. Twenty-six of these studies revealed African-Caribbean pupils were getting lower scores than white pupils on tests of performance. Moreover, the same defined group was over-represented in the category of 'educationally subnormal' and under-represented in the higher school classes. Among the findings of the Swann Report (DES 1985), looking at the educational attainment of most minority ethnic groups, was that racism, mainly unintentional, influenced under-achievement. The incidence of under-achievement was not so prevalent for some Asian groups, who were thought to experience the negative effects of stereotyping to a lesser degree than other groups. In the continuing search for explanations of minority group underachievement, Smith and Tomlinson (1989) showed that investigations revealed school differences in educational achievements by minority group children. The various research teams argued that the differences stemmed not from differing abilities so much as different qualities of teaching and learning. Schools could make a difference to the educational achievement of pupils, whatever their ethnic origin.

What is evident in the foregoing studies is what is referred to as institutional racism. Gillborn (1990) spells out the process clearly. He uses the idea of the 'ideal client', which teachers apply to their pupils. This concept carries a picture of 'appropriate pupil behaviour'; it has dimensions of class, race and gender. The behaviour of African-Caribbean pupils confirmed for teachers the myth about the way the pupils' behaviour and attitudes represented a challenge to authority. The school then became a site of contestation as institutional disciplinary practices were applied at the school. 'Almost any display of African-Caribbean ethnicity was deemed inappropriate' (Gillborn 1990: 29). Gillborn (1995), although suggesting that teachers are not practising institutional racism deliberately, sees them contributing, generally unintentionally, to 'the processes that structure the educational opportunities of minority students' (Gillborn 1995: 42). Gillborn and Youdell (2000) further examine the issue of institutional racism looking at African-Caribbean pupils' experiences and achievements. Their conclusion is that there existed an institutional discourse of race and ability that denied African-Caribbean students any chance of success in school. Youdell (2003) sets out further to investigate how 'the minutiae of everyday life in schools constitutes African-Caribbean students as undesirable learners'. Her conclusion is that in the ordinary conversation of school life the identities of African-Caribbean pupils are 'constituted as undesirable, intolerable, far from "ideal", within the hegemonic discourses of the school organisation'. The 'discursive constitution' of African-Caribbean identities that takes place in 'the apparently trivial moments of everyday life' is the seemingly innocuous way for identities to be constituted. Guillaumin similarly draws attention to the unconscious confirmation of racism when she claims that

> Negations are not recognized as such by our unconscious mental processes. From this point of view, a fact affirmed and a fact denied exist to exactly the same degree and remain equally present in our affective and intellectual associative networks. Just talking about race means that it will always be there in residue. 'Race' is about the least conceptional, cold and abstract of notions, so it appeals from the start to the unconscious side of the mechanisms we have for acquiring knowledge and relating to other human being.
>
> (Guillaumin 1995: 105–106)

Progress or some success

As a result of research on pupil–pupil and pupil–teacher interactions (Wright 1986, 1992); Mac an Ghaill 1988; Gillborn 1990; Mirza 1992; Green 1985) the operationalisation of the concept of race/ethnicity changed its focus. Wright's (1986) classroom study found black boys and girls constructing an anti-school subculture as they reached the fourth and fifth years of schooling. Similarly, Mac an Ghaill (1988) and Fuller (1980, 1983) found that girls from ethnic minority groups, though they disliked school, used it to acquired much needed educational qualifications that would enable them to escape the double disadvantage of both race and gender. Gillborn and Gipps (1996), examining research conducted in the 1970s, 1980s and 1990s, found that teachers who expressed a commitment to equality were still likely to work with negative representations of African-Caribbean pupils.

The idea that minority ethnic group experience of schooling is all bad news is misleading. There are numerous examples that contradict the view that the educational experience of all minority ethnic group children is a failure. The more recent studies of race and ethnicity and educational achievement do show educational success for certain ethnic minority group children. Gillborn and Mirza (2000), in their synthesis of research evidence on race, class and gender, have used a broader range of ethnic group categories than earlier commentators. These categories may still hide much valuable evidence, but there has to be some sort of classification if monitoring of educational achievement is to take place, and the year 2000 amendment to the 1976 *Race Relations Act* insists that it must. Gillborn and Mirza use the categories white, black, Indian, Pakistani and Bangladeshi. This study also attempts to establish 'On the basis of the best available evidence, the relative significance of "race" and ethnicity alongside other factors, especially gender and social class background, so as to clarify an agenda for racial equality in education' (Gillborn and Mirza 2000: 5).

The study quoted above is called *Educational Inequality*, and it acknowledges that minority communities should not be regarded as homogenous, but seen as they truly are: stratified by class and gender. The idea of a single, definitive cultural or ethnic experience is unacceptable. The reality is that educational experience and achievement can only be reliably judged at the conjunction of racial, social and gendered experience. Unfortunately, there are few other studies which take all three variables together. Gillborn and Gipps' (1996) earlier study, which was undertaken on behalf of OfSTED, was one that attempted to take account of 'race'/ethnicity, class and gender. Looking at GCSE grades A–C in England and Wales in 1995, the highest averages went to pupils from advantaged backgrounds, and girls fared better than boys when socio-economic background was the same (Gillborn and Gipps 1996: 17). The Youth Cohort Study (DfEE 1999) referred to by Gillborn and Mirza (2000) addresses the variables of race, class and gender together; this is another rare example. Some interesting, though tentative, conclusions are available:

- No group has been completely excluded from improvement in GCSE attainments during the late 1980s and 1990s.

- By 1995 the gender gap was present within each ethnic group regardless of social class background.
- Ethnic inequalities persist even when simultaneously controlling for gender and class.
- When comparing like with like, in terms of gender, class and ethnic origin, consistent and significant ethnic inequalities of attainment remain clear.

The performance of African-Caribbean pupils has tended to lag behind that of white pupils, though there was an instance when, in the years 1992 and 1994, at Key Stage 1, African-Caribbean pupils in Birmingham were ahead of white pupils as recorded on national assessment tests (Gillborn and Gipps 1996). The general conclusion, however, ran true to form, with the attainments of ethnic minority pupils generally lagging behind those of white pupils. As pupils moved through the junior years, that is Key Stage 2, the gap tended to widen. There are cases of African-Caribbean boys doing better at Key Stage 1 than their white counterparts, but this advantage is soon lost as school careers develop. The declining achievement of African-Caribbean pupils is explained by Gillborn and Gipps as the product of a situation of conflict created between teachers and schooling and African-Caribbean pupils. As a consequence of this seemingly unintentional outcome, levels of achievement of African-Caribbean pupils suffer. As pupils' educational careers proceed through secondary school, to the point where they take GCSE examinations, their achievements are in comparative decline, the average difference being that African-Caribbean pupils are five points lower than white peers. Nonetheless, Gillborn and Gipps reject the idea of total black under-achievement since black African pupils invariably get better results than African-Caribbean pupils. Turning to GCSE grades A–C, which was the benchmark for a pass comparable with the old GCE O-level examination, African-Caribbean pupils are gaining less than half the national average. The results for pupils of Bangladeshi and Pakistani origin are more encouraging since they make up some of the leeway on national averages at 11 to perform in some LEAs at or above the national average (Commission on the Future of Multi-ethnic Britain 2000).

Variations in achievement

Notwithstanding the foregoing reservations, the consistency of much of the data from research projects suggests that the educational under-achievement of many ethnic minority pupils is an outcome of the way the schools deal with these pupils. Gillborn and Mirza's study provides a complex picture of ethnic minority educational performance. In the first place, by claiming that 'all can achieve' – that is 'of the six ethnic minority categories analysed, each one is in the highest attaining category in at least one LEA' (Gillborn and Mirza 2000: 9) Hence the writers' claim that their study is looking at new evidence 'on how different groups share in the rising levels of attainment at the end of compulsory schooling' (p. 5)

There is still some improvement to be made in the monitoring of the educational achievement of minority ethnic groups, and the writers express concern that a number of LEAs applying for the Ethnic Minority Achievement Grant (EMAG) could not give a figure for minority attainment in Year 11. The criticism of the monitoring of ethnic minority achievement has further support in Osler and Morrison's (2000) report for the Commission for Racial Equality (CRE), which claims that OfSTED informed neither schools nor contracted inspectors of OfSTED's responsibility for monitoring schools' procedures for preventing racism. Such strategies were recommended in the report of the Stephen Lawrence Inquiry (Macpherson 1999). A further weakness that Gillborn and Mirza (2000) point out is that only six LEAs provided baselines to GCSE performance by ethnic origin; another was that LEAs had never produced data on performance by ethnic group before and therefore some of their returns were less than adequate. This finding sits well with the OfSTED (1999) report on LEA programmes for raising the levels of minority ethnic group attainments. Fewer than one-quarter of LEAs involved in that survey could provide a clear plan for improving the attainment of minority ethnic groups.

The Gillborn and Mirza study (2000) is mapping attainment at the local level in a number of select LEAs. This leads to a local variability and cannot provide a national picture. However, it does give 'a unique glimpse of variation between localities' (p. 8). The data relate to attainments in the summer of 1998. The report concentrates first on 'local variability' and shows that 'of the six ethnic minority categories ... analysed, every one is the highest attaining of all in at least one LEA' (p. 9), and 'Black pupils are capable of high achievement. In one in ten authorities that monitor GCSE results by ethnicity, pupils in all recorded black groups are more likely to attain the benchmark than their white peers' (p. 10). Pakistani pupils have been recorded as a low-attaining group, but 'in four out of ten LEAs that monitor for ethnic origin, Pakistani pupils are more likely to attain this benchmark than white pupils locally' (p. 10). Again, Bangladeshis who at national level lag behind white averages, do at local level in many cases reverse this pattern. However, this 'snapshot of variations' (p. 11) notwithstanding, 'significant and consistent inequalities of attainment emerge for many of the principal minority groups' (p. 11). Although members of each of the principal minority groups are more likely to gain five higher GCSE grades than ever before, it must be borne in mind that African-Caribbean, Pakistani and Bangladeshi pupils are 'markedly less likely to attain five higher graded GCSEs than their white and Indian peers nationally' (p. 12). Gillborn and Mirza (2000) conclude that ethnic inequalities are 'consistently visible' and that social class and gender differences though 'associated with differences of attainment ... [cannot] ... account for persistent underlying ethnic inequalities: comparing like with like, African-Caribbean, Pakistani and Bangladeshi pupils do not enjoy equal opportunities'. The writers draw attention to the fact that the situation is not static and that for African-Caribbean and Pakistani pupils inequalities have increased particularly in GCSE attainments.

The changing nature of educational achievement of minority ethnic pupils, while showing improvements for some groups, persistently leaves other groups disappointed. Berliner (2003), reporting in the *Education Guardian* on a report by Simon Warren of the University of Birmingham and Professor David Gillborn of the Institute of Education, University of London, says that Birmingham LEA, 'a leader in the field of race equality education', is still employing a strategy that is not resulting in equality of opportunity in all schools, this in particular for African-Caribbean children. Gillborn and Warren suggest that setting, and booster groups to help children reach targets in tests, could be working against black pupils. Typically, girls of all ethnic groups do better than boys.

The *Aiming High* national strategy, reported in the *Guardian* (11 October 2003) was the government's new national strategy to raise achievement levels of minority ethnic pupils and specifically black pupils, whom they saw as one of the main under-performing groups in the country. Central to the strategy was focused work in 30 secondary schools. Each school received a support package including support and advice from an experienced consultant. The National College of School Leadership also contributed and lessons learned were spread throughout England. The strategy involved bringing greater accountability and visibility to the issue. Inspections were to focus deliberately on minority group experience and the school and the LEA were to publish achievement data by ethnic group and LEA. There was to be training for primary school teachers to help them support bilingual pupils from foundation stage to secondary school. The result was a series of guidance documents for LEAs and teachers under the banner of *Aiming High*, which included *Aiming High: Raising the Achievement of Gypsy Traveller Pupils* (DfES 2003a), *Aiming High: Understanding the Needs of Ethnic Minority Pupils in Mainly White Schools – A Guide to Good Practice* (DfES 2004a), *Aiming High: Guidance on Supporting the Education of Asylum Seeking and Refugee Children* (DfES 2004b) and *Aiming High: Guidance on the Assessment of Pupils Learning English as an Additional Language* (DfES 2005).

School exclusions

School exclusions have a long history, but in recent times special concern has been shown for black children and dual-heritage children who are three times more likely to suffer permanent exclusion from school than other pupils. Bernard Coard's (1971) short book with the long title, *How the West Indian Child is Made Educationally Subnormal in the British School System: The Scandal of the Black Child in Schools in Britain*, drew attention to the disproportionate numbers of African-Caribbean children who were being diverted from mainstream schooling into schools for the educationally subnormal. Another early report by the CRE (see Bourne *et al.* 1994), looking into pupil suspensions in Birmingham schools, discovered that from 1974 to 1980 it was recorded that black pupils were four times more likely to be excluded than white pupils. This problematic experience of schooling was further confirmed by OfSTED in a report in 1993, which discovered that the number of African-Caribbean pupils excluded from schools was disproportionately high, and that similar numbers attended referral units that LEAs have to provide for permanently excluded pupils. Osler (1997) claims that the relatively excessive exclusions of African-Caribbean pupils produce an 'educational crisis' since, following exclusion, there is only a 15 per cent chance that a child will be reinstated in mainstream education. Exclusion is not the same for girls as it is for boys, except in the case of African-Caribbean girls, who constitute 9 per cent of female exclusions, and yet only just 1 per cent of all girls in schools. Although permanent exclusions from schools at the turn of the century were lower than they had been six years before, the numbers of pupils excluded had increased for the second year running according to figures provided by the Department of Education and Skills in 2003 (DfES 2003b). Although the total number of exclusions in the DfES report are seen to have risen for the second year running, it is considerably lower than it was in 1997/1998. This exclusion from full-time mainstream schools of a disproportionate percentage of black young people, and African-Caribbean people in particular, shows that little has changed for this group of young people. The CRE had expressed concern on many occasions about what appears to be unfair treatment. There were concerns that the needs-oriented approach recommended in the Warnock Report (1978) was still being overlooked. A further strong criticism is that the Conservative government's *Education Reform Act* of 1988 did nothing for the educational interests of young black pupils on a number of counts. The neo-liberal act created the 'market' for school places, giving parents the opportunity to choose schools; white parents were thus able to avoid schools with appreciable numbers of black pupils. The competition between schools for potentially able pupils to enhance league table positions has taken priority in state education over the aims of equal opportunities for all pupils.

An equally important concern was the content of the National Curriculum. Gundara claimed that the 'National Curriculum, and the Anglo-centric values underpinning it, diminishes the right to knowledge for all Britons in a multicultural society' (Gundara 2000: 39). Adjustments to the National Curriculum subsequent to the 1988 *Education Reform Act* have done little to address the criticism that schooling is in the main 'white, English Christian'. The formal curriculum of schools, together with the hidden curriculum of schooling, is seen by many writers as creating an environment where black pupils are likely to fail (Mac an Ghaill 1988; Gillborn 1990; Osler 1997; Hatcher 1997). As Gillborn and Mirza (2000) and Youdell (2003), among others, claim, institutional racism is still a significant influence on the education of African-Caribbean pupils.

The DfES *Priority Review: Exclusion of Black Pupils 'Getting it. Getting it right'* (2006) is concerned with the 'persistent underachievement of pupils from some ethnic minority backgrounds'. In the DfES's (2004c) *The Five Year Strategy for Children and Learners* it is still the case that black pupils are three times more likely to be excluded from school than their white fellows. In detail, each year 1,000 black pupils are given permanent exclusion status, and almost 30,000 get a fixed-period exclusion. To academics and others exclusion is regarded as a discriminatory action against black pupils. *Getting it. Getting it right* acknowledges that overt racism is unusual so far as staff are concerned, but that discrimination in the form of curriculum content and low expectations is still present, and the excessive exclusion rates of black pupils is further evidence of the presence of racism in crucial aspects of school life. There was some encouraging evidence in the period 1995 to 2000 when the gap between exclusions for black pupils and others closed significantly. But the evidence since 2000 indicates that the proportion of black pupils excluded has increased more quickly than for other groups. In interpreting the quantitative data on black pupils' exclusions, and to draw out a true picture from this evidence, it is also necessary to acknowledge the significant amount of qualitative and anecdotal evidence. In other words, there are 'unofficial exclusions' to be taken into account. Schools are known to use other methods to get pupils off the roll: for instance, to get parents to remove their pupils from the school, or to fail to report exclusions.

The rate of black Caribbean exclusions, which are three times those of white pupils, cannot solely be accounted for by socio-economic inequalities in society; as *Priority Review* suggests, there must be an 'X-factor' connected to ethnicity which explains the exclusions gap; this together with the assertion that the education system deals out treatment to black pupils which is different from that experienced by other pupils (Blair *et al.* 1998). In-school factors and out-of-school factors are offered as explanations, with in-school factors seen as the most likely ones. The case seems to be that schools are likely to exclude black pupils in situations where they would be less likely to exclude white pupils (Majors 2001). The exclusions gap then is put down to institutional racism, that is, that schools are making decisions which ultimately constitute a racist act.

The Joseph Rowntree Foundation, as one of the many research and innovation projects it has supported, produced a school exclusions report, *Learning Partnerships Outside Mainstream Education* (Frankham *et al.* 2007). The project reported on how teachers, with assistance, worked with children and young people who have been excluded from school on a permanent basis. The project describes an approach with hard-to-reach children, young people and parents who experience poverty and multiple disadvantage coming from black and dual-heritage backgrounds. All have experienced a disproportionate number of permanent exclusions. The project team describe how they have thrown light on why there is disproportionality in exclusions, and how education and other agencies can work positively with children and parents most affected. The choice and quality of specialist staff is clearly an important factor, consultation with parents about provision, the 'specialist contribution of the black voluntary sector' and the need for continuing study and research are among the team's proposals. The project team started the project in the knowledge that black and dual-heritage children are three times more likely to be permanently excluded from school than other groups. The approach they recommend 'impacts positively on hard-to-reach children' because the approach requires adults to develop a relationship of care with a focus on social and emotional issues.

Out-of-date traditions

Between its election and the mid 1990s, the Conservative government had visited almost every bit of education. No institution from early years through to higher education went untouched. The urge to reform covered curriculum and assessment, school inspections, parental roles and teacher training. The intention of this modification of the education service was to establish the market ideology in education by promoting parental choice of their children's school. The second right-wing objective was to hand to central government the power to determine curriculum content and its assessment.

The control that local authorities and teachers formerly had over their schools was considerably reduced, and the possibility of a process of selection by ability was promoted under the guise of school diversity. The most obvious example of the latter being the assignation of a title which contained the specialist subject(s) delivered by a school which only a short time before had covered all subjects of the curriculum without the need to 'specialise'. The foregoing changes removed a state system which was moving in the direction of egalitarianism and transformed it into a competitive and divisive system of schooling. Clearly the system that was being replaced would benefit from some planned change, but instead, as Denis Lawton said, the new system was an enforcement of 'ideological prejudices and out of date traditions' (Lawton 1994: 102). The result of this change was that ethnic minorities, although they held high aspirations for their children, were less likely to get their children into schools with good examination results (Tomlinson 2008). Clearly the way that the racially and culturally diverse society was developing, and indeed had been propelled to some degree by the policy of the previous Conservative government, had changed colonial immigrants into black and Asian citizens; youthful citizens who were fit to complain about inequality and discrimination which they suffered in British society, their society. Citizens of the Muslim faith were also ready to assert their identity. Together they were discarding the label of the disadvantage and aspiring to the needs of members of a multi-ethnic society. To complete the picture, while the anti-racists and the multiculturalists were arguing about their aspirations, the media and the white majority were letting multiculturalism pass them by.

New Labour and schooling

The New Labour Party of 1997 was intent upon an identity for citizens which valued cultural diversity, and development of separate schooling was encouraged. This development of separate faith schools, however, tended to threaten the idea of multiculturalism which appeared to be failing both in society and in the education system. However, a significant moment in English race relations came with the publication of the Macpherson Report (1999), where at a public inquiry into the murder of Stephen Lawrence in April 1997 the issue of institutionalised racism was brought to public attention. The definition was based on the Metropolitan Police handling of the murder, where a public institution failed to provide equal, fair and just service to all groups in society. Four of the recommendations in the Macpherson Report related to education. The *Race Relations Act* (2000), for all public institutions, gave education the responsibility to monitor race equality treatment and its outcomes.

The development of education markets together with a wide-ranging selection of schools is more likely to be available to meet the demands of the school itself and to attract certain families which meet its needs and theirs. Ethnic minorities are likely in the main to come off worst in these circumstances since their location in an urban area plus their social status will go against them. The schools that are left for them to choose from will be less in demand, under-resourced and schooling children who are below average measured ability levels. Abbas' book concentrating on the education of British 'h Asians (Abbas 2004) in Birmingham, and using the grammar schools remaining, ...u a take-in thus in 2004: white – 68 per cent; Indian – 14 per cent; Pakistani – 7 per cent; African-Caribbean – 3 per cent; Bangladeshi – 1 per cent. The foregoing figures show that well-to-do Indians took advantage of their status and chose the selective grammar schools, while the Bangladeshis had to make do with local schools where, on the whole, aspirations were less ambitious and resources more restricted.

The newly elected Labour government put in place a number of proposed projects to make up for the previous neglect of pupils from low socio-economic groups. Specifically, the Labour government identified particular targets, conscious as they were of the concerns that ethnic minority parents were expressing about their children's education. Having seen the promise of the Academies programme and then been disappointed by the over-subscription to these selective schools, parents were clearly unhappy about the education provided. Among the projects set were Education Action Zones, set up in 1998, which six years later were amalgamated into Excellence in Cities. The latter was intended to satisfy minority-group parents who were locked into inner city areas that attainment via gifted and talented programmes would be given high priority. The new government also introduced in 1998 a National Childcare Strategy intending to create five million childcare places. There was some concern that in densely populated ethnic minority areas where need was greatest parents were less able to afford places. Craig's report (2007) concluded that local Sure Start programmes had not been as successful as required with minorities because the issue of ethnicity had not been successfully confronted. Further government initiatives to promote an improvement in the attainments of ethnic minority pupils were making scant progress. Gillborn and Mirza (2000) were invited to read 118 submissions on the Ethnic Minority Achievement Grant and the Youth Cohort study. Among a number of important findings was that ethnic minorities, with social class and gender controlled, still presented inequality in attainment.

What was emerging from the study of ethnic minority achievements in schooling was a fact which has been emerging over the years, namely that not all ethnic minority pupils under-achieve in comparison with the norm. In this respect there is additionally a concern for the lower school performance of white working class boys who, like the black, alienated boys of African-Caribbean descent, represent a neglected underclass, a group of under-achievers. Tomlinson (2008) draws attention to the continuing concern of black parents to improve their children's education and refers to a study which examines the support of black parents for their children. Cork (2005) studied five organisations that supported black parents 'and demonstrated the wider issues of institutional racism, cultural stereotyping and the impact of race and class on home school relations. She also showed the way the exclusion of black boys extended to the marginalization of their parents' (Cork 2005).

Conclusion

The education system has had the task of central player in the multicultural society of England since the mid twentieth century. While for a short period in the 1960s and

1970s there appeared to be a commitment to an egalitarian society via a rhetoric of equality of opportunity and a comprehensive system of, predominantly non-fee paying, state education. However, from the 1980s to the present day increasingly the intention has been to encourage a range of different schools at secondary level. The result is an education system supposedly based on meritocracy with equal opportunity for all. As a result of the foregoing the education system is producing greater inequality. Some of these schools have been enhanced by the authority to select their pupils; in effect to have first choice, while others have picked up remaining pupils, invariably children coming from the lower social strata and/or ethnic minority groups. The comprehensive system of the 1960s and 1970s was never given a chance as it strove alongside selective grammar schools which survived without too much fuss until the election of the Thatcher government, which applied the neo-liberal idea to schooling. Education then became a market commodity with the schools who had chosen their pupils in the past continuing to do so. The remainder of pupils, including most of the ethnic minorities, were allocated to less successful schools in urban locations. Some ethnic minority groups, for instance East African Asians, have come from a background of financial and cultural strength and are in a position to compete with the successful indigenous pupils. By comparison, the majority of black Caribbean children will have suffered due to a shortage of what the school perceives as cultural capital. Bangladeshi pupils will have suffered the same treatment. Certainly the lack of success in under-achieving groups is not due to any lack of effort or commitment. The preparation of teachers for work in the multi-ethnic society has not always been appropriate to needs In the mid 1980s most colleges or university departments for teacher training provided some multicultural education courses as teacher training began to realise the lack of experience, expertise and knowledge in a subject receiving considerable attention at the time. The LEAs had their multicultural adviser in post, and teacher training was quick to catch up by having the multicultural tutor in place. Multicultural education became a part of the teacher training syllabus for a while. However, the 1990s saw a decline in the national concern for multicultural education, and the early days of the OfSTED inspections attached little importance to the presence of multicultural education in the schools' curriculum.

The model of the education system for the multicultural society is a long way from realisation, and at the start of the 1990s the right-wing attacks on race equality and multicultural education in schools had eased considerably since interest appeared to be in decline. The presence of inequalities in schools have not been denied, but what has held back the possibility of proceeding towards a level playing field in education in Britain has been a collective insecurity about a shared national identity, with all that that might entail in a multicultural country. Where educationists should come in to help make schooling work for all in a multicultural society is difficult to achieve in a political climate where no consensus seems to be present. However, the complexity of this task means that the development of an education system which promises to be a unifying and successful experience for all pupils seems far from being realised. The reality is that the social status of families and the increasing variety and diversity of our schools combine to produce a range of experiences. We have the traditional private schools, schools acquired by businesses and faith schools. That looks to be an arrangement for diversity, selection, competition, different curricula and distinctly different ways of learning. The need for certain common values in a society together with a common curriculum would help in confronting issues such as racism and inequality which have been discussed here. What we have considered in the foregoing discussion should be seen to come from an ongoing debate on race, education and multiculturalism. Issues raised here continue to be refined and developed in literature and research, and the references have been selected with that purpose in mind.

References

Abbas, T. (2004) *The Education of British South Asians.* London: Palgrave-Macmillan.

Berliner, W. (2003) 'Gifted, but Black', *Education Guardian*, 14 October, p. 2.

Blair, M. and Bourne, J., with Coffin, C., Creese, A. and Kenner, C. (1998) *Making the Difference: Teaching and Learning Strategies in Successful Multiethnic Schools.* London: DfES.

Bourne, J., Bridges, L. and Searle, C. (1994) *Outcast England: How Schools Exclude Black Children.* London: Institute of Race Relations.

Carby, H. (ed.) (1982) *The Empire Strikes Back.* London: Hutchinson/Routledge.

Coard, B. (1971) *How the West Indian Child is Made Educationally Sub-Normal in the English Education System.* London: New Beacon Books.

Cork, L. (2005) *Supporting Black Pupils and Parents.* London: Routledge.

Cox, C.B. and Boyson, R. (1977) *Black Paper, 1997.* London: Temple-Smith.

Craig, G. (2007) *Sure Start and Black and Minority Ethnic Populations.* London: DfES.

Department for Education and Employment (DfEE) (1999) *The Youth Cohort Study.* London: HMSO.

Department for Education and Skills (DfES) (2003a) *Aiming High: Raising the Achievement of Gypsy Traveller Pupils.* London. DfES.

Department for Education and Skills (DfES) (2003b) *Exclusions 1997–2002.* London: DfES.

Department for Education and Skills (DfES) (2004a) *Aiming High: Understanding the Needs of Ethnic Minority Pupils in Mainly White Schools – A Guide to Good Practice.* London: DfES.

Department for Education and Skills (DfES) (2004b) *Aiming High: Guidance on Supporting the Education of Asylum Seeking and Refuge Children.* London: DfES.

Department for Education and Skills (DfES) (2004) *The Five Year Strategy for Children and Learners.* London: HMSO.

Department for Education and Skills (DfES) (2005) *Aiming High: Guidance on the Assessment of Pupils Learning English as an Additional Language.* London: DfES.

Department for Education and Skills (DfES) (2006) *Priority Review: Exclusion of Black Pupils. 'Getting It. Getting It Right'.* London: DfES.

Eysenck, H. (1971) *Race, Intelligence and Education.* London: Temple-Smith.

Fenton, S. (2010) *Ethnicity.* Cambridge: Polity Press.

Foster, P., Gomm, R. and Hammersley, M. (1996) *Constructing Educational Inequality.* London: Falmer Press.

Frankham, J., Edwards-Kerr, D., Humphrey, N. and Roberts, L. (2007) *School Exclusions: Learning Partnerships Outside Mainstream Education.* Manchester: University of Manchester Press.

Fuller, M. (1980) 'Black Girls in a London Comprehensive School', in Deem, R. (ed.), *Schooling for Women's Work.* London: Routledge and Kegan Paul.

Fuller, M. (1983) 'Black Girls in a London Comprehensive', in James, A. and Jeffcoate, R. (eds), *The School in the Multicultural Society.* London: Harper & Row.

Gillborn, D. (1990) *'Race', Ethnicity and Education.* London: Unwin Hyman.

Gillborn, D. (1995) *Racism and Antiracism in Real Schools.* Buckingham: Open University Press.

Gillborn, D. (2008) *Racism and Education: Coincidence or Conspiracy.* London: Routledge Falmer.

Gillborn, D. and Gipps, C. (1996) *Recent Research on the Achievement of Ethnic Minority Pupils.* London: HMSO.

Gillborn, D. and Mirza, H. (2000) *Education Inequality: Mapping 'Race', Class and Gender – A Synthesis of Research Evidence.* London: OfSTED.

Gillborn, D. and Youdell, D. (2000) *Rationing Education: Policy, Practice, Reform and Equity.* Buckingham: Open University Press.

Green, P. (1985) 'Multi-ethnic Teaching and Pupils' Self-concepts', in Department of Education and Science, *Education for All.* London: HMSO, Annex B.

Guillaumin, C. (1995) 'The Changing Face of "Race"', in Bulmer, M. and Solomos, J. (eds), *Racism.* Oxford: Oxford University Press.

Gundara, J. (2000) *Interculturalism, Education and Inclusion.* London: Paul Chapman.

Hatcher, R. (1997) 'New Labour, School Improvement and Racial Equality', *Multicultural Teaching*, 15 (3), 8–13.

Herrnstein, R.J. and Murray, C. (1994) *The Bell Curve: Intelligence and Class Structure in American Life.* New York: Free Press.

Jensen, A.R. (1969) 'How Much Can We Boost IQ and Scholastic Achievement?', *Harvard Educational Review* 39: 1–123.

Jensen, A. (1973) *Educability and Group Differences*, Cambridge, MA: Harvard Educational Review.

Kamin, L. (1977) *The Science and Politics of IQ.* Harmondsworth: Penguin.

Lawton, D. (1994) *The Tory Mind on Education.* London: Falmer.

Mabey, C. (1981) 'Black British Literacy', *Educational Research* 23 (2).

Mac an Ghaill, M. (1988) *Young, Gifted and Black.* Milton Keynes: Open University Press.

MacDonald, I., Bhavani, T., Khan, L. and John, G. (1989) *Murder in the Playground: The Report of the MacDonald Enquiry into Racism and Racial Violence in Manchester Schools.* London: Longsight Press.

MacPherson, W. (1999) *The Stephen Lawrence Inquiry: Report of an Inquiry.* London: HMSO.

Majors, R. (2001) *Educating Our Black Children.* London: Routledge Falmer.

Mason, D. (ed.) (2003) *Explaining Ethnic Differences: Changing Patterns of Disadvantage in Britain.* Bristol: The Policy Press.

Miles, R. and Brown, M. (2003) *Racism.* London: Routledge.

Mirza, H.S. (1992) *Young, Female and Black.* London: Routledge.

Montagu, A. (ed.) (1999) *Race and IQ.* New York: Oxford University Press.

Nei, M. and Roychoudhury, A.K. (1983) 'Genetic Relationship and Evolution of Human Races', *Evolutionary Biology* 14, 1–59.

OfSTED (1999) *Raising the Attainment of Minority Ethnic Pupils: School and LEA Responses.* London: HMSO.

Osler, A. (1997) *Education and Careers of Black Teachers.* Maidenhead: Open University Press.

Osler, A. and Morrison, M. (2000) *Inspecting Schools for Racial Equality: OfSTED's Strengths and Weaknesses.* Stoke on Trent: Trentham Books.

Ratcliffe, P. (2009) *'Race', Ethnicity and Difference.* Maidenhead: Open University Press.

Report of the Committee of Enquiry into the Education of Handicapped Children and Young People (The Warnock Report) (1978). London: HMSO

Sivanandan, A. (1982) *A Different Hunger.* London: Pluto.

Sivanandan, A. (1988) *Communities of Resistance.* London: Verso.

Sivanandan, A. (2000) *Macpherson and After.* London: Institute of Race Relations.

Smith, D. and Tomlinson, S. (1989) *The School Effect: A Study of Multiracial Comprehensives.* London: Policy Studies Institute.

Smith, Z. (2000) *White Teeth.* London: Penguin Books.

Swann Report (1985) *Education for All: Report of the Committee of Inquiry into the Education of Children from Minority Ethnic Groups.* London: HMSO.

Tomlinson, S. (1980) 'Ethnic Minority Parents and Education', in Craft, M., Raynor, J., and Cohen, L. (eds), *Linking Home and School*, 3rd edition. London: Harper and Row.

Tomlinson, S. (2008) *Race and Education: Policy and Politics in Britain.* Maidenhead: Macgraw-Hill Education/Open University Press.

Troyna, B. and Ball, W. (1985) *Views from the Chalk Face: School Responses to an LEA's Multicultural Education Policy.* Coventry: ESRC/Centre for Research in Ethnic Relations.

Troyna, B. and Carrington, B. (1990) *Education, Racism and Reform.* London: Routledge.

Wright, C. (1986) 'School Processes: An Ethnographic Study', in Egglestone, J., Dunn, D. and Anjali, M. (eds) *Education for Some: The Educational and Vocational Experiences of 15–18 Year Old Members of Minority Ethnic Groups.* Stoke: Trentham Books.

Wright, C. (1992) *Race Relations in the Primary School.* London: David Fulton.

Youdell, D. (2003) 'Identity Traps or How Black Students Fail: The Interactions between Biographical, Sub-cultural, and Learner Identities', *British Journal of the Sociology of Education* 24 (1), 2–20.

20

Schooling and social class

Michael Wyness

The history of all hitherto existing society is the history of class struggles.

Marx and Engels ([1848] 1985: 79)

Introduction

Much has been written about the demise of social class and other meta-narratives such as gender and nationality. The advent of consumerism and globalisation and the decline of Marxism as a political and intellectual force worldwide have at the very least complicated the view that our social positions, identities and affiliations are governed by conventional material differences. Similarly, within education, the conventional view that children of different class backgrounds are mapped onto different class trajectories as they move through the school system has been challenged by an educational establishment committed to raising the standards of all children and ensuring that at least half of all young people have access to higher education.

However, despite the rise of the 'individual' and the overall economic well-being of many developed countries, material differences between groups within society are widening. In a UNICEF report on the state of the world's children it was reported

> that the proportion of children living in poverty in the developed world has risen in 17 out of the 24 OECD nations for which data are available. No matter which of the commonly used poverty measures is applied, the situation of children has deteriorated over the last decade.
>
> (UNICEF 2006: 235)

The previous UK Labour government made the reduction of child poverty a key plank of its social policy on coming to power in 1997. The current Conservative–Liberal government took office in June 2010 and renewed the commitment to tackling child poverty. However, the UK still has one of the highest rates of child poverty among developed countries, and the government's target of halving the child poverty by 2010/2011 has not been met (Department for Work and Pensions 2012). Policies more generally designed to tackle social inequality have been unable to reverse the widening gap between the richest and poorest sectors of society (Wheeler *et al.* 2005).

In the past few years unemployment has risen significantly, inflation has eroded the incomes of the poorest paid and the recent tightening up of the welfare system makes it very unlikely that the gap between the rich and the poor will be substantially reduced (Harkness *et al.* 2012)

This chapter examines social inequality as a continuing feature within the UK. It focuses on the role that education and schooling play in England and Wales in reinforcing these trends, while at the same time identifying the way that current governments have used social and educational policy to tackle child poverty and social inequality.[1] In the first section we explore the contention that despite generating policies that set out to equalise conditions for all children, social class differences between children are reinforced through the education system. In the second section we examine a number of factors that mediate the relationship between the children, the school and their future class identities. Among other things we discuss the relationship between the child and the curriculum, the influence of the family and the countervailing importance of the peer group as social frame of reference for particular groups of working-class children. In the final section we analyse government policy and highlight the ambiguous relationship between education policy and social class.

Social class and its reproduction

One approach to researching social inequality is to look at how social class differences are reproduced from generation to generation. In the 1950s and 1960s in the UK there was an expectation that the links between children's class of origin and their social class of destination would be broken as the state invested heavily in trying to ensure that working-class children had opportunities to become socially mobile. Despite these political and economic commitments, the evidence during this period suggested that there was limited movement between the social classes (Halsey *et al.* 1980). More recently, longitudinal studies that follow large samples of children from birth into adulthood corroborate these findings, and report a generational transmission of disadvantage. The Centre for Longitudinal Studies (CLS) at the University of London draws on birth cohort studies from the 1958 National Child Development Study and the 1970 British Cohort Study in making more explicit links between the child's social class of origin and their social class of destination. Researchers referred to size of family, housing and income as indicators of social disadvantage. Drawing on these indicators, they argue that as children get older social disadvantages persist, with 16-year-olds just as likely to experience similar levels of poverty as when they were aged 11, and 'poor' teenagers remaining in poverty once they reach adulthood and well into their thirties (Blanden and Gibbons 2006)

Schooling and social class reproduction

Schooling and education tend to reinforce these class-based trends. A recent Joseph Rowntree report identified relatively poor levels of educational success associated with whether a pupil was entitled to free school meals, parents' employment status, family structure and parents' level of educational qualifications (Cassen and Kingdom 2007). According to 2010 figures, around one-fifth of the poorest 20 per cent of the population managed to gain five or more GCSEs at A*–C grade, as opposed to 75 per cent of children from the most affluent 20 per cent of the school population (Goodman and Gregg 2010). If we refer more specifically to those children receiving free school meals the figure is 25 per cent (DfES 2006).

Recent research has combined assessments of young children's development with socio-economic data in accurately predicting the level of educational attainment by the age of 26 (reported in Evans 2006). The Millennium Cohort Study also focuses on the early years, with language and cognitive development markedly different for children from poorer backgrounds compared with their more affluent counterparts (CLS 2007). The researchers place particular emphasis on a child's 'school readiness', with children from families in poverty up to a year behind more affluent children by the time they reach three and thus less able to engage with the culture and expectations of the early years of primary school.

The relationship between social class and education is a complex one. Ethnicity, for example, is a powerful intervening variable. Social disadvantage is a complex idea, with ethnicity as well as social class being a significant factor. Both factors combined suggest, for example, that a small group of middle-class Afro-Caribbean pupils will do better than their working-class counterparts. However, Afro-Caribbean pupils are the lowest attaining of ethnic minority groupings if we look simply at all middle-class pupils (Gillborn and Safia Mirza 2000). Children of Pakistani and Bangladeshi origins are seen as being particularly vulnerable due to English being a second language. Other research suggests that this is likely to be a short-term problem, with African and Asian children catching up to white children by the time they get to secondary school (Cassen and Kingdom 2007). Nevertheless, educational failure is likely to be located in poor urban areas where there is a predominance of families of Bangladeshi, Pakistani and Caribbean origins.

Class, schooling and the relational dimension

The broader picture of social inequality and schooling tends to focus on material factors such as income, health and employment status. If we draw on social and cultural influences, what we might call relational criteria, we can build up a more subtle and multi-layered understanding of how schooling contributes to the reproduction of inequality. Moreover, a closer look at the everyday lives of thousands of school children and their families reveals an intermingling of social and cultural as well as economic factors that complicate and on occasion contradict the broader picture.

The child and the curriculum

Children's relationship to knowledge through the school curriculum can have a significant effect on their ability to thrive in school. Middle-class children are better equipped to engage with the curriculum than working-class pupils. For middle-class children there is a seamless link between their own lives and interests and school-based knowledge, which is abstract and formal in nature. Knowledge here becomes an end in itself: middle-class children find it easier to enter into an intellectual world of abstract ideas that connect with their own affiliations and identities. Given this relationship between middle-class pupils and the curriculum there is a tendency to take a more negative view with respect to working-class children, with the latter alienated from the school curriculum. Hatcher (2000) argues that the curriculum does not connect with working-class children's everyday lives and relations with their families, as their experiences are more likely to be shaped by more immediate influences from the community and the street. And in some respects working-class children enter an alien environment when they go to school. However, the curriculum also offers more tangible rewards. The dominant ideas and conceptual tools that make up the curriculum can be grasped by working-class children as a means of gaining qualifications. While this still puts working-class children at a disadvantage in the classroom, it does at the very least suggest one possible route to educational achievement for children who lack the cultural means to progress throughout their school careers

Cultural and social capital

The family has been a key resource in both reinforcing and challenging the relationship between 'origins and destinations' since Douglas' (1967) classic analysis of family influences in education in the early 1960s. However, it is the persuasive, if at times opaque, force of Bourdieu's (1997; see also Bourdieu and Waquant 1992) theory of social and cultural capital that locates the family as a primary force in class reproduction. There is still the recourse to material factors in trying to explain the differential education outcomes for working-class and middle-class children. But cultural and social factors are drawn on in explaining how these material differences are passed on generationally.

Social and cultural capital are in many respects the intangible resources that parents and communities pass on to their children. Middle-class parents, in particular, invest these resources by socialising their children into the dominant culture. Social capital consists of the contacts, social networks and friendships that constitute the everyday social relations people possess. The social networks inhabited by middle-class parents, such as the golf club, the private housing estate and the parent–teacher association give them social advantages in providing their children with a wider range of opportunities and a more appropriate social frame of reference as their children progress through the school system.

Bourdieu's (1997) notion of cultural capital is more diffuse in that it includes levels of educational qualification as well as a more embodied notion that includes dispositions, attitudes and speech patterns. In effect an individual's identity and personality reflects their social class position. Thus our taste in music, our dress code, even the way that we carry ourselves in public, all demonstrate in a number of ways our social class and differentiate us from others. But again unlike more conventional Marxist analyses where personal attributes are either ignored or inferred from economic status, an individual has to work at displaying their cultural capital. A more nuanced analysis here focuses on these personal habits and predispositions in terms of the notion of 'habitus'. Bourdieu argues that these cultural resources are deployed by middle-class parents in maintaining their class positions and passed on to their children through processes of socialisation.

In effect what we are saying here is that educational success and failure are governed by parents' access to these social and cultural resources. Unlike more conventional Marxist analyses that emphasise the relative positions of people within the social structure, there is an important relational or interactive component to the theory. In a conventional Marxist sense parents possess their 'capital', but they also need to invest it How they use these resources has important consequences for their children's life chances. Thus working-class children fail because their parents have limited access to the above resources, whereas, middle-class children are more likely to succeed because their parents are in tune with dominant modes of thought and speech found within the school and have the right social frames of reference.

Lareau's (1989) seminal research on the relationship between US families and elementary or primary schools refers to the significance of cultural and social capital in terms of parents' relative 'connectedness'. Applying Bourdieu's model to a class analysis of parental involvement in their children's schooling, she refers to three key dimensions: the extent to which parents see education as a teacher's responsibility; the level of parental support at home for their children's schooling; and the extent to which both parents are reference points when the school comes into contact with the family.

Middle-class parents are said to be more connected to their children's schooling in that they see themselves as being jointly responsible for their children's education with the school; they are likely to 'speak the same language' as teachers and take a more informed and structured interest in their school work; and both parents are likely to get involved with their children's schooling. Not only do middle-class parents take a greater interest in their children's educational progress, they are more informed and more sceptical of educational issues. Relations between working-class parents and the school, on the other hand, are characterised by 'separateness'. Their children's education is seen as the school's responsibility, their interests in their children's schooling is sporadic and largely concerned with social and emotional rather than 'educational' issues, and mothers tend to take sole parental responsibility when it comes to getting in contact with schools. From the school's vantage point this perceived lack of parental responsibility for their children's education is seen as an obstacle to teachers in terms of delivering the curriculum and supporting children's educational and social development (Connell *et al.* 1982). Moreover, this lack of responsibility is rarely viewed as a social class problem in school, with teachers more likely to perceive it as an individual failing on the part of the parent and thus compounding the parent's sense of separateness from the school (Reay 2006).

Parents and risk management

The work of Stephen Ball and his colleagues (Ball *et al.* 1995; Ball 2003) has linked Bourdieu's theory to contemporary UK educational policy. The introduction of a quasi-market in education in the late 1980s and the rise of an audit culture have placed more importance on the role of the parent as an educational consumer: 'The new culture of schooling, a culture of commodification and output indicators which articulates with the culture of choice and relative advantage into which parents are being drawn' (Ball *et al.* 1995: 65–66). While middle-class parents' access to the different forms of capital gives them a clear advantage in comparison with working-class parents, these market opportunities have placed particular strains on the former as they attempt to retain if not improve their social class position. Parents here become risk managers and invest their cultural and social capital in trying to minimise the chances of their children's academic failure. The key point in their children's academic careers is the last year of primary school. Middle-class parents are now more likely to regulate their children's futures by searching the internet for information about the best state secondary schools, 'naturalising' their children's entry into higher education, spending far more time visiting prospective schools and networking with those who are likely to have some local influence in school choice. Middle-class parents are, in general, investing far more of their economic, social and cultural capital in their children's futures. Ball (2003) refers to the emotional and psychological costs: parents report higher levels of anxiety as they commit themselves to 'doing the right thing' for their children. They also refer to the guilt sometimes felt at not being able to make the right choice for their children.

Ball and his colleagues (1995), in an earlier piece of work, distinguish between different 'circuits of choice' that map on to middle-class and working-class households. Parent choice is part of a decision-making strategy undertaken by all parents in one way or another when their child is about to enter secondary school. Middle-class parents have a wider range of schools from which to choose, including in some cases schools in the private sector. They are also in a position to prioritise school choice over other family commitments. They have the time, space and material resources to make 'strategic' choices. Working-class parents, on the other hand, are constrained by time and social geography: getting their children to a more distant school is likely to be a problem if there is limited transport or the school timetable does not mesh with their own domestic or work timetables. Ball *et al.* (1995) argue that working-class parents have to make 'accommodative' choices: they are constrained by local circumstances and their own experience of schooling, which may be less sanguine than their middle-class counterparts' experiences.

Family dynamics and school readiness

While educationalists have acknowledged the school as a socialising domain, social scientists have tended to emphasise the family as the primary socialising agency, with parents being the most formative influence on their children, particularly in the early years (Wyness 2012). This assumption is reinforced on a daily basis by primary school teachers who continually refer to their pupils as the products of their parents. In an early analysis of home–school relations Sharp and Green (1975: 86) argue that primary school teachers generally expect parents to provide them with 'school trained child[ren]', children who have been socialised by their parents such that they easily take on their new roles as pupils in the first few months of their schooling. Their analysis of 'school readiness' confirmed the view that parents with limited social and cultural capital are less likely to be able to produce 'school trained children'. Consequently, teachers are more likely to spend their time managing working-class children's behaviour in class than providing them with a formal education that prepares them for their later school years.

More recently, Gillian Evans' (2006) in her ethnography of working-class life in South London explores the dynamics between parents and children and observes that 'formal learning plays little part in the way that caring relationships are established at home' (2006: 45). Working-class family values conflict with expectations found in school: the lack of school 'readiness' and 'connectedness' here being seen as an important factor in children's educational failure in later years. Thus working-class children are more likely to spend their non-school time on non-educational activities; they are less likely to be pushed by their parents, particularly when they claim to dislike school. Education is effectively seen as a separate sphere of activity associated with what goes on within the school.

Peer group

A final mediating factor is the peer group. The relations that children and young people have with their peers are more likely to be correlated with levels of crime and delinquency (Muncie 2004) However, poverty is often conceptualised in terms of social exclusion which refers to a cluster of risk factors that include educational and public order criteria. There are also a number of well-known pieces of research that link school disaffection among young males to social class and the reproduction of inequality. Thus the work of Willis (1977), Corrigan (1979) and Mac an Ghaill (1988) all argue that the peer group in some way or another both underpins educational failure and provides an alternative set of values that compensates for a young working-class male's anticipated educational failure.

More recent research locates the street and the peer culture as a dominant social and moral frame of reference for many young men in inner city areas. Evans (2006), for example, argues that charismatic rebel peers provide alternative role models for young boys in the absence of appropriate adult male role models in school and where discipline is a problem in some schools and classrooms. The street becomes the location for the development of reputation and social identity: the site where conventional rules on what is appropriate behaviour are inverted:

> Rather than making their behaviour seem pathological, my proposal is for research that might help us begin to understand how it is that young boys in certain kinds of social situations, like on the street and in failing schools, can come to structure their relations with one another in such a way that troublesome, violent and intimidating behaviour becomes a social good.
>
> (Evans 2006: 115)

Evans' research is an ethnography of family life in a local setting and there is no attempt to generalise her data to other young males brought up in similar urban working-class areas in the UK. Nevertheless, within this context we might speculate that school rules, the curriculum, examinations and the compulsory nature of schooling are unlikely to connect with everyday lives of many working-class boys. Other rules and conventions generated in the peer group become more compelling. This view is corroborated by Horgan (2007): findings from her study of primary school-aged children's experiences of poverty in Northern Ireland identify levels of 'disenchantment' from schooling at around the ages of nine and ten among boys from disadvantaged backgrounds. The peer group can act as a conflicting source for young boys that challenges the dominant expectations around schooling, making it more difficult for them to commit themselves to the educational project.

Tackling inequality

Bucking the trend

While the research emphasis has been on trying to establish the relationship between social class inequality and educational achievement, the political context in Britain from the late 1990s until the change of the UK government in 2010 has been one of challenging the deterministic relationship between origins and destinations through the introduction of policies of social inclusion. Contemporary research agendas to some extent have reflected this policy approach. Thus the CLS research not only focuses on the intergenerational transmission of inequality, it also looks at factors that break this cycle of disadvantage. Key factors here in producing 'resilience in the face of adversity' are linked to the parents' positive relationship to education and their children's schooling. Thus the ability of working-class parents to provide a more educationally stimulating home environment for their children (CLS 2007: 2) reduces the risk of them falling into poverty in adulthood. Children from working-class backgrounds are also more likely to do well in school if both parents are involved in supporting their children's education, and where children's schooling is integrated into the routines of domestic life within households. For Blanden and Gibbons (2006) reading was a particularly important domestic activity, with working-class parents being in a stronger position to 'buck the trend' if they read regularly to their children. Parental aspirations are also important here: working-class parents who invest emotionally as well as materially in their children's futures are often driven by a desire to see their children move into higher education (Goodman and Gregg 2010)

UK government policy: challenging inequality

During the tenure of the recent Labour government attempts were made to limit these social class inequalities in education with a view to reducing levels of poverty and social exclusion. While the previous Conservative administration promoted the role of the *individual* in and against the broader society, the Labour Party on coming to power in 1997 made clear undertakings to improving the life chances of particular *groups* within society. The commitment to reducing child poverty, and the setting up of the social exclusion unit to tackle a range of social problems from racism through to teenage pregnancy, were expected to have a significant impact on the well-being of young working-class children. Education Action Zones were created in 1999 in areas where schools were underperforming. With a mixture of support from local businesses and community and parents, schools within these areas were expected to 'create a culture of expectation, achievement and opportunity in areas of significant social and economic disadvantage' (Birmingham City Council 2007: n.p.).

Preschool children were also targeted, with children from the age of three onwards given free access to early years education through the childcare system. There are also a number of initiatives designed to tackle inequalities between families, giving young children from all social class backgrounds the opportunity to thrive within the formal school sector. Children's centres have been opened up in most communities across the UK through the *Sure Start* initiative (Glass 1999). The most recent government child-related project, *Every Child Matters*, offers a more integrated institutional approach to supporting children's physical social and educational well-being. Schools are now to work alongside the health and social services in offering more holistic support for children and their families. While evaluations of Sure Start have identified its failure to reach the most excluded families and communities (Ward 2007), there is undoubtedly here a commitment to equality of opportunity at preschool level with 'school readiness' being seen as a crucial precondition of educational success for working-class children.

The current Conservative–Liberal coalition government has a less consistent approach to tackling inequality. This is partly due to the global economic crisis, which has restricted investment in social and infrastructure projects. While there is a continued commitment to early years education, cuts in funding have taken place in Sure Start, the continued expansion of Children's Centres has slowed down and the *Every Child Matters* initiative has been removed from the policy agenda (Phillips 2011). While it is a little early to assess the coalition government's record on poverty and schooling, the Conservatives, the dominant coalition partner, are less ideologically committed to tackling inequality, with a focus on more conventional 'right-wing' issues such as the market provision for schooling and school discipline.

Government policy: reinforcing inequalities

Despite the previous Labour government's commitment to greater social inclusion, there are important continuities with the earlier Conservative emphasis on individual differences, which arguably reinforce existing social class differences in terms of opportunities and outcomes. The Conservative's earlier attempts to create a quasi-market in education emphasised the role of the individual parent as a consumer of their children's education, with parental choice being promoted against the 'collectivist' powers of the educational establishment, including local education authorities (LEAs) (Whitty 1992). Market values imply a differentiated educational product. Thus the introduction of the City Technical Colleges and 'grant maintained' schools, the retention of grammar schools and the long-held commitment to the private sector created the impression that all parents had a choice of where to send their children when they left primary school. The Labour government extended this approach by introducing foundation schools with subject specialisms, self-governing independent state schools and city academies alongside existing LEA community schools and the government's expansion of the range of faith schools. Moreover, one of the centre pieces of the current coalition government's education policy is the expansion of academies and free schools, which get their funding directly from central government thus bypassing allegedly more bureaucratic LEAs. In principle, all existing primary and secondary schools in England and Wales can apply for academy status and parents can apply to set up their own 'free schools'.

Notable in terms of social class differences are three things. First, as with the previous Conservative and Labour educational regimes, the current government is expanding not simply a market in schooling, but a new hierarchy of schools within the state sector. Specialist schools, city academies and trust schools are being created ostensibly to bring 'more choice and higher standards' but are arguably creating distinctive choices for middle-class parents committed to maintaining their class positions (*BBC News*, 30 November 2006: 1). In creating academies the current government has prioritised schools rated highly by OfSTED, the body that inspects schools. This may have the effect of reinforcing social and economic differences between the high-achieving schools predominantly found in more affluent areas, and less successful schools in more disadvantaged areas.

Second, there is the government's ambivalence towards grammar schools. While there are supporters of grammar schools in the coalition and former Labour governments, there is a fear among proponents of grammar schools that the new academies will usurp the notion of the grammar school as a powerful means of moving the bright working-class child up the social and economic hierarchy ('Academies Bill puts grammar schools at risk, say Tory MPs', *London Evening Standard*, 21 July 2010). The process of introducing more socially inclusive comprehensive schools in the 1960s and 1970s was never completed, with a number of LEAs retaining a hierarchical distinction between 'academic' grammars and other state schools. Thus, far from acting as conduit of social mobility, Chitty (1999) provides evidence that the existence of grammar schools, predominantly populated by middle-class children, has a depressing effect on exam results of other surrounding state schools. Schools in areas without grammar schools do far better than their counterparts in areas with grammar schools. Third, as was noted earlier, it is only parents living in more affluent areas that have the economic, social and cultural capital to take advantage of this choice in secondary schooling. While middle-class parents have greater social and cultural capital, they also tend to live in areas where their local schools tend to be those with the best reputations. Middle-class parents are thus in a much stronger position to take advantage of the policy on 'free schools'.

Individual differences within the classroom

Differentiation also takes place within schools. The Labour Party rejected its long-held support of mixed-ability teaching after the 1997 election: 'The modernisation of the comprehensive principle requires that all pupils are encouraged to progress as far and as fast as they are able. Grouping children by ability can be an important way of making that happen' (Tony Blair quoted in Carvel 1996: 7).

The current coalition government has had less to say about grouping by ability or 'setting' since coming to power. Nevertheless, the Conservatives have been long-time proponents of differentiation by ability. Grouping by ability is standard practice in most UK schools. In most developed countries the teaching of mixed-ability groupings of pupils is the norm, and, as Boaler (2005) notes, ability groupings have fateful consequences for the great majority of children. Eighty-eight per cent of children placed in groups or sets at the age of four continue in the same sets until they leave school. The emphasis on setting generates low expectations among children within lower-status groupings, which work their way through the education system in terms of relatively poor levels of achievement. Moreover, Boaler's research reinforces the link between educational outcomes and social class origins; children taught within mixed-ability classrooms are more likely to do well in school than children taught in single-ability groupings (Boaler 2005). Boaler's work on learning strategies and social class connects with large-scale comparisons of national education systems that suggest the UK, despite its relatively high standard of living, has one of the most unequal education systems compared with other developed countries (Green 2003).

Conclusion

The previous Labour government policy on education acted in a contradictory manner when challenging the problem of social inequality within the UK. As Clyde Chitty (1999) argues, '[T]here are obvious contradictions involved in affirming a commitment to "social justice" and "community" while, at the same time, pursuing competitive market policies in education.' The current coalition government, on the other hand, has taken a more neo-liberal approach to education, expressing fewer obligations to challenging social inequality.

Both governments have vigorously pursued the 'school improvement' agenda which emphasises improving educational standards for all children. In the past few years there have been rising levels of educational performance across the board, particularly in relation to the GCSE examinations taken by 15- and 16-year-olds (*BBC News*, 25 August 2007). However, the educational outcomes of all children tell us very little about the relative differences between groups of children. Hatcher (2000: 184) distinguishes between 'polarising improvement' and 'equalising improvement'. The emphasis on absolute standards has led to the polarising of outcomes for pupils with middle-class pupils and schools doing proportionately better than pupils in working-class areas. While there may be some 'equalising' outcomes in that some schools in deprived areas have been able to take advantage of educational changes, the great majority of children from poor areas have limited opportunities to improve their chances of educational success (Mortimore and Whitty 1997). In many respects many of the initiatives designed to improve the life chances of working-class children, particularly in the early years, are very likely to be monopolised by middle-class parents.

As we have seen in this chapter, material factors still shape the relationship between different groups of pupils within the English and Welsh education system. However, the relationship between social class and education is a complex one. A closer 'micro' analysis of the lives and experiences of young people and their families reveals a number of mediating factors that provide a nuanced account of how class inequality is reproduced from generation to generation. Social and cultural factors are critical, with parents playing a crucial role in acting as a conduit between the child and the education system. How parents understand, experience and relate to the education system has an important bearing on children's life chances. As we have tried to demonstrate, middle-class parents have a number of advantages over their working-class counterparts in ensuring that their children are educationally successful.

Note

1. While the broad trends are similar across the UK, the chapter will only discuss education in England and Wales. There is a quite different education system in Scotland and there are notable differences in assessment in Northern Ireland.

References

Ball, S. (2003) *Class strategies and the education market: the middle classes and social advantage*, London: RoutledgeFalmer.

Ball, S., Bowe, R. and Gewirtz, S. (1995) Circuits of schooling: a sociological exploration of parental choice of school in social class contexts, *Sociological Review*, 43, 1, 52–78.

BBC News 24 (2007) GCSE results rise at all grades, 25 August http://news.bbc.co.uk/1/hi/education/4182006.stm, accessed 25 April 2014.

Birmingham City Council (2007) Education Action Zones, www.services.bgfl.org/services/eic/eazs, accessed 25 April 2014.

Blanden, J. and Gibbons, S. (2006) *The persistence of poverty across generations*, Bristol: Policy Press.

Boaler, J. (2005) The 'psychological prisons' from which they never escaped: the role of ability grouping in reproducing social class inequalities, *Forum*, 47, 2–3, 135–143.

Bourdieu, P. (1997) The forms of capital, in: A.H. Halsey, H. Lauder, P. Brown and A. Wells (eds), *Education, culture and economy and society*, Oxford: Oxford University Press.

Bourdieu, P. and Wacquant, L. (1992) *An invitation to reflexive sociology*, Cambridge: Polity.

Cassen, R. and Kingdom, G. (2007) *Tackling low educational achievement*, York: Joseph Rowntree Foundation.

Centre for Longitudinal Studies (CLS) (2007) The intergenerational transmission of disadvantage and advantage, *CLS Briefings* February, www.cls.ioe.ac.uk, accessed 25 April 2014.

Chitty, C. (1999) The comprehensive ideal, in: C. Chitty and J. Dunford (eds), *State Schools: New Labour and the Conservative Legacy*, London: Frank Cass.

Connell, W., Ashenden, D., Kessler, S. and Dowsett, G. (1982) *Making the difference: schools, families and social division*, London: George Allen and Unwin.

Corrigan, P. (1979) *Schooling the Smash Street kids*, London: Macmillan.

Department for Education and Science (DfES) (2006) *Social mobility: narrowing social class educational attainment gaps*, http://webarchive.nationalarchives.gov.uk/20130401151655/http://www.educa-tion.gov.uk/researchandstatistics/statistics/allstatistics/a00195182/social-mobility-narrowing-educational-social-class, accessed 25 April 2014.

Department for Work and Pensions (2012) *Statistics*, available at http://statistics.dwp.gov.uk/asd/index.php?page=hbai, accessed 20 November 2013.

Douglas, J.W.B. (1967) *The home and the school*, London: Panther.

Evans, G. (2006) *Educational failure and working class white children in Britain*, Basingstoke: Palgrave.

Gillborn, D. and Safia Mirza, H. (2000) *Educational inequality: mapping race, class and gender*, London: OfSTED.

Glass, N. (1999) Sure Start: the development of an early intervention programme for young children in the United Kingdom, *Children and Society*, 13, 257–264.

Goodman, A. and Gregg, P. (eds) (2010) *Poorer children's educational attainment: how important are atti-tudes and behaviours?* London: Joseph Rowntree Foundation.

Green, A. (2003) Is UK education exceptionally unequal? Evidence from the IAALS and PISA surveys, *Forum*, 45, 2, 67–70.

Halsey, A.H., Heath, A. and Ridge, J. (1980) *Origins and Destinations*, Oxford: Clarendon Press.

Harkness, S., Gregg, P. and MacMillan, L. (2012) *Poverty: the role of institutions, behaviours and cultures*, Joseph Rowntree Foundation, www.jrf.org.uk/sites/files/jrf/poverty-culture-behaviour-full.pdf, accessed 25 April 2014.

Hatcher, R. (2000) 'Social class and school: relationships to knowledge', in M. Cole (ed.), *Education, equality and human rights*, London: Routledge.

Horgan, G. (2007) *The impact of poverty on young children's experience of school*, London: Joseph Rown-tree Foundation.

Lareau, A. (1989) *Home advantage: social class and parental intervention in elementary schools*, London: Falmer.

Mac an Ghaill, M. (1988) *Young gifted and black: student–teacher relations in the schooling of black youth*, Milton Keynes: Open University Press.

Marx, K. and Engels, F. ([1848] 1985) *The Communist manifesto*, Harmondsworth: Penguin.

Mortimore, P. and Whitty, G. (1997) *Can school improvement overcome the effects of disadvantage?* London: Institute of Education.

Muncie, J. (2004) *Youth and crime*, second edition, London: Sage.

Phillips, L. (2011) Sure Start funding 'must be ring-fenced to save children's centres, *Public Finance*, 7 April.

Reay, D. (2006) The zombie stalking English schools: social class and educational inequality, *British Journal of Educational Studies*, 54, 3, 288–307.

Sharp, R. and Green, A. (1975) *Education and social control*, London: Routledge and Keegan Paul.

UNICEF (2006) Child poverty in rich countries, 2005, Part I, *International Journal of Health Services*, 36, 2, 235–269.

Ward, J. (2007) Sure Start failing ethnic minorities, says report, *Guardian Unlimited*, 10 July, www.the-guardian.com/uk/2007/jul/10/race.earlyyearseducation, accessed 25 April 2014.

Wheeler, B., Shaw, M., Mitchell, R. and Dorling, D. (2005) *Life in Britain: using millennial census data to understand poverty, inequality and place*, Bristol: The Policy Press.

Whitty, G. (1992) Education, economy and national culture, in R. Bocock and K. Thompson (eds) *Social and cultural forms of modernity*, Cambridge: Polity.

Willis, P. (1977) *Learning to labour*, Farnborough: Saxon House.

Wyness, M. (2012) *Childhood and society*, second edition, Basingstoke: Palgrave.

Gender in education

Jane Martin

When Marjorie was eleven and I nearly eight we were transferred to Pontefract and District Girls' High School. It had been opened shortly after the war to provide secondary education for girls, and at the laying of the foundation stone County Councillor E. Talbot, chairman of the West Riding Higher Education Sub-Committee pontificated on what this should involve. The aim of girls' schools, he told an appreciative audience, should be 'the production of womanliness'.

Barbara Castle (1994: 11)

These are the words of Barbara Castle, born in 1910, in Chesterfield, Derbyshire, arguably the most prominent woman politician in the history of the British Labour Party. The purpose in quoting them at the start is to draw attention to the assumption that an individual's education should be determined by his or her gender. In this chapter I take the long view of differences in educational provision, opportunities and achievements between boys and girls, to try to make sense of current key issues. The narrative is constructed around the use of autobiographical vignettes and empirical research, which is intended to present the groundwork for thinking about forms of policy and forms of equity, rather than an attempt to provide a detailed and comprehensive picture. My intention is to focus on a set of relationships between gender and education, to sketch some of the ambivalences around educational and curricular developments.

In her 1792 classic, *A Vindication of the Rights of Women*, Mary Wollstonecraft asked: what kind of education must women have to become the equals of men? She looked at education from the standpoint of the individual but her vision of equal opportunities did not find favour at a time when the education of children was organised along the lines of social class. In Britain, state intervention into and provision of education developed in the nineteenth century as a response to the requirements of the economy, the social and political problems of the urban working classes (following mass migration into the cities), concerns about empire and 'national efficiency' and the question of the role of the Churches in education. Elementary education was associated with the working class, and secondary education, which was not confined to the three Rs of reading, writing and arithmetic – plus needlework for girls (when the boys did extra maths) – was associated with the middle class.

The 1870 *Education Act* 'plugged the gaps' in the existing system of elementary schooling, which at that point was largely provided by small, private schools (commonly known as 'dame schools'), church societies and voluntary organisations. The Act provided for the development of state elementary schools run by directly elected local school boards (Martin 1999). A system of inspection had been introduced in 1862 based on 'payment by results'. Essentially, this meant that the size of the government grant paid to individual schools was calculated on the basis of how well pupils performed when they were examined annually by an inspector. Payment by results remained in place until 1897. In cities the 'ideal' elementary or board school had different entrances for the sexes, as well as separate playgrounds and separate departments for children aged seven and over.

Family culture provided a rationale for the ways in which girls and women experienced formal and informal schooling and education. Working-class girls often acted as surrogate 'wives' and 'little mothers' on washdays, or if their mother was ill or having a baby (Dyhouse 1981; Davin 1996). Overall there were fewer school places for girls. Middle-class girls were largely educated for the marriage market and Wollstonecraft did not consider the frivolous education they received as any education. Emmeline Pankhurst, born 1858, who led the British suffragette campaign for the vote, records that: 'My parents, especially my father, discussed the question of my brothers' education as a matter of real importance. My education and that of my sister were scarcely discussed at all' ([1914] 1979: 5–6). Likewise, Emily Davies (born 1830, who led campaigns for access to secondary and higher education for women) resented the fact that whereas her brothers all attended private public schools for the ruling class followed by Trinity College, Cambridge she only received a limited education. This included a brief spell at a day school supplemented by occasional paid lessons in languages and music.

State schools had to prepare children to earn their own livings and be useful citizens, but there were distinctions between the education of boys and girls. The period 1870–1914 also saw the promotion of a sex-differentiated curriculum. In 1878, for example, theoretical domestic economy became a compulsory specific subject for girls; four years later the government gave grants for the teaching of cookery. By the 1890s a significant expansion in the curriculum prescriptions for working-class girls saw the inclusion of laundry work and housewifery. Despite the addition of male craft subjects like woodwork, Turnbull (1987: 86) concludes that working-class boys 'did not receive practical instruction equivalent to the girls' needlework, cookery, laundry work and so on'. Further, when national efficiency became a priority in the aftermath of military failures and deficiencies highlighted by the number of recruits declared unfit for call-up in the second Boer War (1899–1902), the Board of Education increased the quota of these lessons (Attar 1990; Dyhouse 1981; Turnbull 1987). Hurt (1979) suggests military drill as the masculine equivalent to the housework and mothering lessons given to the girls, but fails to acknowledge the proportion of time filled by domestic subjects instruction.

Elementary school fees were not abolished until 1891, and only one in 150 working-class children ended up at university. When the 1902 *Education Act* snuffed out the democratic and radical potential of the school boards the division between elementary and secondary education became more firmly defined (Martin 2010). Responsibility for the provision and management of education passed to local authorities, who were permitted to establish rate-aided secondary schools. Fees were set at £3 per annum, which excluded all save the high-ability working-class child who won a free place on the basis of an attainment test. It seems likely that the main beneficiaries were lower middle-class boys (Purvis 1995). By 1938, 88 per cent of children were attending all-age elementary schools up to the age of 14. Overall education policies remained tailored to processes of class formation in the 1920s and 1930s. Beyond that, there was a split between the sexes in terms of access to schooling, curriculum content and years of education.

Born in the 1900s, Gladys Seaman taught at a school in an isolated village in rural Cambridgeshire, England, in the 1920s and 1930s. The school was built in 1848 and until the 1960s it took children right up until school-leaving age. It was the first state school in the county to provide school dinners and the cookery teacher immediately got the older girls to help. This meant they spent all morning cooking. 'Well, it was all their education', Gladys said. 'And they did washing too – we had an old mangle for that. And of course, there was needlework and knitting' (Chamberlain 1983: 58). For many years, traditional expectations that a woman's place was in the home was seen to supersede all other social principles, both inside and outside school. In the 1970s, 24-year-old Rosemary Butler's first teaching post was in the school where Gladys Seaman taught some 40 years previous. Rosemary liked to be 'looked after' and didn't think it was a good idea for girls to become bus drivers or have a career. 'Most girls are interested in clothes and a family and a home.... Their aim is to get married and have a family, and they're learning to do things they can do for themselves later on' (Chamberlain 1983: 64).

In their history of gender in British education in the second half of the twentieth century, Arnot et al. (1999) make the argument that feminist campaigners were able to manipulate the concerns of the Conservative governments of the 1980s and 1990s by integrating equal opportunities work into national debates about educational standards in failing schools. Sixteen-year-old girls were already improving their results in the 1970s, but 20 years on, when improvements in girls' educational performance at 16 suggested girls were behaving against stereotype, even in maths and sciences, the results proved shocking. In the summer of 2011, Jim Sinclair, director of the Joint Council for Qualifications, which publishes the exam results, described the growing gap between the sexes at the top grades as a 'worrying trend' (*Guardian*, 25 August 2011) although it has to be remembered that not all boys under-achieve, and conversely not all girls achieve well at school.

In the twenty-first century gender in education is very much on the policy agenda. Unlike 30 years ago, when 'it took a good deal of persuasion by (mainly) feminists before policy makers would look beyond the innate capacities of girls themselves for explanations' (Mahony 1998: 39), the response is not 'Well, they're just boys'. To understand this cultural change demands that we place it in historical perspective. The chapter begins with a brief policy history within the field of education, viewed through the lens of gender, before moving on to more recent efforts to eliminate gender inequities in the UK. The broad phases I identify are intended to be indicative of policy trends, as opposed to a precise historical chronology.

1944–1976

Under the influence of wartime radicalism, the *Education Act* (1944) established the principle of universal and free secondary education for all children over the age of 11. Although many saw the reform as primarily about the realisation of class equality and the production of a new type of society, this did not mean that all children received what had previously been described as secondary education. Typically, 11-plus attainment testing on the lines of 'age, ability and aptitude' became the principle of allocation of students to different types of post-primary school. Ellen Wilkinson and George Tomlinson, her successor as Minister for Education, were both committed to the idea of three types of school as recommended in the Norwood Report and the White Paper *Educational Reconstruction* (both published in 1943), which were intended to cater for three different 'types' of child.

However, the envisaged tripartite system of grammar, technical and modern schools was largely implemented as a bipartite system with technical schools not set up in the numbers envisaged. Throughout the 1940s and 1950s girls had to do much better than boys to secure a place at a grammar or technical school (Thom 1987). This was justified on the grounds that girls' academic superiority in the early stages made it necessary 'to tilt the balance in the favour of those late-developing boys' (Grant 1994: 37). The accepted theory was that these boys would catch up by age 14. Medical practitioners who warned female students of the risks evoked by too much intellectual work reinforced gender stereotypes about male superiority. As late as the 1930s, it was professed that a girl who worked hard might get brain fever (Rendel 1997: 56).

Whereas too much intellectual work was detrimental for typically 'diligent' and 'industrious' girls who were seen as susceptible to overstrain, the elite male was distinguished by his alleged 'superior' natural ability. Because hard work was construed as a sign of *lack* of ability, the underperformance of boys became 'an index of their mental health' (Cohen 1998: 27). So, when it came to 11-plus scores, the fact that girls frequently outperformed boys at 11 prompted some local authorities to set up different norms, while others added new tests to level the sexes (Thom 1987). Technical adjustment was necessary (generally girls' scores were weighted) to balance the numbers of successful girls and boys; there was also a historic shortage of girls' grammar school places. It has to be accepted 'that there is no such thing as a fair test' (Gipps and Murphy 1994: 273), but girls' achievements were actively resisted from 1947 on, while the question of gender in education was lost in the general problems of the tripartite system.

During the years of Clement Attlee's Labour governments (1945–1951), politicians saw the domestic role of women as crucial for the construction and rehabilitation of social harmony and cohesion (Dean 1991). The notion of a companionate marriage organised around a male breadwinner and dependent wife and mother received further legitimation in the creation of a welfare state which was intended to redistribute social goods and resources more equitably. Women workers who had done men's jobs during the Second World War were made redundant, wartime nurseries were closed and the writings of John Bowlby on the dangers of 'maternal deprivation' for normal child development were a means by which women's caring roles were created, legitimised and justified (Riley 1983).

However, a post-war labour shortage saw governments turn to a 'reserve army' of female labour, with several government recruitment programmes aimed specifically at attracting married women back into a number of occupations, including domestic service, nursing, teaching and textiles. Part-time employment for married women was consistent with the notion of women's dual role, popularised in the 1940s and beyond, in which women's household responsibilities were intended to be constant and central, and paid work was peripheral and sporadic. Another consequence of this governing ideology was to be seen in the distribution of funded places in higher education and training. Most women were denied a university education in the period 1946–1949, since ex-servicemen were given priority (Briar 1997: 97).

In the 1940s, influential school inspector John Newsom published a book, *The Education of Girls*, in which he cast doubt on the value of an academic education for girls. As time passed, Newsom's views on domestic education 'for the average girl (or rather the working-class girl), whose vocation was still seen as marriage and family, were not only still widely accepted, but even became more popular as sex education was introduced into schools after 1956' (Wilson 1980: 36). Social and political expectations of what was appropriate for girls and boys to study persisted. In the secondary modern schools (virtually synonymous with working-class schooling), the Crowther Report (1959) which dealt with the education of 15–18-year-olds, expressed sympathy for the idea that marriage and courtship should influence the education of the adolescent girl. Natural, inherent interests 'in dress and personal appearance and the problems of human relations' were highlighted (quoted in Riley 1994: 37). Crowther also commented on the fact that grammar school girls were more likely to leave school at the statutory age and the Early Leaving Report (Gurney-Dixon Report 1954) found that grammar school girls left school before their male counterparts and with fewer qualifications. Then, as now, issues of participation were cross-cut by class differences. Working-class boys were more likely to go from grammar school to university than working-class girls, especially a prestigious one (Jackson and Marsden 1962).

Cultural attitudes and material provision all worked towards encouraging girls to train as teachers, which cost £255, compared to £660 a year for undergraduates – mainly white, middle-class men. That being the case, teaching was the favoured career goal of many female grammar school pupils and nearly half of the girls Jackson and Marsden researched went to colleges of education: by 1958 there were 100 teacher training colleges for women, 18 for men and 18 co-educational institutions (Heward 1993: 23–24). Ultimately, when universal student grants became available in the early 1960s women represented on average 25 per cent of the university population in Britain: in Oxford they were 15 per cent and only 10 per cent in Cambridge (figures from the Robbins report quoted in Dyhouse 2003: 173). Gendered attitudes also meant that relatively little use was made of women's skills and qualifications, despite there being economic concerns about a shortage of skilled workers. Consequently, women graduates were much more likely to have to accept non-graduate employment than male graduates and 'the proportion of women workers in jobs classed as skilled continued to decline in this period, having fallen from 15.5% in 1951 to 13.9% in 1961' (Mackie and Patullo 1977: 99).

During the late 1950s and early 1960s, government reports and academic research pointed to the 'wasted talent' the divided educational system produced and the inefficacy of intelligence testing as a device for meritocratic selection was highlighted (Chitty 2004). It was now becoming apparent that secondary modern schools were second best and this coincided with a view that a common school, educating all children together, was a desirable aim. Faith in the logic of human capital theory and the central assumption of 'upskilling', where education is seen as crucial to economic growth and development, precipitated a break with the belief that large numbers of people lacked the ability to benefit from a university education (Schultz 1970; see Simon 1991: 222, 229, 291 for a discussion). In 1964, when the Labour Party was returned to office, the new government made the introduction of comprehensive schools a priority. It did so by means of a circular, 10/65, requesting local authorities to choose a development scheme and start the planning process.

Reassessments of the concept of equal access saw a gradual shift to a non-selective system of secondary schooling in England and Wales, a change that accelerated the number of children educated in mixed schools in the state sector. As the Labour government moved towards comprehensive education it made an assumption that boys and girls should be educated together, rather than separately, on academic and social grounds. The feeling was that the presence of female pupils would have a 'civilising' influence on their male peers. As pointed out by Arnot (1984: 54), 'never it would seem has the argument been reversed'. In effect, co-education tries to extend to girls and women an education historically intended for boys and men – the goal of preparing students for life as a worker, a citizen and an individual, not as a member of a home and family (Martin 2011). Overall, the removal of barriers to female success in the 11-plus examination inevitably benefited some, mainly middle-class, girls. Discussion of who benefits academically from mixed- or single-sex schooling rumbles on and will be returned to later.

Change was slow and piecemeal, but Benn and Simon (1972) found that very few secondary schools offered a common curriculum in the early days of the comprehensive reform. Divergence in the content of education continued in the provision of gender-specific courses in subjects like domestic science, typing and childcare, which were not open to boys; and woodwork, metalwork and technical drawing, which were not open to girls. Links between the distribution of educational knowledge and patterns of women's work remained in evidence despite the greater participation of women in the labour force. The effects were carried forward into further study and employment at precisely the point when, for the first time since the Second World War, there was a growing problem of youth unemployment. Education was to take the blame for at least some of the nation's ills resulting from the economic and industrial problems of the early 1970s, as a worldwide oil crisis put increased pressure on public expenditure. Working-class boys and men were particularly affected by the decline of vocational apprenticeships and industrial jobs with release for college training. Cutbacks in teacher training and fierce competition for university places in arts courses reduced opportunities for some young women.

When the Labour government under Harold Wilson passed the *Sex Discrimination Act* in 1975 it made direct and indirect discrimination on the grounds of gender illegal in a number of spheres of public life, including education. It also set up the Equal Opportunities Commission (EOC). Although the then Department of Education and Science was unenthusiastic, the Act outlawed discrimination covering admissions, curricular and non-curricular facilities and extra-curricular activities. Additionally, it covered standards of behaviour, rules regarding pupils' dress and appearance, school discipline and careers guidance, but did not apply to private schools. Stemming from the political impact of the women's liberation movement in the 1970s, equality legislation was a spur to targeted equal opportunities programmes in education and training. It is in the context of an increasing entry of women into higher education, the establishment of women's studies courses and departments, and the performance of girls in examinations, that we have to consider the transformative powers of feminism in educational thinking and practice. That is, the women's movement within the educational system.

1975–1995

In a damning critique of patriarchy, Australian feminist Dale Spender argued that in education women have learnt *how* to lose even though they may have had the ability to succeed academically.

> While the prevailing belief is that women are inferior, and while this is taught within education with all the 'massaging' of the evidence that such teaching requires, women will continue to find themselves devalued, in the lowest paid, least skilled jobs, with least power to change those conditions.
>
> (Spender 1980: 31)

Feminists levelled criticism at schools across a diversity of areas, noting among other things the interplay of gender and leadership embedded within the work of schools, governments and teacher unions. While the great majority of teachers were women, generally men ran the schools, dominating the administrative and policy-making side of education.

Education research, including gender, revealed that teachers at all levels (primary, secondary, tertiary) readily clustered behaviour and attitudes into two categories, one for boys and another for girls, drawing on oppositional constructions of masculinity and femininity (Clarricoates 1980; Stanworth 1986; Riddell 1989). Boys were lively, adventurous, boisterous, self-confident, independent, energetic, couldn't-care-less, loyal and aggressive. Girls were obedient, tidy, neat, conscientious, orderly, fussy, catty, bitchy and gossipy. Pupils and teachers accommodated traditional gender codes. For example, Riddell observed one maths lesson in a rural comprehensive school in south-west England in which a girl produced a large make-up kit, 'spread out the cosmetics on the desk top as if it were a dressing table' and proceeded to apply the make-up. 'Amazingly, the male teacher completely ignored what was going on' (Riddell

1989: 193). Similarly, Irene Payne (1980: 15) wrote about her experience of a single-sex grammar school. Some girls used a stylised femininity as a way of positioning themselves 'in opposition to the "masculinity" of school rules about appearance. I can remember bouffant hairstyles, fishnet stockings, make-up and "sticky-out" underskirts being the hallmarks of rebellious girls'.

Major gender issues of the 1970s and 1980s included the ways in which female pupils were steered away from traditionally 'masculine' subjects. In relation to subject choice by gender, school inspectors found evidence of illegal segregation of craft subjects in 19 per cent of the schools studied in the period 1975–1978 (cited in Pascall 1997: 119). Generally, boys were allocated the limited places in technical areas at the expense of girls and Griffin (1985: 78–79) found that girls who pursued such subjects 'were either presumed to be interested solely in flirting with the boys or discounted as unique exceptions'. Despite the achievements of equal rights legislation, most girls were still sitting examinations in a narrow cluster of subjects seen as supporting 'natural' female interests, needs and choices with respect to personal/domestic life. Fewer girls than boys achieved the three good A-levels needed to gain access to higher education, and there were prevailing inequities in curriculum and attitudes (Arnot *et al.* 1999). Indeed, Arnot (1983: 71) argues the development of co-educational state comprehensive secondary schools 'did not represent … a challenge to the reproduction of dominant gender relations but rather a modification of the *form* of its transmission'.

Therefore, individual feminist teachers and groups of feminists (such as organisations like Girls/Gender and Mathematics Association – GAMMA) tried to act as change agents, by consciousness-raising and encouraging small-scale school-based initiatives. Teaching styles were challenged to avoid a tendency to encourage competition between the sexes in sports, academic learning and examinations, attention also turned to management hierarchies within schools. Most were dominated by male teachers and the proportion of women holding senior posts in secondary schools was highest in such female 'spaces' as home economics and girls' games. One of the best-known projects, the Girls into Science and Technology Project, was set up in Manchester (Kelly 1985). Here researchers worked alongside and with teachers in ten schools to encourage girls to take traditionally 'male' subjects, even after they became optional (then at age 14). To this end, the project team brought adult women scientists to act as role models, tried to raise awareness about the gender dynamics of classrooms and experimented with single-sex classes.

Discussion of strategies to actively challenge gender inequalities in education demands attention to the meaning of equality, explored by Hughes (2002) who asks: does equality mean 'the same' and if so, what measures of sameness should be used? Do you argue for women's rights on equal terms with men or should feminists be arguing that women's difference is at the root of their equality? The implications are evident in legislation redefining responsibility for the curriculum in England and Wales. The 1988 *Education Reform Act* introduced a national curriculum and put in place a system of national testing measured as ten levels of attainment at four Key Stages (ages 7, 11, 14 and 16) based on the programmes of study for each national curriculum subject. Initially mathematics, science and English were defined as core up to

16 years, together with seven foundation subjects – art, geography, history, music, physical education, technology and a modern foreign language (after age 11). As time passed, there were incremental moves to reduce the compulsory elements in favour of greater choice.

Feminist educators supported the notion of a common curriculum experience, albeit one that encompassed the hidden curriculum of schooling and not one posited on a male educational paradigm (Benn *et al.* 1982). On the one hand, the national curriculum gave all state school pupils equal entitlement to develop the same learning skills and experience the same subjects. On the other, the privileging of maths, science and technology reinforced traditional gender hierarchies and did little to break the circulation of stereotypical sex-role expectations. Knowledge is not a neutral commodity, but the emphasis on equal opportunities serves to reinforce the illusion of neutrality.

> In short, while girls must be educated in the skills and attitudes to achieve an academic equality with boys – and to challenge inequalities within the labour market – the education of boys in the skills and attitudes to address their equal responsibilities within the family are of equal if not greater importance. And this is where the formal equality accorded by the National Curriculum is most lacking, in the 'masculinisation' of the schooling of girls with no corresponding 'feminisation' of the schooling of boys.
>
> (Gomersall 1994: 246)

What this position represents is a concern to restructure boys' education in such a way as to break the circulation of stereotypical sex-role expectations. The views expressed emphasise that the majority of schooling operates for a particular form of hegemonic masculinity.

Arnot's (1994) review of gender research in British sociology of education highlights two theoretical traditions. The first is that of the cultural perspective, wherein cultural analyses concentrate on different socialisation processes. The second tradition that Arnot explores is political-economy theories. Key thematic influences and concern that stand out in such approaches are the concept of *social reproduction*, suggesting that schools reproduce the values and ideologies of the dominant social groupings, as well as the status rankings of the existing class structure. Building on this work, Arnot adjusts the theory to enable her to combine a class and gender analysis. Here she develops the concept of gender codes, to refer to 'the principles which govern the production, reproduction and transmission of gender relations and gender hierarchies' (Arnot 2002: 176). The concept of *cultural hegemony* plays a considerable theoretical role, showing the structural constraints or limits that shape a prevailing context in which individuals and groups act. Sociological analysis can provide insight into how powerful groups within society maintain control, while showing how teachers, students and other human agents can and do play a crucial role in moderating or changing existing social norms. Within this spirit, it is accepted that individuals and groups may hold within them different ways of seeing and thereby offer routes to change in the name of, for example, women's rights.

A report produced for the EOC indicated how educational and curricular developments in the late 1980s and 1990s exerted some influence on the gender gap in educational attainment (Arnot *et al.* 1996). Studying the figures for the period 1985 to 1994, the benchmark of exam performance at 16 showed more girls than boys were entered for GCSE examinations and more girls than boys attained five or more A–C GCSE grades. On the other hand, boys continued to predominate in chemistry, physics, CDT (craft, design and technology) besides newer subjects like computer studies. English, mathematics and history all showed a more balanced entry pattern. Post-16 the data showed enduring patterns of sex-stereotyping in subject entry and performance. Far more young men completed A-levels (used for university entrance) in mathematics, physics and technology. Similarly in vocational examinations and the various training schemes, women mostly took the less prestigious types like business and commerce, hairdressing and beauty and service courses. Importantly, although the research sponsored by the EOC noted that girls began to widen the achievement gap post-1987; when the GCSE exam, with a larger coursework element, had been introduced, the elite minority of girls in private single-sex schools enjoyed a substantial advantage. It has to be remembered that gender cannot be abstracted from issues of class, 'race' ethnicity, disability, sexuality, religion, citizenship and spatial location.

In her research, Lees (1993) found that whereas academic girls expect careers, non-academic girls anticipate the need to combine unskilled and part-time employment with the responsibilities of housework and childcare. Pro-school and academically or work-oriented girls were typically white females from middle-class homes with strong parental support. Mirza (1992) comments that the Irish girls in her study saw their futures as homemakers, child-carers and part-time workers, whereas the black girls she interviewed anticipated a career. Clearly, the way in which women perform relative to men varies according to class and ethnicity, as does the value of having or not having educational qualifications. Significantly, the mature women students interviewed by Pascall and Cox (1993) saw education as an escape route from a lifetime of domesticity and low-paid work. However, the gradual abolition of mandatory grants, the introduction of loans and the prospect of incurring high levels of debt had a major impact on this group of students.

The neo-liberal social policy and marketisation of education instigated by the Conservative governments of the 1980s and 1990s was developed with enthusiasm by the 'New Labour' administrations of Tony Blair and Gordon Brown (1997–2010) as a key way of improving institutional, group and individual standards and effectiveness in schooling. In a series of complex provisions, pupils and students become educational clients, with parents the consumers of education systems. Within this policy movement, performance league tables, a more stringent school inspection process (set up in 1992) all served as mechanisms to 'measure' standards, with an unprecedented emphasis on the phenomenon of the failing school.

Contexts, changes and continuities: under-achieving boys?

Governments from the 1980s believed in the application of technical solutions to the problems of so-called failing schools and, a little later on, failing boys. The argument was that schools could be manipulated to make a difference to performance through charismatic leadership. Target-setting persisted, as did a blame-and-shame culture that labelled certain schools as ineffective while playing down the impact of social and economic disadvantages on learning. These new regimes had a dramatic impact on equity discourses that sit alongside dominant educational narratives about school effectiveness. The concept of 'excellence' promoted plays through the dynamic of 'success' and 'failure' and Ball and Gewirtz (1997) pointed to the accretive value of 'successful' girls. Girls were positioned as 'a valuable and sought after resource' by strategies to increase school effectiveness through enhanced levels of performance, because 'their presence in school normally conveys positive impressions to parents about ethos and discipline' (Ball and Gewirtz 1997: 214).

In the 1990s and beyond, gendered reactions to the annual publication of the GCSE results promoted a generalised narrative of female academic success and male failure. Sections of the media turned the issue into a 'moral panic' about the problem of the under-achievement of boys. This received official legitimation in 1996, when Chris Woodhead, then Chief Inspector of Schools for England, wrote a column in *The Times* entitled 'Boys who learn to be losers: on the white male culture of failure'. In it he said that the apparent failure of white working-class boys was 'one of the most disturbing problems we face within the whole education system' (quoted in *TES*, 26 April 1996). Two years later, when the publication of new official statistics showed girls outperforming boys in terms of the proportion of pupils obtaining five A–C grades at GCSE in all but one local authority (Kensington and Chelsea), concern for boys' under-achievement led then Schools Standards Minister Stephen Byers to intervene. In a speech at the 11th International Conference for School Effectiveness and Improvement, he argued that the 'laddish, anti-learning culture' was impeding boys' achievement (*Guardian*, 6 January 1998). Henceforth each local authority was required to address the issue of male disadvantage in drawing up its Education Development Plan.

It may be in modified form, but a powerful fear of working-class masculinity is nothing new. Early sociological texts dealing with the making of male identity through resistance to schooling show how anti-school working-class 'lads' block teaching (Willis 1983). These teenage boys linked their counter-school culture to that of the factory floor, and in so doing they asserted definitions of masculinity that positioned mental work and having girls as friends as effeminate. Similarly, in *Schooling the Smash Street Kids*, Corrigan (1979) used the analogy of a 'guerrilla struggle' to represent the ability of white, working-class, heterosexual boys in the north-east of England to monopolise space in the classroom, despite the 'occupying army' of teachers. Examples of disruptive behaviour included 'running about in classrooms', 'running under chairs' and 'tossing chairs about' (Corrigan 1979: 58). Twenty years on, policy initiatives included a recommendation that teachers appeal to boys' interests (humour, adventure and sport) and a drive to recruit male primary school teachers (*TES*, 23 May 1997; *Daily Mail*, 5 January 1998). Others speculated whether rhetoric about a generation of male losers and the object of the failing boy might lead to a further masculinisation of classroom environments (Raphael Reed 1998).

Anti-sexism work to raise achievement for all pupils might go further. Boys/men negotiate and take up a variety of masculinities and some of these confer power and prestige, while others are stigmatised and subordinate. Take the example of young boys positioned as slow learners, poor at sport and lacking physical strength and skill, who resort to overtly challenging behaviour. Analysis of the labelling process surrounding the category of special educational needs points to the fact that middle-class boys dominate the non-stigmatised category of having specific learning difficulties (Benjamin 2003). In contrast, black Caribbean and 'black other' boys are twice as likely to be categorised as having behavioural, emotional or social difficulty as white British boys. Furthermore, African-Caribbean children of both sexes are more vulnerable to permanent exclusion from school than their white peers (Osler and Vincent 2003).

Arguably the escalating hysteria about the 'growing gender gap' is masking another story. In this story the script is one of rising assessment performance of boys *and* girls, making the phenomenon one of relative rates of improvement for both sexes. This is absent from a common-sense discourse in which mothers and women teachers are often blamed for boys' relative lower performance with girls. Contemporary schoolgirls may have greater career ambition than their 1950s counterparts, they may show an awareness of the gender-discriminatory nature of the adult workplace, plus inequality of housework and childcare, all of which may have provided new motivation for educational achievement, but where will the exam results get them? Will twenty-first century girls have the power to change conditions, and which girls are we talking about? Working-class girls with few or no qualifications are hardly ever mentioned, middle-class girls may go on to resolve the contradiction of 'career' and 'motherhood' by employing other women.

In their study *Growing up Girl* published in 2001, Walkerdine *et al.* offer longitudinal data on UK girls from working-class and middle-class backgrounds, showing how achievement is always a 'class related phenomenon'. Therefore, the meaning of the 'good' girl is constructed across class lines. None of the working-class girls who succeeded in education trod a straightforward academic path, whereas only one middle-class girl did not go on to university entrance. The educational trajectories of two girls, Patsy (working class) and Julie (middle class), who went to the same nursery, infant and junior schools, and whose parents did all the 'right things', may help to explain why. At ten, both girls were doing equally badly at junior school, but whereas the teacher read Patsy's performance as lack of ability, Julie's performance was viewed as a problem of motivation. At 16, both girls got poor GCSE results and Patsy left school while Julie went on to university: 'at 21 Julie was back on track and was likely to become a graduate professional, while Patsy, painfully aware of her lack of qualifications, was equally likely to remain in relatively poorly paid, low-status work' (Walkerdine *et al.* 2001: 125–126).

Conclusion

Boys and girls are both much more successful at school than they were 50 years ago. However, we still need policies to enhance equality of educational opportunity, whether through class, culture, social disadvantage, disability, ethnicity, family, sexuality, gender or race. The last Labour government enacted the 2010 *Equality Act* that enshrined a single public sector equality duty, including for gender, that applies to all maintained and independent schools, including academies and maintained and non-maintained special schools.

A historical perspective shows that girls and women have continued to do better in education when offered more opportunities. It also shows that generations of women, past and present, have failed to translate their academic capital into social and economic capital. The labour market realities confirm sex divisions, with women still in predominantly traditional female employment. Female graduates can expect to earn 15 per cent less than their male equivalents by the age of 24 and it is mostly men on very high salaries who comprise the new elite in the financial and multinational sectors. Although an *Equal Pay Act* was passed in 1970 (it became enforceable in 1975), the gender pay gap in Britain remains among the highest in the European Union. On average, women in the UK earn about 15 per cent less than men. In London, the pay gap stands at 23 per cent (*Guardian*, 16 June 2012). Data from the Office for National Statistics annual survey of hours and earnings shows that male teachers earn more than their female counterparts at every level. However, the gap is narrowest among further education teachers (4.27 per cent) and widest among special needs teachers (9.55 per cent). Figures are dwarfed by the pay gap between male and female education officers and school inspectors (16.11 per cent).

Under this coalition government it is becoming more obvious that the needs of the middle-classes take precedence over a commitment to social inclusion and social justice. When it comes to the question of gender, traditional masculinities seem to be on the ascendance. A perception of elite boys as innately able continues, as does a tendency to imply that girls' academic attainment is the result of compliant hard work. In 2011, commentary on the 'worrying trend' of girls surging ahead at GCSE was peppered with reflections on the structure of GCSE examinations. As journalists and others searched for explanations one could be forgiven for wondering if some found comfort in the fact that from September 2012, pupils will be assessed at the end of their courses rather than at the end of modules, which is allegedly more often a characteristic of girls; noting that in 2011 boys narrowly beat girls at GCSE maths for the third year in a row, following a decision to drop coursework in the subject. It has to be remembered that post-war research and policy documents record that girls had always outperformed boys in public examinations at 16. So we cannot equate GCSE results to shifts in the pattern of gender inequality. Indeed, the 2011 A-level results showed boys narrowing girls' lead at the top grades.

To come full circle and return to the quote with which we started, in the UK gender is no longer accepted as a difference that makes all the difference in education, appropriate because boys were breadwinners and secondarily fathers whereas girls also needed to be prepared for family life and motherhood. Albeit arguable that change has come about *despite* the sexual politics of schooling. Even though equality legislation has been in place for nearly 40 years, research evidence about gender and education suggests the under-representation of women in science remains an issue, as do the sexualisation of girls and women, male dominance in the classroom, the playground and greater demands on teacher time and energy. We have never broken out of the 'toys for the boys' perception of computer science and, to continue with the theme of what changes and what stays the same a little longer, British women still lose out on seniority and wage equality in the workplace. In an age of austerity there are other 'worrying trends' that need to be placed on record when it comes to the so-called gender gap. First, the gender pay gap (already too big) is likely to be widened by public sector pay cuts. Second, women workers, particularly those aged 50 and over, are bearing the brunt of rising job losses and the number of unemployed women stands at its highest level since 1987. Finally, BBC research cited on the Fawcett Society's website shows that men hold two out of three of the UK's most influential jobs (www.fawcettsociety.org.uk).

References

Arnot, M. (1983) 'A cloud over co-education: an analysis of the forms of transmission of class and gender relations', in Walker, S. and Barton, L. (eds), *Gender, Class and Education*. Lewes: Falmer.

Arnot, M. (1984) 'How shall we educate our sons?' in Deem, R. (ed.), *Co-education Reconsidered.* Milton Keynes: Open University Press.

Arnot, M. (1994) 'Male hegemony, social class and women's education', in Stone, L. (ed.), *The Education Feminist Reader*. London: Routledge.

Arnot, M. (2002) *Reproducing Gender? Critical Essays on Educational Theory and Feminist Politics.* London: RoutledgeFalmer.

Arnot, M., David, M. and Weiner, G. (1996) *Educational Reforms and Gender Equality.* Manchester: Equal Opportunities Commission.

Arnot, M., David, M. and Weiner, G. (1999) *Closing the Gender Gap: Postwar Education and Social Change.* Cambridge: Polity Press.

Attar, D. (1990) *Wasting Girls' Time: The History and Politics of Home Economics.* London: Virago.

Ball, S.J. and Gewirtz, S. (1997) 'Girls in the education market: choice, competition and complexity', *Gender and Education* 9 (2), 207–222.

Benjamin, S. (2003) 'Gender and special educational needs', in Skelton, C. and Francis, B. (eds), *Boys and Girls in the Primary Classroom.* Maidenhead: Open University Press.

Benn, C. and Simon, B. (1972) *Half Way There: Report on the British Comprehensive-School Reform.* Harmondsworth: Penguin.

Benn, C., Parris, J., Riley, K. and Weiner, G. (1982) 'Education and women: the new agenda', *Socialism and Education* 9 (2), 10–13.

Briar, C. (1997) *Working for Women? Gendered Work and Welfare Policies in Twentieth-Century Britain.* London: UCL Press.

Castle, B. (1994) *Fighting All the Way.* London: Pan.

Chamberlain, M. (1983) *Fenwomen: A Portrait of Women in an English Village.* London: Routledge and Kegan Paul.

Chitty, C. (2004) *Education Policy in Britain.* London: Palgrave Macmillan.

Clarricoates, K. (1980) 'The importance of being Ernest … Emma … Tom … Jane. The perception and categorization of gender conformity and gender deviation in primary schools', in Deem, R. (ed.), *Schooling for Women's Work*. London: Routledge and Kegan Paul.

Cohen, M. (1998) 'A habit of healthy idleness: boys' underachievement, schooling and gender relations', in Epstein, D., Elwood, J., Hey, V. and Maw, J. (eds), *Failing Boys? Issues in Gender and Achievement.* Buckingham: Open University Press.

Corrigan, P. (1979) *Schooling the Smash Street Kids.* London: Macmillan.

Crowther Report, The (1959) *15 to 18: A Report of the Central Advisory Council for Education (England).* London: HMSO.

Davin, A. (1996) *Growing Up Poor: Home, School and Street in London, 1870–1914*. Hatfield: Rivers Oram Press.

Dyhouse, C. (1981) *Girls Growing up in Late Victorian and Edwardian England*. London: Routledge and Kegan Paul.

Dyhouse, C. (2003) 'Troubled identities: gender and status in the history of the mixed college in English universities since 1945', *Women's History Review* 12 (2), 169–193.

Gipps, C. and Murphy, P. (1994) *A Fair Test? Assessment, Achievement and Equity*. Milton Keynes: Open University Press.

Gomersall, M. (1994) 'Education for domesticity? A nineteenth century perspective on girls' schooling and domesticity', *Gender and Education* 6 (3), 235–247.

Grant, L. (1994) 'First among equals', *Guardian Weekend*, 22 October: 37–46.

Griffin, C. (1985) *Typical Girls? Young Women from School to the Job Market*. London: Routledge and Kegan Paul.

Gurney-Dixon Report (1954) *Early Leaving: A Report of the Central Advisory Council for Education (England)*. London: HMSO.

Heward, C. (1993) 'Men and women and the rise of professional society: the intriguing history of teacher education', *History of Education* 22 (1), 11–32.

Hughes, C. (2002) *Key Concepts in Feminist Theory and Research*. London: Sage.

Hurt, J. (1979) *Elementary Schooling and the Working Classes 1860–1918*. London: Routledge and Kegan Paul.

Jackson, B. and Marsden, D. (1962) *Education and the Working-class*. London: Routledge and Kegan Paul.

Kelly, A. (1985) 'The construction of masculine science', *British Journal of Sociology of Education* 6, 133–154.

Lees, S. (1993) *Sugar and Spice: Sexuality and Adolescent Girls*. Harmondsworth: Penguin.

Mackie, L. and Patullo, P. (1977) *Women Who Work*. London: Tavistock.

Mahony, P. (1998) 'Girls will be girls and boys will be first', in Epstein, D., Elwood, J., Hey, V. and Maw, J. (eds), *Failing Boys? Issues in Gender and Achievement*. Buckingham: Open University Press.

Martin, J. (1999) *Women and the Politics of Schooling in Late Victorian and Edwardian England*. Leicester: Leicester University Press.

Martin, J. (2010) *Making Socialists: Mary Bridges Adams and the Fight for Knowledge and Power, 1855–1939*. Manchester: Manchester University Press.

Martin, J.R. (2011) *Education Reconfigured*. London: Routledge.

Mirza, H.S. (1992) *Young, Female and Black*. London: Routledge.

Newsom, J. (1948) *The Education of Girls*. London: Faber and Faber.

Osler, A. and Vincent, K. (2003) *Girls and Exclusion: Rethinking the Agenda*. London: Routledge Falmer.

Pankhurst, E. (1979 [1914]) *My Own Story*. London: Virago.

Payne, I. (1980) 'Sexist ideology and education', in Spender, D. and Sarah, E. (eds), *Learning to Lose*. London: The Women's Press.

Pascall, G. (1997) *Social policy: A New Feminist Analysis*. London: Routledge.

Pascal, G. and Cox, R. (1993) 'Education and domesticity', *Gender and Education* 5 (1), 17–35.

Purvis, J. (1995) 'Woman and education: a historical account 1800-1914', in Dawtrey, L., Holland, J., Hammer, M. and Sheldon, S. (eds), *Equality and Inequality in Education Policy*. Bristol: Multilingual Matters.

Raphael Reed, L. (1998) '"Zero tolerance": gender performance and school failure', in Epstein, D., Elwood, J., Hey, V. and Maw, J. (eds), *Failing Boys? Issues in Gender and Achievement*. Buckingham: Open University Press.

Rendel, M. (1997) *Whose Human Rights?* Stoke-on-Trent: Trentham.

Riddell, S. (1989) 'Pupils, resistance and gender codes: a study of classroom encounters', *Gender and Education* 1 (2), 183–198.

Riley, D. (1983) *War in the Nursery: Theories of the Child and Mother*. London: Virago.

Riley, K.A. (1994) *Quality and Equality: Promoting Opportunities in Schools*. London: Cassell.

Schultz, T.W. (1970) *Investment in Human Capital: The Role of Education and of Research*. New York: Free Press.

Simon, B. (1991) *Education and the Social Order: 1940–1990* London: Lawrence and Wishart.

Spender, D. (1980) 'Education or indoctrination?', in Spender, D. and Sarah, E. (eds), *Learning to Lose*. London: The Women's Press.

Stanworth, M. (1986) *Gender and Schooling: A Study of Sexual Divisions in the Classroom*. London: Hutchinson.

Thom, D. (1987) 'Better a teacher than a hairdresser? "A mad passion for equality" or, keeping Molly and Betty down', in Hunt, F. (ed.), *Lessons for Life: The Schooling of Girls and Women 1850–1950*. Oxford: Basil Blackwell.

Turnbull, A. (1987) 'Learning her womanly work: the elementaty school curriculum 1870–1914', in Hunt, F. (ed.), *Lessons for Life*. Oxford: Basil Blackwell.

Walkerdine, V., Lucey, H. and Melody, J. (2001) *Growing Up Girl: Psychosocial Explorations of Gender and Class*. Basingstoke: Palgrave.

Willis, P. (1983) *Learning to Labour: How Working-class Kids Get Working-class Jobs*, Aldershot: Gower.

Wilson, E. (1980) *Only Halfway to Paradise: Women in Postwar Britain: 1945–1968*. London: Tavistock Publications.

Wollstonecraft, M. ([1792] 1975) *A Vindication of the Rights of Woman*. Harmondsworth: Penguin.

Debates in educational research

Abdeljalil Akkari and Bernard Wentzel

If we knew what it was we were doing, it would not be called research, would it?

Albert Einstein

Introduction

By way of introduction, we will open this chapter with a few preliminary remarks. First of all, we need to make a distinction between education and schooling. While all human societies, dating back to prehistory, have put in place educational processes, formal schooling, particularly compulsory mass schooling, marks a more recent phase in the history of humanity. One must therefore be aware that educational research is not only research into the process of schooling and the activities that take place in school. However, it is worth noting that for over a century educational research has favoured the school as an institution because of the social context it represents. Second, the history of educational research is also the history of the researchers, authors and, in particular, institutions which have carried out and informed the research. To this end, it is expedient to bring debates on educational research back to a national level, even though the objective of this text is to cover issues which are more international and global in nature. Third, educational research is an area full of controversies and conflicts between different methodological approaches and diverging concepts of research and its status.

All observers agree that research requires systematic and methodical investigation (De Landsheere, 1979). To summarise, we can state that educational research is a process which covers three main dimensions: (1) an attitude: the mindset of the individual educational researcher – in other words, this means having a specific research approach and an uncertainty regarding a given problem; (2) an activity, or a set of completed behaviours (carrying out research) – these behaviours are mobilised with a view to comprehending and understanding an educational issue and/or introducing change with the aim of renewal and innovation; and (3) a result which is the product of the action of research. This is the publication and communication of results to the scientific community.

The main aim of this chapter is to retrace the process of how educational research has historically been constructed. Different eras will be identified along with the continuities and divides which have marked the history of educational research. In the first section, we discuss the philosophical origins of thinking about education. The second part is devoted to explaining the dominance of educational psychology during the first half of the twentieth century. The third part examines the contribution of sociology of education to educational research. The fourth and fifth parts summarise the contemporary challenges faced by educational research. The text is organised into different periods of history to aid the reader's comprehension; it does not signify that a discipline which was dominant in a given era has lost its importance in modern times.

Philosophical origins of thinking about education

As far back as we can go into human history, there has been reflection on education as a tool for transmitting culture and values to future generations. This critical thinking was originally clearly linked to philosophy. In other words, the debates mainly centred on the values and the meaning of educating younger generations. Both Greek philosophy and Christian theology considered education as a search for both meaning and wisdom. Other peoples and civilisations also had their own thinking on education, such as Confucius in China or Al Ghazali in the Muslim/Arab world (Yutang 2008; Al-Ghazali 2010). Socrates was one of the sophist teachers, charged with educating the children of well-off families. But he railed passionately against the Sophists, denouncing the formal and crudely utilitarian nature of their teaching and arguing for an emphasis on truth rather than rhetoric. For Socrates, educating man is to teach him to reason so that he can become a better member of society by adopting the ideal of justice as his guiding value. Plato's text entitled 'Meno' recounts the story of the young slave who was able to work out a mathematical theorem[1] through a simple process of interrogation: anamnesis and recollection. This pedagogical lesson marked a major contribution in philosophical thinking on education. Regardless of the actions of the master, it is the pupil alone who is learning. We can externally awaken the desire to learn, but the decision to learn is internal to the learner. In education, there was the desire to give precedence to the species over the individual, to promote universality over particularity and to favour eternity over death (Meirieu, 1994).

One of the most interesting debates in Ancient times was that of recollection. This centred around the importance of the subject's interiority and exteriority in the learning process: whether learning is to be shaped by external forces or to develop one's inner being. St. Augustin clearly leaned towards the second theory, illustrated by the fact that he favoured the inner master. This Christian disciple of Plato took this theory of recollection further by demonstrating that there is no single person who can teach anything to anyone. The role of the wise man, the master, the educator, the teacher arose in Antiquity as a central issue in education and pedagogy. Rogers (1972) is the contemporary successor of this strain of philosophy, advocating the liberty of the subject in order to learn.

There are three key authors from this first period in the reign of the philosophy of education who must be mentioned: Comenius, Rousseau and Jullien-de-Paris. All three of them caused a major divide in educational research. Comenius, with his comprehensive didactic work, was equally as visionary as Rousseau, putting forward the possibility of the systematic control of teaching and learning processes. Towards the middle of the seventeenth century, Comenius (1627–1632) recommended there be one school for all, not just boys and girls, but children from all social classes. He believed that mass schooling would better identify those who are capable of continuing education to higher academic levels. He proposed that all differentiation during the first years of a child's life be abandoned. This was one of the first ever conceptions of a schooling system in its true sense, since it affects the entire population and we can see the interdependence of elementary teaching and the other levels of education. Rousseau was a pioneer when it came to thinking about education in so far as he was interested in the child as a specific being and not as a miniature adult. In some way, we can say that Rousseau was the first author to look at childhood and its specific psychology. The contradiction between the individual and society was keenly observed by Rousseau, giving rise to his idea of the need to postpone the child's entry into the global social environment by entrusting him or her to a tutor who would act as a filter.

At the start of the nineteenth century, Jullien-de-Paris (1817) used, and was the first in the history of education to define, the term 'comparative education' in a text entitled: *Esquisse et vues préliminaires d'un ouvrage sur l'éducation comparée* (Outline and preliminary view of a work on comparative education). Jullien-de-Paris wanted education to progress with this rigour, for it to become almost a 'positive' science. He advocated the application of a scientific method to deduce set principles and determined rules for the organisation of educational systems on an international scale. Jullien used the method of observation and analysis of the various educational systems in Europe so as to adopt the trends which had proven their effectiveness in terms of school organisation and public education.

This long first stage in educational research (from Antiquity to the mid nineteenth century) is characterised by the fact that research into better education was often connected to philosophical debates without any systematisation of the methods of investigation. The educational research methodology was intuitive and recourse to empirical data was rare.

The emergence of measurements and psychology

We can consider the start of the second period in educational research to fall around the middle of the nineteenth century. European and Northern American societies at this time were undergoing an unprecedented cultural revolution. The idea of compulsory primary schooling had emerged. A large number of countries made compulsory schooling law and introduced a unified public education system. This measure had far-reaching social consequences: mass literacy, increased political participation, economic development. It also provoked a qualitative development in educational research. Philosophy was no longer the main reference discipline, coming increasingly into competition with psychology, a rapidly emerging discipline.

John Dewey can be considered one of the first educational researchers. He straddled the line between philosophy and psychology. Head of the Department of

Philosophy at the University of Chicago between 1896 and 1904, he introduced a new approach to the study of education and became the leading light of the New Educational Theory. John Dewey's research into progressive education was based on testing and analysing the curriculum. He worked to combine philosophy, psychology and pedagogy. Surprisingly, Dewey never put forward any systematic surveys or suggested future directions for educational research to take in his writings. He never published any systematic data on the effects of their experience in the laboratory school on the children.

In 1904, the same year Dewey left the University of Chicago for Columbia University, the psychologist Edward Thorndike published an introduction to the theory of mental and social measurements in which he argued for a solid and positivist theoretical approach to educational research and theory (Thorndike 1904). Thorndike recommended the separation of philosophy and psychology. His aim was not to collect data with a view to creating a census, but rather to use this data to produce accurate statistics and measurements which could then be analysed. Thorndike was behind the introduction of the empirical and experimental approach within educational research: 'We conquer the facts of nature when we observe and experiment upon them. When we measure them we have made them our servants' (1903: 164). Thorndike became a highly influential scientist in the field of educational research and his research method has been broadly accepted and adopted in university settings both in the United States and in Europe. His behaviourist approach to education was a strong influence on Skinner. The success of Thorndike's approach in terms of educational research over that of Dewey marked a key moment in defining a science of education and in anchoring it to the empirical terrain of psychology.

At the same time, in France, Alfred Binet was working in the same direction as Thorndike and contributed to confirming psychology as an academic discipline at the end of the nineteenth century with the creation of the journal of psychology, *Année psychologique*, in 1895. In 1904 the French Minister for Education asked Binet (a doctor and psychologist) to study the measures which could be taken to enable 'abnormal children' to benefit from education. The French Minister for Public Education called on his skills to create a tool which would enable children liable to experience the greatest learning difficulties to be identified. Alfred Binet recruited the services of the doctor Théodore Simon. The Binet–Simon psychometric scale was designed to quickly diagnose retardation by comparing the child's performances with others in his or her age group. Binet (1909) refused to exclude those deemed borderline retarded. Far from seeking to remove certain pupils from the schooling system in the name of segregationist ideology, Binet actually intended to set up an adapted reception structure for them to enable them to be reintegrated into normal classes as quickly as possible. Psychometry and the measurement of the cognitive abilities of pupils then became a central preoccupation, as compulsory schooling must deal with the issue of pupils who do not learn. Therefore, the aim of the systematic measurement of children's cognition was to better understand and adapt schools to different school-going groups.

The cognitive development of the child would occupy a central position in educational research throughout the entire first half of the twentieth century, with the aim of constructing an education based on scientific psychology. Understanding the characteristics of the child should automatically lead to a scientifically adapted school. Behaviourism aspired to be a scientific psychology founded on the empirical observation and testing of behaviour-related phenomena. It studied the observable actions and reactions of any organism in response to observable stimuli. This behavioural psychology hoped to discover the laws which govern the behaviours of living organisms and therefore to predict and control these behaviours.

The Swiss psychologist Piaget (1969) formulated the hope that education could eventually become 'an impartial and objective discipline whose authority would impose factual principles and data'. He forcefully denounced the absence of a 'science of education' which was sufficiently well-developed that any educational action depended on it the way medicine depends on biology. Piaget's interactionism postulates that our knowledge experiences are constructed by the interaction between the subject and object. The links between development and learning in children was one of the issues most thoroughly explored by psychologists. In this regard, the debate between the Swiss psychologist Piaget and the Russian psychologist Vygotsky was a passionate one. Piaget was convinced that development was originally an internal process. The initially egocentric child gradually comes to learn through social interactions. However, Vygotsky believed the opposite: that development is basically sociocentric. The child learns through the mediation of peers and adults, which then becomes a process internal to the subject.

Crahay (1998) shows that, in education, we come across two very distinct trends. Some authors 'discount research as soon as they start thinking about educational actions'. The diametrically opposed view was expressed by the founders of experimental pedagogy and the New School. Authors such as Edouard Claparède (who counted J. Piaget among his pupils), Alfred Binet (inventor of the IQ test) and Maria Montessori (founder of the nursery school educational theory) constantly demonstrated the desire for a pedagogy firmly based on scientific foundations. The methods of the New School, however, were based on Piaget's theory of child psychology. Crahay opted for a conciliatory position:

> It is best to affirm the inherently socio-historical nature of education and simultaneously to claim a right and a duty for the scientific approach to refute pedagogical ideas.... The most securely-held pedagogic convictions must be put to the test according to strict information gathering principles.
>
> (Crahay 1998: 153)

The second step in educational research that we can consider psychology-related is defined by the importance of measurements and a gradual systematisation of research methodologies. The start of the twentieth century coincided with the illusion of a purely scientific pedagogy. This imagined a pedagogy which would be linked to child and adolescent psychology. The understanding of the child's cognitive development would enable scientific teaching methods to be identified. However, the illusion that a scientific psychology, working on the model of the natural sciences, could provide the means for determining effective teaching did not last. The scientific approach to education would largely be defended and illustrated by the singular science that we call psychology. In the twentieth century, it was mainly psychology which would seek to achieve dominance as the science of education. In fact, for a long time, the science of education and psychology of education formed, in least in the minds of psychologists, a single science based on the model of the natural sciences. In terms of methodology, the second period saw the increase in testing and work in the laboratory. Statistics were an effective instrument for supporting or refuting emerging psychological and educational theories.

The contribution of the sociology of education

While the beginning of the introduction of compulsory schooling gave rise to the emergence of tests in educational research, the mid-twentieth century saw another major divide in educational research. Post-war European societies, which were prospering economically, introduced widespread access to secondary education. The sociology of education then clearly highlighted the role of the school in reproducing inequalities. Three authors, among many, can be cited as having contributed to confirming the role played by the sociology of education in educational research: Coleman in the United States, Bernstein in the UK and Bourdieu in France.

The work of James Coleman had a major impact on governmental policy as regards education in the United States and gave rise to a number of controversies. In 1966, he presented a report (*Equality of Educational Opportunity*) to the US Congress in which he concluded that black children from underprivileged areas achieved better results when they were integrated into schools attended by the middle classes. The Coleman report therefore formed the sociological foundation for a vast programme of desegregation, organising a bus system to ferry children to schools in order to achieve a racial balance, a practice which met with strong resistance from white parents in many regions of the United States (Coleman 1966).

Bernstein had a decisive influence on sociological research into education. He carried out several years of empirical research in the UK and in other countries, during which efforts were made to test his theories with empirical evidence. His research was used as a basis for facilitating understanding of the complex relationship between the pedagogic code of the family and the school, the differences in social class among families, the educational development of the child and the child's results and academic behaviour (Bernstein 1996).

Bourdieu highlighted the importance of cultural and symbolic factors in schools' reproduction of social hierarchies. He criticised the emphasis placed on economic factors and underlined the ability of persons in a position of domination to impose their cultural and symbolic production (Bourdieu and Passeron 1970; Bourdieu 1972). Bourdieu believed that the education system transmits knowledge similar to that which exists in the dominant social class. This means that the children of the dominant class have a *cultural capital* which allows them to adapt more easily to academic requirements and, as a consequence, to be more successful in their studies. According to Bourdieu, this ensures the legitimisation of social reproduction.

The main aim of these educational sociologists was to question the school's ability to reduce social inequalities. Compared to the previous period, it was no longer the pupil as an individual which interested researchers, but the pupil as belonging to a social category, an ethnic group or a home environment. Educational research also focused on the role of the school and of the family as social institutions during the second half of the twentieth century. However, a number of criticisms were levelled at the sociology of education. In particular, it was criticised as a form of sociological determinism which considered individuals as passive in the face of social or institutional structures.

In this third stage of research, we can observe that governments, by means of the statistical databases they provide to researchers, have set themselves up as the main actors in educational research. The creation in the United States of the Educational Resources Information Center (ERIC) in 1966 demonstrated the importance of databases in the development of educational research during this period. It exemplified the new role of the state in educational research throughout this period. At a methodological level, this period saw the emergence of both statistical tools used for educational research and also of large pools of subjects.

During this third stage in the history of educational research, this scientific activity brought together several disciplines in the social sciences and the humanities: sociology, psychology, history, science of teaching, economics, ethnology. For this reason, educational sciences were often criticised by their adversaries for their hybrid and multidisciplinary nature, which could call into question the status of the scientific discipline on a par with the traditional academic disciplines. In response to this epistemological question, the defenders of educational research underlined that the main feature of the field is precisely that it is multidisciplinary (Hofstetter and Schneuwly 2004). Charlot (1995) explained that the fact that educational sciences invest in multiple directions is considered either as a modern academic creation, or as a demeaning fragmentation. In either event, the educational sciences now form an integral part of scientific research into education.

Contemporary challenges faced by educational research: guiding educational policies

At the end of the twentieth century, two events occurred which turned educational research on its head: economic globalisation and the move, desired by some, towards a knowledge society in which ICT (information and communication technologies) would play a key role. During the last two decades, educational research has shown significant growth in line with economic development processes and the increased economic competition between countries. The need to have a larger, better trained workforce in the post-industrial economy has given rise to discussions on the role, the implementation and, most importantly, the results observed or expected from the education system (Lessard and Meirieu 2005).

In terms of disciplines used for reference, the trend is no longer towards the domination of a single discipline within educational research, but rather a combination of psychological, sociological, anthropological, pedagogical and other approaches in an attempt to identify the problems in education. The combination of quantitative and qualitative research methodologies is also very much the current trend.

The contemporary period is marked by both an increase in educational research and also by its extreme fragmentation. For this reason, Hargreaves (2007) has rightly called for a radical paradigm shift. By way of illustration, he compares educational research with medical research. He considers research in the medical or natural sciences as cumulative. Research projects explicitly aim to build on previous research, either confirming or contradicting it. Researchers attempt to replace old understandings with better analyses or emerging theories. Educational research is not cumulative, as very few researchers in this field aim to build a knowledge base which has been tested, extended or renewed systematically over a long period of time.

The contemporary era in educational research is also marked by the omnipresence of policy in education. This is not policy as understood by the Brazilian educational theorist Freire (1995) in *Pedagogy of the Oppressed* or by certain Marxist authors, but policy in the sense of educational policies driven by the state. Educational research for some policy makers becomes primarily a decision-making tool for educational policies. The most emblematic phenomenon of this period is the development of international comparative studies such as PISA (Programme for International Student Assessment) and TIMSS (*Trends in International Mathematics and Science Study*). The underlying idea behind these studies is to aid the government of educational systems and to promote a convergence between educational systems, at the very least within OECD countries. This government of educational systems through numbers (Felouzis and Hanhart 2011) is the successor of psychometrics, but also of the sociological databases of the 1960s and 1970s, to which can be added the new concern for evaluation of pupils' learning.

The start of the twenty-first century has also favoured the increased involvement of international organisations, private foundations and pressure groups as diverse as press bodies and employer or trade union organisations in education research. These institutions are all attempting to employ the results of educational research for specific sociopolitical and economic agendas. They also highlight the potential practical applications of educational research, a proposal which until relatively recently has been neglected by academic research. For example, over the last few decades the World Bank has continued to recommend the privatisation of secondary and higher education, particularly for developing countries.

Educators and educational researchers have adopted policies and strategies in response to the concerns and interest expressed by public opinion, by government officials and by philanthropic foundations. The responses made by researchers always have long-term consequences as we can see with the Coleman report, which still exerts an influence in debates on educational research within the United States. Deliberation on the merits of quantitative research, as opposed to qualitative research, the discussion of the differences in academic achievement between sociocultural groups and the emphasis currently placed on value-added research make up the centre ground of debates (Johanningmeier and Richardson 2007).

Over the past decade, developments in cognitive sciences have shed new light on how we learn. Studies of cognition focus on the 'learning subject', his or her memory, his or her conceptions. Taking education and learning to be information processing activities, cognitive sciences analyse the processes which enable the acquisition and reapplication of knowledge to be facilitated.

In parallel to educational research's keen interest in cognitive sciences, research is also focusing on the impact of globalisation. Appadurai (2006) suggests that we reconnect the steps which unite knowledge, globalisation, citizenship and research. His view of the world in which we live is that it is characterised by a growing gap between the globalisation of knowledge and the knowledge of globalisation:

> This is why it is important to deparochialise the idea of research and make it more widely available to young people with a wide range of interests and aspirations. Research, in this sense, is not only the production of original ideas and new knowledge (as it is normally defined in academia and other knowledge-based institutions).
>
> (Appadurai 2006)

Another contemporary challenge for educational research: guiding the development of some human occupations

The job of a teacher, like other occupations involved in education and training, has undergone many reforms over several decades, as part of what we would now call the 'professionalisation process'. While the professionalisation of teachers is a concept with roots in English-speaking countries – in particular the United States – it has now been transformed into a global phenomenon, present in many national contexts. The challenges and the steps of the professionalisation process vary according to each of these contexts; however, elements of international convergence can be clearly identified. By way of example, we can cite social recognition or recognition of status, freedom from competing logics, the rationalisation of practices delimiting a recognised expertise, the increase in societal demands as relates to the school universe, or even the elevation in the level of teacher training.

The impact of the professionalisation process on the different teaching systems remains poorly understood. Educational sciences have gradually appropriated this subject of research by largely taking as reference an Anglo-Saxon sociological tradition of studying human occupations and, more specifically, professions. Comparative approaches, particularly between the different 'academicised' systems of teacher training, have been developed over recent years. Furthermore, an in-depth reflection on 'teacher effectiveness' (Anderson 2004) also emerged in the scientific literature during the same period. This took very different directions depending on the context. In North America, *process–product* type research (on this subject, see in particular Wang *et al.* 1993) was intended to be prescriptive, occupying an even more important position. Extending and sometimes opposing this, a number of researchers focused on the development of cognitive theories to build new intelligibility models for teaching practice.

The learner gradually becomes the active party and the role of the teacher changes, coming to interact with his or her pupils. Holistic 'environmental' models reinstated the importance of the *situation* within which the teaching in question takes place, and the implementation and the management of situations. The concept of *situation* replaces that of *objective* in research, used in the *process–product* paradigm.

The process of professionalisation does not only concern the task of teachers. Educational research was able to highlight the increase in new education-related jobs and professions whose agents have been increasingly taking over the roles and tasks previously entrusted to regular teachers (Tardif and Levasseur 2010). The new forms for organising educational work and the division of jobs and professions in education now provides fertile ground for educational research.

Lastly, educational research cannot limit itself to observing the phenomenon of professionalisation of jobs within education. It is directly involved with and guides the development of the professions through the knowledge that it produces and communicates. The challenges are manifold, but we shall outline four here.

In many countries, the overhaul of initial teacher training constitutes one of the main levers in the professionalisation process. Research makes a major contribution to the modelling and subsequent analysis of vocational training, particularly since educational researchers are themselves involved in training future teaching professionals. One of the goals and challenges of integrating research into the process of professionalising teacher training is without a doubt the control and analysis of the governance of teacher training systems. The place, role and potential benefits of research into education (and into training) are largely yet to be clarified, despite the fact that the professionalisation process is not considered to have been successfully completed in many countries.

The second challenge concerns the integration of knowledge arising from research into the vocational training curriculum, even though theory and practice are systematically set against each other. Educational researchers still largely have to face a two-fold challenge: to ensure the results of educational research can be transposed didactically so that these integrate the reference knowledge for the teaching professions; to contribute to the transmission and construction of meaning for this reference knowledge in the field of vocational training.

Ensuring the model of the reflective practitioner is valued in the definition of teaching as a profession has contributed to the legitimisation of scientific training for future teachers. The goal of educational researchers is to introduce these professionals to social science research methods. This challenge is far from an easy one as it is difficult to make teacher practitioners adhere to research practices that they consider to be disconnected from their professional practices. But, in fact, the main goal is not to create a new generation of scientists. The challenge for research and educational researchers is to guide an ongoing process which must promote the construction of reflective skills thanks to the transfer, in different contexts and experiences, of what was learnt during epistemological and methodological training to research.

The last challenge relates to the participation of educational research in the construction of professional knowledge specific to each teaching and education profession.

This construction cannot be realised without the involvement of the professionals themselves in collaborative research processes aimed at making educational phenomena intelligible and formalising the professional experience, notably to ensure it can be communicated in initial and continuing education institutions.

Conclusion

In this chapter we have attempted to give the reader a brief overview of the development of educational research and its contemporary challenges. Other authors have attempted this complicated task. Knox (1971), in particular, identified four periods of educational research in the United States: (1) the emergence of education as a field of study (1855–1895); (2) the period of empiricism (1895–1938); (3) the assumption of a pragmatic orientation; and (4) the emergence of a major role in research for the federal government. During the first period, curriculum reformers relied upon new European ideas on education, and the federal government disseminated these ideas. Changes based on scientific investigation and controlled experimentation marked the second period, which was highlighted by the founding of John Dewey's laboratory school at the University of Chicago and the rise of education as a field of graduate study. Rapid growth and proliferation of responsibility for the sponsorship of R&D programmes have characterised research since 1965.

This was therefore an attempt to analyse the historical evolution of educational research. This evolution was at the intersection between (1) the strategies practised by

TABLE 22.1 Main historical periods in the development of educational research

	First period From antiquity to the middle of the nineteenth century	**Second period** From the mid nineteenth century to the mid twentieth century	**Third period** From the mid twentieth century to the end of the twentieth century	**Fourth period** Twenty-first century
Reference disciplines	Philosophy Theology Comparative education	Psychology Biology	Sociology Anthropology	Neurosciences Multidisciplinarity Global studies
Dominant debates	Humanism Search for meaning	Measurements and tests	Social inequalities	Accountability International comparison Educational standards Professionalisation
Methodologies	Observation Educational trips	Experimental methods Empiricism	Statistical databases Longitudinal studies	Articulation of quantitative and qualitative methods

the different scientific disciplines to occupy the terrain of education and academic research (philosophy, psychology, sociology, anthropology, etc.); (2) the major socio-cultural events (introduction of compulsory schooling, mass access to secondary schooling, increase in international migration, globalisation); and (3) the interest of public policies in using educational research to drive the desired change to the educational systems. This intersection forms the basis of educational research. This historical overview is summarised in Table 22.1.

Note

1. The slave demonstrates an example of Pythagoras' theorem.

References

Al-Ghazali. (2010). *Le Livre du savoir*. Vevey: Editions de l'Aire.

Anderson, L. (2004). *Increasing teacher effectiveness*. Paris: UNESCO

Appadurai, A. (2006). The right to research. *Globalisation, Societies and Education*, 4(2), 167–177.

Bernstein, B. (1996). *Pedagogy, symbolic control and identity: Theory, research, critique*. London: Taylor & Francis Ltd.

Binet, A. (1909). *Les idées modernes sur les enfants*. Paris: Ernest Flammarion Editeur.

Bourdieu, P. (1972). *Esquisse d'une théorie de la pratique précédée de Trois études d'ethnologie kabyle*. Geneva: Droz.

Bourdieu, P. and Passeron, J.C. (1970). *La reproduction*. Paris: Minuit.

Charlot, B. (ed.). (1995). *Les sciences de l'éducation, un enjeu, un défi*. Paris: ESF éditeur.

Coleman, J.S. (1966). *Equality of educational opportunity (COLEMAN) study (EEOS)*. Computer file. Ann Arbor, MI: Inter-university Consortium for Political and Social Research (distributor), accessed 27 April 2007.

Comenius, J.A.K. ([2002] 1627–1632). *La Grande didactique ou l'art universel de tout enseigner à tous*. Trans. de Marie-Françoise Bosquet-Frigout, Dominique Saget, Bernard Jolibert. 2nd edition, reviewed and corrected. Paris, Klincksieck.

Crahay, M. (1998). Peut-on, et comment, concilier recherche en éducation et réflexion de l'action éducative? In C. Hadja and J. Baillé (eds), *Recherche et éducation: vers une nouvelle alliance. La démarche de preuve en éducation* (pp. 125–159). Brussels: De Boeck Université.

De Landsheere, G. (1979). *Dictionnaire de l'évaluation et de la recherche en éducation*. Paris: PUF.

Felouzis, G. and Hanhart, S. (ed.). (2011). *Gouverner l'éducation par les nombres? Usages, débats et controverses*, Brussels: De Boeck.

Freire, P. (1995). *Pedagogy of Hope: Reliving the pedagogy of the oppressed*. New York: Continuum.

Hargreaves, D. (2007). Teaching as a research-based profession: possibilities and prospects. In M. Hammersley (ed.), *Educational research and evidence-based practice* (pp. 3–17). London: SAGE and Open University.

Hofstetter, R. and Schneuwly, B. (2004). Introduction: educational sciences in dynamic and hybrid institutionalization. *Pedagogica Historica*, 40(5), 569–589.

Johanningmeier, E.V. and Richardson, T.R. (eds) (2007). *Educational research, the national agenda, and educational reform: A history*. Charlotte, NC: Information Age Publishers.

Jullien-de-Paris, M.A. (1817). *Esquisse et vues préliminaires d'un ouvrage sur l'éducation comparée*, Paris: Colas.

Knox, H. (1971). *A history of educational research in the United States*. Washington, DC: National Institute of Education.

Lessard, C. and Meirieu, P. (eds). (2005). *L'obligation de résultats en éducation. Evolutions, perspectives et enjeux internationaux*. Brussels: Editions de Boeck.

Lubienskim, C. and Scott, J. (2011). The rise of intermediary organizations in knowledge production, advocacy, and educational policy. *Teachers College Record*, 22 July, www.tcrecord.org, ID Number: 16487, accessed: 25 April 2014.

Meirieu, P. (1994). *Histoire et actualité de la pédagogie. Repères théoriques et bibliographiques*. Lyon: Université-Lumière-Lyon 2.

Piaget, J. (1969). *Psychologie et pédagogie*. Paris: Denoël.

Rogers, C.R. (1972). *Liberté pour apprendre*. Paris: Dunod.

Tardif, M. and Levasseur, L. (2010). *La division du travail éducatif, une perspective nord-américaine*. Paris: Presses universitaires de France.

Thorndike, E.L. (1903). *Educational psychology*. New York: Lemcke and Buechner.

Thorndike E.L. (1904). *An introduction to the theory of mental and social measurements*. New York: Teachers College, Columbia University.

Wang, M.C., Haertel, G.D. and Walberg, H.J. (1993). Toward a knowledge base for school learning. *Review of Educational Research, 63*, 249–294

Yutang, L. (2008). *La sagesse de Confucius*. Paris: Editions Picquier.

Research in professional contexts

Catherine Matheson and David Matheson

I believe in innovation and that the way you get innovation is [that] you fund research.

Bill Gates

Introduction

This chapter aims to introduce the reader to some basic techniques in how to carry out research not just *in* one's own professional context but *on* one's own professional context to offer you some guidance as to how to put these into practice.

The notion of researching one's own practice goes back, informally at least, to the time when teachers first became aware that their practice need not be fixed. This was the moment when teachers began to realise that they were not obliged to teach as they themselves had been taught[1] but that they could, at least to a degree, be inventive and imaginative in their pedagogy. Depending on one's perspective and preference, this can take us back at least to the great nineteenth-century headmaster of Uppingham School, Edward Thring, who revised and reformed the pedagogy of his establishment, or to such reformers as Thomas Arnold of Rugby School. Arnold improved diet and housing, moral tone, discipline with a new way of using the prefect system, widened the curriculum to include mathematics and languages along with Greek and Latin; he thought about more efficient teaching methods in order to get the interest of the pupils (Staunton 1877).

These, however, were lone figures and their example was not one much followed until the flourishing of progressive education in the twentieth century. However, they showed a willingness to examine their own practice, ascertain where improvement was needed, develop a strategy for improvement and not only put it into practice but also amass evidence to show others how well it had worked.

Since the Second World War, practitioner research and evidence-based practice has come eventually to signify a set of well-defined processes whereby the practitioner – no longer isolated as were Thring and Arnold but working in terms of accepted and established practice – identifies a problem or a situation (and such an identification is a personal decision) and sets about increasing his/her understanding of it. In some varieties of practitioner research, the overall aim of this process is to develop a solution to the problem or an improvement to the situation and to evaluate its effectiveness.

At this point we need to distinguish between two senses of practitioner research. One is concerned simply with research carried out by a person who happens to be a practitioner and which is hoped to have a positive influence (again, this is a personal construction) on his/her practice, although this may be difficult to quantify. After all, if one has increased one's understanding of the impact on learning made by one's students' socio-economic or cultural circumstances, then while it is reasonable to hope that one will have become more sensitive to one's students' needs, it is highly unlikely that one will be able to directly measure the effect this has had on one's students.

A second concerns itself explicitly with researching what goes on in the course of one's practice. It is principally with this and with one variety of it – action research – that we are concerned in this chapter.

Action research

'Action research has been traditionally defined as an approach to research that is based on a collaborative problem-solving relationship between researcher and client, which aims at both solving a problem and generating new knowledge' (Coghlan 2003: 452). Action research demands a degree of involvement with the 'clients' that is not needed in other forms of insider research, such as conducting a policy contextualisation and analysis of one's organisation. From this alone, it throws up ethical issues which require particular attention – but more of this anon.

Action research 'is an increasingly popular approach among small-scale researchers in the social sciences [education, health and social care] in order to improve practice. It offers a systematic approach to the definition, solution and evaluation of problems and concerns' (Blaxter *et al.* 2001: 67).

The idea of action research is attributed to Lewin who, in 1946, coined the term action research and used it as a methodology to investigate and improve major social problems and bring about social change based on democratic principles (Kemmis 1993; Hopkins 1995). Lewin had perhaps grander ideas than the average modern practitioner seeking to improve his/her practice in the classroom or workshop, but his fundamental idea still pertains. For Lewin and his associates, action research involves 'a cyclical process of diagnosing a change situation or a problem, planning, gathering data, taking action and then fact-finding about the results of that action in order to plan and take further action' (Coghlan 2003: 452).

Nunes and McPherson (2003: 431) suggest the notion of the spiral framework, as shown in Figure 23.1, where one begins by diagnosing a problem or an issue. One then plans action, takes action and finally evaluates the action before conducting a second round of diagnosis and each of the subsequent steps. This iterative process is at the heart of Lewin's vision of action research. It does tend to rather assume that one has both the time and the possibility to repeat one's trials. Without elaboration it also implies an assumption that one avoids altering the set-up once one has begun to take action. In this respect, it is somewhat naïve, if not actually dangerous. It is naïve in the

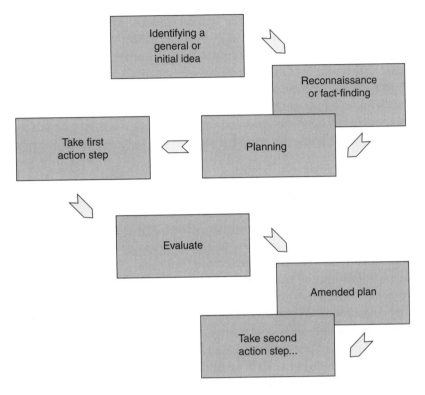

FIGURE 23.1 Lewin's cycle of action research.

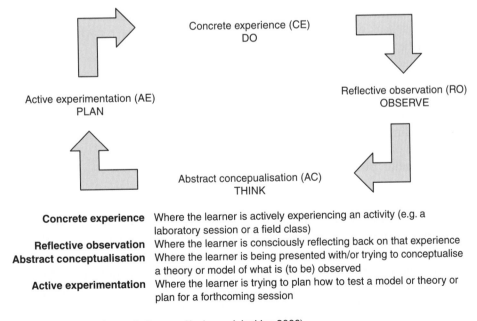

Concrete experience	Where the learner is actively experiencing an activity (e.g. a laboratory session or a field class)
Reflective observation	Where the learner is consciously reflecting back on that experience
Abstract conceptualisation	Where the learner is being presented with/or trying to conceptualise a theory or model of what is (to be) observed
Active experimentation	Where the learner is trying to plan how to test a model or theory or plan for a forthcoming session

FIGURE 23.2 The Kolb learning cycle (source: Healey and Jenkins 2000).

sense that it is a rare practitioner who will be content to sit back and watch a process unfold without intervening. In fact, it is a rare situation where the practitioner would be able to do this as practice by definition usually requires intervention. It is dangerous in the sense that it implies that even if one sees the project going completely awry then one should wait until the evaluation phase before doing anything about it. It would be a rare teacher who would do this.

In some respects, Lewin's notion of action research resembles Kolb's learning cycle (Figure 23.2), which is itself derived from Lewin's cycle of adult learning (Atherton 2002).

Planning action research

As Coghlan and Casey (2001) remind us, 'action research is an approach to research which aims at taking action and creating knowledge or theory about that action' (p. 676). 'It simultaneously involves generating data and analysis together with actions aimed at transforming the situation in democratic directions. It is context-bound producing practical solutions and new knowledge' (Greenwood and Levin 1998: 50). What it does, by definition, is to impinge directly on the lives of those involved in it. It is no exaggeration to say that an action research project can and will change lives, perhaps only to a small degree, perhaps fundamentally.[2] With this major caveat in mind, how does one begin the planning of such an undertaking?

To engage in the 'type of inquiry that is fluid, emergent and cyclical' (Christenson *et al.* 2002: 260) requires careful preparation. One approach is that advocated by Costello (2003), which consists primarily in signing on at one's local higher education institution (HEI) and taking a module involving action research! While there is an undoubted appeal in this approach (especially from the point of view of the HEI, which is ever seeking students), it does not do much for those for whom such modules are impractical. So where to start?

Every action research has a similar set of constituents:

1. an issue or problem to be investigated and/or resolved;
2. an aim and a set of research questions;
3. a grounding in the literature;
4. an action plan;
5. an evaluation plan;
6. revision.

Figure 23.3 shows how these might be arranged. However, nothing prevents steps 1, 2 and 3 being arranged in the order 3, 1, 2. It is not uncommonly the case that in reading the literature one becomes aware of what might constitute an issue and one also increases one's awareness of the language used to describe and delineate that issue. Additionally it is all too easy to assume that how one has always done certain things is the only way to do them and that there are no alternatives. The literature can serve to open one's eyes.

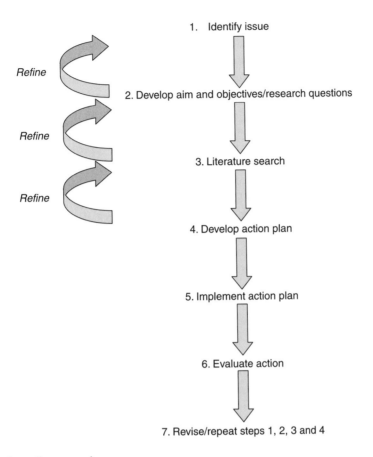

1. Identify issue

Refine

2. Develop aim and objectives/research questions

Refine

3. Literature search

Refine

4. Develop action plan

5. Implement action plan

6. Evaluate action

7. Revise/repeat steps 1, 2, 3 and 4

FIGURE 23.3 Planning action research.

The literature

Education has the wonderful attribute that much, if not most, of its literature is accessible to the debutante. Macintyre (2000) eulogises over the literature and reminds us that the literature can help us pinpoint a topic 'which would be both relevant and interesting for the researcher and contextually available' (p. 3). This is potentially crucial when one finds oneself in the situation where one is obliged to undertake a research project as part, for example, of a degree or of further training/education or as part of an appraisal process.

Macintyre (2000) also reminds us that the literature helps us in focusing our thinking. It lets us see what others have done and gives us examples to follow, or in some cases to avoid. The literature allows us to build on what has already been done (Brown 1990; Stark 1998) and in doing so it gives our research academic credibility since it allows us to show how our present work is extending knowledge.

This term sounds rather grander than it is in reality. Anything which has not been done before extends knowledge. Using someone else's techniques in a new situation –

perfectly acceptable provided you don't pretend it's your own invention and you do this by crediting the source – extends knowledge. Extension of knowledge is frequently quite small in both its impact and its scope.

A major caveat with the literature concerns just how much of it you should use. If you are too parsimonious then you may well miss essential pieces of work. If you attempt to be exhaustive, then you will never get anything else done – unless you land on some obscure topic that no one else has ever researched. What you need is enough to demonstrate that you have a reasonable grip on the topic – and if no one has looked at it before, on neighbouring topics that relate closely to the topic in hand. Spread yourself across not only books (and individual chapters), but also articles in refereed journals on education. There is a not uncommon tendency for students and beginning researchers to avoid education journal articles in the mistaken belief that they are difficult to comprehend. Certainly some are, but most are not. What using journal articles demonstrates is that you are effectively going to the horse's mouth and getting material directly from the source. Journal articles are where researchers like yourself publish their results; books are a common place for others to discuss them. There is of course the internet, that vast repository of every aspect of human experience that it is possible to depict as word, image or sound. There are many serious internet sources, as those in the references at the end of this chapter show and an increasing number of open access refereed journals available for free online. Many researchers also present their findings at conferences and a vast number of conference papers are lodged on the Education-line database, which can be found at www.leeds.ac.uk/educol.

However, there is also a lot of nonsense. Practice and a fair dose of cynicism will help you distinguish between them. As we are talking about evidence-based research, it is appropriate to suggest that a question to ask of any material is simply 'how do you know this?' The lesser sources will use polemic and assertion while the better sources will use argument and evidence.

Finally don't assume that *new* literature means *better* literature and that *old* means *worse*. *Old* means historical and nothing more. There are old publications, even from thousands of years ago (such as those of Plato), which might well be relevant to your research. Relevancy is the key, not age. Do remember, however, that every publication is a product of its age and may well refer to events as contemporary but which from the present perspective are very much historical.

The aim and the research questions

The aim is simply what one sets out to achieve, or to investigate. It is the direction in which one travels. So, for example, a teacher using action research to examine issues around numeracy in her class might have as the aim *to investigate improving numeracy in a pre-nursing course*. The research questions[3] are much more the nuts and bolts of what you are attempting to do. They are, if you prefer, the steps on the way towards achieving the aim. One thing to bear in mind, though, is that the research questions (and indeed the aim) you start off with may well not be the ones you finish with.

As Sally Brown (1990) reminds us, even the most seasoned researchers can get carried away with ideas of what is possible in a given time period. We can all easily get too ambitious or otherwise unrealistic and have to curb our enthusiasm as reality kicks in. However, as Brown further states, such modifications have to be done *consciously*.

For the numeracy example above, research questions might be the following:

1. What is the level of numeracy at the start of the course?
2. What is the attitude of students towards numeracy at the start of the course?
3. What factors during the course affected the students' numeracy and their attitudes towards numeracy?

Notice the use of two base points (questions 1 and 2), while question 3 highlights areas that can be further investigated either with this cohort or with a successor cohort. The action here is the gathering of evidence as to what affects student numeracy. Once this is achieved then you are in a position to suitably modify teaching materials. And at that point, you are also in a position to carry out a further piece of action research to determine whether your modifications are successful.

Data collection

Space does not permit us to delve into the various forms of data collection, and the reader is referred to the references at the end of this chapter. However, whatever the approach you take to data collection, it needs to relate to the research questions. Also of great importance is to only collect data that have some bearing on the research questions. So, if the age of your respondents has no bearing on the research questions, then why ask for it? It may be useful as background material on the participants or it may be wholly irrelevant. If you decide to ask for it, make sure you know why you are doing so. Ethnicity is similar, but with a twist. While there is only one way to label age, there are umpteen to label ethnicity and none is really satisfactory. It is safer, if you need to ask for ethnicity, to ask people to say what ethnic group they feel they belong to – and to permit 'don't know' as a response. This may lead to a plethora of categories but at least no one will feel offended that their group has been left out.

Interviews can be structured, semi-structured or unstructured. Structured interviews are really just questionnaires which are delivered orally. The order of the questions is fixed for all participants. Semi-structured interviews have a more fluid approach. Opening questions may be the same for all participants. Everyone will cover the same questions/topics, but the order can be allowed to vary to suit the participant. Semi-structured interviews resemble a conversation more than do structured interviews. Unstructured interviews are individual conversations around a topic where the conversation goes where it will, within the broad confines of the topic at hand. Questions may be closed, in that there is a limited range of responses possible and the respondent chooses from a list, or open, in that the respondent is free to say whatever she/he feels replies to the question.

Whether you choose interviews (whether structured, semi-structured or unstructured[4]), questionnaires,[5] observations,[6] tests, focus groups or whatever, you absolutely must pilot your instrument. An interview is not just a series of questions and neither is a questionnaire. For one thing, the question you think you are asking may not always be the question your respondent answers. Piloting with respondents drawn from as close a group as possible to the one you will be examining – and this means trying out the instrument on them and discussing with them what they felt about it – will reduce enormously the chances of the whole thing going awry. Similarly for observations. Check out what you are going to observe and make a conscious decision as to how you are going to observe it. Decide whether your observations are going to be structured or not. Decide what you are looking for and from whom you are looking for it – it is well nigh impossible to observe a whole group, and indeed observing a couple of individuals can be hard enough. However, be prepared for surprises (Bell 2002).

Interviews can be conducted with groups as well as with individuals. Often referred to as focus groups, group interviews can be less intimidating for participants than an individual interview, but they can suffer from the garrulous participant who seem never to let others speak. They can also suffer from the participants who are too shy to say a word. What follows is a simple technique which we have used in all sorts of contexts – in schools, in colleges, in hospitals, in universities. We have used it with teachers, with students, with university faculty, with senior medical practitioners. We have used it in research and we have used it with teaching. It is derived from Davies *et al.* (2001) and discussed in detail in Matheson and Matheson (2009).

Metaplanning: a recipe for successful focus groups

Metaplanning can be used as a discussion starter to get participants thinking about issues. It is a variation on *force field analysis*[7] and looks at drivers and barriers. To use metaplanning, you need a topic with pros and cons. Anything dichotomous will do as long as it is appropriate to the research. For example, if you were researching students' expectations of a masters in education, you might set it out as follows:

The material required consists of:

Four colours of square post-its, sticky dots (two colours), four sheets of flipchart paper, board markers, two audio recorders with fresh batteries (this is not just in case one stops working but also to get recordings from two perspectives, an essential point when participants can be moving about as happens when they are categorising their responses – see 1b and 2b below).

1. What are the positive expectations of masters study in education?
    a. Four post-its: what are your positive expectations of doing a masters in education? Each participant to respond as quickly as possible, one positive per post-it. Participants stick the post-its anywhere on the sheet marked *Positives*.
    b. The group puts the post-its into categories and gives each category a name.
    c. Vote (three sticky dots per participant): vote for categories, *not* for individual post-its (this can be done after the negatives have been put up and categorised)

2. What are the negative expectations of masters study in education?
    a. Four post-its: what are your negative expectations of doing a masters in education? Each participant to respond as quickly as possible, one negative per post-it. Participants stick the post-its anywhere on the sheet marked *Negatives.*
    b. The group puts the post-its into categories and gives each category a name.
    c. Vote (three sticky dots per participant): vote for categories, *not* for individual post-its (this can be done after the positives have been put up and categorised).
3. Summary and comment/discussion: to what extent have these expectations so far reflected reality?
4. Fresh post-it: which negative can overcome all the positives? This need not be a repeat of a previous idea. Stick on sheet.
5. Fresh post-it: which positive can overcome all the negatives? This need not be a repeat of a previous idea. Stick on sheet.
6. Discussion.

The post-its give the participants' thoughts in their own words, their own spelling (which might be significant), their own priorities. A metaplanning exercise provides a rich mass of both quantitative and qualitative data. The former comes from the voting, the number of categories, the number of words used. The latter comes from the terms used, the metaphors employed, the categories, as well as from the recordings of the discussions both during and after the post-it exercise.

Data analysis

Data analysis is an essential part of planning the action research. Simply put, if you don't know how you are going to analyse the data you will acquire then you need either to find out how or look for other data-gathering tools.

There are entire volumes devoted to research methods which give much space to data analysis (Cohen and Manion (1996) and Bell (2002) are good examples which are useful for the beginning researcher). Data analysis can be complicated or simple, statistical or not. It all depends on the data gathered and the information that is required from it.

Beginning researchers are frequently drawn to questionnaires and interviews and so it to these that we shall devote a little space.

Most questionnaires contain some questions demanding simple factual answers. These might ask for the respondents' age, gender, ethnicity, previous educational attainment and so on. Analysis of such responses is done most readily by means of simple statistics to give you, for example, the mean age, the most common ethnicity, the gender balance and so on. Responses to open questions can be categorised and grouped according to how the respondents have replied. In this way, themes can start to emerge and you can see the extent to which they are shared between the participants. This begins the process of analysis and you can then discuss just how significant the themes are. It is at this point that the factual data you have gathered can come into its own. For example, is a particular theme spread equally between genders or is it predominantly or even exclusively in only one? What can you surmise from this?

Interviews can be similarly analysed. For detail on the various interview types, you are referred to Bell (2002) and Gillham (2000). Do bear in mind, though, that interviews should always be recorded but only with the participant's permission. Recording allows you to listen more closely to what your participant is saying. It also allows you to listen again to what was said and, as importantly, to *how* it was said. There is much more to an interview than just the words that were used. Lastly, recording allows you to make an accurate transcript of the interview. Metaplanning, as mentioned, has both qualitative and quantitative components which need to be analysed appropriately, while the recordings can be dealt with in much the same way as interviews, except that one needs to distinguish between participants.

Ethics of action research

Action research has the simultaneous advantage and disadvantage of familiarity with both the respondents and the context within which they operate. A major advantage of this is that the researcher does not have to spend large amounts of time getting to know the situation. A disadvantage is that she/he may assume to be obvious aspects of the context which are anything but clear to the outside observer. A greater disadvantage concerns the ethical dimension.

Ethics in this regard can be divided into three categories:

1. confidentiality
2. consent – real and coerced
3. working with the aftermath.

The reader is referred to the BERA Research Guidelines[8] for more detail on some ethical considerations.

Confidentiality

In action research one is dealing with – and frequently experimenting upon – people that one deals with on a daily basis. This can cause stress in terms of confidentiality. You have to take extreme care to avoid, if possible, giving information to anyone and especially in circulated material that will identify particular respondents. Of course, if the respondent is the principal of your establishment then non-identification can be impossible, but in such a case she/he is what is sometimes termed an 'elite respondent'. The usual rules of confidentiality do not apply in such cases but you are well advised to make sure that your respondent is aware of this and agrees to it.

More to the point than the elite respondent is the general group of respondents. Care has to be taken to limit to the absolute minimum the information that is elicited from them as well as limiting the information on them that appears in the final report.

Consistently ask yourself whether you need to include a particular piece of information. If the answer is negative then leave it out. It can be worthwhile asking a trusted colleague who knows the respondents if she/he can identify any individuals. If she/he can, then others might be able to also and so you need to revise what you are saying about them.

Ideally you should maintain confidentiality about the institution as well. However, this is usually impossible as far as your colleagues are concerned. You do need, however, to ensure the institution's confidentiality as far as the wider public is concerned. This may appear quite simple and sometimes it is. Other times, the institution's uniqueness is such that it is impossible. If, for example, you were to have conducted your project on the Liverpool Institute for Performing Arts, you might have quite a job making it disappear in your reported work as it is a somewhat unique institution and this shows through in much of what it does.

Consent: real and coerced

The current received wisdom is that all participants in a research project should either give their consent or that a person in a role of responsibility for them should act as gatekeeper and give consent on their behalf. This latter applies especially in cases of research with children and young people where parents or teachers can fulfil the gate-keeping role. This blanket injunction can create difficulties for the action researcher in particular and for the reflective practitioner in general. Nothing, of course, prevents one from asking children and young people directly for their consent but this needs to be in addition to, not instead of, asking the gatekeeper.

The problem consists of knowing where one's usual practice ends and where the research begins, and this may be a question without an answer. All practitioners observe their learners, whether directly as they undertake tasks or indirectly by looking at assessments, reports, etc.; all informally interview their learners; most modify their practice in the light of what they learn from these observations and interviews. So, should you make clear to your learners that at all times they will be subject to a research-type process since this is what reflective pedagogy is all about? And what to do if someone wants to opt out?

In fact, there's no harm in telling learners what the reflective process consists of and how they contribute to your learning just as you, hopefully, contribute to theirs. Whether they will believe you or not is another matter. As regards opting out, by the logic of this scenario, opting out of being part of a reflective pedagogy can only mean opting out of the class altogether. It is our experience that students adopt one of only two attitudes to being told about the symbiotic nature of teaching and learning: they are either happy to be part of it – especially if a publication might arise or they might contribute to the course improving – or they don't care.

More important in terms of explicit consent is when an experiment – for that is what much of action research consists of – is to be introduced with the class members as participants. In this case, the problem can arise of coerced consent as opposed to that which is freely given.

It is well nigh impossible to be certain that no class member feels obliged to take part in your action research. What you can do, though, is to be open and honest with them and involve them in the planning and execution of the project. We see in Christenson *et al.* (2002) and Fryer (2004) examples of how this might be done. Fryer (2004) mentions the BERA (1992) *Ethical Guidelines for Education Research*, which demand openness and honesty between researcher and participants, a point repeated in the current (BERA 2011) edition. These give a reasonable set of rules of thumb to follow but blind adherence to them may cause problems if your study depends on observing participants. Simply put, when people know they are being observed then they are liable to alter their behaviour. On the other hand, when people are sufficiently observed then they may well cease to be aware of the observer. The problems arise when time is of the essence.

Consent is not a simple procedure, available as a 'one-size-fits-all'. It is complex and needs to be treated with care and attention. In general, though, involving your participants in the project, treating them as responsible persons and taking into account their observations and thoughts – of which there may be many or few – will result in them seeing the project as an occasion to take a hand in determining the shape of their own learning.

Working with the aftermath

One of the problems of any form of the insider researcher is that, at the end of the project, you cannot simply walk away. Your participants, whether they are students or staff, are liable to be around you for some time to come. So, you have to decide whether the action research you undertook with them was a one-off or whether it might be part of a larger process. It is here that the emancipatory aspect of action research (Kemmis 1993) can come to the fore. If carried out in collaboration with the participants then it can be seen as 'a process of systematic reflection upon circumstances to bring about a desired state of affairs' (Schostak 2002: 192). It can act to get people to think about their situation and to see that the status quo is not the only available option. This can open a Pandora's Box or it can simply give a glimmer of hope that can then be extinguished.

In any case, time spent thinking about what happens after the project can be time well spent. Relationships can – and probably will – change during the research process. How you want them to remain needs to be considered.

Developing the action plan

This is where you sit down and decide what exactly you are going to do. The more explicit you are, then in general the better it is. Make sure that you keep the aim and the research questions at the forefront of your mind. Everything that you include in the action plan has to relate to these. It is therefore useful when, for example, you are considering a data collection method, to write down what kind of data you can expect to acquire from this method, what's good about it and what's not, plus how you plan to overcome the negatives. In any case, if your project is destined for submission for an award or for submission to a journal, then you will have to include a discussion of methodology which does exactly this. You may, as Price (2004) does, integrate this discussion into the section on data collection. Price (2004) is an excellent example of the use of, and the reporting of, action research to improve teaching.

You will need more than one research instrument in order to be able to triangulate your findings. So, if your first main instrument is a questionnaire, then you might want to consider doing some interviews or focus groups to allow respondents the opportunity to be more fulsome in their responses. In this way, you triangulate by quite literally setting out to measure the same thing from different directions. The literature will also give you some triangulation by allowing you to see the extent to which what you have found matches what others before you found.

The action plan should also include some kind of outcome that is hoped for. Knowing what you hope for at the end of the process will put you in a far better position to evaluate whether you have achieved it.

For the end of the project

A strategy for improvement?

Depending on the extent of the involvement of your participants in the construction and execution of the project, then the strategy for improvement may be already built-in. A question which needs to be posed, both at this juncture and in developing the action plan, concerns the extent to which improvement is defined by the researcher, by the context within which she/he operates and/or by the participants themselves. If your action research aims at being emancipatory then there is no option but to involve the participants, unless of course you take a paternalistic view of emancipation.

Fundamentally, it all comes down to asking yourself why you are doing this and for whose benefit. What is it that you would like to see at the end of the project that was not evident at the beginning?

A strategy for improvement is often expected in what Agyris (1970) terms 'mechanistic-oriented' research. This is where 'the research is framed in terms of managing change or solving a problem' (Coghlan 2003: 453). As Coghlan (2003) reminds us, this is not the only approach and he highlights Agyris' (1970) notion of 'organistic-oriented' research in which 'enquiry into [participants'] own assumptions and ways of thinking and acting is central to the research process' (Coghlan 2003: 454). Linked to each of these concerns is the action research which is exploratory in nature and which is seeking to better understand the participants, their learning, their context or whatever, before formulating a judgement as to whether improvement is even desirable or possible.

Evaluation of outcomes?

It is quite feasible to enter an action research project without a clear idea, or indeed any idea, of the outcomes that might result. In this case you would have engaged in an action research in which the process itself was the object of enquiry. On the other hand, the opposite is also possible. A frequent, but false, assumption regarding action research is that it must contain a strategy for improvement and that this must be open to evaluation.

If we adopt a mechanistic-oriented approach then such is usually possible. If we are organistic-oriented then it may well not be, at least not in any easily defined manner.

The means of evaluation of outcomes can range from simple pre-test and post-test – if the participants did better on the post-test then the strategy has worked – to in-depth interviews in which the researcher tries to ascertain the manner and extent of changes in attitude. Fundamentally, what it comes down to is looking back to the research questions and ascertaining the extent to which you have responded to them. This may be done by further fieldwork or by argument and discussion of your findings or, indeed, by a combination of these. Remember, though, that not all outcomes are measurable and most of these are not measurable in numbers, no matter how tempting this can be. Numbers can serve to give a semblance of objectivity to the proceedings and this may not be merited at all. However tempting it is to rate pain from 0 (= comfort) to 10 (= agony), it is really quite a meaningless exercise since your slight twinge might be my agony or vice versa.

Conclusion

This has been a brief look at researching practice and in particular at action research – 'a form of self-reflective enquiry' undertaken by practitioners 'in order to improve the rationality and justice of their social or educational practices, their understanding of these practice and the situations in which the practices are carried out' (Kemmis 1993: 177). Action research is currently a very popular pursuit, especially among bodies who see it as a means of creating a reflective workforce, especially in teaching. Quite why they would want to encourage such reflection is open to question but, suffice to say, an inherent danger in action research is that in examining one's practice at a very close distance one loses sight of the bigger picture that surrounds it. With this in mind, it can be very worthwhile considering other approaches to research and using them to expand the picture that one has available.

One might, for example, take a macro-sociological perspective and consider the wider context within which one's learners and one's institution are operating. In this way, one looks at the larger social forces which stimulate and are stimulated by the context of the learners and the institution. What, for example, is the role of social expectation in the lives of the learners? What government initiatives are impacting on their lives and hence on their lives as learners?

One could take a historical perspective and consider how an issue was dealt with, if at all, in previous generations. What we perceive as problems nowadays were very often not so seen in the past. This can impact on the socio-cultural baggage that people bring with them. It can impact on the expectations made of members of society and so on.

One could take a comparative perspective and consider how other places deal with the same issue, if indeed it is an issue for them at all. We could consider how other places view the way in which we treat the issue and go some way towards seeing ourselves as others see us.

One could take a philosophical approach and consider the concepts involved. What does, for example, *numeracy* really mean? What are the implications for further education to have what is easily seen as a punitive inspection system?

There are many more perspectives to choose from. However, regardless what you are researching and why you are doing it, taking more than one perspective will almost inevitably serve to enrich your work and let others see it as more than just a cute example that maybe only pertains to your particular situation.

Notes

An earlier version of this chapter appeared in A. Coles (2004) (ed.) *Teaching in Post-Compulsory Education: Policy, Practice and Values.* London: David Fulton.

1. See, for example, Wells (1918) for a vivid description of the stultifying effect of the teacher who teaches as he was taught and as his own teachers before him were taught.
2. Lest you feel this stance is hyperbolic, consider the fact that within action research one is examining and modifying one's own practice. One is therefore and *per force* impacting on the learning experience of those one is charged to teach.
3. See Lewis and Munn (1997).
4. See Drever (1995); Gillham (2000).
5. See Munn and Drever (1995).
6. See Simpson and Tuson (1995).
7. A useful introduction to force field analysis can be found at www.institute.nhs.uk/quality_and_service_improvement_tools/quality_and_service_improvement_tools/force_field_analysis.html.
8. Available at www.bera.ac.uk/publications/Ethical%20Guidelines.

References

Agyris, C. (1970) *Intervention Theory and Method.* Reading, MA: Addison-Wesley.

Atherton, J.S. (2002) *Learning and Teaching: Learning from Experience.* Available at www.dmu.ac.uk/~jamesa/learning/experien.htm, accessed 23 October 2003.

Bell, J. (2002) *Doing your Research Project.* Buckingham: Open University Press.

Blaxter, L., Hughes, C. and Tight, M. (2001) *How to Research.* 2nd edition. Buckingham: Open University Press.

Brown, S. (1990) *Planning Small-scale Research.* Available at www.scre.ac.uk/spotlight/spotlight27.html, accessed 20 October 2003.

Christenson, M., Slutsky, R., Bendau, S., Covert, J., Dyer, J., Risko, G. and Johnston, M. (2002) 'The rocky road of teachers becoming action researchers', *Teaching and Teacher Education* 18, 259–272.

Coghlan, D. (2003) 'Practitioner research for organizational knowledge', *Management Learning* 34, 4, 451–463.

Coghlan, D. and Casey, M. (2001) 'Action research from the inside: issues and challenges in doing action research in your own hospital', *Journal of Advanced Nursing* 35, 5, 674–682.

Cohen, L. and Manion, L. (1996) *Research Methods in Education.* 4th edition. London: Routledge.

Costello, P. (2003) *Action Research.* London: Continuum.

Davies, P., Osborne, M. and Williams, J. (2001) *For Me or Not for Me? That is the Question: A Study of Mature Students' Decision Making and Higher Education.* London: DfES.

Drever, E. (1995) *Using Semi-Structured Interviews in Small-Scale Research: A Teachers' Guide.* Edinburgh: SCRE.

Fryer, E. (2004) 'Researcher-practitioner: an unholy marriage?' *Educational Studies* 30, 2, 175–185.

Gillham, B. (2000) *The Research Interview*. London: Continuum.

Greenwood, D. and Levin, M. (1998) *Introduction to Action Research: Social Research for Social Change*. Thousand Oaks, CA: SAGE.

Healey, M. and Jenkins, A. (2000) 'Kolb's experiential learning theory and its application in geography in higher education', *Journal of Geography* 99, 185–195.

Kemmis, S. (1993) 'Action research', in M. Hammersley (ed.), *Educational Research: Current Issues*. London and Buckingham: Paul Chapman and Open University Press.

Lewis, I. and Munn, P. (1997) *So You Want to Do Research! A Guide for Beginners on How to Formulate Research Questions*. Edinburgh: SCRE.

Macintyre, C. (2000) *The Art of Action Research in the Classroom*. London: David Fulton.

Matheson, C. and Matheson, D. (2009) 'Déballage d'idées, catégorisations et hiérarchisation comme activités structurées en groupe focalisé', *Pédagogie médicale* 10, 1, 65–68.

Munn, P. and Drever, E. (1995) *Using Questionnaires in Small-Scale Research: A Teacher's Guide*. Edinburgh: SCRE.

Nunes, M.B. and McPherson, M. (2003) 'Action research in continuing professional development', *Journal of Computer Assisted Learning* 19, 429–437.

Price, J. (2004) 'A parent in the classroom: a valuable way of fostering deep learning for the children's nursing student', *Nurse Education in Practice* 4, 5–11.

Schostak, J. (2002) *Understanding, Designing and Conducting Qualitative Research in Education*. Buckingham: Open University Press.

Simpson, M. and Tuson, J. (1995) *Using Observations in Small-Scale Research: A Beginner's* Guide. Edinburgh: SCRE.

Stark, R. (1998) *Practitioner Research: The Purposes of Reviewing the Literature Within an Enquiry*. Edinburgh: SCRE. Available at www.scre.ac.uk/pdf/spotlight/spotlight67.pdf, accessed 20 October 2003.

Staunton, H. (1877) *The Great Schools of England*. London: Daldy, Ibister and Co.

Wells, H.G. (1918) *Joan and Peter: The Story of an Education*. London: Macmillan.

Afterword

Now that I have read about education, how do I write about it?

David Matheson

Writing is a dreadful labour, yet not so dreadful as Idleness.

Thomas Carlyle

The desire to write grows with writing.

Erasmus

Introduction

Each chapter in this book has introduced you to a different aspect of education, with of course some overlap between certain of the chapters. However, reading about the topic is only part of the academic journey. Another, very important, part consists of writing about it. What follows aims to show you how to research an academic essay, how to structure it and then how to write it. The chapter ends with a section on argumentation and the various errors one can make (and which are often employed in error, carelessly or in an attempt to argue in a less than rigorous manner). The same tools can of course be used to research and write an oral presentation, although there you will have to give some attention to visual aids such as PowerPoint.

This chapter is the fruit of helping students over many years and seeing where they can run into problems in writing essays. It is also the fruit of my own experience of writing and of developing as a writer, of remembering where I have had difficulties and how I resolved them. There is of course no such thing as a recipe for an essay. Every essay is (or should be) unique. For this reason, what I am offering here is guidance which, like everything else in this book, you should examine critically. Decide for yourself whether it makes sense. Does the advice offered here agree with your experience? Are the arguments sound? If so, why? If not, why not? When you ask these questions and others like them, you are beginning the journey towards academic creation: you are analysing the prose which is before you. This is something you always have to do in academic writing and it is analysis which makes academic writing stand out from mere description. Description is always necessary but poor writing consists only of that. Good writing is analytical.

Essay-writing: some pointers

This section is in two parts. Part 1 deals with the build-up to writing the essay and gives guidance on carrying out research. Part 2 deals with what to do when you come to put pen to paper or fingers to keyboard. You may very well find some of the statements blindingly obvious. However, sometimes even the most obvious needs to be said since things sometimes only *become* blindingly obvious when they are said.

Part 1 Preparing the ground

And the question is...

IF YOU ARE TACKLING A SET QUESTION

Read the question carefully and thoroughly and make sure that you understand what is being asked of you. It is all too common for students to write very good essays which do not tackle the question as posed. Answer the question as it is actually asked, not as you think it ought to have been asked.

IF YOU ARE SETTING YOUR OWN QUESTION

Read the module/course guide very carefully and ensure that your proposed question is relevant to what you are meant to be doing. Seek advice from your tutor. Read the assessment criteria for the essay to see what you will be judged against. At the end of writing each draft, look back and check whether you have answered your question. If you have not, depending on how your course is organised, you may be able to change the question so that it fits the essay.

Plan ahead

This means several things. First, plan when you are going to start work on your research for the essay. Plan when you are going to write that all-important first draft. Plan when you are going to revise your essay. Plan when you are going to have the final draft ready. Perhaps most importantly: *plan what you are going to put in the essay.* An essay, like all creative writing, has to have a beginning, a middle and an end.

> The White Rabbit put on his spectacles. 'Where shall I begin, please your Majesty?' he asked. 'Begin at the beginning', the King said, very gravely, 'and go on till you come to the end: then stop.'
>
> (Carroll 1886: chapter XII)

The beginning lays out what you are going to say; the middle says it; the end tells the reader what you have said, what conclusions you have drawn. Put another way, the beginning sets the context; the middle gives the content and the end gives closure.

Imagine reading a story that started in the middle and assumed that you knew all the characters; or a story which stopped dead, with no ending. To get the idea, take any fairy story and imagine what it would be like to read it to a child but without 'Once upon a time…'. Then imagine what it would be like without the ending. In either case, the story is lost and the person to whom you are reading the story is left a bit befuddled. Neither of these is very satisfying. Your essay is, in effect, a story; it needs a narrative structure and it needs to take the reader from one place to another. This is why your plan needs to show clearly where you are starting and where you are finishing. But do remember that, at this stage, it is a plan. Nothing more. It is there to remind you of what you are going to write and it lets you see if you have a clear idea of where you are trying to go and how you will know when you get there. But remember: a plan is not carved in tablets of stone. A plan is just what it says it is. It is a series of ideas which you believe, at the time of writing, will lead to a successful and satisfying essay. If you find that a part of your plan becomes redundant then jettison it.

Plans can easily become over-ambitious and I personally have seen essay plans which would have taken a tome the size of *War and Peace* to realise, so strive to keep the plan short and workable. Your plan does not commit you to anything. What it does is to give your thoughts a focus and a direction which show a promising avenue to follow. You can modify it at any time during the writing process.

Whatever the final size and shape of your plan, make sure it flows logically from one point on to the next.

It can help to discuss the essay topic with a friend, just to see if you both have the same understanding of the question.

Research for an essay is critical

Even if your thoughts are entirely original, you lend credibility to them by showing how they are distinguished from previous writings.

Research can open your mind to possibilities which you have not yet considered. *But* do make sure you note your findings so that you can use the most salient parts in the actual writing of your essay. There are many methods for doing this. Popular with adult learners especially is underlining lines of text. This is not recommended for library books. In fact, it is to be seriously discouraged. Annotating library texts can make them unreadable for other library users and usually renders them useless for blind and partially sighted users who rely on scanners and text recognition software.

Putting flags on especially relevant pages is also popular, but note on the flag the page number and what it was on the page that was so appealing. In this way, if you drop the book and your flags fall out then all is not lost and also you have a rapid means of finding out again what it was that interested you in the first place.

My preferred method used to be to make jottings in a notebook. This is more time-consuming than the other two methods listed but it had, for me, the crucial advantage of still being available to me when the book had gone back to the library (I still have occasion to use notes that I made three decades ago). My jottings always started with the full bibliographical data on the book and then I would use either direct quotes (if they are fairly short) or non-quotes (i.e. paraphrasing the gist of what the writer has said). It is essential to note the page number, even for indirect quotes, just in case you ever need to see the setting for your quotation.

Nowadays I prefer to take my notes directly onto a computer, but using the same method as I did with my old notebooks. Advantages are manifest, such as not having to rewrite everything, but there are negatives which are easily overlooked: working from notes already word-processed lends itself to over-use of cutting and pasting and with this comes the real danger of not actually reading precisely what you are copying. Rather one may read what one *thinks* one is copying, rather than what is actually on the page.

Of course, if you are sufficiently clued up then you may wish to use a bibliographical referencing program such as *Endnote* or *Reference Manager*. The principal use of these programs comes when one has to use the same source material for different outputs and these outputs require different forms of referencing. Endnote and Reference Manager are worth trying out, but be warned: there are those who swear by such programs and those who swear at them.

Every method has its good points and bad points and there are certainly others I have not listed. Nonetheless it is critical that you find a method of retaining your research findings so that you can refer to them again at a later date.

Deciding which books and articles to read is a sticky problem

If you can get the books and articles on the reading list, then fine. Otherwise, take a look at the ones on the library shelf which are to either side of where your chosen book ought to be; search online for other writings on the topic. Think creatively. Think laterally (read Edward de Bono's *Lateral Thinking*!). Think around the topic. Use the index at the back of books. Check the table of contents. Use the reference list(s) in the book. These may seem like statements of the obvious but I continue to be amazed at how many people I encounter who do not do them.

Using the Web

With the unbelievable amount of material available online, it is easy to be tempted into viewing the Web as being all one needs for academic writing. Be aware that, while there is much of great value on the Web (e.g. online refereed journals and well-established databases) there is also much which is nonsense. There are no controls whatever on material that gets on to the Web so there may be no indication of the academic validity of anything you may find there. A classic example of this used to be Wikipedia, whose quality ranged enormously and it used to be lampooned and ridiculed for the lack of editorial control over its articles. As time goes by, this is less and less justified as Wikipedia has demanded proper citations and accurate referencing. However, like all sources, a Wikipedia entry has to be read critically. Check the references that are cited and follow up those that look most useful.

Check the journals

Academic journals will give you material that is much more up to date than books tend to – *but* don't assume that just because something is old that it is useless. Neither should you assume that newness means value. There is old nonsense and new nonsense. All of it is still nonsense. Equally there are texts dating back sometimes thousands of years (such as those of Plato and Aristotle) which are relevant and valuable in many education essays. Just because the text is old tells you nothing of the relevancy of the writing.

Most journals are available online and there are increasing numbers of open access journals which can be consulted by anyone, not just those belonging to a institution with a subscription. The Educational Research Global Observatory (www.ergobservatory.info/ejdirectory.html) maintains a list of open access journals in education.

This said, search engines such as Google Scholar (http://scholar.google.com) are invaluable. But, think carefully about the search terms you are using. Too narrowly defined and you may find little of use. Too broadly defined and you might be presented with thousands, or even millions, of hits. These search engines will help widen your horizons and bring you into contact with useful ideas from domains you might never have considered looking at.

Part 2 Writing the essay

How to avoid getting low marks

POOR EXPRESSION AND VAGUENESS

Poor expression and vagueness are invariably the result of haste. There do exist rare individuals who can sit down and write a good essay in one go, but these individuals are either unusually talented or are writing about a topic they have been immersed in for a long time. The rest of us take several attempts and we take time over the thinking about the essay and the writing of it. Simply put, for most people it takes time to crystallise a good argument. You need to take time to immerse yourself in the literature, focusing on the topic you are going to write about and then to mull it over for a little while. A first plan needs to follow shortly afterwards. Get down on paper some ideas of what you are thinking about writing and keeping reading and mulling. Remember, the cure for writer's cramp is writer's block and the only way to get writing down on paper is, funnily enough, to write.

Often, the most difficult part of writing any essay is making a start. You should aim to write a first paragraph at the first opportunity you have after choosing your essay title – once you have done some initial reading and thinking. Managing this will normally make you more receptive to relevant ideas, and it becomes easier to read round a topic purposefully. This first paragraph need only be your plan put into continuous prose, rather than bullet points. After all, your opening paragraph should only tell the reader what the essay is about. This said, by the time you have finished the rest of the essay, you will probably have revised this first paragraph several times and it is often said by writers that the opening paragraph is the last one to be finalised.

Take the time to write the first draft of the essay as soon as you can after the title has been selected. The more you write, the more you can write and the better focused your reading is going to be. The first draft should be re-read and once you have put right its most obvious errors, try to leave it unread for at least a week before you return to it. This way you will read it with fresh eyes, almost as if it had been written by someone else and you will not only be more aware of the mistakes that remain and the parts that don't work, you will also be more aware of the parts that are well written.

The aim is to do what is known as an iterative process: you return to the essay several times and each time you make adjustments to it. This is what each writer in this book has done with their chapter. Between iterations you need to leave the essay and do more reading of journal articles and chapters from books which have some bearing on the argument you are making or which discuss your topic. As you go back and forth to the essay, your readings are much more likely to make sense since you are seeing them in the context of your own work.

As a final check, someone other than you should read through the completed essay to check that it is clearly written and that there are no major grammatical or spelling errors and ideally that there are no such errors at all. Students might well work in pairs for this purpose. Everyone can write gibberish; everyone can miss out letters, words or even whole sentences – and anyone can depend on the sometimes dubious results put out by the spellcheckers that are part of most word-processing programs. When we write, we know what we *want* to say. We can all, however, become blind to what we have actually written.

MUDDLING TENSES, SAYING WHAT YOU FEEL AND WHICH VOICE TO USE

Novice academic writers (and not uncommonly more experienced ones too) can tie themselves in knots over which tense to use when they refer to a piece of writing. Should one say, for example, Winch and Gingell (1999) *term* Education an essentially contested concept or that they *termed* it an essentially contested concept. After all, it was some years ago that they made their claim.

There are two ways of approaching this. One is to always use the past tense since the claim was made in the past, which makes sense. The other is to always use the present tense since the claim is made every time you read it in their book. The essential point here is to decide which way to use (and your course tutors may have their preferences, so check with them) and stick to it ... rigidly and without exception!

In conversation it is common for people to liberally mix opinions and arguments for which they have evidence. They will assert (i.e. say things without evidence) and they will argue (i.e. say things with evidence which is based on facts they cite or based on the logical flow of the argument). In conversation, opinions abound and they are often prefaced by terms such as *I feel* or *I believe*. Problems can arise when this conversational looseness is carried over into essays.

Using terms such as *I feel* or *I believe* reduce what you are saying to the level of an opinion and nothing more. Saying *I feel because* ... gives a reason for your opinion so why not drop *I feel* entirely and just present your reasons?

The exception to this comes when you are writing a reflective essay in which you examine your experience. In this case, what you feel and what you believe are important because you are being reflective. However, don't forget to compare what you thought or felt with what the literature says. That way you show whether others have experienced similar sentiments to you.

This brings us to another bone of contention in essay writing: which voice to use. The tradition in scientific circles is generally to avoid using the first person singular. In social sciences, such as education, writers frequently use the first person and say *I* if they are solo writers or *we* only if there is more than one of them. Some of those from a scientific background will use a passive voice and, rather than writing *I will show that* ... they say *it will be shown that* .... In addition there are those who write *the writer will show that* .... While some of these styles can seem a bit awkward, fundamentally it does not matter which one you use (unless your course tutors say otherwise). What is important is to pick one and to stick to it. Don't be *I* in one line, *we* in the next and *the writer* in the one after that. If you do switch voices, then you may well confuse your reader, if not actually annoy them.

IRRELEVANCE AND POOR ARGUMENT

Irrelevance and poor argument are often the result of students not thinking through what is demanded by the topic or title set. It always helps to write as a first paragraph an explanation in your own words of what the assignment set is actually asking, and how a response will be framed. Any difficult terms in the title/question should be defined briefly in your own words, but not by quoting a dictionary since dictionaries only give the immediate *definition* of a word, not its sense or its implications, unless that is all is needed. Other sorts of introductions ('setting the scene', etc.) should in general be avoided, unless you are specifically asked to provide a background to the essay. The main principle of a good educational essay is that it answers a question directly and in the most economic way (i.e. with no lengthy digressions).

Other impediments to good argument are unnecessary repetition and unsupported generalisations or assertions. Examples of unsupported generalisations or assertions would be when a writer states, without giving reasons for his/her beliefs: 'Comprehensive schools have failed, and should be abandoned'; or 'progressive methods of teaching are unstructured and do not work'. In fact, an acceptable argument may well only make a few major points, which amount to saying that comprehensive schools have failed or that progressive teaching methods do not work. But, in making these, an essay marshals *evidence* in favour of the *argument* and deals with as many possible criticisms of it as possible. The force of a case will, therefore, lie in the illustrations and examples made, clarifying main points, and the other sorts of evidence (i.e. taken from references) used. So, where important points are repeated, they are repeated so that a different criticism can be dealt with, or a different example given to strengthen the argument.

In sum, a good argument is not one which necessarily makes many points, but one where the key points are well supported and criticisms of them are well met. A good essay structure therefore would be as follows:

1. A first paragraph which interprets the question set in the student's own words and defines main terms.
2. A clear summary of a student's answer to the question set, indicating which parts of the answer need clarification (with examples, evidence, etc.) and what sorts of criticisms of the answer need to be faced.
3. A step-by-step discussion of the answer (already summarised). This discussion will be in two parts – first, providing examples and other sorts of evidence supporting the case, and second, stating and dealing with criticisms of it.
4. A re-statement of the answer to the question set, indicating the extent to which it might, still, be questioned in the light of criticisms, and any further problems with it that have been thrown up by examples and illustrations.

POOR REFERENCING

In any academic essay, a reasonable selection of writers who have commented on the topic being discussed must be referred to and named. When they are named, the date of a publication on the topic must also be cited. What follows shows how the 'Harvard' style does this:

Kelly (1981) argues that educational curricula should … etc.

Peters (1966) believes that … etc.

Whenever a writer is named, the date of a relevant publication should follow immediately. This writer and the text cited should then, always, appear in the bibliography or list of references at the end of the essay. When a writer's work is cited by another writer, both texts should be indicated in the essay and appear if possible in the bibliography, as follows:

(in essay text): Piaget and Inhelder (1969, cited Bee, 1992) write that … etc.

(in references): Piaget, J. and Inhelder, B. (1969) *The Psychology of the Child*, New York: Basic Books, cited: Bee, H. (1992) *Child Development*, 3rd edition, London: Harper Collins.

When a point is made in an essay which is not self-evidently true, it must either be argued through (on the basis of a student's own ideas and experiences) and/or be supported by a writer who also makes the same or an equivalent point.

So, for example, a student might write: 'humiliation and harassment continue to be used as a method of teaching in medicine'. This is not self-evidently true (in other words it might, in fact, not be true). Some writers who have found it to be true need to be cited. Therefore, the sentence could read: *research has shown that humiliation and harassment continue to be used as a method of clinical teaching* (Lempp and Seale 2004; Musselman *et al.* 2005). Notice that two articles are referred to (which adds credibility to your claim) and that no page number is given as the sentence is not a direct quote.

Lempp and Seale (2004) and Musselman *et al.* (2005) are then listed in the essay's bibliography. The titles of texts are *not* included in the body of the essay, only in the bibliography, unless you have a special reason for giving the title (as I have done later when I refer to Anthony Flew's 1975 book *Thinking about Thinking*, which I want to emphasise as an important text). With this system (the 'Harvard' system), footnotes are usually not needed, except perhaps to mention a point deriving from the argument but not directly relevant to the direction being taken. Examples can be found in journals. It is worth bearing in mind that footnotes tend to get read; endnotes do not get read to anywhere near the same extent.

Quotations should be as short as possible (a sentence is often quite long enough). The page of a text from where the quotation is taken should be stated following the quotation, as follows:

> For example, Bruner (1963) says 'any subject can be taught effectively in some intellectually honest form to any child at any stage of development (p. 33).'

Where a quotation exceeds about two lines, it should be written as a separate indented paragraph.

There are literally thousands of referencing styles and the list is growing. Unless there is a course requirement to use a particular style, then the style you adopt does not matter. What is important is that you use a referencing style and that you are consistent in your use of it.

How to get high marks

WRITE CLEAR, WELL-SUPPORTED, RELEVANT ARGUMENTS

High marks for essays are obtained by students writing clear, well-supported arguments which deal directly with the topic or question set. Arguments are likely to be clear if they are expressed in students' own words, using simple, non-technical language. There are no right answers in education, but there are better or worse presented arguments. This is not to suggest there are not correct and incorrect ways of executing tasks, which clearly there often are. Rather, it is to suggest that there are multiple interpretations of the same scenario, whereby different arguments my lead to different conclusions. On a basic level, there are many ways to hold a pencil, but not all of them will allow you to write legibly, if at all.

Students may well decide to make a case which is different from that provided by a tutor in a lecture. Tutors are usually pleased to be disagreed with. Indeed, an essential element of academic life is that ideas shift and sometimes even change radically (Kuhn

1996) and debate is at the heart of this, by posing questions and demanding robust answers sustained by evidence and argument.

The quality of the argument will depend on how good the reasons are which support it, and the quality of the evidence cited. Students should not be afraid to state, clearly, their own reasons for believing a particular point of view, but they must support those reasons with examples and references. Examples may well be taken from students' own experiences. Providing these are expressed convincingly, they count as real evidence. The crucial matter will be how well these experiences fit into the general case being made.

A good example would be a student's citing of his/her own experiences of being a person with dyslexia in higher education to argue a view that some forms of academic support for people with dyslexia are more effective than others. Providing these experiences are described clearly, in ways a reader can recognise as valid (that is, other people might well have had the same experiences in similar circumstances), they are acceptable. However, a single experience does not make a case; such an experience will always need further support (usually from books and articles, though more examples and illustrations can help). Students must also recognise positions opposing their own and make some attempt to explain why they do not accept these.

GOOD REFERENCING

Perhaps the single most important feature of a good essay is the quality of its referencing. It is not difficult to find support for most arguments in books and articles on the library shelves, though students may need to browse for a time in order to find these. An easy way of achieving this is to remove potentially relevant texts from the shelves, whether physical or online, and check through indices (usually at the end) or contents pages to find the appropriate section. It is not necessary to read much of a book in order to cite it in an essay. Students may well find only one paragraph in a text relevant to their essay topic: it is still legitimate to cite the whole book as a reference. Books and journal articles relevant to topics on education can be found not only in the Education section of the library, but also in most parts of any library: you should not be afraid to cite texts from Psychology, Sociology, Philosophy, Literature, Linguistics, History and Geography, Law, etc. in support of your argument. The more support that can be stated, taken from a variety of (reasonably up-to-date or acknowledged classic) texts, the better.

It is very important not to be enslaved by course booklists. These are almost always indicative only and, in any case, books listed are usually quickly borrowed by the first students to arrive at a library. Tutors are always pleased to find reference to books and articles which they themselves have not yet discovered. To say that a booklist is indicative means that there are many other books which could have been listed, but have not been, through lack of space. Tutors are not especially looking in essays for references to set books, though where these are easily obtained, it is expected that students will, where relevant, refer to them. Tutors are, more obviously, looking for references to *appropriate* texts. There are very many chapters and articles which are appropriate texts for essays in education and far from all of them appear in books and journals with the word *education* in the title.

You need to become aware of the wealth of material available through online databases, whether public domain (such as ERIC and the British Education Index) or restricted access (for which you may need an *Athens* username and password for which you need to speak to your librarian). Higher education institutions subscribe to refereed journals and most of these can usually be accessed online (though you will usually need a username and password in order to do this).

Research is where the internet can really come into its own and open you up to a range of sources you might otherwise not consider. You need to think of a set of *keywords* to search for using a search engine such as Google Scholar, as mentioned above.

A GOOD ARGUMENT RELIES ON ITS EVIDENCE

Evidence will be of several kinds:

a. An appropriate book, or journal article, properly referred to, provides a form of evidence. This has been discussed extensively above.
b. Policy documents, Acts of Parliament, Statutory Orders, Green Papers, White Papers, etc.
c. Material from archives.
d. Students' own experiences are a form of evidence. Again, this has been discussed above.
e. Empirical research evidence. Where students discover that some research has been carried out which supports (or opposes) the point being made, this may well be discussed at some length (though beware of padding out an essay by simply describing a long research project). It is not always easy to find research evidence to support an educational argument, so students should not worry unduly if they do not discover much. It is, by contrast, relatively easy to discover writers who (for whatever reason) support one point of view or another.
f. A reasoned argument is a form of evidence. Usually, the reasons supporting a point of view will relate to (a), (b), (c), (d) or (e) above.

NOTE

The word *prove* should not be used in an education essay unless you are using the term in a mathematical sense. The mathematical use of the word *prove* is somewhat dodgy, as what is meant is that a proposition has been demonstrated to be true, subject to a long list of caveats which may or may not be explicitly stated. Outside of most mathematics, *prove* is frequently used to mean that it has been shown that there is the greatest likelihood that the proposition is true.

Important educational positions are never proved. We simply provide evidence for them. This is because education is based upon the study of human beings, and we rarely (if ever) *prove* anything about people. The rare exception would be where students turned to a physical science such as biology for evidence, where (possibly) some physical law has been proved which reflects upon an educational idea. This is so rare a likelihood that students are best advised not to use the word *proof* even here, but simply discuss the biological evidence as good (valid) evidence. In short, students should attempt to introduce the word *evidence* (with accompanying ideas) at key points in their essays since a sound argument *indicates* what *appears* to be true. It does not prove anything. This is a crucial concept. They should work to eliminate words such as *prove, proof*, etc.

ANALYTICAL RATHER THAN DESCRIPTIVE

Descriptive arguments are those where points made are not supported by reasons and/or explanations. Few ideas in education are so straightforward that they do not need explanation. As a simple example, students might believe that it is obvious that learning occurs best in happy places, and teachers should be kind to their learners. But writers such as Gramsci (Entwistle 1980) thought that the best learning occurs when learners work hard (pleasure is irrelevant) and that formal learning should be viewed just like a job of work. Other people, such as some of the more aggressive teachers in my primary school in the 1960s, held onto the belief that people will learn best in order to avoid pain or punishment and so dispensed physical punishment with liberal abandon. It can also be argued that the end justifies the means and that the path taken to learning is irrelevant. All that counts is the learning thus acquired. This opens the debate over process versus product.

So anyone proposing that learners should be in happy places to do their learning would need to justify such a proposal and would need to counter the arguments which are either opposed to happy places being where learning happens best or for whom happiness is irrelevant in learning.

ORIGINALITY, UNIQUENESS

Originality is usually stated as the key to being awarded the highest attainable essay grades. In fact, students do not have to be exceptionally able to produce arguments with a degree of originality. Obviously, it is unlikely that any idea will be wholly original, but it may be markedly different from currently accepted ideas. The secret of expressing such a (relatively) original point of view is, first, to try to understand what the current views are, then deliberately fashion an argument which shows a recognition of these before arriving at a deviant position. This position may be difficult to sustain, but by expressing it students will come to a better understanding of current views.

For example, it is easy to see from the figures available from the Higher Education Statistical Agency[1] that few applicants to medical school come from social classes 5, 6 and 7. This problem is usually located in the relatively low rate of academic success generally enjoyed by pupils in schools where social classes 5, 6 and 7[2] predominate; or in the aspirations that teachers in such schools have for their pupils with regard to school examinations and thence further or higher education and that they work to create self-fulfilling prophecies of social reproduction. An alternative argument might recognise these two standpoints but recognise also that many pupils from such schools do in fact attain the levels required for medical school but do not make the application. It might consider the tendency for humans to feel most comfortable in surroundings where they see people like themselves (by whatever criteria). Thus it might argue that the root cause for the low level of applicants from social classes 5, 6 and 7 is in the image potential applicants have of higher education in general (Matheson 2006) and medical school in particular.[3] Considering such an argument side by side with the others might lead to some new insights into educational issues which might then engender ideas for remediation or rectification.

NOTE

A synthesis of ideas, produced from a student's own individual point of view can sometimes reveal a new insight. It is only by writing down a set of ideas that we discover whether or not it is worth expressing. Usually, the best essays arise through students taking risks, trying to fashion some novel case, rather than through students playing safe and trying to write the argument they believe their tutors want.

Argumentation

Argumentation means recognising that your opinion needs to be backed up with, for example, reference to evidence from elsewhere. There are, however, a number of what is termed sophistical devices (after the Ancient Greek Sophists who were paid to write speeches and convincing arguments, especially for people who were going to appear in court). What follows is a list of such rhetorical devices. It is not exhaustive but rather indicative of the kinds of ways that logic can elude an argument. If you listen to politicians, you may well notice much use of such devices. Be careful though: there are occasions when the use of some of these devices can be legitimate

Ad hominem

'Would you buy a used car from this man?' (1968 US Presidential Campaign poster showing Richard Nixon, nicknamed *Tricky Dicky* and reputed to be economical with the truth).

Ad hominem is used to reduce the value of a person's argument or stance by being derogatory about the person. An example of this occurred in 2003 when the Conservative leader of the time, Iain Duncan Smith, referred in a speech to the Conservative Party Conference to Charles Kennedy's alleged drinking habits as a means of attacking the Lib Dems' policies. That Kennedy turned out to have a very real drinking problem is immaterial. In fact, several of the UK's more illustrious prime ministers have also had drinking problems.[4]

Ad antiquitatem (appeal to antiquity)

'We have always done things this way so we must be right.' This asserts that just because something is old then it is valuable/correct/justified.

Ad crumenam (appeal to money)

'Microsoft must be good, otherwise they would not have got so rich.'

Ad lazarum (appeal to poverty)

This assumes that to be poor is to be virtuous by dint of being poor.

Ad nauseam

This asserts that the more often something is heard then the more true it becomes. This is frequently seen in the generation of 'truth' by the media. For example, bird flu, which killed very few people and for which there was no evidence that it would go on to kill many more, filled many column inches in the press and became a perceived threat through being talked about. There is also the case of the measles-mumps-rubella triple vaccine where a very limited trial of dubious methodology and a tiny sample was picked up by the media and taken as the truth[5] (see Wakefield *et al.* 1998 for the original paper that set off the storm and whose evidence base was very weak indeed, and certainly far too small to be generalisable).

The converse of *ad nauseam* is also true: the New Orleans floods of 2005 were seen as more of a disaster than the Kashmiri earthquake of the same year since the former received enormously more coverage in the media than did the latter. The former killed fewer than 1,000 people; the latter killed at least 50,000 people. See Miller *et al.* (1998) for an explanation of how *ad nauseam* and its converse work with the broadcast and print media.

Argumentum ab auctoritate (appeal to authority)

This is fine if the authority is legitimate for the topic under discussion. It becomes fallacious when the authority has little or nothing to do with the topic. See, for example, Enoch Powell's use of Virgil ('Like the Roman, I see the Tiber foaming with much blood') in an attempt to add legitimacy to his argument when he attacked immigration into the UK in his famous 'rivers of blood' speech in 1968.[6]

Appeal to common sense

'Common sense is a set of prejudices acquired before the age of eighteen' (Albert Einstein). What is common sense for you might be complete anathema to me. Common knowledge is equally fraught since what I commonly know might be alien to you. Both common sense and common knowledge are cultural constructs.

Ad misericordiam (appeal of pity)

This is fallacious when it is used to distract from the substance of the argument and to distract from relevant evidence (e.g. 'Don't hit me; I'm just a poor person'). It can, when properly used, be quite legitimate and arguably can have echoes of Aristotle's idea that we should treat equals equally and treat unequals unequally.

Ad novitatem (appeal to novelty)

A new thing is better than an old thing *because* it is new. This reasoning is used (fallaciously) to justify not considering older, but still relevant, sources of material for essays.

Ad populum (appeal to popularity)

'The people are always right.' 'Capital punishment is justified because the people approve of it.' This is one of the greatest failings of Utilitarianism, which took as its bedrock the aim of pursuing the greatest happiness of the greatest number

Ad baculum (appeal to threat)

This is a common way to end discussions in some pubs. It is legitimate when some sort of sanction may be employed and is commonly used in discussions between employers and unions.

Ad ignorantiam (argument from ignorance)

There are two types and they go like this:

1. This proposition is not known to be true, therefore it is false.
2. This proposition is not known to be false, therefore it is true.

It is legitimate to use this in courts of law where one side or the other must establish its case *beyond reasonable doubt* in the case of criminal courts or *on balance of probabilities* in the case of civil courts. In both cases, if a proposition is not established to be true (or false) then it is deemed to be false (or true).

Fallacy of many questions

'Are you still beating your wife, Mr Smith? Please answer yes or no' is the classic of this genre. There are presuppositions built into the question. The only answers are to ask that the question be broken down into smaller questions or to reply 'none of the above'.

No true Scotsman

This term was coined by Anthony Flew in his 1975 book *Thinking about Thinking*. It refers to a form of argument where rebuttal of the opening statement leads to a revision of that statement and this with the aim of the proponent never being 'proved' wrong. It is more than simply refining the proposition (which is usually valid) as it is dependent on an ad hoc change to shore up the assertion. So,

A: 'No Scotsman puts sugar on his porridge.'
B: 'Angus is a Scotsman and he puts sugar on this porridge.'
A: 'Then he can't be a *true* Scotsman.'

Over-generalisation

This is the basis of stereotyping where one takes a limited experience and generalises it to an entire population (or country, or ethnic group, or whatever). This is commonly done where a person uses limited data and applies them, without justification, to a much larger population or group.

Question-begging

Assuming to be true that which remains to be shown. This is not the same as the mundane use of the term, which means simply to suggest a question. In the philosophical sense, question-begging links propositions without showing why (or how) they are linked. A typical one is to claim that raising the price of fuel will reduce global warming. It has to be shown that there is a link between fuel prices, fuel consumption and global warming. Without these links being demonstrated, questions are begged. A category of question-begging founds the argument on its conclusion and is known as *circular argument*, an example being 'The charges of physical abuse are absolutely untrue, because the police would never do something like that.'[7]

Slippery slope

This is also the 'thin end of the wedge'. It is used by libertarians to fend off such initiatives as identity cards. It is used by other groups to protest against such phenomena as immigration. Fundamentally, slippery slope depends on extrapolation from the situation we are in now to one that has yet to come to pass. Its legitimacy is variable since it requires certain prophetic powers, though these may be based on past experiences. However, such inductive reasoning depends on the past being a valid indicator of the future. This it may or may not be. Nonetheless, 'Those who cannot remember the past are condemned to repeat it' (George Santayana[8]).

Stereotyping

This links in with (at least) *ad hominem* and over-generalisation. Individuals are ascribed to groups and certain traits are ascribed to those groups. Examples include the depiction of, for example, the Scots in most popular TV drama as thugs, drunks, thick, psychopaths and so on. This is not to say there are none of those in Scotland, but by applying stereotypes there is the creation of the expectation that all Scots are like that. Stereotyping is never justified in arguments.

This list is a taster of sophistical devices. It is neither exhaustive nor complete. Try to find some more!

Conclusion

Essay writing is a skill. Like any skill, it can be learned. Like any skill, some people find it easier to learn to do well than do others. However, like any skill, it gets better with practice and the only way to practise writing essays is to write essays. This is where the iterative process is so useful: you revisit the same essay several times and in effect have several bites at the cherry. You get to practise your writing skills more times than if you just dashed off your essay in one hectic night of writing. Following the essay-writing pointers will strengthen and develop your writing skills. Paying attention to the various sophistical devices and knowing how to recognise them and how to see when they are being used illegitimately will strengthen not only your writing but also your analytical skills.

Good luck and enjoy the journey.

Notes

1. See, for example, Table SP5 available via www.hesa.ac.uk/index.php?option=com_search, accessed 30 December 2013.
2. Lower supervisory and technical occupations, semi-routine occupations, routine occupations, respectively.
3. See Kamali *et al.* (2005), Heathfield and Wakeford (1994).
4. Winston Churchill was apparently told by Lady Astor one evening at a reception: *Winston, you're drunk.* Without missing a beat, Churchill is said to have replied, *My dear, you're ugly but in the morning I shall be sober.*
5. See http://en.wikipedia.org/wiki/MMR_vaccine_controversy for a lengthy list of research papers debunking the claims of Wakefield *et al.* (1998), as well as an account of the whole affair.
6. The text of this speech is available at www.martinfrost.ws/htmlfiles/rivers_blood2.html, accessed 30 December 2013. It employs one sophistical device after another.
7. With thanks to Andrew R. Davidson, the copy-editor of the third edition.
8. Available from http://en.wikiquote.org/wiki/George_Santayana, accessed 29 December 2013.

References

Bee, H. (1992) *Child Development*, 3rd edition. Glasgow: Harper Collins.

Bruner, J.S. (1963) *The Process of Education*. New York: Vintage Books.

Carroll, L. (1886) *Alice's Adventures in Wonderland*. London: Macmillan.

Entwistle, H. (1980) *Antonio Gramsci: Conservative Schooling for Radical Politics*. London: Routledge.

Flew, A. (1975) *Thinking about Thinking, or Do I Sincerely Want to be Right?*. Glasgow: Fontana.

Heathfield, M. and Wakeford, N. (1994) *They Always Eat Green Apples*. Lancaster: Unit for Innovation in Higher Education.

Kamali, A.W., Nicholson, S. and Wood, D.F. (2005) A model for widening access into medicine and dentistry: the SAMDA-BL project, *Medical Education* 39, 9, 918–925.

Kelly, A.V. (1981) *The Curriculum: Theory and Practice*. London: Harper Row.

Kuhn, T. (1996) *The Structure of Scientific Revolutions.* Chicago and London: University of Chicago Press.

Lempp, H. and Seale, C. (2004) The hidden curriculum in undergraduate medical education: qualitative study of medical students' perceptions of teaching, *British Medical Journal* 329, 7469: 770–773.

Matheson, C. (2006) Optimal cultural distance: a conceptual model of greater and lesser likelihood of participation in higher education by potential entrants from under-represented socio-economic groups. Unpublished PhD thesis, City University, London.

Miller, D, Katzinger, J. and Beharrel, P. (1998) *The Circuit of Mass Communication.* London: SAGE.

Musselman, L.J., MacRae, H.M., Reznick, R.K. and Lingard, L.A. (2005) 'You learn better under the gun': intimidation and harassment in surgical education, *Medical Education* 39, 926–934.

Peters, R.S. (1966) *Ethics and Education.* London: Allen and Unwin.

Piaget, J. and Inhelder, B. (1969) *The Psychology of the Child.* New York: Basic Books, cited: Bee, H. (1992) *Child Development*, 3rd edition, Glasgow: HarperCollins.

Wakefield, A.J., Murch, S.H., Anthony, A., Linnell, J., Casson, D.M., Malik, M., *et al.* (1998) Ileal-lymphoid-nodular hyperplasia, non-specific colitis, and pervasive developmental disorder in children, *Lancet* 351, 637–641.

Winch, C. and Gingell, J. (1999) *Key Concepts in the Philosophy of Education.* London: Routledge.

Index

Page numbers in *italics* denote tables, those in **bold** denote figures.